Culture and Public Action

CONTRIBUTORS

Anita Abraham

Sabina Alkire

Arjun Appadurai

Lourdes Arizpe

Fernando Calderón

Monica Das Gupta

Shelton H. Davis

Mary Douglas

Simon Harragin

Carol Jenkins

Arjo Klamer

Timur Kuran

Jean-Philippe Platteau

Vijayendra Rao

Amartya Sen

Alicia Szmukler

Marco Verweij

Michael Walton

Culture and Public Action

Edited by
VIJAYENDRA RAO
and MICHAEL WALTON

Stanford Social Sciences
an imprint of Stanford University Press
Stanford, California 2004

Stanford University Press
Stanford, California

© 2004 The International Bank for Reconstruction and Development /
The World Bank

1818 H Street, NW
Washington, DC 20433
Telephone 202-473-1000
Internet www.worldbank.org
E-mail feedback@worldbank.org

Printed in the United States of America
On acid-free, archival-quality paper

Library of Congress Cataloging-in-Publication Data

Culture and public action / edited by Vijayendra Rao and Michael Walton.
    p.   cm.
   Includes bibliographical references and index.
    ISBN 0-8047-4786-5 (cloth : alk. paper)—ISBN 0-8047-4787-3 (pbk. : alk. paper)
    1. Culture.   2. Economic development—Social aspects.   3. Developing
countries—Cultural policy.   I. Rao, Vijayendra.   II. Walton, Michael, date—
HM621.C8575 2004
306—dc22   2004001629

Original Printing 2004
Last figure below indicates year of this printing:
13 12 11 10 09 08 07 06 05 04

Typeset by BookMatters in 10.5/12.5 Bembo

Contents

Preface   vii

Contributors   xi

1. Culture and Public Action: Relationality, Equality
   of Agency, and Development   3
   VIJAYENDRA RAO AND MICHAEL WALTON

2. How Does Culture Matter?   37
   AMARTYA SEN

3. The Capacity to Aspire: Culture and the Terms
   of Recognition   59
   ARJUN APPADURAI

4. Traditional Culture—Let's Hear No More About It   85
   MARY DOUGLAS

5. Appendix to Douglas: Cultural Theory
   and Development Studies   110
   MARCO VERWEIJ

6. Cultural Obstacles to Economic Development:
   Often Overstated, Usually Transitory   115
   TIMUR KURAN

7. Cultural Goods Are Good for More than Their
   Economic Value   138
   ARJO KLAMER

8. The Intellectual History of Culture
   and Development Institutions   163
   LOURDES ARIZPE

9. Culture, Poverty, and External Intervention   185
SABINA ALKIRE

10. Participatory Development: Where Culture Creeps In   210
ANITA ABRAHAM AND JEAN-PHILIPPE PLATTEAU

11. State Policies and Women's Agency in China,
the Republic of Korea, and India, 1950–2000:
Lessons from Contrasting Experiences   234
MONICA DAS GUPTA, SUNHWA LEE, PATRICIA UBEROI,
DANNING WANG, LIHONG WANG, AND XIAODAN ZHANG

12. HIV/AIDS and Culture: Implications for Policy   260
CAROL JENKINS

13. Political Culture and Development   281
FERNANDO CALDERÓN AND ALICIA SZMUKLER

14. Relief and an Understanding of Local Knowledge:
The Case of Southern Sudan   307
SIMON HARRAGIN

15. The Mayan Movement and National Culture
in Guatemala   328
SHELTON H. DAVIS

16. Conclusion: Implications of a Cultural Lens
for Public Policy and Development Thought   359
VIJAYENDRA RAO AND MICHAEL WALTON

References   373
Index   415

Some may find it incongruous that two economists who work for the World Bank are editing a book about culture. It reflects an increasing recognition of the centrality of cultural process to the reproduction of inequality and human ill-being among development policy makers and economists. However, we are well aware that economists are newcomers to this field and that anthropology and sociology have made seminal contributions to it for over two centuries. On the other hand, over the last fifty years, economists have been engaged, for better or worse, much more centrally with making policy than the other social sciences. It thus seems obvious that policy would be better served by a cross-disciplinary dialogue among the social sciences—on equal terms—on "why" and "how" culture matters for development and the implications of this for public action. This book is an effort in that direction.

We have targeted the book to a broad audience—anthropologists, economists, political scientists, other academic social scientists, as well as development practitioners and policy makers of all stripes. We are also keen that the book be read by undergraduate and graduate students interested in development. To achieve this, all the contributors to this volume have written their articles trying to stay clear of excessive jargon, and assuming a minimum level of prerequisites. We realize that this may mean that some disciplinary or practitioner perspectives may not be as adequately represented as would be possible in a book targeted to a specialized audience.

Acknowledgments

We have been privileged to have had Amartya Sen as our guru and main advisor through this process. His wisdom and critical guidance have played a central role in shaping the book. We have also greatly benefited from

Arjun Appadurai's deep insights and cogent suggestions on both substance and style. This project would have never been completed without the unstinting support of Nick Stern, who served as chief economist of the World Bank during the time when this book was being produced. Tia Duer was a crucial ally in seeking funding and institutional support, and we are grateful for her help. Much of this effort was sparked by World Bank president James Wolfensohn's vision for a more inclusive and culturally sensitive development.

We would also like to acknowledge our gratitude to Mary Douglas for agreeing to contribute to this volume despite several obstacles. Our contributors were most responsive to pesky requests and policing, and many also served as peer reviewers and commentators on other essays. For this, we thank Anita Abraham, Sabina Alkire, Lourdes Arizpe, Fernando Calderon, Monica Das Gupta, Shelton Davis, Simon Harragin, Carol Jenkins, Arjo Klamer, Alicia Szmukler, Timur Kuran, Jean-Philippe Platteau, and Marco Verweij.

The contributions in this volume served as the basis of a conference held on June 30, 2002, in Washington, D.C. Several distinguished scholars and practitioners participated in that conference as commentators and discussants, and others provided their inputs as peer reviewers. Their insights have contributed greatly to revisions of the chapters and the overall perspective on the book. For this, we express our gratitude to Yonas Admassu, Kaushik Basu, Sarah Berry, Michael Cernea, Kamala Chandrakirana, David Dollar, Andreas Eshete, Ian Goldin, Stephen Gudeman, Isabel Guerrero, Jeffrey Hammer, Keith Hart, Karla Hoff, Michael Kremer, Peter Lanjouw, Glenn Loury, Alexandre Marc, Deepa Narayan, Mieko Nishimizu, Hnin Hnin Pyne, Mamphela Ramphele, Debraj Ray, Jo Ritzen, Gayatri Reddy, Sita Reddy, Andrew Steer, and Michael Woolcock.

There is a Web site that accompanies this book where digital videos of the conference proceedings, discussants' comments, and additional readings and links can be obtained: http://www.cultureandpublicaction.org.

Caroline Archambault did a superb job as the main organizer of the conference, and she and Jerry MacLean were primarily responsible for the initial development of the Web site, along with Saumitra Jha and Mattihias Vom Hau. We thank them all for their excellent work. The project was funded by Dutch Trust Funds provided by the Netherlands government, and we are very grateful for their generous support.

Our colleagues at the World Bank provided input and support without which this project would have never got off the ground. In particular, we thank Martin Ravallion, Anis Dani, Emmanuel Jimenez, Karen Mason, and Lynn Bennett.

At Stanford Press, Patricia Katayama, our editor, was a cheerful, enthusiastic, and patient guide in moving this book through the publication process, and we are indebted to her for her help. We are deeply grateful for thoughtful and insightful comments provided by two reviewers for the press—Keith Hart, and an economic theorist who chose to remain anonymous.

Last, we acknowledge the role of our spouses, Isabel Guerrero and Sita Reddy, whose insights, input, and moral support, as, respectively, a development practitioner and economist, and a sociologist and museum studies practitioner, have contributed immeasurably to our work.

VR, MW

Contributors

ANITA ABRAHAM has wide experience in development research and action both in India and Africa and teaches at the University of Namur, Belgium, on development problems. Her major interests in research are the failure of the state and development aid in Africa and women's right to inheritance and problems of transition from premortem to postmortem inheritance in transitional societies.

SABINA ALKIRE is a Research Associate at the Global Equity Initiative, Harvard University. She received a DPhil in economics as well as an MPhil in Christian political ethics from Magdalen College, Oxford. She previously worked for the Commission on Human Security cochaired by Amartya Sen and Sadako Ogata, for the Poverty Reduction Unit at the World Bank, and with Oxfam and the Asia Foundation in Pakistan. Her dissertation was published as *Valuing Freedoms: Sen's Capability Approach and Poverty Reduction* (Oxford University Press, 2002), and current research interests include value judgments in economic decision making, especially through participatory or deliberative processes, and further development of the capability approach.

ARJUN APPADURAI is Provost of New School University, where he is also John Dewey Professor of the Social Sciences. His research focuses on the cultural dilemmas of globalization, especially those involving violence, diversity, and inclusion. He has served as an advisor to many multinational institutions, including UNESCO, UNDP, and the World Bank, and is a member of the American Academy of Arts and Sciences. He is also the founder and president of a nonprofit cross-sectoral research group based in Mumbai called PUKAR (Partners for Urban Knowledge Action and Research). He is the author of *Modernity at Large* (1996) and has previously held faculty appointments at Yale University, the University of Chicago, the University of Pennsylvania, and Yale University.

LOURDES ARIZPE is Professor of Anthropology at the Centro Regional Multidisciplinario of the National University of Mexico and led UNESCO's first World Culture Report for 1998. She is also the vice president of the International Social Science Council. Her research has focused on issues of culture, development, migration, and women.

FERNANDO CALDERÓN is International Adviser on Human Development to the United Nations Development Programme for Bolivia and Professor of Sociology at the University Oberta of Catalunya. His research focuses on politics, culture, and development. He is currently working on studies on the information era in collaboration with Manuel Castells, a Human Development report entitled "Bolivia in the Information Economy and Society," and a regional report on democracy and development in Latin America. He recently published *¿Es sostenible la globalización en América Latina? Debates con Manuel Castells*, a book of which he is the coordinator and author (two volumes, Fondo de Cultura Económica-PNUD, 2003) and *La reforma de la política: Deliberación y desarrollo* (Nueva Sociedad-Fundación Friedrich Ebert, 2002).

MONICA DAS GUPTA is Senior Social Scientist in the Development Research Group of the World Bank. Trained in social anthropology and demography, she has extensive experience of multidisciplinary quantitative and qualitative research. She is currently studying the organization of public health services and has published extensively on the interaction between state policies, social institutions, and development outcomes. She has served on the editorial boards of several journals, the board of directors of the Population Association of America and the IUSSP, and various committees of the WHO, UN, and US National Science Foundation. Before joining the World Bank, she worked at Harvard University and at the National Council for Applied Economic Research in New Delhi, India.

SHELTON H. DAVIS is Sector Manager for Social Development in the Latin America and Caribbean Region of the World Bank. Dr. Davis is a social anthropologist and did his doctoral dissertation on a Mayan-speaking indigenous community in the highlands of Guatemala in 1970. Since that time, he has written extensively on the situation of Maya-speaking peoples in Guatemala, including the introduction to *Harvest of Violence: The Maya Indians and the Guatemala Crisis* (University of Oklahoma Press, 1988), edited by Robert M. Carmack.

MARY DOUGLAS retired from active university teaching in 1988. Born in 1921, she trained as an anthropologist in Oxford after the war under the supervision of Evans-Pritchard and did fieldwork in the Congo in 1949. She taught in the Anthropology Department of University College, London, from 1951 to 1977, when she went to the United States to join the Russell-Sage Foundation in New York. After four years, she moved to Northwestern University as Avalon Professor in the Humanities, and in 1985, she was Visiting Professor in the University of Princeton. The honors she has received include honorary doctorates from Notre Dame University, Indiana, and the Jewish Theological Seminary of New York, the University of Pennsylvania, and in 2003, a DLitt from the University of Oxford. She is especially interested in cognition and social influences on belief. Her best-known books are *Purity and Danger* (1966), *The World of Goods* (1979), and *Risk and Blame* (1992).

SIMON HARRAGIN, who is based in Paris, is a consultant and writer on anthropology and development issues. His research focuses on the East and Central Africa regions and on the delivery of aid in humanitarian emergencies. He is currently involved in a study looking at the relevance and meaning of "community participation" in emergency situations.

CAROL JENKINS is an independent consultant, based in Bangkok, working on HIV/AIDS issues, primarily in Asia. She has recently served as the Asia/Near East Regional HIV Advisor for USAID and HIV consultant for the World Bank's Middle East/North Africa Region. Her work focuses on HIV prevention and care, especially among marginalized groups. She is currently involved with developing HIV prevention programs in Burma, Thailand, Vietnam, Cambodia, China, and Papua New Guinea and strategies for the Middle East/North Africa.

ARJO KLAMER is professor in the economics of art and culture at Erasmus University. He has previously taught at Duke University, Wellesley College, the University of Iowa, and George Washington University. His research focuses on the rhetoric of economics and the value of culture. His publications include *Conversations with Economists* (1984), *The Making of an Economist* (with David Colander, 1990), and *The Value of Culture* (1996). *Speaking of Economics: How to Be in Conversation with Economists* is forthcoming. He is on the board of various cultural institutions in the Netherlands.

TIMUR KURAN is Professor of Economics and Law, and King Faisal Professor of Islamic Thought and Culture at the University of Southern California. His research focuses on social change, including the evolution of preferences, values, and institutions. His current projects include a multivolume study of the role that Islam played in the economic rise of the Middle East and subsequently in the institutional stagnation that accompanied the region's slip into a state of underdevelopment. Among his publications are *Private Truths, Public Lies: The Social Consequences of Preference Falsification* (Harvard University Press, 1995) and *Islam and Mammon: The Economic Predicaments of Islamism* (Princeton University Press, 2004).

JEAN-PHILIPPE PLATTEAU is Professor of Economics and member of CRED (Centre de Recherche en Économie du Développement) at the University of Namur, Belgium. Most of his work has been concerned with the understanding of the role of institutions in economic development, and the processes of institutional change. The influence of noneconomic factors and various frontier issues at the interface between economics and sociology are a central focus of his research projects. He has written numerous articles in academic journals and published several books, including *Halting Degradation of Natural Resources—Is There a Role for Rural Communities?* (Clarendon Press, 1995) with J. M. Baland, and *Institutions, Social Norms, and Economic Development* (Routledge, 2000).

VIJAYENDRA RAO is a Senior Economist in the Development Research Group of the World Bank who combines his training in economics with an interest in anthropology. Relying on "participatory econometrics," a method that merges economic and ethnographic methods, his publications include studies of dowries and marriage celebrations, identity choice, domestic violence, sex workers, festivals, and community-based development. He is currently involved in research projects on village democracy in India, community development in Indonesia, and urban poverty. He serves on the editorial board of *Economic Development and Cultural Change*, and previously held appointments at the University of Chicago, Michigan, and Williams College.

AMARTYA SEN is Lamont University Professor at Harvard University. Formerly, he was Master of Trinity College, Cambridge. He is a past president of the American Economic Association, the Indian Economic Association, the International Economic Association, and the Econometric Society. His publications include *Collective Choice and Social Welfare* (1970), *On Economic Inequality* (1973), *Poverty and Famines* (1981), *On Ethics and Economics* (1987), *Inequality Reexamined* (1992), *Development as Freedom* (1999), and *Rationality and Freedom* (2003).

ALICIA SZMUKLER is a sociologist (from the University of Buenos Aires, Argentina) and Magíster in Social Sciences (from the Instituto Latino-americano de Doctrina y Estudios Sociales-Pontificia Universidad Gregoriana de Roma). She is Professor in Postgraduate Studies in Development of the University Mayor of San Andrés (La Paz, Bolivia), and her research focuses on urban culture. She has published *La política en las calles: Política, urbanización y desarrollo* (with Fernando Calderón, Plural-CERES-Universidad Andina, 2000); "Globalización, multiculturalismo y migraciones: Los migrantes bolivianos en Buenos Aires y Sao Paulo" (1999); and *La ciudad imaginaria: Un análisis sociológico de la pintura contemporánea en Bolivia* (PIEB, 1998).

MARCO VERWEIJ is Associate Professor of Political Science at Singapore Management University. He is the author of *Transboundary Environmental Problems and Cultural Theory* (2000), and coeditor of *Deliberately Democratizing Multilateral Organization*, a special issue of the journal *Governance* (2003). He is presently organizing a book project, entitled *Clumsy Solutions for a Complex World*, in which political scientists, engineers, economists, lawyers, and anthropologists spell out and test the policy implications of cultural theory pioneered by Mary Douglas. He is also writing a monograph on international policy solutions to climate change and the loss of biodiversity, and organizing a special issue of the *Philosophical Transactions of the Royal Society of London B* on the ways in which brain research and social theory can be successfully combined.

MICHAEL WALTON is an adviser on poverty reduction and human development for Latin America and the Caribbean for the World Bank. He joined the World Bank in 1980 after working for the government of Lesotho. Major publications include the 1995 World Development Report on labor, participation in the 2000 World Development Report on poverty, a book on inequality in Latin America, and a range of country reports, including Brazil, Indonesia, Mexico, South Africa, the West Bank and Gaza, and Zimbabwe. Previous positions at the World Bank include Director for Poverty Reduction, Chief Economist for Human Development, and Chief Economist for East Asia and the Pacific. He holds degrees in philosophy and economics from Oxford University.

Culture and Public Action

CHAPTER 1

Culture and Public Action:
Relationality, Equality of Agency, and Development

VIJAYENDRA RAO AND MICHAEL WALTON

Introduction

Much of the discussion on the role of culture in development has either seen it as a primordial trap, a mystical haze, or a source of hegemonic power. These have not proved very useful as guides for public action. In recent years, however, development thinking has arrived at an interesting crossroads. In the academic world, economists are grappling with models of how social and cultural factors shape human behavior, and academic anthropologists, having grappled with these questions for a long time, are seeing the need to move beyond critique toward a more "facilitatory" anthropology (Sillitoe 1998). Similarly, in the world of policy, culture is increasingly being viewed as a commonplace, malleable fact of life that matters as much as economics or politics to the process of development. But there remains some confusion about *how* it matters. In this introductory essay, we draw on the contributions in this volume to examine some of the positive and normative implications of taking culture on board in improving how public action alleviates poverty and reduces inequality in the world's less affluent countries. We begin with two case studies to place our arguments in context, go on to review past work on the subject (in the worlds of both thought and action), and then distill the contributions in this book toward a conceptual and practical overview of the role of culture in reproducing or alleviating poverty. We end the chapter with some thoughts on the normative implications of this, arguing that it suggests a shift from the individually based principle of "equality of opportunity" to a group-based principle that we call "equality of agency." We should note that the book is primarily concerned with poverty and inequality, and some important topics at the intersection of culture and development are not addressed in detail. Globalization is one of them, and the relationship between culture and economic growth is another one. Both, we feel, have been adequately treated elsewhere.[1]

But what is culture? It has been defined in myriad ways (Kluckholn and Kroeber 1963), and we hesitate to privilege one definition over another. Our general view is that culture is about relationality—the relationships among individuals within groups, among groups, and between ideas and perspectives. Culture is concerned with identity, aspiration, symbolic exchange, coordination, and structures and practices that serve relational ends, such as ethnicity, ritual, heritage, norms, meanings, and beliefs. It is not a set of primordial phenomena permanently embedded within national or religious or other groups, but rather a set of contested attributes, constantly in flux, both shaping and being shaped by social and economic aspects of human interaction.

A focus on culture is necessary to confront the difficult questions of *what* is valued in terms of well-being, *who* does the valuing, and *why* economic and social factors interact with culture to unequally allocate access to a good life. To use Amartya Sen's framework, culture is part of the set of capabilities that people have—the constraints, technologies, and framing devices that condition how decisions are made and coordinated across different actors. There is no presumption that these processes are inherently "good," or inherently "bad," for economic and social development. By reproducing inequality and discrimination, they can be exploitative, exclusionary, and conflictual—resulting in what Sen has called "relational deprivation" (Sen 2000). Cultural processes, however, can also be harnessed for positive social and economic transformation, through their influence on aspirations, the coordination of collective action, and the ways in which power and agency work within a society.

In order to make concrete the relevance of culture for public action, we turn to two examples: in the first example, a failure to pay attention to a group's culture adversely affected a policy intervention, and in the second, a careful attention to culturally conditioned processes led to a highly successful project.

Two Case Studies

FAMINE IN THE SUDAN: HOW MISSING THE CULTURE DIMENSION DIMINISHED AID EFFECTIVENESS

The first case, based on the case study by Simon Harragin in this volume, illustrates how a failure to pay attention to local cultures—in particular, to notions of kinship and social structure—reduced the effectiveness of a response to a famine in Sudan. Blindness to the group's culture caused relief workers to miss the early signs of famine, and to misread as corruption the group's responses to aid.

In early 1998, relief workers began noticing signs of the sudden onset of a catastrophic famine in southern Sudan. Partly because of a debate over the severity of the famine, Operation Lifeline Sudan, which was formed to tackle such problems in the area, did not organize large infusions of food until August 1998. By that point, food deprivation was widespread and famine imminent. A task force concluded that there had been a lack of "contingency planning" in the relief operation and that Operation Lifeline Sudan had "underestimated the total number of people in need" (SPLM/SSRA-OLS 1998b). Why did such a large, and well-intentioned effort fail to intervene in a manner that might have preempted the famine?

The relief organizations were concerned that the famine was being caused by food hoarding, allegedly by corrupt chiefs and the military, rather than by severe lack of food. The concern was highlighted by the observation that food destined for the "vulnerable" was being taken over by local leaders. Harragin's field investigation found that the leaders were, in fact, appropriating the food to distribute it equally to all members of their kin group and that the targeted "vulnerable" members of the group were willing participants in this. For instance, he observed an old lady go to a secret location designated by a local chief and put her ration back into the collective pot to be redistributed among everyone, rather than cook and eat her food alone. Aid workers perceived this as "elite capture" and made attempts to bypass local leadership structures and target aid directly at the most vulnerable. The fact that vulnerable groups were themselves complicit in these practices only indicated to aid workers the degree to which the weak were subservient to the powerful.

Harragin argues, however, that the perception of the aid workers reflected a lack of knowledge of local cultural systems. In particular, they were unaware that the basis of ownership of economic resources in southern Sudanese society were kinship groups. Key economic resources—such as cattle—are owned by a small group of kin with common grandparents. Even in a famine, it is unlikely that a man will approach an unrelated person to ask for food. It is therefore felt to be important that all the separate economic units (the lineages) receive their fair share in a distribution of relief food, before choosing the family members with the greatest need for assistance.

The health of the kinship system depends on having resources to circulate. It is with this aim that food was reassembled and redistributed on a kinship basis. Survival of the kinship system was considered almost as important as physical survival. There were, as with any welfare system, individuals without kin who were left unprotected by this traditional distribution mechanism, but it commanded broad support. This equal sharing of meager and declining resources resulted in the food shortages having an even impact on the population. Thus, the most obvious warning sign of a famine—the incidence of severe malnutrition—was not effective because there were no early, isolated cases of malnutrition. Aid workers were consequently led to believe that the famine was not severe. When malnutrition did appear, it came at a point when the famine had reached an advanced stage, when severe malnutrition was widespread and catastrophic.

What can be learned from this account? This was a well-intentioned "failure." Relief workers may have been attempting to circumvent traditional redistribution mechanisms because they were judged to be inegalitarian. Many traditional allocation systems do indeed have exclusionary features that must be confronted, but in a famine, practical choices have to be made that recognize how individuals and groups actually behave. By not grounding their intervention within local understandings of distributional norms, relief workers also underestimated the impact of food shortages until it was too late. Furthermore, attempting to work around those norms with technocratic targeting approaches proved fruitless and inefficient. A more culturally sensitive intervention would have attempted to investigate local understandings of deprivation and food allocation, understood the cultural logic of why certain decisions were being made by the community, and worked with community members to find a solution. Instead, a more external, one-size-fits-all method was followed where the intervention, initially at least, may have caused more harm than good. The solution to the crisis of 1998 eventually came through sending in more food and not through better targeting, but even a cursory reading of the anthropological literature on southern Sudan could have resulted in a more effective response.

THE HIV–AIDS INTERVENTION AMONG SEX WORKERS IN SONAGACHI, KOLKATA: HOW A CULTURAL LENS IMPROVED DEVELOPMENT EFFECTIVENESS

The second case comes from Kolkata (Calcutta), India, which has been the site of one of the most remarkable transformations among sex workers in recent history.[2] Sex work is arguably even more stigmatized in India than in most parts of the world because of strong social restrictions on sexual behaviors. Women who become sex workers are considered to have fallen into a life of shame. Only about 10% enter the profession voluntarily; most are forced into it either because of poverty, abandonment, or violence by husbands or other family problems (Sleightholme and Sinha 1996). The sex workers are almost always part of a brothel under the ownership of a madam or pimp.

Sonagachi is Kolkata's oldest and best established red-light district, with over 4,000 sex workers working in 370 brothels that service about 20,000 clients a day (All India Institute of Hygiene and Public Health 1997). Because of the intense level of stigma, Sonagachi is a world unto itself, and sex workers have developed their own subculture.[3] There are elites— madams and pimps—often tied to criminal mafias, and an associated set of actors—tea shop owners, restaurants, babysitters (usually retired sex workers)—who provide a hinterland of social and economic support. Stigma induces several strategies to acquire respectability. One of the most common is a form of marriage where women associate themselves with long-term clients called *babus* (who may themselves have "respectable" wives and children living elsewhere) even though they remain active in the profession. This sex worker subculture is self-contained, shaped by a pervasive sense of exclusion from the mainstream, and conditioned by the market for sex work—selling a diversity of services to different clients for a range of prices.

Until the 1990s, interventions in Sonagachi tended to reflect the values of the middle-class bureaucrats who crafted them. They focused on "rehabilitating" the sex workers, "rescuing" them, and taking them to shelters for training in income-generating activities such as tailoring, in an attempt to wean them away from sex work. This usually did not work. The (relatively) high earnings in sex work (Rao et al. 2003), and the harassment and discrimination faced by former sex workers in the world outside Sonagachi, led most women to return to prostitution.

With the onset of the AIDS crisis, public health workers had serious concerns about the potential for sex workers to become vectors for the disease.[4] In this context, the All India Institute for Hygiene and Public Health, led by Dr. Smarajit Jana, initiated a new intervention in Sonagachi in 1992. They began by treating sex workers with respect, as individuals who went about the ordinary business of life, practicing a profession that happened to have unique occupational hazards. After spending many months in the community providing basic health services, Dr. Jana and his team established a good relationship based on mutual respect with the sex workers as well as the pimps, madams, and clients. In the process, the medical team gained a deep understanding of Sonagachi's subculture and of the power structures that dominated it.

Gradually, by 1993, Dr. Jana, through a process of trial and error and in consultation with the sex workers, developed an innovative strategy to increase AIDS awareness and condom use that emerged from a profound awareness of Sonagachi's cultural logic. It was extremely simple and yet very effective. Instead of using health extension workers to spread the message, which was the conventional practice in Indian public health interventions, Dr. Jana decided to train a small group of twelve sex workers as peer educators to pass on information to their coworkers. The only thing that distinguished peer educators from other sex workers were green medical coats worn over their saris when they engaged in public health functions. The green coats also gave the peer-educators a sense of self-worth and a "respectable" identity. But at the same time, as members of the community, they were permitted easy access to brothels and had the credibility associated with being intimately aware of the hazards of the profession.

This process of educating the sex workers and mobilizing them for HIV-AIDS intervention, along with the increasing media attention brought about by the success of the project, led, over a period of two or three years, to a metamorphosis in the sex workers' aspirations. They founded a union to fight for legalization, reduction in police harassment, and other rights. Public events, such as festivals, cultural programs, and health fairs, were routinely organized by them, which contributed to the process of mobilization and the removal of stigma. The program was also remarkably successful as a health intervention, with almost all sex workers using condoms at least some of the time. As a result, HIV incidence in Sonagachi was about 6% in 1999 compared to 50% in other red-light areas (including Mumbai's) that did not pursue such a culturally attuned approach.

The Sonagachi project is thus an example of an intervention where a deep understanding of the local subculture and coordination with the community led to a project design that was extremely effective in meeting its objectives: containing the spread of HIV. It also generated positive externalities by increasing aspirations, reducing stigma, and mobilizing the community in a manner that led to a cultural transformation.

These cases illustrate a number of themes that will be taken up in this chapter and the rest of the book. A culturally aware approach to public action pays attention to factors that may be common sense to the intended beneficiaries but are often exotic, irrelevant, or irrational from the perspective of the policy maker. Ignorance of this contextualized notion of common sense, which James Scott (1998) calls *metis*, has been endemic among policy makers in government and in development institutions. As Scott masterfully demonstrates, by ignoring *metis*, policy makers impose a structured and formulaic set of interventions on societies that ill serve the purpose of improving well-being. Common sense, understood as part of a cultural system (Geertz 1983), is a way of providing a knowledge base that shapes how people understand themselves and provides stability to human interaction. The example of Sonagachi illustrates that an intervention that pays attention to *metis*, by taking pains to understand the local context, and that is able to foster a shift in collective identity in a direction that builds collective aspirations, can be very successful. The flip side of that, illustrated by the example of famine relief in the Sudan, is that an intervention that ignores social norms and imposes a view of the world that is external to the target group can be particularly ineffective.

A culturally informed perspective is thus not so much a prescription as it is a lens—a way of seeing. It sees individuals as driven by a culturally influenced set of motives, incentives, beliefs, and identities that interact with economic incentives to affect outcomes. It sees the initiator of public action—which could be the government, a nongovernmental organization, or an external donor—as not only a change agent, but also as part of the unequal relations that inhere within donor-beneficiary relationships. We believe that incorporating this lens into more conventional economic ways of understanding will, in many situations, lead to more effective policy.

Next, we review some of the ways in which anthropologists, economists, and other social scientists have conceptualized the link between culture and development and briefly sketch the history of how these concepts have been implemented in development practice.

Reviewing the Context: A Brief Overview of the Conceptual and Practical Foundations of the Role of Culture in Development

CULTURE IN DEVELOPMENT THOUGHT

It is beyond the scope of this introductory chapter to provide an exhaustive history of the role of culture in development thinking—Lourdes Arizpe (in this volume) provides an admirable introduction to the role of anthropology in development from the perspective of the UN and the World Bank, as do Haggis and Schech with their more academic focus (Haggis and Schech 2000).[5] Surveys of thought in economic development can similarly be found in Ray (1998) and Basu (1997). What we will instead do is to briefly sketch the work of a few key thinkers to place the contributions to this book in perspective.

Two extreme views tend to dominate the rhetoric on culture and development. The first is a hypermodernist perspective, most recently exemplified in the work of Harrison (2000), Huntington (2000),[6] and Landes (2000a) that "culture matters" because societies steeped in traditional cultures are unsuited to market-oriented development and are thus fundamentally hampered in their pursuit of growth. In this variant of Huntington's "clash of civilizations" hypothesis, poverty and low rates of growth are deeply affected by adverse rules and norms that reduce incentives for mobility and investment (Huntington 1998). The challenge for development is then to reform culture by inculcating more growth- and mobility-oriented perspectives through education or other means of transforming "toxic cultures."[7] Culture here is the enemy—a voice from the past that inhibits societies from functioning in the modern world. Max Weber's thesis on the particular suitability of the Calvinist ethic to capitalism is often evoked, incorrectly, as the distinguished progenitor of this perspective. In fact, Weber, in his celebrated *Protestant Ethic and the Spirit of Capitalism* (1930) was not outlining a causal relationship between Calvinism and capitalism, but merely demonstrating that historically there was an "elective affinity"[8] between them. This is a more subtle argument that does not reduce into the practical diagnosis, implicitly advocated by Harrison and Huntington and others, that infusing more Calvinist values into nonwestern cultures would improve their potential for growth.

At the other extreme are the cultural critics of development (Ferguson 1990, Escobar 1995). Arturo Escobar (1995), for instance, applies techniques of deconstruction, in the tradition of Michel Foucault, to study development as a cultural system, focusing in particular on how economists shaped the modernization perspectives that have dominated development since the 1950s. This dominance is taken to be an aspect of neo-colonialism whereby western ideologies and interests have created a "mechanism of control" that led to the "creation" of the Third World. To Escobar, economists, and through them the IMF and World Bank, are the primary culprits in constructing a development discourse that reified the distinctions between the North and the South which had emerged from the colonial era. Culture here is seen as a system of control that creates and extends existing "macro" inequalities between rich and poor countries, and "micro" inequalities between westernized and indigenous groups in poorer countries.

We do not wish to characterize what we have labeled "extreme" perspectives as extremist, but rather as extreme bounds along a continuum of views. We do not dismiss the idea that there is a culture of development associated with dominant mainstream economic views in the development discourse, and that this has had a powerful, and not always positive, effect on the world's poorer countries. Nor do we reject the idea that culture and history may affect the manner in which societies adapt to markets. However, we take a more moderate middle ground. In our view, Escobar's Foucauldian take on development leaves little room for thinking constructively about how to integrate notions of cultural and economic change to design more effective public action, whereas the "culture matters" perspective exemplified by Harrison and Huntington is overly static and simplistic in its diagnosis of the development problem, with culture treated as an exogenous constraint rather than as one of the realms of everyday life.

The middle ground that we seek has a long and distinguished history that can traced as far back as Smith, Marx, and Weber[9] for whom the social, economic, and moral realms were inextricably linked in understanding the determinants of human well-being. Although disciplinary specialization in the social sciences began in the late 19th century, it was arguably only in the second half of the 20th century that it reached an acute state. However, even within the polarized disciplinary worlds of the postwar era, there were pioneering efforts to find a space within the intersection of economic and social life. Perhaps the most noteworthy in its attempt to influence public action was Albert Hirschman's *Exit, Voice and Loyalty* (1970), which established the three words in the title as central themes in thinking about how cultural and social factors affected the development process.

Frustration with the lack of interdisciplinary communication, particularly in thinking about development policy, led to efforts to facilitate a dialogue across disciplines on development topics. At a conceptual level, WIDER sponsored an influential collection of essays edited by an economist and anthropologist, Stephen Marglin and Frederique Apfel Marglin, which examined economic development as a cultural process (Marglin and Marglin 1990). At an empirical level, Pranab Bardhan edited a pioneering book that brought anthropologists and economists together to conduct a conversation on the measurement of economic and social change in rural India (Bardhan 1989). However, culture, as Kuper (1999) points out, is the "special subject" of anthropology,[10] and in order to illustrate what we mean by a disciplinary middle ground, we will highlight the efforts of three key cultural anthropologists—Mary Douglas, Clifford Geertz, and Arjun Appadurai—to reach out and actively engage with economists.

Mary Douglas, with her classic work on rituals and taboo and the anthropology of the body, and later on a more general form of cultural analysis known as cultural theory, has been among the most influential anthropologists of the postwar period and has actively collaborated and debated with economists throughout her career (Douglas 1966/1984, 1973/1982). With Baron Isherwood, she provided a theory of preference formation that was integrated with economic theories of consumption, and in the process, she provided a cultural theory of goods and markets (Douglas and Isherwood 1979/1996). In her joint work with Aaron Wildavsky, she developed an anthropological theory of risk to bring in cultural notions to a subject that had until then been dominated by statistically grounded individualistic perspectives from economics and the decision sciences (Douglas and Wildavsky 1982).

Clifford Geertz, another iconic figure among anthropologists, has also regularly engaged with economists. He is renowned for his seminal contributions to theories of culture and symbolic interaction (Geertz 1973b), but he was also an early proponent of the use of the (then) new economic tools of game theory and information economics to model cultural phenomena, particularly in the context of development (Geertz 1978).

Among the next generation of anthropologists, Arjun Appadurai has conversed with economists on issues of data collection (Appadurai 1989) and the moral dimensions of economic change (Appadurai 1990). He edited a seminal collection of articles by historians and anthropologists that argued that "commodities, like persons, have social lives" (Appadurai 1986). By emphasizing the transition from social to economic value, his work sheds new light on the relationship between exchange and value. More recently, he has provided a way of extending our understanding of global exchanges by integrating the nature of economic flows with the flows of ideas, people, technologies, and information (Appadurai 1996).[11]

From the other side, some economists have also made influential efforts at constructing a bridge across disciplines in thinking about development. Perhaps the most important is Amartya Sen's reinterpretation of the meaning of development, which has provided much of the intellectual rationale for the movement toward a more holistic vision for development. For most economists, the goal of development has long been the maximization of material well-being. Sen interpreted well-being much more broadly in terms of a person's "capabilities"—the potential she or he has to convert entitlements over goods and services into a range of "functionings"—or all the various things a person may value doing or being.[12] The translation of potential into functionings is a product of active choice by the individual as an agent—"as someone who acts and brings about change" in economic, social, and political domains, making use of their capabilities, and indeed influencing personal and public action in ways that determine the future formation of capabilities. The extent to which such agency can be effective depends on the broader institutional context, and especially the extent to which the political, governmental, and social institutions of a society allow for all agents to have an influence. An emblematic statement of this linkage was Sen's comment that a famine has never occurred in a functioning democracy with a free press.

Work in institutional economics, associated in particular with Douglass North and Avner Greif, integrates the tools of economic, historical, and cultural analysis. Institutions—defined as the "rules of a game in a society or, more formally, the humanly devised constraints that shape human interaction"—are, it is argued, the key determinant of economic change (North 1990, 3).[13] Development policy has tended to focus on formal institutions while paying much less attention to informal institutions[14] that shape what North calls the "informal constraints" that "come from socially transmitted information and are a part of the heritage that we call culture" (North 1990, 37). To North, informal constraints form the "governing structure" "defined by codes of conduct, norms of behavior, and conventions," which shape our "daily interaction with others, whether within the family, in external social relations, or in business activities" (36). Greif translates some of these notions into game-theoretic models (Greif 1994a,b). His most influential work compares "individualist" Genovese traders with "collectivist" Maghribis in medieval Mediterranean trading networks and shows why individualists were more likely to develop formal institutional enforcement mechanisms to manage their activities, whereas collectivists were more likely to develop informal systems, concluding that individualist cultures are more conducive to the development of formal property rights.

Although Geertz was perhaps the first to model the link between culture and the transmission of information (Geertz 1978), a broad literature, pioneered by George Akerlof and by Joseph Stiglitz, recognizes the centrality of relational problems of coordination and of information in economic life (Akerlof 1984; Hoff and Stiglitz 2000). This is especially important because, from a functionalist perspective, many informal institutions, including cultural practices and social norms, can be seen as responses to problems of coordination and information asymmetry. This has become a central concern of recent work in economics that has developed and extended problems of information transmission, coordination, and social interaction to examine a variety of subjects. These include social conformity (Bernheim 1994), ethnic diversity (Alesina and La Ferrara 2003), poverty traps (Durlauf 2002), segregation (Bénabou 1993), and fads (Bikhchandani, Hirshleifer, and Welch 1992). Because such topics continue to be the focus of cutting-edge research in economics, instead of attempting a review of this burgeoning literature here, we briefly revisit it in the conclusion and in the Web site associated with this book.[15]

Looking at the links between culture and economic behavior, however, also requires an understanding of how preferences are formed—an issue that, until recently, most of economics chose to assume away.[16] Economists have now begun to address preference formation in at least two different ways: as part of an evolutionary process, or as the result of fundamental changes in opportunity costs. Evolutionary models of preference formation are "functional" in the sociological sense, attributing the dominance of one set of preferences to fundamental factors that relate to human survivability (Bergstrom 2002). In the opportunity cost approach, pioneered by Becker and Stigler (1977), consumers have stable preferences for a fundamental set of goods, related to what Sen would call functionings. These functionings have "production functions" that affect their relative prices. For instance, a person may have a fundamental preference for "good food," but because good food is a cultivated taste, the type of food she eats will be affected by the type of "food capital" she acquires. If we have a higher level of food capital for French haute cuisine compared to hamburgers, perhaps because our parents were gourmets, we are much more likely to enjoy it. However, if the relative "price" of producing haute cuisine capital falls—say, because of food shows on TV, then it becomes easier to enjoy, and more people will consume it. Therefore, in the Becker and Stigler model, cultural change is a function of relative prices.[17]

Economists are methodological individualists—where the individual is the analytical unit—and interactive relationships with others typically result from some form of linked or interdependent preferences, information transmission technologies, or strategic interactions. Issues of relationality, however, have been addressed for much longer by anthropologists and sociologists, albeit under different labels and analytical frames. Anthropologists and sociologists, particularly those schooled in the Durkheimian tradition, more commonly start from a perspective in which a person's belief systems, dispositions, and behaviors are conditioned and embedded within the group to which they belong. In other words, they adhere to "methodological holism" where the unit of analysis is not an individual but a group. Individuals, like the cyborgs in *Star Trek*, are so deeply conditioned by their group membership that one cannot really think of autonomous individual actors or identities (Douglas and Ney 1998b). This emphasis on the primacy of social structure has been extended by social theorists such as Talcott Parsons and Pierre Bourdieu to allow more room for individual agency, but the relatively greater emphasis on structure still gives social theory, with all its diverse perspectives, an analytical apparatus that is distinct from economics.[18]

Bourdieu's work has particular relevance to understanding how culture affects poverty and the reproduction of inequality. Much of his core thinking begins with what he calls *habitus*, which can be thought of as the set of durable principles—practices, beliefs, taboos, rules, representations, rituals, symbols, and so on—that provide a group of individuals with a sense of group identity and a consequent feeling of security and belonging.[19] Bourdieu argues that this varies systematically across groups. To quote David Swartz interpreting Bourdieu: "Habitus tends to shape individual action so that existing opportunity structures are perpetuated. Chances of success or failure are internalized and then transformed into individual aspirations or expectations; these are then in turn externalized in action that tends to reproduce the objective structure of life chances" (Swartz 2000, 103). An economist may find it helpful to think of this internalization of the perceived possibility of success or failure as a *constraining preference* that interacts with exogenous constraints to affect human action.

To illustrate what we mean by *constraining preferences*, let's take the example of a taboo—a proscription against certain types of behavior. The incest taboo, for example, is a feature of most human societies. Most people would not consider breaking it, not just because of fear of social sanctions, but simply because the taboo is so deeply ingrained within their psyches. Thus the taboo is simultaneously an inherent preference against incest and a social constraint.[20] Although the joint production of preferences and constraints is particularly clear in the example of taboos, it is in the same sense that we refer to culturally produced dispositions, beliefs, and behaviors in the habitus as leading to constraining preferences. For instance, preferences derived from the Hindu caste system may create an acceptance of hierarchy and constrain the motivation for mobility, but these beliefs are also simultaneously external constraints; individuals from lower castes who engage in class struggle may face severe social sanctions (we expand on this point below).[21] Thus, culture not only provides a way to classify *other groups*, but for members of a group to differentiate *themselves* from others. A disadvantaged group can view its status within the hierarchy as correct and appropriate. By positioning a group within the social hierarchy, consequently, culture affects their sense of the possible. For those at the high end of the hierarchy, it provides the means to maintain their high position, whereas for those at the low end, it can limit aspirations, create discrimination, and block mobility. As Bourdieu argues, culture, therefore, is a form of capital.

Bourdieu's conception of cultural capital represents an extension of the idea of capital to all forms of culturally derived power.[22] Cultural, social, and symbolic resources can be drawn on by individuals and groups in order to maintain and enhance their position in the social order. As in the case of physical capital, these are valued resources and often become objects of struggle. According to Bourdieu, cultural capital has three states: it can be *embodied*, as "the ensemble of cultivated dispositions that are internalized by the individual through socialization and that constitute schemes of appreciation and understanding"; it can be *objectified*, as books, music, scientific instruments, and so on, that require cultural capital for their use; and it can be *institutionalized* in the credentialing systems of educational establishments (Bourdieu 1990; Swartz 2000). Once cultural capital is embodied and institutionalized, it can be accessed by others within the group. It can also be used as a form of domination. Bourdieu calls this use of capital "symbolic violence," where dominant groups have the capacity to "impose the means of comprehending and adapting to the social world by representing economic and political power in disguised, taken-for-granted forms" (Swartz 2000, 89).

Bourdieu distinguishes between the different influences that social capital and cultural capital have on inequality.[23] Social capital emphasizes the social networks available to people to access and mobilize resources, and contributes to inequality because elites are able to access internal and external social networks that are more powerful and wealthy. By contrast, the poor have less influential networks that, although helping them cope with the vicissitudes of life, restrict their chances for mobility. Different groups within a social system can have different types of social capital, and because it can be bequeathed, it plays an important role in the reproduction of inequality. It is contextualized—because it comingles with habitus and cultural capital. It can be used for constructive purposes—to facilitate collective action or to improve economic productivity—but also for destructive purposes by perpetuating symbolic or actual violence.[24]

Here we should make an immediate clarification. There is a tradition of work on the "culture of poverty" that attributes the persistence of poverty to the cultural attributes of poor groups. As discussed in this volume by both Mary Douglas and Lourdes Arizpe, such "blame the victim" types of poverty diagnoses have not proved fruitful, either on empirical or ethical grounds.[25] Poor people display a remarkable capacity to adjust to extraordinarily difficult circumstances, and it is incorrect to characterize their poverty as deriving from some unchangeable, inherited attribute. However, it is the case that conditions of poverty and inequality can be a product of cultural processes, and culture, economic conditions, and power can interact to sustain disadvantage. This can be demonstrated by two classic examples: caste and race.

Let us expand on the idea of the Hindu caste system that we touched on.

above. The French anthropologist Louis Dumont (1970), in his seminal but hotly debated work on caste, argued that it exemplifies *Homo Hierarchicus*—where a belief in the rightness of the caste hierarchy is deeply internalized by both upper *and lower* castes (Dumont 1970).[26] In Dumont's view, Hindu beliefs, perpetuated by Brahmin upper castes, attribute the station of a person's birth to the stock of his or her rightness of conduct in previous lives—in other words, to the person's karma. Persons born very low in the caste hierarchy deeply internalize this hierarchy and do little to question it, because they lack an ideology of equality. Any sense of mobility then derives only by behaving according to the conduct ordained for one's particular caste and station, which builds up the stock of good karma and increases the chances of having a more satisfactory birth in the next life. This perpetuates the caste hierarchy with little dissent. Constraining preferences, which are a function of the dominant ideology, foster an internalized acceptance of one's low (or high) birth.

The second example comes from the economist Glenn Loury's work on the perpetuation of racial inequalities in the United States. Loury has assessed the range of mechanisms that underlie persistent differences in well-being between blacks and whites. These are reflected in significantly higher mortality rates for blacks, poverty, victimization, incarceration, and teenage pregnancy. Race is interpreted as a socially constructed phenomenon in which "inheritable body markings . . . have come to be invested in a particular society at a given historical moment with social meaning."[27] Persistent racial differences have to be understood in terms of "the tacit presumption of an essentialist cause for racial inequality, ascribing to blacks the virtual social identity that they are, in some sense, 'damaged goods' " (Loury 2002a, 159). This can work in many ways. Racial stereotyping can help explain how rational responses linked to race can lead to self-confirming patterns of behavior, in interactions between members of the same and different groups, whether in work, on the street, or at school.[28] This can be reflected in the norms and behaviors within poorer black communities, for example in patterns of behavior that are valued on the street that are associated with violence, early sexual initiation, and teenage pregnancy. These preferences and behaviors are not a consequence of a pre-existing "culture of poverty" of the group, but of the historical processes that produced them.[29] The perpetuation of difference, especially in the developmental disadvantage faced by blacks, has to be explained by stigma that "inclines one to look for insidious habits of thought, selective patterns of social intercourse, biased processes of social cognition, and defective public deliberations when seeking a cure" (Loury 2002, 168).

As this brief review shows, although economists and social theorists come from different methodological traditions, developments in both fields have begun to emphasize the implications of relational behavior for the distribution of income and power, and for economic action more generally. This offers the possibility for a constructive cross-disciplinary dialogue, away from the old debates on the relative virtues of methodological individualism and holism to a more fundamental interchange about how best to conceptualize the nexus between social structure and individual action in human agency and how this sheds light on the causes of human deprivation. It is at this level of dialogue that we hope the contributions to this volume can be placed.

THE EVOLUTION OF DEVELOPMENT PRACTICE

We turn next, briefly, to development practice where a number of strands parallel the patterns of thought described above. As Arizpe discusses in her contribution, the UN system has been a central domain for discourse over culture, a discourse that reflects a tension between the universalistic principles of the founders and the practical realities of a club of members with diverse cultures. Attempts to resolve the tension have taken the form of declaring a set of universal rights and principles (some of which seem inconsistent with the "cultures" of its members) and, at the same time, declaring the equal claim of every diverse culture to be respected. A similar ambivalence is seen in the allocation of responsibility for culture to one agency—United Nations Educational Scientific and Cultural Organization (UNESCO)—rather than seeing culture as affecting most of the UN's areas of concern. Although UNESCO is perhaps best known for its work on cultural heritage, it has also contributed to important syntheses of the role of culture, involving respect for diversity and interactions with markets, that are consistent with the themes here (UNESCO 1998). Meanwhile, in its Human Development Reports, the United Nations Development Program (UNDP) has helped popularize Sen's broadened conception of ends and means in the development process.

Within some development agencies, there has long been a practical recognition that good development practice needs to take account of social factors. For example, many European bilaterals—including those from the Nordic countries, the Dutch, and the British—have both advocated and supported attention to social and political conditions. This was facilitated by the work of development anthropologists and sociologists who played an influential role in pressing for more culturally sensitive and socially aware form of policy making (Hoben 1982; Cernea 1984). Also important was the focused attention on respecting the cultures of indigenous groups in the design of policy and projects that might affect them—

with the development of specific guidelines on approaches to engage and debate with such groups (see the chapter by Sabina Alkire). By the second half of the 1990s, World Bank practice was illustrative of broader trends in international development, with widespread use of participation in a range of sectors—from water to social funds—rising attention to issues of social capital, increasing use of participatory research within country-based poverty analyses, and more recently a scaling up of community-based development.[30] Culture as a concept began to make inroads into thinking about policy (Serageldin and Tabaroff 1994) and was explicitly developed as a theme by James Wolfensohn, president of the World Bank (Wolfensohn 1998).

Many of these patterns in thought and practice were synthesized in the World Bank's millennial World Development Report on poverty (World Bank 2001b). This report introduced the concept of empowerment as one of the central pillars of poverty-focused development. To a significant extent, these conceptions merely caught up with thinking that had been current in the UNDP's Human Development Reports for several years. As part of the background work for the 2001 World Development report, the World Bank supervised a broad compilation of participatory research in the "Voices of the Poor," attempting to signal a cultural shift in the World Bank's practice toward seeking to listen rather than to tell.[31]

There remains, however, a large gap between how culture in the development process has been conceptualized and implemented. Cultural notions, sometimes informed more by concerns that arise in the course of managing a project than by the scholarship on the subject, are now routinely incorporated in practice. Yet despite the important exceptions noted above, academic anthropologists seem focused on critiquing development rather than engaging with it constructively. And policy economists, for the most part, either treat culture as emblematic of a tradition-bound constraint on the development process, or ignore it altogether. Summarizing the contributions to this volume, we now turn to some ideas on how to close the gap in both thinking and practice.

The Links Between Culture and Human Well-Being:
Learning from the Contributions to this Volume

Amartya Sen, in the opening chapter, provides an overview of the role of culture in development.[32] He extends his work on capability, freedom, and agency by moving the discussion from *why* culture matters to *how* it matters, both in the ends and means of development. Culture is a constitutive part of the good life and a constructive factor in how life is valued.

It is also an instrumental influence on the behavior of individuals, firms, and governments. He shows how the deterministic view of culture's impact on development, as exemplified by Harrison and Huntington, is inconsistent with the historical record. Societies with distinct cultural experiences have shown a capacity to adapt to new demands and opportunities within the development process, including the demands of capitalist development in an integrating world. But this does not imply that culture does not matter or is simply malleable to material conditions. At a point in time, culture can have a potent influence on the behaviors of groups, of businesses,[33] and of the state, for good and ill. Culture also affects how countries interact with one another. Interaction and trade between countries and the hybrid cultures that result can significantly improve the quality of life.[34] But when trade occurs within global asymmetries of power, then there are two obvious reactions—"submissive supplication," where the economically powerful culture dominates the less powerful one; or a withdrawal into an imagined authentic identity as a resistance to globalization. Both are less preferable to a process of "free and informed choice, aided by public discussion, critical scrutiny, and a participatory political environment." Furthermore, it is important to focus on the "institutional demands for cultural democracy"—basic education, free media, and free participation via elections and basic civil rights.

Arjo Klamer, in his essay, builds on one of Sen's points that culture is an end in itself—a factor in the construction of value. He focuses on the ability of culture to inspire, express, and symbolize collective memory and identity. Although he focuses on cultural products, this has more general application. A cultural lens permits a recognition of this value in a country's heritage—its monuments, museums, sacred sites, and expressive and artistic traditions. They contribute directly to well-being in more than an economic sense. This presents a particular development challenge: how do we assess the inherent value of culture?[35] To what extent should a country invest in taking care of its cultural heritage? The question is particularly difficult for a poor country facing trade-offs in its ability to provide basic necessities of life such as good health, education, and jobs. As Sen argues, sometimes entities with an inherent cultural value may also have an economic value—for example, as tourist sites—but there remains a need to assess their cultural value independent of their economic worth. Klamer emphasizes the centrality of interactions between different actors in the development of valuations within social groups. This echoes a broader theme of the book on the role of debate, participation, and deliberation to make choices.[36]

It is important to keep in mind, however, that the valuation of cultural

goods may differ considerably across social classes and the deliberate prop-
agation of culture and heritage goods that are primarily consumed by the
elite may help reproduce inequality by reinforcing economic hierarchies
with cultural distinctions. Thus, if one of the goals of development is to
reduce the incidence of poverty and inequality, access to cultural goods
should be distributed equally to all groups and classes. Similarly, a monument or a sacred site may be politically charged, a symbol of great importance to a subculture that seeks to become dominant and simultaneously
a symbol of oppression to another group. On the other hand, as Sen points
out, they can also be potent symbols of tolerance. Thus, precisely because
they have a value beyond the economic, cultural goods can have externalities that are both good and bad. Policy makers should take care to understand these externalities well before committing resources to their propa-
gation or preservation.

Mary Douglas provides a new synthesis of her thinking on Cultural
Theory to examine the coproduction of preferences and constraints in the
perpetuation of poverty, and Marco Verweij, in his appendix to the chapter, provides some applications of Cultural Theory to development topics.
Douglas's chapter can be seen as a critique (or an extension) of some
thinking on institutions by economists. She employs a fourfold "grid-
group" classification of subcultures ranging in increasing order from weak
groups to strong groups on the x-axis, and descending from strong grids
(hierarchical structures) to weak grids on the y-axis. Therefore, a subculture on the bottom left cell with a weak grid and weak group would be
"individualist." A subculture on the upper right cell with strong grid and
strong group would be "hierarchical." Douglas argues that her fourfold
classification presents a way out of the methodological individualism/
holism debate because it permits strategy and action to occur within a
social structure, and she critiques the individualist-collectivist dichotomy
prevalent in the work of economists such as Greif and North as incomplete. She further argues that most human societies can be sorted in terms
of their mix of subcultures within this grid-group framework, and that the
interaction and coexistence of their subcultures forms a useful way to
understand the "joint production of meaning" in a society, because the
cells are constantly in a process of contestation, coordination, and collaboration. One possible equilibrium in this process is when "connecting
networks" between the four cells break down—when "trust has been
betrayed, when disappointment has replaced hope," or "when the freedom
to choose has been eliminated." This can lead to a "culture of apathy" that
is "completely incapable of development." Understanding this culture of
apathy is therefore key to understanding the link between culture and

development, and intercultural dialogue is absolutely essential to foster the development process.

In response to Douglas's critique of work in economics, an economist could reasonably say that putting ideas into concise and parsimonious game-theoretic models, as Greif and others do, necessarily requires a compromise toward simplicity. Therefore, Douglas's critique may be a critique of a modeling strategy rather than a paradigm. As Greif, Chwe (2001), and others have shown, game theory, although based on methodological individualism, can still provide powerful explanations of social phenomena, and future work by economists may well come closer to Douglas's multidimensional conception of social and cultural life.

In a different take on what we have called "constraining preferences," Timur Kuran, in this volume and elsewhere (Kuran 1995b), argues that the constraint is not internalized values and preferences, but a suppression of voice. The preferences of groups who are less vocal, but perhaps in the majority, could be suppressed because of "preference falsification," where an unwillingness to engage with a more aggressively enforced dominant perspective restricts their ability to express their true beliefs. In order to avoid the sanctions that come from expressing a perspective that could lead to confrontation, groups with less voice simply lie. This suggests the need for a process of discovery of what different groups believe and value, and a recognition of where there are genuine choices to be made. Kuran's example of a more liberal majority in Islamic societies being silenced by the voices of a radical minority is clearly a case of preference falsification. "Man in the street" interviews conducted by journalists in repressive dictatorships where the interviewees express strong support for the regime are another. When those beliefs are internalized and become part of the value system of all groups, we would call them constraining preferences.

Carol Jenkins provides another arena where such forms of external, and internalized, discrimination and stigma can affect public policy. She examines the recent history of HIV-AIDS, and action to deal with this epidemic, from the perspective of two cultures that lie at the center of both the spread of the epidemic and the shaping of public action to deal with it: the wide variety of sexual subcultures, and the culture of injecting drug users. This is a powerful example for this volume, not only because of the importance of the HIV-AIDS epidemic, but because of its documentation of the nature of subcultures of weak or underrepresented groups and of how these are typically unrecognized or stigmatized by mainstream society. This stigma contributes to the perpetuation of the epidemic. In a vivid demonstration of a broader phenomenon, Jenkins shows how policy interventions are ineffective because dominant actors impose interventions on excluded groups that reflect their biases and stereotypes. Effective approaches, such as those in Sonagachi, would recognize the internal cultural logic of groups at high risk for HIV-AIDS transmission, and engage with affected people directly in a manner that does not require "a slavish adherence to traditional codes."

Note that although cultural and economic factors can mutually reinforce inequality and power differences and make them resistant to change, this does not mean that cultural and economic structures remain static. Mobility and change exist even in the most rigid societies. Household survey data in developed and developing countries have established, for instance, that there can be significant movement up and down the income scale, even while the overall distribution remains stable.[37] Entire groups may also demonstrate collective mobility, but the pace of this is typically glacial. For instance, in the caste system, Srinivas (1966) explores how caste mobility occurs in the form of an identity dynamic where upwardly mobile lower castes gradually acquire the behaviors, markings, and other external attributes of upper castes, so that over the long run, they are indistinguishable from them. The memory of their original lower caste status gradually fades. But this mobility occurs not by challenging the dominant ideology, but by a gradual process of identity switching that results in an ideological transformation. The newly minted upper caste group often loses all memory of ever being lower caste. Its preferences now reflect those of upper castes.[38]

Moreover, constraining preferences do not necessarily impose a passive acceptance of fate on poor and subordinate groups—and resistance is itself often a cultural process. Staying within the caste system, an example of this is in the Virasaiva or Lingayat movement founded by the poet-saint Basava in the 12th century in Karnataka in southern India. Opposition to heredity-based caste discrimination was the explicitly stated ideology of the movement, and this was expressed in a series of devotional poems, or *vacanas*, that created a space within the Hindu way of life that went beyond caste-based divisions. A well-known poem by Basava says, "Oh Look Not to Caste! For who could say, anyway, what he had been in birth's past" (Michael 1992). Thus, Virasaivasism rejected caste by arguing that God does not differentiate across groups.[39] So long as people at both ends of the hierarchy buy into this ideological argument, group-based divisions can be circumvented without conflict—but this is typically not the case.

Scott (1985), drawing on a study of the beliefs and behaviors of Malaysian peasants, has argued that the lack of overt activism by subordinate groups does not necessarily reflect acceptance of the existing social order. Although the poor may view the constraints that they face as inevitable and internalize them, they may also have a strong sense that the status quo is unjust. Scott argues that it is important to distinguish what they view as *just* from what they view as *possible*. This sense of injustice, coupled with a recognition of the inevitability of fate, results in subtle, "everyday" forms of resistance that serve to moderate the authority of dominant groups without completely overturning the system.[40] Moreover, resistance has over the centuries often turned to revolution—as can be seen in the history of social movements, protests, and revolts that have sought to overturn existing social systems. In the Indian context, for instance, 20th-century social movements have confronted caste differentials in favor of more equitable public action, most notably in Kerala (Heller 1999).

Arjun Appadurai's contribution to this volume, cognizant of this potential for mobility and resistance, conceptualizes a way out of constraining preferences or "cultures of apathy"—to use Douglas' term. Building on the work of the philosopher Charles Taylor on the "politics of recognition," he coins a phrase—"the terms of recognition"—to describe the adverse terms by which the poor negotiate with the "norms that frame their social lives." To correct this imbalance, he suggests there is a need to strengthen the capacity of the poor to exercise "voice," treating voice as a cultural capacity—because it is not just a matter of inculcating democratic norms, but of engaging in social, political, and economic issues in terms of metaphor, rhetoric, organization, and public performance that work best in their cultural worlds. The cultural contexts in which different groups live form the framework of what he calls the "capacity to aspire," which is not evenly distributed. "The better off you are . . . the more likely you are to be conscious of the links between the more and less immediate objects of aspiration."[41] This is partly because the better off are better able to navigate their way toward potentially actualizing their aspirations. Thus, the capacity to aspire is, at its core, a "navigational capacity." Voice and the capacity to aspire are "reciprocally linked," with each accelerating the nurture of the other. Development then is about empowerment which has an "obvious translation: increase the capacity to aspire, especially for the poor."

For an economist, one way of understanding Appadurai's concepts is to incorporate the Becker-Stigler "opportunity cost" approach to preference change within anthropological understandings that emphasize the collective aspects of preference formation. For someone born into a social group that faces high levels of social exclusion, discrimination, and material poverty, social interactions are geared toward survival and interactions within one's own group. The opportunity cost of a culture of aspiration and change may be high. One way out of this is to reduce the opportunity cost of acquiring cultures of aspiration by facilitating collective organization in a manner that expands and reinforces cultural and social capital. The "capacity to aspire" is about how a group (and the individuals within it) succeed in reducing the costs of developing a culture of aspiration by collectively envisioning their future, and their capacity to shape this future, through influencing other groups, the government, and other factors in their physical and social environment

Although building the capacity to aspire may help break through the constraining preferences of poor groups, it does not address the problem of how different groups interact with one another within a hierarchy. Where groups have little influence and expressions of voice remain unheard or evince repression, the incentives for the development and exercise of such capacities are substantially reduced. In other words, the subordinate group faces adverse cultural terms of trade that affect its ability to aspire to a better life, while the dominant group faces favorable cultural terms of trade that gives it the ability to maintain its dominant position. This provides a way to interpret Appadurai's second concept of the "terms of recognition." When poor or subordinate groups face adverse terms of recognition from dominant groups or state structures, there is both an inhospitable environment for the development of a capacity to aspire and, to the extent that such voice-related capacities develop, their influence is reduced. The potential for increasing *effective* agency is limited.

Accomplishing this in practice sometimes requires an explicit and direct confrontation with powerful elites. In their contribution, Anita Abraham and Jean-Philippe Platteau provide an example of the difficulties in implementing projects that aim to increase the voice of the poor. They focus on the case of participatory local development, where communities are directly given funds to control and manage. From an extensive review of field experience, they argue that effects of such development techniques will be mediated by the cultural context in which they occur. In the cases of "traditional" communities, typical of much of Africa and "indigenous" communities in Latin America and elsewhere, threats to the established ascribed patterns of cultural difference are resisted by community leaders. Elites often capture resources and use them to further client-patron relationships with poorer groups. In both cases, some benefits can pass to poorer groups, but this can be attenuated or transformed by these culturally based processes. Passing resources to local communities presents a particular development challenge and is likely to have disappointing effects in accelerating development and reaching the poor unless it is designed in a way that takes account of the challenge posed by culturally embedded hierarchies. There are other examples where these hierarchies have been effectively tackled, as highlighted in Appadurai's case study of Mumbai slums or by the Sonagachi sex workers example, but they may require more long-term and contextualized approaches than those typically implemented by development agencies.

Shelton Davis contributes another account of a social movement, the Mayan movement in Guatemala, that attempted to change the terms of recognition of a disadvantaged group in an unequal society. Davis shows how the minority ladinos established their dominance by imposing various forms of political, economic, and religious control on the indigenous Mayan population. Many Mayans reacted to this domination by re-affirming their ethnicity, choosing to maintain highly traditional, religion-based community cultures, rather than "passing" for ladinos and attempting to integrate. This reaffirmation of identity then led to various Mayan resistance movements that questioned dominant interpretations of Guatemalan history and society, and by the 1990s attracted international attention with the awarding of a Nobel Peace Prize to one of their activists, Rigoberta Menchu. This had an important influence on debates surrounding the future of the country, contributing to the peace accord of 1996. It is also hopefully laying the foundation for a multiethnic, pluricultural, and multilingual nation in Guatemala. However, there has been a strong backlash from ladinos, and it is difficult to predict if the accord will ever be effectively implemented. But there is no longer any way that Guatemala can avoid the issues raised by the Mayan movement and the peace accord—and Guatemala's recent development and poverty strategies have been strongly influenced by the principles embodied in the accord. This illustrates the potential effectiveness of using social movements and democratic processes to foster debate in order to equalize culturally based inequities. It also shows that the process can be long and difficult.

Thus, changing inequalities in agency almost always involve *interactions* between groups, with the state playing a key role, either responding to pressures from below or initiating changes in the terms of recognition. This message links the culturally informed perspectives of this volume to work in political science that emphasizes the need to conceptualize change in terms of the joint interactions between state and society, in contrast to either state-centered or society-centered approaches.[42]

The contribution in this volume by Fernando Calderón and Alicia Szmukler further develops the theme, with a particular focus on the role of political cultures as either forces for the reproduction or transformation of inequalities. They argue, like Davis, that most political cultures in Latin America are deeply intertwined with structures of social and economic inequality, which form part of the mechanism for the perpetuation of inequities in income and agency. They interpret these as a product of histories of social and cultural exclusion that can sometimes be exacerbated by the workings of market forces, which leads to an argument for achieving more effective poverty reduction through patterns of cultural change that shift the terms of recognition for different groups and strengthen the voice of poorer groups through the development of "deliberative cultures." This is illustrated with some examples, and we will highlight one— the case of participatory budgeting in Porto Alegre, Brazil.[43]

Participatory budgeting is based on the principle that citizens should be directly involved in the management of public funds and should have a voice in the translation of social demands into budgetary priorities. This is done within a framework of participatory democracy where the target population every year votes on the choice of four policy priorities from a list of eight. Once the priorities are set, there is a round of open discussions, where the policies are debated and delegates chosen for the next round of deliberation. In the next round, the government presents the available budget for the following year and elects councilors to supervise and manage the budget for a one-year term. Finally, these deliberations are implemented by a planning cabinet, which allocates the budget. This process of deliberative democracy has resulted in a redistribution of funds to poor areas of the city, sharply improved the quality and reach of public works and services, and reduced corruption. Thus, providing a forum for meaningful participation and debate results in a closer connection between policy makers and beneficiaries that improves the quality of public action—making policy more commonsensical, to use Scott's term, while equalizing the terms of engagement.

Monica Das Gupta and her colleagues in their contribution explore another case where state intervention played a decisive role in cultural change. They examine the very different contemporary statuses of women in three countries—China, India, and South Korea—which started with very similar kinship and inheritance systems and, consequently, low levels of women's autonomy and agency. Korea successfully achieved rapid economic growth while maintaining fundamental aspects of family organization deeply inimical to gender equity. As a consequence, although women now have high living standards and participate extensively in the formal labor force, they have gained relatively little in autonomy, as symbolized by some of the lowest levels of female legislative representation in the world. By contrast, the Indian state has a disappointing record on raising living standards but has been fairly successful in encouraging gender equity. And the communist Chinese state made substantial strides in improving women's lives, both through raising living standards and through a synergistic mix of policies aimed at creating gender equity. It is noteworthy, however, that some of these gains are being eroded in the period after the opening toward free-market capitalism with the reaffirmation of more traditional patriarchal values. Thus, despite similar initial conditions that are culturally determined, the nature of the state intervention can make a substantial difference in the dynamics of agency.[44]

We turn finally to the role of international agencies—bilateral development agencies, multilateral development banks, and international non-government organizations. Sabina Alkire, in her contribution to this volume, explores the ethical basis for engagement in a society of an external agent, using the World Bank as a case study. An understanding of culture leads to a quite different approach to the relationship between external agents and domestic partners: from old-style advise and invest, to an emphasis on exploration and discovery of local conditions and support for participatory debate on options, including those from international experience. The World Bank has been moving significantly in this direction in many areas in recent years, but it still straddles old and new patterns of thought and engagement. Moreover, all powerful external development agencies have their own strong organizational cultures that have an impact on their deliberations and interactions. Unequal power relationships between donor organizations and their clients can result in policies that reflect the donor's domination of the interaction, with policies that reflect the careless application of current ideological fads rather than negotiations under equal terms of engagement. The role that this plays in development policy needs more attention and understanding from policy makers.

The Equality of Agency: Normative Implications of a Culturally Informed Approach to Development

The discussion so far has been essentially positive, seeking to show how a cultural lens can inform the interpretation of development processes. Normative judgments have often been implicit because these processes have been cast in terms of their impact on human well-being. In this final section, we focus on the implications of a cultural lens for the normative assessment of well-being and of policy.

Combining the terminology of Bourdieu and Sen, a group's cultural capital forms part of its capability set. But the implications of the role of culture on capability have not been fully appreciated.[45] Think of equality of opportunity, which is probably the most important guiding principle for public action toward tackling problems of inequality and discrimination—at least within democratic and market-oriented societies. Although equality of opportunity explicitly recognizes the possibility that group-based attributes may lead to discrimination, the individual is assumed to be an autonomous actor, if at times tagged to a group. In its traditional sense, it has two interpretations, according to Roemer (1998):

- The "level the playing field" view. If two individuals of equal ability are granted the same access to human and physical capital, their chances of success will depend solely on their effort. In this view, the role of policy is to improve access to schools, health care, credit, and so on.

- The nondiscrimination interpretation. Individuals competing for the same job should be judged solely on those attributes relevant to the job. This view acknowledges that individuals may have a social identity and that discrimination can result from the use of demographic characteristics as social markers, with the result that an individual of equal or superior qualifications and ability to another may be passed over because of his or her race, gender, or other group-based attribute.

A cultural lens, however, suggests that this is an incomplete way of dealing with the relational aspects of deprivation. Inequality is not just the result of an individual's affiliation with a group; it is also caused by how members within a group relate to one another and how the group relates to other groups—unequal "terms of engagement." Furthermore, equality of opportunity implicitly assumes a distinction between preferences and constraints, in arguing that human beings are primarily held back not by endogenous cultural processes, but by exogenous obstacles. Again, as we have seen above, some groups, because of the symbolic violence of dominant discriminatory ideologies, may have "constraining preferences" that restrict their "capacity to aspire." Similarly, some groups, because of problems of coordination, may lack the capacity for collective action and access to social networks that they would need to move ahead. Individuals are not just limited by obstacles to their individual effort but by *collectively* determined factors that result from ideological, cultural, historical, and social factors that are beyond their immediate control.

A cultural lens thus leads us to a different principle—"equality of agency"—which builds on "equality of opportunity" but takes into account as well the impact of the relationality of individuals, the social and cultural contexts within which they operate, and the impact of these processes on inequality and poverty. Equality of agency would propose that that in addition to providing equal access to human and physical capital, people are also entitled to equal access to, using Bourdieu's terms, cultural and social capital. But because cultural and social capital are inherently relational concepts, these require group-based interventions, along the lines sketched above, that are different from the more individual-based interventions that derive from the equality of opportunity perspective.

The normative implication of this discussion can now be pulled together. Greater equality of agency is a desirable, and often a necessary condition, for putting societies on a dynamic path toward greater equality of well-being. This is also likely to have at least neutral, and potentially positive, effects on processes of accumulation. This has two fundamental implications for public action:

- Moving from a focus on individuals to a recognition that relational and group-based phenomena shape and influence individual aspiration, capabilities, and agency.

- Providing for debate and decision making when there are several distinct culturally determined perspectives, and in particular, assure that poorer, subordinate groups have voice and opportunities for redress.

To summarize what this book sets out to do: it seeks, through a cross-disciplinary dialogue, an ideological and practical middle ground on how a cultural lens can help improve public action to alleviate human deprivation. As in any cross-disciplinary interchange, there will be different points of view, and there are some important disagreements in the perspectives represented here. For instance, Kuran, and Abraham and Platteau, have a methodologically individualist view of the world that leads to prescriptions that focus on the individual—on understanding their "true preferences" in the case of Kuran, and on freeing individuals from the yoke of oppressive elites in the case of Abraham and Platteau. Douglas, on the other hand, takes a more Durkheimian view; individuals are fundamentally socially embedded beings and are limited in their ability to influence broad trends in behavior. She therefore presents a method by which groups can be categorized and characterized in order to understand the nature of social interactions. However, as Appadurai, Sen, and others in this volume show, this divide is less acute than it might appear. In recognizing the role of culture as fundamentally dynamic, endogenous, changeable, both forward and backward looking, and affecting both the ends and means of development, we see an acceptance of the social embeddedness of economic action and of the economic embeddedness of social action. There is also deep agreement that an important implication of all this is that culture affects power relations within a society and is therefore fundamentally linked with the perpetuation of inequality.

This is a fundamental difference from previous points of view on the role of culture in development policy. The modernization perspectives that permeated development thinking in the 1950s and 1960s focused on using science and technology to break free of traditional cultures; the focus on free markets that was emphasized in the 1980s and 1990s were relatively innocent of social thought, and the views (which we call hyper-modernization) exemplified by Harrison and Huntington were led by a belief that the key to progress was to break "toxic cultures." The authors in this book would not fall into any of these perspectives. The articles in this book also provide some answers to the cultural critics of development with constructive suggestions for moving toward a culturally equitable form of development. The focus here is less on critique and more on providing a conceptual and practical basis for finding solutions to poverty and inequality.

Thus, the contributors to this volume agree on far more than what they disagree about. To some extent, this represents a shift within disciplines—economists have increasingly begun to think about the role of social and cultural interactions in human behavior, and anthropologists and sociologists have increasingly come to recognize the practical light that their disciplinary perspectives can shed on policy and positive change. It is our firm belief that in order to address the central challenge of improving development policy, economists, anthropologists, sociologists, and political scientists need to be more cooperatively engaged in an equal dialogue. We view this volume as a step in this direction. In the concluding chapter, we explore some of the implications of this, drawing on the contributions to this volume, for public action and research.

Notes

We thank Arjun Appadurai, Harold Alderman, Sabina Alkire, Monica Das Gupta, Varun Gauri, Karla Hoff, Saumitra Jha, Daniel Lederman, William Maloney, S. L. Rao, Sita Reddy, Amartya Sen, and J. P. Singh for helpful discussions and comments. Any errors, omissions, and opinions are entirely our responsibility. The points of view expressed in this chapter are those of the authors and not necessarily shared by the World Bank, its executive directors, or member countries.

1. Amartya Sen spends some time on both these topics in his chapter, and the concluding chapter also examines some of the implications of globalization for development policy. Outside the book, Appadurai (1996, 2001), Sassen (1999), Hart (2000), Cowen (2002), and World Bank (2002b) are influential contributions to understanding globalization from different points of view. Lal (1998) provides a sophisticated overview of the relationship between culture and economic

growth—particularly on the role of "cosmological beliefs" and individualism in fostering growth-oriented cultures.

2. See Gooptu (2000) and Jenkins (2000) for more details on the Sonagachi transformation.

3. See the chapter by Carol Jenkins for further discussion of sexual subcultures and their role in HIV-AIDS.

4. An important challenge was that sex workers faced losses of about 60% of their income if they used condoms because their clients had a strong preference for condom-free sex (Rao et al. 2003).

5. Despite this long engagement, Klitgaard (1994) proposes four reasons why anthropological notions have not yet become part of the mainstream practice of development. These are differences in the cultures of economics and anthropology, the fear that taking culture into account will lead to an oversimplification and misguided use of complex ideas, the sheer difficulty of constructing an analytical apparatus for the subject, and a "misguided notion of policy analysis" (Klitgaard 1994, 87).

6. The essays by Harrison (2000) and Huntington (2000) are the opening chapters in the Culture Matters volume that they edited (Harrison and Huntington, 2000). The other contributions to the volume represent a diversity of views that do not necessarily agree with those expressed by the editors.

7. A term used by Professor David Landes, the distinguished economic historian from Harvard, in his talk at the "Culture Counts" Conference in Florence (Landes 2000b, 30).

8. We thank Keith Hart for providing us with this phrase.

9. Who, it should be remembered, was a professor of political economy.

10. An extensive literature review is obviously beyond the scope of this chapter, but summaries of the various strands of thought on culture in anthropology and sociology can be found in http://www.cultureandpublicaction.org/.

11. Among anthropologists engaged with problems of development, we should also note the work of Stephen Gudeman (1986, 2001) on the social "base" underlying economic life in a poor economy and Keith Hart's (1973) important work on the informal economy, as well as his more prescriptive analysis of the potential role of the Internet and telecommunications technology in creating a more equal capitalism (Hart 2000).

12. This can include satisfying hunger, living with dignity, and building social status (Sen 1985a, 1992, 1999, 2000a).

13. See World Bank (2002c) for an extended treatment of the role of institutions in the market arena, which is very much in the tradition of North.

14. Development *research*, on the other hand, has increasingly begun to take note of these constraints. For instance, see Platteau (2000), who links North's notions of formal and informal constraints to problems of economic development, with an emphasis on property rights and social norms (Platteau and Seki 2001).

15. See http://www.cultureandpublicaction.org/. One particularly interesting set of models has been developed by Chwe (2000, 2001), who analyzes rituals and other forms of collective cultural expression as solutions to coordination problems. In order to generate collective action, an individual within a group must

know what others in the group know, they in turn must know what she knows, and she in turn must know that they know that she knows, and so on—what game theorists call common knowledge. This sense of culture as a coordinating system is close to the view of many anthropologists. For example, Geertz (1973b, 5) believes, "with Max Weber, that man is an animal suspended in webs of significance he himself has spun." He takes "culture to be those webs." Douglas and Isherwood (1979/1996, 37) link culture directly to economic life by arguing that "consumption is the very arena in which culture is fought over and licked into shape." For them, the "essential function of consumption is its capacity to make sense" (Douglas and Isherwood 1979/1996, 40).

16. Also see Stern (in press) for a discussion on the relationship between preference dynamics and development policy.

17. Becker, in later work, has developed several variants of this idea of preference formation on the basis of relative prices and applied to a variety of situations—addiction and habit formation among them (Becker 1996). Other approaches focus on the intergenerational transmission of preferences and their implications for cultural diversity within societies (Bisin and Verdier 2001).

18. There are exceptions, such as the late Chicago sociologist James Coleman, who made a case for bringing methodological individualism and rational choice theory to the center of social theory as a substitute for what an "unfriendly critic" might describe as the "current practice in social theory" that "consists of chanting old mantras and invoking nineteenth-century theorists" (Coleman 1990, xv).

19. This is our imperfect account of Bourdieu's definition of habitus, "a system of durable, transposable dispositions. . . . principles which generate and organize practices and representations that can be objectively adapted to their outcomes without presupposing a conscious aiming at ends or an express mastery of the operations necessary in order to attain them" (Bourdieu 1990, 53). For a clear and comprehensive exposition of Bourdieu's body of work, see Swartz (2000). Also see Bourdieu (1998) for a readable synopsis of his own worldview.

20. See Douglas (1966/1984) for a classic exposition on this theme. The incest taboo is now almost universally applied but was clearly not the rule among Egyptian pharaohs or the Inca leaders, who were usually the children of brother-sister unions.

21. The economist Piketty has an interesting model that formally shows that it is possible for societies with the same objective opportunities to forever maintain different beliefs about those opportunities, precisely because the differences in beliefs lead to differences in actions (Piketty 1995).

22. Klamer (this volume) and Throsby (2001) use this term in a slightly different sense more akin to view of capital as an asset unrelated to class structures.

23. It is important to note that Gudeman (2001), among other anthropologists, prefers to use the word *base* instead of cultural and social *capital* because they "make the base, which consists of incommensurate things, into a commodity or resource endowment that actors bring to the bar of exchange," and this "marketize[s]" it (Gudeman 2002, p. 8).

24. This approach to social capital is somewhat different from that of Putnam, Leonardi, and Nanetti (1993), for whom social capital is seen as a "stock" of social

norms and networks, from which people can draw to improve their incomes, which can be "built" to facilitate economic growth and development (Grootaert 1998). This version of social capital has been criticized for not being sufficiently concerned with issues of class distinction and power (Fine 2001), affected by reverse causality (the link may go from wealth to more group activity just as much as the other way around) (Portes 1998; Durlauf 2001), and for not recognizing that it can be both destructive and constructive (Portes 1998). See Woolcock (1998) for a survey of the term *social capital*, particularly in its applications to development; and Woolcock and Narayan (2000) for a discussion of the potential role of social capital in economic development from the World Bank's perspective; Harriss (2001) for a stringent critique of the World Bank's use of the concept; and Bebbington et al. (in press) for a defense.

25. As Arizpe notes, it is probably unfair to attribute such a view, or indeed a reified notion of the role of culture, to Oscar Lewis, who coined the "culture of poverty" phrase.

26. Dumont's analysis has been criticized by various scholars for being too textually derived and not allowing for resistance and mobility among lower castes, but it is recognized as being one of the seminal works of Indian sociology. We use it here more as an illustration of our conceptual argument rather than as an empirical characterization of the modern Indian caste system. For a discussion of more recent work on caste that emphasizes difference rather than hierarchy, see Gupta (2000). Dirks (2001) argues that the modern caste system is largely a product of British colonial rule and should not be mistaken for an entirely traditional form of social organization.

27. For a recent synthesis, see Loury (2002a); the quotation is from page 20. See also Loury (1999) for an elaboration with respect to social exclusion in relation to economic thought and contribution to the conference on Culture and Public Action (Loury 1999, 2002b).

28. See also the work of the social psychologist Steele (1999, 4) on "stereotype threat" among African American students. He presents experimental evidence that poor performance of black students can reflect not ability or training but "the threat of being viewed through the lens of a negative stereotype, or the fear of doing something that would inadvertently confirm that stereotype." Hoff and Pandey (2003) conduct a related experiment with low- and high-caste children in rural north India. They find that when children are made explicitly aware of their caste status, low-caste children perform worse than high-caste children in completing mazes. However, when children are put in anonymous groups where caste status is not announced, the performances of children by caste are not significantly different.

29. See Anderson (1992, 2000) for an ethnographic analysis of the workings of interactions between blacks and whites in poor, violent neighborhoods.

30. This approach has been deeply influenced by views from participatory development, of which Robert Chambers has been an important proponent (Chambers 1997). Cooke and Kothari (2001) and Abraham and Platteau (this volume) are sharply critical of the alacrity with which this approach has been appropriated by development agencies.

31. See Narayan et al. (2001a,b). Brock and McGee (2002) provide a thoughtful critique.

32. The contributions are summarized here in a sequence that reflects the narrative logic of this chapter and are not in the order that they are presented in the book.

33. The study of "business cultures" is an important part of research and teaching in business administration and management. Tushman and O'Reilly (1997), for example, argue that cultural norms of behavior are important to understanding the success of highly successful firms such as the U.S. department store of Nordstrom, or the delivery firm of FedEx. These cultures form part of the "fit" between a firm's characteristics and strategic and competitive behaviors.

34. See Cowen (2002) for more on this. Looking at the relationship between trade and culture, he makes the case that free trade and globalization do not lead to the destruction of traditional cultures but to a new cultural hybridity that is mutually beneficial—and provides several examples where this has happened.

35. See Throsby (2001) for the valuable insights that the field of cultural economics brings to this point.

36. Expressive traditions and heritage are also, of course, a means to an end. Sociologists since Durkheim have argued that collective celebrations and heritage serve an important function by providing a site where communities reify their group identity (Durkheim 1912/1965). Turner (1982), for instance, argues that when a social group celebrates a particular event it celebrates itself by manifesting in symbolic form what it conceives to be its essential life. Thus, cultural events may serve to build social cohesion by reinforcing ties within a community. By providing a space where everyone can view everyone else's behavior, they also generate common knowledge and help solve the coordination problems inherent in collective action (Chwe 1999). In this sense, they help build the capacity for collective action. Thus, at the village level, expressive traditions like festivals and other collective rituals can enhance social cohesion and build trust while providing an arena in which families can maintain and enhance their social status (Rao 2001a,b). For these reasons, "culture as expression" is an important component of "culture as identity" and requires serious attention from policy makers.

37. There is a significant literature in economics on mobility; see Fields (2001) for a discussion; and Bowles and Gintis (2002) for a review.

38. Hirschman (1970, 109) discusses how this may also happen at the individual level in a process of "evolutionary individualism," in which "the successful individual who starts out at a low rung of the social ladder, necessarily leaves his own group behind as he rises; he 'passes' into, or is 'accepted' by, the next higher group." He takes his immediate family along, but hardly anyone else. Bloch and Rao (1993, 2001) have models of these ideas.

39. The Virasaiva movement survives today, and Lingayats are an important political force in the state of Karnataka. However, caste-based distinctions seem to have crept back into the Lingayats over the last millennium—for instance, while conducting fieldwork in a Lingayat village, Rao found that it had a well-defined caste hierarchy with brahmin Lingayats, potter (*kumbhara*) Lingayats, artisan (*achari*) Lingayats, and so on.

40. Scheper-Hughes, in her work on life in a Brazilian shantytown, critiques Scott by arguing that the goal of such "weapons of the weak" is not *resistance* but *existence* (Scheper-Hughes 1992). She believes that calling it resistance "runs the risk of romanticizing human suffering or trivializing its effects on the human spirit, consciousness, and will" (533).

41. Ray builds on Appadurai's ideas from an economist's perspective and argues that the capacity to aspire is affected by two important factors: the ability of the poor to see enough of rich behaviors in order to aspire to them, and whether achieving a higher level can be obtained with a feasible level of investment (Ray 2003). Thus, he argues that "aspirations failures" are more likely in societies with a high level of social polarization—high diversity between the "cognitive neighborhoods" of rich and poor groups, or high levels of inequality where it is impossible for the poor to find the resources to achieve their higher level of aspiration (Ray 2003, 4).

42. Jonathan Fox (1993, 151) reviews the theories of state-society interactions in the context of a Mexican case study and argues that effective change occurs in the context of a "sandwich movement," of enlightened state action from above interacting with social mobilization from below.

43. See also Abers (2000) for a case study on political and sociocultural change in Porto Alegre.

44. While the state can influence culture, culture can also influence the state. Migdal (2001) argues, for instance, that culture needs to be brought more centrally into understanding the endurance of the state despite its gaping failures in addressing problems that affect large numbers of people. He refers to the unquestioned importance to symbolic rituals to both those who govern and the governed.

45. See Sen (1992) for a broad discussion of these issues. It should be emphasized that he discusses the role of group-based structures such as class, caste, or gender as influences on the capabilities of individuals.

CHAPTER 2

How Does Culture Matter?

AMARTYA SEN

Introduction

Sociologists, anthropologists, and historians have often commented on the tendency of economists to pay inadequate attention to culture in investigating the operation of societies in general and the process of development in particular. While we can consider many counterexamples to the alleged neglect of culture by economists, beginning at least with Adam Smith (1776/1976, 1790/1976), John Stuart Mill (1859/1974, 1861/1962), or Alfred Marshall (1891), nevertheless, as a general criticism, the charge is, to a considerable extent, justified.

This neglect (or perhaps more accurately, *comparative* indifference) is worth remedying, and economists can fruitfully pay more attention to the influence of culture on economic and social matters. Further, development agencies such as the World Bank may also reflect, at least to some extent, this neglect, if only because they are so predominately influenced by the thinking of economists and financial experts.[1] The economists' skepticism of the role of culture may thus be indirectly reflected in the outlooks and approaches of institutions like the World Bank. No matter how serious this neglect is (and here assessments can differ), the cultural dimension of development requires closer scrutiny in development analysis. It is important to investigate the different ways—and they can be very diverse—in which culture should be taken into account in examining the challenges of development, and in assessing the demands of sound economic strategies.

The issue is not *whether* culture matters, to consider the title of an important and highly successful book jointly edited by Lawrence Harrison and Samuel Huntington (2000). That it must be, given the pervasive influence of culture in human life. The real issue, rather, is *how*—not whether—culture matters. What are the different ways in which culture may influence development? How can the influences be better understood, and how might they modify or alter the development policies that seem appropriate? The interest lies in the nature and forms of the connections and on their implications for action and policy, not merely in the general—and hardly deniable—belief that culture does matter.

I discuss these "how" questions in this essay, but in the process I must also take up some "how *not*" questions. There is some evidence, I shall argue, that in the anxiety to take adequate note of the role of culture, there is sometimes a temptation to take rather formulaic and simplistic views of the impact of culture on the process of development. For example, there seem to be many supporters of the belief—held explicitly or by implication—that the fates of countries are effectively *sealed* by the nature of their respective cultures. This would be not only a heroic oversimplification, but it would also entail some assignment of hopelessness to countries that are seen as having the "wrong" kind of culture. This is not just politically and ethically repulsive, but more immediately, it is, I would argue, also epistemic nonsense. So a second object of this essay is to take up these "how not" issues.

The third object of the chapter is to discuss the role of learning from each other in the field of culture. Even though such transmission and education may be an integral part of the process of development, their role is frequently underestimated. Indeed, since each culture is often taken, not implausibly, to be unique, there can be a tendency to take a somewhat insular view of culture. In understanding the process of development, this can be particularly deceptive and substantively counterproductive. Indeed, one of the most important roles of culture lies in the possibility of learning from each other, rather than celebrating or lamenting the rigidly delineated cultural boxes in which the people of the world are firmly classified by muscular taxonomists.

Finally, while discussing the importance of intercultural and intercountry communication, I must also discuss the threat—real or perceived—of globalization and the asymmetry of power in the contemporary world. The view that local cultures are in danger of destruction has often been expressed, and the belief that something should be done to resist this can have considerable plausibility. How this possible threat should be understood and what can be done to address—and if necessary counter—it are also important subjects for development analysis. That is the fourth and final issue that I intend to scrutinize.

Connections

It is particularly important to identify the different ways in which culture can matter to development (Rao and Walton, this volume; Wolfensohn 2000). The following categories would seem to have some immediacy as well as far-reaching relevance.

1. *Culture as a constitutive part of development.* We can begin with the basic question: what is development for? The furtherance of well-being and freedoms that we seek in development cannot but include the enrichment of human lives through literature, music, fine arts, and other forms of cultural expression and practice, which we have reason to value. When Julius Caesar said of Cassius, "He hears no music: seldom he smiles," this was not meant to be high praise for Cassius's quality of life. To have a high GNP per head but little music, arts, literature, etc., would not amount to a major developmental success. In one form or another, culture engulfs our lives, our desires, our frustrations, our ambitions, and the freedoms that we seek.[2] The freedom and opportunity for cultural activities are among the basic freedoms the enhancement of which can be seen to be constitutive of development.[3]

2. *Economically remunerative cultural activities and objects.* Various activities that are economically remunerative may be directly or indirectly dependent on cultural facilities and more generally on the cultural environment.[4] The linkage of tourism with cultural sites (including historical ones) is obvious enough.[5] The presence or absence of crime or welcoming traditions may also be critical to tourism and in general to domestic as well as cross-boundary interactions. Music, dancing, and other cultural activities may also have a large commercial—often global—market. The presence of centers of such artistic activities can, in addition, help to attract people to particular countries or regions, with various indirect effects.

There can, of course, be room for doubt as to whether cultural—including religious—objects or sites should be used for the purpose of earning money, and it may well be decided that in some cases, in which the significance of the objects or sites are threatened by commercial use, the opportunity of earning an income should be forgone. But even after excluding commercial uses that can be threatening, there will tend to remain plenty of other opportunities to combine economic use with cultural pursuits. Furthermore, people who come to visit well-administered sites of cultural or religious importance, without any direct commercial involvement, could still, indirectly, boost the tourist trade of the country or region as a whole.

3. *Cultural factors influence economic behavior.* Even though some economists have been tempted by the idea that all human beings behave in
much the same way (for example, relentlessly maximize their self-interest
defined in a thoroughly insulated way), there is plenty of evidence to indicate that this is not in general so. Cultural influences can make a major
difference to work ethics, responsible conduct, spirited motivation,
dynamic management, entrepreneurial initiatives, willingness to take risks,
and a variety of other aspects of human behavior which can be critical to
economic success (Sen 1973, 1982; Basu 1980; Hirschman 1982; Margolis
1982; Akerlof 1984; Frank 1985, 1988; Granovetter 1985; Elster 1986;
Mansbridge 1990; Ostrom 1990, 1998; Greif 1994a,b; Brittan and Hamlin
1995; Fukuyama 1995; Zamagni 1995; Becker 1996; Hausman and
McPherson 1996; Frey 1997a,b; Ben-Ner and Putterman 1998; Akerlof
and Kranton 2000; Throsby 2001).

Also, successful operation of an exchange economy depends on mutual
trust and implicit norms. When these behavioral modes are plentifully
there, it is easy to overlook their role. But when they have to be cultivated,
that lacuna can be a major barrier to economic success. There are plenty
of examples of the problems faced in precapitalist economies because of
the underdevelopment of basic virtues of commerce and business.

The culture of behavior relates to many other features of economic
success. It relates, for example, to the prevalence or absence of economic
corruption and its linkages with organized crime. In Italian discussions on
this subject, in which I was privileged to take part through advising the
Anti-Mafia Commission of the Italian parliament, the role and reach of
implicit values was much discussed.[6] Culture also has an important role in
encouraging environment-friendly behavior (Ostrom 1990, 1998; Putnam,
Leonardi, and Nanetti 1993; Putnam 1993). The behavioral contribution
of culture would vary with the challenges encountered in the process of
economic development.

4. *Culture and political participation.* Participation in civil interactions and
political activities is influenced by cultural conditions. The tradition of
public discussion and participatory interactions can be very critical to the
process of politics, and can be important for the establishment, preservation, and practice of democracy. The culture of participation can be a critical civic virtue, as was extensively discussed by Condorcet, among other
leading thinkers of European Enlightenment (Condorcet 1795/1955;
Hume 1777/1966; Smith 1790/1976).

Aristotle did, of course, point out that human beings tend to have a
natural inclination toward civil interaction with each other. And yet the
extent of political participation can vary between societies. In particular,

political inclinations can be suppressed not only by authoritarian rules and restrictions, but also by a "culture of fear" that political suppression can generate. There can also be a "culture of indifference" drawing on skepticism that turns into apathy. Political participation is critically important for development, both through its effects on the assessment of ways and means, and even through its role in the formation and consolidation of values in terms of which development has to be assessed (Sen 1999).

5. *Social solidarity and association.* Aside from economic interactions and political participation, even the operation of social solidarity and mutual support can be strongly influenced by culture. The success of social living is greatly dependent on what people may spontaneously do for each other. This can profoundly influence the working of the society, including the care of its less fortunate members as well as preservation and guardianship of common assets. The sense of closeness to others in the community can be a major asset for that community. The advantages flowing from solidarity and supportive interactions have received much attention recently through the literature on "social capital" (Ostrom 1990, 1998; Putnam, Leonardi, and Nanetti 1993; Putnam 1993).[7]

This is an important new area of social investigation. There is, however, a need to scrutinize the nature of "social capital" as "capital"—in the sense of a general purpose resource (as capital is taken to be). The same sentiments and inclinations can actually work in opposite directions, depending on the nature of the group involved. For example, solidarity within a particular group (for example, long-term residents of a region) can go with a less than friendly view of nonmembers of that group (such as new immigrants). The influence of the same community-centered thinking can be both positive for intracommunity relations and negative in generating or sustaining exclusionary tendencies (including violent "anti-immigrant" sentiments and actions, as can be observed in some regions of impeccable "within community" solidarity). Identity-based thinking can have dichotomous features, since a strong sense of group affiliation can have a cementing role within that group while encouraging rather severe treatment of nonmembers (seen as "others" who do not "belong"). If this dichotomy is right, then it may be a mistake to treat "social capital" as a general-purpose asset (as capital is, in general, taken to be), rather than as an asset for some relations and a liability for others. There is, thus, room for some searching scrutiny of the nature and operation of the important, but in some ways problematic, concept of "social capital."

6. *Cultural sites and recollection of past heritage.* Another constructive possibility is the furtherance of a clearer and broader understanding of a country's or community's past through systematic exploration of its cul-

tural history. For example, by supporting historical excavations, explorations and related research, development programs can help to facilitate a fuller appreciation of the breadth of—and internal variations within—particular cultures and traditions. History often includes much greater variety of cultural influences and traditions than tends to be allowed by intensely political—and frequently ahistorical—interpretations of the present. When this is the case, historical objects, sites and records can help to offset some of the frictions of confrontational modern politics.

For example, Arab history includes a long tradition of peaceful relation with Jewish populations. Similarly, Indonesian past carries powerful records of simultaneous flourishing of Hindu, Buddhist, and Confucian cultures, side by side with the Islamic traditions. Butrint in Albania as a historical site shows flourishing presence of Greek, Roman, and later Christian cultures, as well as Islamic history. The highlighting of a diverse past that may go with the excavation, preservation, and accessibility of historical objects and sites can, thus, have a possible role in promoting toleration of diversity in contemporary settings, and in countering confrontational use of "monocultural" readings of a nation's past.

For example, the recent attempt by Hindu activists to see India as just a "Hindu country," in which practitioners of other religions must have a less privileged position, clashes with the great diversity of Indian history. This includes a thousand years of Buddhist predominance (with sites all over India), a long history of Jain culture, conspicuous presence of Christians from the fourth century and of Parsees from the eighth, Muslim settlements of Arab traders in South India from about the same time, massive interactions between Muslims and Hindus all over the country (including new departures in painting, music, literature, and architecture), the birth and flourishing of Sikhism (as a new Indian religion that drew on but departed from previous ones), and so on. The recollection of history can be a major ally in the cultivation of toleration and celebration of diversity, and these are—directly and indirectly—among important features of development.[8]

7. *Cultural influences on value formation and evolution.* Not only is it the case that cultural factors figure among the ends and means of development, they can also have a central role even in the formation of values. This in turn can be influential in the identification of our ends and the recognition of plausible and acceptable instruments to achieve those ends. For example, open public discussion—itself a cultural achievement of significance—can be powerfully influential in the emergence of new norms and fresh priorities.

Indeed, value formation is an interactive process, and the culture of talking and listening can play a significant part in making these interactions possible. As new standards emerge, it is public discussion as well as proximate emulation that may spread the new norms across a region and ultimately between regions. For example, the emergence of norms of low fertility rates, or nondiscrimination between boys and girls, or wanting to send children to schools, and so on, are not only vitally important features of development, they may be greatly influenced by a culture of free discussion and open public debate, without political barriers or social suppression (Basu 1992; Sen, Germain, and Chen 1994; Drèze and Sen 1995, 2002).

Integration

In seeing the role of culture in development, it is particularly important to place culture in an adequately capacious framework. The reasons for this are not hard to seek. First, influential as culture is, it is not uniquely pivotal in determining our lives and identities. Other things, such as class, race, gender, profession, and politics also matter, and can matter powerfully. Our cultural identity is only one of many aspects of our self-realization and is only one influence among a great many that can inspire and influence what we do and how we do it. Further, our behavior depends not only on our values and predispositions, but also on the hard facts of the presence or absence of relevant institutions and on the incentives—prudential or moral—they generate (North 1981, 1990; Ostrom 1990, 1998; Douglas 1992; Blau 1993; Goody 1996; Bowles 1998; Platteau 2000; Arizpe, this volume; Sen 1984).

Second, culture is not a homogeneous attribute—there can be great variations even within the same general cultural milieu. Cultural determinists often underestimate the extent of heterogeneity within what is taken to be "one" distinct culture. Discordant voices are often "internal," rather than coming from outside. Since culture has many aspects, heterogeneity can also arise from the particular components of culture on which we decide to concentrate (for example, whether we look particularly at religion, or at literature, or at music, or generally at the style of living).[9]

Third, culture absolutely does not sit still. Any presumption of stationarity—explicit or implicit—can be disastrously deceptive. To talk of, say, the Hindu culture, or for that matter the Indian culture, taken to be well defined in a temporally stationary way, not only overlooks the great variations within each of these categories, but also ignores their evolution and their large variations over time. The temptation toward using cultural determinism often takes the hopeless form of trying to fix the cultural anchor on a rapidly moving boat.

Finally, cultures interact with each other and cannot be seen as insulated structures. The isolationalist view—often implicitly presumed—can be deeply delusive (Goody 1996; Throsby 2001). Sometimes we may be only vaguely aware how an influence came from outside, but it need not be unimportant for that reason. For example, while chili was unknown in India before the Portuguese brought it there in the 16th century, it is now a thoroughly Indian spice.[10] Cultural features—from the most trivial to the most profound—can change radically, sometimes leaving little trace of the past behind.

Taking culture to be independent, unchanging and unchangeable can indeed be very problematic. But that, on the other hand, is no reason for not taking full note of the importance of culture seen in an adequately broad perspective. It is certainly possible to pay adequate attention to culture, along with taking into account all the qualifications just discussed. Indeed, if culture is recognized to be nonhomogeneous, nonstatic, and interactive, and if the importance of culture is integrated with rival sources of influence, then culture can be a very positive and constructive part in our understanding of human behavior and of social and economic development.

Bigotry and Alienation *

However, the "how not" issue does deserve extremely serious attention, since rapid-fire cultural generalizations can not only undermine a deeper understanding of the role of culture, but also serve as a tool of sectarian prejudices, social discrimination, and even political tyranny. Simple cultural generalizations have great power in fixing our way of thinking, and often enough they are not just harmless fun. The fact that such generalizations abound in popular beliefs and in informal communication is easily recognized. Not only are these underexamined implicit beliefs the subject matter of many racist jokes and ethnic slurs, they sometimes surface as pernicious grand theories. When there is an accidental correlation between cultural prejudice and social observation (no matter how casual), a theory is born, and it may refuse to die even after the chance correlation vanishes altogether.

For example, concocted jokes against the Irish (such crudities as "how many Irishmen do you need to change a light bulb"), which have had some currency in England for a long time, appeared to fit well with the depressing predicament of the Irish economy, when the Irish economy was doing quite badly. But when the Irish economy started growing astonishingly rapidly—indeed faster than any other European economy (as it did, for many years)—the cultural stereotyping and its allegedly profound economic and social relevance were not junked as sheer and unmitigated rubbish. Theories have lives of their own, quite defiantly of the phenomenal world that can be actually observed.

As it happens, cultural prejudice did play a role in the treatment that Ireland received from the British government, and had a part even in the nonprevention of the famines of the 1840s, which killed a higher proportion of the population than in any other recorded famine. Joel Mokyr (1983) has discussed the contribution of cultural alienation in London's treatment of Irish problems.[11] As Lebow has argued, while poverty in Britain was typically attributed to economic change and fluctuations, Irish poverty was widely viewed in England as being caused by laziness, indifference, and ineptitude, so that "Britain's mission" was not seen as one "to alleviate Irish distress but to civilize her people and to lead them to feel and act like human beings."[12]

The cultural roots of the Irish famines extend, in this sense, at least as far back as Spenser's *Faerie Queene*, published in 1590, and perhaps even earlier. The art of blaming the victims, plentifully present in the *Faerie Queene* itself, survived through the famines of the 1840s, and the Irish taste for potato was added to the list of the calamities which the natives had, in English view, brought on themselves. Charles Edward Trevelyan, the Head of the Treasury during the famines, expressed his belief that Britain had done what it could for Ireland, even as the famine—with little public relief—killed rampantly, and even as ship after ship, laden with wheat, oats, cattle, pigs, eggs, and butter, sailed down the Shannon, bound for England (which had greater purchasing power than starving Ireland and could buy what the Irish—hit by the potato blight—could not afford). Trevelyan also pointed to some remarkable cultural explanations of the hunger, including: "There is scarcely a woman of the peasant class in the West of Ireland whose culinary art exceeds the boiling of a potato."[13]

The connection between cultural bigotry and political tyranny can be very close. The asymmetry of power between the ruler and ruled can be combined with cultural prejudices in explaining failures of governance, as is spectacularly observed through the Irish famines of the 1840s (O Grada 1989; Eagleton 1995; Mokyr 1983; Woodham-Smith 1962). Similar use of cultural prejudice for political irresponsibility (or worse) can also be seen in the history of European empires in Asia and Africa. Winston Churchill's famous remark that the Bengal famine of 1943 was caused by the tendency of people there to "breed like rabbits" belongs to this general tradition of blaming the colonial victim, and it had a profound effect in crucially delaying famine relief in that disastrous famine.[14] Cultural critiques of the victims can be used by the rulers to justify hugely inefficient—as well as deeply iniquitous—tyrannies.

Cultural Determinism

While the marriage of cultural prejudice and political asymmetry can be quite lethal, the need to be cautious about jumping to cultural conclusions is more pervasive. It can even influence the way experts see the nature and challenges of economic development. Theories are often derived from fairly scanty evidence. Half-truths or quarter-truths can grossly mislead—sometimes even more than straightforward falsity, which is easier to expose.

Consider, for example, the following argument from the influential and important book jointly edited by Lawrence Harrison and Samuel Huntington called *Culture Matters* (to which I referred earlier), and in particular from Huntington's introductory essay in that volume called "Cultures Count":

In the early 1990s, I happened to come across economic data on Ghana and South Korea in the early 1960s, and I was astonished to see how similar their economies were then. . . . Thirty years later, South Korea had become an industrial giant with the fourteenth largest economy in the world, multinational corporations, major exports of automobiles, electronic equipment, and other sophisticated manufactures, and per capital income approximately that of Greece. Moreover it was on its way to the consolidation of democratic institutions. No such changes had occurred in Ghana, whose per capita income was now about one-fifteenth that of South Korea's. How could this extraordinary difference in development be explained? Undoubtedly, many factors played a role, but it seemed to me that culture had to be a large part of the explanation. South Koreans valued thrift, investment, hard work, education, organization, and discipline. Ghanians had different values. In short, cultures count. (Harrison and Huntington 2000, xiii)

There may well be something of interest in this engaging comparison (perhaps even a quarter-truth torn out of context), and the contrast does call for probing examination. And yet, as used in the explanation just cited, the causal story is extremely deceptive. There were many important differences—other than their cultural predispositions—between Ghana and Korea in the 1960s when they appeared to Huntington to be much the same, except for culture. First, the class structures in the two countries were quite different, with a very much bigger—and proactive—role of business classes in South Korea. Second, the politics were very different too, with the government in South Korea willing and eager to play a prime-moving role in initiating a business-centered economic development in a way that did not apply to Ghana. Third, the close relationship between the Korean economy and the Japanese economy, on the one hand, and the United States, on the other, made a big difference, at least in the early stages of Korean development. Fourth—and perhaps most important—by the 1960s South Korea had acquired a much higher literacy rate and much more expanded school system than Ghana had. The Korean changes had been brought about in the post–World War II period, largely through resolute public policy, and it could not be seen just as a reflection of age-old Korean culture (McGinn et al. 1980).

On the basis of the slender scrutiny offered, it is hard to justify either the cultural triumphalism in favor of Korean culture, or the radical pessimism about Ghana's future that the reliance on cultural determinism would tend to suggest. Neither can be derived from the overrapid and underanalyzed comparison that accompanies the heroic diagnostics. As it happens, South Korea did not rely just on its traditional culture. From the 1940s onward, it deliberately followed lessons from abroad to use public policy to advance its backward school education.

And it has continued to learn from global experience even today. Sometimes the lessons have come from experience of failure rather than success. The East Asian crisis that overwhelmed South Korea among other countries in the region brought out some of the penalties of not having a fully functioning democratic political system. When things moved up and up together, the voice that democracy gives to the underdog may not have been immediately missed, but when the economic crisis came, and divided they fell (as they typically do in such a crisis), the newly impoverished missed the voice that democracy would have given them to use for protest and to demand economic redress. Along with the recognition of the need to pay attention to downside risks and to economic security, the bigger issue of democracy itself became a predominant focus of attention in the politics of economic crisis. This happened in the countries hit by the crisis, such as South Korea, Indonesia, Thailand, and others, but there was also a global lesson here about the special contribution of democracy in helping the victims of disaster, and the need to think not only about "growth with equity" (the old Korean slogan), but also about "downturn with security" (Sen 1999).

Similarly, the cultural damning of the prospects of development in Ghana and other countries in Africa is simply overhasty pessimism with little empirical foundation. For one thing, it does not take into account how rapidly many countries—South Korea included—have changed, rather than remaining anchored to some fixed cultural parameters. Misidentified quarter-truths can be dreadfully misleading.

There have, of course, been various earlier attempts at cultural determinism in explaining economic development. Indeed, a century ago, Max
Weber (1930), the great sociologist, had presented a major thesis on the
decisive role of Protestant ethics (in particular, of Calvinist ethics) in the
successful development of a capitalist industrial economy. Weberian analysis of the role of culture in the emergence of capitalism drew on the world
as he had observed it in the late 19th century.[15] It is of particular dialectical interest in the contemporary world in light especially of the recent
success of market economies in non-Protestant and even non-Christian
societies.

Max Weber was particularly clear that Confucianism was quite unsuited
for a dynamic industrial economy. "The Calvinist ethic," Anthony Giddens
summarizes Weber, "introduced an activism into the believer's approach to
worldly affairs, a drive to mastery in a quest for virtue in the eyes of God,
that are altogether lacking in Confucianism," adding: "Confucian values
do not promote such rational instrumentalism."[16] In sharp contrast with
this view, many writers in present-day Asia make the opposite claim that
Confucian ethics is particularly suited for success of industrial and economic progress, as illustrated by the performance of East Asia. There have,
in fact, been several different theories seeking explanation of the high
performance of East Asian economies in terms of local culture. Michio
Morishima (a great economist) has traced the roots of "the Japanese
ethos" to the special history of its feudal system; Ronald Dore (a great
sociologist) has emphasized the contribution of "Confucian ethics"; Eiko
Ikegami (a brilliant young Japanese historian) has focused on the influence
of the "Samurai code of honour."[17]

There is much to learn from these theories, and the empirical connections they have brought out have been insightful. And yet it is also remarkable how the specific aspects of cultural explanations, based on observing
the past, have often foundered in the light of later experience. Indeed, theories of cultural determinism have often been one step behind the actual
world. By the time Max Weber's privileging of "Protestant ethics" (based
on 19th-century experience) was getting widely recognized, many of the
Catholic countries, including France and Italy, were beginning to grow
faster than Protestant Britain or Germany. The thesis had to be, then,
altered, and the privileged culture was taken more generally to be
Christian and western, rather than specifically Protestant.

However, by the time that Eurocentric view of the culture of development got established, Japan was growing much faster than the West. So
Japan had to be included in the privileged category, and there was useful
work on the role of Japanese ethos, Samurai culture, etc. But, by the time

the specialness of Japan was well understood, the East Asian economies were growing very fast, and there was a need to broaden the theory of Japan's specialness to include the wider coverage of "Confucian" ethics and a wider and a more spacious regional tradition, fuzzily described as "Asian values." However, by the time that "Confucian" theory had become well established, the fastest growing economy in the world was Thailand, which is a Buddhist country. Indeed, Japan, Korea, China, and Taiwan too have much Buddhist influence in their culture. The grand cultural theories have a propensity to trail one step behind the world of practice, rather than serving as a grand predictive device.

This record need not, however, be seen as one of embarrassment, since we have learned many things from a closer understanding of the cultural linkages emerging from these specialized studies. But attempts to view culture as a singular, stationary and independent source of development have not—and could not have—worked.

Just to illustrate, consider Korea again, which is often seen as a quintessential exemplification of the power of "Asian values" and of the reach of Confucian ethics in industrial development. Confucianism has indeed been a major cultural influence in this country, but there have been many different interpretations of Confucianism. For example, in the 15th century onward, the "Neo-Confucian literati" (*Sarim*) challenged the earlier readings of Confucianism, and interpretational disputes were powerfully pursued by the different sides. Neo-Confucians themselves divide into different schools, according to different lines of division, including the classic Chinese distinction between *li* and *ch'i* (called, I understand, *i* and *ki* in Korea). In the 17th and early 18th century, the contest between the "Old Doctrine" (*Noron*), led by Song Si-yol, and the "Young Doctrine" (*Soron*), led by Yun Chung, related in part to different views of good behavior and of good social arrangements. Confucianism does not speak in one voice, and the particular emphasis on *li* (or *i*, in Korean) in the authoritarian interpretations of Confucius is by no means the only claim that obtains loyalty.

There are also influences other than Confucianism. Buddhism, as was mentioned before, has been a major force in Korea, as it has been in China and Japan. From the seventh century when Buddhism became the state religion, it has had political ups and downs, but a constant cultural presence in this country. Christianity too has had a major presence in Korea, and from the 18th century, regular intellectual confrontations can be seen between the creed of so-called western learning, which disputed Confucian orthodoxy, along with other challengers, such as the individualist doctrines of the Wang Yang-ming school of Neo-Confucianism, and of course various theorists of Buddhism. The richness and diversity in Korea's cultural past cannot be reduced into a simple story of cultural determinism, woven around an allegedly homogeneous Confucian ethics, or the overarching role of an ill-defined "Asian values" (Han 1971; Henthorn 1971; Lee 1984).

Interdependence and Learning

While culture does not work in isolation from other social influences, once we place culture in adequate company, it can greatly help to illuminate our understanding of the world, including the process of development and the nature of our identity. Let me refer again to South Korea, which was a much more literate and more educated society than Ghana in the 1960s (when the two economies appeared rather similar to Huntington). The contrast, as was already mentioned, was very substantially the result of public policies pursued in South Korea in the post–World War II period.

To be sure, the postwar public policies on education were also influenced by antecedent cultural features. It would be surprising had there been no such connection. In a two-way relation, just as education influences culture, so does antecedent culture have an effect on educational policies. It is, for example, remarkable that nearly every country in the world with a powerful presence of Buddhist tradition has tended to embrace widespread schooling and literacy with some eagerness. This applies not only to Japan and Korea, but also to China, and Thailand, and Sri Lanka. Indeed, even miserable Burma, with a dreadful record of political oppression and social neglect, still has a higher rate of literacy than its neighbors in the subcontinent. Seen in a broader framework, there is probably something here to investigate and learn from.[18]

It is, however, important to see the interactive nature of the process in which contact with other countries and the knowledge of their experiences can make a big difference in practice. There is every evidence that when Korea decided to move briskly forward with school education at the end of the second world war, it was influenced not just by its cultural interest in education, but also by a new understanding of the role and significance of education, based on the experiences of Japan and the West, including the United States (Lee 1984; McGinn et al. 1980).

There is a similar story, earlier on, of interaction and response in Japan's own history of educational development. When Japan emerged from its self-imposed isolation from the world from the beginning of the 17th century, under the Tokugawa regime, it already had a relatively well-developed school system, and in this Japan's traditional interest in education would have played a significant part. Indeed, at the time of Meiji restoration in 1868, Japan had a higher rate of literacy than Europe, despite being economically quite underdeveloped. And yet the rate of literacy in Japan was still low (as indeed it was in Europe too), and no less importantly the Japanese education system was quite out of touch with knowledge and learning in the industrializing West.[19] When, in 1852, Commodore Mathew Perry chugged into the Edo Bay, puffing black smoke from the newly designed steamship, the Japanese were not only impressed—and somewhat terrified—and were driven to accept diplomatic and trade relations with the United States, they also had to reexamine and reassess their intellectual isolation from the world. This contributed to the political process that led to the Meiji restoration, and along with that came a determination to change the face of Japanese education. In the so-called Charter Oath, proclaimed also in 1868, there is a firm declaration on the need to "seek knowledge widely throughout the world" (Cummings 1980, 17).

The Fundamental Code of Education issued three years later, in 1872, put the new educational determination in unequivocal terms: "There shall, in the future, be no community with an illiterate family, nor a family with an illiterate person."[20] Kido Takayoshi, one of the most influential leaders of that period, put the basic issue with great clarity:

Our people are no different from the Americans or Europeans of today; it is all a matter of education or lack of education.[21]

That was the challenge that Japan took on with determination, and things moved rapidly forward.

Between 1906 and 1911, education consumed as much as 43% of the budgets of the towns and villages, for Japan as a whole (Gluck 1985). By 1906, the recruiting army officers found that, in contrast with late 19th century, there was hardly any new recruit who was not literate. By 1910, it is generally acknowledged that Japan had universal attendance in primary schools. By 1913, even though Japan was still economically very poor and underdeveloped, it had become one of the largest producers of books in the world—publishing more books than Britain and indeed more than twice as many as the United States. Indeed, Japan's entire experience of economic development was, to a great extent, driven by human capability formation, which included the role of education and training, and this was promoted *both* by public policy and by a supportive cultural climate (interacting with each other). The dynamics of associative relations are extraordinarily important in understanding how Japan laid the foundations of its spectacular economic and social development.

To carry the story further, Japan was not only a learner but also a great teacher. Development efforts of countries in East and Southeast Asia were profoundly influenced by Japan's experience in expanding education and its manifest success in transforming society and the economy.[22] There is a fund of cultural and economic wisdom there from which the world can draw lessons in development. India today may be immensely more advanced technologically and even economically than Japan in the Meiji period, and yet India is paying a very heavy price for ignoring the cultural lessons on the critical role of basic education that emerged so profoundly in the economically poor and politically primitive Meiji Japan (Drèze and Sen 1995, 2002).

Cultural interrelations within a broad framework does indeed provide a useful focus for our understanding. It contrasts both with neglecting culture altogether (as some economic models do), and also with the privileging of culture in stationary and isolated terms (as is done in some social models of cultural determinism). We have to go well beyond both and *integrate* the role of culture with other aspects of our life.

Cultural Globalization

I turn now to what may appear to be a contrary consideration. It might be asked, in praising intercountry interactions and the positive influence of learning from elsewhere, am I not overlooking the threat that global interrelations pose to integrity and survival of local culture? In a world that is so dominated by the "imperialism" of the culture of the western metropolis, surely the basic need is, it can be argued, to strengthen resistance, rather than to welcome global influence.

Let me first say that there is no contradiction here. Learning from elsewhere involves freedom and judgment, not being overwhelmed and dominated by outside influence without choice, without scope for one's volitional agency. The threat of being overwhelmed by the superior market power of an affluent West, which has asymmetric influence over nearly all the media, raises a different type of issue altogether. In particular, it does not contradict in any way the importance of learning from elsewhere.

But how should we think about global cultural invasion itself as a threat to local cultures? There are two issues of particular concern here. The first relates to the nature of market culture in general, since that is part and parcel of economic globalization. Those who find the values and priorities of a market-related culture vulgar and impoverishing (many who take this view belong to the West itself) tend to find economic globalization to be objectionable at a very basic level.[23] The second issue concerns the asymmetry of power between the West and the other countries, and the possibility that this asymmetry may translate into destruction of local cultures—a loss that may culturally impoverish nonwestern societies. Given the constant cultural bombardment that tends to come from the western metropolis (through MTV to Kentucky Fried Chicken), there are genuine fears that native traditions may get drowned in that loud din.

Threats to older native cultures in the globalizing world of today are, to a considerable extent, inescapable. It is not easy to solve the problem by stopping globalization of trade and commerce, since the forces of economic exchange and division of labour are hard to resist in an interacting world. Globalization does, of course, raise other problems as well, and its distributional consequences have received much criticism recently. On the other hand, it is hard to deny that global trade and commerce can bring with it—as Adam Smith foresaw—greater economic prosperity for each nation. The challenging task is to get the benefits of globalization on a more shared basis. While that primarily economic question need not detain us here (which I have tried to discuss elsewhere, particularly in Sen 1999), there is a related question in the field of culture, to wit, how to increase the real options—the substantive freedoms—that people have, by providing support for cultural traditions that they may want to preserve. This cannot but be an important concern in any development effort that brings about radical changes in the ways of living of people.

Indeed, a natural response to the problem of asymmetry must take the form of strengthening the opportunities that local culture can have, to be able to hold its own against an overpowered invasion. If foreign imports dominate because of greater control over the media, surely one counteracting policy must involve expanding the facilities that local culture gets, to present its own ware, both locally and beyond it. This is a positive response, rather than the temptation—a very negative temptation—to ban foreign influence.

Ultimately, for both the concerns, the deciding issue must be one of democracy. An overarching value must be the need for participatory decision making on the kind of society people want to live in, based on open discussion, with adequate opportunity for the expression of minority positions. We cannot both want democracy, on the one hand, and yet, on the other, rule out certain choices, on traditionalist grounds, because of their "foreignness" (irrespective of what people decide to choose, in an informed and reflected way). Democracy is not consistent with options of citizens being banished by political authorities, or by religious establishments, or by grand guardians of taste, no matter how unbecoming they find the new predilection to be. Local culture may indeed need positive assistance to compete in even terms, and support for minority tastes against foreign onslaught may also be a part of the enabling role of a democratic society, but the prohibition of cultural influences from abroad is not consistent with a commitment to democracy and liberty.

Related to this question there is also a more subtle issue that takes us beyond the immediate worry about bombardment of mass western culture. This concerns the way we see ourselves in the world—a world that is asymmetrically dominated by western preeminence and power. Through a dialectic process, this can, in fact, lead to a powerful inclination to be aggressively "local" in culture, as a kind of "brave" resistance to western dominance. In an important article, called "What Is a Muslim?," Akeel Bilgrami (1995) has argued that the confrontational relations often lead people to see themselves as "the other"—defining their identity as being emphatically *different from* that of western people. Something of this "otherness" can be seen in the emergence of various self-definitions that characterize cultural or political nationalism and religious assertiveness or even fundamentalism. While belligerently antiwestern, these developments are, in fact, deeply foreign-dependent—in a negative and contrary form. Indeed, seeing oneself as "the other" does less than justice to one's free and deliberative agency.[24] This problem too has to be dealt with in a way that is consistent with democratic values and practice, if that is taken to be a priority. Indeed, the "solution" to the problem that Bilgrami diagnoses cannot lie in "prohibiting" any particular outlook, but in public discussion that clarifies and illuminates the possibility of being alienated from one's own independent agency.

Finally, I should mention that one particular concern I have not yet discussed arises from the belief—often implicit—that each country or collectivity must stick to its "own culture," no matter how attracted people are to "foreign cultures." This fundamentalist position not only involves the need to reject importing McDonald's and beauty contests to the nonwestern world, but also the enjoyment there of Shakespeare or ballets or even cricket matches. Obviously enough, this highly conservative position must be in some tension with the role and acceptability of democratic decisions, and I need not repeat what I have already said about the conflict between democracy and the arbitrary privileging of any practice. But it also involves an additional philosophical issue about the labeling of cultures on which Rabindranath Tagore, the poet, had warned.

This concerns the issue whether one's culture is to be defined by the geographical origin of a practice, rather than by its manifest use and enjoyment. Tagore (1928) put his argument against regional labeling with great force:

Whatever we understand and enjoy in human products instantly becomes ours, wherever they might have their origin. I am proud of my humanity when I can acknowledge the poets and artists of other countries as my own. Let me feel with unalloyed gladness that all the great glories of man are mine.

The criteria of understanding and assessment are important, but—as Tagore rightly noted—the inert place of origin has no right to alienate us from what we enjoy and have reason to cherish. Culture, after all, is more than mere geography.

Concluding Remarks

To conclude, I have tried to discuss, first of all, how—in many different ways—culture interacts with development. There are complex epistemic, ethical, and political issues involved in identifying the ways in which culture may or may not influence development. Some specific lines of connection have been identified, particularly related to the demands of assessment and policy.

Second, the acknowledgment of the importance of culture cannot be instantly translated into ready-made theories of cultural causation. It is evidently too easy to jump from the frying pan of neglecting culture into the fire of crude cultural determinism. The latter has caused much harm in the past (and has even encouraged political tyranny and social discrimination), and it continues to be a source of confusion which can seriously mislead assessment and policy in the contemporary world.

Third, what is needed is not the privileging of culture as something that works on its own, but the integration of culture in a wider picture, in which culture, seen in a dynamic and interactive way, is one important influence among many others. Attempts at integration have to pay particular attention to heterogeneity of each broadly defined culture, the interdependence between different cultures, and the vibrant nature of cultural evolutions.

Fourth, there has been much focus, in this essay, on the positive contributions that cultural influences across borders can make. But I have also discussed the cultural provocation that global asymmetry of power generates. There are good arguments for not being overwhelmed by this asymmetry—neither in the form of submissive supplication, nor in the dialectical and negative form of redefining oneself as "the other" (in contrast with "the West"), which makes one lose one's independent identity. Both these reactions can be contrasted with reliance on free and informed choice, aided by public discussion, critical scrutiny, and a participatory political environment.

There is no particular "compulsion" either to preserve departing life styles, or alternatively, to adopt the newest fashion from abroad, but there is a need for people to be able to take part in these social decisions. This gives further reason for attaching importance to such elementary capabilities as reading and writing (through basic education), being well informed and well briefed (through a free media), and having realistic chances of participating freely (through elections, referendums and the general use of civil rights). There are institutional demands for cultural democracy.

A democratic commitment is consistent with assisting local cultures to compete in comparable terms, but does not encourage the arbitrary elimination of options on grounds of their foreign origin or a priori unacceptability. The ultimate test is the freedom of the citizens to exercise their free agency and choose in an informed and participatory way. If that foundational value has priority, then other concerns have to be integrated with its preeminence.

Notes

I draw, in this essay, on three earlier presentations on related themes, respectively, at a World Bank meeting on development in Tokyo on December 13, 2000, at the Pardee Center of Boston University on February 4, 2002, and at the University of Mumbai on February 26, 2002.

1. Douglas (1987), North (1990), and Blau (1993) provide interesting insights on how institutions think.

2. Douglas (1973/1982, 1992); Eliot (1948); Appadurai (1986); Inglehart (1990); Adorno (1991); Mosseto (1993); Greif (1994b); Appiah and Gates (1995); Jessor, Colby, and Shweder 1996); Klamer (1996); Landes (1998); Throsby (1999); Eagleton (2000); Platteau (2000); and the United Nations Educational Scientific and Cultural Organization [UNESCO] 1998, 2000) contain important illustrations of different aspects of these pervasive connections.

3. Cultural capabilities are among the major components of substantial freedoms; on the nature and use of the perspective of capabilities, see Alkire (2002a,c); Sen (1982, 1985a,b, 1999); Griffin and Knight (1990); Nussbaum (1993, 2000); Nussbaum and Sen (1993); Nussbaum and Glover (1995); Pattanaik (1998); Appadurai (2004); Arizpe (this volume); and Osmani (2001), among others.

4. There is a vast literature on the connections between economic rewards and cultural pursuits (Baumol and Bowen 1966; Peacock and Weir 1975; Blaug 1976; Towse 1993, 1997; Peacock and Rizzo 1994; Throsby 1994, 2001; Klamer 1996; Hutter and Rizzo 1997; Bowles 1998; Cowen 1998; Avrami, Mason, and de la Torre 2000; Caves 2000; Frey 2000).

5. See Boniface (1995); Herbert (1995); Hutter and Rizzo (1997); Avrami, Mason, and de la Torre (2000); and Throsby (2001) on the interconnection between the cultural and economic aspects of tourism, among other contributions.

6. My article ("On Corruption and Organized Crime") in the Anti-Mafia

Commission of the Italian Parliament collection (1993) analyses the interdendences between culture, values and institutions, in influencing the prevalence of corruption. See also Zamagni (1993, 1995).

7. The concept of social capital and its uses receive attention in UNESCO (1998, 2000); Dasgupta and Serageldin (2000); Blau (2001b); and Throsby (2001).

8. Often many different arguments can point in the same direction, in terms of needed action. For example, there has been only partial excavation of the ruins of the ancient Buddhist university of Nalanda in India, which had come to its end in the 12th century about the time when Oxford University was being founded (after having flourished for many hundreds of years, and having attracted scholars from abroad as well as within India—Hsuan Tsang from China in the seventh century was one of the most prominent alumni of Nalanda). Further investment in Nalanda's excavation, accessibility, and facilities will not only encourage tourism, and generate income in one of the poorest parts of India, but can also help to generate a fuller understanding of the diversity of India's historical traditions.

9. There are, as a consequence, considerable difficulties in finding suitable indicators of "cultural development" (Pattanaik 1998; Alkire 2002c).

10. Since I don't like chili, I have much practical experience of how hard it is to escape this foreign import in many parts of India. I also frequently encounter the comment that my culinary taste must have become corrupted by my spending a lot of time in the West. To this I have to reply, "No, it is *pre*-colonial—what we Indians ate prior to western imperialism messed up our eating habits." There seems to be little memory left in India of its pre-Portuguese, prechili taste.

11. In *Why Ireland Starved*, Joel Mokyr (1983, 291) argues that "Ireland was considered by Britain as an alien and even hostile nation."

12. See Mokyr (1983, 291–92) for a balanced assessment of this line of diagnosis.

13. See Woodham-Smith (1962, 76).

14. Churchill also explained that his job in governing India was made difficult by the fact that Indians were "the beastliest people in the world, next to the Germans" (Roberts 1994, 213).

15. See, however, Goody's (1996) powerful critique of this reading of history.

16. Anthony Giddens, introduction to Weber (1930, xvi). See also Weber (1951).

17. See Morishima (1982); Dore (1987); and Ikegami (1995), among other investigations of the cultural aspects of Japanese economic success.

18. Given the importance that is attached in Buddhism to the ability of people to read religious and philosophical discourses, there is even a prima facie motivational connection here that can be cogently examined and critically scrutinized. Indeed, one of Buddha's criticisms of Hinduism in his time was that the scriptures were in Sanskrit, which made them inaccessible to the common people of India.

19. See, for example, Cummings (1980), chapter 2.

20. See Passin (1965, 209–11); also Cummings (1980, 17).

21. Quoted in Kumon and Rosovsky (1992, 330).

22. The role of education in the economic development of East and Southeast Asia is extensively discussed in World Bank (1993).

23. See Hirschman (1977, 1982); Brittan and Hamlin (1995); Griffin (1996); Klamer (1996); Appadurai (1996); Bowles (1998); Cowen (1998, 2002); Landes (1998); UNESCO (1998, 2000); Arizpe (2000); Blau (2001); and Throsby (2001) for various assessments of market-oriented cultures, arguing in different directions.

24. On a related issue, in the context of Indian identity, see Sen (1997).

CHAPTER 3

The Capacity to Aspire:
Culture and the Terms of Recognition

ARJUN APPADURAI

The Argument

This essay seeks to provide a new approach to the question: why does culture matter? Let us lengthen the question and ask why it matters for development and for the reduction of poverty. This both narrows and deepens the question. The answer is that it is in culture that ideas of the future, as much as of those about the past, are embedded and nurtured. Thus, in strengthening the capacity to aspire, conceived as a cultural capacity, especially among the poor, the future-oriented logic of development could find a natural ally, and the poor could find the resources required to contest and alter the conditions of their own poverty. This argument runs against the grain of many deep-seated images of the opposition of culture to economy. But it offers a new foundation on which policy makers can base answers to two basic questions: why is culture a capacity (worth building and strengthening), and what are the concrete ways in which it can be strengthened?

Getting Past Definitions

We do not need one more omnibus definition of culture any more than we need one of the market. In both cases, the textbooks have rung the changes over the long century in which anthropology and economics have taken formal shape as academic disciplines. And not only have the definition mongers had ample say, there has been real refinement and academic progress on both sides. Today's definitions are both more modest, and more helpful. Others are better equipped to tell the story of what we really ought to mean when we speak of markets. Here I address the cultural side of the equation.

General definitions of culture rightly cover a lot of ground, ranging from general ideas about human creativity and values, to matters of collective identity and social organization, matters of cultural integrity and property, and matters of heritage, monuments, and expressions. The intuition behind this capacious net is that what it gains in scope, it loses in edge. In this chapter, I do not deny the broad humanistic implications of cultural form, freedom, and expression. But I focus on just one dimension of culture—its orientation to the future—that is almost never discussed explicitly. Making this dimension explicit could have radical implications for poverty and development.

In taking this approach to culture, we run against some deeply held counterconceptions. For more than a century, culture has been viewed as a matter of one or other kind of pastness—the keywords here are habit, custom, heritage, tradition. On the other hand, development is always seen in terms of the future—plans, hopes, goals, targets. This opposition is an artifact of our definitions and has been crippling. On the anthropological side, in spite of many important technical moves in the understanding of culture, the future remains a stranger to most anthropological models of culture. By default, and also for independent reasons, economics has become the science of the future, and when human beings are seen as having a future, the keywords such as wants, needs, expectations, calculations, have become hardwired into the discourse of economics. In a word, the cultural actor is a person of and from the past, and the economic actor a person of the future. Thus, from the start, culture is opposed to development, as tradition is opposed to newness, and habit to calculation. It is hardly a surprise that nine out of ten treatises on development treat culture as a worry or a drag on the forward momentum of planned economic change.

It is customary for anthropologists to pin the blame for this state of affairs on economists and their unwillingness to broaden their views of economic action and motivation and to take culture into account. And economics is hardly blameless, in its growing preoccupation with models of such abstraction and parsimony that they can hardly take most real-world economics on board, much less the matter of culture, which simply becomes the biggest tenant in the black box of aggregate rationality. But anthropologists need to do better by their own core concept. And this is where the question of the future comes in.

In fact, most approaches to culture do not ignore the future. But they smuggle it in indirectly, when they speak of norms, beliefs, and values as being central to cultures, conceived as specific and multiple designs for social life. But by not elaborating the implications of norms for futurity as a cultural capacity, these definitions tend to allow the sense of culture as pastness to dominate. Even the most interesting recent attempts, notably associated with the name of Pierre Bourdieu (1977), to bring practice, strategy, calculation, and a strong agonistic dimension to cultural action have been attacked for being too structuralist (that is, too formal and static) on the one hand, and too economistic on the other (Bourdieu 1977). And what is sometimes called "practice" theory in anthropology does not directly take up the matter of how collective horizons are shaped and of how they constitute the basis for collective aspirations which may be regarded as cultural.

There have been a few key developments in the anthropological debate over culture that are vital building blocks for the central concern of this essay. The first is the insight, incubated in structural linguistics as early as Saussure, that cultural coherence is not a matter of individual items but of their relationships, and the related insight that these relations are systematic and generative. Even those anthropologists who are deeply unsympathetic to Lévi-Strauss and anything that smacks of linguistic analogy in the study of culture, now assume that the elements of a cultural system make sense only in relation to one another, and that these systematic relations are somehow similar to those which make languages miraculously orderly and productive. The second important development in cultural theory is the idea that dissensus of some sort is part and parcel of culture and that a shared culture is no more a guarantee of complete consensus than a shared platform in the democratic convention. Earlier in the history of the discipline, this incomplete sharing was studied as the central issue in studies of children and of socialization (in anthropology, of "enculturation"), and was based on the obvious fact everywhere that children become culture bearers through specific forms of education and discipline. This insight became deepened and extended through work on gender, politics, and resistance in the last three decades, notably through the work of scholars such as John and Jean Comaroff, James Scott, Sherry Ortner, and a host of others, now so numerous as to be invisible (Comaroff and Comaroff 1991; Scott 1990; Ortner 1995). The third important development in anthropological understandings of culture is the recognition that the boundaries of cultural systems are leaky, and that traffic and osmosis are the norm, not the exception. This strand of thought now underwrites the work of some of the key theorists of the cultural dimensions of globalization (Beck 2000; Hannerz 1992, 1996; Mbembe 2001; Sassen 1998, 1999), who foreground mixture, heterogeneity, diversity, heterogeneity, and plurality as critical features of culture in the era of globalization. Their work reminds us that no culture, past or present, is a conceptual island unto itself, except in the imagination of the observer. Cultures are and always have been interactive to some degree.

Of course, each of these developments in anthropology is accompanied by a host of footnotes, debates, and ongoing litigations (as must be the case in any serious academic discipline). Still, no serious contemporary under-standing of culture can ignore these three key dimensions: relationality (between norms, values, beliefs, etc.); dissensus within some framework of consensus (especially in regard to the marginal, the poor, gender relations, and power relations more generally); and weak boundaries (perenially vis-ible in processes of migration, trade, and warfare now writ large in glob-alizing cultural traffic).

This chapter builds on and returns to these important developments. They are of direct relevance to the recovery of the future as a cultural capacity. In making this recovery, we will also need to recall some of these wider developments within anthropology. But my main concern here is with the implications of these moves for current debates about develop-ment and poverty reduction.

Bringing the Future Back In

The effort to recover, highlight, and foreground the place of the future in our understandings of culture is not a matter, fortunately, where anthro-pology has to invent the entire wheel. Allies for this effort can be found in a variety of fields and disciplines, ranging from political theory and moral philosophy to welfare economics and human rights debates. My own thinking on this project builds on and is in dialogue with three important sets of ideas which come from outside anthropology and some from within it.

Outside anthropology, the effort to strengthen the idea of aspiration as a cultural capacity, can build on Charles Taylor's path-breaking concept of "recognition," his key contribution to the debate on the ethical founda-tions of multiculturalism (Taylor 1992). In this work, Taylor showed that there is such a thing as a "politics of recognition," in virtue of which there was an ethical obligation to extend a sort of moral cognizance to persons who shared worldviews deeply different from our own. This was an important move, which gives the idea of tolerance some political teeth, makes intercultural understanding an obligation, not an option, and rec-ognizes the independent value of dignity in cross-cultural transactions apart from issues of redistribution. The challenge today, as many scholars have noted, is how to bring the politics of dignity and the politics of poverty into a single framework. Put another way, the issue is whether cultural recognition can be extended so as to enhance redistribution (see especially Fraser and Honneth 2003; Fraser 2001).

I also take inspiration from Albert Hirschman's now classic work (Hirschman 1970) on the relations between different forms of collective identification and satisfaction, which enabled us to see the general applicability of the ideas of "loyalty," "exit," and "voice," terms that Hirschman used to cover a wide range of possible relations that human beings have to decline in firms, organizations, and states. In Hirschman's terms, I would suggest that we have tended to see cultural affiliations almost entirely in terms of loyalty (total attachment) but have paid little attention to exit and voice. Voice is a critical matter for my purposes since it engages the question of dissensus. Even more than the idea of exit it is vital to any engagement with the poor (and thus with poverty), since one of their gravest lacks is the lack of resources with which to give "voice," that is, to express their views and get results skewed to their own welfare in the political debates that surround wealth and welfare in all societies. So, a way to put my central question in Hirschman's terms would be: how can we strengthen the capability of the poor to have and to cultivate "voice," since exit is not a desirable solution for the world's poor and loyalty is clearly no longer generally clearcut?

My approach also responds to Amartya Sen, who has placed us all in his debt through a series of efforts to argue for the place of values in economic analysis and in the politics of welfare and well-being. Through his earlier work on social values and development (Sen 1984) to his more recent work on social welfare (loosely characterized as the "capabilities" approach) (Sen 1985a) and on freedom (Sen 1999), Sen has made major and overlapping arguments for placing matters of freedom, dignity, and moral well-being at the heart of welfare and its economics. This approach has many implications and applications, but for my purposes, it highlights the need for a parallel internal opening up in how to understand culture, so that Sen's radical expansion of the idea of welfare can find its strongest cultural counterpoint. In this chapter, I am partly concerned to bring aspiration in as a strong feature of cultural capacity, as a step in creating a more robust dialogue between "capacity" and "capability," the latter in Sen's terms. In more general terms, Sen's work is a major invitation to anthropology to widen its conceptions of how human beings engage their own futures.

Within anthropology, in addition to the basic developments I addressed already, I regard this chapter as being in a dialogue with two key scholars.

The first, Mary Douglas, in her work on cosmology (Douglas 1973/1982), later on commodities and budgets, and later still on risk and nature (Douglas and Wildavsky 1982), has repeatedly argued for seeing ordinary people as operating through cultural designs for anticipation and risk reduction. This is a line of thought that helps us to investigate the broader problem of aspiration in a systematic way, with due attention to the internal relations of cosmology and calculation among poorer people, such as those members of the English working classes studied by Douglas in some of her best work on consumption (Douglas and Isherwood 1979/1996).

Finally, James Fernandez has had a long-term interest in the problem of how cultural consensus is produced. In this exercise, he has reminded us that even in the most "traditional"-looking cultures, such as the Fang of West Africa whom he has written about extensively, we cannot take consensus for granted. His second major contribution is in showing that through the specific operations of various forms of verbal and material ritual, through "performances" and metaphors arranged and enacted in specific ways, real groups actually produce the kinds of consensus on first principles that they may appear to take simply for granted (Fernandez 1965, 1986). This work opens the ground for me, in my own examinations of activism among the poor in India and elsewhere to note that certain uses of words and arrangements of action that we may call cultural, may be especially strategic sites for the production of consensus. This is a critical matter for anyone concerned with helping the poor to help themselves, or in our current jargon, to "empower" the poor. With Fernandez, we can ask how the poor may be helped to produce those forms of cultural consensus that may be best advance their own collective long-term interests in matters of wealth, equality, and dignity.

I turn now to asking why such a revitalized tool kit is called for to make real progress on the relationship between culture, poverty, and development. What exactly is the problem?

The Capacity to Aspire

Poverty is many things, all of them bad. It is material deprivation and desperation. It is lack of security and dignity. It is exposure to risk and high costs for thin comforts. It is inequality materialized. It diminishes its victims. It is also the situation of far too many people in the world, even if the relative number of those who are escaping the worst forms of poverty is also increasing. The number of the world's poor, their destitution, and their desperation now seem overwhelming by most measures.

The poor are not just the human bearers of the condition of poverty.

They are a social group, partly defined by official measures but also conscious of themselves as a group, in the real languages of many societies. Just as ordinary human beings have learned to think of themselves as "people" and even as "the people" in most human societies in the wake of the democratic revolution of the last three centuries, poor people increasingly see themselves as a group, in their own societies and also across these societies. There may not be anything which can usefully be called a "culture of poverty" (anthropologists have rightly ceased to use this conceptualization), but the poor certainly have understandings of themselves and the world that have cultural dimensions and expressions. These may not be easy to identify, since they are not neatly nested with shared national or regional cultures, and often cross local and national lines. Also, they may be differently articulated by men and women, the poorest and the merely poor, the employed and the unemployed, the disabled and the able-bodied, the more politically conscious and the less mobilized. But it is never hard to identify threads and themes in the worldviews of the poor. These are strikingly concrete and local in expression but also impressively general in their reach. The multivolume World Bank–sponsored study of "The Voices of the Poor" is a major archive of these threads and themes (Narayan et al. 2001a,b).

This archive and other close observations of poor populations in different parts of the world reveal a number of important things about culture and poverty. The first is that poor people have a deeply ambivalent relationship to the dominant norms of the societies in which they live. Even when they are not obviously hostile to these norms, they often show forms of irony, distance, and cynicism about these norms. This sense of irony, which allows the poor to maintain some dignity in the worst conditions of oppression and inequality, is one side of their involvement in the dominant cultural norms. The other side is compliance, not mere surface compliance but fairly deep moral attachment to norms and beliefs that directly support their own degradation. Thus, many untouchables in India comply with the degrading exclusionary rules and practices of caste because they subscribe in some way to the larger order of norms and metaphysical propositions which dictate their compliance: these include ideas about fate, rebirth, caste duty, and sacred social hierarchies. Thus the poor are neither simple dupes nor secret revolutionaries. They are survivors. And what they often seek strategically (even without a theory to dress it up) is to optimize the terms of trade between recognition and redistribution in their immediate, local lives. Their ideas about such optimization may not be perfect, but do we have better optima to offer to them?

I refer to this ambivalence among the poor (and by extension the excluded, the disadvantaged, and the marginal groups in society more generally) about the cultural worlds in which they exist in terms of the idea of the terms of recognition (building on Taylor's ideas). In speaking about the terms of recognition (by analogy with the terms of trade, or the terms of engagement), I mean to highlight the conditions and constraints under which the poor negotiate with the very norms that frame their social lives. I propose that poverty is partly a matter of operating with extremely weak resources where the terms of recognition are concerned. More concretely, the poor are frequently in a position where they are encouraged to subscribe to norms whose social effect is to further diminish their dignity, exacerbate their inequality, and deepen their lack of access to material goods and services. In the Indian case, these norms take a variety of forms: some have to do with fate, luck, and rebirth; others have to do with the glorification of asceticism and material deprivation; yet others connect social deference to deference to divinity; yet others reduce major metaphysical assumptions to simple and rigid rules of etiquette which promise freedom from reprisal. When I refer to operating under adverse terms of recognition, I mean that in recognizing those who are wealthy, the poor permit the existing and corrupt standing of local and national elites to be further bolstered and reproduced. But when they are recognized (in the cultural sense), it is usually as an abstract political category, divorced of real persons (Indira Gandhi's famous slogan *garibi hatao*— remove poverty—and many other populist slogans, have this quality). Or their poverty is perversely recognized as a sign of some sort of worldly disorder which promises, by inversion, its own long-term rectification. The poor are recognized, but in ways that ensure minimum change in the terms of redistribution. So, to the extent that poverty is indexed by poor terms of recognition for the poor, intervention to positively affect these terms is a crucial priority.

In other terms, returning to Hirschman, we need to strengthen the capacity of the poor to exercise "voice," to debate, contest, and oppose vital directions for collective social life as they wish, not only because this is virtually a definition of inclusion and participation in any democracy. But there is a stronger reason for strengthening the capacity for voice among the poor. It is the only way in which the poor might find locally plausible ways to alter what I am calling the terms of recognition in any particular cultural regime. Here I treat voice as a cultural capacity, not just as a generalized and universal democratic virtue because for voice to take effect, it must engage social, political, and economic issues in terms of ideologies, doctrines, and norms which are widely shared and credible, even by the rich and powerful. Furthermore, voice must be expressed in terms of actions and performances which have local cultural force. Here, Gandhi's life, his fasting, his abstinence, his bodily comportment, his ascetical style, his crypto-Hindu use of nonviolence and of peaceful resistance, were all tremendously successful because they mobilized a local palette of performances and precursors. Likewise, as the poor seek to strengthen their voices as a cultural capacity, they will need to find those levers of metaphor, rhetoric, organization, and public performance that will work best in their cultural worlds. And when they do work, as we have seen with various movements in the past, they change the terms of recognition, indeed the cultural framework itself. So, there is no shortcut to empowerment. It has to take some local cultural form to have resonance, mobilize adherents, and capture the public space of debate. And this is true in the efforts that the poor make to mobilize themselves (internally) and in their efforts to change the dynamics of consensus in their larger social worlds.

The complex relationship of the poor and the marginalized to the cultural regimes within which they function is clearer still when we consider a specific cultural capacity, the capacity to aspire. I have already indicated that this is a weak feature of most approaches to cultural processes and frequently remains obscure. This obscurity has been especially costly for the poor, and in regard to development more generally.

Aspirations certainly have something to do with wants, preferences, choices, and calculations. And because these factors have been assigned to the discipline of economics, to the domain of the market and to the level of the individual actor (all approximate characterizations), they have been large invisible in the study of culture.

To repatriate them into the domain of the culture, we need to begin by noting that aspirations form parts of wider ethical and metaphysical ideas which derive from larger cultural norms. Aspirations are never simply individual (as the language of wants and choices inclines us to think). They are always formed in interaction and in the thick of social life. As far back as Emile Durkheim and George Herbert Mead, we have learned that there is no self outside a social frame, setting, and mirror. Could it be otherwise for aspirations? And aspirations about the good life, about health and happiness, exist in all societies. Yet a Buddhist picture of the good life lies at some distance from an Islamic one. Equally, a poor Tamil peasant woman's view of the good life may be as distant from that of a cosmopolitan woman from Delhi, as from that of an equally poor woman from Tanzania. But in every case, aspirations to the good life are part of some sort of system of ideas (remember relationality as an aspect of cultural worlds) which locates them in a larger map of local ideas and beliefs about: life and death, the nature of worldly possessions, the significance of material assets over social relations, the relative illusion of social permanence for a society, the value of peace or warfare. At the same time, aspirations to the good life tend to quickly dissolve into more densely local ideas about marriage, work, leisure, convenience, respectability, friendship, health, and virtue. More narrow still, these intermediate norms often stay beneath the surface and emerge only as specific wants and choices: for this piece of land or that, for that marriage connection or another one, for this job in the bureaucracy as opposed to that job overseas, for this pair of shoes over that pair of trousers. This last, most immediate, visible inventory of wants has often led students of consumption and of poverty to lose sight of the intermediate and higher order normative contexts within which these wants are gestated and brought into view. And thus decontextualized, they are usually downloaded to the individual and offloaded to the science of calculation and the market—economics.

The poor, no less than any other group in a society, do express horizons in choices made and choices voiced, often in terms of specific goods and outcomes, often material and proximate, like doctors for their children, markets for their grain, husbands for their daughters, and tin roofs for their homes. But these lists, apparently just bundles of individual and idiosyncratic wants, are inevitably tied up with more general norms, presumptions, and axioms about the good life, and life more generally.

But here is the twist with the capacity to aspire. It is not evenly distributed in any society. It is a sort of metacapacity, and the relatively rich and powerful invariably have a more fully developed capacity to aspire. What does this mean? It means that the better off you are (in terms of power, dignity, and material resources), the more likely you are to be conscious of the links between the more and less immediate objects of aspiration. Because the better off, by definition, have a more complex experience of the relation between a wide range of ends and means, because they have a bigger stock of available experiences of the relationship of aspirations and outcomes, because they are in a better position to explore and harvest diverse experiences of exploration and trial, because of their many opportunities to link material goods and immediate opportunities to more general and generic possibilities and options. They too may express their aspirations in concrete, individual wishes and wants. But they are more able to produce justifications, narratives, metaphors, and pathways through which bundles of goods and services are actually tied to wider social scenes and contexts, and to still more abstract norms and beliefs. This resource, unequally tilted in favor of the wealthier people in any society, is also subject to the truism that "the rich get richer," since the archive of concrete experiments with the good life gives nuance and texture to more general norms and axioms; conversely, experience with articulating these norms and axioms makes the more privileged members of any society more supple in navigating the complex steps between these norms and specific wants and wishes.

The capacity to aspire is thus a navigational capacity. The more privileged in any society simply have used the map of its norms to explore the future more frequently and more realistically, and to share this knowledge with one another more routinely than their poorer and weaker neighbors. The poorer members, precisely because of their lack of opportunities to practice the use of this navigational capacity (in turn because their situations permit fewer experiments and less easy archiving of alternative futures), have a more brittle horizon of aspirations.

This difference should not be misunderstood. I am not saying that the poor cannot wish, want, need, plan, or aspire. But part of poverty is a diminishing of the circumstances in which these practices occur. If the map of aspirations (continuing the navigational metaphor) is seen to consist of a dense combination of nodes and pathways, relative poverty means a smaller number of aspirational nodes and a thinner, weaker sense of the pathways from concrete wants to intermediate contexts to general norms and back again. Where these pathways do exist for the poor, they are likely to be more rigid, less supple, and less strategically valuable, not because of any cognitive deficit on the part of the poor but because the capacity to aspire, like any complex cultural capacity, thrives and survives on practice, repetition, exploration, conjecture, and refutation. Where the opportunities for such conjecture and refutation in regard to the future are limited (and this may well be one way to define poverty), it follows that the capacity itself remains relatively less developed.

This capacity to aspire—conceived as a navigational capacity which is nurtured by the possibility of real-world conjectures and refutations—compounds the ambivalent compliance of many subaltern populations with the cultural regimes that surround them. This is because the experiential limitations in subaltern populations, on the capacity to aspire, tend to create a binary relationship to core cultural values, negative and skeptical at one pole, overattached at the other. Returning to Hirschman's typology, this may be part of the reason that the less privileged, and especially the very poor, in any society, tend to oscillate between "loyalty" and "exit" (whether the latter takes the form of violent protest or total apathy). Of course, the objective is to increase the capacity for the third posture, the posture of "voice," the capacity to debate, contest, inquire, and participate critically.

The faculty of "voice" in Hirschman's terms, and what I am calling the capacity to aspire, a cultural capacity, are reciprocally linked. Each accelerates the nurture of the other. And the poor in every society are caught in a situation where triggers to this positive acceleration are few and hard to access. Here empowerment has an obvious translation: increase the capacity to aspire, especially for the poor. This is by definition an approach to culture, since capacities form parts of sets, and are always part of a local design of means and ends, values and strategies, experiences and tested insights. Such a map is always a highly specific way of connecting what Clifford Geertz long ago called the "experience-near" and the "experience-distant" aspects of life and may thus rightly be called cultural or, less felicitiously, a "culture" (Geertz 1973b). This is the map that needs to be made more real, available, and powerful for the poor.

Having suggested that the capacity to aspire requires strengthening among poor communities, it is vital to note that examples of such efforts are already available in a variety of new social movements, many driven from and by the poor themselves. In these movements, we can see what can be accomplished when the capacity to aspire is strengthened and tested in the real world, the world in which development can either fail or succeed. In looking closely at one such movement, we are also able to see the how mobilization can expand and enrich the capacity to aspire within a specific social and cultural milieu.

Changing the Terms of Recognition: On the Ground in Mumbai

I have elsewhere described some results of a study in progress of grassroots globalization, which consists of a detailed ethnographic account of a propoor alliance of housing activists based in Mumbai who are building a global coalition to serve their vision (Appadurai 2001). This movement represents forcefully what happens when a group of poor people begins to mobilize its capacity to aspire in a specific political and cultural regime. It allows me to say something about the lived experience of poverty but also about a specific set of ways in which a specific propoor activist movement is changing the terms of recognition for the urban poor and enriching the cultural capacity to aspire among its members through a strategy that creates a double helix between local activism and global networking. The Mumbai-based coalition, which I focus on in this essay, has been at the heart of a global network of community-based housing activists, called the Slum/Shackdwellers International (SDI), which now has members in more than a dozen countries in Africa and Asia (notably in India, South Africa, and Thailand), with additional alliances in Latin America, Japan, and the United Kingdom. SDI is a major example of the sort of global, nongovernmental network which produces new forms of local politics by innovating strategic forms of activism across borders. While the examples I use come from India, I could cite many similar examples from the activities of the network in South Africa and the Philippines, and other national settings.

The city of Mumbai is in the state of Maharashtra, in western India. The movement here consists of three partners, and as an Alliance, its history goes back to 1987. The three partners have different histories. SPARC is an nongovernmental organization (NGO) formed by social work professionals in 1984 to work with problems of urban poverty in Mumbai. The National Slum Dweller's Foundation is a powerful grassroots organization established in 1974 and is a community-based organization which also has its historical base in Mumbai. Finally, Mahila Milan is an organization of poor women, set up in 1986, with its base in Mumbai and a network throughout India, which is focused on women's issues in relation to urban poverty, and is especially concerned with local and self-organized savings schemes among the very poor. All three organizations, which refer to themselves collectively as the Alliance, are united in their concerns with gaining secure tenure in land, adequate and durable housing, and access to urban infrastructure, notably to electricity, transport, sanitation, and allied services.

Mumbai is the largest city in a country (India) whose population has just crossed the 1 billion level (one-sixth of the population of the world). The city's population is at least 12 million (more if we include the growing edges of the city and the population of the twin city which has been built across the Thane Creek). This means a population of 1.2% of one-sixth of the world's population. Not a minor case, even in itself.

By general consensus, here are some facts about housing in Mumbai. About 40% of its population (about 6 million persons) live in slums or other degraded forms of housing. Another 5% to 10% are pavement dwellers. Yet, according to one recent estimate, slum dwellers occupy only 8% of the city's land, which totals about 43,000 hectares. The rest of the city's land is either industrial land, middle- and high-income housing, or vacant land in the control of the city, the state (regional and federal) or private owners. The bottom line: 5 to 6 million poor people living in substandard conditions in 8% of the land area of a city no bigger than Manhattan and its near boroughs. In addition, this huge population of the insecurely or poorly housed people has negligible access to essential services, such as running water, electricity, and ration cards for essential foods.

Equally important, this population, which we may call citizens without a city, is a vital part of the workforce of the city. Some of them occupy the lowest end of white-collar organizations and others the lowest end of industrial and manufacturing industries. But many are engaged in temporary, menial, physically dangerous and socially degrading forms of work. This latter group, which may well constitute 1 to 2 million people in Mumbai, are best described, in the striking phrase of Sandeep Pendse (1995), as Mumbai's "toilers" rather than as its proletariat, working class, or laboring classes, all designations which suggest more stable forms of employment and organization.

Housing is at the very heart of the lives of this army of toilers. Their everyday life is dominated by ever-present forms of risk. Their temporary shacks may be demolished. Their slumlords may push them out through force or extortion. The torrential monsoons may destroy their fragile shelters and their few personal possessions. Their lack of sanitary facilities increases their needs for doctors to whom they have poor access. And their inability to document their claims to housing may snowball into a general invisibility in urban life, making it impossible for them to claim any rights to such things as rationed foods, municipal health and education facilities, police protection, and voting rights. In a city where ration cards, electricity bills, and rent receipts guarantee other rights to the benefits of citizenship, the inability to secure claims to proper housing and other political handicaps reinforce one another. Housing—and its lack—is the most public drama of disenfranchisement in Mumbai. Thus, the politics of housing can be argued to be the single most critical site of a politics of citizenship in this city. This is the context in which the activists I am working with are making their interventions, mobilizing the poor and generating new forms of politics.

Instead of finding safety in affiliation with any single ruling party or coalition in the state government of Maharashtra or in the municipal corporation of Mumbai, the Alliance has developed a complex political affiliation with the various levels and forms of the state bureaucracy. This group includes its national civil servants who execute state policy at the highest levels in the state of Maharashtra and run the major bodies responsible for housing loans, slum rehabilitation, real estate regulation, and the like. The members of the Alliance have also developed complex links with the quasi-autonomous arms of the federal government (such as the railways, the port authority, the Bombay Electric Supply and Transport Corporation) and to municipal authorities who control critical aspects of infrastructure, such as regulations concerning illegal structures, water supply, sanitation, and licensing of residential structures. Finally, the Alliance works to maintain a cordial relationship with the Mumbai police and at least a hands-off relationship with the underworld, which is deeply involved in the housing market, slum landlordism, and extortion, as well as in the demolition and rebuilding of temporary structures. From this perspective, the politics of the Alliance is a politics of accommodation, negotiation, and long-term pressure rather than of confrontation or threats of political reprisal. This pragmatic approach is grounded in a complex political vision about means, ends, and styles which is not entirely utilitarian or functional. It is based on a series of ideas about the transformation of the conditions of poverty by the poor in the long run. In this sense, the idea of a political horizon implies an idea of patience and of cumulative victories and long-term asset building which is wired into every aspect of the activities of the Alliance. The Alliance believes that the mobilization of the knowledge of the poor into methods driven by the poor and for the poor is a slow and risk-laden process that informs the strong bias of the Alliance against "projects" and "projectization" that underlies almost all official ideas about urban change.

This resistance to externally defined time frames (driven by donor schedules, budgets, and economies) is a critical part of the way in which the Alliance cultivates the capacity to aspire among its members. It is played out in tough negotiations (both internal to the Alliance and with external agencies) about how plans are made, risks taken, commitments solidified, and accountability defined. For example, the Alliance recently succeeded in getting a major contract to build a large number of community toilets in Mumbai, on a scale previously reserved for private contracts and developers, or for government organizations and experts. By acquiring this major contract, the Alliance set itself the challenge of relating its long-term visions of dignity, health, and sanitary self-sufficiency to its short-term capacities for handling contractors, builders, suppliers, engineers, and banks in Mumbai. In this ongoing exercise, which is a textbook case of what "empowerment" could really mean, important segments of Mumbai's slum dwellers are exercising collectively the sinews of the capacity to aspire, while testing their capacities to convince skeptics from the funding world, the banking world, the construction industry, and the municipality of Mumbai that they can deliver what they promise, while building their capacities to plan, coordinate, manage, and mobilize their energies in a difficult and large-scale technical endeavor.

Another arena in which the Alliance (and its global partners in SDI) builds the capacity to aspire is in regard to savings, which they see as a discipline of community building. But it is also a central mode for building the capacity to aspire. Savings is thus a term which means more than what it says in the life of the Alliance. Creating informal savings groups among the poor (now canonized by the donor world as "microcredit") is a major worldwide technique for improving financial citizenship for the urban and rural poor throughout the world, often building on older ideas of revolving credit and loan facilities managed informally and locally, outside the purview of the state and the banking sector. Savings and microcredit have many advocates and visionaries in India and elsewhere. But in the life of the Alliance, savings has a profound ideological, even salvational, status. The visionary of the specific philosophy of daily savings for the Alliance is the president of the National Slum-Dweller's Foundation, A. Jockin, who has used daily savings as a principal tool for mobilization in India and his central strategy for entry and relationship building in South Africa, Cambodia, and Thailand. He is the missionary of a specific idea of daily savings among small-scale groups, which he sees as the bedrock of every other activity of the federation. Indeed, it is not an exaggeration to say that in Jockin's organizational exhortations wherever he goes, Federation = Savings. When Jockin and other members of the Alliance speak about daily savings, it becomes evident that they are describing something far deeper than a simple mechanism for meeting daily monetary needs and sharing resources among the poor. They are also speaking about a way of life organized around the importance of daily savings, which is viewed as a moral discipline (in Jockin's words, it is like "breathing") which builds a certain kind of political fortitude and commitment to the collective good and creates persons who can manage their affairs in many other ways as well. It is something like a spiritual discipline whose spread Jockin and other leaders see as the building block of the local and global success of the federation model.

Mahila Milan, the women's group that is the third partner in the Alliance, is almost entirely preoccupied with organizing small savings circles. Thus, in putting savings at the heart of the moral politics of the Alliance, its leaders place the work of poor women at the very foundation of what they do in every other area. In a simple formula: without poor women joining together, there can be no savings. Without savings, there can be no community building. Without real communities (defined by them as parts of "federations"), there is no way for the poor to drive changes themselves in the arrangements that disempower them. Thus, the act of savings is an ethical principle which forms the practical and moral core of the politics of patience, since it does not generate large resources quickly. It is also a moral discipline which produces persons who can raise the political force and material commitments most valued by the federation.

Sharing and circulating ideas and experiences about savings, in direct exchanges among the poor women of SDI, has been one of the major modes by which the poorest communities in SDI have built a global dialogue based on face-to-face conversation and honest criticism of each other's hopes and failures. These exchanges also facilitate conversations about the differences in the challenges that different communities, in different countries, face in their own environments. They are also the processes through which cultural differences are explored, negotiated, and transcended through laughter, debate, song, and speeches in collective events organized over the years in Mumbai, Manila, Cape Town, Durban, and many other places. These discussions about savings are highly specific occasions for poor men and women to find out what the future truly means for different individuals and groups who are trying to think ahead and struggle for secure tenure, for government loans, for permits for water or electricity, or for the right to police their own communities. Here, local horizons of hope and desire enter a dialogue with other designs for the future and poor persons (often women) crossing massive cultural boundaries are able to discuss their aspirations in the most concrete of forms, in conversations about why some members are unable to save regularly, about why some misuse their access to community funds, about what sorts of consumption are more or less legitimate with borrowed money, and about how money relates to trust, power, and community.

The last key term that recurs in the writing and speech of the leaders of the Alliance is the idea of "precedent setting." I am still exploring the full ramifications of this linguistic strategy. What I have learned so far is that, beneath its bland, quasi-legal tone, there is a more radical idea. The idea is that the poor need to claim, capture, refine, and define certain ways of doing things in spaces they already control and then use these to show donors, city officials, and other activists that these "precedents" are good ones, and encourage other actors to invest further in them. This is a politics of "show and tell," but it is also a philosophy of "do first, talk later." The subversive feature of this principle is that it provides a linguistic device for negotiating between the legalities of urban government and the full force of the "illegal" arrangements that the poor almost always have to make, whether they concern illegal structures, illegal strategies, informal arrangements for water and electricity, or anything else that they have succeeded in capturing out of the material resources of the city. This linguistic device shifts the burden for municipal officials and other experts away from the strain of whitewashing illegal activities to the safety of building on legitimate precedents. The image and linguistic strategy of "precedent" turns the survival strategies and experiments of the poor into legitimate foundations for policy innovations by the state, by the city, by donors, and by other activist organizations. It is a linguistic strategy that moves the poor into the horizon of legality on their own terms. Most importantly, it involves risk-taking activities by bureaucrats within a discourse of legality, and allows the boundaries of the status quo to be pushed and stretched without creating fears of rule-breaking among those bureaucrats who are sympathetic to the Alliance. It creates a border zone of trial and error, a sort of research and development space, within which poor communities, activists, and bureaucrats can explore new designs for partnership. The strategies of precedent setting also constitute spaces for exploring the capacity to aspire and for testing the possibilities for changes in the terms of recognition. For in every discussion about precedent setting, what is involved is a map of a journey into the future, whether in the matter of relocating homes (after demolition of temporary homes by the police) or of arrangements with contractors to provide services for building toilets, or of dealings with funders about deadlines, reports, and accountability. In each of these instances, activists and the poor communities they answer to (or come from) have to practice the arts of aspiration, lending vision and horizon to immediate strategies and choices, lending immediacy and materiality to abstract wishes and desires, and struggling to reconcile the demands of the moment against the disciplines of patience.

But the world does not change through language alone. These key-words (and many other linguistic strategies not discussed here) also provide the nervous system of a whole body of broader technical, institutional, and representational practices which have become signatures of the politics of the Alliance. Here I briefly discuss two vital organizational strategies that capture the ways in which technical practices are harnessed to the Alliance's political horizon. They are housing exhibitions and toilet festivals.

Housing exhibitions are a major organized technique through which the structural bias of existing knowledge processes is challenged, even reversed, in the politics of the Alliance. Since the materialities of housing—its cost, its durability, its legality, and its design—lie at the very heart of slum life, it is no surprise that this is an area where grassroots creativity has had radical effects. As in other matters, the general philosophy of state agencies, donors, and even NGOs concerned with slums has been to assume that the design, construction, and financing of houses has to be produced by various forms of expert and professional knowledge ranging from that of engineers and architects, to that of contractors and surveyors. The Alliance has challenged this assumption by a steady effort to appropriate, in a cumulative manner, all the knowledge required to construct new housing for its members. In effect, in Mumbai, the Alliance has moved into housing development, and the fruits of this remarkable move are to be seen in three or four major sites, in Mankhurd, Dharavi, Ghatkopar.

Housing exhibitions are a crucial part of this reversal of the standard flows of expertise when it comes to housing for the rehabilitation of slum dwellers. The idea of housing exhibitions by and for the poor goes back to 1986 in Mumbai and has since been replicated in many cities in India and elsewhere in the world. These exhibitions, organized by the Alliance and other like-minded groups, are an example of the creative hijacking of an upper-class form (historically evolved for consumer products and high-end industrial products oriented to the middle and upper classes in India) for the purposes of the poor. Not only do these exhibitions allow the poor (and especially the women among them) to discuss and debate designs for housing that suited their own needs, it also allowed them to enter into conversations with various professionals about housing materials, construction costs, and urban services. Through this process, their own ideas of the good life, of adequate space, and of realistic costs, were foregrounded, and they began to see that house building in a professional manner was only a logical extension of their greatest expertise, which was to build adequate housing out of the flimsiest of materials and in the most insecure of circumstances. These poor families were enabled to see that they had always been architects and engineers and could continue to play that role in the building of more secure housing. In this process, many technical and design innovations were made, and continue to be made.

More significant, these events were political events where poor families and activists from one city traveled to housing exhibitions in another city, socializing with each other, sharing ideas, and simply having fun. They were also events to which state officials were invited, to cut the ceremonial ribbon and to give speeches associating themselves with these grass-roots exercises, thus simultaneously gaining points for hobnobbing with "the people" and giving poor families in the locality some legitimacy in the eyes of their neighbors, their civic authorities, and themselves. More important, in these public and ceremonial moments, we can see another remarkable way in which the capacity to aspire is built by changing the terms of recognition. Time after time, in the speeches by the leaders of the Alliance at these events, I have seen the importance of the languages of hope, aspiration, trust, and desire come together in a variety of languages (English, Hindi, and Marathi especially), in speeches built around a core of terms such as *asha* (hope), *bharosa* (trust), *yojana* (plan), and *chahat* (desire), all deployed in speeches about the importance of building more housing for the poor, for increasing their freedom from harassment, and for expanding their spheres of self-governance. As politicians and bureaucrats join these events, in which much speech making is substantially spontaneous, they also find themselves drawn into the lexicon of plans, commitments, hopes, and trust. While it is possible to view these events as mere political charades, I would suggest that they are productive forms of political negotiation, in which poor communities are able to draw politicians into public commitments to expand the resources and recognitions available to the poor. Not all of these promises may be kept (or even meant), but they change the climate of negotiation, place certain commitments on public record, and produce a common terrain of aspiration in which the politics of the poor and the politics of politicians are brought into a common performative space. These are critical steps in strengthening the exercise of the capacity to aspire, among poor communities, not just as a cultural capacity but as a public and political capacity. Words, in such contexts, may not exactly be performatives, which guarantee material outcomes. But they are potent signals and occasions for building the capacity to aspire.

As with other key practices of the Alliance, housing exhibitions are also deep exercises in subverting the existing class cultures of India. By performing their competences in public, by drawing an audience of their peers and of the state, other NGOs, and sometimes foreign funders, these poor families involved enter a space of public sociality, official recognition, and technical legitimation. And they do so with their own creativity as the main exhibit. Thus technical and cultural capital are cocreated in these events, creating new levers for further guerrilla exercises in capturing civic space and pieces of the public sphere hitherto denied to the urban poor. This is a particular politics of visibility which inverts the harm of the default condition of civic invisibility which characterizes the urban poor.

Running through all these activities is a spirit of transgression and bawdiness, expressed in body language, speech styles, and public address. The men and women of the Alliance are involved in constant banter with each other and even with the official world (though with some care for context). Nowhere does this carnivalesque spirit come out more clearly that in the Toilet Festivals (*sandas melas*) organized by the Alliance, which enact what we may call the politics of shit. Human waste management, as it is euphemistically described in policy circles, is perhaps the key arena where every problem of the urban poor arrives at a single point of extrusion, so to speak. Given the abysmal housing, often with almost no privacy, that most urban slum dwellers enjoy, shitting in public is a serious humiliation for adults. Children are indifferent up to a certain age, but no adult, male or female, enjoys shitting in broad daylight in public view. In rural India, women go the fields to defecate while it is still dark, and men may go later but with some measure of protection from the public eye (with the exception of the gaze of railway passengers inured to the sight of squatting bodies in the fields, and vice versa). Likewise, in rural India, the politics of shitting is spatially managed through a completely different economy of space, water, visibility, and custom.

In cities, the problem is much more serious. Shitting in the absence of good sewage systems, ventilation, and running water (all of which slums, by definition, lack) is a humiliating practice that is intimately connected to the conditions under which waterborne diseases take hold, creating life-threatening disease conditions. One macabre joke among Mumbai's urban poor is that they are the only ones in the city who cannot afford to get diarrhea, partly because the lines at the few existing public toilets are so long (often involving waiting times of an hour or more), and of course medical facilities for stemming the condition are also hard to find. So shitting and its management are a central issue of slum life. Living in an ecology of fecal odors, piles, and channels, where cooking water, washing water, and shit-bearing water are not carefully insulated from one another, adds high risks of disease and mortality to the social humiliation of shitting in public view.

The Toilet Festivals organized by the Alliance in many cities of India are a brilliant effort to turn this humiliating and privatized suffering into scenes of technical innovation, collective celebration, and carnivalesque play with officials from the state, from the World Bank, and from middle-class officialdom in general. These toilet festivals involve the exhibition and inauguration not of models but of real public toilets, by and for the poor, involving complex systems of collective payment and maintenance, optimal conditions of safety and cleanliness, and a collective obligation to sustain these facilities. These facilities are currently small scale and have not yet been built in anything like the large numbers required for the urban slum populations of India's cities. But they are another performance of competence and innovation, in which the politics of shit is (to mix metaphors) turned on its head, and humiliation and victimization are turned into exercises in technical initiative and self-dignification. This is a politics of recognition (Taylor 1992) from below. When a World Bank official has to examine the virtues of a public toilet and to discuss the merits of this form of shit management with the shitters themselves, the materiality of poverty turns from abjectivity to subjectivity. The politics of shit (as Gandhi showed in his own efforts to liberate Indian untouchables from the task of carrying away the shit of their upper-caste superiors) is a meeting point of the human body, dignity, and technology, which the poor are now redefining with the help of movements like the Alliance. In India, where distance from your own shit is the virtual marker of class distinction, the poor, too long living in their shit, are finding ways to place some distance between their shit and themselves. The toilet exhibitions are a transgressive display of this fecal politics, itself a critical material feature of deep democracy. They also connect, in the most powerful way, the politics of recognition to the politics of material life and of the link between dignity and the capacity to aspire.

In June 2001, at a major meeting at the United Nations, marking the five years that had passed after the important Istanbul housing meeting of 1996, the Alliance and its partners elsewhere in the world built a model house as well as a model children's toilet in the lobby of the main United Nations building, after considerable internal debate within the SDI and official resistance at the UN. These models were visited by Kofi Annan in a festive atmosphere which left an indelible impression of material empowerment on the world of UN bureaucrats and NGO officials present. Annan was surrounded by poor women from India and South Africa, singing and dancing, as he walked through the model house and the model toilet, in the heart of his own bureaucratic empire. It was a magical moment, full of possibilities for the Alliance, and for the secretary-general, as they engage jointly and together with the global politics of poverty. So housing exhibitions, and toilets too, can be moved, built, reconstructed, and deployed anywhere, thus sending the message that no space is too grand—or too humble—for the spatial imagination of the poor and for the global portability of the capacity to aspire.

In all these instances, a creative repertoire of rituals and performances, both linguistic and technical, creates the sort of feedback loop between general principles and specific goals which is at the heart of all active social change. It applies both to the partnerships which the Alliance seeks and to its internal dynamics. These performances increase the density, variety, and frequency of the loops between nodes and pathways that I discussed when I described the capacity to aspire as a navigational capacity. The more it is exercised, the more its potential for changing the terms of recognition under which the poor must operate. The Alliance has palpably changed these terms of recognition, both internally (for example, in how the men in the movement treat and regard the women) and externally (for example, in how funders and multilaterals now treat members of the Alliance and other similar activists today—less as objects than as partners).

Consensus, Capacities, Capabilities

We are now in a position to pull together some of the themes of this chapter. I have tried to show that specific forms of self-governance, self-mobilization, and self-articulation are vital to changing the conditions under which activists among the poor are changing the terms of recognition, globally and locally, for the poor. I have also tried to show in the case of the SDI that consensus works at two levels and that both require conscious intervention. The first is the transformation of core norms that surround the poor in any particular sociocultural regime. The second is that internal consensus is produced through what many of the SDI activists themselves refer to as their own "rituals" of practice and procedure. In both cases, existing forms of consensus are changed and new forms of consensus are built, as James Fernandez would have predicted, by the deliberate orchestration of forms of language and special social performances which we could loosely refer to as "ritualized."

Ritual here should not be taken in its colloquial sense, as the meaningless repetition of set patterns of action, but rather as a flexible formula of performances through which social effects are produced and new states of feeling and connection are created, not just reflected or commemorated. This creative, productive, generative quality of ritual is crucial to consensus building in popular movements and it is a quintessential window into why culture matters for development.

For many propoor movements, such as the Alliance of housing activists I described in detail, the capacity to aspire (what I referred to earlier as a metacapacity) is especially precious in the face of the peculiar forms of temporality within which they are forced to operate. In this, they are not different from many other poor groups, especially in cities, but also in the countryside in many societies. The paradox of patience in the face of emergency has become a big feature of the world of globalization, as many poor people experience it. The world has a whole operates increasingly in the mode of urgency, of emergency, of dangers that require immediate reaction and attention. The poor, as refugees, as migrants, as minorities, as slum dwellers, and as subsistence farmers, are often at the center of these emergencies. Yet their biggest weapon is often their patience as they wait for relief to come, rulers to die, bureaucrats to deliver promises, government servants to be transferred, or drought to pass. This ability to hurry up and wait (an American joke about life in the army) has much more serious meaning in the life of the poor.

In helping the poor to negotiate emergency with patience, the capacity to aspire guarantees an ethical and psychological anchor, a horizon of credible hopes, with which to withstand the deadly oscillation between waiting and rushing. Here, too, the capacity to aspire is a cultural capacity whose strengthening addresses some of the most peculiar cruelties of economic exclusion.

This metacapacity, the capacity to aspire, is also a collective asset which is clearly linked to what Amartya Sen (1985a) has referred to as capabilities. They are two sides of the same coin, much as recognition and redistribution recall and require one another. The capacity to aspire provides an ethical horizon within which more concrete capabilities can be given meaning, substance, and sustainability. Conversely, the exercise and nurture of these capabilities verifies and authorizes the capacity to aspire and moves it away from wishful thinking to thoughtful wishing. Freedom, the anchoring good in Sen's approach to capabilities and development, has no lasting meaning apart from a collective, dense, and supple horizon of hopes and wants. Absent such a horizon, freedom descends to choice, rational or otherwise, informed or not.

What does this mean for those engaged in the active work of development, as planners, lenders, philanthropists? What does it mean to nurture the capacity to aspire?

Nuts and Bolts

I began by noting that culture is many things, and I have by no means addressed them all. The capacity to aspire is one important thing about culture (and cultures), and it has been paid too little attention so far. Since the work of development and poverty reduction has everything to do with the future, it is self-evident that a deeper capacity to aspire can only strengthen the poor as partners in the battle against poverty. This is the only way that words like *participation, empowerment,* and *grass roots* can be rescued from the tyranny of cliché. But even if this seems intuitively right and true, what exactly can lenders, planners, and managers in an institution like the World Bank actually do to put it into practice?

Here I make a few suggestions, not to provide a detailed blueprint, but to provide a guide to further deliberation about making the argument of this chapter into an actual method of intervention and a principle of partnership between the poor and those who subscribe to the view that the poor must have an active role in changing their situations for the better.

The premise is that the capacity to aspire, as a cultural capacity, may well be a capacity (that is, a metacapacity) whose fortification may accelerate the building of other capacities by the poor themselves. If so, it ought to be a priority concern of any developmental effort and a priority component of any project with other substantive goals (such as health, food security, or job provision) directed to the reduction of poverty. How can this recommendation be concretely explored?

Here, some general principles appear relevant:

First, whenever an outside agent enters a situation where the poor (and poverty) are a major concern, he or she should look closely at those rituals through which consensus is produced both among poor communities and between them and the more powerful. This process of consensus production is a crucial place to identify efforts to change the terms of recognition. And any consistent pattern in internal efforts to positively tilt the terms of recognition of and for the poor should be supported, as either a side benefit or as a major target of the exercise. Such support can take the form of encouragement to report, record, and repeat such efforts, wherever possible.

Second, every effort should be made to encourage exercises in local teaching and learning which increase the ability of poor people to navigate the cultural map in which aspirations are located and to cultivate an explicit understanding of the links between specific wants or goals and more inclusive scenarios, contexts, and norms among the poor.

Third, all internal efforts to cultivate voice among the poor (rather than loyalty or exit) in the context of any debated policy or project should be encouraged rather than suppressed or ignored. It is through the exercise of voice that the sinews of aspiration as a cultural capacity are built and strengthened, and conversely, it is through exercising the capacity to aspire that the exercise of voice by the poor will be extended.

Fourth, any developmental project or initiative, however grand or modest in its scope, should develop a set of tools for identifying the cultural map of aspirations that surround the specific intervention that is contemplated. This requires a method of placing specific technologies or material inputs in their aspirational contexts for the people most affected by them. This will require careful and thoughtful surveys, which can move from specific goods and technologies to the narratives within which they are understood and thence to the norms which guide these narratives. This last proposal also recognizes that aspirations connect to much of the rest of what we may regard as beneficial about culture, including the lifestyle, values, morals, habits, and material life of any community. And this brings us back to culture more generally.

Coda on Culture

I began by noting that we need a sea change in the way we look at culture in order to create a more productive relationship between anthropology and economics, between culture and development, in the battle against poverty. This change requires us to place futurity, rather than pastness, at the heart of our thinking about culture. I have tried to draw out the implications of such a revision and have argued that it is of more than academic interest. It has direct implications for increasing the ability of the poor to truly participate in the aims (and debates) of development.

This does not mean that we need to forget about culture in its broader sense, as the sense of tradition, the fabric of everyday understandings, the archive of memory and the producer of monuments, arts, and crafts. Nor do we need to slight the idea that culture is the fount of human expression in its fullest range, including the arts, music, theater, and language. Culture is all of these things as well. But culture is a dialogue between aspirations and sedimented traditions. And in our commendable zeal for the latter at the cost of the former, we have allowed an unnecessary, harmful, and artificial opposition to emerge between culture and development. By bringing the future back in, by looking at aspirations as cultural capacities, we are surely in a better position to understand how people actually navigate their social spaces. And in terms of the relationship between democracy and development, this approach gives us a principled reason to build the capacity to aspire in those who have the most to lose from its underdevelopment—the poor themselves.

Note

Earlier versions of this chapter were presented before audiences at the World Bank, at Cornell University, and at Witwatersrand University in Johannesburg. I am grateful for thoughtful questions and criticisms on all these occasions. I owe a special debt to Biju Rao and Michael Walton for their prodding, their queries, and their patience in the production of this chapter, and to Amartya Sen for encouraging me to regard this chapter as one more step in my long-standing dialogue with his ideas and concerns. Sidney Tarrow and Achille Mbembe gave me additional, and different, forms of courage to push forward with this project. As before, I owe everything to those friends in the Alliance and in SDI who opened their doors and their worlds to me. A major grant from the Ford Foundation supported the empirical research invoked in this chapter.

The section titled "Changing the Terms of Recognition: On the Ground in Mumbai" draws partly on a longer article I wrote on this grassroots housing movement, entitled "Deep Democracy: Urban Governmentality and the Horizon of Politics," previously published in *Public Culture* (United States) and in *Environment and Urbanization* (UK).

CHAPTER 4

Traditional Culture— Let's Hear No More About It

MARY DOUGLAS

Outrage and Helplessness

Hideous poverty in the margins of massive wealth is a mark of our times, and an outrage. Or at least some take it to be outrageous, but others shrug it off as inevitable. Public outrage is a mysterious thing. To foreground certain crimes means ignoring others. Each generation finds something to condemn in the moral record of its immediate ancestors. The prime example of western wickedness is the slave trade, but many public figures, including Voltaire, 18th-century philanthropist and satirist, were not less esteemed for holding shares in a slave ship. Corruption of 18th-century governments drew the censure of 19th-century moralists. Nineteenth-century colonial oppression draws the condemnation of our own times. But what next?

In the 21st century, the 20th will surely be charged with its distinctive load of grave crimes, the racism of the Nazis, the despoiling of the environment, drug dealers, the traffic in weapons. But I am pondering whether one of the prime horrors of our era, the ghastly poverty that reduces millions to hopeless indigence and starvation, will be on that black list. When the historians compile the toll of our evil deeds, we who stood by and tolerated such extremes of poverty may escape being counted as accessories to one of the major crimes of human history. This will be partly because poverty is the unintended by-product of composite causes, also because the perpetrators are hard to identify, and even the thing itself is hard to define. Every thinking person knows that something is very wrong, but no one knows quite what it is or what to do about it.

Bernard Williams's discussion of the various attitudes to slavery is well matched by the ramification of debates on world poverty (Williams 1993). For the ancient Greeks, whose economy depended upon slave labor, it was impossible to imagine a society without it. Williams describes it as a problem of structural injustice: Aristotle believed that, however imperfect it might be in practice, the world "was not structurally unjust—the world could not be such that the best development of some people necessarily involved the coercion of others against their nature" (Williams 1993, 116). But this belief conflicted uncomfortably with his inability either to defend or attack slavery.

We do not explicitly entertain an idea of necessary injustice, but it is there implicitly in the sense of an arbitrary distributive mechanism that we do not know how to replace or improve. We do suspect that the capitalist world might have to change its whole way of life from top to bottom if causing poverty were regarded as a criminal offense and this, like managing without slavery for the ancient Greeks, is unimaginable. Crying injustice can fade into the periphery of the moral vision if no one knows what to do about it. And indeed, trying to think coherently about poverty is a major difficulty. It is too mixed up with politics and justice to be easy to disentangle.

Bernard Williams's account of the various shoddy excuses for slavery has a familiar ring. Slavery is necessary and natural, slaves are different from free men even when they are born: it shows in their physiognomy and their posture, slaves are physically stronger than free men, they are less well endowed in intelligence and judgment. We have heard it all in our own history, from the beginnings of imperial expansion to the end of Empire. Anthropologists of my generation had lived alongside the holocaust of the Jews; combating racial prejudice was part of our professional vocation. As students we were hotly engaged in refuting theories of inherited intelligence, alleged racial differences, variable capacity for government. We have also recognized the same range of comments on the responsibility for industrial poverty: the plight of the poor is their own fault, they are lazy—and they do not wash (Douglas 1966/1984). There is the crass idea that the poor are happier as they are, to be rich is not to be happy. Williams quotes Seneca's notion that slaves were actually free in spirit, though bodily enchained (Williams 1993).

No Such Thing as Traditional Culture

In the pages that follow I will examine the distracting role that the concept of culture has played in the debates on poverty. The idea of culture as a form of collective thinking is particularly awkward in economics, where thinking is essentially an individual function: rational behavior is axiomatically self-interested. Early economists thought it was unnecessary to consider cultural effects. They assumed that demand depends on individual preferences. The idea of consumer sovereignty started as a methodological position, but soon became a moral principle underpinning a liberal profession. This is why so much of the weight of development theory could be plausibly laid on individual psychology. It does not help that others regarded culture as something mysterious, unanalyzable, even mystical.

Early on an unexpected obstacle confronted development economists. They had accepted axiomatically that rational behavior is self-interested and that gain is always preferable to loss. Then, as they started work they encountered poor people who were not interested in greater prosperity. They were surprised that their intended beneficiaries met their benign offers of economic development with indifference; they met poor who did not want new opportunities, they resisted change. It was mystifying to see poor people not bothering to labor for wages once they had earned enough to pay their tax. And it was frustrating to see poor farmers spending their exiguous incomes on lavish festivals instead of investing in their land. Popular attitudes justified the professionals in thinking that something called "culture" is the adversary of rational economic behavior, and that "traditional culture" was holding the poor nations back from development.

The present argument is that the "traditional culture" does nothing of the kind. Development is often blocked by culture, but the problem lies with the culture of apathy, which is induced by helplessness. There is no denying that there is such a thing as a culture of apathy. Oscar Lewis and Eric Banfield were absolutely right: apathy is a grave problem for economic development (O. Lewis 1968; Banfield 1958). The economist's initial idea of culture as the staunch foe of development, an inveterate turning away from modernity, an irrational force, has got some truth. Development programs have failed in many poverty-stricken parts of the globe because the people were unwilling to take risks and were afraid of new opportunities. But why should these people be apathetic? And how did they become apathetic?

A favorite explanation of economic backwardness used to be an affliction called "cultural inertia." It was a form of irrationality, a preference for living in the past that affected the poor countries and not the rich.

Personal characteristics gave some plausible starting points: "fecklessness," "laziness," "childlike natives" who cannot think of the future. If the people in poverty-stricken areas were described as "apathetic," unwilling to take the opportunities that were presented, the adjective suggests an analogy with a range of personality problems, especially chronic depression. Personality defects took the load of explanation. When it was pointed out that West Indians, who could be called apathetic at home, showed themselves to be a cheerful and optimistic set of people when they left the Caribbean and migrated to London, the answer came that emigration is a selective process: the ones who decided to migrate proved in doing so that they were better human material: they were not tainted by the general apathy which afflicted their relatives at home. So what started as a theory about culture turned easily into a theory of individual psychology. Once the problem of poverty has been located on the irrational side of human life it is presumed not susceptible to cost-benefit analysis. With such assumptions, why should economists take an interest in culture? In practice, people who live in a culture of apathy are not being irrational in their hesitations and fears. They perceive that they are trapped and it is usually difficult to see any way out.

The second part of the thesis to be aired here is that there is no such thing as "traditional culture." It is misleading to speak as if it were definable and recognizable. Culture is the moral and intellectual spirit of a particular form of organization. Culture is a dynamically interactive and developing sociopsychic system. At any point in time the culture of a community is engaged in a joint production of meaning. (This is very different from the ways that culture is described in other literatures, either as based on language, or geography, or on social class, or shared history.) In reality, the connected meanings that are the basis of any given culture are multiplex, precarious, complex, and fluid. They are continually contested and always in process of mutual accommodation. The dialogue leads to concentrations of meanings. It is the process of self-understanding, the way the community explains itself to itself. In this respect the culture of apathy is heavily disabled.

This is not the place for doubts about the benefits of development. Suffice it to say that there may be local reasons for questioning the advantages. For example, development may sometimes be badly managed. Stephen Gudeman's history of a rice-farming subsistence economy in Panama can stand for many anthropological monographs on mismanaged development (Gudeman 1978). In this case development took the form of a powerful competing economy intruding into the Panamanian community. It diverted labor from producing rice for home consumption to producing sugar cane for manufacture and export. The result was the conversion of a viable peasant community into an apathetic, rural proletariat, where the local people had good reason to see themselves as caged with no hope of escape. There was nothing irrational about their responses, nor were they struggling to maintain an irrelevant old traditional culture. Outsiders and landlords had taken decisions about their economy which forced them into a struggle to survive.

Development is always going to destabilize a fragile balance of social forces. The people are understandably reluctant to do the grueling hard work and accept the diversion of resources if the resulting prosperity will only line the pockets of outsiders. Furthermore, if it is going to erode the community's accumulated store of trust, and dissolve their traditional readiness to collaborate, the well-being of the community may be worse after development than before. There certainly is inherent ambiguity about the moral case. At least we can say that what stops development is not traditional cultural so much as the way development is organized.

Why Poverty Is Difficult to Define

Poverty at home is easy to define in material terms. The poor are among us and their material privation is visible. From the point of view of the local poor, and from the point of view of administrators in any country, material scarcity obviously does characterize poverty. Analyzing why they are poor is the daily stuff of local politics.

After World War II the economic development of colonies and ex-colonies was seen as a prime political obligation. A duty to share the wealth of the developed world was recognized, not shared by soup-kitchen handouts, but by empowering the people to improve their own lot by their own efforts. This objective extended the idea of poverty to other regions. Administrative purposes now required it to be measured cross-culturally. A long experience of developing the principles and methods of the Rowntree Survey of English poverty (1901) had been satisfactory for calculating the material necessities of a working class family, determining its cost, and comparing needs with income (Rowntree 1901). But international comparisons needed a new theoretical base. In default, they took individual physical needs to be universal and compared their satisfaction. The false start introduced confusion and contradiction.

The problem is how to generalize, and over what? Where poverty is characterized by long hours of unremitting work it can be indicated by lack of leisure. However, in some poor countries where the calendar of work swings between bouts of intense activity and spells of enforced idleness, leisure may be only too plentiful. In a pastoral economy herders have long hours of doing nothing, during which they can play string games, make music, tell stories. A hunting community can supply its food for weeks by hunting for only a few days; they may not have very much to eat, but they have time for personal grooming, art, music, recitation, dance, song, riddling, ritual, prayer, adjudication, philosophy—occupations which elsewhere are the privilege of the leisured classes (Turnbull 1962). In one place a man would be destitute without possession of a bow and a quiver of arrows, somewhere else a spade and a pestle, or somewhere else a certificate of legal immigration or a work permit are necessities.

The idea of scarcity starts the enquiry off on the wrong foot by considering material things needed by an individual person in order to survive. At a higher level of abstraction we must know that cost and scarcity result from evaluative processes. If nobody likes or wants a particular thing, its possible gluts or shortages arouse no interest: the thing is not valued, there is no demand for it. But if the thing becomes fashionable, then customers sweep it off the shelves, and it automatically becomes scarce. Demand creates value, and the measurement of poverty should take into account the kind of society that generates the values (Douglas and Isherwood 1979/1996). A particular kind of society, by valuing specific goods and services, creates the demand for them, which will create scarcity if it exceeds supply.

The paradoxes of plenty and poverty are compounded by defining human wants and needs in terms of individual requirements. Anthropologists see wants as defined collectively. The community itself defines its needs in the light of its shared objectives, and of its accumulated knowledge and capabilities (Sahlins 1972). This goes against the assumption from utility theory that wants arise in individuals and that there is enough uniformity among individual persons for generalizing. As things stand, the theorizing around the subject of human wants and needs does worse than misconceive culture: it omits culture altogether. It uses an entirely fictitious individual whose solipsist intentions and desires are supposedly generated from within, certainly not a social being, and barely a human (Douglas and Ney 1998b). Surveys of poverty have gradually come to include social and spiritual needs, though the starting point is always individual physical wants.

By contrast, anthropologists assume that society and tastes are coproduced. At the local level, wants are part of a feedback cycle between the relations of production and the relations of consumption. Wants and needs are not ordered according to private preference. Other people collectively try to solve problems of coordination, the solutions impose ordering on ego's preferences. The cultural process defines wants, and poverty is culturally constructed.

A tentative definition of poverty should start from the fact that human persons are social beings who interact and exchange. From this basis social life can be defined as a system of exchanges (market or gift) between individuals and between groups (Mauss 1997). Culture is the series of local debates which thrash out the definition of a well-functioning person. The causes of poverty are various disablements from entry into the exchanges that define a social being. Working with this definition, discussions of poverty should incorporate political culture because it exerts control on distribution (Sen 1999), and it should obviously attend to exclusionary behavior, both local and international. There are a few economists who do not let the idea of culture escape through the meshes of individual profit maximization (North 1981). This may be the right point at which to introduce the technical side of analyzing culture.

Cultural Theory

Nowadays economists readily recognize that culture (variously referred to as "ideology," "informal institutions," "informal rules," "lifestyles," "consensus ideology") is the collective product of rational persons trying to coordinate their lives:

People are not simply individuals. They live socially and their views, their values, and even their beliefs, as well as their abilities, are formed and sustained within social groupings, families, and communities. . . . Perhaps the consideration of lifestyle offers an alternative to the *methodological individualism* that has been held to be a weakness of orthodox social science. (Bliss 1993)

The term *lifestyle* is an advance over *ideology* because implicitly, lifestyle must have an infrastructure. Culture is to social organization as mind is to brain. It is part of an internal interaction within the system of society. Economists if they are interested in culture at all, usually recognize two cultures, one, individualist, progressive, modern, and one, corporatist and traditional. We get four by splitting them. The two corporatist tendencies are either hierarchical or tending to the egalitarian pole; the two individualist tendencies are either in a competitive client-patron environment, or they are loners who do not have occasion to collaborate. On this basis culture can be seen as a dialogue between four opposing tendencies, each emanating from a distinctive lifestyle, or more precisely, from a different position in the organization. The advantage of this starting point is that organization is measurable. It is a theory of culture systematically based on social organization. Since any kind of organization depends on moral commitment, the basic assumption is that the collectively held theories about humans and the world correspond to the form of organization.

Consequently each cultural bias provides its own view of poverty, its causes and remedies.

A community at any one time is constituted, not by one, but by four distinctive cultural tendencies. They are not separate cultures, they are tendencies or biases, or some call them "forms of solidarity" (Thompson, Grendstad, and Selle 1999a). They constitute the community as a fourfold cultural unit engaged in a continuous internal dialogue. At all times a culture is responding to the individual culture bearers and how they are dealing with each other. For an example near to home: economists in a very competitive professional community would tend to assume that human nature is naturally self-interested and competitive, while some civil servants in a very bureaucratic department would assume that human nature is essentially rule-obeying. This follows from the match between the cultural values and the way they are organizing their lives.

Culture is not a mechanical control on the individual members of a community. If enough individuals want to be free to compete, they will abolish the rules that check competition. If they really want competition they will see to it that the incentives for risk-taking are commensurate with the effort, and that probabilities of success are reasonable. If the consensus prefers a society that will honor the old, and care for the infirm, or reduce accidents, or maintain a monarchy, they will set up regulations to restrain free enterprise.

The Cultural Process

The appendix to this chapter by Marco Verweij gives a fuller introduction to the four cultures which subsist together, albeit adversarially, in any community. I summarize briefly the four types of organization. Start with the hierarchical tendency. It is a system of coordination based on authority, precedent, rules, and defined statuses (often hereditary, or based on age and gender). Characteristically, it seeks to limit competition. There are specific functions for which this is the most efficient form of organization. For example, any offices dedicated to the care of funds, the bursar, the treasurer, tend to be hierarchical. Hierarchical families work well for the same reasons. Hierarchy assumes the authority of stewardship, it seeks to define the limits of its responsibilities, so draws boundaries around them, and is inevitably inclined to take an adversarial attitude to the other cultural types. Its upholders justify it by appeal to traditions to be conserved.

The entrepreneurial or individualist tendency stands in direct confrontation with stewardship because it explicitly sanctions individual competition. As a system of coordination it depends on show of power, either by coercive force or by wealth. It has an independent system of incentives, its function as a counterbalance to hierarchy is very important to the survival of any community. These two, the hierarchical and the competitive, constitute the major line of control and command in any society. Though balanced against each other, they need each other, the one cannot do without the foil provided by the other's presence.

Almost any stable society will have generated several varieties of permanent opposition. Strongly motivated sets of people hive off from the mainstream and form minority groups (whether for political protesters, a religious sect, or any countercultural commune). Such a dissenting group has distinctive problems for maintaining its membership (Douglas and Ney 1998b). The solution most readily available is to separate the group from the outside world with a strong boundary. Its cosmology of "saints and sinners" is painted in black and white. It tends to be egalitarian in principle and in practice. To the other cultures, the sectarian tendency presents an opposed identity, it stirs the community conscience.

In any community there are some who have dropped out of the exchanges by which individuals are incorporated. They are isolates. No one is around who wants their advice, they have no chance of persuading anyone of anything because no one else is regularly there. They are not necessarily unhappy (Barrett 1962). When nothing we can do matters very much, our life is relatively stress-free (Douglas 1996). There is usually an intimate personal sphere in which they have some small autonomy. At the same time, they may be very frustrated or lonely. In a large community there is inevitably a penumbra of such people, they don't see much of each other, by definition. Their circumstances being similar, they tend to have similar attitudes to time, history, efficiency, justice. They do not combine for political action. They may suffer injustice and hardship but they consider that nothing will ever be done to help them. They rarely have to sustain a consistent argument, their thinking tends to be erratic. This is the culture of apathy or fatalism.

From here the question is what kind of moral attitudes would be able to uphold each of these four types of organization. How do they justify themselves to their members and so mobilize support against their rivals? The hierarchy, with its custodian morality, favors an economic policy that is redistributive, but only within limits set by its traditionalism. It claims to honor and protect the poor, and at the same time it needs to spend lavishly on its public displays of rank and virtue. As Galbraith said: it is the place where private squalor is found beside public displays of affluence. In debate hierarchy will rest its case on tradition first, and then proceed to defend tradition as corresponding to the order of the universe. For reducing conflict and promoting efficient coordination it will put its faith in boundaries and buffers that keep different classes of people apart.

The entrepreneurial culture is based on a morality of merit. Its economic policy must always be justified by showing that merit is rewarded. It finds it very difficult to raise taxes. The duties of stewardship take second place to promoting trade, so here we see public squalor side by side with private affluence. Individualism will tend to promote more opportunistic, merito-cratic, and shorter-term policies, in the name of freedom and prosperity.

The culture of dissenting minority groups is a political force when it is based on protest. The culture of the enclaves tends to be egalitarian as part of their moral dissidence and in their principles of internal organization. They take the moral high ground by speaking for the poor and disadvan-taged suffering in a regime dominated by traditionalist hierarchs and mer-cantile interests.

Lastly, the culture of the isolates: whether they are pushouts or dropouts, they are generally apathetic, cynical about the motives of politicians, fatal-ist about the certain failure of actions intended to improve their situation. They favor practice over speculation, and often take on good works toward their worse-off neighbors. No matter what the issues are, these will be the four potential points of cultural conflict, one quiescent and three of them likely to be contending actively in any community or workplace.

In a thriving democracy all four patterns of coordination and their supporting cultural biases are actively contending. A slight unbalancing of the equilibrium may encourage apathy, the culture most antipathetic to development. This can subvert the other cultures, and threaten whatever organization was in place. Since apathy is not conducive to collective action, how it gets this destructive power is an important question. I would argue that it comes from the real loss of local autonomy that fol-lows on being conquered in war, or possibly from the downgrading of local influence in face of economic development.

A cultural bias is a collective product. This cannot be repeated too much that it is rooted in the need for coordination (Bourdieu 1990). Culture reflects the arguments that the community is having about the life that they would like to lead together (but the isolates don't have anyone to argue with). Culture encapsulates some current consensus on ethical and aesthetic standards. Isolates are not present when the consensus is being formed, they rarely go to meetings. Culture lays down rational priorities and principles for judging. (This does not hold for isolates who must each be their own judge of what to do, and of right and wrong. Culture is fragile and precar-ious, easily shifted, even in very important effects. Everyone knows it, hence the intense anxiety when a cherished way of life is challenged.)

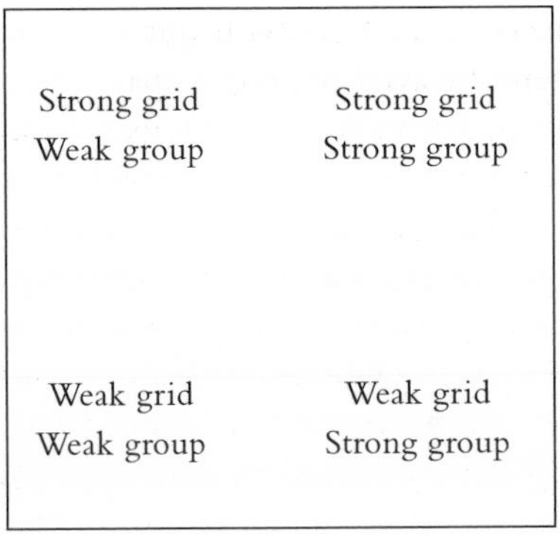

Strong grid Weak group	Strong grid Strong group
Weak grid Weak group	Weak grid Strong group

Figure 4.1. Map of measures of coordination

Ultimately, culture is sustained by a circle of its making. A set of strong arguments presents a particular perception of the world, the results of actions taken on the basis of this perception justify the arguments. So if there is mismatch between the local culture, the local organization, and the way the outside world impinges, both the organization and its culture, will adapt. Cultural theory proposes a method of analyzing the kind of coordination that matches the different cultures.

The method sets up an abstract model of possible organizational forms; this gives a map on which to locate human subjects committed to making one kind of organization rather than another. In a stable society some kind of equilibrium has been found, but it is not inherently stable. If a group can persuade the rest to accept a change, it will happen. If we want to study culture we need to find relatively stable examples and assess the local balance between the different organizational forms in a given society.

Two Dimensions of Coordination

Cultural theory uses a matrix which simultaneously shows the bare form of organization in four varieties and the values that legitimate them.

In a 2x2 diagram the vertical axis (called "grid") indicates regulation, a grid of rules that constrain and separate individuals. The horizontal axis (called "group") indicates incorporation, the rules that incorporate people into groups. On this scheme society is presented as a field of force. It covers the range of social environments in which individuals are moving around, forming groups and being subject to rules. They may have just arrived, or be on their way out, no matter. It is a stochastic view: statistically there should be a big enough population for the exceptions to cancel out. In so far as it is a theory about kinds of coordination, it covers many of the interests of economists (Figure 4.1).

Setting up the two dimensions anticipates the four different cultural biases we have described. In varying degrees they are all available at any time, each in competition with the others, and each liable to dissolve if moral support changes. As a skeletal classification the two dimensions are surprisingly effective for locating individuals at the organizational level, and for raising questions about what kind of cultural bias they are likely to display. For methods of counting and measuring the regularities in behavior that respond to the institutional structures, there is a considerable literature (Verweij 2004).

The map has interesting properties. For example, there is a "positive diagonal" that connects Hierarchists with Entrepreneurs (Ostrander 1982). They form a cultural coalition that runs the town. The individualists bring in the news from outside, they take new initiatives and develop enterprise. The hierarchists have a custodial attitude to the town as a whole, they are the bureaucrats and town officials. The two cultures need each other, but they disapprove and love to hate each other. Their conflicts tend to arise over the uses of space and time. For example, the entrepreneurial individualists are keen on building motorways and fast trains that can rush them to the outside and back. The hierarchists are typically not interested in efficiency or saving time, they are more keen to keep their old meeting places, squares and parks. As the debate continues, both will need to contend with the various dissenting voices in town,

Economists are interested in flows of information. On the left-hand side of the diagram the flow of information is uncontrolled, unclassified and therefore full of noise and triviality. The task of sorting out what matters falls to the individual (Figure 4.2).

On the right-hand side the two kinds of collectivist cultures strictly control incoming information. It is a help to see the group as primarily a receptor and transmitter; it is a funnel whose shape determines what goes through to the members (Douglas and Mars in press). They both systematically monitor news that comes in, but according to different principles. The hierarchies allocate right to know among their various segments according to their preordained roles and functions. The egalitarian enclaves grade the sources of information for all-round reliability. Where the news comes from is the crucial point, its credibility is ranked according to the perceived loyalty of the news bearer.

Similarly for the channeling of wealth, the leveling systems mentioned in Abraham and Platteau work differently in each kind of collectivist culture, but hardly at all in individualist cultures where wealth gives the only

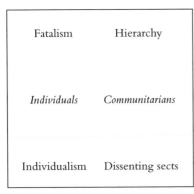

Fatalism	Hierarchy
Individuals	*Communitarians*
Individualism	Dissenting sects

Figure 4.2. Two types of culture:
The right-hand side is collectivist;
the left-hand side is individualist.

form of power (Abraham and Platteau 2001). And no one should make the mistake of supposing that individualism must be absent in a developing country (Douglas 1973/1982). On the left-hand side of the diagram, the individualist system normally allows freedom to accumulate and allocates power according to wealth. However it has to keep a check on big wealthy families who will try to subvert the system and buy up the collective freedoms for the inheritance of their children. The apathetic culture is likely to be jealous of wealth and success.

On the right-hand side of the diagram, the hierarchy channels wealth to support the ascribed statuses. It is not initially friendly to new accumulations of wealth because they threaten to disturb the balance between its hereditary sectors. At the death of the successful entrepreneur it finds ways to enforce redistribution. The dissident group strives continually to achieve an egalitarian distribution, making its own behavior conform to its public policy, no easy matter (Rayner 1988).

Within the cultural theory matrix the very same rational beings who are the subjects of rational choice theory are expected to be alive and well, busily calculating the costs and benefits to themselves of different forms of coordination. They are building the necessary framework of institutional constraints that surround rational beings and affect their choices. Rational choice and cultural theory are compatible and complementary, even more than Douglass North has already shown. This should be good news to economists interested in incorporating a cultural factor into their models. It means that we should always expect to differentiate their attitudes to risk. Hierarchs are predominantly concerned about risk of danger to the whole society, or the whole economy, such as law and order, unemployment, inflations, law and order. Individualists of course are wary of risks that will endanger their own activities. Sectarians are worried about risks to the world or to the large public to who they appeal in their perennial fight against the commercial/industrial governmental powers, so large and remote, low frequency dangers (Douglas and Wildavsky 1982).

Unfortunately most economists are stuck in a past state of the art in which only two cultures count, one entrepreneurial culture, almost a non-culture since it was based strictly on individual rational choice, and the other, traditional, supposed to be an irrational impediment to economic growth. The case exemplifies how a popular fantasy can intrude into the minds of highly rational beings. In that sense, a modern learned profession is in the same case as the subjects they study. They ought to be the first to agree that cultural inertia is not necessarily irrational, it may be a rational move to avoid unprofitable effort. I hope I have sufficiently explained how culture is a part of organization, and how it can be analyzed systematically and how evidence can be supplied for the purpose.

Only Two Cultures, According to North

Douglass North has gone far to bring culture within the range of "the individualist maximizing postulate of economic theory." His achievement is to have provided, over a long period of work, a coherent theory that links culture and development. Sometimes he talks about institutional constraints. Sometimes he prefers the word ideology, perhaps unwisely, because it suggests too much the fashionable, overintellectualized idea of culture (Kuper 1999) to which he does not subscribe in the least. Rather than starting with the individual's thoughts and desires, North's special merit is to scout out the whole social system and focus on the constraints imposed on what may be done, an excellent strategy which expands the concept of transaction costs.

His analysis is worked out within rational choice theory but manages to reconcile anthropological observations about culture with economics (North 1990). He does not have any truck with culture being mystical or irrational or carrying crystallized memories. He treats culture as a robustly practical way of life responding to changes in prices and costs and drawing the economic system along with it (North 1981). He sees that culture is also a resource for finding justifications. He recognizes its forensic function: it provides theories which explain why things must be done thus and not otherwise, it makes informal rules and judges whether they have been breached, and if so, what penalties are due. Culture mobilizes individuals, and turns them into a community with shared norms and values; it does this by setting constraints on behavior. "In the absence of constraints we exist in a Hobbesian jungle and civilization is impossible" (North 1981,

203). "In the absence of restraints" means "in the absence of cultural support." He is particularly talking about the amoral family individualism described by Banfield: a broken down community in southern Italy, where suspicion and resentment were rife, was the kind of moral jungle in which everyone's hand was against his neighbor's (Banfield 1958).

North's argument has the great merit of starting from problems of coordination that beset poor economies (North 1990). Material poverty results from low productivity, which is caused by intractable coordination problems. He sees culture as the poor man's resource for overcoming them. An advanced economy can achieve coordination because it is rich in incentives and rewards, but in a poor economy coordination has to be achieved by culture which can overcome transaction costs but only to a limited extent. A large community can enjoy benefits of scale: this makes it worthwhile to define the basic structure of property rights, ensure that formal contracts are honored, make rules and punish their breach. If benefits of scale are absent all these things must be provided by culture: costs of compliance, of monitoring, of presence, costs of adjudication, costs of measurement, costs of information. Culture reinforces the institutions by normative judgments, it explains why it is wrong to deviate, and it develops theories about the world that justify the feasible choices.

The cultural solutions to coordination problems cost time and resources, and they only work in a small community because they need to be grounded in regular personal interaction. Here are two partners who habitually work together, they rely on each other over their lifetime, and help each other in crises, often at personal cost. How does culture enable them to maintain their impressive solidarity? By organizing things so that the benefits pile up on the side of trust. This involves investing personal and political relations with value, such as family, or monarchy; it uses shame to put individuals under heavy obligations of reciprocity; it builds sanctions around the idea of honor and probity (Davy 1922); it requires proofs of loyalty to kin, such as wildly ostentatious weddings and funerals to which all kinsfolk must be invited (Rao 2001b). It controls envy by redistributive institutions which disperse private accumulation and prevent great disparities of wealth (Douglas and Isherwood 1979/1996). All of this reduces incentives, which is admittedly incompatible with development.

North's model is a self-reproducing system: the small community cannot improve its productivity by division of labor or specialization; it compensates for not being able to enjoy benefits of scale by using institutions that can only thrive by staying poor and small. From here one can extract from North's books a telling list of the coordination problems confronting any poor country, and how the incentives structure works so that the community interests outweigh those of the individual (North 1990).

Development can turn the balance of advantage the other way, it can make the rewards of defection so huge that they easily outbid the local culture, making the collaboration of partners very precarious.

This approach frames development within a cultural contest between individual and social benefits. Development dissolves the bonds of trust and releases the opportunism that the culture was instituted to control.[1] These arguments reveal an inherent conflict between culture and development. In order to develop from poverty to wealth an economy needs to get benefits of scale, and in doing so must weaken culture. This is a very strong argument, but it is not clinching.

Since cultural constraints protect trust and confidence in the future, and since development needs to weaken cultural restraints, a sinister trade-off has appeared. North is an original thinker, not dogged by the old muddles about irrational cultural effects. Yet he arrives at the same old-fashioned view as the others: he thinks that traditional culture is the dead hand that blocks development. In a world of only two cultures his case would be irresistible. Teaching that cultural conflict is a contest between individual and social benefits drives inexorably to the conclusion that, wherever poverty is most deeply entrenched, the old social benefits of nondevelopment have been preferred to the new individual benefits. This would mean that development will inevitably doom the traditional culture, a bleak prospect which in itself accounts for hesitation about plunging into economic advance. However, I maintain that the prospect is an artefact of the model.

North is another of the economists who still recognize only two kinds of culture. One of the two is our kind, individualist, modern, a culture that affords no impediment to rational behavior and is favorable to development. The other kind is collectivist or traditional, resistant to development. The distinction appears to be binary. But it reduces in practice to only one kind of culture, because "theirs" causes all the problems and "ours" is the right one for development and can be ignored. "We" are individualist, independent of culture, and "they" are collectivist, dominated by culture.

We cannot escape from our history. To the anthropologist this talk of two cultures has the ring of old-time imperialist drum-beating: we whites are enlightened, they, the colonial peoples, are benighted. It organizes a desperately confused topic by blatantly imposing a cultural bias. The days when we can dismiss culture as something that other people have, but not we ourselves, have surely gone by. Clifford Geertz wrote of ideology: "I

have a social philosophy, you have political opinions, he has an ideology"
(Geertz 1973b, 194). It is patronizing to impute an unthinking reverence
for tradition to the peoples of the underdeveloped world—as well as misleading. The only hope it can offer would be that the way to end world
poverty is to replace the traditional cultures with individualism (which he
does not count as a form of culture). Alas, when one kind of culture dis-
integrates, its carefully built defenses against arbitrariness are replaced by
the dead hand of apathy, and then development does become impossible.
But cultural failure is nothing to do with the traditional culture.

Everything else that he achieved remains intact. There is a gap in his
argument, and perhaps a contradiction. His questions are: "Why do these
otherwise entirely rational people stick blindly to a cultural form that does
not pay off? Why don't they see their short-sightedness? Why, if they are
so rational, do they defend their culture after it has ceased to serve their
interests?" (Geertz 1973b). The answer eludes because he can only see two
kinds of culture. If he could see four coexisting, some other factors could
be tracked down. The harsh dilemma is irrelevant: people do not have to
choose between development and their own traditional culture, because
the latter can adapt. They just have to avoid apathy.

Utilitarian writings refer to other persons only as they enter and leave
Ego's orbit. Copernicus faced the same problem: studying the sky with the
Earth at the center of the universe made it difficult to construct a systematic view of the relations of the planets. It would help us now to have a
sociocentric way of talking about social beings who are immersed in a culture which they are coproducing, and which then generates a world view
which includes their ideas of justice and their catalogue of human needs
and wants. Should these beings have the misfortune to be reduced to their
basic needs they are indeed in a parlous state, practically subhuman.

Poverty as a Problem of Freedom

To sum up, it does not make sense to consider poverty, wants, or needs,
apart from the form of society which generates and articulates them. The
people together combine to make their list of wants. It is a loop: in the
process of trying to form a kind of society, the people who are cooperat-
ing strive for a consensus about their culture. They argue with each other
about what a human being ought to need and want. The consensus that
emerges confers value on selected items. Amartya Sen has been saying for
a long time that the lack of material goods associated with poverty is
caused by social behavior: rejection, exclusion, and isolation (Sen 1999).
This being so, the theory of poverty should be rooted in a theory of soci-

ety and culture, but for us in the 21st century this grounding is notably absent. The reason for the superficiality of the present debates may simply be that poverty is always too hot politically.

These elusive questions have recently been transformed into cultural problems about freedom and justice. Actually, Amartya Sen made this move a long time ago. A decade before his book on famine and poverty (Sen 1981) he had been considering poverty as an issue of freedom (Sen 1970), and a rich bibliography culminates in *Development as Freedom* (1999). The approach to poverty via freedom must, as he himself eloquently says, recognize the cultural diversity within regional and historic cultural differences (Sen 1999, 247–48). I take this to mean that the problems of measuring differences in culture will be tackled (Gross and Rayner 1985).

Amartya Sen's distinctive contribution to the subject is based on freedom of choice (Sen 1985a). To take this to be the liberty essential to a human person is a radical move away from basic material needs. His theory of poverty requires research to measure the penumbra of potential achievements surrounding each person's life. It is a very original approach, with the understanding that more choice is richer and less choice is poorer. The practical problem is to find some indicator of individual choice.

The analysis of "the quality of life" presents a systematic view of the individual which is intended to apply in any setting. This fits well with the definition of poverty which I am using, the inability to make the exchanges that define a member of society. Disappointingly, "culture" is obliterated, but in compensation a new and measurable factor is introduced. Trying to assess the "quality" of the exchanges in which the individual can take part is a complement to the attempt to identify cultures (Nussbaum and Sen 1993). It is a signal advance on all previous theories as the individual is no longer alone. The enabling environment is the crucial factor in the individual's escape from poverty. Other people are there, the individual in the analysis is not isolated in the theory, even if the other people are only tacked on as adjuncts necessary for exchange and for opportunities. It is a beginning. It provides a strikingly original basis for the comparison of cultures: if there are few options for interaction, the quality of the exchanges is low, high if the choices are many and free.

The concept of poverty had always been confused with that of unhappiness. By this means it becomes a technical term in a theoretical discourse. The measures can use demographic and technological indicators for freedom and scope of choice. Happiness is irrelevant. I surmise that these indicators will always justify the intuitive idea that the forest hunters or the savanna herders are poorer than we are, no matter how much happier their patterns of work and leisure may make them. It would be a whole education in social thought to see how well the criteria of choice apply in various contexts. Paradoxically, though individual happiness is the subject, the individual is in the background, the conditions of social life are to the fore: a complete turn around for utilitarian individualism. You will observe however, that this model of freedom and well-being owes nothing to the idea of culture.

The measurements of the Human Development Index (HDI) keep the individual well offstage, the main focus of the measuring is on the supporting infrastructure which mitigates poverty or promotes well-being. Though it was first produced by the United Nations Development Program in 1990, the history of the HDI refers back to the International Labour Office statistics for the League of Nations. As the old national income figures hid the distribution of income it revealed little about poverty. The object of the HDI is to study the enabling environment, to assess how much it allows people to enjoy long, healthy, and creative lives, with enlarged choices. The HDI uses three indicators of the enabling infrastructure: life expectancy at birth, literacy rates, and purchasing power.

The Human Development Index is related to a human deprivation index, which is amended and updated every year. This index may be crude, but by shifting the focus of poverty studies from material welfare to human choice, away from the individual and toward the social environment, it has transformed the idea of human needs. It is a serious attempt to compare the value of the infrastructure of individuals' lives. A person's chances of schooling, nutrition, life expectancy, and income say much more about well-being than straight comparisons of income.

Political Freedom

Partha Dasgupta took this approach further when he supplemented measures of socioeconomic performance with measures of political freedom. In the usual model of the economy the consumer is the chooser. His model has incorporated the idea of negative freedom (Berlin 1969). No one in the ideal tolerant and liberal society should be telling the individuals what their needs are or what they ought to want. In addition to freedom to choose there needs to be a measure of freedom from political interference: absence of arbitrary despoliation and tyranny. To meet this end, Dasgupta, in *An Inquiry into Well-Being and Destitution* (1993), incorporates two new measures into the comparisons of well-being.

The HDI implicitly treated the activities and achievements of individuals as if they were outputs from some production process that provides the necessary conditions (an infrastructure of public health, education, etc.). Dasgupta makes a Copernican move: he puts the elements of welfare into a cycle, and the model is sociocentric. It takes the whole of human life to be a complex production process that calls for inputs and produces outputs, which themselves influence the next stage of input. The focus is upon the individual's achievements, which in this cycle are inputs into a feedback system. What the collectivity of individuals does or does not achieve in one generation constructs the infrastructure for the welfare of the next generation.

The first inputs in his model are the commodities humans consume: at the most basic level, food, water, shelter, satisfying the basic material needs. Notice the complete reversal of how consumption goods are usually conceived: normally shopping and taking the goods home is the end and object of the whole production process; the economic cycle seems to stop after the human bodies have eaten the food. It is invigorating to have it from an economist that consumption actually produces the kind of society in which the consumer lives. Now we have a dynamic cycle that goes round and round: these inputs are transformed into utilities and functionings, such as survival, health, and exercise of skills; outputs are aggregate welfare and the promotion of vital interests of persons. The outcomes include public goods such as the political and civil liberties to which an individual has access in a given society, and these provide what he calls the "background conditions" of individual choice. What the individuals achieve collectively are the inputs of organization and political effort; these go to make the background conditions of the next round of the cycle.

Dasgupta's first four socioeconomic measures are very like those of the HDI, except that he substitutes income per head for purchasing power. Income is there to represent the input of the human productive process, whereas the infant survival rate, literacy, life expectancy, are its outputs. They correspond to the idea of "positive freedom," freedom to do and be, prominent in Sen's thinking. Looking for indicators of political and civil liberty, Dasgupta introduces two measures of freedom from arbitrary interference. These measures of "negative freedom" would show the extent to which citizens can take part in the decision of who governs and by what laws (Berlin 1969). It shows the freedoms an individual enjoys vis-à-vis the state, such as freedom of speech and the independence of the judiciary.

At last some attention is being directed to culture. The two sociopolitical measures indicate how social institutions confer value on commodities: whether they allocate them fairly or unfairly, and how they permit their safe and peaceful enjoyment. When the four socioeconomic indicators are correlated with the sociopolitical indicators, the comparison of political culture can begin, and the link between democracy and material prosperity can be examined objectively.

As the focus of research has moved away from the tangled paradoxes of the idea of poverty, the nature of the measurements has also shifted away from the individual in poverty to the social mechanisms of allocation. This had to happen once the concern for poverty transcended local boundaries. A model of the social processes of transforming commodities into the conditions of well-being is a long way on from a catalogue of goods that are supposed universally to satisfy individual basic needs. Sen shifted the conversation from the surface of utilitarian individualism to the enabling infrastructures provided by society. The infrastructure (education, transport, communications, public health) gives, or fails to give, to the individual a supporting environment of opportunity for self-realization. Dasgupta added another set of infrastructural conditions to indicate freedom from misrule. Formally, both these developments put the individual to the fore and the rest of society at the rear. The sun is still going round the earth, as it were, but only nominally, for the measures are devised to compare institutional support for the individual.

Humans as Social Beings

The next stage brings the infrastructure further to the fore by attending to the individual's scope for capitalizing on his and her social relations. This thoroughly sociological perception of need is central to the theory of development. Robert Putnam, in *Making Democracy Work* (1993), evaluates the same ideal of well-being in terms of institutional performance. He started by comparing the performance of Italian regional governments from their inception in 1970 up until the mid-1980s. By analyzing institutional responses to policy demands, Putnam looks at how needs are structured, articulated, and satisfied (Putnam, Leonardi, and Nanetti 1993).

Putnam would agree with Dasgupta that "background conditions" are prime factors in providing welfare. In this research he was interested in how the quality of social interaction in the community influences the efficiency of regional government. Does a very solidary community require higher standards from its local government? His surveys showed that in southern Italy, whose vertical structures encourage patronage, clientage and regional isolation, the regional administrations performed poorly. By the same token, in the north the cultures that realized higher standards of administrative performance were more egalitarian and solidary. The northern regions have established horizontal networks of civic interaction thanks to which the community values, "solidarity, civic engagement, cooperation, and honesty" make the government work (115).

Like Dasgupta, he also presents a dynamic cycle of well-being. Instead of citizens being controlled from on high, by their governments, he is assuming that the quality of government is dependent on the quality of civic interaction at even the most informal level. We must applaud this dynamic approach to culture.

For Putnam the civic community has three defining qualities, of which the first is civic engagement in public affairs. The second is political equality ensured by horizontal relations of reciprocity and cooperation. Norms of trust, solidarity, and tolerance mark public life in the civic community. Last, the civic community is associational: citizens are not isolated individuals but take part in diverse forms of organizations and associations in which they are educated in the art of citizenry and learn to appreciate the quest for collective goals. In the classical liberal model civic virtues are held to be inherent in the individual, but here individuals are endowed with social capital by other individuals—again an advance to applaud.

In Dasgupta's terminology, Putnam tries to find measures for outputs and background conditions, though of course a direct assessment of the normative factors, such as trust and solidarity, is always elusive. Putnam obviously wants to study culture, but he is hampered by lack of a theoretical framework. Having started with a piecemeal list of virtues, finding ways of assessing how well they are practiced has to be piecemeal too. They have no overarching theory to frame any arguments.

It is a great advance on earlier writings on culture that these three initiatives take humans as essentially social beings whose behavior contributes to one another's welfare. They have restored inherent sociality to the concept of the human being, and restored it in a sense that invites us to measure influences received from other persons. But this work has only let culture in by the back door; there is no explicit theory of culture. The focus on opportunities (Sen), or liberties (Dasgupta), or civic virtues (Putnam), only shows bits of culture here and there. Culture, as an ardently debated, flexibly responding, system of values, escapes through our fingers.

None of these three researches pretend to account for economic development. In my opinion, this is difficult for them. Either they see culture as rigid, or they do not see it as closely linked with social organization. To their credit, they still stand above the crowd because they do not think in terms of only two cultures. They are not interested in different kinds of culture.

To recapitulate: a culture is a way of thinking that justifies a way of living. Consequently it must be dynamic, and so capable of change. The cultural process is a continuous interaction between four tendencies, and in any community these tendencies are locked in agonistic postures. Some circumstances can bring one of the four to dominate over the others. It might be the hierarchy, it might be the entrepreneurial individualists, it might be a god-fearing, austere sect. The fatalist tendency is by its nature very unlikely to dominate the cultural scene. The indifference of the isolates can dissolve the tension and loyalties in the whole society, making it a nonfunctional, apathetic culture.

The culture of apathy can become completely incapable of development. This is the biggest cultural problem. It is possible that people fail to recognize a way out of a locked-in situation, or it is possible that there is no way out for them. But their hopelessness is nothing to do with the traditional culture. Another culture has expanded in response to the cultural destruction brought by development. It shows in many ways; in graph theoretical terms we would say that the culture of apathy arises when the connecting networks have broken down. Or, it may arise when trust has been betrayed, when disappointment has replaced hope. To adopt Amartya Sen's terms, the culture of apathy develops when freedom to choose has been eliminated.

Apathy and Cultural Failure

Not all isolates experience apathy. Some persons show up on the grid/group diagram as isolates (top left corner) because they live alone. Their isolation may be voluntary or involuntary, either way their social intercourse is very restricted. Nevertheless, their culture tends to be fatalist. They are the people deplored by developers. They have had reason to believe that hard work will not do them any good, they don't believe in politicians' promises, they may not bother to go to the polls. I am supposing that they probably would not have accepted withdrawal or exclusion if they had not had bad experience of corruption and chicanery. However, they would not necessarily be prepared to move into another cultural slot if they were individually offered opportunities to realize their potential. Often the personal cost of joining in the economic development is too high. They are caught in a situation from which they cannot see any escape. They consider all their options have been closed and they are probably right. The context for behaving rationally is absent. The fatalist may be nominally free to speak out, but he is unused to public speaking and has nothing coherent to say. These fatalists are the very people whose negative attitude cancels the best efforts of philanthropists and administrators.

How a culture of apathy emerges should be a priority topic for research in development studies. A community is able to function efficiently only thanks to the saving intercultural dialogue. In any community one of the politically active cultures generally leads the others. If it completely dominates all the rest, we can expect apathy to develop. It largely depends on external factors whether the hierarchy, the market, or the egalitarian enclave, will be the dominant one, or whether creeping apathy rots them all (Verweij 2004). It could be fatal for the development agent to encourage one local culture (probably the individualists) to squeeze out the others. If that happens he will notice how easily the apathetic community is excluded and how quickly it is growing as a proportion of the population.

It is in the nature of things that development is always destabilizing. No one can be surprised that in many poor places economic development is viewed with misgiving. A culture is as strong as the people's commitment to it. The erosion of social capital can put cultural viability at risk. The list of dangers is long: uncertainty about justice, loss of morale, general disorientation, destruction of credit, loss of authority, loss of the commons, destruction of property rights. When these appear in force, something worse than apathy is on the doorstep, cultural failure. This is the point at which the analysis of a culture has to stop because there is no culture left; at this point neither economics nor psychology apply. Rationality is irrelevant. The things that are going to happen are unheard of. Reading Paul Richards's account of the recent civil war in Sierra Leone, the atrocities committed by and against child-soldiers enrolled in the revolutionary force are so appalling, one may well think that understanding is impossible (Richards 1996). Richards uses cultural theory to gain insight into the original exclusions, abuses and corruptions that led hopeless men and women to counter their despair in these horrendous ways.

As a recommendation, it would be possible to apply cultural theory in advance of total breakdown. A cultural audit could be set up to watch how the contest of cultures is unfolding in a community where development is noticeably slow. Policy could be better informed about the desperate conflicts of culture and poverty, and be aware of the dangers of general failure. It would not be difficult to identify the dark pall of apathy descending on the people, and the unintended recruitment to the class of isolates. Cultural failure is beyond poverty, it threatens the basis of civil society.

Conclusion

It turns out that economic development is a very delicate topic. It is as difficult to talk about the causes of poverty without putting blame on the poor as it was difficult for the Athenians to talk about slaves being physically and mentally born to slavery. Learned criticisms of traditional culture sound like comforting ways to avoid talking about the structural injustice of our own time.

We defined poverty as the condition of not being allowed to enter the system of exchanges. If exclusion within a community causes poverty, the principle applied to the global level says clearly that exclusionary tariffs which block the entry of poor countries to the trading exchanges of the world are responsible for world poverty.

Cultural theory applies to the international community. At one level the international civil servants and research officers are behaving as thwarted hierarchs, would-be custodians who wring their hands over the plight of the poor nations and try in vain to persuade the big powers to be generous. At a higher level, the national governments are behaving like cultural individualists, too hotly involved in competition with one another to put the poor nations high among their priorities. At another lower level, the academics, including the writer of this article, are distressed, but can only waver helplessly between fatalism and active dissidence.

Note

1. I recognize this as a central theme of Africanist research in economic anthropology in the 1960s. In the sphere of money, the solidarity-enhancing effects of local (specialized and restricted) currencies were contrasted with the disintegration of social ties produced by an all-purpose monetary instrument (Bohannan and Dalton 1962).

Appendix to Douglas:
Cultural Theory and Development Studies

MARCO VERWEIJ

A Cultural Theory

The "cultural theory" pioneered by Mary Douglas (Douglas 1973/1982, 1978, 1987), and further developed by a group of anthropologists and political scientists (Thompson, Ellis, and Wildavsky 1990; Adams 1995; Hood 1998; Wildavsky, Chai, and Swedlow 1998), sets out four ways of organizing, justifying, and perceiving social relations: individualism, hierarchy, egalitarianism, and fatalism. It postulates that these four cultures are in permanent contention in each conceivable domain of social life. Hence, any such domain (say, the way in which a school operates, or in which the international regime to protect the ozone layer functions) can consist of any mix of these four forms. Thus, the theory makes it possible to perceive a wide, and ever-changing, cultural and social variety while still allowing for general propositions about social and political life. The approach has successfully been used to classify the divergent ways in which people act and think in the domains of public housing, traffic policy, environmental protection, electricity supply, pension reform, treatment of the mentally ill, Internet regulation, hazardous waste siting, and welfare provisions (Thompson, Grendstad, and Selle 1999b; Coyle and Ellis 1994).

The theory's typology can be illustrated for the raging debate on globalization. The Meltzer Report to the U.S. Congress (2000) offers an individualistic perspective on how to organize globalization (Meltzer Commission [International Financial Institution Advisory Commission] 2000). It states that private markets efficiently provide most developing countries with adequate amounts of capital. Offering funds to these countries at favorable rates through the International Monetary Fund (IMF) and World Bank creates "moral hazard" problems, breeds corruption, and stimulates unprofitable economic activities. The report concludes that the roles of these two international bureaucracies should therefore be reduced to a bare minimum in favor of unfettered global markets. The IMF should only serve as a short-term lender of last resort to emerging economies, whereas the World Bank should merely give small grants for infrastructure projects in the poorest of countries. This proposal would significantly reduce the current scope of international bureaucracy.

Radical citizens' groups, such as Earth First! and the International Forum on Globalization, espouse egalitarian views. They oppose the integration of the third world into the world economy, arguing that this threatens local accountability and democracy, erodes environmental standards, and creates a skewed competition between small southern producers lacking in capital and information and large and powerful northern multinationals. Instead, these groups advocate the egalitarian ideal of modest, local consumption and production patterns that are subject to local forms of participatory democracy. Localization, rather than globalization, is their demand.

The United Nations Development Program finds fault with both positions. Its *Human Development Report, 1999*—prepared by "a team of eminent economists and distinguished development professionals"—states that global markets will be beneficial to the majority of the world population, but only if they are strictly regulated by global bureaucracies and treaties (United Nations Development Program [UNDP] 1999a).

Cultural Failure

According to cultural theory, the prevention of massive fatalism requires all four cultures to be interacting. Each culture encompasses a particular way of defining and solving social problems, supported by alternative ways of generating information, learning, and motivating people. None of them contains more than a kernel of wisdom. Policy solutions that are effective, equitable, and efficient are therefore creative and flexible combinations of these alternative perspectives. Moreover, the pure forms are not viable. Each culture needs all others in order not to become a perversion of itself.

Hierarchy is apt to be prey to corruption, throttled by its bureaucracy. It tries to monitor information and to suppress deviant opinion. The hierarchy would slide into chaos unless checked by egalitarian and individualist criticism. The egalitarian concern for the downtrodden checks hierarchy's repression of deviants; the competition provided by individualism checks its ossification. And it needs the distrust of central control and the insistence on transparency that is prevalent in individualism and egalitarianism, to keep itself honest and accountable. Economists recognize the perverse forms of individualism as opportunism. It stands for unfettered competition without externally imposed rules and roles. Even if it does not lead to dishonesty, massive income inequality tends to result. Egalitarianism protests against inequality, and hierarchy organizes the continuous redistribution of resources that will prevent ongoing competitions from becoming increasingly unfair. In its turn, egalitarianism lacks authoritative procedures for settling conflicts. The resulting state of indecision undermines its institutions; deadlock is resolved by threat of expulsion, starting a justificatory process of vilification. The frequent splintering of radical left-wing movements makes the point. Furthermore, egalitarianism rejects activities that would give rise to inequality, and so risks inhibiting economic development. It needs some hierarchical institutions to settle disputes, as well as individualism's vibrancy.

From the above, a general principle for checking widespread fatalism emerges: each of the competing cultures needs to be represented in the debates about every public issue. As Michiel Schwarz and Michael Thompson (1990, 13) put it: "divided we stand, united we fall." Cultural theory posits that even within the most fatalized social domains, there will always be some people around who (want to) adhere to other cultures. Enabling development does therefore not require any import of "appropriate" norms and attitudes, as other cultural approaches to development claim (Harrison and Huntington 2000). Cultural theory calls instead for deliberative political institutions that contain checks and balances guaranteeing that each form of culture is incorporated into public decision making. This at a minimum requires full adherence to human rights and democratic procedures.

Dipak Gyawali (2001) has applied cultural theory to the efforts to generate electricity from the rivers that hurl down the Nepali parts of the Himalayan. In the early 1980s, the feudal *Panchayat* rulers, Nepali bureaucrats, and international aid donors decided to construct Arun-3, an enormous hydroelectric project on the Arun River. This project was officially estimated to cost $1.1 billion, or more than twice the annual internal revenue of the Nepali government. It was supposed to turn Nepal into a second Singapore. Gyawali details the many drawbacks that were overlooked in this massive undertaking: the risks of pouring almost all development and other public funds of a small and poor country into one enormous electricity project; the many indications that cost-and-benefit estimates of the dam were far too rosy; the availability of cheaper, medium- and small-scale alternatives; the regional imbalances that would arise from a concentration of development efforts within one area of Nepal; the increased dependence upon India (the main consumer of the hydropower generated by the dam); and the opportunities for corruption that this mammoth project would provide. Various nongovernmental organizations, local entrepreneurs, and a few civil servants frequently voiced these concerns. Gyawali shows that the Nepali and international decision makers strictly adhered to a hierarchical perspective that remained blind to any drawbacks of their technocratic plans. Local entrepreneurs (who were constantly inventing cheaper, small-scale ways of generating electricity) were acting out the individualistic solidarity, while grassroots movements (who protested the social inequalities, corruption, and environmental degradation created by the project) were advocating egalitarian policies. The unrepresentative Nepali decision-making structures filtered out their dissenting opinions. The restoration of democracy in 1990 allowed egalitarian and individualistic voices to be heard louder. But only after Nepali grassroots movements teamed up with the Oakland-based International Rivers Network could they match the coalition of Nepali ministries and foreign aid donors that had been pushing the dam. In 1995, World Bank President Wolfensohn pulled the plug. By means of counterfactuals, Gyawali shows that a more representative set of institutions and policies would have better served Nepal's development efforts.

Convergence with Development Studies

Cultural theory is in line with three insights that have recently emerged within development studies. A first concerns the social conditions that development strategies should target. One particular proposal has gained ground: development projects should aim to transform those social relations in which lack of trust and cooperation, as well as faltering institutions, bar individuals from leading the lives that they deem worthwhile. Cultural theory's concept of fatalism overlaps with the notion of "destitution" (Dasgupta 1993) and lack of "social capital" (Putnam 1993).

A second nascent insight regards the end goals of development strategies (Rodrik 1999; Sen 1999). No longer should development efforts merely focus on economic growth and poverty alleviation. Other important goals should include democracy, human rights, employment, literacy, health, and justice. This is congenial to cultural theory's emphasis on dem-

ocratic and human rights. These rights are necessary to ensure constructive engagement and disagreement in the cross-cultural dialogue.

A third theme deals with the ways in which this wider variety of development goals can be achieved. Various development economists (Stiglitz
1999; Dasgupta 1999) have taken up the idea that only a balance between
different institutional forms will allow societies to develop: state bureaucracies, markets, and civil society can only flourish *together*. It is often
added that deliberative forums can forge the appropriate linkages between
different institutional forms (Stiglitz 2003; Sen 1999). This view appears in
the World Bank's *Proposal for a Comprehensive Development Framework*
(Wolfensohn 1999). In cultural theory, civil society is the institution cherished by egalitarianism, free markets are extolled by individualism, and
bureaucracies constitute the favored allocation mechanism of hierarchy.
Open, deliberative forums should bring about institutions and policies in
which these organizational forms are creatively combined. Cultural theory
adds that democracy and human rights, though necessary for the proper
functioning of polities and economies, may not always be sufficient.
Gyawali's study (2001) illustrates this. In predemocratic Nepal, the political and bureaucratic elites, hand in hand with aid donors, viewed the
opportunities and problems of hydropower through the lens of only one
culture: hierarchy. This unrepresentative manner of policy making led to
high energy prices, corruption, and stagnation. The advent of democracy
allowed alternative perspectives on Nepali electricity supply to be heard
more in public debates. But democracy has thus far not turned this particular issue-area into a constructive interplay of opposing solidarities.
After the huge Arun-3 project was halted, Nepali bureaucrats (as monocultural as before) proposed an even bigger dam, the Pancheswar High
Dam, as the only possible remedy for Nepal's plight. So formal democracy
may not always be sufficient to bring about the necessary, never-ending,
creative struggle between alternative cultures that can further development. One of cultural theory's aims is to let some light into the black box
of democracy and deliberation.

CHAPTER 6

Cultural Obstacles to Economic Development: Often Overstated, Usually Transitory

TIMUR KURAN

Economic Development and Its Cultural Discontents

In ongoing debates on economic development, a steady source of controversy is the accommodation of cultural particularities. Although the arguments are highly diverse, they may be grouped in two broad categories: multiculturalism and globalism. Multiculturalists generally maintain that globalization, by destroying local cultures, harms the affected communities, even humanity as a whole. There is a need, they say, to resist the homogenizing influences of modern civilization by nurturing cultural differences. For their part, globalists consider the march of civilization unstoppable. Cultural change is an unavoidable fact of life, they suggest, and in periods of economic transition, it inevitably accelerates. Besides, cultural achievements belong to everyone, and it is harmful to block cultural diffusion for the sake of protecting traditional values and practices.

On both sides of the debate, the overwhelming majority of the participants are well educated and well-off by the standards of their own societies, if not by global standards as well. Writings, speeches, and images that grab attention are generally produced and disseminated by elites, such as journalists, novelists, broadcasters, filmmakers, educators, and politicians. Seldom do the pertinent public communications expose us to an opinion column by a Pakistani bank clerk, or a documentary conceived by a Mexican laborer, or the monograph of a Senegalese grocer. Hence, one should be skeptical of the claims that dominate the ongoing "culture wars"; they do not necessarily reflect widely felt sentiments. Arguments on the economic merits of globalization could serve as smokescreens for the disproportionate benefits reaped by multinational corporations based in the West. By the same token, campaigns for the preservation of traditional cultures might be advancing the interests of multiculturalist spokespersons, as opposed to those of the downtrodden they claim to represent.

This chapter explores such possibilities, with a focus on exaggerated claims made on behalf of multiculturalism. It uses an analytical framework that accommodates preference falsification—the misrepresentation of desires under perceived social pressures. In the presence of cultural preference falsification, the *public* support given to a multiculturalist agenda may differ from its *private* support. In particular, the agenda may appear more popular, or less popular, than it really is. My framework also accommodates the fluidity of private cultural preferences. It thus allows the variability of tensions between private and public cultural demands. Insofar as the pertinent private preferences are malleable, a cultural change initially coded as a loss may come to be viewed a gain. Although adjustments in wants can be counteradaptive, ordinarily they lessen, rather than augment, the tensions between genuine wants and actual possibilities.

The traits that define a culture serve aesthetic, psychological, and social needs. They also influence economic performance. Sometimes these various effects present trade-offs, as when a custom cherished for its contribution to a nation's identity harms productivity. However, the economic consequences in question are rarely self-evident, and they are subject to deliberate misstatement. Powerful groups may exaggerate the economic costs or benefits of an aesthetic value. Likewise, the media may ignore a consequence of major significance to the poor. On these grounds, I argue that the effects of cultural traits should be identified through techniques that encourage people to speak for themselves rather than through the intermediation of self-appointed cultural spokespersons. Moreover, all evidence on the welfare effects of cultural transformations should be factored into relevant policy decisions.

If dispassionate investigation of a community's private cultural preferences reveals an authentic conflict between economic performance and cultural satisfaction, the warranted policy implication is not necessarily that the preferences take precedence. One should keep in mind, I suggest, that private preferences are not fixed in stone. Because they are malleable, growth-compatible policies that reduce cultural satisfaction in the short run, even ones that harm social welfare for a while, may serve the community's long-run interests. Losses in cultural satisfaction can be temporary; they may wither away as beliefs and preferences adjust to the new circumstances generated by economic growth.

This is significant, because "cultural lock-in" is among the causes of persistent underdevelopment. By the logic just sketched, one need not refrain from efforts to overcome entrenched cultural obstacles to economic growth. Any burdens of the resulting cultural transformation, even where not imaginary, may well be transitional. There are sound reasons, then, for denying present cultures the *blanket* protections often demanded in the name of multiculturalism. Policies detrimental to genuinely and widely wanted cultural traits could be defensible, provided they serve to dampen the burdensome cultural attachments.

Culture and Its Inner Tensions

The term *culture* carries a huge variety of meanings.[1] For our purposes here, a community's culture consists of the beliefs, preferences, and behaviors of its members, along with the mechanisms that link these traits to one another. These traits give the community a unique identity that distinguishes it from other communities. This identity is subject to change, for a culture is a living organism. Through their interactions and their reactions to external influences, the members of a community transform their behaviors and ultimately also the underlying beliefs and preferences. By the definition adopted here, such changes amount to cultural change.

Unlike most of its alternatives, this definition allows for diversity within any given cultural community. The perceptions and desires of individuals need not be uniform, and their choices may vary. Nor are these traits restricted to those considered proper, correct, or just. Within any given cultural community, there will exist beliefs, preferences, and behaviors considered acceptable, and others considered deviant. Such heterogeneities may give rise to distinct subcultures, and some of these may enjoy greater esteem than others. The present concept of culture also allows for tensions within the individual members of the community. The convictions, sentiments, and actions of a person may harbor contradictions. For example, a person eager to retain social acceptance may follow a custom that he despises. Alternatively, he may heap scorn on a practice that he considers useful. To allow people's behaviors to conflict with their private beliefs and preferences amounts, of course, to recognizing that every culture is, to one degree or another, "incoherent" and "repressed."

Nothing here precludes shared elements within a cultural community. As a matter of practice, people bound by a common culture will share many beliefs, hold similar preferences in a range of contexts, and behave in ways that everyone, insiders as well as outsiders, consider similar. Yet even a behaviorally rather homogeneous community will include individuals who act in ways uncharacteristic of that community. It will also include people who would like, in their hearts, to deviate from prevailing social norms. By itself, then, widespread adherence to a particular custom does not imply a genuine consensus in favor of retaining that custom. Determining the actual popularity of a shared cultural trait requires additional data, in particular, information on the determinants of individual choices, including social pressures.

As certain formal models of cultural evolution emphasize (Cavalli-Sforza and Feldman 1981; Boyd and Richerson 1985), beliefs and preferences (when used without qualification, these terms will refer to their private variants, as opposed to their public variants, which are influenced by reputational considerations) are shaped by the learning and personality formation processes known collectively as socialization. Socialization transmits models of the good and honorable life through records of past achievements as well as through ongoing interpersonal relations. Nothing guarantees that the resulting beliefs and preferences will be "economically functional," in the sense of inducing behaviors favorable to wealth creation. Contrary to an assumption implicit in much cultural anthropology, the normative models contained in a society's heritage, like those promoted by living political leaders, may be ill suited to future economic growth. Therefore the task of maximizing a society's well-being goes beyond uncovering disguised preferences and beliefs. Although every policy should be based on a sound reading of individual understandings and sensitivities, it is also essential to assess how such cultural traits affect economic performance.

Linkages Between Culture and Economic Development

Economic development is influenced both by economic desires and by perceptions of economic opportunities. In addition, the behaviors driven by such variables determine how individuals and communities respond to available opportunities.

Two concrete examples will be useful. India's age-old caste system fosters a notion of hereditary inequality that dampens the aspirations of the "ritually impure," limits occupational choice, and hinders efforts to escape from poverty (Ghurye 1961; Human Rights Watch 1999). It thus causes economic harm through mechanisms that shape Indian beliefs, preferences, and behaviors. For our second example, consider the now-global habit of drinking carbonated drinks. As societies make the transition from homemade beverages like tea to factory-bottled beverages like Coca-Cola, their members become more marketized, more inclined to seek employment outside the home, and more eager to earn money. At the same time, the advertising that fuels this transition alters perceptions about what consumption patterns are socially esteemed. A common cost is that people who cannot afford the new consumption patterns become frustrated and resentful. Other transitional costs fall on producers with a stake in the continuation of old consumption habits; some are forced to change sectors or occupations.

Switching to a new beverage may seem of minor relevance to economic development. However, there is a mechanism by which even routine consumption acts may have huge, albeit indirect, influences on economic performance. What people eat, drink, and wear serve as means to certify their communal memberships. Consumption patterns maintain links with ancestors and offspring, forge bonds among friends, and sustain traditional relationships. The consequent communal solidarity facilitates the production of collective action, which does not necessarily favor economic growth. It also serves to keep outsiders at a distance, even to sustain economically destructive intercommunal animosities.

As George Akerlof and Rachel Kranton (2000) show, an individual's sense of self, which is inextricably linked to the social categories to which he belongs, often contributes critically to his personal economic performance. The identities he develops in the course of socialization—"man," "Indian," "Gujarati," "Hindu," "untouchable"—will shape his later experiences, constrain the pool from whom he chooses his friends, limit the groups with whom he trades, restrict his job opportunities, and affect his earning power. Personal identities also influence the pressures one encounters. In every society, the behaviors expected of women differ from those expected of men. Although the pertinent pressures are variable, nowhere have they ever lost all economic significance.

The cultural elements that strengthen communal ties and forge collective identities do not necessarily become instruments of strife. Under the right conditions, they stimulate mutually beneficial interactions among communities. Think of Turkey's diverse folk dancing traditions and its rich cuisine. These cultural traits contribute to what makes Turkey a different, exotic place to visit. As such, they stimulate tourism, provide employment, and create bonds between locals and foreigners. Or think of Iran's rugs, avidly sought because of their elegance. Both Iranians and their trading partners have benefited from the Iranian rug industry. Cultural treasures carry a potential, however, of becoming vehicles of exclusion and destructive competition. During the Balkan wars of the 1990s, the religious identities of the region's Muslim peoples turned into symbols of pernicious cultural difference, causing them to be treated as heinous foreigners. All across the globe, efforts to sustain minority languages have rankled majorities, fostering political disunity and divisiveness.

My illustrations demonstrate the diversity of the linkages between culture and economic development. Some elements of any given culture are clearly harmful to development; others are manifestly beneficial. Some promote intercommunal mistrust and hatred; others fuel peaceful interactions. The persistence of a cultural trait may enrich certain groups while keeping others impoverished; by the same token, cultural transformation, whether fueled by indigenous forces or foreign interactions, often results in gains for some and losses for others. The payoffs in question involve both material and psychic elements.

Complicating matters further, I return to the possibility of cultural preference falsification. The *perceived* payoffs of a given cultural trait may be clouded by political rhetoric and by social pressures that discourage honest expression. So public opinion on any given cultural matter—the distribution of public cultural preferences—may misrepresent the community's genuine attitudes regarding cultural preservation. A related problem is that private opinion—the distribution of private and usually unobserved cultural preferences—is itself influenced by the factors that shape public opinion. The informational distortions that accompany intimidation and propaganda campaigns rarely leave popular perceptions untouched.

To sum up thus far, although culture matters enormously to economic development, the relevant linkages are diverse. From the standpoint of development, this calls for considerable flexibility. In crafting development policies, one should also recognize that cultural barriers to material growth, where they exist, are generally neither unalterable nor insurmountable.[2] The components of culture can form any number of social equilibria, with possibly different effects on economic development. However, the effects do not speak for themselves. Social pressures may keep any effect from public view, just as they may exaggerate its significance.

Inauthentic Cultural Resistance

Consider a custom that is clearly harmful to economic productivity. There may exist no simple way to modify or eradicate it. We may still want to investigate whether it makes sense even to try. For an answer, one must determine, among other factors, the extent to which the population wants the custom preserved. If it turns out that most people cherish the custom and consider it integral to the local culture, we will have discovered that the material gains from destroying the productivity-reducing custom would be accompanied, at least initially, by a loss in cultural satisfaction. It may turn out, alternatively, that genuine support for the economically dys-functional custom is narrowly based, that calls for protecting the custom are being orchestrated by a politically well-placed minority, and that the less vocal majority hardly cares. Indeed, the self-appointed spokespeople for a community need not even be among its members; especially in the case of poor communities, they are likely to consist of foreign academics, think tanks, and journalists. So the community's *own* and *genuine* loss from erad-icating the dysfunctional custom could actually be minimal. If the protests of cultural activists are ignored and efforts are made to weaken the custom, the masses might consider their lives improved.

Yet uncovering a preference distribution is a tricky task, even in dem-ocratic countries with constitutional protections for speech. A basic reason is that for controversial causes, social pressures, ubiquitous everywhere, can make people conceal, even misrepresent, their privately held, genuine preferences. In nondemocratic countries, the challenge is even greater because people are accustomed neither to speaking for themselves nor to organizing in pursuit of their interests.

The foregoing logic draws on my 1995 book, *Private Truths, Public Lies: The Social Consequences of Preference Falsification.* I show there that in the interest of gaining and retaining social acceptance, we routinely engage in preference falsification, along with belief falsification, which is the mis-representation of beliefs to signal a socially approved disposition. In the presence of social pressures against honest public expression, such forms of insincerity do not occur automatically. To one degree or another, and depending on the context, we all benefit from speaking our own minds. Hence, where the relevant social pressures are sufficiently mild, we put up resistance. Nor are the pressures that induce preference and belief falsifica-tion fixed. They themselves depend on the expressive choices of the rele-vant community. Specifically, the distribution of public preferences con-cerning an issue will affect the pertinent expressive incentives. Given a distribution of public support among rival agendas, some members of society will feel pressured to feign sympathy toward the agenda that appears most popular. In so doing, these preference falsifiers will com-pound the perceived popularity. Moreover, under diverse situations, oth-ers will then be induced to lend the agenda their own public support. In this manner, an agenda's apparent popularity may grow through a reputa-tional cascade fueled by individual efforts to remain within the main-stream. Much of society may come to support an agenda that few would favor if given a chance to vote by secret ballot or to fill out an anonymous questionnaire.

When public preferences are interdependent, public opinion typically features multiple equilibria. Whatever one's definition of optimality, there is no guarantee that any of these will be socially optimal. The interdependence will be strong and, hence, social pressures especially influential wherever the typical individual's ability to mold the overall outcome is negligible.

This condition is satisfied with regard to matters of cultural policy such as historical preservation, language purification, women's social rights, the educational curriculum, art subsidies, and media content restrictions. On these matters individuals typically feel powerless, and nothing other than the need for truthful self-expression induces resistance to social pressures.[3] Therefore, activists who promote definitions of the "national culture," the "regional culture," or the "ethnic culture" may see their interpretations become practically unchallengeable. The public approval bestowed upon their interpretations bolster the social pressures fueling the approval itself. Their success in manipulating society's publicly affirmed cultural identity is thus self-reproducing, perhaps even self-reinforcing.

Market and Migration Tests of Cultural Anxiety

There are powerful forces, then, that distort public opinion on cultural matters. Nevertheless, there exist methods to differentiate genuinely widespread cultural anxieties from those limited to vocal minorities.

One simple test is the *market test*, which relies on personal choices exercised through essentially competitive markets that give individuals some anonymity. In undertaking exchanges through such markets, people advance their individualistic objectives rather than communal goals or the goals of groups they wish to impress favorably. In so doing, they need not participate in public debates concerning the merits of their actions. Remaining silent, they may ignore the chattering of politically vocal groups. Alternatively, if it seems prudent, they may pay lip service to the need for banning the transactions they actually consider beneficial. Either situation causes public discourse to conflict with the realities of the marketplace. As such, one may infer that the requested prohibition would impose hidden costs that merit attention.

For an illustration of the market test, consider the ongoing campaign, most visible within regimes formally committed to Islamization, to ban interest on the ground that it violates a sacred Islamic command. The claim that Islam categorically prohibits all interest, regardless of form, purpose, or magnitude, drew objections from the earliest days of Islam, and in no large community have Muslims ever ceased dealing in interest. Nevertheless, in this century, the notion of an interest-shunning "Islamic bank" emerged through campaigns aimed at differentiating the "Islamic way of life" from other lifestyles, particularly from those identified with the West. For reasons presented elsewhere (Kuran 1998b), it eventually became the conventional wisdom among both Islamist and secular intellectuals that Muslim piety involves shunning interest. Yet in countries with both Islamic banks, which ostensibly avoid interest, and traditional banks, which openly pay and charge interest, only a minority of the Muslim population maintains accounts at Islamic banks. In fact, a quarter century after the advent of Islamic banking, in certain majority-Muslim countries that allow both types of banks, the market share of Islamic banks remains around 1%. Significantly, savers, investors, borrowers, and lenders who refrain from taking a public stand against the anti-interest campaign are usually willing to deal in interest even when given the opportunity to use Islamic banks (Kuran 1995a). In the present context, the market test thus indicates that the drive to prohibit interest and Islamicize all banks lacks mass support.

The last observation is relevant to the controversy over whether governments, firms, and international agencies dealing with countries that have officially prohibited interest—Pakistan, Iran, and the Sudan—should strive to deal with them through "culturally sensitive" means. Given that the promoters of Islamic banking consider "profit and loss sharing" the "Islamic" alternative to interest-based financial contracts, should lenders to such countries make a point of using equity contracts? More concretely, when the World Bank funds a Pakistani forestry project, should it necessarily do so as an equity investor that will share in the profits as well as in the losses? Should it offer Pakistan a financial option that it would deny to Turkey, Thailand, or Mexico?[4] The market test requires us to answer each question in the negative. It indicates that the intended beneficiaries of special privileges, the Pakistani people, generally have little to gain from such a move, or at least that their economic goals trump their cultural objectives. The test thus suggests that the promoters of mandatory Islamic banking hardly speak for the masses. Imagine that for some reason the World Bank agrees to profit and loss sharing. If this special arrangement exacerbates moral hazard in the project's local management, diminishing the return from the forestry project, the Pakistani nation will pay dearly the sake of satisfying its small minority genuinely offended by interest.

Interest-free financial instruments play an important economic role, of course, in various economies, including the most advanced. Witness the economic significance of venture capital firms and stock markets in today's richest countries. However, it is one thing to recognize the usefulness of equity-based finance, quite another to dispense with interest-based lending. Risk preferences vary in every known economy, so there are always individuals willing to lend for a fixed return or borrow at a fixed cost, along with others happy to carry risks that most people would rather avoid. Therefore, an interest ban would block voluntary transactions beneficial to all parties; at the very least, by making people use time-consuming stratagems to disguise interest charges, it would raise the costs of negotiating and monitoring financial agreements. If interest aversion were genuinely widespread, and enough people were offended by interest-based transactions of third parties, such economic costs might be acceptable for the sake of upholding a cherished cultural principle. However, if discomfort over interest is actually minimal, the cultural-sensitivity case for accepting the burden of an interest ban becomes unjustifiable.

For another application of the market test, let us move to the Balkans, scene of bloody conflicts involving indigenous Muslims. Among the justifications given for the Serbian-nationalist campaigns that dismembered Bosnia is that the peoples of this multireligious state have long pursued mutually incompatible lifestyles and despised one another. The global media, while condemning Yugoslavia's Serbian-nationalist regime for the ensuing violence, generally accepted this interpretation of history. They tended to believe the claim that the Balkan peoples have always fumed with "ancient hatreds." Yet various statistics from the former Yugoslavia, and Bosnia in particular, belie the notion of sharp cultural boundaries among the religious communities. A frequently noted sign of harmonious assimilation is the growing acceptance of ethnoreligious intermarriages; in urban Bosnia, one-third of all the marriages were mixed.[5] By virtue of such statistics, in the 1980s, Yugoslavia was portrayed as a shining example of multiculturalism and pluralistic nation building. Indeed, the Yugoslav nation seemed to be becoming socially, economically, and culturally as integrated as European Americans now are.[6]

Against this background, we may ask whether the international community had reason to look favorably upon Yugoslav cultural separatism. If outsiders had accepted the segregation of Yugoslavia's ethnoreligious groups into "cleansed" regions, would the local populations have benefited? According to our market test, the cleansing could not have enjoyed widespread support at the outset; insofar as it gained significant mass appeal, this was a by-product of the violence unleashed by Yugoslavia's post-Tito regime. Therefore, external endorsements of the adopted separatist policies would merely have helped to reverse the long-standing process of cultural mixing and homogenization.

Another test for measuring the accuracy or genuineness of cultural demands is the *migration test*. The logic here is that voluntary migration indicates how people rank alternative lifestyles. Thus, the steady northward flow across the Americas points to a widespread desire for living more like North Americans than like Latin Americans. In any given year, of course, the number of Latin American migrants is small in relation to the population of Latin America. However, this is partly because of barriers to migration. According to surveys, if the United States and Canada were to open their borders, at least half of all Latin Americans would abandon their countries for northern amenities lacking in their ancestral lands (Montaner 2000).

What such migrants are seeking, it might be said, is employment and income rather than a North American lifestyle per se. True, but for the migrants themselves, material wealth must matter more than anything else. In any case, migrants expect to make behavioral adjustments to fit into their new social environment. They also know that new opportunities will present themselves, that they will want to take advantage of these, and that their new cultural milieu will influence their children's beliefs and preferences. Of course, cultural adjustments do not occur smoothly or costlessly. On the contrary, they typically generate confusion, frustration, and resentment (Thomas 1995; Baptiste, Hardy, and Lewis 1997; Kim 2001). Yet in "voting with their feet," or simply signaling that they want to do so, Latin Americans are indicating that they expect the benefits of migration to dominate any costs of cultural adjustment.

Opinion Surveys to Uncover Hidden Resistance

The market and migration tests rely on observed patterns and trends. Additional information regarding cultural demands may be gleaned from *anonymous surveys* designed to identify genuine wants. Anonymity is critical, for it enhances the credibility of responses. Fears of giving offense distort public expressions wherever powerful elites have defined what cultural traits deserve appreciation, what cultural legacies are sacrosanct, and what cultural differences should be celebrated and defended—in short, what is "culturally correct." Depending on the prevailing definition of cultural correctness, in public settings individuals may feel pressured to downplay or exaggerate certain wants, compelled to express one belief or another about what defines their culture, and follow customs either more conservatively or more liberally than they would like.

The purpose of an anonymous opinion survey on cultural issues would be to determine whether, and in what contexts, private and public preferences are in conflict. It would also help to ascertain whether the spokespersons for indigenous cultures are faithful to the interests of their ostensible constituents. At a 1999 symposium on linkages between culture and economic development, an American cultural anthropologist clashed with several participants from Africa and Latin America on the merits of resisting westernization. The American scholar charged that poor societies are being forced to westernize, with lamentable consequences. His critics, accusing various western groups of trying to freeze dysfunctional cultures for romantic reasons, responded that their peoples *genuinely* aspire to the privileges of westerners (Schweder 2000; Montaner 2000; Grondona 2000; Etounga-Manguelle 2000). Who is right, and how would we know? Unfortunately, the answer cannot be obtained simply by turning to the public discourses of underdeveloped countries. As in the developed world, the pertinent public discourses are dominated by the educated, the wealthy, and the powerful. To compound the problem of interpreting the signals generated, the contributors to these discourses do not necessarily speak their own minds. Even elites avoid appearing culturally incorrect.

The activists who try to achieve broad public agreement on the characteristics and boundaries of the local culture need not be members of the local cultural community. As the reported conference exchange suggests, outsiders may play important roles. There is an intellectual tradition that considers "traditional societies" more harmonious and more content than modern industrial societies. Robert Edgerton (1992) critiques this tradition, including its functionalist justifications for practices that offend modern sensibilities or appear economically harmful. For a gripping example of such a justification, murderous witch hunts have been portrayed as socially beneficial instruments for building communal solidarity. In the hands of certain cultural anthropologists, Edgerton shows, functionalism of this kind has gone along with the assertion that all disorder in underdeveloped countries stems from industrialization and urbanization, themselves consequences of modern cross-cultural contacts. Given the West's influence on global intellectual trends, such interpretations have given cultural protectionists within underdeveloped countries a rationale for resisting modernization. In effect, western-based philosophies of cultural relativism are serving to bolster economically dysfunctional social structures.

One reason why sub-Saharan Africa has far more AIDS-infected people per capita than any other region is that, until recently, most of its political and intellectual leaders turned a deaf ear to calls for aggressive reeducation to modify the region's sexual habits. If their avoidance policy was successful, this is partly because, as the epidemic spread, the world's opinion leaders generally stood by in silence. There are many reasons, of course, why African regimes endured only minimal criticism from abroad.

One factor is plain indifference; another is that western intellectuals generally refrain from questioning nonwestern lifestyles in public, muting any criticisms for fear of appearing "racist," "elitist," or "opposed to cultural diversity" (Lawson 1999; Sibanda 2000).

It is precisely such distortions that make anonymous surveying a useful instrument for identifying private thoughts and preferences. Suppose that a few years ago the world's opinion makers had been surveyed on the matter of the global AIDS epidemic. This survey would probably have revealed far more support for encouraging African lifestyle changes than could be gleaned from the media. In Africa itself, the masses appear to have remained genuinely unalarmed, except perhaps in the hardest-hit areas. However, anonymous surveys of African health professionals would have documented deep concerns that the political system was suppressing. By itself, of course, knowledge of unexpressed disapproval does nothing to change the course of events. However, it can stimulate movements for change.

It may seem like a simple exercise to prepare and administer an anonymous survey. There are two common problems, one political and the other logistical. An establishment with a stake in the cultural status quo has much to lose from opinion studies likely to expose cultural preference falsification. So where the government can block any research project it deems harmful, credible anonymous surveying may prove impossible. In any case, researchers fearful of reprisals may avoid even questioning the authenticity of public opinion, to say nothing of undertaking anonymous surveys. The logistical problem involves the administration of anonymous written surveys. Although the anonymity condition is easily satisfied in regard to well-educated populations accustomed to answering questionnaires, it is practically impossible to meet with illiterate populations, even with minimally educated people unable to fill out the simplest application form without assistance.

In certain areas of research, investigators dealing with uneducated populations compensate for this difficulty by questioning subjects individually, using interviewers likely to evoke trust. For example, a Pakistani household survey of the 1990s made a point of interviewing each man and woman separately, with male interviewers administering the questionnaires of the former and female interviewers those of the latter (Pakistan Integrated Household Survey 1990). In the same vein, a study of wife-beating in rural India relied on individual interviews in order to promote sincerity (Rao 1997). Although such approaches yield helpful information, they do not guarantee frankness. An abused wife may fear that her answers will be leaked to her relatives. Likewise, an illiterate African farmer questioned about his sex life, or about the sexual habits of his community, may refrain from opening up to the interviewer in the belief that promises of confidentiality might not be kept.

Alternatives to Surveys

Fortunately, there exist several other techniques that can be used to uncover preferences and beliefs on sensitive subjects. One is to conduct a *hypothetical scenario experiment* designed to identify concealed dispositions. This experiment involves having a trained experimenter present a certain hypothetical scenario separately to each member of the subject pool. The scenario features an individual who endures humiliation for expressing a view on some well-defined issue. Let us say the issue is Islamic banking. The experimenter asks subjects to speculate on what the scolded individual might have said to provoke retaliation. The purpose, of course, is to identify the prevailing expressive pressures without requiring respondents to take personal responsibility for articulating an unpopular viewpoint. The responses of the subjects are expected to yield insights into the genuineness of public opinion.[7] Suppose that we apply a version of this experiment to the Islamic banking controversy in a country officially committed to economic Islamization. The dominant response, suppose further, is that the scolded individual must have opposed the interest ban as unenforceable. We may infer that in the investigated community, public opinion on interest reflects more than private preferences and beliefs.

A second alternative to the anonymous opinion survey is the *biased interviewer experiment.* This experiment relies on interviewers whose outward characteristics make them appear committed to one social agenda or another.[8] If the responses of the subjects vary by interviewer, and the variations are positively correlated with the communicated agendas, the issue in question is obviously considered sensitive. By itself, of course, evidence of pressures against expressive honesty does not indicate what is genuinely believed or wanted. But it establishes that investigations relying on other methods might turn up useful information.

A final alternative to anonymous surveys is the age-old anthropological technique of close observation. The key to this technique, whose successful applications include James Scott's investigations in rural Malaysia (Scott 1985, 1990), is to gain the confidence of a community in order to learn about thoughts and preferences that its members are reticent to express in the presence of strangers. Researchers using this technique do not take expressions at face value. Alert to conformist social pressures, they look to hidden meanings, perceptions, aspirations, anxieties, and resentments.

Returning again to the controversy over interest, we may ask what evidence exists with regard to the depth and sincerity of Pakistani support for economic Islamization. In public settings, most Pakistani politicians and intellectuals, including ones known as modernizers, pay lip service to their country's commitment to comprehensive Islamization. Yet it is well known that many have serious reservations about Islamization and, in particular, low opinions of Islamic economics and Islamic banking. It is also known that many ordinary people hide their misgivings about Islamization.[9] This evidence of hidden opposition to Pakistan's official Islamization agenda is consistent with the poor results that the Jamaat-i Islami, Pakistan's main Islamist party, achieves in national elections held by secret ballot. Although such data are not conclusive, they offer reasons to expect anonymous surveys on economic Islamization to uncover considerable opposition. To date, no such surveys have been conducted.

Imagine that through some combination of methods it has been demonstrated convincingly that nine out of ten Pakistanis are either indifferent or opposed to a ban on interest. In and of itself, supporters will say, this hardly matters. Islamization is essential, they will argue, because it sustains the Pakistani identity by differentiating Pakistanis from other peoples of the Asian subcontinent. Islam is certainly a central component of what, to most Pakistanis, it means to be a Pakistani. Yet economic Islamization has never been central to Muslim-Pakistani perceptions of what it means to be pious. To a Pakistani committed to living as a good Muslim, achieving this goal may require praying five times a day, fasting at Ramadan, being steadily generous, showing solidarity with other Muslims, and instilling the same sense of religious dedication in the young; seldom does it involve avoiding interest. So the claim that interest aversion is critical to the Pakistani self-definition enjoys little empirical support, and the identity justification for prohibiting interest lacks credibility.

Authentic Conflicts Between Economic Development and Cultural Satisfaction

The policy implications of the reported findings on the interest controversy are straightforward. Because they present no significant conflict between cultural objectives and the financial requirements of economic development, no compromise is necessary. In particular, agencies dealing with Pakistan need not go out of their way to avoid interest. Of course, a diversified Pakistani or foreign investor may have reasons for taking an equity share in a Pakistani firm as opposed to making an interest-bearing loan; and the firm itself may want to shift some risks on to the investor. But the fact that some agents benefit from financial instruments other than interest does not mean that these are suitable to all transactions. Even a simple economy requires diverse financial instruments, including interest.

We face a challenge where large groups cherish a practice harmful to economic development as indispensable to their ancestral culture. In various impoverished countries, ethnic segregation and discrimination, schooling restrictions for girls, harmful dietary customs, and unhygienic medical procedures enjoy considerable public support. In theory, such cultural features could rest on contrived behaviors, and their supporters need not act or speak out of conviction. In actuality, even people arguably victimized—members of oppressed ethnic groups, girls denied schooling and their equally uneducated mothers, the consumers of unhealthy foods, the patients of folk doctors—believe in the merits of many such practices and want them passed on to their descendants. Moreover, as Mary Douglas observes, consumption activities may be valued because they structure social relations and provide a sense of identity (Douglas 1984). Quotas, tariffs, and other measures taken to protect local industries offer additional examples of economically harmful policies justified partly through cultural considerations.

The justifications in question may be as ludicrous as the usual excuse for subsidizing American agriculture: "saving the traditional family farm."[10] Yet just as the "family farm" argument resonates with millions of Americans who naively subsidize wealthy corporations through higher food prices, so in many underdeveloped countries protectionist arguments command broad appeal. Vast numbers of Mahatma Gandhi's fellow citizens shared his reverence toward India's indigenous products and local technologies; and the inward-oriented development strategy that India pursued until recently was popular among the very people it condemned to chronic poverty. Likewise, in many Middle Eastern and African countries, including the poorest, resistance to foreign investment carried out under the banners of anti-imperialism, decolonization, nativism, and nationalism have made sense to the very victims of economic isolation.[11] Many unemployed people still support protectionist policies under the illusion that they prevent exploitation, preserve local lifestyles, and reduce economic disparities, when their usual effect is to cover up corruption and tyranny.[12]

In view of the guidelines introduced earlier, such cases pose difficulties. The clash between the globally widespread desire to achieve material prosperity and the equally common desire to shield local cultures from globalization cannot always be dismissed on the ground that the observed cultural resistance is feigned. Nor will the market and migration tests necessarily come to the rescue. Consider first the latter test. Although huge numbers may want to emigrate, under existing restrictions on international mobility, only a small share will succeed. Remaining at home, most will seek to advance economically without significant lifestyle adjustments. Given a single binary choice between becoming rich and preserving their customs, the majority of these people would probably opt for enrichment. But in actuality, each person faces trade-offs in multiple spheres of life, and in certain contexts, some loss of productivity and profitability is considered an acceptable price for cultural continuity. In and of itself, then, the migration test does not dispose of the trade-offs in question. As for the market test, every underdeveloped country harbors people trying to live differently, often through adjustments typically characterized as westernization. But not even these culturally mobile groups are prepared to make unlimited adjustments. Many Egyptians who dress like westerners remain attached to their traditional Egyptian cuisine. In any case, along with westernizing Egyptians, one finds groups genuinely committed to preserving Egypt's cultural particularities. We see again that trade-offs between economic development and cultural preservation are unavoidable.

The Malleability of Cultural Preferences

Where the goals of economic development and cultural continuity are manifestly incompatible, would it be socially beneficial for policy makers to accommodate all genuine cultural demands? This question has no all-purpose answer, for the malleability of beliefs and preferences implies that the pertinent trade-offs are variable rather than fixed. The very foreign contacts perceived as cultural threats are likely to alter personal perceptions, sensitivities, and behaviors. It is no coincidence that the official dismantling of India's caste system began under leaders educated mostly in British schools. Although deeply influenced by Indian culture, these leaders had learned to view the world through a moral prism shaped by the prevailing European conceptions of justice and equality (Srinivas 1966; Sharma 1999). Nor is it coincidental that in the 19th century the massive expansion of trade between Turkey and western Europe was accompanied by an unmistakable westernization of Turkish perceptions, aspirations, and lifestyles. Although individual Turks of the era suffered well-documented identity conflicts, this westernization set the stage for a series of reforms critical to economic development (Berkes 1998; B. Lewis 1968).

Perceptions of cultural loss need not be permanent. What is once considered an offensive cultural borrowing will often come to be treated as indigenous. Most Turks of the 21st century see nothing "un-Turkish" about various institutions and practices that their ancestors had transplanted from other cultures. Examples include specialized secular courts to adjudicate commercial disputes (originally based on a French model), traffic regulations (developed in accordance with international norms), the local cuisine (influenced over many centuries by the cuisines of neighbors, including Greeks, Slavs, and Arabs), and even the local music (now often played with electric and electronic instruments).[13] Also, the perception of cultural loss can be minimized by grafting a new institution onto an old one. Modern Middle Eastern trusts, which enjoy legal personality, have been introduced into the region by grafting it onto the *waqf*, the traditional Islamic trust that lacked legal personality (Çizakça 2000).

The point remains that trade-offs exist. As long as cultural adjustments impose even transitory costs on *someone*, policies aimed at improving social welfare must take account of these costs. Moreover, the adopted policies may involve concessions for the sake of cultural preservation.

Such concessions do not require critics of the protected cultural traits to keep silent. On the contrary, the goal of social welfare maximization calls for anyone with reservations, cultural insiders or outsiders, to speak their minds loudly. A case can be made, in fact, that specialists in economic development—government employees, officers of international aid agencies, academics—have a professional duty to express their honest views on cultural obstacles to growth and efficiency, regardless of the sensitivities involved. By publicizing their perceptions, they will enhance their effectiveness.

Truthful expression on obstacles to economic efficiency is entirely consistent with cultural tolerance and diversity; it implies no disrespect toward the communities whose institutions and practices come under criticism. In fact, thoughtful criticism may reflect nothing more than genuine concern. Consider the finding that when a society denies girls an education it loses economic competitiveness, if only by condemning all children, including boys, to be raised by ignorant mothers in households deficient in intellectual stimulation (LeVine 1980; Schultz 1993). Suppose that this pattern is publicized in Pakistan, where about half as many women gain literacy as men (World Bank 2001b). Within Pakistan, this dissemination could contribute to an economically productive change in private beliefs about the value of education and private preferences regarding female intellectual achievement.

To recognize the malleability of private beliefs and preferences (which, by definition, are free of distortions instigated by the *prevailing* social pressures) is to note that attitudes incompatible with economic development may themselves be social constructs. Indeed, the troublesome attitudes may be the end products of a historical process that impoverished public discourse by inducing massive knowledge and preference falsification. Accordingly, cultural characteristics now regarded as harmful to development may be the vestiges of bygone social conditions.[14] To invoke yet another concept from modern institutional economics, the private beliefs and preferences now considered barriers to development are "path-dependent" variables: had the cultural community's history, perhaps its distant history, followed a different course as a result of different historical accidents, contemporary perceptions, and wants would also be different (North 1990; David 1994; Platteau 2000).

Against this background, let us revisit three of the controversies raised earlier. The doctrinal basis for the contemporary drive against interest is a financial restriction imposed fourteen centuries ago on a preindustrial and largely nomadic economy. This restriction is Islam's prohibition of *ribā*, an ancient Arabian practice whereby debtors who failed to make timely restitution saw their debts double, and then redouble if they defaulted again. Because it pushed hungry people into enslavement, *ribā* was a steady source of unrest. So its prohibition must have been motivated by a quest for social harmony.[15] In a modern industrial economy, even a relatively poor one, conditions are vastly different from those that led to the ban on *ribā*. First of all, we have bankruptcy laws that protect defaulters from enslavement. Second, only some contemporary loans are taken for subsistence needs; many finance luxury consumption and still others, nonconsumption activities such as production, trade, and research. Finally, in economies with well-functioning financial markets, interest rates are far lower than those that apparently prevailed in seventh-century Arabia; borrowers who delay restitution hardly see their debts double. In view of these fundamental differences, the ongoing anti-interest campaign is an anachronism. Hence, resistance to it, however sincerely some consider interest avoidance the sine qua non of an "Islamic economy," may be separated from challenges to Islam itself. In rejecting calls for an interest ban, one is not limited to the pragmatic argument that interest is critical to modern finance. Contemporary conditions differ markedly from those responsible for the ancient horrors of *ribā*.

India's caste system is thought to have arisen through violent intercommunal struggles that relegated the vanquished to undesirable occupations. Over the subsequent millennia, this initial division of labor apparently served as an infectious social model that brought most Indians into a stratification system based on heredity. Responsible for vast inequalities in wealth, status, and rights, the system's remarkable stability has rested partly on beliefs that rationalize its discriminatory features as just retribution for sins committed in previous lives. The ideology of the caste system molded the private beliefs and preferences of many generations of materially disadvantaged Indians, effectively sapping their resistance, even ensuring their willing loyalty (Hutton 1963; Lal 1988). Today, long after the struggles that put Indian culture on its characteristic trajectory, caste-based prejudices and social segregation have still not vanished. Moreover, these continue to limit economic efficiency by distorting educational and occupational choices. To criticize the caste system is to find fault, of course, with a pillar of traditional Hindu culture. Yet recognizing that this pillar rests on a long historical process, one may express opposition in a way that treats contemporary India as the *victim* of insidious cultural lock-in. The purpose of this strategy would be to shift the focus of ongoing debates from the short-run benefits of cultural preservation to the lingering effects of past inefficiencies.

Finally, let us reconsider the ethnoreligious distinctions that served as pretexts for dividing Yugoslavia into ethnically quite homogeneous successor states and essentially autonomous regions. We saw that the country's major groups had been remarkably integrated by global standards. Indeed, many perpetrators of the bloody events were motivated less by ethnic hatred than by fear of isolation from their own groups. This does not mean that no one was driven by ethnic animosity. Even before the bloodshed, some Yugoslavs were privately, if not also publicly, committed to ethnic separatism. And the ranks of such separatists swelled in the course of the hostilities, which propaganda machines of the warring parties blamed on others while casting their own groups as innocent victims (Glenny 1993). What matters here is that the resulting climate of interethnic mistrust stemmed partly from genuine feelings of victimization and fears of insecurity. The consequent economic harm is enormous: losses to fighting, missed opportunities for trade and tourism, low productivity due to the fragmentation of production. So the strictly economic case for resisting the region's "balkanization" is overwhelming. Nevertheless, opposition to disintegration need not rest on economics alone. One may appeal also to the fluidity of perceptions of difference and feelings of mistrust. Just as ethnic fears and animosities ballooned in the course of the hostilities, so they are bound to shrink with the restoration of interethnic peace.

Making the World Safe for Development

The foregoing three examples may suggest that the requirements of economic development must always trump demands for cultural preservation and differentiation. The campaign against interest threatens financial efficiency. The caste system distorts labor markets. Finally, ethnic separatism can turn an integrated regional economy into a patchwork of disconnected minieconomies. Although there exist additional justifications for opposing the cultural features in question—in the case of the Balkans, the threat to global political stability—a common economic thread runs through these illustrations. In each case, the malleability of culture has been used to justify favoring economic development over cultural continuity or differentness. Over the long run, I have proposed, the benefits of economic development are bound to swamp the transitional costs of the consequent cultural changes, because preferences and beliefs will adapt accordingly. Cultural changes that look harmful today may seem beneficial when evaluated with respect to tomorrow's preferences.

In fact, I have stopped short of arguing that economic development is the only goal worth respecting. Nor have I suggested that growth-minded policy makers should have unrestricted authority to restructure cultures as they see fit. Taken as a whole, this chapter has made four points. First, conflicts between local cultures and economic development are *often* artificial. In particular, the apparent demand for cultural protectionism may vastly overstate the extent and intensity of the actual demand. Where knowledge and preference falsification are rampant, as they commonly are on politically charged cultural matters, what meets the eye need not mirror reality. Second, cultural diversity per se poses no obstacle to economic development. Various practices, customs, and conventions are compatible with growth and efficiency; some of these even boost global social welfare by servicing the human desire for variety and novelty.

These two points obviate the need for difficult choices. In many cases, they remind us, we need only to listen to unfiltered voices and respect the cultural outcomes produced by genuine choices. The selected policies will then be democratic, as they will reflect the knowledge and tastes of the masses, rather than those of powerful elites.

By contrast, the next two points *do* present difficult dilemmas. I have suggested, thirdly, that demands for cultural protection and preservation are *not necessarily* contrived. Throughout the world there exist groups whose members resent the lifestyle adjustments required by new commodities, ever-changing fads and fashions, and interactions with cultural outsiders. Insofar as the ultimate goal of economic development is to enhance personal fulfillment, such needs may call for cultural restrictions on economic policies. For instance, they may necessitate measures to limit urban growth, preserve architectural masterpieces, and support ancestral customs. The justification for such measures would be analogous to those for, say, mandatory pollution controls: the cost of collective action makes it advantageous to endow a central authority with certain coercive powers. Finally, some cultural traits are so fundamentally incompatible with a materially prosperous social order based on liberty and tolerance that they should be overridden whatever the extent of their genuine support. One should pursue economic development, I have proposed, even in the face of sincere complaints about threats to particular cultural traits. One may even welcome the weakening of these traits, for they would be accompanied by preference and belief changes that attenuate conflicts between cultural and economic objectives.

The last point has purposefully been stated bluntly and without apology. From the Stone Age to the present, economic development has encountered resistance from groups trying to preserve ancestral, traditional, and familiar lifestyles. It has also entailed, along with a myriad of incremental adjustments of no intrinsic significance, massive institutional changes imposed by visionaries on largely unreceptive societies. The development drive of our own time fits these historical patterns. Whatever their differences, most government planners, international aid officials, development economists, and other such specialists consider such growth more or less essential to achieving happiness in a rapidly integrating world containing some already prosperous societies. Insofar as they are right, much of the ongoing cultural resistance merely postpones the inevitable.

Current debates over economic development are rife with controversy. Witness the ongoing disagreements on the benefits of trade protectionism, the unintended consequences of economic regulation, and the value of economic freedoms. Such controversies point to the multiplicity of ways to join the club of economically advanced countries. Therefore, removing cultural obstacles to economic development will not necessarily extinguish disputes over development policy. But it will undoubtedly enhance the fruitfulness of debates over development.

Notes

For useful comments on this chapter, I am grateful to Vijayendra Rao, Michael Walton, and two anonymous reviewers.

1. Two influential anthropologists, A. L. Kroeber and Clyde Kluckhohn, counted no fewer than 161 formal definitions, and that was before the explosive growth of cultural studies and the advent of postmodernism (Kroeber and Kluckholn 1952; Kluckholn and Kroeber 1963). Many of these consisted of long inventories of disparate traits. The lists typically included only traits presumed to be fully acquired: knowledge, beliefs, art, morals, law, customs, capabilities, and habits. For a critique of the currently popular definitions within cultural studies, see Kuper (1999). The rediscovery of the concept within analytical segments of the

social sciences has produced further definitions. These generally highlight one or more social functions, such as the reduction of transaction costs, the prevention of free riding, and the facilitation of coordination. See, for instance, Kreps (1990); Putnam (1993, esp. 180–81); Greif (1994b, esp. sect. 2); Fukuyama (1995, 34–48); and Bates, Rui De Figueiredo, and Weingast (1998).

2. Even barriers with evolutionary origins may be overcome, because response patterns hardwired into the brain are sensitive to context (Barkow, Cosmides, and Tooby 1992; Pinker 1997).

3. A person engaged in preference falsification in favor of a cultural policy may violate the policy in his own life. A teacher who lends public support to the goal of language purification may continue to use loan words herself.

4. The World Bank's current policy is to offer all borrowers the same menu of contracts.

5. See Malcolm (1994, 222). It is true that until the 1980s Yugoslavia's federal government tried to promote multicultural coexistence. Because citizens were rewarded for endorsing the official vision of cultural pluralism, public discourse and formal opinion surveys on the matter cannot be taken at face value. But intermarriage statistics prove that substantial numbers were genuinely committed to multiethnic coexistence. See Kuran (1998a) for further details as well as an interpretation of Yugoslavia's subsequent ethnic clashes.

6. Few Americans of European ancestry, not even many of those who provide hyphenated answers when asked to state their ethnicity, show much interest in pursuing ethnically distinct lifestyles. This is why intermarriages among different whites are now rarely considered intermarriages (Alba 1990).

7. This testing method was developed by Noelle-Neumann (1984, chaps. 2 and 3).

8. For a stunning variant, see Bischoping and Schuman (1992).

9. See Ahmad (1991, 474–79); and Kuran (1997, 79–80, 90–93).

10. On American agricultural protectionism, see Gardner (1990).

11. In countries with more or less free elections, the mass appeal of inward-oriented policies is evident in the electoral successes of their promoters and in the abysmal showings of parties openly advocating economic liberalism.

12. Said (1994, esp. 15–19, 209–20) provides many examples of "cultural resistance" that serves to cover up the faults of contemporary regimes. Ahmad's polemic on "occidentosis" is representative of a vast literature that blames the West for the shortcomings of underdeveloped countries (Ahmad 1982).

13. On the assimilation of foreign cultural borrowings, see Lowenthal (1985); and Cowen (2002).

14. On the mechanisms at play, see Kuran (1995b, esp. chaps. 10 and 11).

15. For evidence, see Rahman (1964, esp. sect. 1). Because *ribā* had numerous variants, Rahman also shows, many controversies erupted over the scope of the restriction stated in the Qur'an.

CHAPTER 7

Cultural Goods Are Good for More than Their Economic Value

ARJO KLAMER

It may be a bridge, a piece of wood. Or a temple, a windmill, a painting, a piece of furniture, a mask, a jewel, a bead. It may even be a language, a ritual, or a practice. Whatever it is, it differs from other goods because people may consider it a symbol of something—a nation, a community, a tradition, a religion, a cultural episode—and endow it with various meanings over and above its usefulness. They may ascribe to it artistic, aesthetic, or sacred qualities. They may draw inspiration from it or value it because it gives rise to hatred in some and antagonizes others. Let us say, then, that the good has cultural value in that it is a source of inspiration or symbol of distinction. Therefore, we call it a cultural good.[1]

Things cultural draw intense media attention. Ample space in local newspapers is given not only to cultural performances, exhibitions, and parades, but also to disputes and conflicts over cultural goods. Even people unaware of the plight of refugees in Afghanistan in March 2001 probably read or heard about the Taliban's demolition of two giant Buddhas.

For weeks, western newspapers had held readers in suspense with stories alleging the intentions of the Taliban. When the news finally broke that the Buddhas had indeed been destroyed, it summoned up apocalyptic notions for humanity. (The actions of the Taliban contributed to the impression that they were a barbarian regime that had to be removed.) During the war in Bosnia in 1993, the destruction of the ancient Mostar Bridge seemed more devastating than the day's loss of human life.[2]

Travel pages lure readers to cultural artifacts around the world, whether it be to the Great Wall in China or a burial place on Bali. Other pages tell about programs to save national cultural heritage, or about conflicts over the possession of cultural heritage. Governments seem more eager than ever to reclaim cultural goods lost during wars long past. The Greeks want the British Museum to return the so-called Elgin Marbles. This sculptured frieze, once part of the Parthenon, has been in British possession since the early 19th century. The British authorities maintain that Mr. Elgin, a British diplomat, acquired the marbles in a legitimate manner. The Greeks insist that the sculptures are their cultural heritage and, as such, should be in Greek possession. Aboriginals in Australia fight to keep tourists away from sacred grounds that United Nations Educational Scientific and Cultural Organization (UNESCO) has declared World Cultural Heritage. All this ado is about things whose value is mainly symbolic.

Even so, these cultural disputes do not seem to affect the thinking about and design of economic development strategies. They certainly do not figure in conventional accounts of economic development. When economic hardship is the foreground, cultural concerns recede. In the face of poverty and deprivation, spending on things cultural seems wasteful and is quickly judged immoral. Wealthy rulers of poor countries cause dismay with their sumptuous palaces, cathedrals, and prestigious cultural objects. Cultural needs, like the need for identity and aesthetics, tend to be perceived as luxuries, most distant in Maslow's hierarchy of needs. If basic needs come first, securing them is what development is about. People need food, clean water, and shelter before they can address cultural needs. Or so we are led to think.

Even a perfunctory glance tells us something is amiss in this account. From cavemen to Australian aboriginals, from African American slaves to contemporary African tribes, people in the most deprived conditions find time, resources, and energy to make music, build religious temples, maintain sacred places, engage in extensive burial ceremonies, cherish icons, and fashion all sorts of art. Cultural activity *matters*. And indeed, what would a life be without music, rituals, ceremonies, icons—without sources of inspiration?

Cultural here refers to "culture as expression" as opposed to "culture as identity," using the distinction that Rao and Walton make in this volume. Cultural goods, like temples, burial grounds, bridges, and ceremonies, may relate to culture as identity—a monument may stand for a community— but they generally have meanings over and above the social. When Sen states in this volume that culture matters, he is referring to culture as identity. If we were to follow his argument, cultural goods matter insofar as they affect culture as identity. And culture as identity matters insofar as it affects development. So we need to establish that cultural identity affects development, *then* determine that there is a clear relationship between cultural goods and cultural identity before we can conclude the relevance of cultural goods for sustainable development.

Yet "culture as expression" appears to have significance beyond any social and economic impact. The cultural disputes tell us that they may have a value regardless of any social or economic connection. Yes, the Mostar Bridge is an important social symbol as the connection between the Bosnian and Croation communities of the town of Mostar. But it is more: it has a presence in the history of architecture; it has inspired poets, novelists, citizens, and visitors. The furor of belonging and destruction tells us that people need to realize certain cultural values, and that they can clash in doing so.

I will argue that the ubiquitous instrumental mode of reasoning—where all goods need to have value as an instrument toward the goal of economic development—prevents us from acknowledging the special role that cultural goods play in the lives of people. The disputes alert us to the uncertainties involved, the sensitivities that are in play, and the clashes between values. I am seeking to develop a framework that invites us to recognize the complexities that characterize the life of cultural goods, that shows their importance to groups of people, and that eventually will stimulate a reevaluation of development strategies.

Culturalists Versus Economists

CASE 1: THE TALIBAN AND THE BUDDHAS

For centuries, Islam has been the dominant religion in Afghanistan.[3] The giant Buddha statues of Bamiyan dated back to pre-Islamic culture and were considered idols of a pagan king and queen by the local population ever since it had been converted to the Islam. It was probably during the ruling of the Mughal emperor Aurangzeb (1658–1707) that the faces and hands of the statues were sliced off and their feet destroyed by cannon fire. For the locals, the Buddhas had lost the original religious connotations.

In the 19th century, British travelers glimpsed and described the relics of the pre-Islam era. They were especially struck by these unusually large Buddhas. Thus western involvement in the exploration and preservation of Afghanistan's cultural heritage began. Since 1975, UNESCO has become increasingly involved in the archeological preservation of Afghanistan's cultural heritage, listing the statues on its World Heritage List.

When the Taliban announced its intention to destroy the statues, UNESCO reacted strongly. The UN High Commissioner for Refugees,

Ruud Lubbers, went to Afghanistan not only to attend to the plight of its refugees, but also to plead for the conservation of the statues. Buddhist countries such as Japan and Sri Lanka sent personal envoys. Even Islamic countries such as Egypt condemned the Taliban for their plans. The Taliban did not renege. It was confirmed on March 12, 2001, that the statues had been blown up.

Six months later, on September 11, 2001, two airplanes crashed into the twin towers of the World Trade Center in New York, killing nearly three thousand people. On October 7, the United States attacked Afghanistan; around December 12, the Taliban regime disappeared. UNESCO considered allocating foreign money to restore the statues, but experts concluded there was no use.

Those of us who explore the interconnections between the economic and cultural worlds (both identity and expression) get tossed between the two. Culturalists—archaeologists, art historians, historians, theologians—acknowledge the cultural values of things and understand scenarios in which cultural goods figure prominently, regardless of their relationship to the economics of development. To them, the fate of the Bamiyan Buddhas is of such great historical, religious, and aesthetic significance that it justifies any effort to save or restore them. Culturalists are especially adept in analyzing and describing what those values are. They stress the uniqueness of the good and its exceptional quality, and they look in dismay at the economist who brings up issues of costs and benefits. They are Oscar Wilde's romantics, seeing the value of everything and the price of nothing.

Most of my fellow economists inhabit the other world that, together with politicians and civil servants, has adopted the economic way of thinking.[4] They are Wilde's cynics, who see the price of everything and the value of nothing. They want to know what price a good fetches in the market place. They want to know how much people are willing to pay for it. If they had had an opportunity they might have presented to the Taliban the argument for preservation of the statues in terms of costs and benefits. The costs would surely have been high, including the costs of international sanctions that most likely would follow the demolition and the loss of tourist income. (The costs of their demise would have been prohibitive, so I presume, but such outcome could not be foreseen.) The benefits would comprise the emotional relief of knowing that the statues were gone. When put in those terms, a cultural good is like any other good (Grampp 1989; Cowen 1998). Its value is captured in its price. That makes all talk about historical, aesthetic, spiritual, and other substantive values superfluous. The price says it all, and we don't need culturalists to tell us otherwise.

But you're not considering imperfect markets, the culturalists may retort. Shouldn't we make an exception for cultural goods because markets often price them insufficiently? Aren't they often public goods? Surely governments can correct markets with subsidies, tax breaks, conservation programs, and the construction and exploitation of national museums and monuments. But although economists readily acknowledge imperfections in markets, they deny that this makes cultural goods necessarily exceptional because many other goods are financed that way—armies, police forces, clean air, road maintenance, and the like. The risk is, presumably, the chance that culturalists will influence politicians by impressing upon them the enormous value of a cultural good, justifying any amount of spending on it. Economists, therefore, have designed a research strategy aimed at the elimination of the role of culturalists. Their goal is to develop methods and approaches that "objectify" the valuation of cultural goods and thus render the subjective valuations of experts superfluous.

The first line of attack was an estimate of the economic impact of investments in cultural goods, like monuments and museums. This scheme, however, has languished because the results were meager and dubious (van Puffelen 1992; Klamer 1997; Klamer and Throsby 2000). The economic impact of cultural goods is often marginal, and in comparison with the impact of alternative investments, it is not obviously better. Culturalists continued to be convincing with their argument that more than economic values are at stake in the provision of cultural goods. People may want the preservation good because they may eventually enjoy it (the so-called option value of the good); they simply like to know it is there, even if they will never enjoy it themselves (existence value), and they want it be there for their progeny (bequest value).

This alerted economists to the range of values in play. But instead of consulting culturalists, they wanted to know the values of the potential "consumers" themselves.[5] The (implicit) argument was that such a procedure was more democratic. Thus economists went about investigating what people were willing to pay for the cultural good—as in the costs of travel to a cultural site, or the extra expense for a house in a historic center. In willingness to pay and contingent valuation studies, economists are even prepared to ask people what they would be willing to pay for a good. Because of the danger of bias in the responses, economists have resisted such studies for a long time, but after the commendation of a committee headed by two Nobel Prize winners (Arrow et al. 1993), we have seen a flood of contingent valuation studies. The reservations remain in force, however. Investigators acknowledge the problem of leading questions and free riding (those who do not actually pay the amount that they said they were willing to pay). The same applies to more recently developed choice modeling approaches in which respondents are asked to rate various characteristics of cultural goods (Mourato and Mazzanti 2002). Bruno Frey (2000) champions referendums like the ones in use in his native Switzerland, because only there do people have a direct say on the allocation of collective sources. Whatever method economists have proposed, they all have in common the aim of sidelining culturalists by rendering the valuation of cultural goods objective and democratic. Their argument is that only then will politicians, organizations like UNESCO, and private foundations be able to make rational choices concerning the selection and financing of cultural projects.

However desirable and admirable the democratic aspirations of economists, reality defies their dream. As the disputes indicate, deliberations on cultural matters involve a great deal more than "objective" valuations. Where the impact of economic studies on them is dubious, to say the least, the voices of culturalists and their interest groups tend to be loud and clear. Those involved *do* want to know about the historical relevance of the Mostar Bridge and the culture of the aborigines—more than they want to know someone's willingness to pay. Moreover, the disputes about Buddhas, old bridges, the Elgin Marbles, and the sacred grounds of Australian aboriginals suggest that economic concerns can succumb to cultural concerns, with "cultural" referring both to culture as identity and culture as expression. The disagreements furthermore illustrate—more than any economic analysis—that cultural goods can play a constituting role in the life of individuals and their societies. They may conceivably figure prominently in what people consider a good life and a good society.

Even so, economic concerns cannot be tossed to the wind. Scarcity is a fact of life that even the hardest romantics cannot deny. Choices have to be made. The value of one good must be weighed against others. The Taliban made choices. Those campaigning for the restoration of the statues are choosing to allocate resources away from construction of schools, the improvement of the Afghan infrastructure, and other worthwhile projects. So how do we acknowledge the economic dimension while not undermining the cultural one, and vice versa? How can we account for their often contentious role?

To answer these questions, I propose a cultural economic perspective that stresses the role of values and allows for a combination of economic and other values. The following exposition intends to show (1) that cultural goods may be exceptional; (2) that their values are subject to change; and (3) that the realization of their values by means of markets may alter those values. Rather than presuming that values are fixed and only need to be measured, as in a standard economic approach, the cultural-economic method considers the discursive context wherein values of cultural goods evolve. As the disputes indicate, valuations of a cultural good are subject to change because of attention paid to the good, education, policies, the mode of financing, and the like. I will call this phenomenon valorization (or devalorization, whichever be the case). An important argument that follows is that the way in which the values of cultural goods are realized (think of market pricing and government subsidies) matters to their valuation. Call it the Heisenberg principle of economics: an attempt to measure the value of a good will affect that value. Accordingly, the cultural economic perspective claims to account for the dynamic lives of cultural goods that include both economic moments of cultural valuations and (de)valorizations.[6]

VALUATION, EVALUATION, AND VALORIZATION

The controversy about the Buddhas, described in Case 1, revolves around values. At least, that is one way to make sense of it. (In everyday life, most "values" are implicit, expressed in arguments, statements, emotional utterances, stories, and the like, and need to be pointed out.) For the Taliban, the statues stood for values that were an affront to their deeply held religious values. Their response was comparable to the erstwhile Protestants who stormed Roman Catholic churches to rid them of Maria statues, crucifixes, and other icons that they had abjured in their newly found faith. The valuations of other Afghans may have differed. Some people may have been attached to these statues just because they had been with them for centuries, or they may have been proud of the foreign appreciation. The people of UNESCO valued the Buddhas as part of the world's heritage. Historians are drawn to their rich histories. Visitors may have considered them a good destiny for a day trip. The stronger the identification is with one's values, the stronger the emotions will be when those values are ignored, compromised, or overruled. Tourists may not be particularly disturbed at losing a destination for an outing; to the Taliban, the statues evoked such apparently negative values that they were willing to incur the potentially high costs of demolishing them. Many readers of newspapers may have discovered that they cared more than they knew about UNESCO's World Heritage sites.

Values are not a given, nor does the economist provide a neat process of calculation. The disputes in establishing them reflect the deliberations and negotiations involved. Values evolve during the process. The disputes compel people to justify—and perhaps amend—their own values and pro-

vide arguments that render them compelling. ("There are no other spec-
imens like these." "You, too, destroy statues that conflict with your values.") Deliberate, negotiate, weigh, rank—and then do it again.

Uncertainties and questions abound in this process. Why would westerners care about statues that represent eastern religious values? Why
would the Taliban risk international isolation to destroy statues that had
been in their country for centuries? There is plenty of reason for doubt.
People may be uncertain about their own values and can only speculate
about the values of everyone else. Is profit the motive? Is it a power game
that motivates the others? Are there hidden agendas? Are the emotions
genuine? The dispute is meant to clarify each other's positions.

The lived experience of disputes like this tell us how misleading the
assumption of "given preferences" is. People are in need of talk, deliberation, controversy to sort out what they and others believe, think, feel,
know, value. At the end of what may seem like endless talking is a moment
when UNESCO, the Taliban, the American government, tourists, and
interested bystanders are ready to make up their minds and advance and
articulate an opinion—after which the talking usually continues. But the
talking is needed because agents do not know what they prefer or how
they value. As the moral philosopher Stuart Hampshire (1983) so nicely
put it, in his own head is an agent—a committee that consists of different
voices, conflicting values. Moral reasoning is like a committee meeting in
which the differences are worked out in order to reach a common opinion that represents the moral judgment of that agent. If we want to understand the whys and hows of that judgment, we do well to know what
went on in that committee meeting.

One could ignore the intricacies of the process by which people individually and in groups reach decisions and focus on what they do.
Economists do so by focusing on the moment of exchange. Everything
that matters is the number that determined the trade an equal one, not the
controversy that went into its process. All valuations and evaluations, all
deliberating, negotiating, and conversing, all dealings are at that moment
congealed in a single value: price. This shortcut is interesting, and it certainly keeps the community of economists busy. If we consider the case of
the Buddhas, it is not a great help, however, because there is no moment
of exchange. UNESCO could have offered the Taliban a sum of money to
dissuade them from the demolition, but that would have been absurd and
probably would have backfired. Religious values generally do not lend
themselves to monetary measurement. The process comes to a head when
one party, in this case the Taliban, acts upon its intentions. Then the other
parties have to reveal the weight of their values. If the demolition was a

factor in the later decision to oust the Taliban regime, the weight of those values must have been considerable.

The standard economic approach is quite hopeless when the objective is to understand what is going on in this case. Any effort to make use of it in the course of discussion will be met with resistance and, most likely, indignation. Neither the Taliban nor culturally minded people take well to an analysis in terms of costs and benefits. A more helpful approach would be to focus on values, to sort out which ones are in play and with what intensity, and which values determine, and are expressed in, the outcome.

David Throsby, a cultural economist, has come to recognize the multiple values that are at play. Although his survey article in the *Journal of Economic Literature* (1994) still advances a standard economic perspective on the arts with given preferences, in his most recent book, *Economics and Culture* (2001), he argues that economists need to take the culturalists' perspective seriously. To that end, he draws attention to cultural values, such as aesthetic, spiritual, social, symbolic, and historical values. Yet as an economist is wont to do, he subsequently treats those values as given, as inputs in an economic valuation process. Cultural values become like preferences that people hold—as if they would know those. In reality, people have to find out how to sort through values, how to evaluate, revalue, or devalue them. The process of valuation is a dynamic one, as the case of the Buddhas illustrates.

"To value something is to have a complex of positive attitudes toward it, governed by distinct standards for perception, emotion, deliberation, desire, and conduct" (Anderson 1993, 2). Elizabeth Anderson stresses the plurality of our values: we can value a good for all kinds of reasons. The plurality of values may account for internal conflicts, as when we laugh at a sexist joke and are embarrassed at that. To evaluate is to make sense of a valuation. Whereas valuing something is often an unconscious process—as in when a musical piece surprises us or a painting strikes us—evaluation is the conscious reflection on the reasons for a valuation.

Values may change. People develop values and adopt new values. They may learn to develop a positive attitude. In the language of economists, we would say that they acquire their taste (Throsby 1994). I will call this process one of valorization, that is, the enhancement and affirmation of a value.[7] Valorization appears to be particularly important when cultural goods are the objects of interest. Westerners usually dislike Arabic music when they hear it for the first time, but if immersed in the Arabic world, they may begin to appreciate the music, especially when they become knowledgeable about it and learn to distinguish different variants. People in a modern art museum for the first time tend to have some difficulties appreciating the abstract works by Mondrian, Newman, Twombly, and the like; they, too, need to learn to value modern art. The context matters. When immersed in an academic setting, even the most practical students ("I'd like to make some money, you know") may learn to appreciate the value of reading and even "studying" texts. The academic setting, one hopes, affirms and intensifies the values of reflection, critical inquiry, and other such academic values. (I would argue that my most important task as an academic teacher is to express and, I hope, impress those values on the students, more so than to instruct them in the principles of cultural economics.)

In each deliberation, some valorization is going on. Confronted with a report on giant Buddha statues, I may appreciate something I did not even know existed. When people in my environment want to share their indignation about the imminent demolition, I may feel compelled to go along lest I am made out for a philistine. I may actually look up articles on Buddha statues on the Internet and learn about their variety, their history, and their meanings. Who knows, I may even adopt a firm opinion on the matter because of all this and feel a sense of great loss when the demolition occurs, my initial ignorance notwithstanding. Something similar may happen when foreigners point out to indigenous people that the piles of old stones are actually cultural treasures and that they are willing to pay to conserve them. Because of the foreign intervention, the indigenous people may change their perception of those stones and may even begin to value them. Declaring a cultural good worthy of being on the UNESCO World Heritage List causes people to value it more. The same may happen when a painting ends up in a museum, or when it gets sold for millions of dollars at auction.

Noting the role of values in cultural disputes helps us to see the complexity of the various positions as well as the dynamics as values are negotiated, weighed, and evaluated. How high is the value of the Buddhas for the World Heritage List? And what is the value of that list? How about the integrity (value) of the Taliban? Over the course of the deliberation, values change. The Buddhas have become more valuable because of their turmoil. They have gained a history.

ECONOMIC, SOCIAL, AND CULTURAL VALUES

Having established the prominent role of values in cultural disputes, it will help to differentiate between three types of values: economic, social, and cultural. These groupings are a first step to substantive and interpretive studies of the deliberations in which valuations come about.

Economic values occupy a significant portion of the value sphere.

Usually, these values refer to the prices of things, or their exchange value. When economists speak of valuing a good, they mean the pricing of the good. It is a special kind of valuation because it focuses on the moment of exchange. (When the exchange does not actually take place, the economist will figure out price by reasoning as if the transition took place.)

Economic values can take all kinds of forms and expressions. The gross domestic product is a measure of the flow of economic values that a national economy generates. The economic value of a cultural good is what people are willing to pay for it. The economic value of knowledge is the income that can be earned by applying it. Economists speak of human capital to indicate that knowledge is a stock of value that generates a flow of value. In general, economic capital is a stock that will generate a flow of economic values.

At certain moments and during certain periods, economic value will be the center of attention. As such, everything appears to revolve around "profit," "wealth," "income," "economic growth," and so on. "It's all for the money" seduces most people into acquiescence. In such a climate, profits are key, people are valued by their income (or wealth), and the purpose of getting an education is to be worth more in the labor market. When cultural producers have to justify a new theater, the expansion of a museum, or the conservation of an archeological site in this climate, their best argument is to point at the income that the investment will generate by way of jobs created and additional tourist spending in the local economy. Such justification requires economic argument. Economists have complied and developed "economic impact" analyses, contingent valuation methods, and willingness-to-pay studies (Throsby 1994; Klamer and Throsby 2000). They are all intended to determine the economic value of a good.

In the conventional economic frame, there is no reason to look further. The presumption is that all kinds of values are embodied in the price of a good. A demand-supply analysis brings together values in the production process, such as technology, the price of labor, real assets, and financial capital; and values on the demand side, which are expressed in the form of preferences. Grampp (1989) and Cowen (1998) are therefore consistent when they argue that the price of a good is its value. End of story.

But it is not. Even if we chose not to depart from the sphere of economic values, a wide range of other values intrude (Anderson 1993; Lane 1991). Among positive values are "commercial," "businesslike," "results-oriented," "ambitious," "entrepreneurial," "markets," "freedom." Examples of negative values are "cold," "ruthless," "unjust," "immoral," and "constraining." "Freedom" pops up when people associate economics with "markets," and link them to "freedom of choice" (thanks to Adam Smith, Friedrich Hayek, and Milton Friedman). These values, however, are not strictly economic values; "ruthless" is not a price that can be attached to something. One might say they are spillovers of the engagement in exchange relations (van Staveren 2001). To economists, they are externalities. Interacting in such relations implies the valorization of the values that are common to all such relations, that is, to the culture of the market. Keep working the market and you learn to appreciate the uninvited values that accompany it. These values, distinct from economic values, are better grouped in the separate category of social values.

Social values operate in the context of interpersonal relationships, groups, communities, and societies. People appeal to them in negotiating relationships with other people and groups of people. Social values have a broad range and comprise the values of belonging, being a member of a group (Walzer 1983), identity, social distinction, freedom, solidarity, trust, tolerance, responsibility, love, friendship, and so on. In everyday conversations, these values preoccupy people far more than economic values. We are constantly deliberating our relationships with others, weighing the values that are important to us, and assessing relationships in the light of those. "Should I spend time with my children when I feel responsible to finish this article?" "Can I trust those people to be sympathetic and caring?" "Is she friendly out of friendship or because she expects to gain something from knowing me?" "Shall we eat out or make our own dinner?" Examining and reexamining our social values is a consuming process. We spend little time, in comparison, determining and evaluating our economic values.

It is no different in controversies like those over the aboriginal grounds and the Buddha statues of Bamiyan. Insofar as economic values are at play, they play reticently. Most clearly heard are the negotiations about identity, heritage, justice, obligation, and so on. In the case of the Buddha statues, the Taliban wanted to assert their religious identity and national identity. Critics appealed, in vain, to their sense of responsibility toward world heritage. Snubbing international opposition was an important part of their resistance.

The capacity to deal with social values and adhere to social norms is nowadays called social capital.[8] The assumption is that certain people, organizations, or societies have more of it than others. At least, that is how Robert Putnam et al. (1993) applied the concept in their study of the vitality of democracies: those with a greater ability to trust and a stronger sense of belonging and responsibility do better in making a democracy then those with less of such social capital.

A poignant issue has proven to be the relationship between social and economic capital. In a world where economic values and economic capital dominate the political domain, social capital is easily perceived as subservient to economic capital. Politicians and businesspeople argue that investment in social capital is good for economic growth and profit. Students presumably need to learn social skills to better succeed in their future occupations. After all, the goal of all things social is economic gain. Or is it? Would it not make more sense to think of economic values as being instrumental toward social values? What motivation do people have in seeking wealth, other than faring better in their relationships with others? Even if people have stupendous income, the question is what to do with it. Whether they go out for sumptuous meals, buy an extravagant car, yacht, or house, or indulge in exotic travel, the matter is always with, and possibly for, whom and in what way. Lounging around in a luxurious house with a pool and a couple of cars can be quite depressing without meaningful relations. A better life has to be evaluated in large part by its measure of social values. Economic values are instrumental at best.[9]

In the case of cultural goods, satisfaction comes more from their social rather than economic meaning. Yes, local merchants are pleased when a cultural attraction draws customers to their shops, but that particular value will not ascribe to the attraction—a museum or coveted bridge—its cultural value. Its social value, that is, what it does for issues of identity, heritage, culture, pride, and so on, will be far more important. Yet, what permits us to call a good "cultural" is cultural value, that is, the good's evocation of things cultural.

Cultural values, I propose, are those that evoke qualities above and beyond the economic and the social. Throsby includes in this category aesthetic, spiritual, social, historical, symbolic, and authenticity values (Throsby 2001, 28). I would go along except for the social values, which I prefer to categorize separately. Confusion occurs because "cultural" in the anthropological sense refers to social values, that is, values pertaining to the relations between and among people. I use "cultural" to express a value that transcends social, relational, or, for that matter, economic values. A temple has cultural value in that it connects with a religious practice and evokes the religious and spiritual values of that tradition. Because of its architectural properties, it can appeal to an aesthetic sense. It has historical and symbolic value if it restores the memory of something of grave importance to a group (community, organization, society). Aboriginal art has spiritual meanings apart from its decorative and aesthetic qualities. The latter appears to enchant western visitors and has recently attracted the attention of western museums. A temple may have social value by being a meeting place or functioning as a national heritage and economic value if it generates income. But such values are distinct from the cultural values that the goods represent.

A cultural valuation includes the attribution of sacredness to an icon, statue, or temple. A good that a group considers sacred has a special meaning and receives special treatment. The special treatment may exhibit viscerally in response to the good's imminent sale or destruction. American Indians have gone to extremes in defending their sacred burial grounds. Because of the cultural values attributed to them, people must have felt similarly aggrieved about the destruction of the Buddha statues. According to Kant, the quintessential cultural value of a good is its ability to evoke an experience of the sublime. It has a quality that causes awe and "stirs the soul." Kant purports that this quality is disinterested; it does not serve a social or economic goal.

When I follow this characterization of cultural values, I come to the conclusion that cultural capital is the power to inspire or to be inspired absent social and economic influence. It is the inbred, acquired, and developed ability to experience the sublime or sacred character of a good, to see its beauty, or to recognize its place in cultural history. Cultural capital, then, lends us the ability to realize a meaningful life over and beyond its economic and social dimensions. It is one thing to have good social relationships, yet quite another to be in awe of sight or sound when strolling through a museum, attending a religious ceremony, or struggling across a mountain ridge.

In this interpretation, cultural capital is more than the symbolic knowledge that Bourdieu (1986) claims it to be in that inspiration is not an emblem, and less then what Throsby (2001) defines it to be in that he includes all tangible and intangible cultural goods. Throsby furthermore advances the notion of cultural value to mean that it generates both cultural and economic values. In my definition, cultural capital is the ability to deal with cultural values without regard to possible economic returns.

The metaphor "capital" has become somewhat confusing as it encourages an economic interpretation. Like human capital, social and cultural capital would represent economic value in the form of additional income and profit, and so we would drift once again to a sense of life that revolves around economic values. Yet if we take the metaphor to mean something like power, capability or "a person's ability to do valuable acts or reach valuable states of being" (Sen 1993, 30), the focus is rather on what enables people to strive for a good and valuable life, that is, a life in accordance with relevant economic, social, cultural, and other values.

To be sure, the possession of certain social capital and cultural capital can contribute to the generation of economic value. Inspired people may work better. Then again, it also may impede the buildup of economic capital, as in the Amish religious community, which is opposed to the application of modern techniques. The influence is mutual. The amount of economic capital that people have appears to be positively related to their cultural capital (Bourdieu 1984). The reason is that income is positively related to the level of education, and the latter is again an important condition for the level and nature of cultural capital that a person has. This is not to say that people with no education have no cultural capital. The aboriginals of Australia may have little education and income, but they have developed, with their rituals and practices, a cultural capital so rich that it inspires highly educated and wealthy westerners.

Whether and how the relationship between cultural and economic capital can be exploited remains a question. When people "invest" in their cultural capital for the purpose of economic gain, the efficacy of their investment will be less then if the investment had only a cultural purpose. It would be akin to becoming Christian in the expectation that God will bless you with greater richness for believing in Him. When economic motives surface, credibility is lost. For example, a friend who turns out to have engaged in friendship in the hope to benefit from it economically will not be my friend anymore.[10]

By claiming a separate category for cultural values and cultural capital, I am arguing—and culturalists are ready to demonstrate—that they are distinct from economic values, require special skills, and operate in a unique sphere. Cultural capital has nothing to do with economic capital, although it may incidentally add it to it (people working better) or take away from it (the doings of a fanatically pious group).

The notion of capital has the advantage of reminding us of the need to invest in social and cultural capabilities. Like economic capital, they require attention and a great deal of work. People usually "build up" cultural capital by participating in cultural activities; it may require discipline, study, and all kinds of sacrifice in order to achieve insight, wisdom, enlightenment, piety, or the ability to experience the sublime. People may also lose cultural capital in, say, leaving their country, shifting religion, or neglecting a cultural practice. Unlike economic capital, however, cultural capital (and also social capital) does not depreciate with use, but rather increases in value. When I visit a museum, I use my cultural capital in order to make sense of what I am seeing and experiencing, and by doing so, I add to my cultural capital: because of this experience, I may have a more intense experience the next time.

The ephemeral character of notions like social capital, values, and cultural capital make them virtually impossible to pin down. Aristotle insisted that our actions are emotionally homeostatic: geared to negotiate adequacy and to prevent us from doing too much or too little of a good thing. Soldiers can be courageous, reckless, or cowardly, and no one can tell in advance which they will be. Every action calls for evaluation before it can be declared courageous or not. Accordingly, we can write down our values, assert them ("I would give my kingdom for that painting!" "Honesty is *all* that counts." "To live longer for my children, I will eat only healthy foods."), but values are expressed only in what we do. We do not own them, we can only try to work with them.

An inadequate measurement system stands in the way of establishing the roles of cultural and social capital more explicitly. Economic values and capital dominate contemporary public discourse (at least in the western world), possibly because they can be measured so much better. During the previous century or so, economists have worked hard on statistical measures of economic values, such as gross national product, profit, income, and wealth. The accounting for economic value has become quite sophisticated, although it has not been without problems. It has generated an entire industry of statistical offices and accounting firms. Measurements of social capital are being developed but are still in the pioneering stage. Measurements of cultural capital, if possible at all, are far off. UNESCO has been gathering a range of cultural indicators, but its compilation of data on all kinds of cultural activities does not yet add up to a meaningful measurement of cultural capital (United Nations Educational Scientific and Cultural Organization [UNESCO] 2000). Additional subjective measures are called for that can account for the experiences and perceptions of various cultural stakeholders such as local people, visitors, experts, politicians.[11] Deficient and lacking measurements make it difficult to take cultural values into account when developing policy or considering action, their relevancy notwithstanding.

The Realization of Values

When people produce art, they usually have no idea of its value. Family and friends may be in awe, but such valuation is relative. The issue is rather how other artists, experts, and consumers respond. Whatever the case, artists seek to realize the values of their art. (Putting a cultural good up for sale in a market may not only be an imperfect method but may also be impossible, inconceivable, or immoral.)

When goods become candidates for exchange, they become commodities (Appadurai 1986). In this phase—possibly an important one—

their economic value is being realized. What economists may see as the
beginning and end of a good is actually a good in its nascence. The initial
shaping of its economic value is just that, a phase: its being a commodity
is but one moment in its biography (Kopytoff 1986; Appadurai 1986).
Things have a life and pass various stages in which their values are being
realized, sustained, affirmed, questioned, and so on in characteristic ways.

During gestation, goods are the subjects of conversations dealing with
their production. A painting comes about in conversations about technique, the world of artists, and art in general. In those conversations, the
producer and others involved value its qualities and evaluate the values
that are being applied. For example:

"I wanted to paint again as an antidote to the technique."
 "But why in this way? This is really cliché."
 "No, it's not; I'm elaborating on earlier work."

When the good enters the phase of exchange, it becomes the subject of
totally different conversations, like those of the marketers, gallery owners,
and, of course, consumers. Now price, use, and consumer appeal will be
major subjects. One exchange might be:

"It's a pretty large painting, and considering past sales, I'll price it at 10,000 euro."
 "But don't you run the risk of missing the buyer who is looking for an interesting piece above the couch? And why would my work be priced less than that
of A——'s? Maybe I should take it to another gallery that will appreciate it
more."
 "It has nothing to do with that. We just assess where the market is. We can do
no better than this. In the end, the buyer will determine whether the price is
right."[12]

Some goods, however, will never be in such a phase because they are
"blocked from exchange" (Walzer 1998, 100). Goods like friendship, freedom of speech, divine grace, and, in the western world, marriage and
political office are examples. The valuations of such goods take place in
conversations that are distinct from others:

"You are not going to risk imprisonment to defend your freedom of speech! I
don't want to lose you!"
 "It's a worthy cause; it's something I have to do."
 "So that freedom is worth more to you than our relationship?"

The consuming of the good constitutes yet another stage of the good.
In the conventional economic account, consumption is it; as soon as the
good ends up in the hands of the consumer, the story ends, as does the
analysis. For quite a few goods, the consuming process is a lingering one,

involving various people and comprising a variety of experiences, valuations, evaluations, and so on. When people visit a museum, they are said to consume the services of the museum—that is, the exhibition. Yet what actually happens? They may visit the museum with their family, so the outing may actually be important for the life of the family. They may have used the visit to have a nice lunch in the museum or to enjoy being in the building itself. They may have gone to the museum in the hope of meeting certain people. They may experience something in the museum that has a longtime impact. They may have conversations about their experiences afterward, so that the museum visit may have a longer life than the mere visit. People may have learned something; and they may have to account for what they did. So it is not immediately obvious what the consumption is all about. It is obvious, however, that the valuation of the museum visit, that is, its consumption, is an entirely different matter, and subject of again different conversations, than its economic valuation.

The cases below illustrate the stages through which goods may pass. Case 2 describes how goods become enchanted because of the purchase and create the need to be disenchanted. Case 3 shows a nice reversal of value. Beads once symbolized the dominance of western culture to Africans and served as a means of payment. Now beads have become a desirable object for westerners as a sign of African culture. Having been part of African culture has added particular value to the beads; it made them special. We could speak of a valorization in this case: the beads have been reevaluated and appreciated in value because of the life they once had.

CASE 2. ENCHANTMENT AND DISENCHANTMENT OF COMMODITIES IN AFRICA

In the course of her fieldwork among the Peki of southeastern Ghana, the anthropologist Birgit Meyer (1999) encountered a fervent Pentacostalist preacher who had a special experience with a pair of underpants. He had bought them at the local market. After the day he began wearing them, he was frequently disturbed by erotic dreams about having sex with beautiful ladies. It took him some time to realize that the underpants caused these dreams. The preacher told the story not only to Meyer, but also to many members of the church. He warned his people about the possible demons in the goods they bought and offered to exorcise these demons by means of prayer. Thus the enchanted goods would become disenchanted.

Meyer learned that such ideas of enchantment and practices of disenchantment were widely shared in Ghanaian Pentecostalist circles. She found that "in order to retain control over Western goods, a person has to strip them of their fetishist properties, thereby making use of religion in order to produce them as commodities in the sense of Western economists' prose" (Meyer 1999, 151).

CASE 3: AN EXAMPLE OF THE VALUATION OF ART: BEADS

As early as the 15th century, European traders introduced colored glass beads in the African markets. These beads functioned as a means of exchange through which Europeans could purchase African goods. The beads also played an important role in the realm of diplomatic relations. They were desired because they came from far away, could not be produced locally, and were not available on the local markets. The beads were incorporated in local African cultures and came to symbolize status, rank, affluence, and membership. The end of this practice came with the introduction of monetary currency (Steiner 1994).

During the past few decades, African demand for beads has been replaced by European demand:

To the travelers who now buy old trade beads in the markets of West Africa, their appeal, at least in part, stems from the fact that their long presence in Africa has again made them exotic. Once more, they have been packed with a symbolic charge. This time, however, their symbolism communicates encounter with a romanticized vision of traditional, pristine Africa. Hence, at one time beads were popular because they were foreign and European, now they are again fashionable because they are considered "ethnic" and therefore, by definition, *still foreign*. (Steiner 1994, 128)

Accordingly, the notion of "the life of things" alerts us to the valuations and valorizations outside the commodity phase. Indians realize the cultural value of a cow when they refuse to remove it from the road or slaughter it when they are in need of food. The cow has significant value, yet no market has a role in determining that value. Daily religious practices bring out the cultural value of a temple or church; critical discursive practices as well as institutions like museums account for the cultural value of Van Gogh. And the value of a flag may prove itself in the heat of battle or grief of death. Accordingly, we would not do justice to the life of any good, or its values, if we were to focus on its commodity phase alone. Valuations and evaluations take place in different settings and in distinct spheres.

THE MODE OF FINANCING MATTERS:
DIFFERENT VALUATIONS ARE POSSIBLE

The exceptional character of cultural goods may be related to the nature of the conversation in which its cultural values come about. Their valuation, therefore, may call for conversations that are incongruent with those that constitute the market. Having it subjected to the discipline of the market may affect its values, and possibly alter them for the duration of its life. Pricing a sensitive value—friendship, love, courage, truth, perhaps even art—alters the value of the good. Realizing a value by means of market exchange causes it to be a different good from the one whose value had been realized in the form of a gift or as part of a collective program.

In this line of argument, I deviate once again from standard economic analysis, with its implicit assumption that the mode of valuation does not affect the values of a good. In the standard approach, the value of a good is ideally realized in a market; an alternative is a realization by means of a grant from the government or a foundation. Whatever method is followed, the economic value of the good is presumed to remain the same. Yet when we take into account the full range of values, this presumption becomes dubious. As Anderson (1993) argues, "To realize a good as a particular *kind* of good we place it in a particular matrix of social relations . . . [G]oods differ in kind if people properly enter into different sorts of social relations governed by distinct norms in relation to these goods." The context in which a good is placed to realize its value(s), may matter.

When we submit a cultural good for sale in the market in order to realize its economic value, we subject it to conversations that are characteristic for the sphere of markets (which come in all varieties, producing a host of distinct conversations). Comparison with other goods is a good starting point in setting a price. Its economic value may be stressed: potential to generate tourist income, ability to attract customers, and so on. Anonymous buyers may enter the bidding. The rigor of being placed in the sphere of commerce, measured, compared, discussed, priced, and treated like any other commodity may very well affect its *subsequent* evaluation. If the price was exceptionally high, the valuation may increase accordingly (called the crowding-in effect; Frey 1997b). Alternatively, because of a sale, the good may be branded "commercial" and may lose some or all of its cultural value in the eyes of those who care (the crowding-out effect). In both cases, the fact that the economic value was realized has an effect on the value of the good. It is a case of (de)valorization: some values get enhanced, others diminished.

The valorization may also work on the social values that are associated with the market, like freedom of choice, consumer sovereignty, efficiency, commercial value, greed, and ruthlessness. By transforming a good into commodity, people affirm and possibly enhance such market values. Such are the external effects of any valuation. By subjecting a good to the regime of the market, people contribute to, or valorize, the values that those who operate in this market have in common. This is a general feature of human action: even if it is thought of as individual or incidental, any human action will affirm and enhance a sense of the common values. By fathering my children, I contribute to the values and institutions of fatherhood, family, and the like. Similarly, when artists try to realize their art by means of a market exchange, they (willingly or unwillingly) affirm and enhance the values that this market sphere have in common. Thus the method of realizing the value of art will not only affect the valuation of art as a cultural good, it will also affect the larger, common values. The effects may be small, but when more and more artists do the same again and again, they become significant. In the end, the culture of the world in which they operate may change.

Another option is to realize the values of cultural goods by means of government subsidies. Instead of being subjected to the conversation of markets—and its consequences—they become items in bureaucratic and political discussions. Here the consequence is that they become connected to other values, such as political expediency, national interest, justice and fairness, and bureaucratic discipline. Cultural entrepreneurs who seek the financial support of the government adjust their rhetoric and play to whatever values currently dominate the political realm. If politicians are concerned about national identity, accessibility, sustainability, or the integration of minorities, cultural entrepreneurs will cater toward such interests. The valorization in such a case concerns public accessibility, national identity, sustainability, and other values of the collective, integrating the good's values with values beyond those the museum curator wants, or expects, to realize. Accordingly, subjecting a good to the government sphere involves supporting the common that constitutes it.

Ideally, a good that is financed in this sphere has the status of a public or collective good and is appreciated accordingly. The subsidized temple becomes common property and is freed from the regime imposed by the market. Government officials and their consultants determine its value— not consumers and clients. In practice, certain valuations that governmental financing imposes are suspiciously similar to those of the market. But the government has to be objective in adjudicating between competing claims and is compelled to dole out in accordance with well-specified rules; civil servants want measurements. And so subsidy-dependent museum directors count the number of visitors, point at the value of additional tourist spending, and reference the number of jobs the museum creates. These measurements, all economic in kind, will help them to stake their claims in the next round of subsidies.

The social sphere, too, provides a place for goods to be realized (Klamer and Zuidhof 1999; Klamer 1996). Obviously, this is where goods like friendship function, but less obviously, a great deal of artistic value is realized in personal and informal interactions devoid of contracts, measurements, rules, and accounts. How do so many artists paint, draw, make music, and the like without any financial compensation? They often are supported by parents, partners, spouses, or friends. They realize the value of what they do in social settings by sharing their art with others. Their art is then a form of a gift. This makes for different conversations and appeals to different values from those conducted in the spheres of the government and the market. In the social sphere, people may talk about loyalty, responsibility, solidarity, care; they may also mention dependency, charity, and sacrifice. (These values may be interpreted as positive and as negative; how they are understood depends on the cultural context.)

By placing the good in a social setting, we ask for negotiations in social terms and shelter them from the blunter effects of market, political, and bureaucratic values. By barring a good like friendship or religious ceremony from the commodity phase, we lock out the values that would be realized in that phase. The good takes on a life that is different from the one it would have had if exposed to a commodity phase. That makes something like friendship exceptional. One consequence may be that such a good cannot be used as a commodity. Another is that such a good is not commensurable with commodities: there is no way in which we can establish the quantitative equivalent of price (Radin 2001; Anderson 1993).

So What?

In Mostar, both local and international efforts are under way to reconstruct the Mostar Bridge. Italy, Turkey, France, and the Netherlands financed a great deal of the $15 million required to rebuild the bridge (plus some of the old buildings that also were destroyed during the war in Bosnia). The Mostar town council contributed $2 million, and the Croatian government has committed $660,000. Restoring items on the World Heritage List is important enough to involve the economic participation of poorer locals as well as distant countries whose constituency may never have seen the Mostar Bridge—and never will. An important part of the project is the conscious attempt to include workers from the Bosnian-Muslim community that dwells on one side of the bridge, and the Croatian community that dwells on the other. They work side by side in quarries and excavation sites. In this way, the rebuilding of the bridge will inevitably contribute to the bridging of the two camps that were on opposite sides during the Bosnian war. Accordingly, the realization of the values of this bridge does not only involve financial deals (the economic values) but also the social and cultural values that are generated in the process. The bridge is expected to contribute to the social capital and the cultural capital of the town, the organization and implementation of the project a crucial factor.

I advance the cultural economic perspective to break the hold that the economic perspective has on public discussions concerning the role of cultural goods. It embraces the culturalist perspective with its emphasis on the various values that constitute cultural goods while acknowledging the continuing importance of the economic dimension. The economic perspective provides a useful framework (Throsby 2001; Cordes and Goldfarb 1996; Frey 2000), but it is a limiting one—at least when we want to make sense of the functioning of cultural goods. The focus on values, valuation, and valorization serves to sensitize economists and policy makers to the exceptional role that cultural goods can play in the life of individuals, communities, and societies. Cultural goods are the carriers of important social and cultural values.

The cultural economic perspective compels us to distinguish social and cultural values from economic values. It furthermore points us to consider the various spheres in which the values of a cultural good are realized. Cultural goods are exceptional because they often resist the commodity phase, and for good reason, so we found. For when cultural values are involved, actors need a sphere in which they can realize values that have not and should not suffer the rigor and discipline of government and market spheres. We merely need to point to religious institutions like churches, synagogues, and temples: only in rare cases are they realized by means of government programs or market exchange. People who found a temple or develop sacred ground generally do not apply for government grants, find sponsors (in exchange for advertisements), or place a cash register at the entrance. Such cultural institutions rely mostly on the informal sphere and its main instrument: the gift, or donation. Insofar as reciprocity is involved, it is ill defined, not stipulated in a contract, and requires an enduring relationship (Zelizer 1997).

The cultural-economic perspective has several consequences for cultural policy in particular and development policies in general. As cultural goods come about and attain their value in conversations among people who know and care, their sustenance requires the support of such groups of people. The problem with the Buddha statues in Afghanistan was that they were an affront for the locals, yet were cherished by groups of people far removed from the scene. The latter group failed, understandably so, to persuade the local people of the cultural and possibly economic significance of the statues. This is a reason why cultural policy needs to be, at least partially, focused on education and ongoing discussions in journals and newspapers and on the Internet. Controversies like the one about the Buddhas can give a great impetus to the (re)valuation, and therefore valorization, of a cultural good.

Many cultural goods will be financed by means of markets and governments. Performance companies apply for government grants (especially in continental Europe); auction houses and galleries sell visual art. It is necessary, however, to thrive in their own value spheres in order to realize their cultural values. Therefore, a cultural policy that is geared solely to the market or government fails to see the point.

This is not a practical message to translate into actual cultural policy. Take the policy of the World Bank toward an integral approach to cultural heritage. The correct premise is that cultural heritage needs to be considered in development programs (World Bank 2001a). As may be expected, these programs give a great deal of attention to the economic values of the projects under consideration. Their methodologies stress the importance of contingent valuation studies and the like to determine these economic values.

The analysis I propose attempts to contribute to these efforts by calling attention to (1) the importance of cultural goods for people in all stages of development; (2) the process of valorization; (3) the various ways by which the values of a cultural good may be realized; and (4) the knowledge that—as Adam Smith already saw for the economic good in general—governments and international organizations are limited in their power to generate the values that are really important to people.

Notes

Cases 2 and 3 have been provided by Dr. Ellen Bal. I am very grateful to her for this material and for various other suggestions she has made to this article. I also thank Arjan Appadurai, the editors, participants of the seminar in cultural economics at Erasmus University, David Throsby, and Michael Hutter for their critical comments.

1. Culture is, of course, a contested concept. As I try to make explicit here, the "cultural" in cultural goods has the connotation of the artistic, aesthetic, and sacred and refers to culture in the sense of high culture. This is "culture as expression," as the editors call it. Later I also will use culture as identity—that is, culture in its anthropological sense as the set of values, stories, memories, and traditions with which a group of people (a community, a nation, an organization) distinguishes itself from other people. See, for example, Eagleton (2000).

2. The bridge dates from 1566. Built by the Ottoman architect Mimar Hayreddin, it was for years a symbol of Muslim culture.

3. For more information, see UNESCO's Web site (http://www.unesco.org/).

4. The characterization of economists in this article is a caricature for the sake of contrast. Even so, I would be willing to defend it as pretty accurate for the average economists while acknowledging that there are many exceptions. Economists like David Throsby, Deirdre McCloskey, Michael Hutter, and Amartya Sen, to name only a few, do not fit this caricature and will readily admit the importance of including culturalist arguments into the analysis.

5. For overviews, see, for example, the report of the Getty Foundation on the values of cultural heritage (de la Torre 2002; Klamer and Throsby 2000).

6. This project is not original. I see myself following in the footsteps of Adam Smith and other classical economists, Thorstein Veblen, Max Weber, Karl Polanyi, and to some extent the institutionalists. In the contemporary field, I recognize a similar perspective in the works of Deirdre McCloskey, Amartya Sen, David Throsby, Michael Hutter, and Bruno Frey, as well as socioeconomists such as Marc Granovetter, Amitai Etzioni, Viviane Zelizer, and Paul DiMaggio. The research trespasses adjacent fields of philosophy (Michael Waltzer, Elizabeth Anderson, Martha Nussbaum), anthropology (Mary Douglas), sociology (Pierre Bourdieu, Jean Baudrillard), and cultural studies, among others. And even though my discursive strategy deviates from the standard economic approach, it also benefits from that approach, in particular its accounting metaphor and the structure that that metaphor imposes (McCloskey, Donald, and Klamer 1995).

7. Economists like Gary Becker (1996) stress the learning that is going on. By listening to music over and over, people learn to appreciate it. You might say that they build up a particular cultural capital. Before you know it, this all becomes a matter of information. By focusing on values and using the term *valorization*, I want to call attention to the discursive characteristics of the process and its embeddedness in social and cultural contexts. People talk and deliberate a great deal, and they do so for good reasons (McCloskey, Donald, and Klamer 1995).

8. See James S. Coleman (1988, S98), who introduces the concept: "Unlike other forms of capital, social capital inheres in the structure of relations between actors and among actors."

9. When people argue that their goal in life is to make money, the researcher may notice that they actually spend a great deal of their time negotiating and maintaining relationships. Money seems a topos to indicate desire and ambition.

10. See van Staveren (2001) for an interesting analysis of the interactions between the various spheres of value.

11. As is done for the ranking of universities in the United States.

12. For an analysis of the meanings that pricing can have in the market for contemporary art, see Velthius (2002).

CHAPTER 8

The Intellectual History of Culture and Development Institutions

LOURDES ARIZPE

Introduction

This chapter will discuss the intellectual debates on culture and development in international programs and institutions. We know that culture, a concept with many meanings, is used not only to describe certain kinds of empirical phenomena, but also to evoke sentiments of historical ancestry, political loyalty, and emotional attachment. This is why culture is a very sensitive issue in politics and policy debates, as anyone who has dealt with development programs will know. It also helps explain the polarized views that have considered culture alternatively as a positive instrument or as an obstacle for development.

The complexity in dealing with culture in development in the last fifty years has to do with the failure to distinguish the constitutive, functional, and instrumental aspects of cultural discourse. As the report of the United Nations (UN) Commission on Culture and Development explicitly stated, it is not culture that is embedded in development; it is development that is embedded in culture.

The concept of culture, as defined and used by anthropology for more than a century, derived from the need to find order in its increasing knowledge of immensely varied human ways of life. Culture, as understood in the western world of art and intellect, refers more narrowly to a universal longing for meaning and quality in human existence. Both connotations have been constantly entwined and confused in discussions on culture and development.

In the last three decades, cultural policies and development actions about culture have become ever more urgent as intellectual "culture wars" and real "ethnic cleansing" wars have proliferated, the former usually in developed countries and the latter in some countries in transition or developing ones. Of the approximately one hundred sixty wars that have occurred since 1945, most have taken place within nations, and, especially since the end of the cold war, a very great number have been driven by ethnic, religious, or cultural discourses. Why is this so? Is the underlying cause of such conflicts the unequal development that has favored some cultural minorities or ethnic groups at the expense of others? Or is it the other way around: do such cleavages exacerbate the inequality in development by pushing culturally distinct peoples toward power and wealth and others into intolerable poverty? This is the unresolved debate that began even as the foundations of the UN were being put into place. At that time, in 1945, horrified by the devastation brought about by the Nazi belief in their cultural and religious supremacy, war-torn nations set forth the foundation for the international concern for culture by recognizing in the UN Educational Scientific and Cultural Organization (UNESCO) Constitution that "wars begin in the minds of men."

Indeed, the attack of September 11, 2001, in New York and the subsequent military interventions were initially couched in terms evoking strong religious and cultural claims on all sides, although such claims were later carefully denied by western governments. Culture, an ignored factor in the second half of the 20th century in politics and policy, seems to have come back with a vengeance as the new century opened, we had all hoped, to an era of rational negotiation. Now cultural and religious factors have been placed prominently in the world political agenda while development thinking is still moving too slowly in incorporating such factors into their models.

At present, national and international institutions are not yet equipped to take full account of cultural processes. The intellectual ambiguity in the use of the concept of culture and early international geopolitical negotiations in setting up international institutions led to a splintering of culture from development actions among different UN agencies, national ministries, and international and nongovernmental development organizations. As Mahatma Gandhi once explained it, development thinking requires "a recognition that economic activity, at every stage of technical development, has no value except as a contribution to a social aim."

What, then, is an operational definition of culture? My own definition is that culture is the flow of meanings that human beings create, blend, and exchange. Cultures are philosophies of life that hold together all the social practices that build and maintain a capable, creative human being. Such practices also hold together well-functioning, balanced societies. In this sense, cultures function as primary regulating systems that help to keep peoples' feelings and actions within the bounds of institutionally acceptable behavior. Guidelines for behavior are expressed in discourse as values. When such systems are ignored in development, they tend to create unsocial behavior.

It is very important to emphasize that cultures do not exist except through the thoughts, actions, and performance of real people. There is no essence to cultures, except the beliefs that people decide to place on them. Something special, however, is happening in our present world with people's representations of cultures. A threshold is perceptible, created by the new scale and intensity of certain cultural phenomena, but more precisely by the synergy among them. This cultural transition, as I term it, requires developing new concepts and a new intellectual framework to reflect this changing reality. Clearly, culture is more important than ever before.

The First Step: Defining Culture as a Human Right

As the devastation wrought by World War II came to an end, several ideas went down in the rubble. The first among them was the linear evolutionist paradigm, in which "civilization" represented the apex of political, intellectual, and moral achievement. The second was the German romantic ideal of the superiority of sentimental attachment to a community over the search of universality based on reason. Germany, the nation that had most highly held aloft the values of sentimentalized "culture" and that had considered itself one of the most "civilized" in the world, had perpetrated the most deliberately planned genocide in history against many of its own and other citizens in the name of racial and religious identity.

The foundations for peace were set in the UN Universal Declaration of Human Rights of 1948, which states that every individual "is entitled. . . . to the economic, social and cultural rights indispensable to his dignity and the free development of his personality." It also states that everyone is entitled to freely participate in the cultural life of the community and to have protection as an author of literary or artistic works.

The Splintering of Culture in the United Nation Institutions

During this same period, the Marshall Plan, applied to the reconstruction in war-devastated western Europe, became the blueprint for economists at the UN to begin to create development thinking ahead of the curve (Emmerj, Jolly, and Weiss 2001). One of its aims was the formulation of economic development policies for "underdeveloped" nations, many of which were already on the path to decolonization. However, intrinsic to this economic model was the implicit assumption that the cultural structures of Western European societies in terms of values, ethical and political checks and balances, symbolic representations, and civil society traditional organization could be found everywhere or would arise mechanically through the application of economic policies. All the pioneering UN reports on development of the beginning of the 1950s referred to measures for international economic stability and growth; culture was subsumed under the heading of "social development" and was perceived as being related mainly to education and to civil rights—promoted by the western powers—or social rights—championed by the socialist bloc.

A different set of assumptions intervened in the creation of UNESCO as the UN institution explicitly charged with preventing "wars that begin in the minds of men." In the publication of the first UNESCO Conferences of 1946, its organizer, Stephen Spender, set forth the question, "Can a world organization such as UNESCO contribute to aiding development in education, science and culture around the world" to provide "the certainty of peace?" (UNESCO 1947, 2).

The conferences, in fact, bear witness to the "immense menacing shadows," in the words of André Malraux—shadows that European intellectuals felt were falling across Europe as the atomic bomb raised the specter of another world war in which "the end of the world is possible" (UNESCO 1947, 73). In such a setting, Malraux affirmed that "whatever the particular form of a culture, however far it may be from us, it touches us exclusively through its supreme form." He ended by saying, "we are confronted by the heritage of a European humanism. How does this heritage appear to us? First, as the bond with a permanent rationalism, with an idea of progress" (80).

It wasn't until 1948 that a program under the rubric of "culture" was approved at the second UNESCO General Conference, held in Mexico City. Under chapter 2 on "Free Flow of Ideas," a major section addressed the theme of "Interchange Between Cultures" that read, "Channels for the free flow of ideas cannot and should not be used to promote a uniform world culture. UNESCO's goal is rather unity-in-diversity; to aid in using these channels so that one culture can be interpreted to other cultures; so that men can learn first those common elements in the other culture that can serve as the basis for common thought and action; but, of equal importance, that they may learn respect for other divergent elements" (UNESCO 1948, 15).

UNESCO programs on culture, given the intellectual climate, were oriented toward the conservation of cultural heritage, support for artists, promotion of the arts and "folk" arts, and questions of copyright. In parallel, decolonization became an exclusively political question, linked to development as understood only in economic terms. Both concerns were addressed at UN headquarters, while financial planning was assigned to the Bretton-Woods institutions. In this way, the academic structuring of knowledge between disciplines became the architectural blueprint for the organizational structure of international institutions. In consequence, the international discourse on development was constructed exclusively in terms of economic growth, while the discourse on culture followed the more restricted definition of this term, with reference to the arts and the "supreme forms" of cultural heritage.

Culture in Development Theories

As other chapters of this book explain, in the 1950s, emerging development theories, among which Sir Arthur Lewis's *The Theory of Economic Growth* (1955) set the pace, were concerned primarily with economic growth, employment, capital-intensive technology, and productivity.[1] A few authors, such as W. W. Rostow, did refer to concerns related to culture, stressing that, for development to be successful, associated changes must be made in local institutions and values (Rostow 1960). Daniel Lerner's influential book, *The Uses of Literacy*, argued that all modernizing societies had gone through a linear process of increasing urbanization, literacy, mass media exposure, and participation.

Whereas consensus theories were based on the assumption that values and attitudes were part of the necessary components for harmonizing the development of societies, a different school of thought, derived from Marxism, considered conflict, albeit class conflict, not cultural or ethnic conflict, as inherent to the development of societies.[2] Marx's ambivalent definitions of culture led many left-wing intellectuals, especially in developing countries, to reject the use of the term *culture* as an analytic category for social research. It was only much later, when the work of Antonio Gramsci was brought to light, and with British scholars such as Perry Anderson, that culture began to emerge as a legitimate field of analysis in Marxist studies.

One historical study that has had considerable intellectual influence in the 1950s was Karl Polanyi's 1944 book, *The Great Transformation*. He provided historical evidence to establish that "previously to our time no economy ever existed that, even in principle, was controlled by markets"

(Polanyi 1944/1965, 43). Insisting that "economic motives spring from the context of social life," he instead considered reciprocity and redistribution to be the basic principles of organization of economies and societies (47).

A different perspective began to be built by looking at how rural villages were, in fact, being incorporated into expanding capitalist structures in developing countries. A decade earlier, Robert Redfield, an anthropologist, had defined progress as a "folk–urban continuum," a linear process through which peasants in agrarian societies went from isolation and homogeneity, to "disorganization of culture, secularization and individualization" (Redfield 1941, 339). The title of one of his most influential books, published in 1950, *Chan Kom: A Village that Chose Progress*, marks this new perspective, which became highly influential in development thinking and policies in developing countries.

In the 1950s, Mexican anthropologist Gonzalo Aguirre Beltrán and Eric Wolf converged in arguing that rural "closed corporate communities" that had been isolated were now increasingly subject to exploitation through center-periphery relations that constant drained economic resources from their communities (Aguirre Beltrán 1961). It was at that time that anthropologists also began to study some of the effects of development in urban settings. Oscar Lewis had revisited Tepoztlán, Redfield's original site of study, and had followed Tepoztecan migrants to Mexico City to look at the urban side of the "folk–urban continuum."

The "Subculture of Poverty"

Oscar Lewis himself was surprised at how the phrase he originally coined in his 1959 book, *Five Families: A Mexican Case Study in the Culture of Poverty*, had become "a catchy one and has become used and misused" (Lewis 1964, 67). In intensive fieldwork studies that he later continued with the urban poor in Cuba and Puerto Rico, Lewis dealt with poverty not as a "culture" but, more accurately, as he himself defined it later on, as a "subculture."

He described this "subculture of poverty" in terms of some seventy interrelated social, economic, and psychological traits. Among the traits he described are chronic unemployment and underemployment leading to low income, lack of property ownership, absence of savings, and a chronic shortage of cash. He emphasized that the poor lack effective participation and integration in the major institutions of the larger society; that they have high illiteracy rates and low levels of education; and that they tend not to participate in national welfare agencies, labor unions, or political parties. As a result, they have a critical attitude toward some of the basic institutions of the dominant classes, a hatred of the police, a mistrust of government and those in high position, and a cynicism that extends even to the church. Further, they live in poor housing conditions; they live in crowded conditions; and they experience gregariousness with a minimum of organization beyond the level of the nuclear and extended family. He notes, however, that there may also be a sense of community and esprit de corps in urban slums and in slum neighborhoods (Lewis 1964, 71). As defined by the traits he describes, the subculture of poverty is a statistical profile, the traits of which fall into a number of clusters that are functionally related to each other.

In Lewis's thinking, the subculture of poverty is both an adaptation and a reaction of the poor to their marginal position in a class-stratified, highly individuated, capitalistic society. It represents "an effort to cope with feelings of hopelessness and despair which develop from the realization of the improbability of achieving success in terms of the values and goals of the larger society" (Lewis 1964, 69). Less well known than his famous phrase and his important contributions to anthropological knowledge is the difference he perceived in kinds of poverty. In another essay, he explained that the poverty of peasant communities

seemed a natural and integral part of the whole way of life, intimately related to the poor technology and poor resources or both. In fact, many anthropologists have taken it upon themselves to defend and perpetuate this way of life against the inroads of civilization. But poverty in modern nations is a different matter. It suggests class antagonism, social problems and the need for change; and often it is so interpreted by the subjects of the study. (Lewis 1964, 427)

"When Is a Culture Not a Culture?"

The notion of a "culture of poverty" spread like a *llamarada de petate*—the flame of a straw mat, as we say in Mexico.[3] It was quickly picked up in antipoverty public debates in the United States through Michael Harrington's 1962 book, *The Other America*. It also meshed with E. Franklin Frazer's negative views of "lower-class culture" later taken up by Daniel Moynihan, especially in relation to African American family life. It was strongly opposed, though, by other authors, especially anthropologists. Already in 1966, at a meeting of the American Anthropological Association, the notion of a "culture of poverty" was deemed to distort the reality of life among the poor, prejudice our understanding of that life, and encourage policies that tended to perpetuate the disadvantages associated with poverty (Harrington 1962, 17).

Charles Valentine, in his influential 1969 book, *Culture and Poverty*, attacked this concept on two counts. First, he argued, the culture of poverty notion and related ideas contradict all important positive aspects of the culture concept, establishing that "these formulations support the long-established rationalization of blaming poverty on the poor" (15). Second, because the essence of poverty is inequality, he believed that many of the distinctive traits that Lewis identified as culture patterns, rather than being cultural creations of a subculture of poverty, were, in fact, "externally imposed conditions or unavoidable matters of situational expediency" (129).

In a 1972 book of selected readings on poverty, the concept of a "culture of poverty" was dismissed for its "hazy descriptive value" and "lack of explanatory significance" (Roach and Roach 1972). According to Ron Dore (1976), that material deprivation may produce similar cultural traits in different societies was accepted by structuralists in development studies, mainly neoclassical economists and Marxists, but that cultural traits could have an independent influence in perpetuating the condition of poverty was considered inadmissible.

Robert Wade (1976) added that although identifying the "poor" as an analytical category by defining them in terms of statistical income distributions could be acceptable for purely descriptive purposes, it could not be useful to explain the systematic nature of poverty. Within the "current orthodoxy" at the time, he explained, across the academic and political spectrum, from Marxian scholars to neoclassical economists and social anthropologists, the critical factors were the distribution of resources and power and the material and physical constraints. He made the point that "concepts such as 'utility' and 'leisure preference' in neo-classical economics, 'false consciousness' and even 'exploitation' in Marxian analysis, are used as question-stopping devices, to insulate the paradigm, to justify ending the enquiry before entering the realm of culture" (5).

"Cultural Readjustment" in Economic Development

A parallel discussion was being held in development thinking in the 1960s on the need to take into account "cultural readjustment" in economic development planning. In the field, resistance had been encountered "in attempts to introduce technical improvement in communities governed by principles which run counter to such improvements . . . but the problem is now becoming a live issue, owing to the repercussion of the desire for independence (in developing countries) and the eagerness for development" (Meynaud 1963, 4–5). The author, Jean Meynaud, writing in 1963 in a UNESCO publication, then suggested that "the study of cultural models helps us to situate the individual again in his social context" (6). Regarded in this way, he goes on to say, economic and technical changes represent no more than one particular aspect of the general theme of "cultural readjustment."

A decade later, Paul Kennedy explained that the inability of capitalist enterprises to keep their workers in the case of the Ghana was partly linked to the workers' desire to be their own boss, a trait valued in the workers' traditional culture; in addition, the demands of kinship and community could effectively weaken the capacity of entrepreneurs to accumulate capital (Kennedy 1976). He concluded that constraints to development are "partly structural ones of a kind which economists conventionally handle, but partly stem from the particular culturally conditioned behavioral dispositions of the people with whom they have to deal. But the latter, too are not just traditional legacies. They can be modified—and reinforced—by features of the economic structure characteristic of the dependent economies of the Third World" (21).

In spite of a widening interest in culture in development studies, in the 1970s, according to Ron Dore (1976), there was a "flight from culture" in intellectual terms. One element of this flight, he wrote, was the scientific desire to deal with hard, quantifiable, "structural" data (1). "Perhaps," he mused, "there is an element of machismo involved . . . in the sense that a model of man activated exclusively by motives of material self-interest may be taken as an actual picture of reality" (1). Moreover, he noted that the flight from culture could also stem from white man's guilt. "The underlying ethnocentrism and exclusion of realities of control of international monetary and trading systems by powerful countries of economic development models" was rightly opposed by third world social scientists on the rise; "Peru's sociologists or Senegal's or Tunisia's, were not so happy to have their country's troubles diagnosed as basically laziness or narrow-mindedness, however jargonized the diagnosis might be in terms of achievement-orientation scores or empathy ratings" (2).

Culture and Internal Colonialism

Indeed, as a new generation of intellectuals in developing countries began to examine the failures and uneven effects of foreign-assisted modernization in their countries, many turned to culture as an intellectual tool as a way to emphasize "endogenous" development.

Building on Aguirre Beltran and Eric Wolf's thesis of center-periphery relationships, Rodolfo Stavenhagen went further to define the concept of "internal colonialism" to refer to the condition of autochthonous peoples in third world countries. He later proposed "ethnodevelopment" as a policy that would allow such peoples to incorporate capitalism to their lives in their own terms.[4]

By then, Indians were no longer conceptualized as holders of dying traditions, but as peoples who had gone through a passage from tribal Indian to generic Indian, following Darcy Ribeiro (1970). Still, the category of "Indian" is a colonial category, Guillermo Bonfil (1985) argued, part of the oppression, the *México Profundo*, that must be revitalized. Furthermore, Indians were seen as holders of a "negative identity," according to Judy Friedlander. Independently of the content of the villagers' culture, they were defined by that fact that they continued to lack what the elite continued to acquire (Friedlander 1975).

My 1978 study of why Indian families were poorer than mestizo families although they had received equal amounts of land under agrarian reform in the 1930s also gave some answers. The stigma attached to Indianness was used by mestizo families to monopolize jobs and business opportunities, resulting in moderate economic growth for their own children. Yet Indians themselves also told me they refused to send their children to school to learn the necessary Spanish because they did not want to lose their language and way of life (Arizpe 1978).

The same dilemmas of conserving traditional cultures while eradicating internal colonialism were pervasive in countries of Asia and Africa. In the latter in particular, apartheid represented the most brutal continuation of colonial oppression, justified predominantly on the basis of culture. The extent to which it fostered a great mistrust for cultural explanations and for ethnic motivations among development thinkers and practitioners cannot be minimized. Indeed, the policy of apartheid was based on the recognition of cultural difference and the desire of every cultural group to live separately—a fact too often forgotten in contemporary discussions—and was used to legitimize the exclusion of the African population from South African development.

African intellectuals reacted by attacking colonialism and rallying support among their communities for national liberation. Frantz Fanon was one of the first writers to denounce the colonialist experience as one of trying to impose "white masks on black faces." The widespread "Negritude" movement led by poet Leopold Senghor and later president of Senegal, and by writers such as Aimé Cesaire in the Caribbean, vindicated black African cultures and their many artistic achievements. In his speech on "National Liberation and Culture," Amilcar Cabral expressed their view as follows: "The experience of colonial domination shows that, in the effort to perpetuate exploitation, the colonizers not only create a system to repress the cultural life of the colonized people; they also provoke and develop the cultural alienation of a part of the population, either by so-called assimilation of indigenous people or by creating a social gap between the indigenous elites and the popular masses" (Cabral 1970).

In Asia, debates on culture and development took a different turn. The Congress Party of India, followers of the enlightened path of Gandhi, opposed the violent riots brought about by culturally and religiously defined "communalisms" and embarked on locally driven development. The Bandung Conference of 1955 set the stage for the subsequent debate on the "Asian" values of filial piety, honesty, loyalty, and diligence in work. They were highlighted in the 1980s as the reason for the success of economic development in East Asia, only to be recast a decade later as part of the reason for the economic crisis in that region, having to do with nepotism, cronyism, and passivity.

Women, Culture, and Development

Although Ester Boserup's pioneering study *Women's Role in Economic Development*, published in 1970, did not explicitly deal with culture in analyzing women's labor force participation, it nevertheless opened a new intellectual domain in development. It reflected new knowledge about population and contraception, as well as the impact of feminism and the civil rights movement in placing women prominently in the social and political development agenda. The International Labour Organization (ILO) and some governments—for example, the Indian government—began to sponsor studies and seminars on women's economic participation (Indian Ministry of Labour 1964; Indian Council for Social Science Research 1977; Ahmad, Zubeida, and Loufti 1980; Savane 1981). Other studies, especially in Latin American, showed that women were indeed predominant in what were perceived as the three main imbalances in development in the region: tertiarization, rural-urban migration, and the growth of the informal sector (Arizpe 1975; Saffioti 1978; Hewitt de Alcántara 1979; Arizpe and Aranda 1982). Cultural factors were implicit in the heuristic concept of the sexual division of labor, which created distinctive gender patterns in urbanization, industrialization, and labor force participation (Deere and Leal 1982; Safa and Leacock 1981).

The impact of cultural patterns was evident, particularly in comparative studies of women's labor force participation in different developing regions. For example, it showed the influence of cultural and religious factors in Islamic countries, where economic growth had had little effect in increasing women's labor force participation, or in India, where women outnumbered men in migration only in those regions, like Kerala, that had a majority non-Hindu population.

Cultural Policies

The idea of cultural policies had first been proposed in a 1969 UNESCO preliminary study in which criteria were formally recommended to define this concept and to link culture to the fulfillment of personality and to economic and social development (UNESCO 1969). Policy guidelines were suggested in the UNESCO 1977–82 Medium Term Plan, which consolidated a Program on Culture having the following aims: (1) promotion of the appreciation and respect for the cultural identity of individuals, groups, nations, and regions; (2) promotion of cultural identity as a means to achieve independence and solidarity; (3) promotion of cultural identity in the framework of a global development strategy; and (4) promotion of respect for the cultural identity of individuals and groups, particularly those who are marginalized in developed and developing countries (UNESCO 1977).

The most important and successful cultural programs in UNESCO, however, have promoted the conservation of cultural heritage. The 1972 Convention for the Protection of Natural and Cultural Heritage, which created the World Heritage List, is the second most ratified international convention of the UN, after the Convention of the Child.

The challenge of relating "culture" to "development" was taken up for the first time by governments at the World Conference on Cultural Policies held in Mexico City in 1982. Mondiacult, as it came to be known, established an international working concept based on a broader anthropological definition of culture: "the whole complex of distinctive spiritual, material, intellectual and emotional features that characterize a society or social group. It includes not only the arts and letters, but also modes of life, the fundamental rights of the human being, value systems, traditions and beliefs." The Mexico City Declaration highlighted the cultural dimension of development, stating that "Balanced development can only be insured by making cultural factors an integral part of the strategies designed to achieve it; consequently, these strategies should always be devised in the light of the historical, social and cultural context of each society" (UNESCO 1982, 42).

By the mid-1980s, social and cultural factors were beginning to be taken into account in development planning in other UN institutions, especially the United Nations Development Program in the areas of indigenous peoples, women and development, and community development. This was also happening at the World Bank, although, as Michael Cernea expressed it, too slowly. Cernea, who pioneered such studies in the World Bank, explained that such variables were now being taken up because of the inconsistencies or failures of many development programs (Cernea 1995). A major obstacle, Cernea pointed out, was the lack of a comprehensive theory on *induced development*, making it difficult to convince economists who were resistant to incorporating cultural values into their development models of the importance of social and cultural variables.

In 1987 the Group of 77, representing a majority of third world countries and with the support of key European countries, passed a resolution declaring 1988–97 a "Decade for Culture and Development." In a Decade-sponsored publication entitled *Culture: Hostage of Development?*, its contributing authors warned that the opposition of the two concepts revealed itself to be a simplification, "since the assumptions of development themselves are the expression of a culture" (Rist 1994, 12). For example, the western assumption that social change is determined everywhere by the search of maximization of profits or accumulation of goods, Emmanuel Dione noted, is not even uniformly shared in western societies (Rist 1994). Hassan Zaoual, another of the authors, points out that through development, "the Third World is simply (being) decultured: it no longer believes its own myths (except in their fundamentalist forms) and they are offered only simulacres to nurture their imaginaries" (Rist 1994, 58–59).

Cultural Diversity and Modernization

As growing environmental concerns made sustainability the central strategy for development at the end of the 1980s, in my 1995 article "On Cultural and Social Sustainability," I insisted that these two processes necessarily had to be a component of general sustainability (Arizpe 1995). I described four analytically different processes evident at that time: (1) cultural groups that consciously and willingly tried to stay out of modernizing development, (2) cultural groups that were retrenching because they were being marginalized from development, (3) cultural groups that were using culture to fight for political advantage, and (4) groups that were using culture to protect their own national markets. All four trends, it seems to me, have increased notably in recent times.

A few years later, the breakup of the Soviet Union and the end of an alternative political philosophy opened the door to the resurgence of traditional ethnic and religious groups and to explorations into spiritual and environmental New Age philosophies. Amid the diversity, three major currents are having an impact in development thinking, concerning the relations between "cultures" and "civilizations," cultural studies and multiculturalism, and the discursive deconstruction of the ideas of development. What began in the 1970s as an argument for "ethnodevelopment," that is, development which incorporates local cultural differences, was elevated in the 1990s to a large-scale "clash of civilizations" couched in cultural terms but strictly political in its oversimplification and confusion of terms.

Samuel Huntington, in his article "The Clash of Civilizations and the Remaking of the World Order," initiated a most confusing international debate that has fostered retrenchment into ill-defined cultural and religious categorizations. This happened because instead of using the broader, more inclusive term of *western civilization*—since many of its achievements were based on those of other civilizations—or that of *Middle Eastern civilization*—which would have allowed the generosity of reference to the primary cultural foundations provided by Egypt, Greece, and Byzantium— he narrowed the terms to religions: Christianity, Judaism, and Islam. In fact, by ignoring science and political philosophy as the most vital aspects of the hegemony of the West, he reduced it to the position of one religion among many, none of which could possibly claim greater legitimacy. One cannot help but conclude that if moral, political, or scientific legitimacy is removed, the only power left is military.

Huntington distinguished modernization from westernization, arguing that any civilization can benefit from the economic and technological advances of the former without having to westernize. He also suggests that China—which, it must be pointed out, now has a secular "civilization"— may become the potential dominant power in East and Southeast Asia.

A fascinating counterpoint to the above is that precisely during this same period, anthropologists were redefining culture as a "site of contestation." As Stuart Hall argued, "We are living through the proliferation of the sites of power and antagonism in modern society" (Hall 1992, 20). Cultural studies shifted to multicultural urban environments in which the mass media are the main medium of transmission of cultural messages.

A different picture emerged in relation to autochthonous peoples. International organizations had already given prominence to issues of indigenous peoples: the World Bank in terms of their dam and economic development projects in indigenous regions (World Bank 1982), ILO with respect to self-determination, and UNESCO in terms of the conservation of their cultures and the arts. Among many other indigenous movements, the Zapatistas in Mexico became internationally emblematic as a political movement that inserted the demands of autochthonous peoples in relation to globalization processes.

In the quest for culturally pluralistic models in the 1990s, the concept of transnationalism is also used to describe the diasporic creation of cultural communities (Ghosh 1989). Massive outmigration both disrupts and renovates the social fabric of rural communities. It also accelerates cultural change in urban groups, especially among the poor.[5] Such fluidity and uneven integration of migrants having different cultures in urban contexts would make it practically impossible to abstract a single pattern of a "subculture of poverty" for analytical purposes. Such deterritorialization of cultures and creation of these new transnational cultural spaces poses a difficult new conceptual challenge (Kearney 1995).

The new patterns of "segmented assimilation" (Zhou 1999), separation of community and culture through an alternative "demotic discourse" (Baumann 1996), and reethnicization of many immigrant communities in developed countries point toward a new diversity of cultural attitudes, particularly after the first generation of immigrants in what may be called "minority cultures of mobility."

The Evanescence of Culture: The Debates of the 1990s

At the end of the 1970s, Edward Said's book *Orientalism* had cracked open the black box of cultural discourse by examining the idea of "Orientalism" as "the corporate institution for dealing with the Orient: dealing with it by making statements about it, authorizing views of it, describing it, by teaching it, settling it, ruling over it" (Said 1979, 3). Influenced by Foucault and other French postmodern analysts, Said opened a new critical trend, couched in terms of deconstructing regimes of discourse and representation, applied to cultural development. In the 1980s, several authors in developing countries, for example, V. Y. Mundimbe in *The Invention of Africa* and Chandra Mohanty, used the same conceptual tools to challenge current development thinking (Mundimbe 1988; Manzo 1991). Postcolonial studies also challenged such narratives by reading them as colonial discourse whose predominant strategic function, in the words of Homi Bhaba, is "the creation of a space for 'subject peoples' through the production of knowledge in terms of which surveillance is exercised" (Babha 1990, 75).

Arturo Escobar, in his 1995 book *Encountering Development: The Making and Unmaking of the Third World*, also emphasized that the corpus of rational techniques of the development discourse organizes both forms of knowledge and types of power applied to bring under control peoples in developing regions. "Development," he argues, "is at the same time self-destructing and being unmade by social action, even as it continues to destroy people and nature" (217). Such social action by local communities may develop more creative and autonomous practices conducive to renegotiating class, gender, and ethnic relations at the local and regional levels. He calls for a post-development cultural politics that is critically engaged in neutralizing the dominant economic discourse (Rahnema and Bawtree 2001).

In parallel, the development of interpretive and textual-analysis methodologies initiated in the 1980s in anthropology led to a general intellectual questioning of the term *culture* itself in anthropology. For many years, this concept had been critiqued because it creates hierarchy, it tends to homogenize cultural patterns, and it flattens levels of cultural understanding. By contrast, others, such as Christopher Brumann, argued instead that even in highly fluid situations, cultural patterns form valleys and mountains that create conceptual landscapes, or, as Arjun Appadurai would term them, ethnoscapes, that give people a sense of identity and a certain understanding of the world (Brumann 1999).

While such debates raged in university and art circles, however, international organizations began to react to pressure from member states to develop policies and actions to deal with three rising cultural trends. The main ones were perceived to be the rapid loss of cultural traditions associated with globalization, the reemergence of cultural clashes and religious fundamentalisms as state and secular political philosophies lost strength, and the need to protect conditions for continued cultural production in countries as telecoms and mass media flooded cultural spaces with nonnational cultural content. It was then that the independent UN World Commission on Culture and Development carried out its important work.

The UN World Commission on Culture and Development

The UN's independent World Commission on Culture and Development, established by the General Assembly of the UN in December 1992 and chaired by former UN Secretary-General Javier Pérez de Cuéllar, included thirteen international respected figures and six honorary members.[6] After some thirty-one months of work, in November 1995, the Commission presented its report, *Our Creative Diversity*, both to UNESCO General Conference and to the UN General Assembly.

The all-pervasive message emerging from the report is that development embraces not only access to goods and services, but also the opportunity to choose a full, satisfying, valuable, and valued way of living together. Looking at development as a process that enhances the effective freedom of people everywhere to create cultural expressions and to exchange them broadens the widely accepted notion of human development. Culture's role is not to serve the ends but constitutes, in fact, the social basis of the ends themselves. In other words, culture is not a means to material progress; it is the end and aim of "development" seen as the flourishing of human existence in all its forms and as a whole.

In *Our Creative Diversity*, the Commission articulated, first, the notion of a *global ethics* that needs to emerge from a worldwide quest for shared values that can bring people and cultures together rather than drive them apart. It then explored the challenges of *cultural pluralism*, reaffirming a commitment to fostering coexistence in diversity both nationally and internationally. *Creativity* was recognized as a lever of development in relation to technology, new political and social forms, empowerment, and artistic production. The report explored the cultural implications of the world *media* scene, focusing on whether the principles of diversity, competition, standards of decency, and the balance between equity and efficiency, often applied nationally, could be applied internationally.

The Commission also addressed the many processes that are changing the cultural perceptions of *women's* life cycles and social participation. It proposed to broaden the discussion and propose strategies to encompass fundamental changes in women's roles in societies all over the world and to develop agendas against intolerant cultures that deny women their basic human rights. Redistribution of income, assets, and power from men to women requires the consolidation of a political base, empowerment, and cultural change. *Tangible and intangible cultural heritage*, the report went on, embody the collective memory of communities across the world. This heritage is made up not only of sites and monuments, but also of a multitude of arts and crafts objects, documents and manuscripts, oral traditions, and expressive culture in all its forms, including the performance arts. Safeguarding these creations of our ancestors must go hand in hand with fostering the creation of our contemporaries.

The Commission also recognized that the *cultural dimensions of environmental management* should be considered in relation to indigenous knowledge, the built environment, urban culture, population growth, poverty, economic growth and the biosphere, sustainability, and cultural diversity. New *culturally sensitive development strategies* were proposed to fully take into the human factor of development.

Several of the Commission's recommendations had immediate results. UNESCO began to publish the *World Culture Reports*. The Intergovernmental Conference on Cultural Policies for Development was held in Stockholm in 1998; its plan of action emphasized cultural policies, creativity, respect for cultural diversity, and the use of the new communications and information technologies for cultural programs. The UN

Volunteer Services for assistance in the conservation of cultural heritage sites received an enthusiastic response all over the world.

The World Culture Reports

To support and inform the development of new policies, the Commission also saw the publication of an independent world culture report as a vehicle for exploring, clarifying, and updating key world issues. The first *World Culture Report*, published in 1998, explored the themes of culture, markets, and creativity.[7] It gave more precise definitions of culture and explored strategies to create statistical indicators on culture and development. All available data and statistics on culture were aggregated for world, regions, and subregions. The work on indicators of culture and development was continued at a "Culture Counts" seminar held during the World Bank meeting that took place in Florence in October 1999.

The second *World Culture Report* dealt with cultural diversity, conflicts, and pluralism. Its first section argued that diversity, including not only that related to culture, but also to gender, race, and sexual preference, need not threaten stability, as long as citizens are able to adhere to values and cultural practices that are sufficient to secure general compliance and support for the institutions of governance.

Cultures, as explained in this report, must be conceptualized as a constantly flowing process, like a multicolored river in which no current is pure, yet at any point in time, it may be perceived as different while still flowing as a river (UNESCO 2000). In detaching people from their geographical territories, historical places, or semantic self-adscription frameworks, modernization is creating a new world context. Cultural adscriptions are resemantized as "folkloric" in a new global framework in which the cultural narratives transmitted through the media and now the Internet establish a cosmopolitan frame of reference. For example, Indonesian Gamelan music, even if mixed with western music, must continue to sound like Gamelan music in order to keep its niche in the market of world music (UNESCO 1998). The economic aspects of cultural heritage conservation, the construction of knowledge through the new information and communications technologies, and the construction of culture and development indicators were also explored in this report.

The main challenge for this new century, as stated in the first section of the 2001 *World Culture Report*, is to find strategies so that "nations and the global community [may] prevent and remedy the deepening of inequality, especially along fault lines, new and old, that coincide with cultural diversity" (Arizpe et al. 2002, 23).

The Cultural Deficit in Development

In my introduction, I quoted the report of the World Commission on Culture and Development that explicitly stated that culture is not embedded in development but that development is embedded in culture. My discussion of culture and development has clearly shown the inability of mainstream development models to incorporate a basic understanding of culture, especially its constitutive purpose.

Economics has no theory about how human beings become functional members of societies. It only deals with how already constituted members exchange things and intangibles. The practices that are needed to keep human beings in good mental, emotional, and physical balance individually are constantly disregarded. All such practices are social in nature, that is, they depend on the familial, conjugal, amical, community, and national relationships that give individuals the capacity to understand their personal wants in the setting of collective well-being. The effects of leaving such considerations out of development models and policies, even in developed countries, are evident in many instances of loss of trust, social disintegration, delinquent behavior, and greater violence against women and children. Too much competition leads to no cooperation, and the latter is essential for development.

The loss of social integration is not just a question of values but of the systemic nature of feelings of belonging, reciprocity, and responsibility that human beings need to make sense of their lives, even as they participate in markets. These integrative social practices cannot be reintroduced into society through fragmentary political strategies or through religious revivals. Neither will be successful, for reasons that fall beyond the scope of this chapter.

Culture and development issues are rapidly evolving in new directions. In the 1990s, as many developing countries tried to cope with cultural pluralism in the setting of democratization, attention has shifted to the interaction between culture and democracy (Przeworski 1998). The economics of cultural heritage, cultural industries, and intellectual property is also in the forefront of the international agenda (UNESCO 2000). On indigenous peoples, June Nash captures the key process in the chapter title "Pluricultural Survival in the Global Ecumene," defining the task as "no longer one of salvaging waning traditions, but of catching up with the frontiers in global integration now being forged by indigenous social movements" (Nash 2001, 219–20).

By far the greatest intellectual challenge on culture arises from the unprecedented cultural interaction in the world today brought about by the transmission of images and texts in the blink of an eye. Cultural industries and international trade in commodities having cultural content also pose one of the major cultural challenges in the world today.

After years of trying to expand a homogenous "technoculture" or "business culture" around the world so that firms and corporations could function in a seamless economic sphere, there is a new trend now toward multigendered and multiethnic staff in business corporations. This may be interpreted as an attempt at keeping up the creative spirit that comes only from contrasting and confronting alternative ways of doing things. If this is already happening in corporate culture, why hasn't it as yet permeated economic development models of international economic institutions?

The Cultural Transition

History shows that a cultural deficit usually points toward the end of an epoch. A better understanding of the current difficulties of globalization requires acknowledging that, as I contend, we are living through a cultural transition. I believe that it marks the end of an epoch of forever expecting that alternative knowledge, technologies, philosophies, and art existed out there, in other cultures, ready to be brought in to enrich western productions and markets or to be used as a mirror to better define the western sense of universality that leads the world. A culturally monotonic world would mean the end of creativity. Fostering creativity, then, becomes a priority for culture and development policies, and freedom to create, a priority for human development.

At the beginning of the 21st century, culture has become central to building the new geopolitics of a global world. People are rebuilding their perceptions about other cultures as part of a major shift in relations between nations, regional cultures, and cultural, ethnic, and religious groups. This shift, combined with the failures of development, are deepening the perceptions of inequality and unfairness in development.

Globalization is driven by trade and finances, but it is also being shaped by cultural choices that influence political and social actions. As different groups reposition themselves in a global setting, they are recasting their cultural representations and forms of symbolic display. This explains why so many new debates and initiatives related to culture and development have emerged since the waning of the ideologies of the cold war. They deal with social capital and art and humanities policies, with cultural heritage and memory. It also explains why even some old, discredited concepts such as "civilizations" or "race" have been dusted off and used to try to make sense of disquieting contemporary trends.

If we understand development as a means to find alternative solutions for economic growth, then the loss of cultural diversity represents a serious threat for the future. Normally discussed in relation to ethnicity, gender, race, or sexual preference, diversity is now even being brought up in relation to technology (Arizpe 2002). A 2001 research article entitled "The Loss of Diversity" that appeared in the *Economist* warned that "For all its single-minded predictability, technology has always flourished on a diversity of opinion and an unerring ability to invent alternative solutions" (3). The article argued that industrial concentration, the high cost of developing high-tech products and the trend toward globalization are limiting the search for alternative solutions. Is it only coincidence that this is happening exactly at the same time as peoples having different cultures are losing millennia-old philosophies, knowledge, and technologies?

Amartya Sen brings together the different strands in this debate by affirming that social identities are important, so there are reasons to reject the view of individuals merely as self-concerned islands (Sen 1998a,b). Further, he goes straight to the heart of the matter by stating that it is people who must decide whether to sacrifice material goods for the preservation of a culture or to sacrifice certain cultural features for greater prosperity. He says, "In the freedom-oriented perspective, the liberty of all to participate in deciding what traditions to observe cannot be ruled out by the national or local 'guardians'—neither by the ayatollahs (or other religious authorities), nor by political rulers (or governmental dictators), nor by cultural 'experts' (domestic or foreign)" (1998a, 45).

To conclude, I note that the research and policy experiences in culture and development, in spite of their richness over the past fifty years, have not been reflected in the reform of existing institutions dealing with this field—neither at the national or international levels, nor in the creation of new institutions better equipped to help governments and civil societies deal with the multiple phenomena related to culture and development.

The ambiguities in the definition of culture and the implicit assumptions about culture in economic development models led to culturally blind rather than culturally sensitive development policies and programs and to generally well intentioned, yet frequently insubstantial, institutional responses, both nationally and internationally. As a consequence, the cultural deficit in current development activity translates directly to a deficit in the quality of life of those groups such activity is meant to improve.

Notes

1. For an excellent history of UN development ideas, see Emmerj, Jolly, and Weiss (2001).

2. Karl Marx used the term *culture* with different connotations. In the *Grun-*

drisse, he referred to culture as the superstructure of society, which was tied to changes determined by shifts in the structure of relations of production. In other writings, he implied that culture was the cement or glue necessary to bind social institutions together.

3. Title of a chapter in Valentine (1969).

4. Rodolfo Stavenhagen's writings on Indian peoples is vast (Stavenhagen 1968, 2001).

5. The first comprehensive discussion of this field of studies can be found in Basch, Glick-Schiller, and Szanton-Blanc (1994). A useful reader is Vertovec and Cohen (1999).

6. Among them, Keith Griffin, Niki Goulandris, Yoro Fall, Celso Furtado, Elizabeth Jelin, Mahbub ul Haq, Nikita Mikailkov, Leila Takla; honorary members: Claude Lévi-Strauss, Ang Sang Suu Chi, Elie Wiesel. Lourdes Arizpe, also a member of the Commission and at that time UNESCO assistant director general for culture, was in charge of the secretariat for the Commission. Secretary to the Commission, Raj Isar; Guiomar Alonso, Jean-Ives Lesaux, and Vladimir Skok also carried out the work of the secretariat. The Commission adopted an active international approach, holding nine regional meetings around the world. At each one, local experts, social scientists, policy makers, artists, cultural policy and development experts, and nongovernmental organization activists presented their own concerns and ideas.

7. A scientific committee supervised the making of the *World Culture Reports*: chair, Lourdes Arizpe; members: Louis Emmerj, Keith Griffin, Yoro Fall, Elizabeth Jelin, Mohan Rao, Paul Streeten, David Throsby; executive director: Ann-Belinda Preis; researchers: Paula Leoncini and Isabelle Vinson.

CHAPTER 9

Culture, Poverty, and External Intervention

SABINA ALKIRE

Historically growth has expanded choice only in some dimensions while constricting choice in others. . . . Not only can't you go home again, but you can't figure out whether or not you want to until it's too late to change your mind.

—F. Apffel-Marglin and S. A. Marglin, *Dominating Knowledge*

The pointer to any real conflict between the preservation of tradition and the advantages of modernity calls for a participatory resolution, not for a unilateral rejection of modernity in favor of tradition by political rulers, or religious authorities, or anthropological admirers of the legacy of the past.

—A. Sen, *Development as Freedom*

If economic policies designed by economists affect, which they do, the whole of society, economists can no longer claim that they are solely concerned with the economic field. Such a stance would be unethical since it would mean avoiding the moral responsibility for the consequences of an action.

—M. Max-Neef, *Human Scale Development*

A Buddhist monk once told a visiting Dutch priest this story:

There was a man on a horse galloping swiftly along the road. An old farmer standing in the fields, seeing him pass by, called out, "Hey rider, where are you going?" The rider turned around and shouted back, "Don't ask me, just ask my horse!"

The monk looked at the priest from the West and said: "That is your condition. You are no longer master over your own destiny. You have lost control over the great powers that pull you forward toward an unknown direction. You have become a passive victim of an ongoing movement which you do not understand." (Nouwen 1971, 1)

It would be an oversimplification to imply that economic progress is like a lunging horse topped by a feeble rider, who is powerless to direct the muscular economic horse according to the rider's aspirations rather than the other way around. Yet this might be an oversimplification worth pondering. For some, impetus to direct "the great powers that pull you forward"—to transform the passive rider into a reflective and effective agent—appears to motivate many who challenge or block externally supported poverty reduction initiatives on cultural grounds in particular.

This chapter addresses the following normative question: if we understand culture in the ways that various contributions in this volume have sketched it; if we see cultures sometimes as a source of meaning, identity, and aspiration, sometimes as a source of oppression and inertia, always as a dynamic, permeable, heterogeneous, incomplete, and contested set of interrelated social structures, practices, assets, and beliefs, and if we understand cultures to be at times generative of and at times gouged by "poverty reduction" processes, then what, practically, *should* an international development agency such as the World Bank do with this knowledge? In other words, how does the rich and complex analyses others have put forward help poverty-focused World Bank projects and policies and people to "address" culture?

Lest this be unclear, in terms of the foregoing image, the question is *not* how should the rider undertake a flying exit from the horse, falling and rolling so minimum harm ensues. Rather, the question is whether external agencies have a role in enabling the rider to direct the powerful horse—poverty reduction—to goals of the riders' choosing.

This question is far from academic. The World Bank is a prime example of this controversy. Our question arises from those who complain about the World Bank (henceforth the Bank) because of its cultural clumsiness and those who write that it has no comparative advantage to engage in culture and should not try to build such an advantage.[1] It festers in the gap between the Bank's ambitions to empower partner institutions and government, and the sure swift recommendations of its "technically correct" policies (Stiglitz 2001). It lurks beneath analyses in this book, which fail to address the motivation and personalities of the external actors—be they Bank staff or elites—who have the power to expertly fashion poverty initiatives to their own whims.

The chapter proceeds as follows. First, the focal problem for this chapter is identified. Then, building on the work of Amartya Sen, the chapter sketches desirable characteristics of externally assisted development processes—public debate, decisions that remain open to ongoing public scrutiny, information on risks, trade-offs, and "unintended" yet foreseeable consequences; and value judgments. Third, the chapter works back into the World Bank as an institution. It assesses the "level" at which an institution like the World Bank can realistically address culture, then proposes that external actors pursue a two-pronged approach of informed participation and information provision. It sketches how this approach to some extent coincides with certain Bank processes, for example with indigenous persons, and in recent rhetoric related to resettlement, grassroots development ("community-driven development" in Bank parlance), and national planning processes. Fourth and finally, the chapter observes that the proposed two-pronged approach, were efforts made to implement it, is quite certain to fail unless the culture of the World Bank changes, both structurally and in terms of staff dispositions.

Problematic

At first glance, the intersection between culture and externally assisted poverty reduction appears to be treacherous and already strewn with mishaps. Taking a broad view, we can identify four distinct criticisms that are commonly raised against the World Bank and similar institutions on the grounds of their alleged (and often documented) neglect of culture:

1. Inefficient or failed projects. Bank activities have failed or not realized potential gains because staff did not accurately understand cultural influences and made inaccurate assumptions about behaviors or values. Because of these assumptions or other miscommunications, Bank counterparts (be they policy makers or poor communities) behaved differently than anticipated. In retrospect, if staff had responded to culture, the projects would not have failed or the outcomes would have been better.[2]

2. Unrealized resources. Bank activities have not realized the potential propoor economic gains from cultural industries and culture-based skills and knowledge, be it performance or handicrafts or tourism industries in niche markets. Not only might these activities be lucrative and labor intensive; they may also have an aspect of "meaning" and history that some jobs lack (Feldstein 1991; Frey and Pommerehne 1989; Klamer 1996; Serageldin 1999; United Nations Educational Scientific and Cultural Organization [UNESCO] 1995, 1998; Throsby 2001).

3. Imposition of values. Bank activities have deliberately tried to change cultural norms or practices that staff considered negative (nomadic lifestyles, gender discrimination, nonmarket worldviews, caste barriers) to those it supports (markets, individualism, materialism). Even when many agree that certain traditional practices are oppressive, the staff's unilateral authority to judge and impose measures to change those practices is disputed. The justification and limits of such authority bear examination, as does the process by which behavioral changes are pursued (Price 1989; Apffel-Marglin and Marglin 1990, 1996).[3]

4. Valuable cultural aspects undermined. Bank activities—at both the project and policy level—have had unintended and unanticipated cultural impacts that are widely viewed to be negative. Some groups judge that the negative cultural impacts outweigh or deeply compromise the positive outcomes of certain activities. This criticism is common among those who oppose globalization, westernization, or materialism on cultural grounds.

This chapter confines itself to the last two criticisms and in particular the last. This is not to imply that the first two issues are not important. Rather, they are *too* important to be treated only in passing, and the constraints of this chapter do not permit a satisfactory discussion. Of course, the four issues are not neatly divisible in practice; they overlap, and several may be present at the same time. Nonetheless, the chapter concentrates on the fourth problem and the third insofar as they overlap.

CULTURE AND POVERTY: ALWAYS INTERMINGLED

One way of identifying "cultural impacts" is to focus not on the particular cultural practices that slip in and out of focus, but on general categories of values (which are constituted by many influences including culture, gender, faith, family, education, experience, and personal choice). These categories might include life itself, relationships, meaningful work, and so on.[4]

Consider a community in Pari Hari in the Tharp Desert in Pakistan. Pari Hari did not have electricity or sanitation; the women in the women's organization there had not been to Diplo, the nearest market town, nor did they know the name of their country's prime minister. In Pari Hari, a nongovernmental organization (NGO) had recently supported the formation of male and female organizations. These groups were visited on a monthly basis by a male and female social organizer, who discussed issues such as savings, health, hygiene, and education. With the assistance of the NGO, the community had bored a sweet-water well that saved hours each day from women's workload and decreased outmigration in the dry season. They had also started a girls' school.

The men's and women's groups were asked to consider what changes—beneficial or harmful—had ensued from the NGO's activity in Pari Hari. The women identified six categories of beneficial impact (the order following is that in which the women identified the impacts chronologically): their daughters were going to school and becoming *educated*; *savings* had increased, bringing security and longer-term planning; their *health* and knowledge of health care had improved from the water and training; women had not met together previously, and so after the formation of the women's organization, their *unity* with each other increased (before, they had bickered often); when they met, they learned the needs of others in the village—which family did not have enough money to buy a school-book for their daughter, who was ill, in which household someone had died—so were able to *help each other*; and finally, their daughters and they themselves learned more about their *religious faith*—and in particular how women can pray (this was not known before)—from each other and from the school.

The women then compared the six different impacts they had identified and discussed how important the impacts were relative to each other. They decided on the following ranking. The most important impacts were health and prayer instruction. Very important impacts were helping others, savings, and unity. The less important impact was girls' education.

Although this example has many facets, one observation that is relevant to our problem is that in Pari Hari, which by all accounts is very deprived, the women valued social and cultural impacts (unity, helping others, religious instruction) as well as impacts that affected their material well-being (health, savings, education). Furthermore, as girls' education had not yet had a visible beneficial impact, it was valued mostly because of unintended side effects (in this case, the teachings on courtesy and cleanliness, and the training on "how women pray" that the girls brought home). But what is even more interesting is that the "poverty" changes did not categorically outrank the "cultural" changes as more valuable or vice versa; both were *interspersed* (I put both "poverty" and "cultural" in quotation marks because obviously culture influences both to some degree).

Now as an isolated example, this pattern could be due to any number of factors: poor quality of education, a charismatic religious social organizer, a ranking in which the facilitator made leading suggestions, domination by one woman, and so on. And it is likely that the rankings would evolve considerably over time. Yet when this exercise was repeated in a number of different communities in Pakistan, by a number of different facilitators, in initiatives that ranged from agricultural to income genera- tion to literacy to health clinics, using different ranking techniques and different ways of asking questions, a similar result emerged: respondents (men and women, urban and rural, young and old, poor and lower middle class) identified and valued both poverty-related and sociocultural impacts of development initiatives (the particular valued impacts varied tremen- dously), both impacts that directly affected their standard of living and ones that had no effect whatsoever on material well-being, but rather affected their relationships or frameworks of meaning.[5] I will discuss how "culture" fits into this picture in a moment, but first, I will pause one more moment on the issue of value diversity.

DIMENSIONS PEOPLE VALUE: MULTIPLE AND DIVERSE

The observation that communities value many different dimensions of well-being has become quite familiar (although its relevance to our focal problem is not often traced). A team including Deepa Narayan led a pio- neering study of the values of poor persons, entitled *Voices of the Poor*. The study gathered and analyzed subjective data and quotations of the poor, regarding what "the poor"—people who were identified as poor by other members of the community and by themselves—considered to be dimen- sions of poverty and dimensions of well-being. It is pioneering because it is the only cross-cultural study of this magnitude (about 60,000 respon- dents) that includes primarily poor respondents.

A major finding of the study was that poor persons have a complex notion of well-being, with plural constituents, ranging from the tangible (food, health) to the intangible (a lack of security, a lack of self-respect, an inability to bring up children, a lack of peace of mind, a lack of happiness, and a lack of harmony or spirituality) (Narayan et al. 2001a,b).

How does culture relate to these different definitions? First, culture affects to some extent the "instantiation" or local expressions of dimen- sions (the way in which food is cooked or marriage is undertaken or dis- putes are settled). Second, it affects the relative importance of different dimensions (for example, security versus freedom of choice). Third, certain aspects of culture are valued for their own sake (aesthetics of hairstyle or clothing, relational traditions of honor and duty, spiritual practices).

As Sen points out, a person's culture is not the sole influence guiding that person's perspectives and values. Rather, cultural aspects are con- tributing factors alongside a capacious list of other affiliations ranging from the athletic to the political to the ethical to the musical (Sen 1998b).

Thus not only is it the case as all authors have argued, that one cultural view does not have an "absolute priority" over other considerations; but also cultural priorities can usefully be assessed in and among other priorities ranging from physical needs to freedom to peace to family relationships. In particular, it is helpful to return to what Appadurai refers to as the "cultural map"—the configuration of aspirations that describe the good life in relation both to "a larger map of local ideas and beliefs" and to "more densely local ideas about marriage, work, leisure, convenience, respectability, friendship, health and virtue" (this volume). Although there may be some confusion because there are plural definitions of culture at different levels of specificity, the point to be made is clear: culture is not a decisive domain of life whose relationship to poverty reduction can be worked out in isolation from other influences. This point will color the entire analysis that follows.

IDENTIFYING TRADE-OFFS

The story of Pari Hari, in which sociocultural and poverty-reducing capabilities are mingled in importance, and the analyses of *Voices of the Poor*,[6] in which the values of poor persons are demonstrably wider than material poverty alone, clarifies our question. Our problem is this: how can the World Bank, the primary aim of which is to support material and bodily well-being, and which does not know the precise configuration of local cultural values (which are plural, permeable, dynamic, contested, etc.), address poverty in a way that allows cultural aspirations to be among the guiding forces? The first step is to identify what is at stake in a decision.

It will prove useful to restate this problem in the language of capabilities. As is well known, Sen argues that the objective of development (and by implication of poverty reduction activities) should be to expand people's freedom or capabilities. The capability of a person "represents the various combinations of functionings (beings and doings) that the person can achieve." The capability set reflects "the person's freedom to lead one type of life or another . . . to choose from possible livings" (Sen 1992, 40; 1999). The capability set may well include nutrition, basic education, and physical security as well as the freedom to speak one's mind, or to go about without shame, or to attend a dancing festival, or to live an unbothered life. In other words, the capability set reflects both poverty-related freedoms as well as the wider freedoms jointly.

The Pari Hari example is felicitous because the capability set expanded *more* than in simple material capabilities. The problem arises when basic capabilities improve but sociocultural capabilities are eroded—when there is a significant trade-off. For example, a large and vibrant literature opposes development and globalization. The critique is typically not directed against the impetus to reduce poverty. As authors wrote in the introduction to one such a book: "The chapters that follow have nothing to say against longer life-spans, healthier children, more and better-quality food and clothing, sturdier and more ample shelter, better amenities. Nor is any criticism leveled against the luxuries that people buy when their incomes grow enough to permit discretionary purchases, such as the radios and television sets that one sees even in very poor Third World villages" (Apffel-Marglin and Marglin 1990, 1). Rather, the major problem addressed by that book (and a great many others) is that development initiatives, even if they try to reduce poverty, defined as exogenous (out of their field of concern) other capabilities *that people really valued* and allowed them to be nonchalantly undermined.

Examples abound (although they are likely to be contentious)—complaints that the social fabric of mutual caring is destroyed and filial duties are disregarded because of individualism; complaints that local histories are forgotten or devalued; complaints that traditional art forms are lost; complaints that the indigenous institutions of dispute resolution, or traditional medicinal practices are undermined without a trace. This "contraction" of freedoms that people value (and which are often identified with culture) seems to account for much dissatisfaction with externally assisted poverty reduction. Others may protest the accuracy of the criticisms, or may be of the view that what is being protected is precisely what must be dismantled. But it is on this disputed terrain of cultural practices that are displaced by poverty reduction activities (or globalization, or . . .) that much more attention and largeness of mind could fruitfully be focused.

In sum, external poverty reduction activities that try to "take culture into account" have the following features:

1. The subset of poverty-reducing capabilities are positively valued by persons they will affect ("nothing against longer life-spans, healthier children . . .").

2. The cultural aspirations of the community or communities in question include the poverty-reducing capabilities, but also contain other capabilities that are more or less important.

3. The decision-making authority as regards the poverty-reduction activity is usually partly or purely held by an external institution or individual.

The situation is a trade-off between two options, neither of which have all of what the other one has.

Informed Participation

But how can externally assisted poverty reduction activities focus more attention on these trade-offs? This section argues that external actors should support informed participation and decision making. External agents can facilitate informed participation in several ways. They can convene or support participatory processes; they can provide information on unintended but foreseeable consequences of a proposed project; they can use their power to counter local domination and support pluralism; they can relinquish the final decision-making authority, because certain indeterminate value judgments *should* be made by the communities involved.

Setting up the problem as we have in the first section—as a trade-off between sets of capabilities that include poverty-related capabilities and impacts on other (culturally) valued capabilities—is clearly an oversimplification. There are issues of dissensus because people value different capabilities differently. There are issues of morality and oppression because some of what a vocal or powerful group values deeply may oppress others. There are issues of justice and distribution, and many other complicating factors. These issues are common to all participatory decision making, whether it is related to culture or to decentralization or to the identification of community priorities. And these issues of power and voice and oppression must be treated. I will leave aside how they can be treated for the moment but return to this key question in the last section.

The account of informed participation developed below may be stated succinctly as follows: the persons whose lives will be affected by a poverty reduction intervention should know, insofar as is possible, the alternative scenarios that are open to them, and the important trade-offs that are likely in each scenario with other capabilities they value very highly, and the probability of success. Those whose lives will be affected should have a persuasive voice in how to proceed. The dynamics of power must be managed such that minority views are taken into consideration.

EXPLICIT VALUATION OF TRADE-OFFS

Informed participation entails explicit and widespread assessment of *which* capabilities will change, given that "the overall ethical objectives of a society can include concerns *other than* the elimination of economic deprivation" (Sen 1997e, 166). Because capabilities are diverse, Sen commends the "valuation," the process of prioritizing a range of capabilities, as part of ongoing social and political processes. Which proposal is better for equity, which is better for the environment, and which will have an immediate impact then fizzle out? This enables communities to study the trade-offs and make value judgments when there is no best alternative. Sen writes:

> In the case of functionings and capabilities, since there are no markets directly involved, the weighting exercise has to be done in terms of explicit valuations, drawing on the prevailing values in a given society . . . This explicitness is not, in itself, a bad thing, since it gives the public a clear opportunity to question the values and to debate the decisions. (Sen 1996, 58)

It is not in every person or group's style to undertake their value judgments in a detailed rationalist manner of course, nor is this kind of discourse implied. Benjamin Disraeli may have stretched the term somewhat when he referred to being explicit as "the right line to take when you wish to conceal your own mind and to confuse the minds of others" (Disraeli 1845/1998, book 6, chapter 1). But the point is that if one option is better for certain dearly cherished cultural traditions and another option is better for economic return, the case is *indeterminate*—neither option dominates the other. There is no first-best scenario. Thus the decision of which option to adopt is a value judgment, the creation of an alternative future.[7] Sen proposes that the decision be undertaken as a value judgment, rather than hiding behind some other rationale, such as maximization of some good or another. He further proposes that the decision be open to and responsive to public debate.

ONGOING AND PUBLIC DEBATE

We may at this stage reframe the central question as follows: How should economic institutions aim to expand a *subset* of valued capabilities (namely, those related to poverty) if their efforts may have overwhelming negative impacts in other dimensions people treasure? Sen argues that in this case, the decision of whether to proceed should not be left to the market or to the development specialist or to the elite; it requires public debate:

> There is an inescapable valuational problem involved in deciding what to choose if and when it turns out that some parts of tradition cannot be maintained along with economic or social changes that may be needed for other reasons. It is a choice that the people involved have to face and assess. The choice is neither closed (as many development apologists seem to suggest), nor is it one for the elite "guardians" of tradition to settle (as many development skeptics seem to presume). If a traditional way of life has to be sacrificed to escape grinding poverty or minuscule longevity (as many traditional societies have had for thousands of years), then it is the people directly involved who must have the opportunity to participate in deciding what should be chosen. (Sen 1999, 31)

Later in *Development as Freedom* (1999), when discussing "Globalization: Economics, Culture and Rights," Sen restates the need for participation when a proposed project entails rather more painful cultural change. I include this lengthy quotation in order to underscore that it is not only discrete policies but also broader macroeconomic policies that may be subject to scrutiny and public discussion.

In the case of culture . . . lost traditions may be greatly missed. The demise of old ways of living can cause anguish, and a deep sense of loss . . . This is an issue of some seriousness, but it is up to the society to determine what, if anything, it wants to do to preserve old forms of living, perhaps even at significant economic cost . . . There is, of course, no ready formula for this cost-benefit analysis, but *what is crucial for a rational assessment of such choices is the ability of the people to partic-ipate in public discussions on the subject.* We come back again to the perspective of capabilities: that different sections of the society (and not just the socially privi-leged) should be able to be active in the decisions regarding what to preserve and what to let go. (241−42, my italics)

This point is also made by Appadurai who writes that "all internal efforts to cultivate voice among the poor (rather than loyalty or exit) in the context of any debated policy or project should be encouraged rather than suppressed or ignored. It is through the exercise of voice that the sinews of aspiration as a cultural capacity are built and strengthened, and conversely, it is through exercising the capacity to aspire that the exercise of voice by the poor will be extended" (Appadurai, this volume).

What this step requires is public discussion. This might take the form of a community meeting, or opinions on the newspaper and radio, or debates before elections, or large-scale consultations funded by a donor agency, or a dynamic relationship between social movements and elected officials, or some other place where people can form and improve their views.

These analyses seem to overlook the elements of power. What would be needed, one might ask, in order for heterogeneous publics to deliberate and decide these trade-offs without resorting to an oppressive majoritar-ianism or elite domination? This question is valid; however, let it not obscure the point of this section, which is to establish that the authority to judge trade-offs between alternative projects with complex implica-tions should *not* reside with the external agent.[8]

INFORMATION ON UNINTENDED CONSEQUENCES

Advocating explicit valuation and public debate takes for granted what cannot be taken for granted: that communities know the trade-offs they face. Although some cultural impacts may be surprises and sheer accidents (for good or ill), many are foreseeable. Sen argues that when "causal analysis can make the unintended effects reasonably *predictable*" (Sen 1999, 257), then these predicted effects should be identified and considered explicitly. What is odd is not this requirement so much as the silence on this issue by development agencies. Every field worker knows the difference between the city and the countryside; most have heard stories of how villages or neighborhoods have been transformed within one generation. Many even write up and publicize their case studies in glossy print for fund-raising purposes. Some call themselves "change makers." And yet the communities are not themselves dignified with so much as a forthright discussion of what is coming so that they can address the changes reflectively and protect what is most treasured. They are left to their own resources—which can be rather spry, even against all odds.

A case in point: there was an unusually mobilized community in the northern areas of Pakistan well into the Himalayas. Tourist hikers began to come and disrupt their way of life by their dress and habits. The community wished to welcome tourists and wanted the income they obtained from carrying their luggage up the mountains. So the elders identified and contacted the tour bus operators and informed them of a tourist dress code (no shorts or bare chests). They also came up with a local enforcement strategy: anyone who saw an underdressed tourist was not to confront him but rather to summon the English-speaking person in the community who would approach them respectfully, explain the situation, and lend them some clothes. Thus this community endeavored to enjoy the tourist business while maintaining their sense of propriety.

The informed participation approach entails that communities should know the alternative scenario and be informed sufficiently that they are able to judge trade-offs. They need this information in order to balance the different concerns they have and to maintain a local cohesion as necessary (it will not always be possible). There are a battery of participatory mechanisms for communicating these trade-offs at local and national levels. For example, Oxfam supports exchange visits between a community that is interested in a particular initiative (be it a breed of goat or a new crop) and a community that has recently adopted it. Field workers regularly tell stories late into the night of what happened in other communities (the good and the ill) or instigate role plays, acting out what people most want their grandchildren to remember. Formal meetings employ case studies or a panel of speakers from different backgrounds analyzing a society's future, or scenario-building or futures analysis presented by facilitators (in an accessible manner, one hopes). Yet remarkably few of these participatory mechanisms have been employed deliberately for the purpose of identifying cultural consequences of poverty-reduction activities explicitly.

INFORMATION ON THE PROBABILITY OF SUCCESS

Information on the likelihood that the proposed poverty-reduction activity will indeed realize the benefits it promises is a second crucial kind of information for informed choice.

"Probability of success" information can be precious if it is presented to decision makers who are trying to undertake the "explicit valuation" described above—between a universal primary education product (that they now know has a 25% to 30% chance of being realized within three years in the province) and some other capability contraction. Similarly, it could be helpful to know that a recommended policy regime has successfully controlled inflation in 35% of the cases in similar countries, and that at worst, and at best, these have been the actual outcomes.

Such information actually not only enables communities and societies to make more informed decisions, it also empowers them to understand more precisely the advice and authority of the technical advisors. Furthermore, if an institution supports informed participation—a small but important point—it is arguably necessary for its technical advisors to include in their briefing something about the limits of their expertise and of their product.

Some window salesmen claim that their windows will cure everything from draughts to sneezes to the brooding unhappiness of the family pet, and bully one into buying. Others brief one on the benefits and strengths of the company's windows, but also on their weaknesses in comparison with others on the market. If the buyer wished a different variety, the second salesman would cheerily suggest a reliable dealer (the first would try to change one's mind then express irritation as he packed up). In a similar fashion, the acquisition and sharing of existing analyses on the past record of similar poverty-reduction projects and policies could actually build trust and rapport and a shared attitude for problem solving and partnership.

SUSTAINABLE PLURALISM

Finally, informed participation has its own set of prerequisites. It can proceed only in certain social climates. When disagreements are more often resolved by violence than by vote; when dissensus is interpreted as disloyalty; when the majority will gladly dismantle minority cultures; when differences of opinion compete and plural views are not tolerated—then informed participation will not work, will do grievous harm, or will work only if carefully orchestrated with external support. Because social situations are usually spiced with strong personalities and power interests, informed participation will rarely unfold neatly. Cultural disagreements may heighten the need for stable pluralism because they tend to fall along passionately defended ethnic or religious borders. Many have dealt at length with managing power and value conflicts in participatory settings because these are basic and unavoidable in all participatory approaches and not simply those that concern cultural aspirations. But external actors can use their power actively to support power sharing, and in some cases are already doing so.

The requirements for pluralism may also at some times be diametrically opposed to informed participation. If a particular issue is too divisive, too volatile, too dogmatically held by one group or another, then the open-ended, multifaceted discussion of many views that characterizes informed participation may alienate some participants, solidifying disagreements or provoking explosive conflict. Thus informed participation itself cannot be evenly recommended without regard to the parent situation. Similarly, sometimes conclusions are easier to come to on very concrete plans (roads rather than the value of the imported magazines roads bring in); sometimes conclusions are only possible if the propositions are vague (Sunstein 1996).

The first section of this chapter caricaturized the focal problem as a trade-off between a projected poverty-reducing capability and changes in a cultural capability or set of capabilities. The second section argued that the appropriate response to this focal problem is a locally appropriate adaptation of informed participation by the persons concerned. Although these two sections were painted with a rather broad brush, this third section will argue that this broad-brush analysis is still sufficiently different from current Bank practice to identify needed changes: information provision and participation that evoke cultural aspirations.

The World Bank

The World Bank, whose mission is to fight poverty, wages this struggle by means of a heterogeneous arsenal of instruments that range from grant facilities and policy-based loans to projects, technical support, knowledge sharing, and training. Given the size of the institution, with over ten thousand workers, the size of the loans, which total $15 to $30 billion annually, the geographic spread of operations, the diversity of operations and research, the time, thoroughness, local knowledge, and rapport that is required to support culturally reflective decision-making processes such as informed participation seems distinctly out of reach. Furthermore, World Bank staff may be strongly involved with counterparts in project preparation and supervision but do not undertake day-to-day work with communities. This calls into question whether the development of such capacities would be an appropriate use of resources. But how *should* an actor of this scale address culture while supporting poverty reduction? Clearly, no single approach will address all issues satisfactorily, and the heterogeneity of the Bank would make a precise answer irrelevant. But it might be possible to identify a general strategy for proceeding.

STRATEGY

Most critics appear to argue that the Bank would be more culturally adept if it issued ten thousand sandals to its staff and sent them out to attune themselves to local cultures. But is this the most effective strategy?

Sunstein and Ullmann-Margalit (1997) discuss how institutions address recurring problems and decisions. Some institutions set up rules, routines, and standards. These procedures need a lot of planning and preparatory training in advance to set up, but then they can be implemented in a relatively straightforward manner. They name these high-low (high amounts of thinking in advance; lower amounts of thought at the moment of decision). Other procedures are easy to set up (for example, delegating a decision to a trusted associate) but require considerable effort on the part of the associate to address the problem or decision. These are called low-high. Finally, of course, low-low processes need little forethought and little effort, but may be high in mistakes (always pick the first option someone mentions; proceed slowly). The authors suggest that institutions should choose the level of procedure that will minimize two costs: the cost of making the decision, and the cost of making wrong decisions.

Goal = minimize [(costs of making decisions) + (costs of errors)]

For example, the Schumacher "small is beautiful" approach is of the low-high variety: development is delegated to committed agents, who expend considerable time, energy, shoe leather, and care in catalyzing positive changes in a local cultural environment. This is clearly the ideal, as is also articulated in various ways by other authors in this book. But would it be appropriate—or more to the point, feasible—for the World Bank?

Sunstein writes that a high-low mechanism is "appropriate when an agent faces a large number of decisions with similar features and when advance planning is especially important" (Sunstein and Ullmann-Margalit 1997, 4). The World Bank faces a "large number of decisions with similar features." For example, it tries to advance primary education programs among poor populations worldwide, and yet it must do so in different languages, in collaboration with different existing educational institutions, with different cultural understandings of childhood, different traditions of school attendance, different local histories. Advance planning is important to provide research findings on common issues (does education in local languages marginalize the poor or better equip them in later life?), as well as to set up multiyear, multistate programs. There may even be partially standardized ways of supporting culturally appropriate curricula, or of varying school hours and architectural designs. Bank-supported participatory exercises, such as the production of Poverty Reduction Strategy Papers, exemplify the high-low approach by preparing tool kits, standard procedures, and some standardized delegation to other agents. The World Bank's characteristic strengths and method of approach would, I argue, augur for a high-low approach.

This being said, as we will soon see, if the Bank's way of supporting informed participation is to set up broadly consistent information provision and participatory processes for decision making, this still implies that it must be flexible enough to respond to the demands that are identified by communities, and that the authority of local decision makers should not be summarily usurped by higher-level World Bank staff, as it so very often is.

Most advocates of culture argue that development institutions should become massive "small is beautiful" institutions, investing staff time very heavily in the adaptation of projects to sociocultural surrounds. Although this would be appropriate were it realistic, and in practice multiple approaches coexist within any institution, an intermediate high-low approach alone seems feasible for the World Bank.

SUPPORT ONGOING PUBLIC DEBATE

The Bank's rhetoric already supports participation. In the course of the 1990s, participation came to be supported to varying degrees within projects and within policy exercises, from the planning stage through to *ex post* evaluation.[9] Significant participation is now widely advocated, and some Bank projects achieve it. Many do not, as a recent internal evaluation of participatory processes showed.

However fewer, far fewer, participatory approaches explicitly scrutinize the overall "capability set" and raise issues of cultural aspirations, of longer-term goals and of the relative importance of noneconomic activities (that may be cultural), such as celebrations or faith traditions or family duties. For example, one of the fastest-growing strands of Bank project loans are community-driven development projects. In these projects, a large Bank loan is on-granted or on-loaned in very small sums to community groups. These groups identify their own requests, so long as they are not requests for liquor stores, firearms, religious objects, or a few other things. For example, some groups may take loans or grants for livestock; others for irrigation systems; others for sewing machines; and others for professional equipment like table saws or musical instruments. Periodically, the community may gather to discuss longer-term initiatives, such as roads or cemeteries. This is called an "open-menu" approach, in which the agenda is set from below, and it frames one very hopeful cutting edge of Bank work. Yet even this cutting edge does not provide space for communities to come together and talk about longer-term cultural changes, whether it be the excitement of travel and better communications, or dissatisfaction that a traditional craft is dying out. Such conversations happen, if they happen at all, on the margins.

Two high-low processes partly move in this direction and could be strengthened: the comprehensive development framework and the approach to indigenous people.

Comprehensive Development Framework

At the policy level, the Bank now requires and directly supports participatory discussions of coordinated long-term goals in a process known as the comprehensive development framework (CDF) and poverty reduction strategy programs (PRSPs). I will focus here on the CDF, but the conclusions would be similar for the PRSPs that have sought to codify some of the CDF principles and apply these to planning in low-income countries.

Since 1999, the Bank has begun to encourage countries to implement a CDF. The CDF was developed by the Bank's president, James Wolfensohn, and is based on the following principles:

- A long-term holistic vision of needs and solutions.

- Ownership by the country.

- Country-led partnership among internal and external actors.

- A focus on development results (Wolfensohn 1999).

Having completed CDF pilots in twelve countries, the Bank (2001c) published the following introduction to the approach, and because it embodies so much of the informed participation model, I will quote at length:

Fundamentally, the CDF is a means of achieving greater effectiveness in reducing poverty. It puts forward a holistic approach to development, which seeks a better balance in policymaking and implementation by highlighting the interdependence of all elements of development—social, structural, human, governance, environmental, macroeconomic, and financial (Wolfensohn 1999). This approach requires a transition from donor-led development assistance strategies to the development of a country strategy led by a country itself, with vigorous participation of government at all levels, including representative institutions, civil society and the private sector, and with the support of multilateral and bilateral organizations.

Although the CDF is a *potential* conceptual space for countries to address the multiple dimensions of poverty—and very importantly it raises issues of power and multidimensionality—it is unlikely to raise the cultural trade-offs we have discussed. For example, the CDF documents use a "matrix" to chart "each nation's development essentials." According to the CDF update, "each country will have its own unique priorities that should be included and become the focus of the matrix, as it evolves over time." But in this matrix, culture is raised only in the context of physical heritage sites. The CDF matrix that is the basis of participatory discussions does not raise, for example, perceived problems or negative trends from globalization or cultural aspects such Klamer's "capacity to be inspired," whether by one's work or the architecture of a new school. Thus, although the CDF has the potential to provoke discussion, it would require *reinterpretation* of the CDF process to institutionalize such a discussion and communicate the results in a way that they are considered seriously.

Informed Participation and Indigenous People

Within the World Bank, the operational directive (OD) on indigenous peoples already uses the language of informed participation. In 1982, the World Bank approved a policy for indigenous or tribal peoples (a revised policy was issued in 1991).[10] The *Operational Directive 4.20* (1991), relating to indigenous persons, contains guidelines that are applicable wherever cultural identity becomes important: to avoid negative impacts and to ensure culturally compatible social and economic benefits. For example, the OD requires that all Bank projects should respect persons' "dignity, human rights, and cultural uniqueness"[11] and that participation is to be "informed"[12]—which means that particular kinds of knowledge must be gained and/or shared with project participants. Particular attention to indigenous knowledge may increases project effectiveness.[13]

The OD's elaboration of informed participation is of particular interest: "The Bank's policy is that the strategy for addressing the issues pertaining to indigenous peoples must be based on the *informed participation* of the indigenous people themselves." The elements of informed participation are described in section 14 (on Indigenous People's Development Plans):

1. "Full consideration [must be made] of the options preferred by the indigenous people."

2. Participants must "anticipate adverse trends."

3. Local forms of "organization, religious beliefs, and resource use" must be respected.

4. "Production systems that are well adapted to the needs and environment of indigenous people" must be supported.

5. There must be "early handover of project management to local people."

6. There must be "long lead times."

7. "Incremental funding" (possibly) must be used.

The concept of informed participation in the Bank's OD on indigenous persons is very similar to the one proposed in this chapter. Although its implementation has been varied, it has had some remarkable successes. Indeed, Bank critic Jonathan Fox writes that "Here the Bank's paper policies become potential weapons for grassroots organizations. They . . . use the Bank's commitment to public information access and informed participation by indigenous peoples in policies that affect them as levers to open up space in their 500 years of struggle with the state" (Fox 2000, 6). Were the recommendations of this chapter to be undertaken, the high-low procedure at the project level would be an adaptation of this operational directive. But it should not be limited to indigenous peoples. People who are not indigenous also have culture and wider-than-economic values.

Thus, both the approach to indigenous projects and the CDF/PRSP processes could be developed to support ongoing and public debate. However, as was mentioned earlier, two additional kinds of information would be required.

INFORMATION ON CULTURAL TRADE-OFFS

One is information on what "capabilities" might contract. First, it would be necessary to research, anticipate, and share information on foreseeable cultural trade-offs. The cultural reverberations of poverty reduction interventions are vastly underresearched. The World Bank does not regularly investigate what Sen referred to as foreseeable if unintentional cultural changes that accompany poverty reduction policies and projects, except for a small set of changes along gender lines, and changes affecting an erratic sample of indigenous groups. Although the Bank invested a great deal of energy in producing a response to the antiglobalization groups' complaints against increasing inequality, the complaints about perceived cultural changes that globalization has brought were mentioned only in passing (World Bank 2002b, 128–30).

This might be considered a new competence, but similar activities have been under way for more than twenty-five years, pioneered by Michael Cernea, the Bank's first sociologist. He and other social scientists have developed World Bank procedures such as beneficiary assessments (developed by Larry Salmen 1995, 1999), participatory poverty assessments (Norton and Stephens 1995), social assessments (World Bank 1996), and social impact assessments. These procedures are supposed to evaluate the negative as well as positive social impacts of a planned change and mitigate negative social impacts. Hence, some attention is already being paid to these capability contractions.

Yet an unwillingness to share information is an issue that Bank critics still mention, despite the enormous progress that has been made. Cernea et al. carefully documented the Bank's inadequate "informing" of populations to be displaced by the Narmada dam. Within the last two years, "public information" regarding a Bank project was posted in Rajasthan in English rather than a local language. A prominent Bihari author wrote that, "'Information control' is the main weapon by which this development violence is perpetrated. . . . The fact is that the people whose lives and environment are to be affected have no clear prior information. Why is it treated as a military secret?" (Carter 2000, 60). Michael Horowitz gives an example that any discussion of an ongoing practice of slavery in Mauritania was omitted from the Bank's poverty assessment. When Horowitz commented on this omission, he "was told that such mention would be considered offensive by the Beydan elite that controls the Nauakchott regime, and the report would be rejected." Horowitz had a similar experience in Pakistan, where Bank social scientists objected to an identification by "caste" on the grounds that "its government might find this contentious" (Horowitz 1996, 5–6). Within the World Bank, David Ellerman argued without success that the World Bank could best foster informed participation by not taking an official position but rather airing the considerations for and against a range of defensible positions (Ellerman 2000).

Furthermore, the impacts identified by these social instruments do not necessarily pertain to the sphere of meaning and value that we have discussed. They tend to focus on very necessary but different issues of discrimination, displacement, and so on (Alkire 2002c).

INFORMATION ON THE PROBABILITY OF SUCCESS

In addition to information on trade-offs, the Bank's identity as a knowledge bank should be strengthened by including information on the probability of success of policies or projects. The World Bank, although it is praised for its *ex post* self-criticism by many critics, including Robert Chambers, does not regularly research or proactively communicate the probabilities of success (or failure) of poverty-reduction initiatives it supports *prior* to their implementation. This means that Bank clients are not able to judge how likely it is that a proposed policy or project will realize its goals exactly, and of the risks and error margins that surround estimations. Unlike the previous kind of information, the Bank *does* collect this information; it does not, however, disseminate it in a constructive fashion. If the Bank were to support informed participation, clients would receive this information.

For example, in 1981, Jeremy Swift observed, "A major World Bank livestock development project in Mali is based, for crucial calculations of sustainable grazing pressure, on the report of a highly competent ecologist in 1972; the calculations were redone in 1977/78 by a different, equally well-qualified ecologist, who halved the earlier carrying capacity. Nobody is to blame; the science is inexact. But the consequences could be disastrous for the project, and more so for the pastoralists involved" (Swift 1981, 487). On a larger scale, economists at the World Bank calculated the reestimated rates of return for over a thousand projects at the close of the project cycle and observed considerable discrepancy between the planned and realized benefit streams (Pohl and Mihaljeck 1992). The critical literature on the World Bank as well as its own evaluations of closed projects provide a litany of such examples where the "optimistic" projections of Bank staff bore little resemblance to what the projects or structural adjustment policies actually achieved (Caufield 1996). It would be helpful for communities to know how accurate benefit projections might be in their case.

Information, including information on the probability of success, is crucial to making informed decisions; it is coherent with the Bank's ongoing efforts to be a knowledge Bank, and its absence is certainly noticed.

AUTHORITY AND CULTURE OF THE WORLD BANK

Earlier I mentioned that the power issues of participatory discussions would not be treated in depth in this chapter because the way that power imbalances affect informed participation for culture and poverty does not significantly differ from how power imbalances affect a multitude of other development issues.

It cannot pass notice, however, that efforts to enlist the major development institutions and governments are stymied to the extent that they fall
upon persons who are accustomed to deference, and who retain power for
its own sake. Humility—which is essentially honesty about one's strengths
and limitations—is often regarded as a weakness, not a strength. So staff of
the World Bank (for example) at all levels are caught in the crosswinds of
conflicting incentives. On the one hand, they are chosen because of their
excellence, their intelligence, their ambition, their insightful commitment. On the other hand, they are not supposed to impose their good
ideas, their energetic motivation, their own visions. Rather, they are to
defer and support and empower others (who may seem less capable) and
help them walk by their own lights. These conflicting incentives are
difficult to manage. People who do this the best use a very different
method of operation from the "expert."[14] The dignity of such a supportive position might be more satisfactory if the alternative (providing accla-
mation and power to those with ambition who get things done their way)
were not so thoroughly rewarded. But it is.

Because the tensions between the "expert" and "enabler" are so great, it
may be worthwhile to signal that the Bank or any other institution's support
for informed participation *assumes* that the staff who facilitate such participation have the enabling approach. It assumes that they will communicate
information in a way that does not impose their own views; it assumes that
they will be astute enough to require a balanced group of "stakeholders" in
a participatory discussion, that facilitators will not allow it to be subverted
by an elite; it assumes that statisticians will have the honesty to present the
limitations of projected benefits, and task managers will have the composure
to let their project be rejected in favor of a more home-grown alternative
that people decide to try. These assumptions are fragile and regularly inaccurate. But informed participation will not work well unless they are met.

I have elsewhere argued—and would have liked to do so here as
well[15]—that informed participation is incomplete if it does not clarify
decision-making authority. At present the degree to which decisions
reflect participatory processes rests very significantly on the personality of
the people involved. For example, a handful of Bank staff and government
counterparts still have the de facto authority to decide almost anything
about "their" projects should they so choose—and use that authority. No
decisive authority is accorded to priorities developed by participatory
processes, even if these were widespread, democratic, and generated a
clearly preferred course of action. This lack of authority is clearly visible
in the Bank's *Empowerment Sourcebook*, which hopes that "participation"
will increase the "accountability" of decision makers.[16]

In view of the unfortunate wideness of that gap between those voicing their views and the actual decision makers, the World Commission on Dams required "free, prior, and informed consent" before the initiation of dams and other displacement-inducing development interventions. The term *consent*, in opposition to the more acceptable term *participation*, raises the key and topic of decision-making authority, which participatory processes should not avoid.

The Achilles heel of the "informed participation" paradigm as I have been able to sketch it is that many people could participate in discussions, could consider the trade-offs, could independently consult, reflect, and come to a value judgment regarding what they would like to do. Yet the World Bank or government or other development institution has the power and authority to choose to ignore their discussions. By keeping the "authority" of participatory discussions utterly unclear, the higher-level actors maintain the real power to impose whatever policies they wish. Hence, informed participation is not an effective check on the power of development institutions and their government counterparts, unless the authority of these decisions is clarified.

Conclusion

We began with the image of a passive rider on a runaway horse, and drew the connection between the runaway horse and externally assisted poverty reduction. For various reasons, including the disinterest in predicting cultural externalities, the need for simplifying assumptions of human behavior, and the fact that rigorous treatment of cultural impacts does not often fall within the decision makers' professional competence, cultural impacts of externally supported poverty reduction initiatives are normally disregarded. The boundaries of the problem are drawn so as to exclude them; the question of who is responsible for such effects does not seriously arise. Furthermore, in comparison with the other big issues of development—such as the impoverishment of certain population groups because of resettlement or development failures, or the violation of human rights, or the decimation of valued environments—culture seems a rather minor issue, a luxury to be dealt with after the big issues are worked out. So societies are assumed to be passive riders whose job is to hang on, not to guide poverty reduction energies to their preferred destination.

The sharp end of the question, to which this chapter has been directed, is not whether cultural changes have and will continue to arise and trouble communities deeply (a question that seems well enough answered in the positive), or what erroneous assumptions in standard theory cause them to be excluded, but, prospectively and normatively, what role can external actors such as the World Bank have in reducing poverty while supporting cultural aspirations? One suggestion is that the Bank support reflective participatory exercises (such as CDFs and indigenous people's projects). A second suggestion is that they provide information regarding the probability of success, and regarding foreseeable but unintended consequences on cultural practices. Finally, the authority of decisions that are made by informed participation should be binding, and the Bank should have a public procedure for dealing with situations in which these decisions are set aside or challenged.

The need for this information is not confined to cultural issues alone. Joseph Stiglitz, former chief economist at the World Bank, described these wider informational needs in an article entitled "Ethics, Economic Advice, and Economic Policy":

> One of the main activities of the international financial institutions is giving advice. In assessing the way that international financial institutions dispense advice, I feel that all too often they fall short . . . They push a particular set of policies, as loan conditionalities, rather than outline the range of policies and trade-offs and encourage the countries themselves to take responsibility for choosing among alternative policies. They fail to clarify the uncertainties associated with the policies they promote, making assertions about the policies' efficacy that cannot be supported by evidence. Most importantly, at least in the past, not only have they failed to pay due concern to the possible adverse effects of the policies on the poor, they have not even disclosed the likely risks. (Stiglitz 2001, 4–5)

This chapter proposes that development institutions and the advisors within them undertake their role differently, both in relation to poverty-related capabilities in general, and to cultural trade-offs in particular.

Notes

1. In the process of identifying culture-related information that is in Bank records, a delightful piece of Bank trivia emerged: of the 51 Bank documents published between 1969 and 1979 having the keyword *culture*, 46 of these referred to "fish culture" and only 5 to our cultures. The percentage increased somewhat in the next decade, in which only 35 of the 53 "culture" documents referred to fish. By the 1990s, humanity had finally taken the lead, with 82 of the 103 "culture" documents referring to human beings; fish netted a mere 21.

2. Elements of this view have been argued elsewhere (Anderson and Huber 1988; Bergensen and Lunde 1999; Blackburn and Holland 1998; Caufield 1996; Danahar 2001; Price 1989). Weiss substantiates and discusses the stylized fact that 25% of projects fail (Kirkpatrick and Weiss 1996). Even the World Bank's Strategic Compact, issued in 1997, contains as one of its four key elements "attention to issues of social and environmental sustainability" (point 15, p. iii). See also North (1993); and Cassen (1986).

3. There is a considerable literature on ethics and multiculturalism that is not

specific to development activities (Appadurai 1996; Arneson 2000; *Daedalus* 2000; Gasper 1996; Kymlicka 1995; Nussbaum 1998, 2000; Nussbaum and Glover 1995; Qizilbash 1996a,b; Sen 1997a,b, 1998a,b, 1999; Drèze and Sen 2002).

4. I have tried to discuss the basis and usefulness of such categories (Alkire 2002a,b).

5. Impact diagrams and rankings have been documented by the Asia Foundation and also in case studies of twenty-four Oxfam projects. It is diverting to record that the *men* of Pari Hari identified the most valuable impact to be the decrease in bickering among women! They also liked the fact that their daughters were taught cleanliness and courtesy.

6. Alkire (2002b) surveys some of the literature that tracks the range of human values in cross-cultural psychology, social indicators, and philosophy.

7. Of course there would also be trade-offs between different ways of realizing each category. "Art" might be realized by a trip to a modern art museum in the capital city, by a folkloric festival, or by a classical dance. People may have equally strong views *between* these alternatives as they have between alternative dimensions. Each of these trade-offs may at times be very important.

8. This does not mean that participation is always appropriate. For example, in decisions as to which technical plan to pursue when the side effects are limited, the technical experts should have a far greater say.

9. Participation is not new to the Bank operations, but historically the participation of primary stakeholders—individuals and community-based organizations that are directly affected by Bank activities—has been quite limited. That began to change in the late 1980s with the creation of the Bank's NGO team, which in December 1990 proposed creating the Participatory Development Learning Group (PDLG). The PDLG's September 1994 final report, endorsed by the Board, is the closest document the Bank has to a participation policy or strategy. The report concluded that "There is significant evidence that participation can in many circumstances improve the quality, effectiveness and sustainability of projects, and strengthen ownership and commitment of government and stakeholders" (World Bank 1994, i).

10. OD 4.20, for which a revision was also prepared in 1998–99. Other documents of note include *ILO Convention No. 169, Concerning Indigenous and Tribal Peoples in Independent Countries* (1989), and the *UN Declaration on the Rights of Indigenous Peoples*.

11. The quote is at point 6 and reads, "The Bank's broad objective towards indigenous people, as for all the people in its member countries, is to ensure that the development process fosters full respect for their dignity, human rights, and cultural uniqueness."

12. At point 8. See also Davis and Soeftesad (1995).

13. At 15(e). "Plans that draw upon indigenous knowledge are often more successful than those introducing entirely new principles and institutions."

14. David Ellerman (2002) has identified this position with increasing clarity and acuity.

15. Alkire (2002c, chap. 4). A previous draft of this chapter developed the framework of informed consent.

16. The definition of participation in that sourcebook does include the term *control*, but it is unclear how this control is to be exercised.

CHAPTER 10

Participatory Development: Where Culture Creeps In

ANITA ABRAHAM AND JEAN–PHILIPPE PLATTEAU

Introduction

Increasing dissatisfaction with the effectiveness and equity effects of aid programs, particularly in sub-Saharan Africa, has led major donors to reconsider their strategy for supporting development in poor areas. Low performances of national states convinced them that the new strategy ought to give an important role to local agencies, whether municipalities or communities. For the first time, officially, participation of beneficiaries came to be considered as the cornerstone of sustainable development. The underlying motive for this change of approach is rather straightforward: better than external agents, including the state and foreign organizations, beneficiary groups, such as rural communities, know the prevailing local conditions (such as who is poor and deserves to be helped, or the characteristics of the local microenvironment), and are able to monitor the activities related to interventions and to mitigate incentive problems (Hoddinott et al. 2001).

Given the considerable effort presently undertaken by many donor agencies to implement the participatory approach, the huge amount of resources involved, and the speed as well as the enthusiasm with which the new approach has been embraced, it is essential to take a critical view of the aforementioned advantages ascribed to local communities. Indeed, if participatory development is seen as a new magic pill that can cure most of the present ills, and if existing community imperfections are not properly taken into account, serious future disillusionments are unavoidable.

To take a critical view of the participatory approach, we need to probe into various aspects of the social and cultural fabric of the societies concerned. The purpose of this chapter is precisely to propose a cultural perspective on traditional rural societies with a view to gaining a better understanding of the pitfalls that may undermine community-based development. This will be done with special reference to the rural societies of sub-Saharan Africa (and other tribal societies in Asia and Latin America).

A cautionary remark is worth making at this preliminary stage. It is not because we adopt a critical standpoint that we are opposed to community-based development. In point of fact, we consider such an approach to be too important to be jeopardized by a precipitous and ill-thought implementation move that underestimates the complexity of the task and runs the risk of perverting participatory processes. Our critique is thus destined to provoke thinking so that the cost and time required to make decentralized development work are duly assessed. Note also that our diagnosis is grounded in personal experiences of involvement with community-based development as attempted by various nongovernmental organizations (NGOs) in sub-Saharan Africa. Because, unfortunately, freely accessible, written material reporting and evaluating such attempts in a satisfactory manner is hardly available, we believe that it is important to temper present-day excessive optimism about the short-run prospects of community-based development in the light of the field knowledge that we have personally accumulated over the past twenty years.

The outline of the chapter is as follows. First, we unfold the logic of traditional village societies by looking at various interdependent aspects of their functioning, starting from the simple fact that relationships among community members are highly personalized. The critical role of other-regarding and redistributive norms, as well as the presence of a strong authority pattern in tribal societies are emphasized. Next, we examine the problems that unavoidably arise when external values and objectives, the fulfillment of which is a condition of success of the new participatory approach, come into conflict with the local culture and socioeconomic structure. A distinction is made between rather traditional tribal communities and those that have gone through significant processes of socioeconomic differentiation. The experience of participatory development in Asia and Latin America becomes highly relevant for Africa when it comes to address the case of the latter rural societies.

Next, we draw attention to two important dilemma of participatory development. The first dilemma arises from a conflict between the need for sustained institutional support to communities, on the one hand, and the particular stakes of donor agencies, on the other hand. The second dilemma can be stated thus: for a participatory development to be successful, the active intervention of an effective state is required whereas the need for participatory development is greater when or where the state is actually weaker.

The Institutional Logic of Tribal Societies

PERFECT INFORMATION, PERSONALIZED RELATIONSHIPS, AND OTHER-REGARDING NORMS

Communities are dense networks of human relationships that ensure the easy circulation of information among members. In the context of continuous interactions, good information allows reputation effects and sanction mechanisms to operate which induce players to think of the long-term consequences of their present actions. In particular, the threat of ostracization acts as a powerful disciplining device. When interactions among people are close and continuous, they are inevitably characterized by a high degree of personalization. Such features are typically observed in close-knit village communities, yet are especially evident in tribal societies where the clustering of rural dwellings tends to be more dense than in the peasant societies of Asia and Latin America. One immediate implication is that the spheres of private and social life are not neatly separated as they are in modern societies based on wider and more anonymous interactions. As a consequence, any disagreement about a rule or a decision is bound to spill over into the sphere of private relations and to generate personal antagonisms. In the other way around, the wrangles that occur in the sphere of private relations are likely to percolate through to the social sphere where decisions may prove difficult to reach owing to the interference of ill feelings at the level of interpersonal relations.

This kind of situation creates pervasive opportunities for tensions, frustrations, and conflicts that are capable of poisoning the social climate prevailing in the community. Because interpersonal conflicts in small-scale settings can easily get out of control and threaten to undermine the social fabric of the community, mechanisms must be devised to prevent them from arising or to contain them as much as possible.

A central feature of lineage-based societies is that other-regarding values are inculcated in every individual from early childhood and carefully nurtured throughout his or her life—hence their characterization as "group-focused" societies by Albert Hirschman (1958). Individualistic proclivities are accepted only to the extent that they are considered as necessary for the advancement of the group as a whole (von Braun and Webb 1989; Sylla 1994; Ortiz 1967). Unlike what we find in the "Invisible Hand" doctrine, which is at the root of the market-based view of the economic system, the presumption is that the pursuit of individually selfish ends runs counter to the collective good in the general case. Evidence to the contrary must therefore be adduced before exceptions to this rule can be granted.

The emphasis on other-regarding values and codes of conduct is done not only on each and every possible moment of ordinary life but also under exceptional circumstances. Rituals and ceremonies in the course of which the unity and harmony of the group are strongly asserted and celebrated provide these exceptional moments (Godelier 1974). These are privileged occasions during which social norms and values stressing the collective good and the necessity for the individual to sacrifice his own self-interest for the benefit of the community are put in the foreground and intensely felt through dances, songs in unison, and the sharing of abundant food and drinks (Gyekye 1996). During such events, all participants are called upon to manifest regularly and openly their concern for the collective good and their willingness to contribute to it. To the extent that such internalization of other-regarding values through nurturing and rituals succeeds, any reference to self-centered considerations tends to be suppressed from consciousness (Polanyi and Pearson 1977; Wright 1994).

Internalization processes are never complete, however, and hence external reward and sanction mechanisms are needed to complement the work of collective rituals and education. Severe sanctions are thus meted out in case individuals promote their own interest at the presumed expense of the group. Among these sanctions, fear of public humiliation often plays an important role (Badini 1994). Another sanctioning mechanism consists of ideological beliefs regarding the causes and cures of illnesses, accidents, and other misfortunes. Unfortunate events that befall particular individuals are indeed ascribed to violations of other-regarding social norms that aroused the anger of supernatural powers overseeing human affairs. The implication is that more altruistic behavior must be followed to appease these powers and eventually cure the illness or prevent new accidents from occurring.

Finally, much attention and efforts are devoted by elders and specialized mediators to arbitrating and settling interpersonal conflicts so that they do not disrupt the social order of the community and undermine its collective activities and decision-making processes. Conciliatory attempts, repeated reminders of the group's tenets and values, and pressing invitations to behave reasonably, compensatory payments, and judgments allowing all the parties involved to save face play an important role in traditional village societies, especially in the tightly knit societies based on lineage. Face saving is an essential characteristic of conflict settlement insofar as people are expected to live continuously in close contact with each other. If resentment and frustrations are not adequately tamed or suppressed, there is a serious risk that pent-up interpersonal tensions will one day reemerge and perhaps erupt into overtly aggressive acts. Yet in case soft methods do not succeed, beating and fining the culprits may be the ultimate way to bring them back to their senses (Bourdieu 1990). Sheer demonstration of force is then resorted to by the persons endowed with the required status and power.

The above is a good description of the formation and maintenance of preferences in traditional lineage-based societies. In other agrarian societies where class differentiation is marked (the so-called peasant societies), many of the aforementioned mechanisms are also at work even though they are typically not as effective. The following characterization, which applies to Japanese village communities of the Tokugawa era, can be readily extended to other peasant societies of Asia and Latin America:

Tensions were more quickly and intimately felt, but overt expression of them was more resolutely suppressed in favor of an appearance of community harmony—and they were the more explosive for that reason. Deep beneath the everyday appearance of propriety and friendliness there were in many Japanese villages suppressed hatreds that merely needed some shock, some momentary lapse of customary restraint, to send them boiling to the surface. Perhaps it had always been this way; perhaps when the village had been more tightly knit and harmonious the secret antagonisms had gone even deeper and been more powerful. But if so they had also been more effectively suppressed, and it was only as village organization loosened that they were given vent. (Smith 1959, 172)

PERSONALIZED RELATIONSHIPS AND REDISTRIBUTIVE NORMS

Whenever issues of wealth distribution arise, other-regarding values and social norms prescribing other-regarding behavior assume special importance. As a matter of fact, when people continuously interact in close proximity to each other, they have a spontaneous inclination to look at the situation of their neighbors or acquaintances to assess their own situation. Invidious comparisons are thus a constant feature of small groups and tightly knit societies. When social and economic differentiation is low, such as is observed in tribal societies, such comparisons by arousing jealous and envious feelings create a highly charged emotional climate that can easily lead to serious conflicts and eventually to the implosion of the group itself. To counter such an ominous threat, these societies do not rely only on other-regarding values and associated preferences, but they also have recourse to strictly applied redistributive norms that enjoin enriched individuals to share their surplus with their brethren. This is done on the ground that solidarity is the cement which ties all the members of the community together and enables them to survive in the long run. As one old Bosnian saying goes: "If the whole society is prosperous, each of its members gains from it, but when one individual is too powerful, he harms his fellow members, whether he likes it or not. When a hand is too big, swollen and painful, it is because it has been bitten or invaded by bad spirits. In order to restore the health of the hand's owner, the swelling must be reduced or the hand will need to be cut off" (Karahasan 2000, 191, our translation).

As a rule, generosity and hospitality are highly praised behaviors in traditional rural communities, and successful individuals therefore gain social prestige and esteem when they redistribute their surplus. A careful look reveals two mutually reinforcing motives that drive individuals to put pressure on successful individuals to share. First, if a prosperous individual were allowed to stop making gifts to fellow villagers, the size of the informal insurance network formed by the community would be reduced, and the group's ability to spread risks would be correspondingly diminished. Private wealth accumulation is perceived as an antisocial behavior because it is an attempt to break away from traditional solidarity networks (Fafchamps 1992; Platteau 1991). Here are "levelling societies, in which attempts by equals to gain individual advantage are constantly suspected and bitterly resented" for "fear that the fundamental security of the village will slowly be lost if one individual after another can reach a platform of prosperity from which he might not need the help of the community and could therefore excuse himself from helping them" (Hunter 1969, 40).

"Forced mutual help," as Raymond Firth (1951) has called it, is then used to maintain the status quo, which has the potential effect of discouraging exceptional individual performances on the grounds that they can only take place "at the expense of other members and of the cohesiveness of the group" (Hirschman 1958, 23). Mutual help is forced unless dynamic individuals are interested in gaining the social prestige accompanying wealth redistribution (for a modern example of this, see Platteau and Seki 2001).

The second motive underlying social norms of sharing is the following: because the effort of any individual to improve his lot generates positional externalities that negatively affect the welfare of fellow villagers, redistributive norms that enjoin economically successful individuals to share their surplus appear as a form of taxation designed to curb positional race for status. In other words, the presence of sharing norms prevents a chain reaction of emulating efforts from being triggered off. This is a happy outcome insofar as efforts to improve one's lot are mutually offsetting and inefficient equilibria arise precisely because investment in status enhancement is more attractive individually than collectively (Frank 1995, 1998; Congleton 1980).

That the insurance-based explanation is insufficient to account for sharing norms in tribal societies is evident from the fact that the hierarchy of ranks may not be called into question. Typically, while one of their functions is to redistribute wealth toward the needy, the chief or the elders do not accept that commoners rise above them by acquiring old or new symbols of wealth and status (like cocoa plantations, mechanical devices, or roofs made of corrugated iron). All efforts to accumulate such symbols are unavoidably viewed as conscious attempts to compete with traditional leaders and to overturn the existing social order. As a consequence, they are strongly condemned, and the prosperous commoner is immediately coerced into handing over to the chief his newly acquired riches (Geschiere 1994).

Tribal communities thus appear as societies prone to resist any differentiation process whereby relative status positions are modified. Social reshuffling is actually perceived as a dangerous force capable of jeopardizing the fragile social equilibria typical of small-group societies based on highly personalized relationships. As hinted at above, the prevailing redistributive norms are often backed by powerful sanctions that include social pressures, constant harassment, and the use of effective mechanisms of ideological intimidation, most notably witchcraft accusations and practices. Witchcraft accusations are especially threatening when they are based on the allegation that economic success of a particular individual is the result of some hidden and treacherous exploitation of fellow villagers (Evans-Pritchard 1937, 1940; Platteau and Hayami 1998). Although transient or ordinary luck is believed to result from the normal course of natural events, persisting or exceptional luck is attributed to the obscure and ill-intended manipulation of supernatural forces, a very serious misgiving inasmuch as such manipulation is perceived to be thwarting others' projects and even jeopardizing the survival of the entire social group (Elster 1989; Platteau 2000).

In accordance with what has been said above, accusations of sorcery are not only professed by villagers against a prosperous individual of similar rank, but they are also used by traditional authority figures against any maverick who dares challenge the erstwhile hierarchical structure (Peters 1994). Of course, witchcraft accusations against social superiors are excluded (Evans-Pritchard 1964).

THE AUTHORITY PATTERN

A rigid hierarchy of ranks, based on age, gender, and lineage, prevails in many tribal societies. At the top of the hierarchy, the council of elders typically comprises old men belonging to the dominant lineages, foremost among which is the lineage descending from the man who cleared the bush and founded the village. The chief is usually taken from that founding lineage. Moreover, legitimacy of power comes from supernatural agents (the ancestors, gods) who are assumed to be in charge of the day-to-day affairs of the community, seeing to it that order and prosperity prevail. The elite of the society, whether chiefs, notables, or priests, constantly seek advice from the ancestors and gods, and they interpret this advice for the group.

A direct consequence of the supernatural source of their legitimacy is that their actions may neither be called into question nor be susceptible of any sanction or punishment. Because the council of elders embodies the will of supernatural agencies (the ancestors' souls), lower people are inclined to believe that their decisions and rulings have an incontrovertible force. And if they would nonetheless feel that the elite are erring in their judgments or abuse their power, they have no choice but to comply. It is out of the question for them to speak out their possible disagreement, and out of fear of retribution, they may pay lip service to decisions or rules that they do not like.

Another consequence of the supernatural legitimacy of the elders' power is that no open disagreement can arise between them. Any disagreement among the elite is bound to cause serious suspicion about its ability to represent, or act on behalf of, the ancestors who supposedly share a common view about how human affairs should be run. Moreover, as mentioned above, disagreements in the public domain unavoidably percolate to the sphere of private relations and thereby threaten social peace. A way must therefore be found to prevent open manifestation of internal splits within the power elite and to contain or reduce disagreements.

Consensus-seeking procedures provide the required solution. They imply that the viewpoint of everyone is attentively listened to and that all elite members come to adopt a common position however long is the time needed. It is in the course of interminable, never-ending discussions (the "palabres") that opinions or attitudes are being slowly transformed so as to ensure better convergence between initially differing standpoints. And because communication helps modify preferences and beliefs, no one among the elite is asked to act against his own belief. The risk is therefore avoided that an elite member violates a rule or a decision because he does not feel tied by it. Here are the fundamental reasons why the principle of majority voting is not deemed acceptable in close-knit societies: because it would make official the existence of disagreements, and because the minority would thereby feel justified in behaving as it likes, such a principle is perceived as a potential threat both to the effective enforcement of rules and decisions and to the continuation of amicable relations on which the reproduction of the group depends so critically.

Insofar as the notion of democracy presupposes the possibility of dissent and the peaceful handling of divergent opinions and behaviors, one can safely say that it is alien to the societies under consideration. In effect, the democratic concept is not straightforward because it implies that one is ready to act according to the will of the majority and not necessarily according to one's own belief or perceived self-interest. To be established, it therefore requires the development of a sense that social order cannot exist in its absence. The fact of the matter is that in small groups or communities, it is possible to establish social order with the help of unanimous agreement that is the most natural way to proceed. In larger and more complex societies, this rule is no more feasible for obvious reasons, and people have to learn that continued adherence to it will unavoidably lead to social chaos and its most obvious outcome, dictatorship.

Finally, systematic recourse to voting through a show of hands is another striking characteristic of decision-making procedures in lineage-based societies. The rationale for this method has to be seen in conjunction with the above-described logic of the unanimity rule. Indeed, because the purpose of the discussion is to reach unanimous agreement and to have all participants tied by the expression of their personal consent, secret balloting is unacceptable. The vote is actually a public commitment made in front of witnesses, and as such, it must be manifested in the most unambiguous manner.

The Participatory Approach Under Test in Tribal Societies

Rather than idyllic "village democracies" whose members interact in a free atmosphere of trustful cooperation, tribal societies appear as strongly structured entities based on powerful socialization processes stressing the welfare of the group at the expense of the individual, where mutual control is constantly exercised, individual initiative and capital accumulation tend to be repressed, suspicions are continuously entertained about others' intentions, jealousies, rivalries, and interpersonal conflicts are pervasive, and a rigid rank-based hierarchical structure governs peoples' lives. In an environment fraught with production and other types of risks, rural dwellers have no other choice than to accept this constraining social arrangement to be able to survive in the short and the long run.

Insofar as the participatory approach to development aims at channeling substantial amounts of resources to communities considered as levers of economic growth, democratic accountability, and equitable distribution of wealth, a problem unavoidably arises. In keeping with the analysis proposed above, various facets of this problem are discussed and illustrated below.

PROBLEMS ARISING FROM THE GROUP-FOCUSED IDEA OF CHANGE

For Hirschman, the world image congenial to genuine economic development is the so-called group- and ego-focused idea of change—that is, the idea that "the individual can advance at his own speed within an expanding economy" without obstructing the progress of other people. This modern ideology cannot be imposed *ex abrupto*, and it "is likely to be adopted only after a considerable span of experience has convincingly shown the possibility of such a development" characterized by all-around growth and mutual benefits (Hirschman 1958). In other words, traditional images of change, themselves largely the product of constraints and material determinants that characterized these societies for a long time, will remain a critical bottleneck of constructive action for economic development until experience modifies them in the appropriate direction. A culture built on a worldview incompatible with modern economic growth cannot instantaneously evolve to suit the needs of an environment of changing individual aspirations and new economic opportunities.

Various sorts of problems can arise from the persisting influence of a group-focused image of change. If participatory development takes place through rural communities acting as decentralized decision-making bodies endowed with considerable allocation responsibilities, there is a serious risk that the available resources will be spread thinly over many people and projects. Priority setting will therefore be eschewed and efficiency considerations may easily be sacrificed in order to satisfy all members of the community, or, at least, those who matter (Drijver and van Zorge 1995), who speak about the utmost concern of villager groups in northern Cameroon that "the others should not benefit more than them."

If the external agency that supplies the funds specifies guidelines or instructions as to how they ought to be disbursed and used by the communities, or if participatory development involves channeling resources directly through beneficiary groups rather than through community institutions, those who feel excluded tend to react by exercising pressure on the beneficiaries so that they redistribute the benefits of the external intervention. In case this pressure is ineffective, they may go as far as sabotaging the projects selected. Such outcomes may happen not only when some groups are favored within a given community but also when a community itself is given precedence over other communities in the access to development resources—for example, on account of the greater extent of its needs. Thus, the economic success of the inhabitants of Kalengera along Lake Kivu (Republic of Congo), who on account of their relative poverty had received priority access to a new gill net technology supplied by a development project, has been deeply resented by the inhabitants of neighboring villages. To express their frustration and anger, the latter did not hesitate to steal gill nets from the beneficiaries, as well as other equipment and goods from the project premises. Even more tragically, some of them went so far as systematically catching juvenile fish with the apparent purpose of sabotaging the (future) productive performance of gill net operators, regardless of the cost entailed for themselves. By acting thus, "they believed that they will one day succeed in emptying the lake of its entire fish stock and thereby block the progress of gill net owners." As a result, the project's beneficiaries would be compelled to abandon their contemptuous attitude vis-à-vis their brethren and the project's staff would be compelled to correct the injustice they had committed by favoring a special segment of the local fishing population (Melard, Platteau, and Watongoka 1998).

PROBLEMS ARISING FROM PERSISTING TRADITIONAL PATTERNS OF AUTHORITY

More serious than the above redistributive pressures (after all, the group-focused ideology may be helpful when efficiency losses are small compared to equity gains) is the negative impact resulting from the existence of a stratum of chiefs and notables whose status and power are reflected in a greater amount of material possessions. To protect their status and power, traditional elites are ready to oppose any disturbing outside intervention. There are innumerable instances attesting that they frequently claim priority access to new resources brought by development programs. If their request is not satisfied, they attempt to appropriate the coveted assets by force or by guile, and if this strategy does not succeed, they do not hesitate to sabotage the external intervention by inciting community members to boycott it.

For example, in Canhabaque (Bijagos Islands, Guinea Bissau), dynamic youths were targeted by an NGO to receive training and fishing assets with a view to better exploiting the surrounding fish resources. Yet the local traditional king could not agree with the fact that young members of his community received boats, nets, and engines when he himself had to go without them. All the attempts to enlist the youths into the project and transform them into independent professional fishermen met with passive resistance. The only individual who dared challenge the king's authority by keeping his equipment and operating it productively had to leave the island and resettle on the continent (personal field observations).

In Yalogo, in the northeastern part of Burkina Faso, a women's group acquired a mill through the support of another NGO, yet it was soon confiscated by the local chief. That, in this instance, the mill was conceived by him as a status symbol rather than as a productive asset was evident from the fact that it was lying unused in his backyard. All the efforts undertaken to get the mill back and return it to the intended beneficiaries proved unavailing.

In the same area, irrigated rice cultivation was introduced and villagers were asked to organize themselves into village-level peasant associations in order to manage the irrigation schemes (maintenance of water-control infrastructure, collective purchase of modern inputs, collective disposal of produce, and the running of a credit scheme). In doing this, they were required to elect an executive committee composed of a chairman, a secretary, and a treasurer. As the NGO soon discovered, the local chief was systematically chosen to act as the chairman of each association. Moreover, in the only village for which detailed information was available regarding the internal functioning of the local association, it appeared that all important decisions were made by the chief without consulting the members and the other persons in charge. The secret character of some of his dealings aroused serious misgivings about his honesty—in particular, his refusal to disclose the names of the persons to whom he claimed to have granted loans, as well as the amounts and repayment terms involved. Such an attitude was all the more detrimental to association members because the loans have never been repaid.

Another serious problem arose from the fact that the chief decided to sell the rice produced in the irrigation scheme to a trader who turned out to be his own brother and who tried to cheat the farmers by underpaying them (setting purchase prices at levels much below the current market prices). Revealingly, the chief was unable or unwilling to compel his brother to pay the farmers their dues in spite of the latter's grumbling. When asked why they did not react by removing their mischievous chairman, the members' typical answer is that such a step is inconceivable precisely because he is their chief.

As the last above example shows, insofar as it aims at promoting the values of equality and democracy, the participatory approach to development runs into major obstacles that result from the persisting influence of traditional patterns of authority. In particular, that the chairman of an association can be freely chosen among its members, that the most competent should be the most liable to be elected, and that an incompetent, ineffective, or corrupt leader should be removed from his responsibility position are all ideas still difficult to accept in many tribal societies. Also problematic is the idea that the same rules and the same sanctions should apply to all members, irrespective of their personal identity and their place in the local sociopolitical hierarchy. As a matter of fact, the associated logics of ascriptively fixed status and power positions and of particularistic ethics and unequal treatment of different people continue to hold in the minds of both the elite and the common people. Following the first logic, competence criteria are not allowed to guide the choice of leaders and office holders, whereas, following the second logic, privileges and rights, duties and obligations, sanctions and awards are neatly differentiated in accordance with positions occupied in the social matrix.

By imposing rules and institutions embodying modern values of democratic governance, protection of the poor, as well as transparency of decisions and accounts, the participatory approach to development operates a disjunction between the patterns of behavior that people have always experienced in most sectors of their life, on the one hand, and those which they are expected to follow within the ambit of a decentralized program, on the other hand. Under the latter, formal rules and general principles are adopted that reflect the objectives pursued by the participatory approach (for example, democratic election and voting mechanisms, division of labor between chairman and treasurer, accountability of the executive committee before the general assembly of members, predefined accounting procedures and reports, use of competence-based criteria for the selection of office holders, uniform treatment of members), yet in actual practice, they are being ignored, circumvented, or subverted. For example, how can a youngster talk on an equal footing with an elder in a meeting of a participation-minded village association while he simultaneously has to address himself to the leader respectfully and humbly as soon as he steps out of the meeting? And could the elder who has always been accustomed to deference accept such a shift in behavior?

To the extent that subversion of the above rules and principles is the result of a sheer failure to grasp their meaning and requirements, it cannot be considered as a deliberate attempt to undermine the new approach. The fact of the matter is that, rather than the general society being influenced by the institutional experience of a decentralized program, people tend to behave in the new institutional setup according to norms and patterns prevailing in the general society: primacy of personal relationships and loyalty to kith and kin, particularistic ethics, respect of traditional authority and its status symbols.

SOCIOECONOMIC DIFFERENTIATION AND EXCLUSION OF THE POOR

In the above analysis, we have considered the case of tribal societies that have not been exposed (yet) to new market opportunities (often as a result of physical isolation) and have therefore undergone only low levels of socioeconomic differentiation. In some parts of Africa (for example, the northern Guinea Savanna in northern Nigeria), however, market penetration and the availability of new technologies have brought about increasing levels of differentiation. Typically, the new entrepreneurial elite has arisen from the womb of the chieftaincy, including the educated groups that have often been coopted by the colonial powers. Precisely because they come from the traditional elite, these new entrepreneurs are able to shake off the old structure and, in particular, to call customary redistributive norms into question.

They tend to devote a growing part of their energies to the pursuit of private wealth accumulation, and in the process, they evade their erstwhile mission of assuming responsibility for keeping the forces of individualism in check and thereby preserving stability of the social order. If they keep on making transfers to the common people, it is important to see that the logic is different from the one prevailing in traditional tribal societies. As a matter of fact, the beneficiaries of such transfers are a limited segment of the community that now comes to form a particular clientele with special economic and other obligations toward the new self-seeking capitalist elite. In other words, what we witness is the gradual emergence of a patron–client system (Platteau 2000, 216–21; and, for a particular illustration documenting the rise of marabouts in Senegal, Cruise-O'Brien 1971; Boone 1992).[1]

When socioeconomic differentiation has proceeded far enough, the problems encountered by the participatory approach to development are somewhat different from those that we have discussed above. To see this, we consider two types of situations. In the first situation, village associations or more restricted groups are given external resources for some predetermined purposes, whereas in the second situation, communities are left free to make important allocation decisions.

First, it is in the logic of participatory development that funds are channeled through communities with a view to enabling them to construct social and economic infrastructures. At the same time, it is taken for granted that communities will show their willingness to "own" their projects by providing operating funds and carrying the burden of infrastructure maintenance. In short, through their active involvement, communities are expected to make the projects concerned sustainable. However, what the evidence shows, whether it relates to Africa or to Asia and Latin America, is that communities often do not meet these expectations, or when they meet them, they do it in such a way that the poor are excluded.

An illustration of the former possibility is provided by the Philippines, where the National Irrigation Administration has been pioneering efforts of devolution, and where, contrary to expectations, there have been more cases of failure than success. Indeed, reduction in state agencies' operation and maintenance activities has not been compensated for by the activities of irrigators' associations, with alarming consequences for agricultural production (Fujita, Hayami, and Kikuchi 1999; Landes 1998). As an example of the latter possibility, think of the well-documented cases of health and education projects that do not eventually benefit the poor. This is because when the community is confronted with the task of ensuring the proper functioning and the regular maintenance of the social infrastructures (including the payment of decent salaries to the teachers or the health staff in order to keep them motivated), it has to require from the beneficiaries the payment of appropriate fees and contributions. Because the poor cannot afford such payments, they gradually drop out of these projects, which were initially intended for the benefit of the whole community (Swantz 1997; Tendler 2000). In this case, clearly, the poor are deprived of the benefits of decentralization owing to a process of self-selection that operates to their disadvantage.

If the maintenance and functioning expenses are sufficiently low, and if the rich internalize a large portion of the benefits accruing from the establishment of a new infrastructure (say, because they own much land in an irrigation system, or many boats anchoring at a jettee), instead of being the victims of a process of self-exclusion, the poor may actually see their incomes increase as a result of significant wealth disparities. In these conditions, indeed, the rich have an incentive to supply the leadership, and bear the associated organizing costs, required to construct the local public good and carry out the repair and maintenance tasks (Baland and Platteau 1998, 1999). Even when the above two conditions are met, however, the benefits of the poor ought not to be taken for granted. Thus, if the rich enjoy the advantages of a strategic location because they have succeeded in getting hold of the best lands, the interests of the poor are likely to be neglected. This is particularly evident in the case of an irrigation system. If the parcels of the rich are located near its head end, close to the water-control works, while those of the poor are found near its tail end (and are usually not well leveled), repair and maintenance efforts will be concentrated on the best-situated portion of the irrigated area, and the flow of the water will be directed mainly to this portion, especially in times of scarcity (Wade 1988).

Second, when the external agency devolves to communities the task of allocating budgets to projects to which they choose to give priority, or when the purposes for which the money is to be used are fixed but the identity of the beneficiaries or the methods to achieve the objectives are to be decided by the communities, the problem of collective decision making arises in the context of socioeconomic inequality. Because of large wealth disparities, there is likely to be divergence of interests among community members when such choices have to be made. What will then happen depends in particular on whether inequality in wealth or income is also associated with an asymmetry in the distribution of voting power.

Under a first scenario, where all people, rich and poor, have an identical voting power, there is a serious possibility that economic inequality will prevent members of the village association from reaching a satisfactory agreement. For example, it has been shown by Baland and Platteau (1998, 1999) that, under such an assumption of equal voting power, wealth or income inequality complicates the reaching of an agreement about more effective ways to manage village-level common-property resources. More precisely, because regulatory instruments are often imperfect, being limited to uniform quotas or constant tax rates, they cannot be tailored to the particular situation of each resource user, implying that they will have to be calibrated for average characteristics. As a consequence of this constraint (and the impossibility of compensatory transfers), if we require the collectively regulated management of the village resources to result in greater efficiency, it is more likely to hurt the interests of some users, and therefore to be opposed by them, if inequality among users is larger.

In the more realistic scenario where the voting power is asymmetrically distributed, the rich use their leverage to impose on others a solution that meets their own interests. They may even decide to participate in a collective action with a view to influencing it in a direction suitable to their private needs. From evidence pertaining to Latin America and Asia, it is thus evident that village-level elites tend to appropriate for themselves whatever portion of the resources that they need and to let the poor have the leftovers only (Galasso and Ravallion 2000). The advantages of community-based (welfare) programs—namely, the better knowledge of local conditions that communities possess, and their better ability to enforce rules, monitor behavior, and verify actions (Hoddinott et al. 2001)—can therefore be outweighed by the accountability or "capture" problem—communities may not be as accountable to their poor as state agencies. The poor are then better targeted through a state distribution system than through a decentralized mechanism (Bardhan and Mookherjee 1999, 2000a,b).

To exercise their power, the rich need not necessarily have recourse to intimidation or other forms of more or less overt coercion over poorer members, particularly their clients. Their greater influence on the allocation decisions may thus be the natural consequence of the fact that they can pose themselves as the benefactors of the community because they have played a critical role in obtaining the new resources. The economic elite typically enjoy privileged relations with key persons in funding agencies (official or private), thanks to their wealth, education, and exposure to the outside world through work, schooling, and other experiences. Their leverage may manifest itself in their ability not only to get external funds but also to influence the purposes for which these funds are granted to their community. In these conditions, the potential problem of interest divergence among members is eliminated even before the funds reach the village.

All this, it should be remarked, does not prevent poor people from drawing some benefits, however small compared to those obtained by the rich, from programs of decentralized development. Precisely because of such Pareto-improving outcomes, poor people may feel sufficiently rewarded to be inclined to give their support to the rich patrons, whom they believe are behind what they perceive as favors granted to them. In a context where the ability to deal with external sources of funding is concentrated in a small elite group, the bargaining strength of common people is inevitably limited, and hence their ready acceptance of highly asymmetric patterns of distribution of programs' benefits. The situation is akin to a ultimatum game in which the elite have the right to make a proposal about how to divide a pie that would be lost in the event that no agreement would be reached with the other villagers. As we know, the predicted equilibrium outcome of such a game is a division that gives a trifle amount to the latter, who are deprived of any leverage because they cannot make the first move.

Also worthy of emphasis is the following fact: the ability of the rich, in overt or covert, direct or indirect ways, to make their own preferences prevail over those of economically weaker people may or may not impair efficiency. The latter possibility is illustrated by Banerjee et al. (1999) in their study of sugar cooperatives in Maharashtra. There, they reach the conclusion that the weight of wealthy and influential users in collective decision making tends to distort collective regulation toward their interests at the cost of efficiency. Their empirical estimates show that distortions (and inefficiency) in collective regulation tends to be highest when inequality is high among users. Likewise, a number of empirical studies of irrigation schemes in developing countries conclude that higher inequality in landholdings (or farm income) tends to reduce the overall level of maintenance, even though it simultaneously induces larger agents to support a bigger share of the collective costs (Tang 1992; Dayton-Johnson 1998; Bardhan 2000).

Two Central Dilemmas of Participatory Development

THE CONFLICT BETWEEN THE NEED FOR SUSTAINED INSTITUTIONAL SUPPORT AND THE STAKES OF DONOR AGENCIES

A key problem today arises from the fact that most donor agencies, including governments from developed countries, are rushing to adopt with a lot of enthusiasm the so-called participatory approach to development. In order to persuade their constituencies or supporters that the new strategy works well, they need rapid and visible results. Moreover, they have sizable financial resources at their command that they want to disburse within a short time. The temptation is great to spread them widely so as to reach as large a number of village communities as possible. As should now be evident from the previous discussion, especially that pertaining to lowly differentiated tribal communities, such a rush is problematic insofar as communities need to evolve and be institutionally strengthened if they are to achieve the objectives of the participatory approach: economic growth, democratic governance, sustainability, equity, and protection of the poor. The risk is then high that the decentralization approach will be subverted and deflected from its intended purpose.

Confronted with such a hard dilemma, donor agencies have the tendency to maintain their "diluted" approach, which implies that they downplay the task, and minimize the cost, of institutional support to target communities. It is revealing, for example, that lack of capacity building, especially the building of organizational skills at community level, and lack of "ownership" of the projects by the beneficiary groups, are among the main limitations of the World Bank's social funds program. As a consequence, the program remains too much driven by a supply-led approach rather than being responsive to the needs of rural people, as a participatory approach should be (Narayan and Ebbe 1997; Tendler 2000).

In addition, when strong local communities or organizations do not exist or when the required leadership is not available, there is a big temptation to ask communities or specific groups within them to "elect" leaders. For a reason well explained by Esman and Uphoff (1984), however, such a solution is bound to produce perverse results and to be self-defeating:

> The most prominent members are invariably selected and then given training and control over resources for the community, without any detailed and extended communication with the other members about objectives, rights, or duties. Creating the groups through these leaders, in effect, establishes a power relationship that is open to abuse. The agency has little or no communication with the community except through these leaders. The more training and resources they are given, the more distance is created between leaders and members. The shortcut of trying to mobilize rural people from outside through leaders, rather than taking the time to gain direct understanding and support from members, is likely to be unproductive or even counterproductive, entrenching a privileged minority and discrediting the idea of group action for self-improvement (249)

If acting through local leaders enables outside agencies to channel considerable amounts of resources toward rural communities in a short span of time, it increases the probability of misuse of these resources by local elites that stand reinforced in the process. In lineage-based societies, local chiefs and elders from dominant lineages are ideally positioned to thus capture the benefits of decentralized development programs or projects. As noted above, instead of father figures clinging to their traditional duties of guaranteeing people's livelihoods, redistributing wealth and settling conflicts in such a way as to maintain the existing social order, the erstwhile elite become greedy individuals who show all the less restraint in enriching themselves at the expense of their community as they are actually legitimated by outside actors.[2] By virtue of their dominant position, they can thus manipulate participatory methods by subtly representing their own interests as community concerns expressed in the light of project deliverables (Mosse 2001; Platteau and Abraham 2002). In Senegal (in the Petite Côte and Casamance, in particular), for example, municipal bodies or rural councils used the new prerogatives accorded them under the decentralization scheme to get involved in dubious dealings such as sales of rural lands to tourist and other business interests without consulting the communities concerned, as they should have done.

The traditional elite are not the only category of persons to benefit from the newly channeled resources because they are frequently involved in tactical alliances with educated persons and politicians operating outside the village domain. In actual fact, the urban rather than the rural elite may be responsible for initiating the process that deflects the participatory development program from its intended purpose. Witness to it is the rapid

multiplication of national NGOs that are created at the initiative of educated unemployed individuals, politicians, or state employees who may
have been laid off as a result of structural adjustment measures. These people, acting as "development brokers," have been quick to understand that
the creation of an NGO has become one of the best means of procuring
funds from the international community (Bierschenk, de Sardan, and
Chauveau 2000). It is thus ironical that budget cuts in the public sector at
the behest of international multilateral organizations may be made good
for through the capture of resources intended for the grass roots, possibly
by the same organizations.[3] As pointed out in the context of non-African
countries, NGOs often constitute "an opportunistic response of down-
sized bureaucrats, with no real participation or local empowerment" and,
inevitably, program officers themselves become involved in the creation of
community institutions (Conning and Kevane 1999; Meyer 1995; Bebbington 1997).

BYPASSING THE STATE IS SELF-DEFEATING

When rural societies become economically differentiated, the "elite
capture" problem becomes acute. Also, as the above discussion attests,
external intervention in the form of channeling substantial amounts of
money through communities has the effect of triggering or speeding up
processes of socioeconomic differentiation within African village societies.
The experiences of Asian and Latin American countries are then more
relevant for Africa.

Probably the main lesson that we can learn from these experiences is
the following: in order to curb the obnoxious influence of vested interests
of local power holders, a strong and effective central government must
exist that is determined to confront the clientelism of rural areas in an
environment rife with rent-seeking opportunities. Thus, one of the most
interesting findings of Tendler's detailed inquiry into the reasons underlying Brazil's success in decentralization of public service from state to
municipal government (in the state of Ceara in the northeast) is that "it
had at its core a strong and new role played by central government"
(Tendler 1997, 73). More precisely, the (state) government "kept an iron
hand" on some crucial components of the decentralized programs so as to
substantially reduce the opportunities for mayors and local power holders
(especially large landowners) to exercise patronage. Simultaneously, it
worked actively (through educational and information-spreading campaigns) to raise the hopes of rural communities about what to expect from
their government. The result was a profound change in the dynamics of
patronage politics as it related to public service at the local level.

That the ability of the central government to set directions and strictures regarding how programs of decentralized development should operate locally can create much-needed constraints on rent-seeking behavior by local elites (and government workers) is also evident from the experience of Bolivia's Emergency Social Fund (ESF). Here, we are told that "Decentralization worked because centralization worked. The ESF centralized the appropriate things: information, negotiations with international donors, and incentive systems for ESF employees. This in turn enabled it to decentralize the design and construction of rural projects" (Klitgaard 1997, cited in Hoddinott et al. 2001, 12; see also Stavis 1982).

By contrast, in Jamaica, where the government does not exercise a significant measure of control over the mode of functioning of the Social Investment Fund at the local level—the Fund just screens the applications on the basis of its target criteria, which mandate a focus on the poorest communities and the selection of projects within a rather flexible list of priorities—the whole process appears to be elite driven and decision making to be dominated by a small group of better-educated and better-networked individuals (Rao and Ibáñez 2001).

The experience of Kerala state (in southwest India) with decentralization is especially instructive.[4] As a matter of fact, the government (the State Planning Board, more precisely) is ultimately responsible for setting the national and regional priorities under which the program is to operate (for example, priority to productive investments), defining the eligibility criteria, fixing the representation of various population groups or strata in the local decision-making bodies as well as their mode of operation, providing guidelines on what village reports should contain, and so on (Isaac and Harilal 1997; Isaac 1998; Veron 2001). On the other hand, it must be borne in mind that, after a long period of intense social struggles (starting in the 1930s) and a widespread literacy and conscientization campaign, the weakest sections of the rural population—especially agricultural laborers (always belonging to the lowest castes) and women—learned to articulate and express their aspirations, assert their rights, and bargain with local power holders.

These two factors provided seemingly ideal conditions for an effective operation of a program of decentralized development. Yet unfortunately, such a program has rapidly become a platform for political favoritism in a country plagued by excessive party politicization down to the local level. When a political party dominates a *panchayat*, it thus tends to reward its sympathizers exclusively, with the result that many villagers became disillusioned with the participatory process and began to absent themselves from meetings in the *gram sabhas* (village forums) (Das 2000).

What the above discussion suggests is that no participatory development can achieve its objectives and realize its potential, especially in the context of economically differentiated rural societies, first if an effective and impartial state, genuinely devoted to the protection of the poor, is not available to impose and enforce directions and strictures regarding the modus operandi of the decentralization program, and second, if no real empowerment of the weaker sections of the population takes place that enables them to obtain relevant information, influence policies, and monitor the state's instructions at the local level. A genuine dilemma actually arises from these conditions. Indeed, participatory development is deemed especially necessary in countries where the state is inefficient and corrupt and where the civil society is weak (such as numerous countries of sub-Saharan Africa)—that is, in countries where it is the least likely to be successful. The fact of the matter is that participatory development is no ready-made solution to circumvent or overcome the drawbacks resulting from the absence of an effective state and the lack of organization among the poor. If the latter are not present, such an approach is bound to be perverted and to miss at least some its main objectives.

Conclusion

To try to implement in great haste a participatory approach in order to get visible results in as short a time as possible is treading a dangerous path and is very likely to prove a self-defeating strategy. This is especially so in societies, typically tribal or lineage-based societies, whose culture is essentially based on a high degree of personalization of human relationships, on the pervasive presence of other-regarding norms, on strong beliefs in the role of ancestors and supernatural powers, and on a strict respect of status and rank differences. If such cultural characteristics are ignored, numerous institutional anomalies are bound to occur as a result of the superimposition of imported norms, values, and behavior patterns that are not compatible with erstwhile beliefs, mores, and habits. The expected outcome is the missing of most objectives of the participatory approach. In societies where a great deal of socioeconomic differentiation has taken place, the main obstacle to the participatory approach is the "elite capture" problem. Here, for such an approach to be successful, there needs to be an effective state at the helm of the decentralization program so that local patrons and doubtful intermediaries can be prevented from subverting the participatory logic for their own benefit.

It might well appear that a less hasty approach toward participatory development, one that lends a lot of attention to institution building and capacity training, will lead to disappointing conclusions. We may overrate the possible impact of training programs, and supporting a corrupt and ineffective state is likely to be an exercise in self-delusion. If that is the case, a drastic strategy shift will be called for: it will then be better to give up any significant financial support for community-based development through aid programs and let trade unions, rural organizations, and the like in advanced countries share their experiences with similar emerging organizations in poor countries. In actual fact, by disbursing funds that eventually bolster the rise of a class of greedy rentier capitalists, donor agencies obviate the necessity for the local elite in poor countries to bargain with their own people for the mobilization of state resources. As a result, they retard the moment at which autonomous development can start on the basis of an effective state and a thriving capital-accumulating bourgeoisie. An alternative way would be to support small- and medium-scale entrepreneurs or artisans without channeling resources through community-based development programs. When the state is ineffective and deeply corrupt, it is indeed advisable to avoid backing big projects and enterprises that can only arouse envy and invite predation, or, conversely, can exercise considerable leverage through extensive patronage networks beyond the control of a strong-enough central agency.

Notes

Our thanks are due to the editors of this book as well as to Michael Kremer (Harvard University) for their valuable comments and suggestions.

1. It is also important to note that by guaranteeing the day-to-day survival of his clients, a patron somewhat exculpates himself in the eyes of other villagers. In other words, regular transfers to a personalized set of poor people are not only a service that patrons provide in order to win the effective support of these people in many walks of life, particularly in promising economic activities and in political enterprises. By evoking tradition, they are also part of a strategy that allows patrons to pursue their private wealth accumulation objectives without arousing too much hostility from common people (including nonclients) (De Lame 1996). In the words of David Szanton, "the fact of differential wealth and power, although readily visible, was frequently phased (disguised? glossed over?) by participants in a 'we are all in this together' rhetoric that was at once egalitarian and communal." This traditional discourse of patronage, "cast in moral terms of reciprocity, mutuality, sharing, generosity, and redistribution," is precisely what allows the emergent businessmen to prosper without arousing too much anger from their own community (Szanton 1998, 259; Peters 1994).

2. In some areas, they have been accustomed to just doing that since colonial or precolonial (slavery) times (Bayart 1989; Boone 1994).

3. Whereas before, state assets were often put to private use by state officials,

the same officials can now manipulate local NGOs or other types of associations to get access to cars, computers, telephones, foreign travel, and various perks.

4. Kerala's left-coalition government decided in 1996 to allocate 35% to 40% of its annual budget for new development plans to projects designed by the local bodies themselves (Veron 2001).

CHAPTER 11

State Policies and Women's Agency in China, the Republic of Korea, and India, 1950–2000: Lessons from Contrasting Experiences

MONICA DAS GUPTA, SUNHWA LEE, PATRICIA UBEROI,

DANNING WANG, LIHONG WANG, AND XIAODAN ZHANG

Introduction

Strong commonalities in their lineage-based systems of kinship and inheritance generate a stark and extremely effective logic of marginalizing women in China, northern India, and the Republic of Korea above and beyond the more global issues of women's burden of domestic work and inadequate access to productive resources. This is reflected in some of the highest rates in the world of excess female mortality before birth and during early childhood (Das Gupta 1995; Das Gupta and Li 1999).

What makes a comparison of these countries especially interesting is the fact that they all had a new beginning as modern nation-states around 1950, after the end of colonial rule or revolution. At that time, they were largely poor agrarian societies with a large agenda of nation building and development ahead of them (Table 11.1). Women's lives were also fairly similar: they worked long hours to help make ends meet in their peasant households and suffered maternal depletion from high levels of fertility. In addition, they coped with the powerlessness imposed by their position in the family.

Since then, these countries have taken very different political and developmental paths, resulting in quite different developmental achievements (Table 11.1). Today, the Republic of Korea is highly urbanized and industrialized, with high levels of per capita income, life expectancy, and

Table 11.1. SOCIAL AND ECONOMIC INDICATORS, INDIA, CHINA,
AND THE REPUBLIC OF KOREA, 1950 AND 1995.

	India	China	South Korea
GNP *per capita*			
c. 1950 (US $)	52	31	76
1995 (US $)	340	620	9700
Percentage rural			
c. 1950	83	89	83
1995	73	70	19
Female adult illiteracy rate, 1995	62	27	3
Female labor force participation, 1995	32	45	40
Infant mortality rate	68	34	10

Source: For 1950 data: Per capita income from Kansal (1974); PRC State Statistical
Bureau (1985); The Bank of Korea (1971). Percentage rural in national census held
nearest to the year 1950, from Lee (1980); Census of India (2001); PRC State
Statistical Bureau (1985); The 1995 data are from World Bank (1998).

education. India is still largely rural, with relatively low levels of income,
life expectancy, and education, and China is somewhere in between
these two countries. The three countries also differ enormously in the
kinds of policies used to incorporate women into mainstream society, as
a result of which the position of women has also taken quite divergent
paths. These contrasts offer the opportunity to examine how different
developmental and policy settings have affected women's living conditions and autonomy.

We argue that the Republic of Korea has sought successfully to achieve
rapid economic growth while maintaining fundamental aspects of family
organization deeply inimical to gender equity. As a consequence, women
now have high living standards and participate extensively in the formal
labor force but have gained relatively little in autonomy—as symbolized
by some of the lowest levels of female legislative representation in the
world (United Nations Development Program [UNDP] 1998). By contrast, the Indian state has a disappointing record on raising living standards
but has been fairly successful in encouraging gender equity. The communist Chinese state has made substantial strides in improving women's lives,
both through raising living standards and through a synergistic mix of
policies aimed at creating gender equity, but some of these gains are being
eroded since the opening of the market economy.

Below, we describe the broad outlines of the system of kinship and inheritance in these settings, which so powerfully inhibit gender equity. We then discuss some key dimensions along which gender issues have been addressed in the development policies pursued by the three countries during the second half of the 20th century: education and employment, women's health, family law, mass communication, and the space created for women's organizations (Sen 1999).

Kinship Systems and the Construction of Gender

Northern India, China, and South Korea have rigidly patrilineal kinship systems whose basic organizational logic is strikingly similar, despite considerable local variation in detail. Because gender analyses often discuss the problems of patriarchy, it is necessary to clarify what is so exceptional about these particular family systems and why they are so effective at marginalizing women. *Patrilineality* means that group membership is passed on through the male line. Typically, this involves passing on the main productive assets through the male line, which constrains women's ability to be economically viable without being attached to a man. *Patrilocality* means that it is normative for couples to live in the man's home. The combination of rigid patrilineality and patrilocality essentially means that women have little independent social or legal personhood.

A THUMBNAIL SKETCH OF CLAN AND LINEAGE ORGANIZATION IN THESE SOCIETIES

The traditional social organization prevailing in these settings in the early decades of this century (and to a large extent also today in rural areas) was one in which clans had their own territories. Villages had their dominant clans, to which the majority of men belonged. Strict exogamy was maintained by these clans, so wives would be brought in from elsewhere. A strong sense of clanship pervaded the village, making men from other clans feel like interlopers. Such interlopers are referred to caustically as "wild ducks" (as opposed to home-grown ducks) in northern China (Xie Zhenming, personal communication). A man who lives as a member of his wife's home is subject not only to humiliation, but also to the threat posed by other villagers who resent his usurping clan property.

Thus it is that only men constitute the social order, and women are the means whereby men reproduce themselves. Women are the biological reproducers, but it is through the father that a child acquires a social identity and is incorporated into the social order.[1] Because only boys remain in the lineage, the significant social reproduction is that by the father of the son. Nowhere is this more apparent than in a genealogical record or in an ancestor worship hall: one can literally see each generation of men, and the generations of men to whom they gave rise. Access to key economic and social assets depended on one's position in a lineage, so enormous importance is placed on carefully recording the precise lineage ties between men for generations. Women are recorded, if at all, only in the capacity of the wives of the men who gave rise to succeeding generations of men.

Men are the fixed points in this social order, and women are the moving points because lineages are strictly exogamous. When women marry, they leave their home and lineage, to be absorbed into their husband's lineage. Neither in her father's nor her husband's lineage can a woman ever aspire to the central position that is the simple birthright of any boy born into the lineage. When she marries, a woman is perceived to have been permanently exported from the family: her (temporary) slot in the household ceases to exist, and a new (permanent) slot is created for incoming brides. In the rare cases when women do return, they and their parents have to struggle to make it work because other members of the village resist the incursion on their property rights (Das Gupta et al. 1997; Das Gupta and Li 1999).

WHAT MAKES THESE KINSHIP SYSTEMS SO UNIQUELY BIASED AGAINST WOMEN?

Yet many other societies around the world also have patrilineal inheritance and patrilocal residence. This description would broadly fit many 19th-century European peasant societies and some African societies. So what makes these particular kinship systems so uniquely biased against women? The answer is that they are structured so as to allow for very little flexibility in actual practice of inheritance and residence rules.

In peasant Europe (as also in Japan), parents without sons would typically have their daughter and her husband inherit the property, rather than seeking to adopt a brother's or cousin's son (Arensberg and Kimball 1968; Nakane 1967; Sieder and Mitterauer 1983). The emphasis was thus more on reproducing the household rather than the father's lineage. By contrast, in these societies, a man without sons would typically seek to bear one by remarrying, adopting the son of one of his male kin, or even (as in China) negotiating with the daughter's husband that at least one of his sons will bear his father-in-law's family name. The driving motivation is to continue the patrilineage by whatever means possible.

The potential for support from daughters is also very different. In large parts of rural Europe, it was completely acceptable for a grown daughter to remain single for many years as part of their parents' household, supporting and being supported by the aging parents (Arensberg and Kimball 1968; Sieder and Mitterauer 1983). In Asian settings, an adult woman has no socially acceptable role in her parental family except as a visitor: her appropriate position is that of a wife in another family. This is reflected in the negligible proportions of women never married in their thirties in the censuses of these countries.

Women's relationships with their husbands are also very different (Das Gupta 1995). Among northern European peasants, the conjugal unit was central for economic, social, and emotional purposes. Marriage was the central event in the domestic life cycle, marking the formation of a new and independent economic unit. By contrast, the Asian kinship systems discussed here make for strong intergenerational bonds and deemphasize the conjugal bond. The household and property management is conducted by the unit of the father and his sons. Thus marriage does not create a new partnership that is of much significance, other than importing another woman into the household to bear children and provide labor. The central event in the domestic life cycle is not marriage but the birth of a grandson, which signals the continuation of the family line.

Field interviews reveal how these Asian kinship systems make younger women isolated and vulnerable (Das Gupta et al. 1997). Here is a part of the life story of a seventy-year-old woman in the Hebei Province of China:

My mother-in-law was a very harsh woman. My husband did not live at home, he worked elsewhere and visited home from time to time. I had to serve my mother-in-law hand and foot. In the morning I had to wake up and begin work before she woke up. I also had to empty her chamberpot in the morning. Then I worked all through the day, and could only go to sleep after she did. . . .

My first child was a son, but she would not let me hold him. She insisted that I just lie him flat on the bed and leave him alone all day while I worked.

She would not let me eat rice, only inferior grains. Once at the Spring Festival my husband noticed that I did not get rice and asked her why this was so. She agreed to let me have some that day, but my husband couldn't help me much with my problems in the home.

When the Communist youth meetings began in the village, I attended a couple of them. They made me feel as though I had some group to which I belonged, outside my husband's household. But my mother-in-law forbade me from going to any more meetings, and I did not dare oppose her.

REGIONAL DIFFERENCES IN INDIA AND CHINA

There are thus some critical points of similarity in the customary rules of kinship and marriage in northern India, China, and the Republic of

Korea that distinguish them from most other settings that could also be characterized as patrilineal and patrilocal. However, India and China are very large countries, and there is significant regional heterogeneity in their kinship systems.

In the case of India, a very substantial proportion of the population lives in regions with other types of kinship systems. There are even pockets of matrilineal kinship in northeastern India and Kerala. Although most of south India is formally patrilineal, women have considerable interaction with their parental family after marriage and can return to stay with the parents if necessary. Many studies have emphasized how different kinship rules are in southern India (Karve 1953; Kolenda 1987; Trautmann 1981). Women can function as independent social and legal entities in ways virtually unthinkable in the north.

Similar regional differences exist in China, but the Han, with their rigid clan-based patrilineages, constitute the overwhelming majority of the population. Some of the non-Han minorities have more flexible kinship systems. This includes the Tibetans (Levine 1988) and the Muslim minorities of western China. It also includes the ethnic minorities in Yunnan, who share cultural patterns with bordering societies of Burma and Thailand, with their bilateral kinship systems. These also include small pockets of matriliny (Hua 2001).

Gender and Development Policies in China, 1950s–1990s

The Chinese state has for centuries sought to manipulate and adapt its people's lineage organization to serve its own ends. Tightly knit clan organization offers the state the possibility of reducing the costs of managing a large and far-flung empire by passing on much of the burden of microadministration to the lineage (Gates 1996; Fried 1969; Schurmann 1968). This possibility has been formally exploited for centuries. For example, entire groups of families could be punished for one member's crime—a powerful incentive for people to keep their kinfolk compliant with state directives. At the same time, the state has always had to contend with the possibility that lineages could become large and powerful enough to challenge state authority (Faure 1989; Hu 1948), a consideration that has kept the state vigilant and in some ways antagonistic toward the lineage system.

This ambivalence has continued after the Revolution. On the one hand, the state had many reasons to want to reduce the power of the family and lineage. It wanted to collectivize property ownership and production, and to make people obedient directly to the state instead of to their lineage superiors. This could not be achieved without smashing lineage political organization, as well as age and gender hierarchies within the household. To achieve these goals, the Communist Party launched a frontal attack on lineage organization, along with genealogical records and ancestor worship, and went far toward breaking age and gender hierarchies. The commune took over many traditional familial functions in social, economic, and political life (Andors 1983).

And yet the communist state could not bring itself to abandon the strengths of the family system for ensuring social stability, caring for the old and disabled, and raising new generations of useful citizens. It left virtually untouched the system of exogamy and patrilocal residence, whereby a man stayed in his own village and obtained rights to live and work there by dint of birth, whereas a woman moved to her husband's family, losing her rights in her parents' village and looking after his parents instead of her own.

Radical changes have taken place in gender relations outside the household. Since the May Fourth movement in 1919, women's liberation has been inextricably linked with the thrust toward building a modern state. This was strongly reinforced by the communist ideology of gender equality, which became the dominant ideology after 1949. The communists used the power of a totalitarian state to transform gender relations and encourage women's full participation in economic, social, and political life. During the 1950s women were brought out of the home to be paid for their work, to participate in political meetings, and to exercise their newly acquired legal right to choose their own husbands. During the Cultural Revolution, this process accelerated. Since 1979, the state has given up some degree of interventionism to encourage private enterprise, which has brought some reversals for women. Yet this period has also opened up new opportunities for the women's movement, as described below.

EDUCATION AND EMPLOYMENT

Universal education was a priority for the communist regime, equally for girls and boys, and impressive strides were made in providing basic education to all people. Emphasis on this diminished with the advent of economic reforms. As a consequence, there is a growing gender gap in schooling, especially in rural areas (Honig and Hershatter 1988; Wolf 1985). There is also a gender gap in higher education.

Production was collectively organized, and women were formally incorporated into the workforce in both agriculture and industry. Women gained both materially and psychologically from the replacement of family-based production by collective units, which radically altered the balance of power in the household. As a village woman explained:

It wasn't the work that changed much: we had always worked hard in the fields. The difference was that earlier we would go alone to work on our husband's family's fields, and got little recognition for our contribution. After collectivization, we worked along with our brigades, which gave us a chance to participate as members of the community in our own right. Moreover, our work points affirmed our economic contribution to our families and the community.[2]

Since 1979, there has been a major change of direction as China shifted from collective production to a market economy, which raised incomes sharply but sometimes adversely affected gender equity. The work point system in the rural areas was given up, and the family became the production unit once again under the "household responsibility" system. In the vast agricultural sector that continues to absorb the majority of China's population, women's work is once again becoming invisible, which can potentially erode their intrahousehold bargaining power. The sexual division of labor has deepened, with men migrating to higher-paying jobs outside the agrarian sector and women remaining to take care of agricultural production. Women are also gaining employment in the mushrooming private sector in urban and rural areas, but this involves mostly young, unmarried women with poor working conditions and insecure jobs (Andors 1984; Gu 1997; Wolf 1985), supplementing their parents' income until they marry.

In urban areas, reform of state-owned enterprises has led to discriminatory practices against women. With increased pressures to be efficient, enterprises are decreasingly willing to make concessions for women's reproductive roles. Efforts to protect women's access to maternity and child care benefits[3] make employers less likely to hire or promote women, and more likely to lay them off in difficult times.[4] For some women, the reduction of income has caused a marked drop in family and social status (Woo 1994). Another gender gap is introduced by mandatory retirement for women five years earlier than for men. This does little for gender equity, but helps the state by freeing up middle-aged women to look after aging parents-in-law, grandchildren, and the home while their daughters-in-law go out to work.

WOMEN'S HEALTH

Communist China has consistently placed high priority on public health, and many of the efforts have targeted women in an effort to improve household health and sanitation (Parish and Whyte 1980; Sidel and Sidel 1982; Whyte and Parish 1985). A prenatal health care campaign was launched to modernize midwifery practices (Goldstein 1998), and infant and maternal mortality was radically reduced. Women's health also benefited from interventions driven by other agendas, notably population control, which was viewed as a top national priority since the mid-1960s (Peng 1989). Although this program has sometimes been harsh in implementation, it was accompanied by strenuous efforts to ensure good conditions for pregnancy, delivery, and child health, leading to rapid improvements in maternal and child health (Sidel and Sidel 1982).

FAMILY LAW

The Communist Party has tried to give women equal legal rights as men, including in many aspects of family law. These laws constituted frontal attacks on the traditional family system, and crucial aspects of these reforms elicited strong popular resentment. Faced with threats of popular uprising, the state compromised in its implementation of new policies and laws.

The Marriage Law of 1950 was truly radical. It sought to eliminate arranged marriages, bride-price, and child marriage. Women were given the right to choose their own partners and demand a divorce, and rights to inherit property and control of their children. Female cadres attached to the Women's Federation were given the task of implementing these policies at the village and household level, with the active cooperation and support of other cadres. The law met deep-seated and violent resistance from men as well as older women, both of whom stood to lose control over their young daughters and daughters-in-law (Croll 1981; Davin 1995; Andors 1984), and resulted in an estimated 70,000 to 80,000 suicides and murders of women between 1950 and 1953 (Davin 1976). Widespread peasant opposition threatened social and political instability, and the state slacked off on implementing these controversial aspects of the law (Andors 1983).

A fundamental clash between the peasants' and the state's views on women's rights created problems in implementing the state's family laws. The 1950s and 1980s marriage laws also sought to give women equal control over productive resources. A further attempt to give women equal rights of inheritance was made in the inheritance law that came into force in 1985 and prohibited gender discrimination in inheritance. However, the state has avoided directly indicating what share of property married-out daughters should inherit. In reality, land is allocated on the basis of village residence, and residence continues, with few exceptions, to be determined patrilineally. Although the 1980 New Marriage Law made it much easier for rural women to obtain a divorce and leave a difficult marriage, women still face obstacles of financial viability and social stigma in the villages.

A similar ambivalence is evident in the campaign to reduce domestic violence. Local cadres are expected to mediate in resolving disputes, raise consciousness regarding how women are oppressed within the household, and specifically address issues such as husbands spending too much on alcohol. This has given women much support in domestic matters and increased their self-confidence. However, cadres are much less likely to support women when lineage interests are threatened. For example, villages may act jointly to prevent the return of women kidnapped for marriage; their sympathies tend to lie with their male kinsman, who needs a wife and has paid good money to the kidnappers for his wife (Das Gupta and Li 1999; Zhang and Xiaojin 1993).

The 1950 Marriage Law sought to change the custom that only sons can provide old age support by implying that both sons and daughters have the duty to support their parents. In reality, however, many practices reinforced traditional norms of old age support. For example, when parents had no work unit to reimburse their medical expenses, the oldest son's work unit would generally contribute because it was perceived to be his responsibility. The 1980 New Marriage Law reinforced this social custom by requiring children to assume responsibility for their aged parents. Women are once again encouraged to be good daughters-in-law (Honig and Hershatter 1988). In the face of a rapidly aging population, the state encourages stable familial support for the aged and is unlikely to alter course on this issue.

CHANGING SOCIAL NORMS THROUGH MASS COMMUNICATION

In communist China, the media and publishing industries are under the strict control of the Communist Party and the state, and all channels of communication were actively used to promote their policies on women. This was successful in demolishing many of the bases of women's oppression. For example, to spread awareness of the new marriage law and to reduce cultural resistance to its implementation, extensive use was made of the story of a young girl (Xiao Qin) who fought her mother, the matchmaker, and other villagers in order to marry her lover.

Massive propaganda efforts used female role models to make people think of women as intellectually and otherwise the same as men, with the same rights and duties. In the 1950s, a few outstanding urban workers received much public attention and later went on to be elected as political leaders. The same was true of what came to be known as "Iron Girls Teams": groups of young women who took on the most difficult and demanding tasks at work to show that they could be as strong as men. This received enormous publicity and quickly became a standard fixture in every factory and collective farm. The Cultural Revolution brought a new twist to this effort by conveying the message that real heroines are totally committed to the revolution and disinterested in being wives and mothers (Honig and Hershatter 1988).

Changes in women's lives in the new market economy of China are mirrored in how women are portrayed in literature, newspapers and journals, television programs, commercial advertisements, movies, and soap operas. These sometimes portray women as housewives and sex objects and introduce female stereotypes adept at manipulating men for financial gain, despite a law against using sexually charged images of women in advertisements (Bu 1998; Zhao 1997). Counterbalancing this are portraits of successful career women awkward with the roles the family prescribes to them (Rofel 1994).

WOMEN'S ORGANIZATIONS

The first tide of the modern women's liberation movement in China emerged after Britain invaded China in the Opium War of 1840. This national crisis triggered a serious examination of how to strengthen the society and polity. The Constitutional Reform and Modernization movement advocated reforms to improve women's lives, such as educating women and discouraging polygyny and foot binding. This movement failed (Lu and Zhen 1990), but gender issues were reopened in 1919 as part of a broader movement for political reform. The agenda was broadened to include women's right to choose their husband, their right to be sexually active before marriage and after widowhood, rights of inheritance, women's education and work, prostitution, and foot binding (Li and Zhang 1994).

These efforts at social reform were interrupted by the political and administrative chaos generated by internal wars between warlords and between the communists and the Kuomintang, as well as by the Japanese invasion during World War II. In the regions controlled by the communists, efforts were initiated to break age and gender hierarchies along the lines developed further after 1949. With the establishment of communist control over the entire country, these efforts were spread across China, as described above.

The economic reforms carried out since the late 1970s brought an end to the era of intense proactive support by the state of women's liberation. The state continues to be active through organizations such as the Women's Federation. However, more independent women's organizations have also come up under the leadership of educated women,[5] which maintain a working relationship with the Women's Federations areas (Li and Zhang 1994). Both the Women's Federation and women's non-governmental organizations advocate women's independence gained through means such as education and skill training programs. They are concerned with minimizing the negative implications for women of the market economy, including job insecurity, growing gender gaps in schooling in rural areas, the return of prostitution, and the misuse of women's images in advertisements. Thus women's movements in China today are returning to the forms of women's movement common in other countries and emergent in China before the Revolution.

Gender and Development Policies in the Republic of Korea, 1950s–1990s

The Republic of Korea has had rapid economic growth since the 1950s. The initial industrialization process began during the Japanese colonial occupation (1910–45), creating a modern infrastructure in the areas of finance, production, transportation, and commerce. Radical land reform was carried out, starting in 1947 during the American occupation and completed after the Korean War. This enhanced the process of breaking traditional Korean power structures to create an egalitarian society, which was a crucial basis for subsequent development (Lee 1982; Koo 1987).

After the devastating Korean War, successive governments had a strong commitment to rebuild the war-torn country into a prosperous industrial country. Poor in land and natural resources, the government concentrated on building a skilled and healthy workforce to lay the basis for rapid industrialization. During 1960–95, the economy grew at an average annual rate of 9%. In the late 1950s, the country's gross national product (GNP) per capita was less than $100, and over 40% of the population lived in absolute poverty. By 1995, it had become the world's 15th largest economy, with a per capita GNP of over $10,000 (UNDP 1998). This stunning pace of development has included rapid improvements in people's levels of education, health, and living standards.

This emphasis on human development and economic growth has dramatically transformed the living conditions of women as well as men. However, women's position in the family and society has been slow to change. The land reform redistributed land to male heads of household and had little implication for gender equity. State policy has made considerable effort to protect Korean culture in the face of rapid industrialization and urbanization. Patrilineal social organization and segregated gender roles are perceived to be central to Korean culture, and consequently, state policy has sought to preserve them. The social, economic, and political participation of Korean women are still among the lowest in the world (UNDP 1998).

EDUCATION AND EMPLOYMENT

From the 1880s, modern education for girls and boys was introduced by Christian missionaries, and many schools also began to be established by Korean intellectuals. The Japanese colonial government organized a modern educational system, and when Korea became independent in 1945, the enrollment rate at the primary level was about 45% (McGinn et al. 1980). Much destruction took place during the Korean War, but immediately after the war, the government concentrated on primary education, with the explicit objectives not only of increasing people's skills but also of inculcating anticommunist thought and "moral education." Primary schooling became universal by the mid-1960s, but a substantial gender gap in educational attainment persisted at the higher levels. The gap in middle and high school enrollment rates began to narrow only in the 1970s and did not close completely until 1980 and 1995, respectively. Although there is still a wide gender gap in enrollment in higher education, women's enrollment has risen sharply in recent decades, from below 9% in 1980 to 45% in 1996.

Women's participation in the labor force has risen substantially in recent years. However, women in most occupations face gender discrimination, including hiring practices, wage differentials, limited opportunities for long-term employment, and male-oriented culture of the workplace. The earnings differential by sex was one of the largest in the world in the 1980s,[6] but the female–male wage ratio has improved steadily from 46.7 in 1985 to 61.7 in 1998 (Korean Women's Development Institute 1999). The wage gap by sex narrows with education: in 1998, the female–male wage ratio was 57.6 for those with less than junior high school and 74.3 for those with university education (Korean Women's Development Institute 1999).

The Equal Employment Act of 1987 has made explicit discrimination against married women illegal, but strong cultural norms regarding women's proper role as wife and mother continue to prevail, and many employers and employees alike expect that female staff will leave their jobs when they marry. Given their relatively poor prospects in the job market, one major incentive for women to enroll in higher education has been to increase their chances of marrying men with higher incomes (Kim 1990; Lee 1997; Park 1991). This is also reflected in parents' responses to the question of why they want to educate their children. In the case of sons, they emphasize "good job," while for daughters, they stress "marriage and connections" (National Statistical Office 1997).

WOMEN'S HEALTH

The government's development strategy has included a heavy emphasis on improving levels of health and reducing fertility (Kim 1990; Lee 1997; Park 1991). Extensive efforts in preventive health services combined with improvements in nutrition and living conditions to bring about a rapid decline in mortality (UNDP 1998). From 1962, a nationwide blitzkrieg was launched to reduce population growth, enabling women's reproductive health and child survival to improve rapidly. The life expectancy at birth for women increased from 53.7 years in 1960 to 77.4 years in 1995, and that for men increased from 51.1 to 69.5 years (UNDP 1998).

The state's commitment to family planning had some other indirect benefits for women. First, it provided an acceptable forum for women to coalesce into some formal organizations. During the 1950s, some women's organizations had already formed around this issue (Kim, Ross, and Worth 1972). During the 1960s and 1970s, this process received state backing as the state encouraged the formation of mothers' clubs nationwide at the grassroots level to disseminate contraceptive information and supplies.

Another indirect benefit for women from the family planning program came in the mid-1970s, when it was perceived that in order to maintain the pace of fertility decline, it was necessary to try to reduce the strong cultural preference for sons. This made the government more receptive to women's organizations' demands for changing the family law to reduce the hold of patrilineal social structure (Kim 1991). Since the late 1980s, the government's receptiveness to these demands received a further major boost from strong concerns that the high sex ratios at birth will lead to a shortage of future wives (UNDP 1998).

FAMILY LAW

In principle, the legal rights of Korean women were ensured by the 1948 Constitution, which stated that all citizens are equal before the law. This was a great improvement over the previous situation—in which, without their husbands' approval, women were legally debarred from credit or property transactions, mediating disputes, initiating lawsuits, or making donations (Kim 1993). In practice, however, there has been very slow change in women's legal rights during this century.

The customary family law, which severely restricts women's legal rights, was given legal backing by being formalized in the Civil Code of 1962. It is based on the patrilineal clan system, so a woman's social and legal identity is derived from her relationship to the male head of the family, even if this is her grandson. In the event of divorce, a woman had little chance of obtaining child custody, alimony, or a share of joint marital property unless the husband consented to it. This gave women strong incentives to avoid divorce at all costs.

The Civil Code of 1962 did improve some aspects of women's lives, in that people were permitted to formally adopt girls if they wished to; women were allowed to inherit what the family head might want to give them; and male and female adultery were treated equally as grounds for divorce. The family law was mildly amended in 1977, but key changes required for gender equality were ignored. Under pressure to avoid the demographic result of the strong preference for sons, as well as the cumulative pressure of decades of effort by women's organizations, the government substantially revised the family law in 1990 (Kim 1991; UNDP 1998). Yet even today, it contains some key provisions effective in curtailing women's autonomy.

With the 1990 revision of the family law, divorce is easier for women because child custody is no longer granted automatically to the father. Moreover, women and men have equal rights to any property acquired during marriage and are entitled to claim for its division upon divorce. Women's right to inherit parental property is also expanded. In the absence of a will, the property is to be distributed evenly among the children, regardless of sex. Clearly, it is still easy for parents to contravene this law by making a will. However, parents may be less reluctant than in the past to allow their daughters some inheritance rights because the population is now overwhelmingly urban. The real sticking point on women's property rights hinges around inheriting land, which is completely incompatible with customary norms of exogamy and patrilocal residence. In urban areas, it is possible to have more egalitarian inheritance without threatening the very fabric of social organization. Thus there is, in principle, scope for the new laws to be implemented with little of the mayhem encountered in China and in northern India, described below.

However, it continues to be the case that only men can be heads of household, and marriage continues to be prohibited between people of the same clan. These continue to be key concerns for women's organizations because they are central to the continuation of patrilineal social organization and consequently women's social marginalization. The insistence on male headship in particular is perceived as the principal source of gender inequality in the family and in the workings of other social institutions.

CHANGING SOCIAL NORMS THROUGH MASS COMMUNICATION

As in the case of education and employment, the state encouraged women's emancipation to the extent that it helped meet national development objectives, while making sure that the emancipation did not go further than strictly required. Thus women were encouraged to play an active role in the national drive for community development (*Saemaul Undong*) during the 1970s and also participate in the decision-making processes in the village general assembly. This was a radical departure from custom, and women participated actively in programs for savings, nonformal education, and agricultural extension, as well as family planning, environmental improvement, and income generation (Whang 1981).

The state had less interest in broader emancipation of women—for example, through the use of the mass media, which was under the strict supervision of the government until the mid-1980s. In the 1960s, popular dramas usually portrayed women as virtuously and resolutely enduring domestic problems. For instance, one popular drama focused on a woman who was being treated very badly by her mother-in-law while also making sacrifices for her son's success. Over time, career women have increasingly come to be represented in TV dramas. However, they are generally portrayed in "acceptable" female occupations, and their primary concerns still revolve around men and marriage. Career women are typically portrayed approvingly only if they also succeed in fulfilling their traditional familial roles well and can keep their husbands happy (Lee 1989).

A hopeful trend in recent dramas has been a rise of support given to women's pursuit of their careers by their parents, parents-in-laws, and husbands—for example, by raising the subject of how a woman should not waste her education by withdrawing from the labor force after marriage. Recently, there has been more open discussion of some critical gender issues, such as rape, domestic violence, and sexual harassment in the workplace. This helps give some legitimacy to women's growing concerns about their lives and increased awareness of gender equity issues among the audience (Lee 1989).

Other TV programs such as news or entertainment programs have maintained a more traditional orientation. For instance, female anchor positions on news programs are confined to good-looking single women, who mostly leave their position when they get married, while their male counterparts continue for decades. These highly visible forms of gender differentiation further reinforce the already prevalent views of women's limited roles in public life. In sum, although portrayals of Korean women in TV programs have gone through some changes over the years, they still appear to reinforce conventional stereotypes of women's social position.

WOMEN'S ORGANIZATIONS

A number of women's organizations were established in Korea during the period of Japanese colonial occupation, mostly as part of a wider political movement for independence, but also with an agenda for women's welfare (Kim 1986). Some socialist women's organizations also sprang up, advocating gender equality more strongly. Since the 1950s, a variety of women's organizations have been formed. Some have been directly concerned with immediate issues of equal pay or legal concerns, others have focused more on political changes and human rights reforms, while still others engage in voluntary community activities (Palley 1994). However, their effectiveness has depended heavily on the extent to which their roles have meshed with the priorities of the state, as evidenced by the progress of efforts to change Korea's family law.

The 1970s and 1980s brought international efforts to improve the status of women across the world. This encouraged women's organizations to push for further reforms in the family law. On its part, the government also became more proactive. It established a Special Advisory Commission on Women in 1983, and in 1986 it added a plan for women's development to the Sixth Social and Economic Development Plans. At the same time, organizations such as the Korean League of Women Voters began to lobby political candidates to vote for a family law reform and exhorted women not to vote for candidates who did not support this (Kim 1991). All these efforts combined with economic and demographic exigencies to bring about the 1990 revision of the family law, which, for all its limitations, represents a significant break from the past.

Gender and Development Policies in India, 1950s–1990s

From around 1800, there was a series of Indian social reform movements against gender- and caste-based injustices (Heimsath 1964; Nair 1996). A series of efforts have been made since then by the Indian political and social leadership to improve women's position in society, including demanding female suffrage at about the same time as it was granted in Britain (Forbes 1996). The circumstances leading up to independence played an important role in shaping the state's policy imperatives, including those concerned with women's empowerment. The independence movement included a serious interest in integrating women into main-stream public life (S. Sen 2000).

At the same time, the independence movement sought to create a dem-ocratic and secular polity and was successful in achieving this goal. This has constrained efforts to empower women because the political leader-ship has had to keep an eye on the demands of different constituencies, especially those of religious groups seeking to maintain their identity in the secular society.

India's achievements in gender equity are quite mixed. On the one hand, considerable effort has been made to use legislation and more direct interventions to bring women into the mainstream of society. Women's own efforts to mobilize to improve their lives have mostly received official encouragement, albeit sometimes not as actively as could be wished. As a result, women have come a very long way in India from the position they were in the early 1900s. Yet the pace of improvements in levels of health, education, and income has been painfully slow, in turn hampering women's ability to avail of the state's gender-equitable laws and policies.

EDUCATION AND EMPLOYMENT

Women's education was undertaken by Christian missionaries from the early 19th century, and it was soon taken up by the social reform move-ments, Hindu religious reform movements, and the state (Forbes 1996). Yet progress has been very slow: only 54% of girls and women were literate in 2001 (Census of India 2001). Budgetary allocations have been diverted to tertiary education at the expense of primary education. Consequent gaps in educational attainment by income level, gender, and rural–urban resi-dence are high, and the most neglected are people living in the rural areas of northern India (Filmer and Pritchett 1999). There are small signs of improvement here: of all children enrolled in school, girls constituted 28% in 1951, and this had risen to 42% by 1991.

A similar picture emerges of women's employment. The most serious problem is not a gender gap, but the lack of growth of employment opportunities. The legal system offers several kinds of protection to women workers. The constitution guarantees women's rights to equal opportunity in employment, and to maternity and other benefits. In prac-tice, these attempts are limited not only by uneven implementation, but mainly because they apply only to formal sector employment, which accounts for only a small fraction of total employment. Moreover, they serve to make it less attractive for employers to hire women in the indus-trial workforce.

WOMEN'S HEALTH

The health transition in India has been hampered by much the same factors as the education transition: the elites have diverted resources to provide for the expensive tertiary-level facilities that serve their own needs. The needs of rural areas and of the urban poor are consequently neglected, except in a few states committed to overall social development. This neglect combines with poverty, malnutrition, and illiteracy to produce a slow pace of improvements in health (Shiva, Goyal, and Krishnan 1992). Women and children have borne much of the brunt of poor health conditions because of the poor conditions of childbearing.

Family planning has received much more serious attention than health. A major crop failure during the mid-1960s alerted the government to the urgent need to raise food production and simultaneously reduce the number of mouths to feed. Both objectives were embarked on with much seriousness of purpose, creative organization, and considerable success. The consequent fertility decline has greatly improved maternal health.

FAMILY LAW

Colonial policies reinforced the strength of patrilineages in northwest India by basing their land revenue and administration system on their genealogical records. For maximizing revenues with minimum management, it was difficult to beat the cost-effectiveness of this system, where peasant owner-cultivators had high incentives to invest in increasing production and were organized into units that could be mobilized to ensure that revenues were paid. This was what the Chinese state had also discovered. This system received much administrative support,[7] and northwest India became the source of massive food exports to the rest of India and the world, while reinforcing a kinship system that marginalized women.

The legal systems established by the British and the Indian elites who replaced them were essentially patriarchal in their orientation to property and family law. Successive legislative measures radically transformed the property relations and social systems of the matrilineal communities of southwest India, effectively dismantling them (Dube 1997; Nair 1996; Sangari and Vaid 1989; Saradamoni 1996; Uberoi 1996). This process is still ongoing in the matrilineal societies of northwest India and in the Yunnan Province of China (Nongbri 1993; Hua 2001).

At the time of independence, a subcommittee of the National Planning Committee of the Congress Party recommended the adoption of a civil code applicable to all citizens, under which women would have equal rights of inheritance and equality with men in respect to marriage and divorce laws. However, as mentioned above, India's cultural diversity is mirrored by enormous heterogeneity in family systems, which greatly complicates efforts to modify family law. One critical obstacle is the principle of religious freedom, whereby family or "personal" law was different according to individual religious affiliation.

Because Hindus could not claim protection as a religious minority, the state exercised greater initiative in amending Hindu family laws to improve gender equity despite vociferous opposition (Paraschar 1992). A series of radical laws comprising the Hindu Personal Law Code were passed in 1955 and 1956 banning bigamy, facilitating divorce, and countering child marriage. Widows were given full rights to their husbands' property, and children of both sexes were to inherit equally. However, all this applies only if there is no will, so in practice, people are free to implement their own cultural norms with regard to children's inheritance (Agarwal 1994; Sarkar 1999). In northwest India, there have been cases in which brothers have murdered a sister who has dared lay claim to their father's land.

There are other serious obstacles to reforming family law and enforcing constitutionally guaranteed rights to equality before the law. For example, the principle of federalism gives states have the power to legislate on many issues, including health, education, social welfare, and agricultural land, the latter being a particularly critical issue in overwhelmingly agrarian India. As a result, women continue to have little control over land, particularly in the northern states (Agarwal 1994).

Notwithstanding resistance, legislation has sought consistently to enter the private domestic sphere to protect women from various abuses. During the colonial period, Hindu social reformers and colonial administrators combined to pass a series of laws, including laws banning widow immolation (1829), enabling Hindu widows to remarry (1856), banning female infanticide (1870), and banning child marriage (1891, 1929). These efforts continued after independence. Alarmed by a rise in dowry pressures, a law in 1961 sought to ban dowries. Despite this, the problem of dowries and associated violence continued to grow, and new laws were passed in the mid-1980s facilitating prosecution of people for receiving dowries and for dowry-related violence against women.

CHANGING SOCIAL NORMS THROUGH MASS COMMUNICATION

The Indian government has developed a range of mass communication channels and has actively used them as an instrument to further its development policies and programs. By the early 1990s, an estimated 93% of the population was reached by radio and 54% by television (Planning Commission—Government of India 1992). The state has enormous capacity to organize communication campaigns, using a variety of highly creative methods. Entertainment serials and soaps are designed to carry an explicit social or developmental message as well as to entertain.

Efforts to increase gender equity in norms and values have been built into many levels of communication. One example is a lively radio drama about a childless woman, in which messages are woven in through folk songs to point out that childlessness is more often caused by male than female sterility, and mocking mothers-in-law who refuse to believe their precious son can be deficient in any way. Popular soap operas portray women who interact confidently and effectively in the public domain.

Since the early 1990s, foreign-based satellite TV and local cable networks have mushroomed, providing mass entertainment without the handicap of weaving in social and educative messages. To avoid losing its audience altogether, the state has been forced to adopt more commercial criteria in its programming. As a result, there is less emphasis on messages to improve gender equity, both in the programs and in their accompanying advertisements.

The Indian film industry consists largely of movies created for mass entertainment, in which "good women" are typically portrayed in roles of chaste, self-sacrificing wives and obedient daughters-in-law. Scenes portraying violence against women are also common in these films. Sensitive to the power and outreach of the media, an increasingly vigilant network of critics has been engaged in monitoring and critiquing the media in its portrayal of women.

WOMEN'S ORGANIZATIONS

Through the 19th century, women's causes were championed mostly by male social reformers, some of whom also founded women's organizations. In the early 20th century, some influential women's organizations were set up by upper-class women, which became active in mobilizing opinion for reform of various kinds, including demanding universal female suffrage. From the 1930s, people were increasingly swept up in the independence movement, in which women of all classes were centrally involved (S. Sen 2000). At the time of independence, women's organizations actively lobbied for reforms and were successful in obtaining a strong official commitment to gender equality.

The women's movement also received a boost from the international interest in the UN Decade for Women. The government was active in this endeavor, setting up a high-powered Committee on the Status of Women in India to assess the effects of government policy with reference to women's legal status, educational levels, economic roles, and health and family planning, as well as to make policy recommendations in these regards. The ensuing report (Government of India 1974) helped set the agenda both for a more interventionist approach by the government and for political activism by women's organizations.

As a result of combined efforts of women's groups, a series of laws or legal amendments were passed during the 1980s on issues such as rape and dowry violence (Gandhi and Shah 1992; Kumar 1993). In line with the recommendations of the Committee on the Status of Women in India, a commission was set up in 1987 to review the working conditions of women in the informal sector. Its task was to recommend measures to improve labor legislation and to ensure women greater access to credit facilities (National Commission on Self-Employed Women and Women in the Informal Sector 1988). However, with the increased market orientation of the economy in the 1990s, these concerns are receiving less attention.

Excess Female Child Mortality in China, India, and the Republic of Korea

Although there have been considerable improvements in women's lives in these three settings, levels of sex-selective abortion and excess female child mortality are among the highest in the world: approximately 7% of girls are estimated to have been removed through sex-selective abortion, and other means, in China and the Republic of Korea around 1990, and around 4.5% in India (Das Gupta et al. 1997). These rates of "missing girls" have risen sharply in recent decades (Das Gupta et al. 1997), while by contrast, adult women's life expectancy has risen steadily relative to that of men.

This is a sharp illustration of the fact that there is no simple relationship between the way in which girls and women are affected by social and economic changes. For example, efforts to integrate women into education and formal employment may not decrease parents' incentives to avoid raising daughters. In principle, these give women greater ability to function independently and offer support to their parents. But in practice, women's earnings are likely to accrue to their husbands' families instead.

As long as daughters continue to be totally absorbed into their husband's home and cannot contribute to their parents' welfare, son preference will continue to persist. Under these circumstances, efforts to raise the status of women as a whole will remain a somewhat indirect route to reducing discrimination against daughters. More rapid reduction in son preference requires measures to raise the value of girls to their parents relative to boys—thereby reducing the incentive to discriminate against girls.

Even the most strenuous efforts to improve women's autonomy in these countries have not focused enough on these issues. For example, communist China did much to help women become full social actors, but did relatively little to alter the rules of inheritance and residence that underpin son preference. Thus, although women's situation is enormously improved in modern China, parents continue to seek to bear sons rather than daughters.

There are, however, some important forces of change at work that increase flexibility in the kinship system and thereby help equalize the value of sons and daughters. Urbanization is a powerful force in this direction. The organization of urban life differs enormously from that of rural areas, reducing the centrality of sons in their parents' lives. Daughters may live in close proximity to their parents, and sons' employment may take them to a city other than that of their parents. Whether urban parents derive support from a child often depends more on who lives nearby and the nature of their relationship than on the sex of the child.

Much can be achieved through the mass media, women's organizations, and other civil forums to reduce the gender gap in children's value to their parents—as a conscious additional dimension to their effort to increase gender equity in social values. The media has been shown to powerfully influence group norms—for example, with regard to childbearing (Mari Bhat 1998). Soap operas can be used to portray women (and also their husbands) helping their parents, emphasizing that this is socially acceptable. Parents can be shown dividing inheritance equally between children of both sexes. The fact that the relationship with a daughter is often emotionally more rewarding can be emphasized, and parents can also be portrayed living with married daughters.

Comparisons

At the beginning of the 20th century, the educated elites in all three countries were preoccupied with similar concerns arising largely out of contact with the outside world. They all felt the threat of modern military power of powerful colonizing forces, and the elites in these countries felt that their societies urgently needed to "modernize" to enable them to assert their identity and engage on more equal terms with the outside world. It was perceived that improving women's welfare was a key element of modernization. Some of the worst iniquities perpetrated on women were targeted for change, and the principle of educating girls was accepted.

Around 1950, all three countries had new beginnings with new regimes in power. Their attention focused on how to transform their poor agrarian societies into modern industrialized economies. By the 1960s, they perceived that this required urgent efforts to reduce population growth. They launched intensive and successful family planning programs, which have frequently been insensitively implemented but nevertheless have substantially improved women's reproductive health and helped closed the gender gap in adult survival. They have all been influenced by the growing trend of international attention to issues of gender equality.

Here the broad similarities end. Shaped by the circumstances of their birth, these three nation-states took quite different paths of economic and social development. The Chinese Communist Party was deeply committed to equity, including gender equity. The Republic of Korea's government chose to focus on rapid economic growth, while preserving its culture and family system with all its implications for gender inequity. India became a democracy in which the influence of a modernizing leadership and social movements for gender equity remained strong, but where the process of setting and implementing development agendas was constrained by the need to balance the competing political demands of an enormously heterogeneous people.

It is well known that these different paths have profoundly affected development outcomes in these countries, but they have also had tremendous impact on gender outcomes. Differences in political systems have also played a role in shaping the nature of women's movements. In China and the Republic of Korea, women's movements are in relatively early stages of development. By contrast in India, democratic regimes have facilitated the rise of a civil society in which strong women's movements could grow—with some far-reaching successes in drawing women into the mainstream of public life, such as the legislation requiring that at least a third of elected local government representatives must be women.

Conclusions

States affect women's capabilities in a multitude of ways. Some of these are fairly direct, such as legislation pertaining to the family and to the workplace, rules of political representation, and forms of affirmative action. Others are quite indirect but nevertheless important, such as development strategies and the institutions of governance. Here we discuss how these influences have played out in China, the Republic of Korea, and northern India in order to understand how states can be more effective at reducing women's social marginalization and increasing their capabilities.

These case studies illustrate the subtle ways in which states influence the manifestation of cultural beliefs and values: most actions and policies are not gender neutral; they either increase or decrease gender equity. They also illustrate the constant tension and negotiation between state ideologies, state interests, and social norms.

They also present some notable points of caution. One is that even when states are interested in promoting gender equity, their actions are often constrained by the desire to maintain stable family structures in order to maintain social stability; to support the old, the infirm, the unemployed, and disabled; and to raise good citizens for the future. Moreover, in these rigidly patrilineal settings, it is very difficult for the state to make peasant rules of residence and landownership more gender equitable. This complex system of roles and rights forms part of the moral order of the society, and efforts to alter it are perceived as deeply invasive. Transition out of an agrarian economy loosens up these constraints to gender equity.

A second note of caution is that states' legislative and other policies tend to homogenize the cultures of their citizens, which can work against gender equity in some ways. Especially striking in these settings is the demise of matrilineal and matrifocal kinship systems, under pressure from patriarchal legislative and policy settings—as noted in studies in southwest and northeast India, and in southern China. Even well-intentioned efforts at introducing gender equity can be implemented in ways insensitive to cultural heterogeneity. For example, reform of family law focused on gender inequities in north India can, in the south, serve to spread and legitimize the less gender-equitable cultures of the north.

A third cautionary note is that despite improvements in women's autonomy, levels of sex-selective abortion and excess female child mortality have been rising in these settings. A very substantial part of efforts to increase gender equity has focused on issues such as education, employment, and political representation—which impact relatively slowly and indirectly on the underlying motivations for son preference. Much more needs to be done through social movements, legislation, and the mass media to focus specifically on increasing the scope and social acceptability of daughters helping their parents, thereby reducing parents' incentives to avoid raising girls.

Notes

This is a revised version of World Bank Policy Research Working Paper No. 2479. It draws on country reviews funded by the World Bank's Gender Sector

Board. The reviews were prepared by Danning Wang, Lihong Wang, and Xiaodan Zhang (on China), Sunhwa Lee (on the Republic of Korea), and Patricia Uberoi (on India). It also draws on fieldwork conducted by Monica Das Gupta in north India in 1975–90, and in China and the Republic of Korea in 1995–96. Comments from Judith Banister, Lyn Bennett, Gillian Brown, Hill Gates, Elizabeth King, Mick Moore, Vijayendra Rao, and Michael Walton are gratefully acknowledged.

1. In India, the mother's caste may affect that of her child in the rare event that her caste status is very different from that of her husband.

2. Interview conducted in 1998 in a mountain village by Monica Das Gupta and Li Bohua.

3. The 1986 Health Care Regulations, and the 1988 Labor Protection Regulations (Woo 1994).

4. Lu (1988) and Danning Wang's fieldwork in Tianjin 1996–97.

5. The term *nongovernmental* is used to describe any institute or organization not set within the official network according to the will of party authorities. This kind of organization was allowed to exist legally only after the late 1970s.

6. 1989–90 ILO Yearbook of Labor Statistics, cited in Bai and Cho (1996).

7. The colonial administration even endorsed the

levirate system as an "enforceable" custom, undermining widows' independent claims to family property (Chowdhry 1994).

CHAPTER 12

HIV/AIDS and Culture: Implications for Policy

CAROL JENKINS

[C]ommunities, like individuals, cannot respond to the challenges
of HIV unless they can express the basic right to be involved in
decisions that affect them.

—Jonathan Mann

World is crazier and more of it than we think, incorrigibly
plural.

—Louis MacNeice

Introduction

No phenomenon in recent history has presented as great a challenge to
the formal and informal institutions of society as has the pandemic of
HIV. The obvious links between culture and sexual transmission of HIV
have been highlighted repeatedly as countries attempt to grapple with the
pandemic. Yet it is not always clear what is meant when people use the
word *culture* in this context. In this chapter, the term will be used in two
senses. The first is a classical type of definition referring to all the cognitive and social traits, as well as artifacts, associated with a human group.
The second sense emphasizes that culture is itself a biological, genetically
inherited capacity of the species *Homo sapiens*, evolved through time and
presumably still in the process of doing so. All members of the human
species possess this capacity through the inheritance of a brain capable of
learning and creating. Hence, cultures change and the cultural attributes of

human groups are always in a process of change, albeit at different paces, in different directions, and often with contradictory components.

The latter sense of the term *culture* is especially important to conceptualize in a discussion of HIV/AIDS. On the one hand, we are told that good HIV prevention or care should be based on culturally appropriate strategies and messages, that respecting local culture is essential, and that only culturally competent personnel working in HIV prevention and care can expect success. On the other hand, we are told that cultural traits must be changed, because some aspects of culture are maladaptive in light of the HIV epidemic, leading to greater spread of the infection and stigmatization. Many people simply stress that behavior must be changed, leaving out the larger issue of cultural norms, competing priorities, and other factors contributing to vulnerability. Still others believe biological drives associated with many of the social and behavioral factors contributing to the spread of HIV are essential to the species and intransigent to change. These might include male sex drive and male dominance, the social mechanism of stigmatization, and the propensity of humans to become addicted to chemicals that produce pleasure.

What are the implications for policy and the design and implementation of HIV prevention and care strategies of such apparently opposing positions? Should culture be manipulated in directive ways, and who has the right to do so? What is the role of government in this regard? And how can investors decide where to place their HIV funds? Although there is widespread agreement with overall development aims that could have an impact on HIV, such as reducing poverty and improving girls' education and reproductive health, there is far greater contention, implicit as well as explicit, over whether to uphold cultural codes that are perceived to be protective (abstinence before marriage, antihomosexual tenets, laws against prostitution, zero tolerance for drugs) or to show people how to make sex of all kinds safer, treat all sexually transmitted diseases, and reduce the harm in illicit drug use as a public health strategy, without direct concern with existing cultural values.

Culture and Behavior Change

Much of the current emphasis on behavioral change derives from a psychology-driven full or partial separation of behavior from all other associations (affect, ideas, social structures, places, objects, etc.) and seeks simply to alter particular behaviors or practices without altering many of the pertinent cognitive systems, social norms, or structures associated with those practices (Odets 1994). It derives from the behaviorist branch of psychology that has developed in the West. It could be viewed as a culture-sparing strategy, one that requires less interference with cultural issues, although it often doesn't work that way. For example, simply in order to design and implement a behavior change project with a socially marginalized group, a considerable amount of advocacy may be required, which in itself becomes a culture-changing activity. Vaccine development is also hailed as the final answer to the HIV pandemic, mainly because vaccines do not require complex behavioral or social change. It is clear, however, that this is a vast oversimplification of what will be required to test a vaccine, then manufacture, purchase, and distribute it. There is real danger that "vaccine optimism" could set in, increasing exposures and overriding vaccine effects.

Another issue of importance is the oversimplification of accepted psychological or social psychological techniques for application to people from hundreds of different cultures. This is highly questionable. Further, behavior change communications, a recent offspring of the older information, education, and communications approach, has become an essential part of most HIV programs. Although it may be possible, in a simple and direct way, to apply these methods to convince people to buy a different brand of condoms, convincing enough people to adopt condom use itself as a consistent, lifetime practice is likely to require far more complex and far-reaching sociocultural change. Neither behavior change communication nor its companion, social marketing, can ensure long-lasting change alone, or even in combination, without continued investment and allied interventions (Population Services International 2000).

Whose Culture?

Anthropologists have long cautioned each other to pay attention to intracultural variability, having been stung by frequent criticisms that ethnographic accounts of a culture are often written as if everyone thinks, feels, and behaves in the same ways. Yet the ethnographic record demonstrates that even very small and simple human groups, numbering no more than 300 persons, are likely to divide themselves into subgroups with different food taboos, marriage rules, beliefs, dialects, or clothing. In larger societies, where wealth accumulates, labor specialization and socioeconomic class then emerge, creating additional modes of social differentiation. The current great disparity in wealth and opportunity among the world's countries drives increasing levels of migration, as do numerous internecine and interstate conflicts. Population dynamics today suggest increasing levels of migration in the future, with the ensuing processes of ethnic and language loss and/or diversification. Coupled with the numerous new ideological and behavioral options that contemporary globalization makes possible, the variegated face of humanity increases. The HIV pandemic has been especially sensitive to migration and to the globalization of technology as it affects a widening drug epidemic and sex trade. Sexual cultures, that is, a particular configuration of ideology, practice, meaning and context, are created and recreated as people move and the virus moves with them.

Although many forces are working toward homogenizing the globe, tribal and ethnic identities remain strong. Even if people of a particular ethnic group actually behave more or less the same most of the time as others in their nation, they may emphasize different values, and they usually have different rituals, arts, and language. There are many important purposes for maintaining ethnicity in the face of homogenizing forces, and sexual cultures reflect this as well. In less industrialized nations, such as Papua New Guinea, much of China, Southeast Asia, and Africa, ethnic or tribal groups may significantly differ from each other in their sexual cultures. Although highland New Guinea is characterized by many ethnolinguistic groups with marked sexual antagonism between men and women built into the structures of marriage and reflected in frequently brittle relationships, high levels of extramarital sex, and sexual violence, the societies found on the nation's coasts and surrounding islands are very different. Many are matrilineal, women and men have more equitable relations, sexual violence is less marked, and sexuality as a whole is more relaxed and permissive. Within the modern nation of Namibia, there are !Kung (Bushmen) people, who now work as ranch labor and also hunt, small farmers in the north of different tribes living under their chiefs, many migrant laborers who go to the coast to work in fish processing or mining, urban dwellers living as students, wage earners, and traders. The contexts in which these people live their sexual lives differ greatly, and no simple scaled-up, national HIV prevention program can be expected to be effective with all of them.

The importance of integrating a fuller understanding of what culture means, in all its variability and dynamism, to the development of informed HIV policy and effective prevention and care cannot be overemphasized. This chapter will seek to make several observations on the relationship of culture and HIV, using examples from selected sexual and drug-using subcultures—those arenas through which HIV is most often transmitted—from the literature, as well as from my own work in Papua New Guinea, Bangladesh, and Namibia. These will be discussed in relation to forces and policies that either abet or diminish vulnerability to HIV infection.

Sexual Cultures

SEXUAL CULTURES AND SOURCES OF CHANGE

Sexual cultures vie in variability with the world's cuisines. The one major difference is that although we can watch what our neighbors eat, we rarely see them having sex. Most people simply do not know the range of human sexual behavior that is going on around them. Young people almost everywhere learn whatever they can from peers, often only slightly older and with as little correct information as they have themselves (Rivers and Aggleton 1999). In much of the world, a significant part of what may be called sexual culture is the deliberate withholding of information from youth. Although the discourse of biological reproduction dominates, the majority of sexual acts taking place anywhere at any time are nonreproductive. Basic field biological research reveals that most animals, from birds to whales, engage in erotic behavior that is not reproductive (Begemihl 1999). Linking all erotic behavior to the requirement of a species to reproduce threatens to confine explanatory models and delay understanding of what is really going on.

Culture is the primary process by which the human being meets biological needs, both organic and perceived. Thus, sexual cultures can be understood to be those constellations of ideas, practices, and artifacts and their meanings and contexts in which people participate, either as a life-long involvement or at various times of their lives, that are adapted to meet felt erotic needs. The erotic components are linked to the body through gender or role presentations, expectations and actions, larger kinship and social roles and structures, demographic dynamics, economic environments, beliefs and attitudes, political forces, and, as we are becoming increasingly aware, disease and its meaning. Sexual cultures vary through time and place and are thoroughly influenced by a myriad of factors. The HIV pandemic can be counted on to be a major factor influencing changes in various sexual cultures as time passes.

Sexual cultures change through time even without the pressure of fatal sexually transmitted disease. In 1994, after considerable political wrangling and delays in funding, the results of a major and representative sex study on Americans were revealed, showing that the majority of adult opposite-sex couples had experienced oral sex (both fellatio and cunnilingus), and nearly half found it very appealing (Laumann et al. 1994). Anal intercourse was less common, particularly among white Americans, but reached as high as 19% in the last year among Hispanic Americans. In fact, the whole report made certain aspects of the social organization of sexual repertoires abundantly clear, with religion having less influence compared to education and ethnic group. Most importantly, it showed a dramatic cohort effect for oral sex, with an increase from 62% for men born between 1933 and 1937 up to 90% of those born between 1948 and 1952. These data point to the influences of various sociocultural forces moving oral sex up in popularity through the 1950s, peaking in the mid- to late 1960s. The authors of the report suggest that the emergence of a distinct singles sub-culture in urban centers where unmarried women could move and work in the 1950s and early 1960s was the demographic shift leading to an increasingly widespread sexual consumerism. They also refer to the increasing concern over the decades with foreplay and lengthening of the duration of the entire sexual event. Studies such as this one make it possible to begin examining the social, economic, ideological, and political influences on sexual cultures and can help enlighten us about possibilities for HIV prevention.

HETEROSEXUAL, HOMOSEXUAL, OR SIMPLY SEXUAL

Many men and women in no identifiable sexual "community"—people thought by everyone else to be heterosexuals—are likely to have had or have a current same-sex relationship. Although the available evidence seems to suggest that men who never have sex with women (and the con-verse, women who never have sex with men) tend to represent a very small proportion (1% to 4%) of any population, men who at some time experience sex with both male and female bodies represent a far greater portion of humanity. The most representative studies in the western world, that is, in the United States (Laumann et al. 1994) the UK (Wellings et al. 1994), and France (ACSF Investigators 1992), show between 5% and 10% of persons report a same-sex relationship at some time in their lives, although some studies in the United States have been higher, ranging from 10% to 14% (UNAIDS 2000). In the United States, greater levels of education (and therefore class and income) are associated with a wider set of sexual experiences, but elsewhere, the sociocultural dynamics of these associations are likely to differ. In a recent study of university students from the poorer classes of Mumbai, 18% of males and 4% of females stated they had had same-sex relations, with only slightly different proportions, 23% of males and 3% of females, having experienced opposite-sex rela-tions (Abraham and Kumar 1999). In Papua New Guinea, 12% of a national sample of rural and periurban males stated that they had experi-enced sex with another male (National Sex and Reproduction Research Team and Jenkins 1994). In another study, 50% of male university students in Sri Lanka reported that their first sexual experience had been with another man (Silva et al. 1997). A recent UNAIDS document on men and boys reports the proportions of young men who have had same-sex relations as 15% in Botswana, 5% to 13% in Brazil, 6% to 16% in Thailand, and 10% to 16% in Peru (UNAIDS 2000). Simply put, many men have sex with other men.

But what is another male? In Brazil, one sex-related identity is called a *travesti*, that is, a male who alters his body with silicone injections to appear female and attract the men he desires. He nonetheless can and does perform insertive sex with "heterosexual" males (not his main boyfriend) and does not consider himself either female or "gay" (Kulick 1998), but an "effeminate homosexual." His clients consider themselves heterosexual. Frequently, where transgendered males dress as female and are engaged in sex by a man having a standard male self-presentation, they are often thought of as "like females" by their partners, suggesting a complex interaction of gender presentation and erotic tastes in determining practice.

Hijras in Pakistan, India, and Bangladesh are thought to be eunuchs, with their sexual organs removed by ritual surgery, but around two-thirds are not (Jenkins and Nahar 1999; Government of Bangladesh 2001). Dressed as women, they often work as sex workers. Unlike transsexuals in the West, *hijras* do not consider themselves females born into the wrong bodies. They usually emphasize a third gender status instead. Male sex workers, even if dressed in female garb, often vociferously distinguish themselves from *hijras*. Yet another South Asian configuration is the *kothi*, a male who does not cross-dress but prefers to be the penetrated partner in sex, affecting female gestures to attract other male partners (Jenkins 1998). A sizable proportion of *kothis*, even sex-working *kothis*, marry, have children, and may have other female partners as well. The clients of sex-working *kothis* and *hijras*, called their *pantis*, are the average policemen, businessmen, vegetable sellers, university students, and rickshaw pullers on the streets of South Asian cities. In one probability sample of these mostly married rickshaw pullers, 60% stated they had engaged in sex with both males and females in the previous year (Government of Bangladesh 2001).

Concepts of the meaning of sexual acts have a real influence on practice where no other body of information exists to challenge them. They may be embedded in physiological understandings, concepts of hygiene and morality (Mogensen 1997), or even associated with sorcery and magic (Jenkins 1998). In addition to a widespread belief in South Asia in the dangers of semen loss (Dewaraja and Sasaki 1991; Mane and Shubhada 1992), there are simultaneously beliefs that heat can build up, especially from being close to motors (as with truckers) or through physical exertion. If this heat is not released, it is thought, illness, especially of the head or brain, could ensue. In South Asia, many men engage in same-sex activities with no implication for western-derived identities and are frequently married or will be. Elsewhere, as in the Caribbean and Latin America, male-male sex is hidden under a cloak of machismo and the myth of the penetrating male, cultural values that have been well documented and discussed (Paraschar 1992; Parker 1991; Prieur 1998; Gutman 1996). It is highly likely that a large component of male-male sex goes underreported in cultures where the possibility exists of masking a stigmatized behavior either through sex with transgenders, homophobic behavior, or violent and aggressive acts directed toward women. These features of sexual cultures are very likely to play havoc with the validity of reporting in surveys. All of this needs to be understood when developing HIV behavior change programs.

The types of sexual collectivities discussed above, whether *gay* as in the West, *fa'afafini* as in the South Pacific, or *waria* as in Indonesia, can function like little tribes, attaching people to groups for protection and security, among other social, mental health (Kippax et al. 1993), and biomedical benefits (Stall et al. 2001). Effective HIV prevention and care among these groups is highly dependent on subcultural competence—that is, people in the know should be directing services and messages specifically to the context and meanings of these lifestyles. Even if actual sexual practice has only partial congruity with the public rhetoric of identification, communications must aim at self-imagery (Bockting, Rosser, and Coleman 1999). While commercial advertisers and small local nongovernmental organizations often recognize this, government programs rarely do, either brushing these hard problems under the rug or subsuming all the variation under a broad label such as MSM (men who have sex with men). Worse, there are clear signs of renewed violent oppression of people with alternate sexualities in many nations, especially in the Caribbean, Africa, and the Near East, presumably in response to the threat of AIDS, and conveniently linked to nationalism or religion. Repression simply does not work as HIV prevention, and to date, few countries have scaled up their prevention programs enough to reach the majority of these critical small sexual tribes or the millions of men who are their partners—men who identify with no sexual group at all, as well as their female partners. In order to do this, the larger societies' fears of homosexuality have to be reduced by education and leadership. The level of homophobia in a society is itself a major risk factor for HIV (Ross 1989; Stokes and Peterson 1998). Even though small projects have been carried out in certain difficult political regimes, for example, Morocco, Bangladesh, Zimbabwe, and Malaysia, these are always under threat and cannot scale up to the extent needed. Homosexuality is often couched in terms of a cultural import from the West when leaders wish to denounce it and deny its importance. The public, however, is usually a bit wiser, and strong indigenous leaders, many hailing from religious institutions, can and have taken a stand on these issues.

SEXUAL CULTURES AND HIGH-RISK SEXUAL PRACTICES

From a strictly bioepidemiological point of view, it is sexual practice, not sexual identity or orientation, that actually places people at risk of acquiring the HIV virus. Anal intercourse, the most efficient sexual mode of HIV transmission, is the highest risk behavior in male–male sex but also not an uncommon practice in male-female sexual repertoires. Cultural preferences for anal intercourse because it avoids pregnancy, connotes a greater sexual conquest, and has a tighter or drier feel, and even as a mode of avoiding HIV, have been documented in numerous countries, for example, in Brazil (Parker 1991) and Bangladesh (Government of Bangladesh 2001). Even where male-female anal intercourse has been an uncommon sexual practice, it may be on the rise, as reported in Sweden (Reuters 2000), Bangladesh (Government of Bangladesh 2001), and the United States. In 1995, 10.6% of males 15 to 19 years old in the United States reported ever having anal intercourse (Gates and Sonenstein 2000) with females. The U.S. national study of adults discussed earlier found that 25.6% of men and 20.4% of women reported experience of anal intercourse at some time during their lives, with 9.6% men and 8.6% women reporting this practice in the last year. Rates were slightly higher for younger cohorts and markedly higher among Hispanics than among others, reflecting an increasingly well documented cultural preference.

Is anal or oral intercourse really seen as sex? Where the cultural rule states that sex is what you do to make babies, neither practice would qualify. Where abstinence is the imposed rule for avoiding HIV, anal and oral sex may be seen as "fooling around" or "play." Nearly universally, penile-vaginal intercourse remains the privileged adult sex act, much like rice is the cultural superfood in Asia or wheat in the Middle East. It dominates most people's thoughts such that they do not *feel* like they have had sex if they did not have penile-vaginal intercourse. Abstinence messages for youth, although morally acceptable to many, cannot meet the challenge of creative manipulation of action and desire. In Sri Lanka, West Samoa, and other cultures where female virginity has been highly prized and guarded for centuries, oral, anal, and manual sex are common practices as a way around the technical restrictions (Silva et al. 1997). The U.S. National Survey of Adolescent Males in 1995 showed that 17% of boys who had not had vaginal intercourse had experienced either receptive oral sex or insertive anal intercourse with girls (Gates and Sonenstein 2000).

High-quality sex education for youth has repeatedly shown the capacity to convince some youngsters, particularly young women, to delay initiation of sexual intercourse (Rivers and Aggleton 1999), but, at some point, nearly all young women will engage in sex. The simple fact that it may be within the confines of marriage is no protection at all where young men are not similarly delaying sexual initiation or where the average age of husbands is considerably older. Studies assessing the impact of virginity pledges have shown that among pledgers, when they do have sexual intercourse, they are significantly less likely to use a condom or any contraceptive (Bearman and Bruckner 2001). HIV can defeat these "culturally appropriate" approaches very easily when programs are carried out based on short-sighted interpretations of sexual safety and denial of the range of normal sexual activity. Serious gaps in coverage, support, and service provision are likely to follow.

MARRIAGE PATTERNS AND NONMARITAL AND COMMERCIAL SEX

While frequently brushing aside or denying the sexual activities of youth and variant sexual subcultures, the presentation of problematic sexuality in the AIDS era has focused on multiple partnership. From the epidemiological point of view, concurrent or overlapping multiple partnerships represent the greater risk, because recently infected persons more efficiently transmit HIV. All studies seem to report higher levels of concurrency among males than among females. In Europe, across eight countries, 1% to 11% of females and 10% to 33% of males reported more than one opposite-sex partner in the past year (Leridon, vanZessen, and Hubert 1998).

Multiple concurrent partnerships commonly occur in several types of contexts. Across the life cycle, this may first appear as premarital sex, when young people are searching for long-time partners, sometimes keeping one for future marriage and a few on the side for money or other purposes (Meekers and Calves 1997). In a recent study of youth in Cameroon, 27% had multiple partners at the time of the survey (Rwenge 2000). Polygyny (one man with multiple wives) and polyandry (one wife with multiple husbands) are the classic examples of marriage forms with multiple partners. Once HIV enters such systems, it can spread easily if fidelity is not practiced by all partners. Concurrent multiple partnerships may be common in polygynous societies as men search for additional wives, particularly if their current wives respond in revenge by taking additional lovers (National Sex and Reproduction Research Team and Jenkins 1994).

Serial monogamy is a more common marriage form characterized by high levels of divorce and remarriage. In these societies, marriages break up relatively easily and entail a period before, during, or after the break when people search for new partners. This period may be especially tricky for emotional reasons, and researchers report lower condom use in sex with both new partners as well as with the previous partner during this period (Bajos and Marquet 2000).

A much higher risk of HIV spread is present whenever relatively moderate to high levels of commercial sex are normative, as in South and Southeast Asia; or where high levels of casual or short-term sexual affairs (not necessarily seen as "commercial") are normative before and/or during marriage. In much of Africa, men have a variety of girlfriends, some of whom are paid, without either party considering the interaction to be strictly commercial. The frequently recounted pattern of "sugar daddies" among young women, "road wives" among truckers, and other arrangements for consensual sex exemplify this. Along with main girlfriends, bar pick-ups, wives, and acknowledged commercial sex partners, there is ample room for concurrency of partnerships to drive a serious HIV epidemic.

In today's globalizing world, macroeconomic factors influence the levels of commercial sex, including the degree of poverty among women and their families, the organization of the sex trade, rates of male migration, labor policies and job markets, and communications technology. The global sex trade is not diminishing in response to the HIV pandemic and may even be growing in some areas to involve younger women and girls and increasing numbers of young men. In Thailand, many women have generally accepted that it is normal for their husbands to visit sex workers, as long as this does not threaten the marriage and family (Saengtienchai et al. 1999). The government of Thailand and its civil partners have managed to bring down the overall national HIV prevalence. Reports circulate, however, of men's changing strategies, such as having more casual sex with lower condom use than in commercial sex, and a greater diversification of the sex trade, including the appearance of brothels around construction sites and along borders with Laos and Cambodia. These are the sorts of shifts in sexual culture that could undermine the national success story. Sexual culture in Thailand is clearly under pressure and, given the danger of a recrudescence in HIV rates, bears careful watching.

Many male and female sex workers, speaking out through researchers, reveal that they are a significant part of the out-migrant labor pool to supplement the incomes of families back home in agricultural areas suffering from population pressure, indebtedness, sociopolitical disturbances, and land loss (Hu 1948; Hull, Sulistyaningsih, and Jones 1998; Kempadoo and Doezema 1998; McCamish 1999; Odzer 1994). Too often women and some proportion of men find little opportunity to earn and either become sex workers or supplement their small incomes with cash raised through sex in one way or another. Exchanging sex to survive today, to feed oneself and perhaps one's children, to repay parents in order to gain merit and status are frequently the aims of sex workers, who are trying to improve the family unit in which their own ultimate security might rest. It may be a gamble, but millions of people are simply too poor to have better options to actualize these important cultural values.

There are obvious policy implications in this scenario; they have been noted before, but remain inadequately operationalized by decision makers. If the aim is to diminish the attraction of prostitution, then women need to stay in school longer, have greater job opportunities, more power over their own bodies, and improved legal equity in marriage. Outright forced trafficking and other exploitative forms of labor migration are also present and must somehow be differentiated from voluntary migrant labor and reduced. But the structure of the existing job market is critical. Even where women are better educated and have employment opportunities, some are likely to choose to sell sex because of the relative costs and benefits among their options, as is more clearly seen in developed nations both in the East and West (Lim 1998).

The functioning of many sexual cultures, as well as quite a few local and national economies, are dependent on prostitution. The growing sex industry, viewed as a whole with all its components, including pornography and a myriad of small services, suggests that millions of men and women choose to spend a significant portion of their increased disposable incomes on erotic entertainment (Business Wire 2001; Rich 2001). The volume of sexual services is not likely to diminish any time soon, though its character is likely to change toward greater safety.

Given an evolving sexual consumerism globally, it seems far more culturally appropriate to improve the rights of sex workers to organize themselves as a labor pool and to help them improve their capacity to assure their own safety. However, many persons oppose such a strategy on the grounds that any prostitution is an affront to the position of women in society. The issues surrounding the rights and safety of male or transgendered sex workers are generally off the screen entirely. The lack of adequate information, a great deal of righteousness and hypocrisy, and considerable cultural ambivalence combine to form a powerful block to developing safe and civil arrangements to assure HIV prevention for sex workers and their clients. Sex workers of all sorts are rarely specifically mentioned in recent UNAIDS declarations, research, or donor programs and have been given little voice in their own future.

One disturbing trend that may be related to the fear of HIV is an apparently increasing demand for younger sex workers. The price of a night with a virgin is high, and in some areas, recruiters may be aiming at younger women for a niche market. Many thousands of vulnerable children from homes broken by poverty in both rural and urban areas form an accessible pool for recruitment. Defining the "child" aside, these young people are likely to require special interventions. At the well-documented Sonagachi brothel program in Calcutta, older sex workers have organized a system to discover young women as they enter the trade and to remove them to safer environments (Jenkins 2000).

SEXUAL COERCION AND HIV RISK

Male dominance and sexual privilege are very widespread. In many cultures, indigenous mechanisms to safeguard the status of women have been eroded by the economic forces of colonialism, and more recently by the combination of changing labor markets and natural resource impoverishment. In much of the world, a woman has few options but to accept that her husband has the right to demand sexual satisfaction when he wants it and the right to go outside of marriage as he chooses. This is the usual scenario. There are, in addition, sexual cultures that assure men the right to use violence to achieve their sexual aims. In cultures such as these, male dominance and sexual privilege are often so unfettered as to make it extremely difficult for young women to refuse sex to a man without the threat of violence, blackmail, and other frightening consequences. In a survey of 178 young men in highland Papua New Guinea, when asked that they would do if they proposed sex to a woman who refused, 1.1% said they would kill her, 5.6% would beat her up, and 17.4% would rape or force her anyway (Jenkins 1997). In South Africa, the levels of coercive sex from schoolteachers as well as male classmates drive many young women out of school (Human Rights Watch 2001). In a large community-based study in Johannesburg, 20% of men stated they had had sex with a woman without her consent, and 6% thought jack-rolling, the term for gang rape, was either good or just a game (CIETafrica 2000).

In Papua New Guinea, line-ups, or gang rapes, are common in both rural and urban areas, and when girls of a particular clan or similar urban group (defined in the urban setting by home region or language) are gang raped, the boys of their groups retaliate with the same against girls of the offending clan or urban group (Jenkins 1996). Sexual violence, such as jack-rolling and line-ups, are the far end of a continuum of male sexual dominance that keeps women under threat and sexually accessible. These may be seen as mechanisms by which male bonding, possibly evolved for defense of the homestead, is rewarded and enforced. Men who may not want to join are often coerced by the others, not unlike similar customs among fraternities, militia, police, and other paramilitary forces in a wide variety of societies. Such violent customs are not found absolutely everywhere, and studies of "positive deviance," that is, those in which rape and sexual coercion are low or absent, would be enlightening.

Although no societies openly approve of such extremes, few male politicians or other decision makers in developing countries have had the courage to invest in strong programs to diminish violence against women, possibly because it could affect lesser rights of control. Few societies have laws that specifically punish a husband's right to physically chastise his wife or demand sex coercively. Despite considerable opposition, the possibility of culture change is, in fact, fairly great around these issues, and women's groups, gender education, research, and a host of other efforts instigated by outsiders and insiders alike in many countries around the globe are already starting to show small to moderate success (*Innocenti Digest* 2000). Education and mentoring for political decision makers has been less emphasized but may be critical to move social change processes forward. Support for leaders from religious and secular domains to communicate the need for change to others is also likely to resonate positively with alternative culturally acceptable values, even if these exist at the moment as minority views. The benefits to society of diminished sexual violence are easy to defend against so-called cultural arguments, particularly where HIV is a threat.

The Social Ecology of Injecting

THE MACRO FACTORS

Although it has been a struggle to persuade most governments to face the reality of their sexual transmission patterns, responses to prevention issues concerning injecting drug users (IDUs) have been far worse. Many countries in Asia and the disbanded Soviet Union are now severely affected, with rapidly rising HIV epidemics among their IDUs. Recreational drug use as a whole has been increasing worldwide, reaching levels at which the phenomenon must be considered statistically normative among adolescents in several nations. Widely held notions that poverty, frustration due to lack of opportunities, and dysfunctional families are the principal factors influencing drug use do not explain all the realities on the ground or the history of drug use. On the macro level, there is ample evidence of powerful political forces supporting the international drug trade, assuring supply and distribution (Marshall 1991). This phenomenon has been growing over the past 200 years, at least since the British East

India Company established a monopoly on the opium trade in India (Booth 1996). Accessibility is now so great in many of the world's communities that simply being there is a risk factor for addiction, and these are by no means only the inner cities of the world. Gradually, middle- and upper-income communities are also becoming affected in the United States (Centers for Disease Control and Prevention [CDC] 2001), as well as elsewhere. Whatever conditions prevail among law enforcement officials—for example, discretion to ignore offenders, accepting bribes for protection, or active complicity with the drug trade at any level—these have obviously undermined any attempts at diminishing supply (van der Veen 2000; Kane 2001). The number of countries reporting injecting drug use has increased from 80 in 1992 to 134 in 1999 and, predictably, those with known HIV among their IDUs from 52 to 114, a rise from 65% to 85% (Ball 1999; Strathdee 2001).

Mind-altering drugs have a long history in a wide array of human cultures. Traditional patterns of use, often sacred and highly managed, have shifted considerably (Grob and Dobkin de Rios 1992). As the number of these substances has increased, access has become increasingly controlled by the state, and negative health and social consequences have risen. The criminalization of opium in the Indian subcontinent is widely considered to be responsible for the growing intensity of social and health problems associated with its present forms of use. But it is unlikely that history can be reversed. When Dr. Alexander Wood of Edinburgh first discovered in 1843 that his patients got a massive "kick" if he administered morphine with a needle and syringe, the story began to change. In Asia, opium smoking, first introduced by the Portuguese, gave way to heroin smoking ("chasing the dragon"), and as the price of heroin rose, to injecting, the most efficient mode of drug administration. In some local areas, shifts back to smoking heroin or opium have taken place, but their total magnitude has not been great enough to affect world trends. It has only been 103 years since heroin was first introduced to commerce, and the world has not yet grappled with its effects. Drug use in modern societies is not well managed culturally and hence is far more often destructive.

CULTURE AND DRUG POLICY

Few Asian or ex–soviet bloc nations have mandated any strategy of demand reduction, other than prohibition. The United States has imposed legal and trade-linked antidrug trafficking requirements on most of the world, while it has at times abetted the drug trade in other ways for political or economic reasons (van der Veen 2000). The "war on drugs" approach, supporting an increasing army of crop eradicators and drug police, has not reduced heroin or cocaine availability in the United States to the present day (Kane 2001). While some crops are destroyed, others are planted elsewhere. There is often little relationship between the nature of a drug and its effects to the degree of prohibition; more often, political and economic forces determine which drugs humans have access to than do concerns about health or well-being. This is as true today as it was in the past, when coffee was outlawed by Prussia's King Frederick to bolster sagging beer prices. Although there is a serious scientific effort to sort out exactly what different drugs do to the human mind and body, official drug policies do not ordinarily base their premises on science. Logic and evidence notwithstanding, nicotine, the most addictive substance known, remains legal throughout the world, whereas drugs with little documented harm or addictive potential, such as marijuana, are widely prohibited. This has created a serious gap in the credibility of drug education efforts in the United States. Consequently, few have shown any success at all in reducing demand (Botvin et al. 1996; Kreft and Brown 1998).

With neither drug supply or demand on the wane and rapidly rising rates of HIV among IDUs in many countries, the world faces some hard choices. The most contrary symbolic image to the dominant values of achievement and success is the slovenly, sickly, and manipulating drug addict. Although a sizable proportion of drug addicts in many societies are working or in school, the popularized negative image is supported by the large number of persons who become socially and physically disabled through their addictions. Few politicians have the courage to defend the need for investment in people so widely considered to be unproductive drains on society. Yet the cost of *not* investing in programs that could diminish the negative health and social consequences of injecting drug use can only lead to far greater expense to society in the future. HIV, hepatitis B, and hepatitis C are all commonly and efficiently spread through injecting. It is not unusual for prevalence rates of HIV to range between less than 5% to more than 80% and rates of hepatitis C to reach 50% to 90% in IDU populations around the world (Hagan and Des Jarlais 2000). Evidence is clear in India, Brazil, and the United States of spread from IDUs to their female (and male) sex partners and children. In the United States, a third of all HIV infections and half of all hepatitis C infections are now related to IDUs, either through injecting or sexual contact with injectors (CDC 2001). Elsewhere, over time and without adequate prevention services, the impact of the HIV epidemic among IDUs can easily become catastrophic. In Indonesia, the prevalence of HIV in blood donors is rising in tandem with those in IDUs (US Census Bureau 2001). China's severe epidemic among IDUs smoldered for several years in Yunnan and nearby provinces and now shows evidence of spread throughout much of the country (US Census Bureau 2001). Myanmar, India, Vietnam, Kazakhstan, Nepal, Indonesia, Belarus, Ukraine, Iran, Dubai, Russia, and Tajikistan are only some of the nations now seriously affected with HIV among IDUs. Rapid and extensive responses are called for, but there are numerous barriers, not least of which is the moral disapproval of recreational drug use. Simple prohibition, exemplified by "zero tolerance" strategies, as in the United States, have already been shown to be thoroughly unrealistic in the face of the enormity of this public health problem (Kane 2001).

EFFECTIVE APPROACHES TO REDUCING HIV AMONG IDUS

Effective control of the spread of HIV among IDUs and from them to their sexual partners and children has been demonstrated repeatedly in a variety of countries or cities, for example, Australia, New York, New Zealand, and the United Kingdom. This has been accomplished primarily by providing education and making clean injecting equipment easily available (National Institutes of Health [NIH] 1997; Des Jarlais et al. 2000). Drug substitution programs have also contributed in most settings and have been shown to be effective in reducing HIV risk behaviors as well as HIV incidence (Sorensen and Copeland 2000). A major obstacle to achieving broad and effective HIV prevention for IDUs is an inadequate supply of needles and syringes almost everywhere. Depending on whether the drug injected is cocaine, heroin, a mixture of the two, buprenorphine, or other drugs, the average IDU uses differing numbers of needles and syringes per day. In Bangladesh, where men (rarely women) inject buprenorphine, the average IDU needs three new syringes per day, but current programs are only able to offer about two per year for each IDU in the country. Where cocaine is injected, as in Vancouver, IDUs binge at times and may require 10 syringes or more in a single day. These are needed 24 hours a day, and people have to feel free to give them to friends because they are placed under pressure at the time of injecting to share equipment. Even with this level of demand, in Asian countries where syringes and needles are less expensive than in developed countries (Lurie et al. 1998), the maximum cost of equipment amounts to less than $100 per year. This is, however, far greater than most governments want to invest in people whose social value is perceived to be so low. Only a few Western European nations even approach the level of investment in equipment and programs that is needed.

SUBCULTURES OF DRUG USE

Numerous writers have documented the drug-use patterns, demographics, socialization into drug use, peer networks and pressures, secrecy and rituals, codes of conduct and reciprocity, dominance and hierarchical relations, deceit and interpersonal violence, and special linguistic codes, among other aspects of the social context in which drugs are used in different societies (Faupel 1987; Grund 1993; Gamella 1994; Mata and Jorquez 1988). Numerous local factors influence these subcultural traits. In most areas, however, the nature of the drug being used, the degree to which users are persecuted by police and others, and economic circumstances stand out as highly salient determinative features. Shooting galleries and the use of professional injectionists substantially increase risk of HIV transmission but simultaneously provide a social context in which IDUs can be reached with prevention services (Jenkins et al. 2001). Although stigma is a feature of drug-using cultures nearly everywhere, its burden is far lighter in some groups than in others. In north Bengal, injecting drug use is common, fairly openly known to all, and the majority of users are married and working. Among the hill tribes of Southeast Asia, injecting drug use takes place in rural agricultural settings, in contrast to the far more common highly urban settings where unstable housing, illegal incomes, and small shifting social networks prevail. Native Americans, Australian aborigines, and other tribal peoples who are IDUs have a different set of concerns with regard to their connections to traditions and life on the reserves, reservations, or other segregated spaces to which their people have been confined (Baldwin et al. 1999). Women IDUs in western nations develop different coping strategies than men, more often resorting to exchanging sex for drugs and depending on a denser social network to deal with pregnancy, children, regular partners, and violence (Baldwin et al. 1999; Brook et al. 1999; Estebanez et al. 2000). IDU prisoners comprise a very important subgroup internationally, whose highly constrained situation greatly heightens HIV risk. Whatever the social adaptations are that emerge in these groups, their most important function is to cope with the craving induced by addiction, a biophysiological fact that tends to homogenize their local cultural differences.

COMPOUND EFFECTS AND NEEDS

Being lower class, a sex worker, a prisoner, a foreigner, of a minority ethnic or tribal group, or even simply being female—all of these disadvantaged and stigmatized identities in a host of countries around the globe compound the difficulties of HIV prevention among IDUs. The sum total of legal and social condemnation functions to drive these people further into hidden, secretive, and mobile subcultures, distant from any helping services, should any exist. For stalwart HIV/AIDS workers who seek to diminish HIV among IDUs, the breadth and depth of their needs soon becomes apparent. Simply providing enough needles is a first and essential step to reduce HIV transmission, but is clearly not enough. Opiate substitution—the use of methadone or other fairly effective and less harmful drugs—has great value for many addicts, stabilizing their habits and lives, with attendant reduction of local crime rates and disease transmission. (For cocaine and the amphetamines, no effective substitute drugs are yet in use.) Skin abscesses, an "occupational hazard" of IDUs, are widespread and often severe, particularly in developing countries with deplorable hygiene conditions. Treatment for these must be made available. Some proportion of addicts is also mentally ill and require assessment and mental health services. Others need job skills and housing. Basic to all of these services is good professional counseling. No developing or even medium-income country yet has the capacity to meet these needs for all of their IDUs, let alone all of their substance abusers.

The majority of research into drug addiction is carried out in the United States, so it is difficult to know if the findings on deaddiction can be generalized to other countries and various drug subcultures. There are clearly no magic bullets, and few programs show major success in terms of a high proportion of ex-addicts maintaining a long-term drug-free life. An unknown proportion do manage to become drug-free and rebuild their lives without enrollment in specific programs, but little is known about how that takes place or how many such persons there are. Overall, the best-documented predictor of success in managed deaddiction has been the length of time in treatment (Bell, Richard, and Feltz 1996). For the difficult combination of drug addiction and mental illness, frequently associated with severely abusive life histories, increased length of time spent off of drugs has been found to be associated with the presence of four elements: (1) a significant caring relationship with someone sober; (2) improved stability of housing; (3) a meaningful, enjoyable occupation or activity; and (4) a long-term regular relationship with a professional counselor (Alverson, Alverson, and Drake 2000).

These findings would not surprise elders of traditional Plains Indian tribes. Their strategy for handling "deviants" was not to push them out but to pull them in closer, placing them more firmly under the guidance of the chiefs and elders. Cultural differences in management strategies for those who somehow get lost in a society bear examination. Modern technological societies, while having advantages for the individual in many domains, tend to lose sight of strategies that maximize societal benefits. Replacing the "tribe" with other social arrangements that confer similar bonds and benefits has often been rediscovered in urban and other modern environments. This is probably what happens naturally in drug-using subcultures, explaining how peer socialization into drug use is so strong, argots form and are disseminated, and associated dress or music styles and other markers of group cohesion develop. However, any group cohesion is undermined by the need for mobility to escape police, self-preservation, and having enough money for drugs. For example, many heroin addicts overdose at some time in their drug-using careers, particularly when combining heroin and alcohol or other drugs. This often occurs in the presence of others who are reluctant to call an ambulance for fear of the police (Darke, Ross, and Hall 1996; Powis et al. 1999).

Users groups, or groups of addicts able to come together to discuss the types of actions needed to improve their lives, offer the model of a typical interest-based association. Such groups have emerged where the pressure from law enforcement agencies is less severe, as in the UK, the Netherlands, and Australia (Crofts and Herkt 1993), and are facilitated by government commitment to decentralized community health strategies. In some developing countries, rural values still prevail to a considerable extent in many communities in which addiction is widespread. Although families of addicts suffer as a result of the economic pressure of a father's addiction, they are often still together. Community-based drug substitution, needle/syringe access, and family-oriented support groups, implemented with income generation and other social development components, have been shown to be highly effective in such settings (Gray 2001). Few, however, have been maintained, and the model has not been scaled up, usually because of lack of political support.

Opening up the problems of opiate and other addictions to the social processes of self-interest group formation may offer a way forward in helping addicts and their families to help themselves. With adequate understanding of the local social ecology of injecting, prevention programs can tap into existing networks to involve addicts and their families in the design and implementation of their own prevention activities. If done well, the outcome should benefit the individual, his or her group, and the surrounding society. Building more prisons or rehabilitation camps, and increasing a person's separation from society are both ineffective and expensive (Kane 2001). Imprisonment is a simplistic state-level solution that runs counter to most societies' cultural preference for family cohesion. Far greater education of the wider public is needed, as is a thorough overhaul of drug policies in relation to the HIV pandemic and other health consequences of drug use. The voices of addicts and their families have not played a part in drug use and HIV prevention policies to date, and hence culturally appropriate solutions for the management of these interrelated problems have yet to emerge.

Policy and Cultural Change

Long-term cultural change can and does take place under pressure from severe and massive disruptions such as the HIV pandemic. Influencing the direction of some of those changes is possible through enlightened policy. Investing in policy development processes that open discussions to a wide array of stakeholders, including those whose very identities have been stigmatized and problematic, has worked, as Brazil's recent experiments in participatory governance and HIV policy have demonstrated (Buckley 2000) and as Australia appears to have managed early in its HIV epidemic (Ballard 1992). In Uganda, the groundswell of concern and action by affected people impelled political leadership to support strong national action, and although the epidemic was quite widespread, HIV prevalence rates are coming down.

Effective HIV prevention requires cultural sensitivity based on in-depth knowledge but does not require a slavish adherence to traditional codes. When major social institutions cannot move, smaller, closer to the ground agencies often can. Donors who pass all their funds through the main political channels should know better. A wise government would not wish to control all AIDS prevention funds. The most direct way to avert cultural blockades and contribute to long-term cultural change is to engage with the affected people directly. Change emerging from within is far more likely to be lasting. When we do manage to get rid of AIDS, we do not want it to come back.

CHAPTER 13

Political Culture and Development

FERNANDO CALDERÓN AND ALICIA SZMUKLER

How does political culture affect development processes? How do the identities, values, ideas, prejudices, and feelings that are predominant in a society and are expressed in the political sphere (in the recognition of institutions and in the practices, outlooks, and broadly shared political norms) act on development? In particular, how do they act upon the possibilities of development of people's and societies' capabilities?

The political cultures that historically have been dominant in Latin America limit the development of people's and communities' capabilities, especially their political capabilities. They do so by emphasizing differences and by stigmatizing and lowering the other (whether poor, woman, indigenous, migrant, black, or mestizo). This pattern, which is expressed in the practices and projections of political cultures of inequality, was later reconstructed by oligarchies during the era of the republic and subsequently by populist governments. Recently, it has been implemented through market fundamentalism, which tends to exclude those who have limited or no access to consumption, education, and employment.[1] This pattern of inequality naturally presents obstacles to more equitable and sustainable development.

In the context of the democratization that is taking place in the region, however, some social and institutional experiences show that a more egalitarian political culture seems to be emerging. By recognizing differences, it strives to create a democratic framework of citizen participation and to foster conditions that allow people and societies to develop their capabilities. The potential of this political culture is based on the fact that it allows for a rethinking of development from the perspective of people's

and communities' own interests and actions. Given the problems of legitimacy of the exercising of democracy—in the region specifically, and in
contemporary societies in general—a particularly important avenue of
democratic renovation is the expansion of deliberative culture and deliberative politics. This means (in gross oversimplification) the construction
of options that permit diverse actors to reach agreements for achieving
development results.

Deliberative politics, which can have effects on culture, is based on a
pluralistic notion of justice that seeks the recognition of equality in difference. This, in turn, can promote socially shared economic development,
starting with the idea that development must include many distinct
groups, and with a reexamination of the notions of the common good and
public responsibility. Moreover, deliberative politics tries to link in a
renewed way the local, the national, and the global, striving to use information technology in new forms, and to participate in globalization in an
advantageous way.

Our discussion emphasizes the contributions of deliberative culture to
the democratic procedures and values that are necessary for achieving levels of social and political participation that promote socially inclusive
development. Two analytical sources support our perspective: the historical experiences and processes of empirically demonstrated cases and situations, and the new literature on deliberation and development.

The Political Culture of Inequality

Political culture is understood as the combination of ideas, feelings, values, information, attitudes, and political capabilities that is expressed in the
way in which citizens, groups, leaders, and communities practice politics,
create historical memory, and process the political, social, cultural, and
economic situations of a country. It is also expressed in behaviors that give
meaning to the political life of specific contexts. Political culture includes
the distribution of knowledge of institutions, practices, and political
forces; predominant attitudes and political perspectives (levels of trust,
rationality, bureaucracy, clientelism, paternalism, tolerance, legal obedi-
ence, respect [or lack thereof] for the other, etc.); and societal norms and
the ways in which they are determined (what rights and duties citizens
have regarding participation, the obligation to accept the decisions of the
majority, etc.). The history and inclusion of specific subcultures are other
factors that have an important impact on political culture (Almond and
Verba 1963; Bobbio and Matteucci 1985; Touraine 1997).

Two particular traits of Latin American political cultures that we would like to explore are the exclusion of the other and the denial of difference. These are expressed in the inequality that has manifested itself in many ways throughout the region's history. As we discuss below, political cultures of inequality are based variously on origin, on a rationalized homogeneity of culture and society, and on the fetishization of the market. These cultures are also strongly influenced by the "dialectic of the negation of the other." This refers to the cultural rejection that places the other (whether indigenous, woman, marginal, or campesino) on an inferior plane and superimposes inferiority on social, economic, and political exclusion. The negation of the other in Latin America took root with conquest, colonization, and evangelization, and was later entrenched by the processes of modernization that created marginality and rejection, which in turn weakened democracies and limited the exercise of citizenship (Calderón, Hopenhayn, and Ottone 1996).

Political cultures of inequality are reinforced by cultural, economic, and political factors: the culturally or ethnically different are often poor, and experience obstacles to the exercise of their political citizenship. Membership in a discriminated-against class, ethnicity, culture, or gender subjects individuals to the consequences of these political cultures of inequality—political cultures that are manifested in political action, education, access to markets, and daily social relations. The foundations of these cultures will be analyzed below. Though they are presented separately, in reality they coexist and should be understood in terms of their interaction.

ORIGIN AND INEQUALITY

A political culture of inequality fundamental to Latin American sociopolitical patterns is the one shaped by the negation of equality and discrimination based on origin. In the case of the elite, it defined certain dispositions toward the system, processes, and policies based on paternalism and authoritarianism, combined with disrespect for, or simple negation of, origin. This justified the denial of political, social, and cultural participation to indigenous people and to women, the complete neglect of these groups in the content of public policies, and their lack of knowledge of their political rights and of political institutions and practices.[2] In Latin America, this type of culture was counterbalanced, to a certain but limited extent, by an extensive vision of citizen rights resulting from various movements (mainly national-popular in nature).

Inequality conferred by origin or "designated state" carries a colonial and caste mark, under which equality is understood as membership (by heredity or designation) in a specific ethnic, socioeconomic, political, or cultural group, and tends to negate the other for not sharing a common origin. The regime of the hacienda, first colonial and then republican, provided the social basis for this type of culture.[3]

Political cultures of inequality have their roots in the rejection of indigenous people during the conquest. This rejection came to be expressed in the concepts of mestizo and mulatto—in essence, anyone who was considered to be inferior both for belonging to a different culture and for being economically exploited. This discrimination is not only ethnic—it also reflects a general pattern of relations with the other (women, youth, homosexuals, etc.), and is a source of the region's complexity of cultural identities. Discrimination against women is especially significant, because the current dearth of women's rights in Latin America extends back to the colonial era, and the patriarchal pattern of colonial origin is a common thread through the different political cultures of inequality. Various studies show how class, gender, and ethnicity were superimposed upon each other in order to discriminate against women in this era (Stolcke 1993; Silverblatt 1990; Behar 1993).

In Latin America, discrimination against the other has proven a major obstacle to economic development, to the strengthening of democracy, and to the exercise of universal citizens' rights. It thus also limits the possibility of real freedom, because it prevents the broadening of the capabilities of various groups. In general, political projects and a pattern of authoritarian social relations in daily life were built on the foundation of an origin-based culture of inequality. This perception of inequality had consequences for the exercise of citizenship, because negating the other also meant excluding him or her from the community.

NATIONAL HOMOGENEITY AND INEQUALITY

National-popular regimes in Latin America tended to reduce the rifts between members of different socioeconomic and cultural groups, and have recognized, within a unified national subjectivity, different ethnicities and cultures. The extension of citizens' rights to broad masses who, until then, had been unprotected and relegated to a position outside the national political community offered these groups a degree of integration and belonging, as well as more equal opportunity.

However, the identification of the people as the state resulted in their being viewed as a homogenous population: political definitions took precedence over social and cultural ones. Thus, even as the authoritarian culture acknowledged the existence of discrimination against the other, it suppressed expressions of political and cultural diversity. In this way, the complexity of the social fabric was denied. The attempt to construct a national community headed by the state and the party prevented the creation of a community that was differentiated politically and socially, and that surely would have allowed for advances along a different path of integration, transformation, and national development.[4]

Corporatist and paternalist regimes naturally favored those who supported the system and excluded those who rejected it, so political and cultural recognition remained incomplete. Social equality, though broad-based, depended to a large extent on one's agreement with the nationalist ideology and membership in the national-popular party, or at the very least the refraining from the promotion of confrontational ideas. The evolution of campesino unions established during the Bolivian revolution of 1952 offers a good example of a relationship skewed by the clientelistic state system. Although the revolution brought to campesinos and indigenous people rights and a level of citizenship that they had not been able to achieve before, the state promoted a favor-trading logic that was closely tied to the ruling party.[5] Beginning in 1956, the campesino unions began to identify with the interests of the ruling party, and became its official voice. The distribution of property titles in exchange for political support became the main activity of the campesino unions, and other issues that were crucially important for their future, such as production methods and the relationship with cities, were neglected (Calderón and Dandler 1984).

The national-popular regimes established clientelistic relationships between public institutions and civil society organizations (CSOs). Through the latter, the regime satisfied the social needs of the population in exchange for political loyalties that gave it legitimacy. At the same time, the regime took advantage of the weakness of the party system, which failed to meet the demands of representation of all of the population. This bureaucratic clientelism controlled the flow of jobs and favors as well as the mechanisms of intermediation between the interests of the state and of society.

The national-popular regimes managed to effect considerable change in Latin American societies, giving new value to victims of discrimination, providing opportunities for upward mobility, and destabilizing the self-image of the socioeconomic elites. However, clientelism and the state's homogenizing vision presented major obstacles to full integration and recognition of the other, and defined a political culture that excluded dissenters while offering social citizenship in exchange for political loyalty.

The globalization of markets, the reevaluation and crisis of democracy and politics, and the influence of market ideology have spawned a new type of political culture in Latin America, in which the excluded are those who have no access to markets. It is a political culture that takes the form of a new type of negation that adds layers to the extant political cultures of inequality discussed above.

Inequality, Globalization, and Democratization

DIFFERENTIATION IN GLOBALIZATION

Social differentiation is not a new phenomenon, but it takes on specific characteristics because of the processes of cultural, political, and technoeconomic globalization.[6] Though these processes provide countries and regions with new opportunities to interact on their own terms, they also promote unequal access to their benefits and limit chances of integration for developing countries. Globalization's strong mechanisms of economic concentration result in a growing distance between core and peripheral countries,[7] and these mechanisms have accelerated processes of socially exclusive modernization and put limits on democracy.[8] At the same time, on the national level globalization has complicated and, to a certain extent, increased the gaps between social classes, regions (rich and poor), cultures (making the indigenous the most excluded), and genders (for example, women experience considerable salary discrimination). Differentiation takes place between countries and within them, and in both developed and developing countries. Some examples of unequal distribution of income within countries are presented in Table 13.1.

At the socioeconomic level, differentiation manifests itself in growing social inequality, in unequal income and distribution of wealth, and in increased poverty, which affects indigenous people, women, and youth most severely. At the political level, it is expressed in a growing fragmentation and weakening of political and social actors, and in the fragility of the institutional system of representation and citizen participation. This, in turn, weakens social ties and feelings of belonging, creates apathy, and relegates individuals to the private sphere. Differentiation at the functional level brings increased autonomy to the different spheres of society (political, economic, judicial, scientific) and blurs the vision of a modern culture of progress, freedom, and integration.

Globalization reinforces the processes of social and functional differentiation in Latin America, because it creates high expectations and aspirations (especially in terms of consumption) among all groups, yet does nothing to help integrate societies. This problem is exacerbated by the shrinking of the state, which has increasingly unburdened itself of social responsibilities. The task of integration has been left to the market, which also fails in the task. Poverty, exclusion, and social instability end up becoming more entrenched and complex, and this has very negative effects on social relationships.

Globalization has provoked a relative loss of sovereignty of nation-states

Table 13.1. PERCENTAGE OF INCOME OR CONSUMPTION OF THE RICHEST
10% AND 20%, AND OF THE POOREST 10% AND 20%.

Country	HDI ranking 2001	Year	Poorest 10%	Poorest 20%	Richest 20%	Richest 10%	Gini/ year	Gini/ year
			Percentage of income or consumption of:				*Gini coefficient*	
USA	6	1997	1.8	5.2	46.4	30.5	...	40.8 (1997)
Japan	9	1993	4.8	10.6	35.7	21.7	...	24.9 (1993)
Slovakia	35	1992	5.1	11.9	31.4	18.2	...	19.5 (1992)
Chile	39	1996	1.4	3.4	62.0	46.9	46.0 (1988)	57.5 (1996)
Belarus	53	1998	5.1	11.4	33.3	20.0	21.6 (1993)	21.7 (1998)
Colombia	62	1996	1.1	3.0	60.9	46.1	51.3 (1991)	57.1 (1996)
Brazil	69	1997	1.0	2.6	63.0	46.7	63.4 (1989)	59.1 (1997)
Bolivia	104	1997	0.5	1.9	61.8	45.7	42.0 (1990)	58.9 (1997)
Honduras	107	1997	0.4	1.6	61.8	44.3	52.7 (1992)	59.0 (1997)
Pakistan	127	1996-97	4.1	9.5	41.1	27.6	31.2 (1991)	31.2 (1997)
Guinea-Bissau	156	1991	0.5	2.1	58.9	42.4	...	56.2 (1991)

Source: Prepared by the authors, based on data obtained in United Nations Development Program (UNDP) (1993, pp. 188–89; 2001, pp. 186–89, 282–83); World Bank (1997, pp. 222–23).

and a weakening and questioning of proposals for social progress that in turn has led to a certain amount of disorganization in sociocultural terms. At the same time, it is important to understand that politics are becoming purely pragmatic. This is an increasingly internationalized trend that serves the interests of the hegemonic power of the United States, particularly on the level of military and economic politics. Meanwhile, business interests amass and concentrate power, and inequalities of income distribution grow as corollaries to this concentration of power. The globalized world appears to be relatively depoliticized and internationalized, but it is increasingly less integrated in terms of values. The effects of these changes on political culture are of a magnitude that demands responsible reflection on the content and possibilities of democracy.

Increased information flow and globalization of culture bring together, into a common cultural market and industry, people from cultures and regions historically very different from each other.[9] Borders are increasingly blurred. This does not mean that the nation will disappear, but rather that it must redefine its role, taking into account the situation of its citizens, their cultural identities, and their particular collective memories in order to strengthen democracy and promote development in a globalized context.

In light of this, how does economic globalization affect the patterns of social differentiation in Latin American societies, societies historically characterized by tremendous internal social inequality? We are living in the time of a dismantling of classical class relations and patterns of social organization; of increased social inequalities and reduced social integration; of a weakening of the classic social movements (nationalist, labor, campesino); and, at the same time, of the emergence of multiple actors in the arenas of subjectivity and identity. These factors make it impossible to reproduce the industrial state order of the past, and characterize a type of emerging multicentric, pluriconflictive society.

In cities, a series of factors have exacerbated differentiation: deindustrialization and industrial reconversion (which weakened the labor movement); the presence of a growing rural migrant population; increasingly limited social mobility; the growing tertiarization and informalization of the economy[10]; and the failure of urban policies to address the needs of the population. In recent years, unemployment and unstable employment have increased throughout Latin America (Comisión Económica para América Latina y el Caribe [CEPAL] 2000). Employment problems inhibit the exercise of citizenship and negatively affect individual perceptions of the future, of social and symbolic integration, and of aspirations of social mobility—aspirations that were widespread especially during the second half of the 20th century, when urbanization was traditionally associated with social integration. As a consequence, people in the region live with high levels of insecurity caused by reduced access to goods and services that are now privatized, and by a growing distrust of others because of the fear of unemployment (United Nations Development Program (UNDP)– Chile 1998; Karasimeonov 1997; UNDP 1994; Pronagob/UNDP Bolivia/ ILDIS 1996).

In rural areas, the rift separating agribusinesses and campesinos is ever wider. And these groups are sharply segmented within themselves. Agribusinesses include, at one extreme, those that have incorporated high technologies, and at the other, large landholders characterized by precapitalist forms of production. The campesinos, for their part, range from those who have been able to integrate some new technology into their productive systems, to those who are semisalaried or unpaid, landless, and have immense difficulties in reaching the market (the latter represent the vast majority). This economic-productive differentiation has corresponding social and political implications. The campesinos with greater advantages in productive terms have a certain degree of organization through which to defend and negotiate their interests, but the organizational capability of the weakest campesinos is very limited, making it difficult for them to articulate their needs (Calderón, Chiriboga, and Pinero 1992).[11]

The social actors historically active in the political arena have also become fragmented and have become more reactive than proactive. Moreover, the party systems face serious challenges in handling increasingly complex social processes, while the new role of the state has exacerbated the negative effects of differentiation and weakened citizen participation in decision-making processes. Structural adjustment programs (which included reforms aimed at stabilizing the economy, transforming productivity, opening markets, and privatizing state companies) have reduced the state's direct role in the economy and society, but clientelistic relationships between state and society remain. A new axis of power has been formed that unites transnational corporations, more concentrated national groups, and the party system and the political enterprise. Although this has allowed for the implementation of important reforms, and has brought the region into the global community, it has not eliminated the paternalism and bureaucratic clientelism that are peculiar to these populist regimes. Processes of functional differentiation (which are based on growing autonomy of the economic, judicial, scientific, technological, and political sectors) reinforce the feeling of dismantling by making it difficult to form an overall picture of the social order.

In sum, we are living in a highly complex context of modernization-globalization, characterized by growing social and functional differentiation that impairs social change; an increase in economic and social exclusion and fragmentation; extreme structural social inequality that limits social integration; and a crisis of the state, which highlights the fragility of the institutions that make possible the exercise of citizens' rights.[12]

All of the factors we have discussed are closely tied to poverty, which we understand not only as low income, but also as a product of unequal social relations and the inability to exercise citizenship. Poverty can be best understood in terms of the capabilities a society has to act upon itself, and in terms of a notion of justice that promotes equality and pluralism in practice, while recognizing the different meanings that equality can have in different cultures.[13] It is therefore crucial to rethink development in terms of the relationship between poverty, culture, inequality and the exercise of citizenship. The issue of poverty is inseparable from that of inequality and the expansion of political freedoms (and therefore from political cultures), because both are the main resource on which societies and people can rely in order to develop (Sen 1999). In this perspective, the values, aspirations, and subjectivities of individuals and communities have a fundamental value. It is in this framework that analytical and political judgments on poverty must be made. A renewed conceptualization of poverty should consider limits to citizenship and limits imposed by highly unequal socioeconomic structures. It should take into account the fact that high levels of exclusion reinforce a perception of inequality as a phenomenon that is worsening, and in which the weakening of the exercise of citizenship is an effect of exclusion.

In some countries, economic restructuring allowed for a partial recuperation of growth, but in general created neither sufficient levels of employment nor a more even distribution of income. The social costs were also very high. Social spending became more focused, and to a certain extent, a progressive structure was achieved. However this achievement is only quantitatively significant when social security spending—which increased in almost all Latin American countries and which has a regressive effect on the distribution of total social spending—is excluded from the analysis (CEPAL 2001). Although the efforts to focus spending enjoyed a certain amount of success, their overall results show them to have been insufficient for confronting the complexity of modernization processes and the key problems of the social structure.[14] And it is important to keep in mind that the poorest populations are excluded not only economically, but also politically and socially. This limits their ability to exert pressure and to participate in political dialogues, and thus reinforces a cycle of inequality, lack of citizenship, and poverty.

In this region in which the processes of social differentiation and exclusion are complex and persistent, it seems urgent to reconsider the issues of social exclusion and poverty in terms of citizenship and deliberative culture. In this context, the poor live in conditions of precitizenship, and poverty is thus a key element in political cultures of inequality. Latin America is experiencing a perverse paradox: on one hand, a process of democratization, though limited, is moving forward; on the other hand, the application of structural adjustments has resulted in widespread economic and political exclusion. In this general framework a new political culture of inequality caused by market fundamentalism has emerged.

MARKET FUNDAMENTALISM AND INEQUALITY

Political cultures of inequality generated by market fundamentalism have various antecedents in Latin America. These include the political defeat of the left after the transition to democracy; the implementation of structural adjustment programs that carried high social costs; and processes of economic globalization that the majority of countries in the region were not prepared to exploit. These cultures look to the market as the natural and only distributor of opportunities. They assign subordinate roles to the state, to society, to the regime of parties, and to democracy itself (Hinkelamert 1984). However, the market has not been capable of effecting social or economical integration because of its failure to achieve high growth rates, especially in Latin America. Thus, it has been converted into an ideology more than a reality. Although the processes of structural adjustment and reform have rationalized various economic institutions, they also have forced national economies to integrate in a limited way into a globalization that is essentially monopolized and has protected markets, especially in developed countries.

The market is based on the rational principal of maximization of individual benefits, and it promotes a society bereft of the notion of the common good. Individuals are more consumers than they are citizens, and they retreat to private life and hold a self-centered concept of the future. The closed logic of the market tends to weaken social ties, and it gives equality an abstract character, without affording market access to all of the population and without even assuring egalitarian treatment to those who do have access.

An effect of the market's new culture is a fracturing of the notion of equality of opportunity based on abilities acquired through education. The rise in unemployment rates and labor instability foster an understanding of equality as being increasingly unjust and dependent on luck or possibilities of influence. This is because conditions for participation in the market are different for each person, even for those with similar levels of education (Sen 1995; Fitoussi and Rosanvallon 1997). This critical vision of the market does not deny its fundamental importance in development and its modernizing role in society. Rather, it only highlights the market's limitations in terms of equality and social, political, and economic integration. The automatic equality proposed by neoliberalism seems to lead to a weakening of citizenship and to a setback in individual betterment. The state and the market should instead work for the sake of that which is public.[15]

How does one respond to these global changes that lead to a restructuring of our societies? How can we improve access to the benefits of globalization and reduce socioeconomic exclusion? To what extent do political cultures of inequality constitute obstacles to integration in this new era? We propose that only by means of a pluralist deliberative culture, capable of recognizing all "others" on equal terms, will it be possible to achieve more inclusive development.

Political Culture and Development: Toward a Deliberative Political Culture

The limits of economic restructuring, as well as those of the democratic process, make necessary an examination of the relationship between political culture and development. The ideas of pact, deliberation, and commitment must be reevaluated in light of various factors: popular demand for ethics in politics and for social justice; the experiences of local participation in several places and demands for participation in various countries, as several surveys show; and the new understanding of deliberation, of commitment, and of the social, cultural, and economic complexity in Latin American societies. This reevaluation should come from the perspective of the political culture of equality, in order to reconsider development and connect it to culture and democracy.

First we analyze deliberative political culture, in terms of both the empirical evidence that supports its implementation and the ideas on which it is based. Next, we consider examples of deliberative political culture in the region that are linked to the development of communities and people's political capabilities. We argue that in societies with deep socioeconomic and cultural heterogeneities, as in much of Latin America, the options for fertile connections between democracy and development seem to come from deliberative practices that create options, consensus, agreements, and results for the sake of a better society.

AN EMPIRICAL AND CONCEPTUAL OVERVIEW

Heterogeneity and Participation

The cultural, structural, and social heterogeneity of Latin American societies are central to our argument. These characteristics are integral to political cultures of inequality and, at the same time, integral to demands for participation and to the variations in ability to achieve political and social consensus-building that were experienced during the periods of redemocratization that took place in the region (dos Santos 1987). Regarding *cultural heterogeneity*, the three types of political cultures of inequality discussed above are based on the recognition of a historical, complex social heterogeneity in the region, especially present in Andean societies. The *structural heterogeneity* of the region's economy has a direct impact on political cultures of inequality thanks to its marginalizing character. Finally, *social heterogeneity* has been expressed with emphasis since the 1980s, with the explosion of diverse sociocultural demands (regarding gender, indigenous rights, ethics, and improvements in standard of living) promoted by social movements. Although they did not posit an overall proposal for society and have been highly fragmented, these movements managed to lay on the table the need to include difference and diversity as central aspects of a democratic plan for Latin American society.

The region's cultural heterogeneity dates to the precolonial period, which saw highly unequal societies. Indigenous societies ranged from tribal groups with a rudimentary level of organization to the extremely complex empires of the Maya, Inca, and Aztec. This complexity increased with the arrival of the colonizers, for they did not see the indigenous peoples as equals and tried to subjugate them through religious conversion and economic exploitation.[16] The subjugated cultures, despite being negated by the politically powerful, survived underground through rituals, beliefs, crafts, food, and art. A new culture began to form in which the indigenous cultures, despite their subordination, managed to resist complete assimilation and to persist within the new culture. This complexity of the Latin American cultural fabric still exists, though today there is a broader acceptance of the indigenous cultures.

Latin America's cultural heterogeneity became tied early on to a highly concentrated economic structure that associated occupation with ethnicity. Thus, for example, it can generally be said that the campesinos were indigenous, marginalized people; informal urban commerce workers were mestizos; and most of the bureaucracy and economic leadership was in the hands of white colonists. The ethnically and economically segregated groups eventually came to occupy new spaces as society began to modernize. However, they continued to be segregated, because subordinated groups were not given the tools to integrate themselves into the broader market, despite the passage of major legal measures such as land reform and emancipation of slavery. Thus there has been a tension, especially in the past twenty years, between cultural recognition and discrimination.

With the expression *structural heterogeneity of the economy*, we refer to a growing polarization of Latin American societies due to accelerated urbanization and incomplete processes of industrialization and modernization. This phenomenon has been characterized by an opposition between those who are included in these processes because of their participation in the labor force (industrial workers), and those who are marginalized (informal urban workers, campesinos, and employees in unstable work situations in the formal sectors of the economy); tensions between the modern and traditional sectors of the economy; and the gap between transnational and national businesses. Another main characteristic of this polarization is the growing concentration of income, which has negatively influenced social investment in national economies, and results in lavish consumption by the rich few in contrast with basic consumption by the majority (Touraine 1989).

In the middle of the 20th century, national popular regimes stimulated a massive incorporation of the populace into the culture industry, along with very rapid social mobility. The regimes invested in education and the general welfare of the population, strengthening a middle class that had been impoverished by state cutbacks. Meanwhile, land reforms provoked sharp social differentiation. However, the former oligarchies did not cease to exercise power, though they did diversify their activities by investing in industry and in the financial sector. The guarantor of development was the state. This was an interventionist state that provided employment, owned businesses, and increased economic growth. With the end of this state role, and the strengthening of a globalized economy in which information technology plays a central role, the region entered a deep social and economic crisis in the 1980s.[17]

Social heterogeneity refers to the multiplicity of social actors who made their presence felt strongly in the 1980s. They put forth a variety of demands ranging from the ethical to the economic, and their rise coincided with the increasing lack of representation by classic social movements (such as unions), which had been weakened by the restructuring of the economy. These new actors generally argued for a new means of representation of social diversity, and questioned the traits of exclusion present in the party system (which was in crisis) and of the authoritarianism of societies that continued to deny difference in social relations. In most cases these social actors were defensive regarding structural changes, and their demands were mostly of a practical nature—this diminished their strength and ability to form alliances. However, they managed to force the discussion of a series of unresolved problems linked to citizenship, including social, territorial, and cultural diversity; the value of pluralism and difference; the recognition of the other; the need for these social actors to achieve greater autonomy from state; the tendency to self-administration; the reaffirmation of a collective culture in light of the growing individualism of the market society; and the need for institutional transformation of the region's democracy (Calderón and dos Santos 1987). For the most part, these movements have lately become very fragmented and weakened.

With this specific historical background, what would an egalitarian political culture be like? What is the relationship between equality and deliberation? What basic elements are necessary for deliberation? We will try to present a critical overview of a deliberative political culture in order to then analyze specific cases from the region.

Conceptualizing Deliberative Political Culture

Deliberative political culture opposes political cultures of inequality—it strives to make the central public issue be general equality and respect of the pluralism of Latin American societies.[18] This political culture requires the construction of options that ideally culminate in collective decisions made with universal participation in the decision-making process, either directly or through representatives. Here, deliberation among actors, regardless of the power relations to which they are subjected, is based on rational and impartial arguments. These arguments represent a starting point that allows actors to promote forms of cooperation, to search for autonomy, and even to dispute outlooks on development in order to achieve more freedom, tolerance, and justice in their daily lives.[19]

Deliberative political culture requires the construction of diverse public spaces in which actors and individuals—with their specific cultural and socioeconomic backgrounds—can interact with each other as equals, and in which they can reach agreements that favor the common good and that are possible to evaluate collectively. Deliberative political culture requires, at the least, an acknowledgment of the existence of political equality, equity in speech acts, and a certain reflective capability on the part of society.

RECOGNITION OF EQUALITY

The perception of equality held by any society depends on that society's priorities. This is because equality is not general and abstract, but involves specific issues such as equality before the law, equality of income, and equality of opportunity (Sen 1995).[20] However, given that differences among people (be they economic, social, cultural, or individual) have a strong impact on inequalities, the issue is how to achieve equality while respecting differences.

Deliberative political culture, while it recognizes power relations, should also allow for the manifestation of multiple voices in order to create new development horizons that are more equitable and efficient for all. Such inclusiveness will yield an institutional seal that inspires confidence and commitment, and, based as it is on democratic values, will ensure the manifestation of differences. The agenda and solutions of problems are also built around public deliberation by the participants, collectively and through free debate of the issues.

Equality and justice are the result of a successful deliberative construction of the political community. Only in the framework of a deliberative political culture do the vision and practice of equality make sense. Admittedly, inequality exists inevitably on many levels because of the logic of power. However, in the community of citizens, the logic of majority interests makes for a tendency toward equality based on actors who are taking into account the larger aims of the society in their interactions with others (Miller and Walzer 1995; Walzer 1998). This requires the construction of argumentative collective action that optimizes the achievement of individual interests while extending them to the whole of society. The greater the opportunities of a broad group of actors, the more effective will be the results of this process (Sen 1999).

EQUITY IN SPEECH ACTS

The common good requires that people develop the ability to express themselves publicly: to make themselves heard but also to listen to and respect the voice of the other, and to be given equal consideration for their public expressions. This promotes greater political equity in decision making, increased democratic legitimacy, and a new way of processing and institutionalizing conflicts. The aim is to construct a new culture of deliberative communication, while being conscious of the prevalence of authoritarian and antimodern cultures in Latin American societies and exclusive logics in developing countries in general.

The speech act is deeply contextual. Actors try to understand the meaning of others' actions in light of myriad factors, including their own cultural history, the others' interactions, and their own interpretation of the others' personal histories. Inequity cuts across socioeconomic and political lines and takes hold in that which is subjective and cultural. It expresses itself in the speech acts of everyday situations—family, work, recreation—and thus is a constant reinforcer of deeply rooted and longstanding patriarchal patterns. Moreover, equity in speech acts cannot exist unless the actors are able to make critical objections and are willing to make demands of the political-institutional system and transform these demands into concerted plans of action by means of speech acts.

REFLECTIVE CAPABILITY

In addition to requiring universal equality, a deliberative political culture also requires considerable reflective capability. Reflection must apply both to changes in the "risk society" and also to the possibility of modi-

Table 13.2. BENEFITS AND LIMITATIONS OF DELIBERATIVE CULTURE.

Potential Benefits	Potential Limitations
Creates options for political choice and development	Risks manipulation of options
Reinforces public space	Reinforces corporate interests
Requires that all individuals be considered free and equal, and ideological debate in which the most efficient and fair option wins	The culture of inequality may not be discussed because it requires deliberation among free and equal subjects
Facilitates preparation of demands and achievement of consensus	Achievement of consensus may be difficult, and debates may be decided by vote rather than by the preferable process of debate
Is a moral end in itself, which should inspire a reexamination of the ideas of the common good, public responsibility, and the basic principles that political decisions rest upon	Not all participants share this moral end, and debate may be confined to political instruments rather than values
Improves collective decision making because it gives legitimacy to processes and choices based on efficiency and distributive justice	The most efficient or fair option is not always chosen, or debates can reach dead ends, undermining the legitimacy of the process
Requires that information be equitably distributed and as transparent as possible	Information may be manipulated in order to influence preferences and decisions

fying the arguments of others, taking into account their subjectivity, their sociability, and their reflection. Deliberation requires an increase in the quality of the decision-making system in democracy and fundamentally in the exercise of distributive justice that is self constructed by the political community and that increases the capabilities of citizens and actors in order to better understand society and modern transformations. However, deliberative political culture also carries with it many risks (Stokes 2001). Table 13.2 outlines some limitations and possibilities offered by this political culture.

Deliberative political culture undeniably has its limitations and potential for conflict, but it also offers great possibilities. It can be an efficient and legitimate resource against exclusionary political cultures of inequality, and it also can redirect development toward a common good built around consensus, and toward equality that respects differences in the highly complex and inequitable context of globalization.

Latin American society has a variety both of obstacles and of openness to deliberative political culture. The obstacles include internal processes of structural heterogeneity; social gaps, high levels of fragmentation, and the effects of social and functional differentiation; the coexistence of diverse subjectivities in conflict with industry and the cultural market; the crisis of politics and systems of representation; and the malaise of the citizens. All of this gives primary importance to the need to build a public space of interaction. Some factors that make the region open to deliberative culture include demands for participation and conflict resolution through dialogue; communitarian, union, territorial, and participatory experiences with deliberative elements; and the experiences of reaching agreements and political and sectoral pacts.

TWO LATIN AMERICAN PROJECTS WITH DELIBERATIVE AIMS:
THE PARTICIPATORY BUDGET OF PORTO ALEGRE, BRAZIL,
AND THE POPULAR PARTICIPATION LAW IN BOLIVIA

The Participatory Budget of Porto Alegre

The participatory budget (PB) of Porto Alegre, Brazil, is a decision-making framework for issues of public policies and urban budgets that tries to increase the efficiency of resource distribution based on the oversight of expenditures and on citizen participation in policy making by means of deliberative democracy.[21] The system has been in place for fifteen years in several municipalities of the city of Porto Alegre and was initiated in response to a crisis of representation within a general national context of decentralization, vast socioeconomic inequality, political favor-trading and corporatism, and free-market reforms implemented through adjustment policies with high social costs.

The PB is based on six principles: (1) direct inclusion of citizens in an empowering process; (2) complete autonomy of the social movements involved; (3) shared management of public funds by local governments and civil society; (4) the translation of social demands into priorities; (5) mobilization and organization of social groups with the goal of gaining access to available resources; and (6) previous identification of the resources involved in the process (Pires 1999, 94).

Porto Alegre's PB was proposed as a way of democratizing the distribution of public spending. The efficiency of public policies was thus linked to local decisions made in a framework of participatory democracy, in which citizens put forth their demands and make decisions. It is a plan for modifying the state from the bottom up, based on a new type of relationship between citizens and the state, in which the former are more committed to public policies and the latter decentralizes power and resources. PB is not intended to oppose representative democracy, but rather to broaden the exercise of deliberative democracy as a means of redistributing the urban budget and promoting development options that favor the common good.

How does the PB work? Its structure is revised periodically, but basically it is an informal process for annual budgetary planning within municipalities. After agreements reached in 1989 with all of its social organizations, the city of Porto Alegre was divided into sixteen zones. Once a year, the population of each zone chooses four policy priorities from a fixed list of eight.[22] The zone then determines the public works and services that will be necessary to address each of the four priorities. In addition, five annual assemblies are held at which specific citywide issues are discussed, with the objective of establishing a long-term vision. A variety of social actors, including unions, students, and the private sector, participate in the assemblies.[23]

Once the priorities for each zone have been set, a first round of discussions is held in which any citizen may participate. This is an important event for CSOs because it is here that individuals choose delegates to participate in subsequent rounds. Thus this initial event determines the bargaining power that each CSO will have. The government presents the results of the expenditures from the previous year alongside the budget for the current year that was prepared in previous activities of the PB. In the first round of discussions, the tasks and budget for the coming year are always addressed—in other words, the decision-making process takes place one year ahead of its corresponding actions. The first round is followed by several intermediary rounds, in which the chosen public works and services are analyzed and prioritized in detail. In the second round of discussions, the government presents the available budget for the following year and elects councilors (who serve a one-year term) to assemblies for each zone and work area. After these deliberative processes take place, the demands are channeled through the planning cabinet, which analyzes them, in coordination with the government secretaries, according to legal, technical, and financial requirements, in order to determine final priorities and allocate the budget.

The PB process has yielded impressive results. Citizens' participation in the process of preparing and prioritizing public policies has increased strikingly. Municipal funding has been redistributed in order to fund works in poor areas of the city. Transportation has expanded to outlying zones. The quality and reach of public works and services (such as road paving, housing, and urban development projects) have improved. Corruption has decreased. And there has been a general increase in both the quantity of public works and the responsibility of municipal government and its employees.

How has this deliberation and participation process achieved such positive results? Various factors contributed to the program's success. The actors participating in the deliberative processes can clearly see the benefits that they confer—not only in terms of improved material quality of life, but also as a means of increasing human, social, and institutional capital in order to reduce poverty and stimulate development. The actors can also see in these processes an opportunity for overcoming the economic crisis in a more efficient way. The high level of social organizations' representation in this society is an enormous advantage for deliberation and consensus-building because many interests and demands are represented; it also helps that the procedure by which agreements are reached has been institutionalized (although the degree of institutionalization is not very formal). In this context, state actors have begun to decentralize power, form a positive opinion of consensus building, and make room for new actors in participatory processes, thus separating themselves from traditional clientelism. Consensus building in this case has been greatly promoted by the trust developed among the actors involved, as well as by the concrete results that have resulted directly from the agreements reached (which, in turn, materialize the deliberative process).

Porto Alegre's PB does have its deficiencies, and there is always room for improvement,[24] but it has proven that it is possible to attack poverty while taking into account the opinions of the stakeholders, and to reach agreements in the short, medium, and long term aimed at promoting shared development. This starts with a deliberative process in which local organizations, CSOs, and social movements all participate. The process fosters the trust that is necessary among the representatives, and this trust is maintained by procedures. Most importantly, it is based on building consensus to deal with problems that have been prioritized by the population.

Popular Participation in Bolivia

In recent years, Bolivia has stood out among Latin American countries for its especially large number of conflicts stemming from economic adjustments and the ineffectiveness of social policies. The most recent conflicts have been in response to an economic crisis, to a general political and cultural malaise (a phenomenon that is closely tied to the political cultures of inequality discussed above), and to a market model whose high social costs are severely deleterious to social integration.

However, not everything is negative, and there has been progress with some of the reforms implemented in recent years. Among these, the case of popular participation (PP) at the municipal level combined with decentralization stands out. The Popular Participation Law, passed in April 1994, is intended to provide channels of representation and participation to groups (especially rural indigenous communities) that had previously been marginalized at the municipal level. It does so by recognizing local grassroots organizations (*organizaciones territoriales de base*, or OTBs).[25] The law established a new type of relationship between the state and society that, from that point on, gave priority to local actors. It also specifies a redistribution of fiscal resources based on population density, with the aim of promoting distributive equity by allocating an equal amount of resources per number of inhabitants of each municipality, be it a large city or a small rural town. In addition, the PP law broadens the scope of municipal activities. Not only does it transfer resources, it also decentralizes the physical infrastructures of education, healthcare, sports, local roads, irrigation, and culture. With this law, municipal governments assumed responsibility for the planning and execution of programs intended to promote individual betterment at the local level.

The PP law has been criticized on several levels. First, it gives priority to local organizations and thus ignores the importance of Bolivia's historic organizations, such as unions and civic committees. Also, there is a wide range of organization levels and inequality among OTBs that makes it difficult for them to participate regularly and equitably. The power of local elites can also present obstacles to participatory processes. Finally, the many responsibilities transferred to municipalities from the state are often beyond the fiscal capacities of the municipalities' limited coffers. However, the crucial point of this law is that it puts municipalities at the center of a new, locally focused process of democratic participation.

The results in terms of empowerment of different populations have been uneven, especially for those populations that are poorest. The varied results seem to be due partly to the ideological histories of the populations themselves, and partly to their levels of social capital and political capabilities (in other words, the organizational and institutional capabilities as well as the ideas that make possible effective political action). The work of Whitehead and Gray-Molina (2000) illustrates this issue nicely.[26] Blackburn's (2001) study of PP in Sucre takes a similar approach, although it does not emphasize the historical context.[27]

The PP law is an important instrument that provides procedures and structures that promote increased citizen participation, and it represents important progress as a proposal for democracy. But, as the cited studies have shown, the outcomes of its application in terms of real participation depend on the people, their political culture, their social capital, the knowledge and consciousness they have of their rights, and on the political capabilities of their organizations. Generally speaking, two contradictory tendencies seem to exist in Bolivian society. On the one hand, there is a high level of conflict; on the other hand, there is participation and interest in dialogue in order to find solutions to problems.[28] The actors who protest, paradoxically, are often the same ones who dialogue. There are signs that the internal tension may be broken, but this can only happen through dialogues that produce agreements and, most crucially, concrete results. This must take place in a difficult context of minimal economic, social, and political efficiency. If it does *not* take place, a new cycle of protests will begin, and the legitimacy of dialogue and of the culture of deliberation itself will be lost.

The complex processes of participation highlight at least three important phenomena in Bolivia: first, a poorly coordinated structural economic heterogeneity; second, sociocultural diversity (ethnic, but also religious), that leads to inequalities; third, the search for solutions to conflicts, for the presentation of demands, and for the creation of proposals based on open dialogues and the building of consensus. At the same time there is a clear inability of the system of political party representation to provide for broader citizen participation, and a clear need to create new structures of participation that are essentially local. How is Bolivia to bring together fragmented actions and demands within a deliberative political culture based on reaching consensus for the sake of the common good? Municipal structures seem to be best suited to the task of deepening democracy and enabling processes of deliberation and dialogue due to their proximity to local citizens and institutions. They have greater credibility than national and departmental institutions, and citizen auditing is more viable at the local level.

The two cases we have examined—Porto Alegre's PB and Bolivia's PP—show that these populations have a predisposition toward deliberative political culture that, through participation and consensus, can provide a framework of equity, tolerance, and acceptance of others in decision-making processes. The effectiveness of these processes will be determined by how efficiently decisions are implemented. Success puts in motion a virtuous cycle of participation in deliberative culture, the reaching of consensus, and the execution of decisions. The intention of deliberative political culture is not to idealize the processes by which actors and individuals at different hierarchical levels participate. Rather, the goal is to accept a minimum base upon which it would be possible to dialogue, without negating the conflicts. The issue is how these processes are conducted and in what framework they take place—in short, whether they tend toward fragmentation and the resulting inefficiency for all, or whether they tend toward consensus building and agreement, toward the discussion of a better and shared development, and therefore toward greater well-being, equity, and the respect of differences.

Notes

This chapter is to a large extent a summary of a book (Calderón 2002).

1. By *market fundamentalism*, we mean reification of the market in all areas of social life.

2. This does not mean that there has been no resistance to this discrimination and exclusion.

3. The central traits that Medina (1980, 56) found in the hacienda regime are political-military and economic concentration; power linked to families that manifests itself in the institutions of society; being a model of authority; and giving birth to a "type of human with a peculiar character." In comments on these ideas, Faletto (1988, 79) argues that the hacienda was "the foundation of a . . . political culture."

4. A series of factors makes it possible to sociologically interpret the political culture of inequality as being linked to a clientelistic system. These include the rapid processes of urbanization experienced in the region with limited growth of industrialization (which resulted in the development of cities without industry); the high levels of symbolic integration by means of popular cultural consumerism; proposals for the construction of a national community in which the state was the main actor; and weak institutionality. Latin American cities produced semicitizens and political citizenries that were later subjugated by authoritarian regimes (Medina 1980; Di Tella 1965). *Zapatismo*, for example, is a political-cultural response to this type of negation, as are the current protests of the *Mapuches* in the south of Chile.

5. *Favor trading* is a rough translation of the Spanish *prebendal*, which refers to the exchange of privileges, jobs, or favors, often (but not always) in a political context.

6. Globalization is understood as a mainly economic process with sociocultural and political effects promoted by information technologies, telecommunications, and transportation. These factors connect the world through a network of information flows that function in real time in all aspects of life. A new social structure with global features of a network society seems to be emerging. Castells' trilogy, The Information Age, is obligatory reading for understanding the changes in contemporary society and economy (Castells 1997, 1998).

7. World inequalities have increased constantly during the past two centuries. An analysis of the long-term trends in world income distribution (between countries) shows that the distance between the richest country and the poorest country was around 3 to 1 in 1820, 11 to 1 in 1913, 35 to 1 in 1950, and 44 to 1 in 1973, and 72 to 1 in 1992 (UNDP 1999a, 38).

8. The dynamic of the processes of modernization seem to take on strong authoritarian characteristics, as suggested by Germani (1985). It reduces the access of societies to the political system of decision making, in which everything is delegated to specialists, thus eroding democracy itself.

9. The impact of the culture industry and cultural market is crucial to the redefinition of cultural identity, of politics, and of the economy. According to Calderon and dos Santos (1987), in Latin America, education, science, technology, and the national cultural industries are in clear decline as a result of the impact of the internationalized cultural market on people's daily lives. This segments sophisticated tastes and creates mass cultural consumerism for the majority. This phenomenon is linked both to the progress in information technology and to the global economic restructuring and is a new are of domination.

10. *Tertiarization* refers to the dominance of a tertiary sector over other sectors of the economy. *Informalization* refers to the informal sector of economy—small activities, outside of recognized businesses, that normally use little capital, rudimentary techniques, and unskilled hand labor, and generate income but lead to unstable employment.

11. Along these lines, it is worth mentioning that the state policies in the cycle of economic adjustments reduced the prospects of diversification and social reproduction in rural areas (Chonchol 1990; Bartra and Otero 1988; Warman 1988).

12. On the complexity of the process of modernization-globalization, see Dahrendorf (1995); Germani (1985); Giddens (1995); and Haferkamp and Smelser (1992). For Latin America, see Calderón and Lechner (1996).

13. In European culture, for example, the word for poverty comes from the Latin *paupertas*, which means "poor" or "unproductive." In Andean Quechua culture, the word for poverty is *waqcha* or *waycha*, which means "orphan," without father, mother or community—in other words, without social ties. Thus it is different to be poor in northern Potosí than it is in the streets of Manhattan.

14. Data from CEPAL (2001, 14) show that between 1990 and 1999 the fight against poverty in the region achieved moderate success, and a slow tendency toward poverty reduction can be seen later. However, although some countries had more success than others, none managed to reduce poverty to 1970s levels.

15. Some measures that can favor a market that serves the public are investments in health care, education, and individual betterment; equitable distribution of assets, especially of land in poor agrarian societies; the availability of credit to the poor; access to information regarding the opportunities provided by the market; sufficient physical infrastructure and support for research and development; a clear legal framework; the removal of barriers linked to cultural factors, gender, or religion; macroeconomic stability; systems of incentives and a just fiscal regime; protection of competition, consumers, workers, special groups (women, children, and ethnic minorities) and the environment; and social security networks that aid the transitory victims of market forces and help them reintegrate (UNDP 1993b).

16. However, this notion of the other was not homogenous; within the church, there were differentiated attitudes.

17. The factors that seem to have led to the crisis include external pressures on the economy (the worsening of terms of trade, interest payments on foreign debt);

the increase of demands and necessities of the population that had previously been satisfied to a large extent by the state; the force of an antistate conservative ideology; the growing inefficiency of the state structure in satisfying people's demands, in making the administrative functions more efficient, and in eliminating corruption (Calderón 1995).

18. For an overview on the discussion on this topic, see Elster (2001); and Bohman and Rehg (1997).

19. Several historical examples in the region illustrate this possibility, among them the communitarian traditions with deliberative traits, especially among the indigenous and workers, and the option of dialogue as a way of resolving problems in different Latin American societies.

20. According to Sen, the demand for equality is justified, above all, by an ethical consideration (Sen 1997c, 1999).

21. For a summary of this experience, see Franché (2000).

22. These eight are basic sanitation, housing, road paving, education, social aid, health care, transportation and traffic, and urban planning.

23. The issues addressed in these assemblies are traffic and transportation; health care and social aid; education, culture, and sports; economic development and fiscal codes; and urban planning and development.

24. A major limitation of this proposal is the difficulty of implementation at the national level because of different levels of trust among actors and because of national structural limits that can negatively impact the possibility of resolving certain local issues; also, in this case, the initiative was promoted by a specific political party, and there was a failure to make reforms that would ensure its continuity after a change in the ruling party of government.

25. The law creates spaces and procedures that allow OTBs to participate in planning, discussion of problems, preparation and implementation of solutions, and oversight of their execution.

26. Whitehead and Gray-Molina (2000) describe the cases of the Upper Valley of Cochabamba, northern Potosí, and northern Santa Cruz, which is based on a historical analysis of the political capabilities of these three populations. In the Upper Valley of Cochabamba, the social movement, especially regarding campesinos, was historically very strong. During the land reform of 1953, rural unions united into a single federation of unions that provided guidelines for action to the country's other campesino federations. These campesino unions organized popular political participation, out of which came political leaders who had previously led unions. In the 1960s these unions participated in the military-campesino pact that was promoted by General Barrientos. However, in the 1970s the unions began to gain autonomy from the state. And in the 1980s they took a stance that was quite independent from the government, turning to international organizations and nongovernmental organizations for support. The PP law, in this context, managed to bring together the different campesino unions. In this area, levels of participation in municipal planning are presently very high, and the leadership of the unions has a high percentage of indigenous people and campesinos. In northern Potosí, the organizational duality of the rural structure (indigenous communities organized according to their traditions alongside agricultural unions

created in the 1950s) created conflicts in rural areas. With the military–campesino pact this division became wider, at a time when the relationship between the two types of organizations was either clientelistic or nonexistent. Although there were attempts to overcome this kind of division and create relationships of solidarity among communities and unions, the social and political panorama of the 1980s was highly fragmented. PP was implemented in this context. It is interesting that in Cochabamba, a place with a history of high levels of social and union participation, the results of PP are very positive. In Potosí, an area with traditionally low levels of participation, the PP law was taken advantage of by the different organizations in order to obtain more power without allowing for genuine participation of grassroots organizations.

27. Although this study recognizes that poor sectors of society can, by means of certain provisions established by PP, obtain some degree of power, its main argument is that the less democratic the extant political culture, the more likely it is that the powerful elites will gain further advantages from the process. Meanwhile, the more democratic the political culture (the greater the transparency and trust among actors), the more the PP process will increase the power of citizens and their capability to act in local governments. In the case of Sucre, the persistence of a favor-trading culture (characterized by clientelism, *caudillismo*, and racism) and the shortcomings in social capital of the poorest populations (mainly of Quechua origin) present obstacles to genuine participation in decision making and to discussion of priorities in local government programs.

28. The indigenous movement locally based in the Amazon Basin region is an example of an attempt to achieve political participation and a presentation of demands by means of agreements and negotiation processes. On the state level, another example is the undertaking of the National Dialogue in Bolivia (first in 1997 and then again in 2000). This process had the goal of reaching consensuses with different CSOs on general policies that the state needed to address (economic development, the fight against drug trafficking, state-society relations, and human development). The survey presented in the *2000 Bolivian Human Development Report* demonstrates that 59% of people responded that in their organizations decisions are made by means of dialogue to reach consensuses; and that obstacles to problem solving are due to a lack of dialogue and ignorance (56%) and to discrimination (50%). More than 83% said that it is possible to reach agreements on the country's development (UNDP-Bolivia 2000). This demonstrates a strong predisposition toward deliberation.

CHAPTER 14

Relief and an Understanding of Local Knowledge: The Case of Southern Sudan

SIMON HARRAGIN

Introduction

The aim of this chapter is to cast an anthropological eye over the issues of local knowledge, famine relief, and development theory, using the case of southern Sudan to reveal structural weaknesses in the ways local people are seen and represented in conventional development discourse. Information produced by anthropologists has often been praised but subsequently ignored by development practitioners (Saleem-Murdock 1990). Anthropologists have done little to resist being pushed aside on matters of policy as a result of the increasingly introspective direction that overtook the subject in the 1970s and 1980s.[1] However, that period of introspection did produce a heightened awareness of the structures of power that lie behind the production of anthropological knowledge[2] and subsequently gave anthropology the opportunity to examine the power structures that lie behind development discourse (Gardner and Lewis 1996).[3]

If current theories concerning development and famine relief fail to exert power over poverty, then that is either because they fail to explain accurately the *causes* of such poverty or because their findings are simply not put into practice by those countries with the power and the wealth to address the problem.[4] Where there is the political will, famine can be avoided[5]; where there is no political will, inaction can often be justified by recourse to theories that see foreign aid as "doing harm" (Anderson 1996). Such theories are critically examined in the context of the 1998 famine in Sudan to decide whether they accurately represent reality from the point of view of those who suffered a famine or whether, in the way they are interpreted, they simply lend intellectual credibility to inaction.

The first section of this chapter attempts to locate outside economic assistance in a meaningful local economic and cultural context. Such outside assistance must be incorporated into local concepts of economic ownership if it is to be successfully absorbed—but the most appropriate economic form that aid can take (that of a common property resource to which all kin groups have access) does not accord well with the amount of aid available and the way that aid agencies want to see themselves—as the saviors of the most vulnerable. There is a conflict over ownership and definition of the "vulnerable." In the case of the donor culture, this means being "conspicuous" in the way it helps that particular group and in the case of local cultures they try to win by passive resistance, disengagement, and corruption to remove the corrosive intrusion of another culture into their own—the kinds of technique called by Scott (1985) the "weapons of the weak"—giving the donor culture further leverage to see poor countries as unable to manage their own affairs. The victims in all this are the poor people who could potentially benefit from aid, and the result is the kind of fiasco that emerged in the early stages of the 1998 famine in Sudan—described in the second part of this chapter.

The third part goes on to describe how aid agencies have their own bureaucratic culture that explains in meaningful terms how it is justified to delay reacting to a potential famine—for the good of local people (so they do not become dependent), in order that the outside world does not reward those leaders who might be starving their own people for personal gain, and because they do not have accurate systems that can predict famines (they might therefore go away or simply not materialize without any extra mobilization of funds). Anthropologists need to describe this culture, as well as indigenous cultural beliefs, if we are to arrive at a better fit between culture and public action.

Understanding the Cultural Context

Behind any emergency is a cultural context, "a set of social, geographical and economic circumstances on which some damaging event has been superimposed" (Seaman 1994). Only by understanding that context and seeing things through the eyes of local people can one understand how to provide relief to them (De Waal 1989). The southern Sudan has had only eleven years of peace since the creation of an independent Sudan in 1956. The south itself is a complex mix of ethnic groups, ecological conditions, and differing histories. The present analysis concerns itself with the Nilotic groups, and more particularly the Dinka ethnic group, which suffered most during the 1998 famine.[6] The Dinka, with approximately 2 million people out of the estimated 6 million in the south are the largest ethnic group. They cover a swathe of territory from Bahr-el-Ghazal on the west bank of the Nile to Blue Nile and Bor County on the eastern floodplain of the Nile. Their history has been intricately bound up with that of the Nuer ethnic group, with whom they share many linguistic and cultural attributes.

The present phase of the war reignited in 1983 after the abandoning by President Jafaar Nimeiri of the terms of the 1972 Addis Ababa peace agreement, and precipitated, among other things, by the discovery of oil in the south and the construction of the Jonglei Canal. The western Nuer are currently engaged in fierce fighting over the oil-rich territory around the government-held town of Bentiu, although this situation could be changed by the recent negotiation of a peace agreement in the Kenyan town of Machakos. These oil fields recently started pumping oil through a pipeline to Port Sudan on Sudan's Red Sea coast, a development that ensures the continuation of the conflict. The Jonglei Canal was designed to benefit northern Sudan and Egypt with greater flows of water but provided little tangible benefit to the south. In other words, the war is a war about control over resources—especially fertile land, water, and oil—with a strong economic logic in addition to historical and political factors, not an irrational war about lines on maps.[7]

Cattle are the mainstay of the Dinka economy and vital to the nutrition of the Dinka particularly in years when the sorghum crop fails. Raiding of cattle has been an important military strategy to impoverish the people of the south. Cattle define the predominant political entity in Dinka life—the *wut*, or cattle camp. Within the physical cattle camp, there are individual fires (*gol*; pl. *gal*), around which family groups tether the animals they own. The *gal* represent the kinship groups that share a territory. Different kinship units have differing numbers of cattle in the cattle camp—that is, different levels of wealth—but they all have equal rights to grazing.

Economic resources (including cattle as well as agricultural products) are therefore owned by family groups, but territory is shared by many different family groups that combine together for political representation, ceremonial purposes, and the collective defense of grazing land against outsiders. They do not share cattle or food together, and it is the responsibility of each kinship group to care for its own members. Members of the same kinship group combine for receipt and payment of bride wealth.[8] In times of economic hardship, members will demand help from other extended family members but will rarely go to anyone outside the

kinship group to request help.⁹ There are also various taboos associated
with accepting food prepared by another kinship group.

Such practices indicate the extent to which different kin groups are
considered to be independent economic units. However, because such
units band together to share a common territory, there must be some form
of political organization to organize the combination of family ownership
with territorial protection of grazing rights. Before the arrival of the
British, there were only religious, military, and kin group leaders, aside
from the old men in the cattle camps who made decisions on when to
migrate. In order to run their civil administration during colonial times,
the British appointed executive chiefs (*alama thith*) and subchiefs (*alama
chol*) on the basis of territory—a structure that continued after independence to the present day. These chiefs do not have economic control over
the kinship groups that share their territory; this role is taken by the family or *gol* leaders. Their role is a mainly political one—to keep the peace
and calm the tensions between kin groups, which are sometimes in an
almost permanent state of feud. It is all such chiefs can do to keep the
peace within their own territorial units. Relations between such units
(neighboring tribes and subtribes) are openly acknowledged to be characterized by competition—for grazing, water, and now relief food.

What is significant is the split between territorial resources and family-
owned resources. Grazing and aid are seen as belonging to a territorial
group, whereas cattle are seen as being family owned. Such a split is far
from being unusual, particularly among pastoralist groups. In brief, aid has
been absorbed into the local structure is as a common-property resource
for a territorial group, like grazing, not for any particular individuals
within that territory, be they poor or wealthy.

Given such a background of underlying tension between the economic
power of the kinship structure and the territorial and political power of
the executive chiefs and subchiefs, it is unsurprising that one of the major
priorities of local leaders, since the start of large-scale food relief deliveries in southern Sudan in 1989, has been to ensure that the distribution of
such food does not exacerbate existing tensions. The targeting of aid by
relief agencies to certain zones in preference to others has sometimes
caused tension (it was cited as a major reason for clashes between Nuer
and Dinka groups in 1991 east of the Nile). Within their own areas, territorial chiefs have the opportunity to use food relief as a way of reducing
tension by distributing it fairly to all the kinship groups in an area according to their size, and then allowing the leaders within each kin group (the
gol leaders) to distribute it to their family members according to need.

The local perception is that large, powerful family groups contain a majority of the population, and so deserve the largest share. Having a large family is the ideal to which Dinka aspire (*cieng*). In practical terms, having more than one wife allows a man to have many sons to bring fame to the family name, many daughters to bring bride wealth cows into the family, and plentiful labor in an unmechanized subsistence economy where the main constraint to increasing production is labor shortage. Penalizing those who have attained the kind of success to which people aspire and rewarding the unsuccessful has a questionable logic in a war where aspiration and hope of better times sometimes seems to be all that remains. The feeling is that all kin groups are separate economic units and should have equal rather than preferential rights to access resources—whether in the form of grazing or relief—be they rich or poor. Such economic units are the indigenous welfare system (there is no cross-cutting local system that encompasses all kin groups, such as widows groups or soup kitchens), and it is not seen as politically fair or wise to sustain the welfare system of some lineages and not others purely on the basis of differential need. More than all this, though, is the sense that the problems of the south, and the reason that relief is needed in the first place, are caused by an ethnically divisive war and that it is better to use relief to encourage group solidarity rather than to exacerbate difference.

The final benefit of seeing relief as a common resource is that it converts aid from being an owned resource like cattle into being common property and thus freed from the idea of debt or stigma. In other words, it situates "foreign aid" into a meaningful local frame of reference, and even if this is different from the cultural context in which it is given, the significant point is that the items have adopted a meaningful identity (*kake UN*—the things of the UN, therefore belonging to everyone).

In summary, therefore, an individual cannot be seen in isolation from a complex web of kinship and territorial obligations. The "vulnerable" in a given territory are not seen as a category able to claim special rights separate from those that come from membership of a specific kinship group within that territory. On the other hand, favoring the vulnerable could legitimize a system that favors a particular kin group and encourage the kind of preferential treatment that could be used to justify corruption, whereas at least treating aid as a common-property resource ensures that even the poor have access.

The 1998 Famine

Operation Lifeline Sudan (OLS) was set up in 1989 as a tripartite agreement between the government of Sudan, the United Nations, and the Sudan People's Liberation Army (SPLA, the main rebel faction in the south). It was established in response to the disastrous famine of 1988. OLS's "negotiated access" to areas controlled by both sides in the conflict was "the first formal acceptance of unresolved conflict by the international community" (Royal Anthropological Institute 1995). Under the OLS umbrella, specialized UN agencies—including the World Food Program (WFP) and UN Children's Fund—UNICEF—and nongovernmental organizations (NGOs) provide a basic level of assistance to areas of Sudan both under government control and under rebel control. The south is still in a state of ongoing war, and the donor funds available for southern Sudan are precarious and inadequate for such a huge area with such enormous needs. As a result, OLS has been unable to build up the long-term resistance of communities to cope with crises on their own and exists in a reactive capacity rather than to anticipate and prevent crises.[10]

This was the scenario in 1998, with only 48% of the $109.4 million proposed budget for OLS approved by donors, in part because there had been ten years without a famine to match the one that had launched OLS (Deng 1999). The factors that led up to the famine were various—some having built up over a series of years and others being more spontaneous. Not least among the causes were many years of raiding by renegade Dinka commander Kerubino Kuanyin Bol and the People's Defense Forces, his subsequent defection, and a failed attempt by the main rebel group—the SPLA—to take the government-held towns of Wau and Aweil, causing massive displacement. In addition, there had been consecutive years of failed harvests, in 1997 caused by particularly low rainfall (Disasters Emergency Committee [DEC] 1999; Deng 1999). In late 1997, there were no signs of famine, according to the Dinka, because the part of the population that had suffered years of cumulative stress to their livelihoods since 1994 were sharing food with the part of the population that still had assets. What happened at the start of 1998, though, was that these remaining assets became exhausted as a result of the number of people relying on them—particularly the increased numbers of displaced people fleeing fighting in Wau town and staying with relatives in the countryside—and tipped families over the edge. The number of people in need in Sudan increased exponentially overnight as the host population was no longer suppressing a famine but actively becoming part of one. Once this stage had been reached, there were no local resources left to turn to, and large numbers of people needed outside help quickly.

Even the most inexperienced relief worker could clearly see what was happening. In one area, local people called the hunger *cok macok gaar*, meaning that it had a bell attached to its foot and could be heard coming from afar (Deng 1999). By May 1998, it was clear that there were large numbers of people, not just isolated individuals, in south Sudan without enough food. A Joint Task Force on Targeting and Vulnerabilities was created with representatives of the political and relief wings of the Sudan People's Liberation Army (the SPLM and the SRRAa[11]) and OLS to investigate and try to solve the problem. By the end of August 1998, the final report of the task force was able to conclude that there had been a lack of "contingency planning" in the relief operation and that OLS had "underestimated the total number of people in need" (SPLM/SSRA-OLS 1998a).

The task force noted that there is "a belief [by local people] that all are now in a vulnerable situation and thus should receive equally—even if it is a cup each" (SPLM/SSRA-OLS 1998a). Local people were thus challenging the idea of targeting assistance only to that group that were actually manifesting signs of advanced malnutrition. As a result, relief distributions that were planned by aid agencies to go to the vulnerable minority in a given territorial area were often reassembled by local authorities after the official distribution and redistributed subsequently to the general population through their kinship leaders and along kinship lines rather than on a territorial basis. Not only was such redesignation a necessary process to allow relief to enter into the kinship welfare system, it was also necessary because larger numbers were facing famine than aid agencies were targeting. This was interpreted by outsiders as diversion. When food had been given out to a child that qualified for supplementary feeding, the family would take it home and divide it among all the other children in the family that, although hungry, did not qualify for the center.[12] Thus the malnourished child received only a subdivided share of what aid workers had intended. It seemed logical to such aid workers to assume that the family were keeping the child starving as a way of accessing food, and Médecins Sans Frontières accused local people of doing this (Duffield et al. 2000).[13] In the same way, the task force argued that diversion to the army was starving civilians of aid that would have kept them alive.

The task force argued a strong case for better management of limited resources and recommended training local institutions and WFP field staff on the need for focused targeting of the most vulnerable. There were problems with shortages of planes, food, fuel, staff and trucks, as well as problems with the roads, but these were compounded by problems in the distribution system (meaning a failure of targeting). The fact that the local distribution system sought to provide a general ration to the majority of the population rather than targeting according to needs was seen as a problem to be overcome in the same way as the shortage of planes. Local

Table 14.1. NEEDS AND DELIVERIES FOR THE FIRST EIGHT MONTHS
        OF 1998.

Month	Local authority estimate of population in need (SRRA)	World Food Program estimate of population in need	Amount delivered (tons)	Ration per person (kg)[a]
January	1.2 million	250,000	140.1	0.56
February	1.2 million	350,000	494.6	1.41
March	1.2 million	350,000	1,225.7	3.50
April	1.2 million	595,000	984.1	1.65
May	1.2 million	595,000	2,750	4.62
June	1.2 million	701,000	3,439	4.91
July	1.5 million	701,000	4,731	6.75
August	1.5 million	1,000,000	14,937	14.9

Source: Figures from WFP (1998); SPLM/SSRA-OLS (1998)
[a] Actual amount divided by WFP population estimate.

authorities, on the other hand, blamed OLS for underestimating the number of people in need. There was thus a fundamental difference in opinion between agencies and local people, each accusing the other of being responsible for the starvation of the vulnerable.

Table 14.1 shows the amount of food being delivered did not peak until the month of August, six months after the threshold had been reached when local people could cope on their own shared assets. The ration per person increased exponentially only in that month. However, the number of deaths in one relief camp were at their highest for the week June 26 to July 2, when there was an acute shortage of food in the area (Harrigan and Changath 1999). It also shows how the WFP increased their estimate for the population in need in August, only when it could finally deliver the amount that was needed to the population that the local authorities (the SRRA) had already predicted in January. The improvement in conditions after August was brought about without any change to the distribution methodology in most places, but by an enormous increase in OLS capacity to deliver food, as well as a partial harvest and increasing supplies of fish. It was not achieved by successfully adopting a targeted distribution strategy.

A joint statement by the military and civilian wings of the Sudan People's Liberation Army released on July 27, 1998, expressed their appreciation for the assistance provided by the international community, but requested that they increase support from a target population of 700,000 "currently targeted" to 1.5 million (Table 14.1). It also complained that "UNICEF/OLS is mounting a concerted media campaign to divert attention from its inability to mount an effective response to avert the humanitarian crisis by accusing the SPLM/A of food diversion." The thing that seemed to cause more offense than the poor administration of relief was "the impression which UNICEF/OLS is attempting to portray, that it cares more for our people than the SPLM itself," an impression that is "unfortunate, unfounded, untrue and is deplorable."

In 1996, the Operation Lifeline Sudan *Review* wrote, "If targeting towards malnourished sections of the population is to take place, it should be done in addition to a general ration that makes up for the structural food deficits which exist" (Karim et al. 1996). What would have been of more use would have been to take local estimates of the needs more seriously in the early stages—with, of course, cross-checking by agency staff at the site. In 1998, even untrained eyes could see the most obvious evidence of needs on the ground.[14] As has been shown, it is also a false economy if the international community later has to pick up the cost of a failed targeted intervention—estimated at $1 billion for 1998 (DEC 1999). In Sudan in 1998, there simply wasn't enough food for the people who were genuinely vulnerable. Admission criteria for Supplementary Feeding Centers—an internationally agreed definition of malnutrition set at a ratio of 80% body mass to height—were reduced to 70% because the relief system could not cope with the number of people that, in an objective sense, were malnourished. The definition of vulnerability was thus a moving goalpost.

The people left out of this argument taking place at a political level are those who are actually vulnerable—what Duffield (1998) calls "the disappearing beneficiary"—to whom both the aid agencies and the SPLM are only questionably accountable. These are the people who know most about what is happening to them, how vulnerable they are, and what they most need. What was of most concern to them in 1998 was to build up their resilience to the risks to which they were exposed. An early intervention was therefore very much in the interests of these people. Local people were saying in 1998 that the UN would only give aid to people who were already too feeble to do anything for themselves, instead of intervening before the situation became desperate (*kake UN ee koc hoc*—literally, the things of the UN force people to starve). The relief effort of OLS did not really have any effect until most of the damage had been done. It is estimated that between 60,000 and 100,000 people died as a result of the emergency in 1998 that would not have died normally (DEC 1999).

Famine Theory and Famine Practice

If famine theory accurately explains the development of famine and is put into practice in famine prevention policy, then it should be possible to control famine. As Luka Biong Deng (1999) writes, "with famine theories mushrooming and after almost two decades of entitlement theory, the real challenge is to test how far these theories have benefited famine victims." However, Deng continues, "there is little evidence that the proliferation in the 1980s and 1990s of theories of famine has been translated into practical policies to prevent or control famine"(3). Massive amounts of food arriving in Sudan in March 1998 would have prevented a famine. But food aid, the most powerful weapon at the disposal of famine relief, arouses concerns that it fuels war, damages markets, is subject to corruption and political manipulation, and encourages dependency. Often that means that its use is kept to a minimum and is restricted to curative rather than preventative use. Such explanatory frameworks are cultural constructs and as such can usefully be examined in terms of the culture of the bureaucracies that use them, and can be understood in terms of the function that they perform to justify current public action rather than their efficacy in resolving famine.

DEFINITIONAL QUESTIONS

The way we look at famines today has essentially been defined by Sen's theory of entitlements, summed up in the 1981 book *Poverty and Famine*, and the reaction to that book by writers such as Rangasami (1985) and De Waal (1989). Important contributions by Keen (1994) and Duffield (1994) deal specifically with Sudan. These writers all sought to apply a high degree of empirical rigor to their work, and they use the experience of people who had actually suffered to inform the actions of policy makers. The activities of relief workers in 1998 in the field were vaguely informed by such debates about famine, but in an unsystematic way that transformed the debates into forms that corresponded with the agenda of relief workers. Collier refers to "an information cascade" where opinions "can be widely held without most of its adherents being able to justify it in terms of supporting propositions" (Bikchandani et al. 1992, cited in Collier 1999). Most relief workers do not read any of the books or journals that are produced by the policy departments of their own organizations, let alone universities or research institutes, although they are broadly aware of current debates when it comes to justifying themselves before donors or the media. However, they do, in general, now believe, following Sen, that lack of food does not in itself cause famine.

De Waal (1989) wrote of the danger of relief technologies such as nutritional surveillance giving aid agencies the power to define famines rather than allowing them to be defined by local people. His work sought to clarify the issue of famine, rather than to consign it into a definitional maze—"the Sahel [in 1973] *did* suffer famine," he comments (28, my italics). Sen writes that "much about poverty is obvious enough . . . one does not need elaborate criteria, cunning measurement or probing analysis" (Sen 1981, vii). In fact "one can very often diagnose [famine]—like a flood or a fire—even without being armed with a precise definition" (Sen 1981, 40). Neither author was encouraging the reaction to a famine to be delayed while definitional questions were clarified; nor did either author claim that it was not possible for famines to be caused by direct food entitlement failure.[15] In the case of Sudan in 1998, though, agencies chose to delay launching a fund-raising appeal while they addressed the definitional question of whether 1998 was a famine or not and clung to the idea that it was not the availability of food that was the problem but its poor distribution (London Times 1988). By creating a task force to try to understand what was happening, agencies were attempting to gain intellectual mastery of a problem that was fast escaping their control on the ground. It was clear in April 1998 that there *was* a famine, and the definitional battle was quickly lost by the judgment of television cameras.[16] An appeal was launched on May 21, 1998, and the food pipeline massively reinforced (DEC 1999).

POLITICALLY INFORMED RELIEF

Famines in Darfur, Sudan, in 1984–85 and Bahr-el-Ghazal in 1988 were, without doubt, part of an intentional policy that led to benefits accruing to certain sections of the population (Keen 1994). Analyses of these events were intended, at a time when famines were considered to be exclusively natural phenomena, to show that these famines in Sudan had been man-made. Keen wrote, "unless donors address themselves to the underlying processes creating famine and to the local power structures that shape famine and famine relief, their interventions might serve to reinforce these power structures and exacerbate famine" (Keen 1991). At around the same time, Macrae and Zwi observed that "the use of food as a weapon of war by omission, commission and provision has contributed to the creation of famine in recent decades" (Macrae and Zwi 1992, 299). Such analyses came to be accepted by most aid agencies toward the end of the 1990s.

However, as greater political consciousness was beginning to be shown in the policies of donors and relief workers, the pendulum began to swing in the opposite direction among academics. Writers began to criticize the way that aid policy was now being driven by a political vision of conflict management and liberal democratic transformation that was mixing political and humanitarian objectives (Duffield 1998). In an article entitled "Purity or Political Engagement," Macrae argued that "the pressure on humanitarian agencies to extend their range of activities into conflict resolution and developmental programming is a further indication of the trend towards delegation of responsibility from the political domain into the aid domain" (1998, 16). She goes on to recommend acting in a way that is politically informed rather than politically driven, and continuing to supply basic relief goods, in spite of donor fatigue and disengagement. By their reluctance to understand and work with the local political structure and by trying to establish systems parallel to the state structure, NGOs were failing to see the long-term importance of the local political structure and thereby limiting opportunities to negotiate its reform (Macrae 1998, 8).

This was the scenario in Sudan in 1998, where there was a complete breakdown in communication between relief agencies and the de facto state (the Sudan People's Liberation Movement). Agencies were operating on the 1988 model, where the Sudan government were seen as the cause of the famine, but OLS, operating out of Kenya, was relatively free of the kind of state interference that left relief wagons languishing in railway sidings at Meiram in 1988. The government of Sudan flight ban in Bahr-el-Ghazal in 1998 had little effect compared with the insidious government noncooperation experienced in 1988.[17] Issues such as who was responsible for protection of the vulnerable and who defines the vulnerable (or even *whether* they define them) are important political questions. "Care for the vulnerable" seems to imply political canonization, whereas their neglect leads to criticism and accusations from the media. "Finding" or "reaching" a vulnerable group despite the lack of cooperation from local leaders is a recurrent theme in emergencies. However, sometimes "targeting the vulnerable" can just be a disingenuous way of identifying a number of people that corresponds to the amount of a relief item that happens to have been sent in, because of the unpredictable nature of relief pipelines, and is not an attempt to do more politically informed relief. This is not, I believe, the result of malevolence on behalf of aid agencies. There are very real institutional issues—including chronic underfunding—that explain why agencies take the pragmatic decision to target aid. However, in this context, political activism could more usefully take the form of lobbying donors to speed up their response as well as improving their own capacity to respond. In addition, relief agencies should realize that engaging with local authorities and encouraging them to distribute relief in a fair and accountable manner is the best way of eventually producing a long-term civilian as opposed to purely military structure.[18] Failing to engage with the appropriate local structures also increases the chances of producing a corrupt, unsympathetic leadership accountable to neither their own people nor relief agencies.

They had very real difficulties to overcome, including funding problems, aircraft shortages, fuel shortages, and the destruction of a road bridge on the road to Mombassa. Such problems were understandable, but under the glare of the world's media, it seemed easier to go on the offensive and blame the military. OLS therefore launched the Task Force on Targeting and Vulnerabilities in a cynical exercise that invited the Sudan People's Liberation Movement to join in on a study to prove that its military wing (the SPLA) was responsible for diverting food. The whole process was itself a diversion.

CORRUPTION

A European Community evaluation report, examined below, concluded that the scale of diversion in Bahr el Ghazal was "much lower than in some conflicts" (for example, Somalia) (Duffield et al. 2000, 191).[19] It is unrealistic to imagine that the food eaten by civilians and soldiers can really be kept apart in the context of a nonprofessional army. Combatants and civilians in Bahr-el-Ghazal are often related, and food given to wives and daughters will probably feed combatant sons and brothers even without exploitation. The insistence that food be given only to vulnerable women and children encourages subterfuge and cover-up rather than genuine accountability (Duffield et al. 2000, 191). The choices are hard ones, but the open system of taxation to support the military (*tayeen*) used now is preferable to soldiers extorting food from locals at night with guns (Deng 1999).[20]

Systematic diversion to the army is just one possible form of corruption of relief goods. It has been established above that food aid among the Dinka, like grazing, is not seen as belonging to anyone, even to the extent that someone accused of stealing aid can reply, "what did I take from your mother?" (Deng 1999). The potential for corruption is therefore enormous. The only way to address the problem is to use a model of ownership of resources that is understood and respected by local people (that is, relief is owned by all) and to ensure that the rights of ownership over aid are asserted as soon as possible by inserting aid into the kinship system. Only then can those rights be protected by the indigenous legal system that exercises little jurisdiction over "unowned" relief goods.[21]

FOOD AND FAMINES

Deng argues that the 1998 famine was a result of "direct food entitlement failure" rather than the result of a "health crisis model" suggested by De Waal (De Waal 1990; Deng 1999). De Waal (1990) argues himself that there are rare cases where it is likely that there is a direct link between "food availability decline and famine." The 1998 famine was one that could have been averted with timely delivery of food, despite De Waal's reservations about the impact of food aid. That is not to suggest that food is enough to sustain meaningful human activity: there is music and dance and myths and marriage and a host of important social and political activities. However, it is important to have confidence in local ways of incorporating relief food into local cognitive systems. Cultures can be amazingly creative at absorbing a foreign influence that is beneficial to them, as well as ignoring one that is not in their interests.[22] Deng (1999) shows that where needy people were reluctant to come forward to accept relief in Abyei in 1952, Dinka chiefs took away the stigma attached to relief food by registering their own families to receive relief, and then encouraging the food to be widely shared rather than targeted. The way that food was widely distributed in 1998 showed that food was significant not just as a source of nutrition, but as a way of expressing group solidarity. It *is* possible to build up a model—especially at a theoretical level—that sees food aid as being harmful in a famine, but at an empirical level, it is much more difficult to sustain such an argument in the face of imaginative local indigenization of aid.

Too little food causes starvation, whatever distribution system is used. The number of people defined as needing food should not depend on the amount of food there is to distribute. It should reflect the scale of the problem that needs to be overcome and should be delivered as soon as these needs start to manifest themselves.[23] It should also be delivered in a professional way that reflects the capacity of the modern world to react rapidly when it chooses, and reflects the amount of time and money that is spent studying famine. An early reaction is much cheaper than one that comes too late, and fears that such an early reaction might be premature can damage markets or cause a "dependency culture." The poor should be trusted to use any surplus that a generous intervention might give them in a sensible way to build up its defenses against future crises. In addition, a clearer understanding of the nature of agricultural production in south Sudan makes it clear that the majority of production is for subsistence rather than the market, so food aid has a smaller possibility of having negative side effects on markets.

In the advanced stages of a famine, nutritionists are united in stating that it is pointless to provide "supplementary feeding" only for those showing visible signs of malnutrition if there is insufficient food for the majority of the population (Young 1992; MacAskill 1994). Supplementary feeding programs in such contexts suffer not only from high numbers of readmissions once patients have left feeding centers and returned to their families, but they are also unable to do anything about preventing the majority of the population descending into a state where they are vulnerable to malnutrition. However, despite their questionable effectiveness, in most major famines—including the 1998 famine in southern Sudan—such centers are set up. The reason is fairly simple: there is often insufficient food aid available in the early stages of a famine, and targeting of a group defined by objective nutritional criteria seems the fairest way to share that assistance.

SMALL AMOUNTS OF ASSISTANCE AND DEPENDENCY

Conversely, too much food given out does not necessarily cause people to become dependent; nor should limiting the amount of food distributed to encourage people to fill the deficit themselves be seen in such simplistic instrumental terms. The dependency model has its origins in studies of welfare recipients in the West, where up to 80% of household incomes were derived from welfare payments. However, Collier (1999) demonstrates that although welfare recipients might receive up to 80% of household income from welfare payments, gross aid flows to Africa "peaked at around 12%." In a "good policy environment," aid continues to have beneficial results for growth "until the share of aid in GDP is around 30%" (531). In a report entitled *Sudan: Unintended Consequences of Humanitarian Assistance*, for the European Community Humanitarian Office, the authors note that the average contribution of WFP food to the annual food requirement of individuals targeted in south Sudan between 1992 and 1998 was only 7.5% (Duffield et al. 2000). They write that "in south Sudan, there is no evidence that people are becoming dependent on food aid in any prolonged or permanent way." They are "in fact surviving this war largely by their own efforts and the natural resources available to them" (Duffield et al. 2000, 47). Sudanese people do not lay down their tools and wait for UN food to arrive. Instead, the one point that the massive airlift of 1998 made absolutely clear was the sheer amount of food that gets produced by the sweat and toil of local farmers in a normal year, and in 1998 needed to be replaced by food brought in from outside by plane.[24] According to Duffield et al. (2000), relief, on the other hand, can actually "reduce dependency in the sense that it enables households to conserve their assets and remain in their home areas, thereby supporting their agricultural and livestock systems" (47).

There is a danger that listening to the local value system and adopting a distribution system that targets the majority of the population will result in an inadequate amount of assistance going to the most needy. A finite amount of aid spread thinly across the whole population reduces its value to almost nothing. There is also the mandate of certain aid agencies to address the needs of particular groups such as children or the elderly. If a local value system reproduces gender inequalities, should it be supported? The arguments are valid ones, and the counterarguments sometimes sound like one is taking sides or idealizing the egalitarian nature of non-western societies. However, in a poor country in the throes of a civil war, the needs are going to be greater than the amount of aid available, and there are going to be some victims that slip through any welfare net, so there is something to be said for using a system where people are fully aware of their rights and responsibilities, and are familiar with how it functions. There are mechanisms that uphold the responsibilities of Dinka society to the most marginalized, especially through the courts (although this might take time).

It has not been shown that aid agencies, with their targeted approach, are any better at reaching these people than would be the case with the local system. This system at least gives the poor the strongest case for inclusion on the locally acknowledged principle of *equal* if not preferential treatment. Therefore, the idea that aid should be minimized to prevent dependency should not be seen as a valid argument, especially in a mainly subsistence economy. The slow reaction to the 1998 famine was in many ways caused by such a reduction in budgets (Duffield et al. 2000).[25] If it is an anthropologist's job to point out the dissonance between expressed reality and observed reality, then the idea of cutting budgets to save the most vulnerable must be a glaring example of this phenomenon.

THE FAILURE OF LOCAL COPING MECHANISMS

Declaring that local coping mechanisms have failed is a good excuse to ride roughshod over them. The widespread sharing through the kin network in 1998 caused the effects of the emergency to be felt throughout the population. The problem was that the kin groups had simply run out of resources to circulate. People from all walks of life had died in 1998—including men, the displaced, widows, and children. The people who suffered were from small kinship units, particularly those who were cut off from a larger kinship group, such as widows and estranged wives; those from small, fractured families; and the displaced or those who were away from home when the problems erupted. If anything, the statistics, and the general feelings expressed, indicate stronger adults were not collectively leaving their older and younger people to go hungry while they fed themselves (Harragin and Changath 1999). There was not a general collapse in moral standards. Deng's study on the 1998 famine concludes that the effects of an ongoing war "did not trigger absence of law and order amongst the communities in Bahr el Ghazal region, and nor did famine itself" (Deng 1999, 106). However, declaring that local moral standards have collapsed legitimizes the intervention of outside agencies with different cultural practices, ethics predicated on running an aid program rather than preserving the values of a society. Events were to show, though, that the international community *did* seriously underestimate the number of people in need in the early stages, and ended up finally demonstrating, by a massive food relief operation lasting almost two years, that it had in fact been all the population that had been in need (Duffield et al. 2000).

CONCLUDING THOUGHTS ON THE USE OF "FAMINE THEORY"

There is strong feeling among relief workers that they should speak out on behalf of the oppressed in the places where they work—for example, for Médecins Sans Frontières, *temoinage* (literally "witnessing") is written into the mission statement of the organization. However, there is a danger that overzealous "representing" of their opinions leaves the poor without a voice and leaves relief agencies believing that the poor cannot think or act for themselves. It is dangerous when relief agencies start to make calculations on the basis of the image of the poor they have themselves created—for example, the myth that giving less relief will make people diversify away from relief. The test of models that seek to represent the behavior of the poor is simple: do they represent the poor, or do they present the theory of being poor according to relief workers?

The model relief agencies used in Sudan was defined by what relief workers could do about the situation rather than the situation itself (De Waal 1989). Inaccurate representation is unimportant if the object is to create "powerful, pervasive and long-lasting moods" that one is helping. If, however, one looks at a model *of* reality in south Sudan on the basis of what really happens, rather than what we would like to happen or what we fear *might* happen, we see the following: food given out before a famine prevents that famine from occurring, and food given out in anticipation of a reasonably likely famine that never materialized allows people to build up their defensive strategies, rather than causing them to become dependent. In creating a model *of* reality, it is vital to take as a starting point the self-interested nature of each society's encounter with another society. One must allow for the misrepresentation by each party

of the other's point of view, both voluntarily and involuntarily, as a necessary process of developing and justifying their own identity.[26] In other
words, one must accept that the West will delay reacting to a famine as
long as it can possibly avoid it, hoping it will simply go away so that it can
avoid the genuine cost of an emergency relief operation and hoping those
crying "famine" have misread the situation.[27] There *will* be conflicts of
opinion—and the opinion of the West will not necessarily be right,
although it will often be the most influential. Given the self-interested
nature of aid, it should not be for one party—in this case, the donor—to
define what is in the interest of the other party.

The Social Scientist's Role as Cultural Interpreter

The message communicated by most anthropologists to respect local
knowledge and allow people to speak for themselves is not just neglected
but actively ignored by nonanthropologists (Warren and Brokensha 1980).
In 1932, Sir Harold MacMichael (civil secretary in the Sudan government)
wrote in the introduction to *The Pagan Tribes of the Nilotic Sudan* that
anthropologists were of help to administrators to explain how local
requests that seemed "idiotic" at first sight could be shown to be reasonable when "explained by the applicant in his own tongue" and "understood in the light of the local viewpoint (Seligman and Seligman 1932,
xviii). Half a century later, the message still does not seem to have gotten
through. Although anthropology has spent a lot of time examining its relationship to colonialism and feels an ambiguous engagement with the
whole development process, it continues to call for the same improved
understanding and awareness of the nature of local cultural complexities
(Bennett 1988). Even the most basic anthropological consciousness could
benefit the work of development agencies, what Ryle referred to as "a
diffuse anthropological sensibility" (in Benthall 1995). Anthropologists
are, in the words of Dyson-Hudson, "essentially translators" motivated by
"the conviction that it is both necessary and possible to explain human
groups to each other" (1991).

Anthropologists who take part in development projects tend to call for
the same solutions—"local participation, awareness of social and cultural
complexities, and the use of ethnographic knowledge in the planning
stage" (Gardner and Lewis 1996). They also recommend "a recognition of
ones own ethnocentricity" as well as an understanding of "the problems of
intercultural communication (including racism, nationalism, xenophobia
and ethnic conflict)" (Shore 1996).[28] According to Zulkuf Aydin, such
conclusions about the role of social science "are not new or original and

are well known to planners in agencies like the World Bank. . . . yet in each new development project they are not taken into full consideration" (quoted in Saleem-Murdock 1990, 333). It will be ignored as long as donors are not prepared to understand or accept their own ethnocentricity (the natural tendency to be attached to ones own solutions).[29]

The lesson that anthropological self-consciousness can teach the practice of relief work is the benefit of constantly reexamining the personal and institutional prejudices that lie in the way of an objective understanding of a phenomenon on the ground. Anthropology has occupied itself for twenty years with analyzing its own misrepresentation of other societies, rather than focusing on how such societies are subjected to much more obvious caricature in other areas such as "development." It is time it realized that such introspection risks failing to engage with global forces that will sweep on with or without anthropological insights.[30] It is a local person's own definition of what constitutes well-being that ultimately counts, and it should be the job of an anthropologist to express that person's definition as faithfully as possible. A well-meaning outsider's best intentions to provide aid will be futile if none of his or her priorities corresponds with those of the person being helped nor engage with his or her culture and political or economic institutions. It is all too easy and too human to forget that there are also the good intentions of a local welfare mechanism that existed well before the invention of humanitarian assistance, and a humane value system that does not depend on outsiders to tell people to take care of their weakest members.

Notes

The fieldwork for this chapter was undertaken between June 1997 and December 1998 as part of a project funded by USAID for Save the Children (UK)—the Southern Sudan Vulnerability Study—which aimed to take an anthropological look at the idea of targeting of vulnerable populations in south Sudan. The views reflected in this chapter are those of the author and do not represent the views of these organizations. Helpful comments were also received on an earlier draft of this chapter from Mary Douglas, for which many thanks are due.

1. This trend was encouraged by Talal Asad's *Anthropology and the Colonial Encounter* (1973); Edward Said's *Orientalism* (1979); and Clifford and Marcus's collection *Writing Culture* (1984).

2. Foucault (1980) describes how an explanation of a phenomenon imparts power over it.

3. Gardner and Lewis write (1996, 153), "discourses of development are produced by those in power and often result (even if unintentionally) in reproducing power relations between areas of the world and between people."

4. Note that "relief" is shorthand in aid work for emergency humanitarian intervention and is seen as opposed to "development" as part of the questionable "relief-development" continuum.

5. See Deng (1999, 66): "Famine is a tragedy that can easily be prevented; it is recurrent simply because of a lack of public action with effective policies to contain it."

6. Much time was spent debating the definition of *famine* in 1998, mainly by those furthest away from events on the ground. The *London Times* of April 30 headlined its editorial "There is no famine in Sudan yet," taking its lead from major British NGOs. De Waal (1989) recommends that famines are called by the terms of those who experience them. The general term that was in use by local people (*cong dit*) can be translated in current usage as "famine," although each area gave the famine a different name (De Waal 1989; Deng 1999).

7. Relief workers tend to see conflict as "an interruption" to the normal state of society and as an irrational obstruction that prevents them from doing their work, rather than being a logical response to a dispute over resource allocation and the fundamental reason they are there (Duffield 1998).

8. Girls must be married outside the family group, and this circulation of bride wealth represents one of the only economic transactions between nonrelated groups in a subsistence economy.

9. Kinship groups can be huge, and there are different levels of sharing within the group. At the level of economic ownership of cattle—the *mac thok*—sharing is considered to be without question. This is the group that collects and shares bride wealth together. At a higher level—the *gol*—food is shared ceremonially as a way of reinforcing kinship solidarity.

10. Ironically, better preventative work would reduce the funds available to OLS as donors perceive that there is no longer a crisis.

11. SRRA (Sudan Relief and Rehabilitation Association) and SPLM (Sudan Peoples Liberation Movement).

12. The initial admission criteria for supplementary feeding centers was less than 80% ratio of body mass to height.

13. "An unfortunate tendency to see the people as 'the problem' and the technicians, bureaucrats and planners as 'the solution'" (Cernea 1991, 466).

14. "Formal early-warning techniques appeared to have played only a minor role in famine prevention . . . early response has been much more a matter of political incentives and motivation than one of informational or predictive wizardry" (Drèze and Hussain 1995, 290).

15. Sen (1981) writes, "one of the major influences on the actual prevention of famine is the speed and force with which early hunger is reported and taken up in political debates."

16. This was also a feature noted by Rau for India in Drèze and Sen (1990).

17. "The argument that denial of access by the [Government of Sudan] was the major cause of the delayed humanitarian response is weak and a smokescreen, as the denial of access occurred only during the months of February and March and was relatively normal for the rest of the year" (Deng 1999).

18. A senior Sudanese official comments: "We acknowledge the positive role

of OLS in our struggle, but not because it provides food. It is primarily because it helps us run a state" (Duffield et al. 2000, 181).

19. The desire to see "diversion" all around is a self-fulfilling prophecy that has much to do with the insecure feeling of foreignness and paranoia aid workers feel in Sudan. For some cases where there genuinely was corruption due to failure to insert aid into an accountable local structure, see Harragin and Changath (1999).

20. It is also worth noting that the famine was occurring in the core area of support for the SPLA, and the political costs of hoarding food for the army during a major famine are much greater than they are when food is plentiful.

21. In fact, it is very rare that agencies use local courts to follow up pilfering of relief goods.

22. The Dinka resisted the influence of missionaries for a hundred years until Christianity became a useful way of getting health care, education, and a corporate identity against the Muslim north.

23. Obviously the calculation of numbers is particularly difficult in an emergency, but it is uncanny how relief operations consistently estimate a figure that is too low ("statistics that owe more to guesswork and imagination than research"; Keen and Ryle 1996).

24. "The ethnocentric inference that rural war-affected populations in the Third World will make effective responses only when outsiders tell them not to become dependent on outside assistance, and that self-reliance will be instilled in people by being told so" (Jok 1998). Geertz also showed that the dependency model did not work in rural Java (Turton 1988).

25. According to Deng (1999, 70), the small amount received as a result of the 1997 appeal (50% of the amount pledged) "was inconsistent with the claim made by the head of DfID that lack of money was not the problem in the Sudan crisis."

26. "The formation of groups and societies depends upon the unequal treatment of members and non-members" (Banton 1999).

27. "When administrators or rulers do not know what to do, they usually ignore the problem in the hope that it will go away. This has been the history of southern Sudan throughout the 20th century" (Collins 2000, 4).

28. Anthropology looks at things from different points of view and is "not so much interested in matters of fact as perceptions and expression of reality" (Ellen 1984).

29. "*Our* customs do not hinder efficiency . . . this is not because we have particularly distinct customs, but because we define efficiency in the context of our customs" (Cancian 1974, quoted in Turton 1988, 147, my italics).

30. Ahmed and Shore (1995) argue that the crisis affecting anthropology is not about lack of representation but about lack of relevance.

CHAPTER 15

The Mayan Movement
and National Culture in Guatemala

SHELTON H. DAVIS

Introduction

In 1981, the Mexican anthropologist Guillermo Bonfil Batalla published a collection of statements by a number of young indigenous leaders and organizations that highlighted the emergence of a new form of ethnic consciousness among Latin America's more than 40 million indigenous people (Bonfil Batalla 1981). During the previous decade, these leaders and organizations began to question the conventional notion that the region was composed of monolithic nation-states that were on their way to socially and culturally assimilating or integrating their large indigenous populations. Throughout Latin America, intellectuals of indigenous background and leaders of newly formed indigenous organizations were questioning the generally accepted interpretations of the historical and cultural roots of their countries, affirming their rights to their ancestral lands and cultures, and calling for a formal recognition of the multiethnic, pluricultural, and multilingual nature of Latin American societies. Bonfil Batalla highlighted the significance of the viewpoints of these new indigenous intellectuals and movements for the future of Latin American countries and warned that policy makers would be wise to take into account their claims in terms of official recognition, human rights, and participation as distinct peoples with their own identities and cultures in national politics and decision making (Bonfil Batalla 1981).

Since the publication of Bonfil Batalla's book, many of his predictions about the new indigenous movements in Latin America have come true.

In fact, one of the results of the rise of the new indigenous movements has been the transformation of the national political cultures and the recognition of the realities of ethnic diversity and cultural pluralism by many Latin American countries. Throughout the 1980s and 1990s, as many Latin American countries reestablished democratic polities and liberalized their economies, new political spaces opened up for the recognition of the claims of indigenous peoples. The nature of these changes took many forms from the rewriting of national constitutions and the ratification of International Labour Organization (ILO) Convention 169 on Indigenous and Tribal Peoples, to the setting up of national bilingual/intercultural education programs and the creation of a Hemispheric Fund for Indigenous Peoples. In countries such as Argentina, Bolivia, Brazil, Colombia, Ecuador, Paraguay, Peru, and Venezuela, these changes came about through democratic protests and lobbying of their governments and parliamentarians by indigenous organizations. In other countries, such as Nicaragua and Guatemala, and in Mexico as a result of the Zapatista rebellion in Chiapas, it was mainly through armed movements that the rights of indigenous peoples were brought to national attention and eventually recognized within the context of peace negotiations between governments and insurgent groups (van Cott 1994).

Here, I look at the social and historical roots of one of these indigenous movements, the Mayan movement in Guatemala, and I analyze some of its implications for Guatemalan national culture, legal reform, and public policy making. Although the Mayan movement in Guatemala has its own peculiarities and is not as unified at the national level as in some other countries (for example, Bolivia or Ecuador), it has had a significant effect on both the 1990s peace process in that country and more recently on national policies relating to education and culture and the discussion surrounding the preparation of a national poverty reduction strategy. Most significantly, the Mayan movement has been relatively successful in bringing to public attention and gaining some formal recognition of Guatemala's multiethnic, pluricultural, and multilingual character (LeBaron 1993; Fischer and Brown 1996; Warren 1998).

By way of introduction, it is important to note that Guatemala, unlike some of the other Central American countries, still has a relatively large indigenous population. Depending on the source or means of identification, between 40% to 60% of the country's 11 million people still speak an indigenous language (either one of twenty-one Mayan Indian languages or two smaller indigenous languages, Xinca or Garífuna) and/or identify as indigenous people. These contemporary indigenous peoples, most of whom reside in the western highlands or the northern parts of the country, maintain strong social and historical ties to their communities of origin, possess traditional agricultural and land-use practices, and have a world-renowned arts and crafts tradition, as reflected, for example, in the colorful textiles produced by Mayan women.[1]

The past several decades have seen major transformations in the rural economy of Guatemala brought about through demographic growth, land fragmentation and scarcity, and urban and international migration. At the same time, extreme poverty and lack of access to basic services continue on a massive scale. More than half of the Guatemalan national population (56.7%) and nearly three-quarters of the rural indigenous population (73.8% as compared to 40.6% of the nonindigenous population) live in conditions of poverty. On almost all indicators of social and economic welfare—household income and consumption, literacy and schooling, child health and nutrition, access to potable water and decent housing, etc.—the Guatemalan rural indigenous population is among the poorest in Latin America and ranks with many of the poorest populations in the world.[2]

Added to this poverty profile is a pattern of social exclusion and racial and cultural discrimination that Guatemalan national society inherits from its colonial and postcolonial past. Until 1945, most land and labor legislation in Guatemala discriminated against the country's majority indigenous population. Throughout much of its national history, the Guatemalan agrarian economy was characterized by a type of structural dualism in which indigenous land and labor were exploited for purposes of capitalist agricultural development. This was basically large-scale, plantation-based coffee production for export markets.[3]

At the same time, the country's dominant political and social ideology, especially from the late 19th century onward, was one of an "exclusive nationalism." This ideology, represented in legal codes and the writings of prominent Guatemalan intellectuals, did not recognize or respect the cultural diversity of the country's Mayan-speaking indigenous population. Denied access to education in their own languages and unable to vote for national office holders if they were not literate in Spanish, the Mayan-speaking population had no formal "citizenship" rights well into the second half of the 20th century. National political power and social ideology were dominated by a small ladino (the term used for the Spanish-speaking, nonindigenous population of Guatemala but comprising a great variety of class and ethnic groupings) elite that had little respect for the languages, cultures, beliefs, or knowledge of the Mayan-speaking population.[4]

The following essay traces the historical and sociological antecedents of the contemporary Mayan movement's response to this "exclusive nationalism" and shows how this movement has created a new discourse of a multiethnic, pluricultural, and multilingual state in Guatemala. The essay opens with a brief historical discussion of the rise of coffee production in Guatemala, its effects on the lands and labor of the Mayan population, and its relation to the social and ideological construction of Guatemalan nationhood. After this, the essays turns to a discussion of some of the most important social, economic, and political changes that affected the Mayan population in the period after World War II. In particular, the essay focuses on the implications for the Maya of the national revolution that occurred in Guatemala in October 1944 and ended with the United States–supported military coup that overthrew the socially progressive government of President Jacobo Arbenz Guzman in June 1954. In the aftermath of the 1954 coup, a further process of what might be called "sociological awakening" took place within Mayan Indian communities, led this time by foreign missionaries of the Roman Catholic Church. At the same time, a general process of pauperization took place among the indigenous peasantry, spurred on by population growth and increasing land scarcity. The combination of the militarizing of the Guatemalan state, the sociological awakening and mobilization of the indigenous population, and the increasing poverty and deterioration of the rural peasant economy set the stage for the widespread political violence and civil war that gripped Guatemala in the late 1970s.

In the third section of the essay, I discuss the emergence of the Mayan movement, its lobbying for the ratification of ILO Convention 169, and its effects on the drafting and eventual signing of the Guatemalan peace accords in the mid-1990s. In terms of the latter, the major agreement is clearly the Accord Relating to the Identity and Rights of Indigenous Peoples signed by the Guatemalan government and the National Revolutionary Unity (URNG, the umbrella organization of the Guatemalan guerrilla groups) in Mexico in March 1995. Although there have been numerous setbacks in the fulfillment of the Guatemalan peace accords, including a May 1999 referendum that failed to provide public support for constitutional reform, the Mayan movement has played a significant role in promoting a new conception of the Guatemalan nation that is based on the idea of a multiethnic, pluricultural, and multilingual state. Using this notion as a central theme, the last section of the essay focuses on the role that this new vision of the Guatemalan nation has had on recent educational and cultural policies and the emerging debate surrounding the preparation of a national poverty reduction strategy. A major argument here is that the Mayan movement, despite its internal divisions and difficulties in generating more fundamental constitutional reforms as in some other Latin American countries, has had a significant effect on Guatemalan national culture. To understand the significance of this change in national culture, however, it is necessary to go back more than a century and a quarter and trace the effects of the rise of coffee production on the Mayan-speaking population.

The Coffee Republic and the Creation of the Guatemalan Nation

Most historians agree that the rise of coffee production in Guatemala in the second half of the 19th century had a profound effect on both the national economy and the country's indigenous population. As the Guatemalan sociologist Edelberto Torres Rivas notes in his classic study of the economic and social history of modern Central America, the insertion of Central America in the world market economy began with the late 19th-century production and export of coffee on a major scale. By the mid-1880s, coffee comprised 75% of the value of all exports in Costa Rica, 85% in Guatemala, and 53% in El Salvador. Yet there were major differences in the domestic effects that coffee production had on the social structures of these three Central American countries. In Costa Rica, where the crop was first planted as early as the mid-19th century, coffee was produced on small estates owned by immigrant farmers and with a salaried, non-Indian labor force. In contrast, in Guatemala and El Salvador, the expansion of coffee production depended on the private expropriation of Indian communal lands and the forced mobilization by the state of Indian labor.[5]

Guatemala, with a population at the end of the 19th century estimated to be 1.5 million people and with 64.7% of the national population categorized as Indian, led the way in preparing the legal groundwork for the growth of coffee production. In the 1870s, President Justo Rufino Barrios, the architect of the late 19th-century Guatemalan liberal reform, promulgated a series of decrees promoting the early development of coffee production in the Alta Verapaz and Pacific Piedmont regions. Between 1871 and 1883, the Barrios government sold over 397,000 hectares of "public lands" to coffee planters in what are today the richest and most productive areas of the country. Many of these lowland coffee areas, such as the famous Costa Cuca above the Pacific coast, had previously been cultivated by highland Mayan subsistence farmers.[6]

Barrios also reinstated the colonial labor institution of the *mandamiento*, which enabled regional political authorities to force a given number of persons from each of the highland Indian communities to work for the new coffee planters. A special rural labor law of 1877 compelled all rural workers to carry a document showing their labor obligations, legalized the system of *mozos colonos*, or resident tenants and sharecroppers on coffee plantations, and regulated the flow of Indian laborers from the highland townships to the coastal coffee farms. At the same time, the national government also called for the registration and titling of all municipal and communal lands. Over 45% of the land grants that were given by the government to individuals in the seven most highly populated Indian departments between 1896 and 1918 were to persons with Spanish or European surnames. These were essentially non-Indians—either ladinos or recently arrived Europeans—who had migrated into the highland Indian departments at the turn of the 20th century and who were trying to profit from the national coffee boom as local merchants, liquor salesmen, and labor contractors (Davis 1997b).

From a cultural perspective, two things are important to note about this period of increasing incorporation of Guatemala and its Mayan-speaking indigenous population into the world economy for coffee and other agricultural commodities. The first was the emergence of an ideological current among the Guatemalan political and social elite (many of Spanish or recent European immigrant background), which saw the indigenous population and their cultures as obstacles to national progress. One of the most prominent of these elite figures was a Guatemalan lawyer, writer, and diplomat named Antonio Batres Jáuregui. In 1892, to mark the fourth centenary of Columbus's discovery of America, Batres Jáuregui wrote a prize-winning essay on the history of the Mayan Indians. In his essay, Batres Jáuregui noted that although the Indian population of Guatemala had nearly tripled since the beginning of the century, it still lacked the economic dynamism of the non-Indian, or ladino, sector of the population. Citing John Stuart Mill's *Principles of Political Economy*, Batres Jáuregui argued that the forced labor laws reintroduced under the liberal regime of Justo Rufino Barrios held the Indian population in a condition of virtual slavery and prevented its members from experiencing individual liberty. These laws, Batres Jáuregui claimed, explained the low level of productivity in the Indian sector of the agricultural economy and the fact that the country failed to produce sufficient food crops and basic grains (Batres Jáuregui 1893).

In his essay, Batres Jàuregui also attacked indigenous systems of communal property and the ineffectiveness of Spanish land laws, which recognized such communal land tenure. He claimed that even those laws that were instituted after the reform period in 1871 to promote commercial agriculture benefited only the large landowners and the ladino sector of the population. The Indians, he wrote, continued "to live under a primitive system of communal property ownership, which represents epochs of poverty and backwardness" (Batres Jáuregui 1893, 72).

After surveying the general backwardness of several Indian townships, Batres Jauregui suggested that the government should follow the examples of Chile and Argentina, introducing a new rural code that would integrate Indians into the wider society. Such a code, he said, would abolish Indian communal lands, regulate the contracting of rural laborers, and prepare Indians to become members of modern society through the teaching of Spanish and the introduction of new agricultural and industrial arts. "It is necessary," Batres Jáuregui wrote, "that the agrarian laws, along with fomenting the development of agriculture, should bring the aborigines along the road to civilization" (Batres Jáuregui 1893, 159). He wrote,

We need to give the Indians the means to leave their communal system, their common and unchanging dress, their barbaric diet of totopoxte [large corn cakes] and chili; their antediluvian languages; their rural, primitive, and rustic homes. In a word, Indians need to be removed from their manner of being—immutable and oriental. It cannot be doubted, then, that Indians are very able to develop their civilization and promote progress.[7]

Batres Jáuregui's views, as well as those of a number of other prominent Guatemalan political leaders and intellectuals of the late 19th and early 20th centuries, led to a series of laws calling for the private titling and distribution of the last remaining indigenous communal lands. They also called for the education of the rural population, their learning of Spanish, and their assimilation into the ways of western commerce, work habits, and culture. The reigning theory of education during this period—although seldom put into practice outside of the major urban centers—was based on the notion of a homogenous nation rooted in western European culture and the suppression of aboriginal languages and cultures. It was also based on an exclusionary idea of citizenship that, from the first liberal constitution of 1879 until the passage of a new democratic constitution in 1945, provided that only men who were literate in Spanish had a right to vote and hold national political office.[8]

The second point that needs to be emphasized about this period in Guatemalan history is that Indians did not respond passively to either the rise of coffee production or the attempts to ideologically negate the worth of their languages, cultures, and traditions. For example, numerous anthropologists who did research in Guatemala during the 1920s and 1930s recognized the profound effects that the coffee plantation system was having on the Mayan peoples. Yet these same scholars also discovered that the modern Mayas still maintained a fairly vibrant and cohesive community culture and a strong sense of local ethnic identity. Each highland Mayan community had a unique style of dress and dialect, practiced local village or township endogamy, and maintained a rich ceremonial life based on remnants of the ancient Mayan calendar and community worship of the Catholic saints. Mayan culture and ethnic identity, in other words, had persisted at the local township or community level despite strong pressures for acculturation from the plantation system and Guatemalan national society.[9]

In 1941, anthropologist Sol Tax of the University of Chicago, who had just completed several years of field research in the Indian townships surrounding Lake Atitlan, tried to explain why there was so little ethnic passage or so-called ladinoization of the Guatemalan Indian population. Tax noted that the minimal degree of acculturation of Guatemala's Mayan-speaking Indians could not be explained simply by social barriers to ethnic passage or a lack of physical proximity between the Indian and ladino populations. For although ladinos comprised less than 10% of the population in most highland Indian townships, they lived in almost every town where there were major Indian social, religious, and marketing centers, and they were in almost continuous interpersonal contact with the Indian population. Yet despite this intense, day-to-day personal contact between ethnic groups, there was very little passage of Indians to the ladino class, demonstrating that it was possible, according to Tax, "to live in continued physical contact with the suburbs of modern urban civilization" and still maintain a strong sense of ethnic identity and a highly traditional, religiously based, community culture (Tax 1941).

Although Sol Tax and his contemporaries never phrased the phenomenon in these terms, it can be argued that, at least at the community level, a movement of ethnic resistance and revitalization arose among the Mayan Indians of Guatemala during the period that historians call the *siglo de café*, or "century of coffee." Anthropological studies conducted during this period show that indigenous peoples do not necessarily vanish or disappear in the face of sustained contact with what is today called the "modern world system." On the contrary, these studies indicate that indigenous peoples have often tended to reaffirm their native ethnic identities and cultural traditions as a collective defense mechanism when faced with the loss of large amounts of communal lands and the transformation of large numbers of people into a seasonal rural proletariat for capitalist agricultural estates.[10]

In the case of Guatemala's Mayan Indian population, three important aspects of this ethnic affirmation process occurred during this period of agroexport growth and liberal political reform. First, as Tax pointed out, traditional ethnic identity in Guatemala at this time was locally based and focused on the township or municipal unit, rather than on a larger language or ethnic group. Second, the major organizational way in which ethnicity was expressed was through participation in local religious brotherhoods (*cofradías*) or other organizations dedicated to the worship of Mayan gods and Catholic saints. And third, the social ideology of traditional Indian ethnic identity tended to support, rather than challenge, the ethnic division of labor (Indians as peasants and rural workers and ladinos as large landowners) on which the national economy was based. As we shall see, new social and economic conditions emerged in Guatemala after the October 1944 national revolution, and these in turn led to a rephrasing of both national social ideology and Mayan ethnic identity. Nevertheless, many aspects of Guatemalan social structure and culture remain as inheritances of the agroexport economy and the late 19th-century period of liberal reform.

The "Sociological Awakening" and Impoverishment of the Mayan Indian Population

On October 20, 1944, a group of young army officers and university students deposed General Federico Ponce, the hand-picked successor to the dictator Jorge Ubico (1931–44), and launched what was to become a new but brief era of democratic government and social reform in Guatemala. From the early days of the government of Dr. Juan José Arévalo (1945–51), a former schoolteacher and the first democratically elected president after the October Revolution, the new government focused attention on the social and economic conditions of the country's indigenous population and rural poor. The discussion leading up to the drafting of the 1945 political constitution, for example, contained a lively debate about the appropriate policies for incorporating indigenous communities into the new national project of social reform. Among other things, the 1945 constitution outlawed all forms of discrimination (Article 21); called for the providing of adequate housing, sanitation and working conditions for "indigenous workers" (Article 67); declared the need for the government to formulate an integral policy for the economic, social, and cultural benefit of the indigenous groups (Article 83); recognized popular arts and industries as essential elements of national culture (Article 87); and provided for government recognition and protection of what remained of indigenous communal lands (Article 96).[11]

As a follow-up to the 1945 constitution, the government introduced other laws and programs that were intended to improve the socioeconomic conditions and incorporate the indigenous population into national politics. These included a new municipal law that provided for local democratic elections, a law of forced rental of farm lands to tenants and squatters, a social security law, and laws providing for the protection of indigenous textiles and recognizing special orthographies for the writing of the four major Mayan languages, K'iche', Kaqchikel, Mam, and Q'eqchi'. The Ministry of Education also began a national literacy program (the first in the country's history), and the government created a National Indigenist Institute. The latter was established to focus greater attention on the "ethnic problem that confronts the social constitution of the country" and to search for the most appropriate methods of "incorporating the Indian into national culture."[12]

The National Indigenist Institute, which was part of a hemispheric movement to incorporate indigenous peoples into national social reform efforts, played a particularly important role in investigating the social, economic, and cultural conditions of the Mayan communities during this period. One of the most important of these efforts was the institute's conducting of a series of community studies, using modern anthropological field techniques, which provided ethnographic and socioeconomic profiles of more than a hundred Mayan communities. These studies found that there was great variability in the degree of traditionalism or acculturation among (and within) the indigenous communities, as well as in their land tenure and productive systems.[13]

In preparation for a congressional debate surrounding a proposed agrarian reform law, the government also conducted the first national agrarian census. The 1950 Agrarian Census demonstrated the strong dualism of Guatemalan agriculture, especially between the small-scale *minifundia* agriculture of the indigenous peasantry in the western highlands and the large-scale export agriculture along the Pacific coast. It also documented the great differences in land ownership between the Indians and ladinos. The 1950 Agrarian Census, for example, found that 72% of the farmland in the country was controlled by 2% of the farm units (mainly large coffee and banana plantations or cattle ranches); 88% of the farm units (mainly small subsistence farmers) controlled 14% of the land; and only 10% of the farms were family-sized units. Many of the small farm units were barely able to provide for subsistence, although a number of the large farms possessed lands that were uncultivated (there were over 1.75 million hectares of "unused" land on privately held estates according to a 1947 Ministry of Agriculture survey) (Handy 1994, 13, 82).

Just as revealing were the findings of another set of surveys carried out by the government's statistical bureau that revealed the continuing dependency of rural smallholders (most of them Mayan farmers) on municipal and communal lands. The surveys carried out in 1951, just before the introduction of the agrarian reform law, and on the basis of interviews with local municipal authorities found that there were still 505,129 hectares of municipal lands and 294,458 hectares of communal lands distributed across the country's twenty-two administrative departments. The municipal lands served an estimated 56,120 "comuneros" and were either being rented out by the municipal corporations to local residents for purposes of cultivation, maintained as forest reserves, or being used for pasturage or other purposes. The communal lands, although not as extensive as those controlled by municipal governments, comprised 124 *comunidades* and served an almost equal number of *comuneros* as those served by municipally held lands. The departments that had the largest amount of such municipal and communal lands were mainly in the areas of indigenous occupation, both in the western highlands and eastern sections of the country.[14]

The Agrarian Reform Law (Decree 900) was introduced by the newly elected government of Colonel Jacobo Arbenz Guzman in 1952 and became the most controversial policy of his administration. Decree 900, as many commentators have noted, hardly posed a radical solution to Guatemala's agrarian problems as it had as its explicit goal to introduce "agricultural capitalism" in the Guatemalan countryside, a goal that, interestingly, was shared by a World Bank mission that visited Guatemala and presented a study to Colonel Arbenz Guzman three months after he assumed office in June 1951. However, the agrarian reform legislation and some of Arbenz's main advisors supported a mass mobilization of peasants, tenant farmers, and rural workers into peasant leagues, syndicates, and agrarian committees. The agrarian reform legislation also provided for the expropriation and eventual distribution to peasants (albeit only in usufruct) of lands that were privately owned but not in cultivation. In addition, it contained one article (Article 9) that stated that uncultivated municipal lands (except those that were designated as "forest reserves" and under the control and management of the national government) could be denounced by agrarian committees; and another article (Article 33) that provided that those lands that were in conflict between municipalities and agrarian committees would be adjudicated in favor of the latter.[15]

Not surprisingly, given the political turmoil and tense nature of interethnic relations that existed in many Indian townships, conflicts arose between municipal governments and agrarian committees, as well as between these entities and recently formed peasant committees. The nature of these conflicts depended on the ethnic composition and politi-

cal history of each Indian township, as well as the meteoric way in which
political parties were being formed on the national and municipal levels.
The issue of control over municipal lands and their distribution under the
agrarian reform also got entangled in religious disputes at the local level
as new Protestant sects began to have an increasing presence in the countryside and as a reform movement called Catholic Action began to
counter and come into conflict with more traditional forms of Mayan-
Catholic religious belief. What is clear from the archival record, the writings of observers in the countryside during this period, and the oral testi-
mony of surviving peasant activists is that the struggle for land became a
source of intense political conflict both at the national level and in local
Indian townships during the implementation of the short-lived agrarian
reform.[16]

Along with this general political environment, another factor that
clearly fueled much of the intense intra- and intercommunal conflicts
during this and subsequent periods was of a demographic nature. Namely,
from 1950 onward (when more modern national censuses were available),
population began to grow rapidly in Guatemala. The 1950 population
census enumerated a national population of 2.9 million inhabitants, but
almost every census since this date has indicated intercensus population
growth rates of between 2% and 3% annually, with even higher growth
rates among the indigenous population. Among the social and ecological
consequences of this population growth have been fundamental changes
in land use within indigenous and other rural communities (for example,
reduction of traditional fallow and crop rotation cycles) and increased land
fragmentation, landlessness, and internal migration. Population growth has
also affected the integrity of municipal and communal lands as more people looked toward such lands for subsistence and as greater pressure was
put on them for pasture and forest and firewood resources.[17]

In summary, by the early 1950s, a process of political mobilization had
taken place in most of Guatemala's Mayan-speaking communities. At the
same time, as a result of population growth and other factors, there was a
general deterioration in the living conditions of most Mayan farmers as
increasing land fragmentation and scarcity forced them to seek other
means of maintaining family subsistence and survival, including increasing
internal migration as seasonal laborers to the coffee and new cotton plantations on the Pacific coast. The military coup of June 1954 brought to an
abrupt end both the agrarian reform and much of the political mobilization that took place during the Arévalo and Arbenz years. However, rural
impoverishment continued in Guatemala, and new forms of social and
political mobilization occurred in subsequent years.[18]

Perhaps the major factor in the continuing social and political mobilization of the indigenous population was the Catholic Action movement, which was established in Guatemala in 1948 and began to grow significantly after the 1954 military coup. Originally, the Catholic Action movement was an attempt by the Church hierarchy to stem the tide of Protestant fundamentalism and radical peasant politics (in the cold war context of postwar Latin America, it was strongly "anticommunist") that were then gaining popularity among the Mayan population. As the religious movement grew, however, it became the basis of a strong ethnic revitalization and rural modernization movement.[19]

Foreign Catholic missionary societies, which were banned from Guatemala during the liberal period, played a major role in the extraordinary growth and the tremendous social and cultural influence of the Catholic Action movement. Between 1950 and 1965, for example, the number of Catholic priests in Guatemala increased from 132 to 483, while the number of sisters increased from 96 to 354. Most of this growth in religious personnel came from foreign orders sending missionaries to Guatemala. Initially, these missionaries conducted fairly conventional activities aimed at converting traditional Mayan religious believers (that is, members of the *cofradías* or religious brotherhoods) to a reformed Catholicism that was based on ritual participation in the sacramental life of the Church. However, through the training of Indian catechists or lay religious leaders, the clergy began to transform the social and political outlook of Indians, while at the same time going through radical changes of consciousness themselves. They also began, under the philosophical influence of Vatican II and the emerging liberation theology movement in Latin America, to link their new converts to budding cooperatives and peasant movements; and in some areas, they established the conditions for what during the 1970s became known as a "people's Church."[20]

In the early 1970s, opposition political parties, especially the Christian Democratic party, also began to organize and to gain influence in the Guatemalan countryside. Although the military denied the Christian Democrats an electoral victory in the 1974 presidential contest, it and other opposition parties were successful in municipal elections in several Indian townships.[21] After the earthquake that struck Guatemala in February 1976, a surge of political activity also took place in the urban trade union movement, and this also had an effect on the outlook of the rural indigenous population. Although the trade union movement never acquired the degree of unity and organization it had experienced under the Arévalo and Arbenz regimes, it did begin to reach out to newly industrialized sectors of the urban population as well as to farm workers and peasants in the countryside. Perhaps the major event in the revitalization of the Guatemalan labor movement was the formation in April 1976 of the National Committee for Trade Union Unity (CNUS). From its inception, CNUS maintained close links with peasant and rural worker organizations, while at the same time guarding its independence from radical political parties and a nascent guerrilla movement. In 1978, CNUS, along with a number of other religious, labor, and popular organizations, began to protest the increasing presence of the military in rural areas. Lawyers from CNUS also assisted peasant cooperatives in frontier areas that were encountering difficulties in obtaining land titles from the government, and federation members joined mine workers who were striking in such indigenous areas as Huehuetenango and Alta Verapaz.[22]

The late 1970s also saw the formation of the Committee of Peasant Unity (CUC), which was established to link the urban and rural labor movements with the country's large indigenous peasantry. CUC was the first Indian-led labor organization in the history of Guatemala and the first to bring highland Indian peasants together with poor ladino farm workers. Although it was forced to function in secrecy, it was reported to have had the support of thousands of seasonal and permanent farm workers. Perhaps its major achievement, before its affiliation with the guerilla movement, was the organization in February 1980 of a strike of 70,000 cane cutters and 40,000 cotton pickers, an action that, along with another CUC-initiated strike of coffee workers in September 1980, forced the government to raise the minimum wage of farm workers from $1.12 to $3.20 per day.[23]

To summarize, by the end of the 1970s, the first steps of a generalized social and political mobilization had taken place among Guatemala's rural indigenous population. Although the degree of mobilization varied among regions and ethnolinguistic groups and within individual indigenous communities, there is little doubt that the social, economic, and political aspirations of the Mayan Indian population had been expanded by the activities of foreign missionaries, rural development workers, opposition political parties, and the urban and rural trade union movements. Under different sociopolitical conditions (ones more conducive to political democracy, social reform, and inclusive economic development), this mobilization could have naturally evolved into greater Indian participation in Guatemalan society and public life. As it was, however, the Guatemalan military was not ready to allow Indians to participate as free and independent actors in national politics. Nor were the recently reorganized guerrilla movements, of which there were four in the late 1970s, ready to accept a nonviolent path to change in Guatemala. Thus, as the

Central America region became embroiled in political and military turmoil, Guatemala entered into a full-scale civil war in which the Mayan Indian population became its most displaced and victimized population. In was on the ashes of one of the most brutal counterinsurgency campaigns in the modern history of Latin America, and after a return to democratic rule in 1985, that the contemporary Mayan movement emerged on the political stage in Guatemala.[24]

The Mayan Movement and the Peace Accords

Throughout the course of the 1970s and increasingly into the 1980s, a growing number of young indigenous persons began to rediscover the historical significance of their Mayan cultural roots and reaffirm their ethnic identities. Several factors played a role in this rediscovery and reaffirmation of Mayan culture and ethnic identity on the part of this new generation of Mayan-speaking leaders and intellectuals. Throughout the 1970s and 1980s, a small number of Mayan-speaking young people gained access to secondary and higher education and began to question among themselves and publicly some of the reigning ideas about the history and dynamics of Guatemalan politics, society, and culture. In particular, these more educated Mayan young people strongly reacted to theories then being espoused by North American anthropologists about the supposed "ladinoization" of the Mayan-speaking population and by Guatemalan historians and sociologists about the identification of the indigenous population with the intensifying "class struggle" in rural areas. At the same time as these new Mayan leaders were questioning standard interpretations of Guatemalan history and society, a number of other young people were placing greater value on their linguistic and cultural heritage through contacts with foreign linguists and anthropologists. Many indigenous leaders were also influenced by Professor Adrian Chávez, a K'iche'-speaking Mayan educator in Quezaltenango and one of the first native-speaking translators of the Pop Wuj, the sacred book of the K'iche' Maya. Thus, beginning in the 1970s and increasingly throughout the 1980s, these young indigenous leaders began to reaffirm their Mayan cultures, languages, and identities, as well as to form into new indigenous associations and organizations. By the early 1990s, a highly diffuse but growing Mayan movement existed in Guatemala. This movement, in turn, had an important influence (for the first time in the nation's history) on the debates surrounding the future of the country.[25]

Three points are worth emphasizing about the social dynamics and influence of the Mayan movement. First, like other indigenous movements that arose in Latin America during this period, it has been greatly influenced by the international attention being given to indigenous peoples rights, especially within the context of the United Nations Human Rights Commission and the International Labor Organization. Many of the leaders of the Mayan movement participated in discussions at the United Nations Working Group on Indigenous Populations (established in 1982) on the Draft Declaration on the Rights of Indigenous Peoples and in the debates leading up to the ratification of ILO Convention 169 in 1989. There were also contacts between the Mayan leaders and indigenous leaders from other parts of the Western Hemisphere who were preparing a response to the celebration by Spain and several of the Latin American governments of the "Fifth Centenary of Columbus's Discovery of the Americas" in 1992. The indigenous organizations called their response to the Columbus Discovery celebrations "Five Hundred Years of Resistance" and held a hemispheric meeting on the subject in Quezaltenango in 1991. The announcement of the Guatemalan indigenous rights activist Rigoberta Menchú as the Nobel Peace Prize winner in 1992 also gave impetus to the Mayan movement and reflected the growing amount of international attention that was focusing on the human rights situation of Guatemala's indigenous population by that date.[26]

Second, as mentioned previously, the Mayan movement is highly fragmented and is not represented by a single ideological current or organization that can speak for the movement as such. In fact, as several observers have noted, there are often deep rifts within the movement between those who take an essentially "cultural" position, such as many of the Mayan intellectuals and writers, and those indigenous leaders who continue to maintain strong affiliations with some of the class-based popular organizations that existed before the civil strife of the late 1970s and early 1980s. The nature of these differences were highlighted at the Second Continental Meeting for Indigenous, Black, and Popular Resistance, which took place in Quezaltenango in 1991, and which some Mayan intellectuals denounced as being captured by the popular movement and the left. There are also differences within the Mayan movement along other lines, including those of language, residence (rural- versus urban-based organizations), and religion. In terms of the latter, the late 1980s and early 1990s saw a rediscovery of traditional Mayan customs, values, and religious beliefs on the part of several Mayan leaders; and this in turn caused further fragmentation within an indigenous population that was already divided among traditional Mayan religious believers, reformed Catholics, and mainstream and evangelical Protestant groups. At various times during the 1990s, and especially during and after the signing of the peace accords, attempts were made to unify the various Mayan and popular organizations, but unlike other countries (for example, Bolivia, Colombia, and Ecuador), no national indigenous organization emerged to represent and speak for the large and by that time quite socially heterogeneous indigenous population of Guatemala.[27]

Finally, as the Mayan movement became more public in its demands for both human and indigenous rights and sought a new vision of Guatemalan national culture and society, it created a backlash among political, intellectual, and other elites. The new emphasis on Guatemala as a multi-ethnic, pluricultural, and multilingual state and the claims for the recognition and protection of both the identities and the rights of the indigenous population caused fears within some sectors of the politically and socially dominant ladino population that the Mayan movement would lead to a fragmented and nonunitary Guatemalan state. Although several leaders of the Mayan movement disclaimed that they wanted to separate themselves from the Guatemalan nation or create another form of "exclusive nationalism," fears emerged within the nonindigenous sector of the population and increasingly formed part of debates within Guatemalan political and intellectual circles and the national press.[28]

These issues came to a head in the public debates in Guatemala surrounding the ratification of ILO Convention 169 and the implementation of the peace accords, especially the Accord on the Identity and Rights of Indigenous Peoples. Although the 1985 Guatemalan Constitution contained several articles and a special section dealing with indigenous communities, relatively little happened in terms of implementing these provisions in the following years. In fact, it was not until the late 1980s and the early 1990s that a fairly heated public debate took place in the Guatemalan congress about the ratification of ILO Convention 169. The latter was ratified by the parent body of the ILO in 1989 and includes a more pluralistic and participatory framework for dealing with issues relating to indigenous peoples than ILO Conventon 107, which was ratified in 1957. It also contains relatively strong provisions concerning the recognition and protection of indigenous lands and natural resources, and the recognition of the customary law and legal procedures of indigenous communities (Dandler 1999).

During the early 1990s, a series of discussions took place among indigenous and civil society organizations about the nature of ILO Convention 169 and its importance for Guatemala. These discussions were supported by the Guatemalan minister of labor but did not have the full support of either the government or prominent members of the Guatemalan congress. In fact, as the Mayan organizations began to demand the ratification of ILO Convention 169 by the national congress, a political backlash took place within the congress and among certain factions with the Guatemalan military, the legal profession, and the political elite. The debate between the congress, in which Mayan-speaking deputies were severely underrepresented, and the Mayan movement over ratification of ILO Convention 169 lasted for nearly four years, and it was not until 1996, based on a recommendation in the peace accords, that the Guatemalan congress finally ratified the convention. However, even in providing such ratification, the congress attached an amendment to the legislation stating that the convention would be subordinate to the constitution. This left open the possibility of further legal debate and interpretation on the meaning of the convention's provisions for Guatemala's treatment of its indigenous population.[29]

The internal political disputes among the Mayan movement, the government and national congress, and the various powerful sectors of Guatemalan national society provide a context for understanding the debates that took place after the official signing of the peace accords in December 1996. As mentioned previously, clearly, the major document from a Mayan perspective was the Accord on the Identity and Rights of Indigenous Peoples. Although the accord was drafted by the government and the URNG without the direct participation of the Mayan organizations, the latter did have some influence on the substance of the accord through their representation as a special sector in the Civil Society Assembly, which was created as a mechanism to ensure some degree of civil society participation in the peace accords process and included the participation of the Coordinator of Organizations of the Guatemalan Mayan People Saqb'ichil (COPMAGUA) as one of eleven civil society sectors contributing to the peace process. By means of a consensus-building approach characteristic of traditional Mayan decision making, COPMAGUA and its various affiliated Mayan organizations had a significant impact on the substance of the Accord on the Identity and Rights of the Indigenous Peoples, as well as on the follow-up discussions with the government, civil society organizations, and the international community for its implementation (Presidencia de la República Comisión de la Paz 1996; Saqb'ichil COPMAGUA 2000).

Among other things, the Accord on the Identity and Rights of the Indigenous Peoples outlines the institutional basis for the creation of a multiethnic, pluricultural, and multilingual nation in Guatemala. To achieve this, it calls for the recognition of the historical identities of Guatemala's Maya-, Xinca-, and Garífuna-speaking language communities and highlights the primacy of the struggle against all forms of racial, cultural, and gender discrimination. It also promotes the cultural rights of indigenous peoples, including the rights to maintain their languages, personal names, spiritual beliefs, religious and ceremonial centers, sacred places, traditional dress, and indigenous science and knowledge.

A major aspect of the Indigenous Peoples Accord is in the area of "educational reform," which, among other things, provides for a new vision of education in Guatemala that is more consistent with the multicultural and multilingual nature of the country. Among the measures called for are greater government support for the expansion of the National Program of Bilingual/Intercultural Education (PRONEBI), more decentralization and regionalizing of the educational system to take into account the linguistic and cultural specificity of the country, and fundamental reforms of the national curricula to take into account indigenous conceptions of education. A special bipartite commission comprising representatives of the government and Mayan organizations was established under the accord to provide more concrete recommendations for such reform in the educational sector, and it functioned throughout the period from 1996 to 1999.[30]

In terms of civil and political rights, the Indigenous Peoples Accord highlights constitutional changes that would be necessary to bring about a multiethnic, pluricultural, and multilingual nation. It also addresses issues relating to the recognition of local indigenous communities and their traditional leaders, the role of these communities in administrative decentralization, the participation of indigenous peoples and their organizations at all levels of governance and administration, and the recognition of customary law within indigenous communities and as part of the national judicial system.[31]

Finally, the whole question of the land rights of indigenous communities is given prominence in the Indigenous Peoples Accord. Specifically, section IV F of the accord is devoted to the "Rights Relative to the Lands of Indigenous Peoples." "These rights," the accord reads, "include the communal and collective, as well as the individual tenure [of these lands]; the rights of property, possession and other real rights, as well as the rights to the use of natural resources in benefit of the communities and without prejudice to their habitat."[32]

Special attention is also given in the Indigenous Peoples Accord to the need to juridically protect the rights of indigenous communities. This is mentioned as including the development of special legal norms for indigenous lands, the training of local judges to deal with the resolution of land conflicts within and between communities, legal assistance to deal with indigenous land claims, and bilingual interpreters and the dissemination of information on agrarian rights and legal procedures among the indigenous population. Although a separate accord between the government and the URNG was signed on socioeconomic aspects and the agrarian situation, there are a number of overlaps between the latter accord and the section of the Indigenous Peoples Accord dealing with indigenous lands.

With issues of this scope included in the Indigenous Peoples Accord and other peace accords, it is hardly surprising that a major political debate arose within Guatemala about the implementation of the accords. Perhaps the major point of contention was the constitutional reforms that would be necessary for the peace accords to be effectively implemented. In the case of the Indigenous Peoples Accord, several fundamental changes would be needed in the 1985 Constitution in order to produce the conditions for a multiethnic, pluricultural, and multilingual nation. Once the scope of these reforms became known, a major debate arose in Guatemala that pitted the indigenous and other civil society organizations against numerous vested interests in the political, military, and economic elites of the country. With the government in power immediately following the signing of the peace accords unable to establish a consensus within its own political party and with opposition parties in the national congress, it was forced to call a referendum on the issue of constitutional reforms.

Fifty different proposals for constitutional reform were initially submitted for discussion to the national congress, and among these were several relating to indigenous lands, the official recognition of indigenous languages, and the rights of indigenous peoples to practice their customary law. There was also a proposal for a redefinition of Guatemala as a multiethnic, pluricultural, and multilingual nation that would have fundamental implications for the political and administrative structure of the country.

The referendum on constitutional reforms took place in May 1999. During the months preceding the referendum, there was a major campaign in the national press and media on the implications of the Indigenous Peoples Accord and the proposed constitutional reforms. Resistance to the proposed constitutional reforms came from the opposition Guatemalan Republican Front political party, and several conservative "constitutionalist" organizations such as the Center for the Defense of the Constitution, the Pro-Fatherland League, and the Association of Dignitaries of the Nation. The powerful Coordinating Committee of Agricultural, Commercial, Industrial and Financial Associations also spoke out against the proposed reforms arguing that the full package of fifty reforms as well as the four questions being put before the citizenry (one of which dealt with the rights of indigenous peoples) was a "violation of the people's will." When the referendum was finally held, less than 18.5% of the country's registered voters actually went to the polls to vote on it, and of those who did vote, 55% voted against the constitutional reforms. As pointed out by Susanne Jonas, one of the major outside observers and analysts of the peace process in Guatemala, the defeat of the May 1999 constitutional reform referendum provided a sense of triumph for the forces who had opposed the peace process from its inception. It also led at least one newspaper in the United States to carry an article after the referendum headlined, "Guatemalans Turn Thumbs Down on Multiculturalism" (*Wall Street Journal*, May 28, 1999).[33]

Although the May 1999 constitutional reform referendum was a setback for both the Mayan movement and the evolution toward a more pluralistic society in Guatemala, it must also be understood historically and in terms of the contemporary politics and culture of the country. For more than a century and a half, Guatemala's majority indigenous population—comprising twenty-three distinct ethnolinguistic groups, hundreds of townships, and thousands of small communities—had been systematically excluded from citizenship rights and national politics. This "exclusive nationalism," which had characterized Guatemala, was deeply rooted in cultural attitudes, interethnic relations, and systems of stringent political, administrative, and most recently, during the counterinsurgency campaign of the late 1970s and early 1980s, military control. To change this structure of social, political, and cultural domination, especially within a new framework of democratic debate and electoral politics, was a major challenge for the Mayan movement. This was even more the case given the fragmentation of the movement and the powerful control that traditional elites continue to have over the political party apparatus and media in Guatemala. Therefore, one can see the May 1999 referendum not as a defeat for the vision of a new and more culturally pluralistic and inclusive society in Guatemala, but rather as one of many obstacles in the path of implementing this vision espoused by the Mayan movement and its allies in civil society, some parts of the government apparatus (particularly the Secretary of Peace and the National Peace Commission established to implement the peace accords) and the international human rights community. As we shall see in the concluding section, although this vision of a new society has still not been fulfilled in Guatemala, it is influencing several aspects of the public policy debate including new initiatives in bilingual/intercultural education, culture and development policy, and the recent discussion and debate surrounding the country's poverty reduction strategy.

Education, Culture, and the National Poverty Reduction Strategy

Despite the setback of the May 1999 referendum, in at least three areas both the Mayan movement and the Peace Accord on Identity and Rights of Indigenous Peoples have had a significant effect on public policy discussions in Guatemala. The first area where the Mayan movement and the peace accords have had an influence is in the field of bilingual/intercultural education and proposals for the general reform of the education system. As documented in several studies, Guatemala ranks among one of the most backward countries in Latin America in terms of adult literacy rates and primary school attendance rates. Ministry of Education statistics indicate that 29.6% of the country's adult population or an estimated 2.2 million people were illiterate in 1999. The major part of the country's illiterate population lives in rural areas (77%), belongs to indigenous groups (61%), and are women. Similar geographical, ethnic, and gender differences characterize the school-age population attending primary school in Guatemala. Although some improvements in primary school enrollment took place during the 1990s, the gross primary school enrollment rate in the year 2000 was 95%, and the net enrollment rate was only 84%. In the year 2000, Ministry of Education statistics indicated that 164,032 girls between the ages of seven and twelve years old were not attending school. The Guatemalan departments that had the highest illiteracy rates and lowest primary school enrollments (in some departments only 73% of the primary school-age population attended school) were in the northern, northwestern, and southwestern parts of the country. These regions also have the highest concentration of indigenous people. This educational deficit of the rural indigenous population (including, most importantly, indigenous women and girls) has been highlighted in every recent poverty and human development report on Guatemala. On average, persons who speak indigenous languages have attended 1.6 years of school as compared to 2.4 years of schooling for nonindigenous persons (both rural and urban) and 5.4 years of schooling for nonindigenous urban dwellers (Gobierno de la República de Guatemala 2001).

Although these statistics demonstrate the challenges faced by Guatemala in providing literacy training and universal access to education to its ethnically and linguistically diverse population, on the positive side are the pioneering steps that Guatemala has taken in the field of bilingual/intercultural education. From the 1970s onward, there has been a very active and increasingly influential bilingual education movement in Guatemala comprising Mayan-speaking schoolteachers and linguists. Bilingual/intercultural education programs were initially supported by international donors but have increasingly been taken up by the national government. In the mid-1980s, for example, Guatemala established a national bilingual education program (PRONEBI), which provided special training for bilingual teachers and translated parts of the national curriculum for the early years of primary schooling into the four major Mayan languages. By 1991, there were 96,194 indigenous children enrolled in PRONEBI schools out of a total population of 653,413 rural indigenous children (or about 14.7% of the indigenous primary school-age population). At the same time, a number of Mayan schoolteachers established their own private schools for the education of indigenous children, many of which combined bilingual education with the incorporation of Mayan values, customs, and spiritual beliefs into the school curriculum. By 1995, when the Indigenous Peoples Accord was signed, Mayan schoolteachers and linguists had formed into several national and regional organizations for the promotion of a broader program of bilingual/intercultural education. This led to the establishment of a new General Directorate for Bilingual/Intercultural Education in the Ministry of Education. The Mayan educational organizations also participated actively in the debate in the Educational Reform Commission set up under the Indigenous Peoples Accord. The report of the latter focused on the need to scale up the bilingual/intercultural education program, to further regionalize and decentralize Ministry of Education functions to correspond more closely with the ethnic geography and language characteristics of the country, and to incorporate Mayan history and values into the national curriculum. Perhaps more than in any other area, the debate surrounding educational reform has reflected the growing power of the Mayan movement and its more general influence on debates surrounding public policy in the country.[34]

A second area of public policy where the Mayan movement and the Indigenous Peoples Accord have had a significant influence is in the field of cultural policy. Although Guatemala has had a cultural patrimony law since the mid-1940s, it was not until 1985, with the drafting of the new political constitution, that it established a special Ministry of Culture and Sports. In its early years, the new ministry mainly continued to carry out its traditional functions of conserving the archaeological and historical patrimony of Guatemala, and in supporting artistic, sports, and other activities mainly directed at the urban and ladino population of the country. After the signing of the Indigenous Peoples Accord, some of the archaeologists affiliated with the Ministry's Institute of Anthropology and History also became involved in a highly contentious debate over indigenous participation in the administration and control of the country's archaeological heritage. Issues also rose about the role of the state in the protection of contemporary Mayan ceremonial and sacred sites. In January 2000, however, a new government took office in Guatemala, and newly elected President Alfonso Portillo Cabrera, an economist by training, surprised many observers by announcing the selection of Otilia Lux de Coti (a well-known Mayan educator and one of the members of the Truth Commission set up under the peace accords) to be the new Minister of Culture and Sports. The new minister, in turn, selected another Mayan leader, Virgilio Alvarado Ajanel, as her vice minister, and the two made it known publicly that they were dedicated to reforming the ministry's policies and administrative structure in order to better reflect the values of multiculturalism and iintercultural understanding contained in the peace accords. In fact, in March 2000, just two months after taking office, the new minister announced that in the next month, a national congress on cultural policies would be held in the colonial city of Antigua to develop guidelines for the new cultural policies of the government. "We live in a multi-lingual, pluri-cultural and, therefore, multi-ethnic country," the new minister told the press in announcing the national congress. "This situation, combined with the fact that we are at the portal of the 21st century, obligates us to look for and study guidelines for a cultural policy which our nation requires" (de León 2000).

The April 2000 National Congress on Guidelines for Cultural Policies was intended to bring together about 250 people with interests in the fields of culture and development policy. However, once announced, over 600 persons registered for the congress, representing nearly 200 organizations and institutions. Most of the people in attendance were professionals who were actively involved in the areas of culture, education, and development. However, there were also a large number of leaders of Mayan organizations in attendance, as well as representatives of local governments, including municipal mayors and members of town councils from rural areas. Along with the Mayan-speaking attendees, there was also a delegation of Garífuna-speaking (or Afro-Caribbean) representatives from the Atlantic coast of Guatemala, and a large number of young people (many of them secondary school or university students) who reflected the relatively youthful demographic profile of the country (44.8% of the national population is younger than fifteen years old and 64% is younger than 25 years old).

The congress was opened by President Portillo, who highlighted the role that culture and identity should play in an increasingly global economy and society. He also stressed the need to incorporate the proposed guidelines for cultural policies within the framework of the country's broader goals of democratization, decentralization, and sustainable development. Other speeches followed by the Minister of Culture and Sports, the United Nations Development Program representative in Guatemala, and the Regional Director for Culture of the United Nations Educational Scientific and Cultural Organization for Latin America and the Caribbean. Once the opening speeches ended, the participants formed into a series of working groups to discuss a broad range of topics relating to culture and development issues. These included discussions of legislative and juridical aspects of culture, the promotion of social and cultural development, the conservation of cultural and natural patrimony, the economics of cultural industries and production, information and communication for cultural development, and sports and recreation. The results of these working groups were presented at a plenary session opened by the Ministers of Culture and Sports and Education and were followed by a set of recommendations for moving ahead with the preparation of a new cultural policy for the country. One of the major recommendations was the establishment of a Citizens Monitoring Committee for accompanying the cultural policy development process and made up of representatives of civil society, the academic community, and the private sector and with adequate ethnic and gender representation (Ministerio de Cultura y Deportes 2000a).

In November 2000, the Ministry of Culture and Sports published the proceedings of the national congress and reached a consensus with the Citizens Monitoring Committee on a set of principles and policies that would guide the government's actions in the cultural field. The document of policies is relatively short and opens with a set of principles that are based on the recommendations of the national congress and other documents such as the 1985 political constitution, the peace accords, and various international statements on cultural rights and their relations to human and social development. The most fundamental of these principles is the recognition, respect, and promotion of the cultural and linguistic diversity of Guatemala. The document also highlights other principles such as the values of "liberty, civic participation, solidarity, responsibility and equity; and, the right of all persons to participate in the cultural and inter-cultural life of the country." The basis of such a cultural policy is seen as being rooted in the cultural values, cosmologies, modes of behavior, beliefs, and actions of the various peoples of Guatemala, and as being a fundamental ingredient in the struggle for sustainable human development. "For this reason," the policy document states, "the State is obliged to incorporate the cultural dimension in its policies, plans and actions directed at improving the quality and sustainability of the life and personal realization of each of the inhabitants of the country" (Ministerio de Cultura y Deportes 2000b, 3).

The new cultural policy released by the Ministry of Culture and Sports also highlights the need for a decentralized approach that incorporates the cultural dimension into all government social programs at the departmental, municipal, and community levels. This would include the integration of cultural promoters associated with the Ministry of Culture and Sports into departmental "development councils." Other aspects of the policy include statements relating to the creative arts and social communication, the protection and conservation of cultural and natural patrimony, the institutional strengthening of the ministry and its coordination with other ministries, the need to promote the revision and actualization of cultural legislation, the formation and training of cultural professionals, and the promotion of investigation in the cultural fields. Perhaps one of the most important aspects of the new policy is the recognition that the "cultural dimension should be incorporated into development through collaboration with other governmental and nongovernmental institutions, especially those responsible for development planning" (Ministerio de Cultura y Deportes 2000b, 4).

The third and final area of public policy where the Mayan movement and the Indigenous Peoples Accord have had some (albeit still limited) influence is in the formulation of a national poverty reduction strategy. Responsibility for preparation of the national poverty reduction strategy (NPRS) has rested with the Office of the Presidency's Secretary of Planning and Programming (SEGEPLAN) and has drawn heavily on the support of international donor agencies and the academic community. Much of the work of SEGEPLAN in preparing for the preparation of the NPRS has been in increasing the information base on poverty and human development indicators in Guatemala. In February 2001, for example, SEGEPLAN published a short report titled *El Drama de la Pobreza en Guatemala: Sus Rasgos y Efectos Sobre la Sociedad* [The drama of poverty in Guatemala: Its characteristics and effects on society]. This was followed by the publication of a poverty map of Guatemala that highlights the conditions of poverty in the various regions of the country and identifies 102 of the townships that have the highest poverty and lowest human development indicators. As in several previous reports done by the government and international agencies, both poverty (and in many cases extreme poverty) and lack of access to basic social services are highly correlated with rural townships and geographical regions that contain large numbers of indigenous language speakers (SEGEPLAN 2001 a,c).

Given the attention being placed by the Ministry of Culture and Sports on the cultural dimensions of development, especially within the context of the recognition of the multicultural nature of Guatemalan society, the former began to open up discussions with SEGEPLAN for incorporating a specific cultural dimension into the NPRS. In June 2001, for example, a special two-day workshop was held in Guatemala City on the subject of "Culture and Poverty" sponsored by the Ministry of Culture and Sports, SEGEPLAN, the Latin American Faculty of Social Sciences (FLACSO-Guatemala), and the Institute of Economic and Social Investigation of the Rafael Landivar University. The workshop, which included both national and international specialists, was a first attempt to see how an explicit cultural dimension, based on the ministry's new policy of promoting cultural diversity and pluralism, could be incorporated into the national discussion for a strategy for alleviating poverty and promoting sustainable human development. A background paper prepared by the ministry outlined the details of such incorporation of a cultural dimension into the NPRS and provided plans for three projects in the areas of regional language training institutes, the promotion of artisan production and other cultural industries, and the comanagement of parks and other protected areas by indigenous communities. At the seminar itself, emphasis focused on the role of culture in human development interventions (health, education, social funds, etc.); culture, decentralization, and environmental management; and the importance of culture in social and political development. "The seminar," the final document states, "provided a space for multi-cultural, multi-sectoral and multi-disciplinary participation and dialogue concerning such fundamental themes for sustainable human development in Guatemala, as poverty, cultural marginalization, national identity, the economic potential of cultural resources, environmental conservation, social participation and the ways in which multiculturalism and inter-cultural understanding could be inserted in the Poverty Reduction Strategy" (Ministry of Culture and Sports and SEGEPLAN 2001).

Since the June 2001 Workshop on Culture and Poverty, SEGEPLAN produced an initial draft of its NPRS that contains as one of its cross-cutting or transversal themes a focus on multiculturalism and intercultural understanding, the two major pillars of the Ministry of Culture and Sports' new cultural policy and the Indigenous Peoples Peace Accord. The fundamental objective of the NPRS is to promote equity in the orientation of public expenditures by assigning a greater percentage of resources to programs and projects directed to the country's large poor population, especially in rural and indigenous areas of the country. Among other things, this would demand a modernization of the current system of public expenditure management, greater transparency in such expenditures, increased citizen participation, and greater decentralization of poverty alleviation programs to the municipal and community levels. Strategically, the NPRS calls for the modernization of the financial system and macroeconomic stability, increased investments in human capital (particularly health and education), and increased investments in physical capital, including the construction and maintenance of rural roads, rural electrification, and water and basic sanitation. Cross-cutting each of these activities would be a set of transversal themes, including a respect for cultural diversity and intercultural understanding, environmental quality, gender equity, and improvement in the management of natural risks and hazards (SEGEPLAN 2001b).

The current political and economic situation in Guatemala is such that it is difficult to predict whether a future government will actually implement the poverty reduction program as outlined in the NPRS document. To do so would demand a significant increment in public resources dedicated to poverty reduction, their more efficient and transparent use, and types of citizen participation and decentralization of resources and activities that have not been traditionally characteristic of public policy making and implementation in Guatemala. However, even given these political constraints (which are real and reported daily in the national press), Guatemala is one of the first countries in Latin America to explicitly incorporate a cultural dimension into its proposed strategy for poverty reduction. Other countries in Latin America, such as Bolivia, Ecuador, Mexico, and Peru, also have the constitutional and legislative capacities and relatively strong indigenous movements to fully incorporate such a multicultural and intercultural perspective into their national poverty reduction strategies. In these countries, as in Guatemala, much will depend on the political will of those individuals, parties, and elites who continue to control power in these countries. Nevertheless, whichever way Guatemalan politics turns in the future, there seems to be no avoiding the issues raised by the Mayan movement and the Indigenous Peoples Accord. Guatemala, like these other countries with large indigenous populations in Latin America, is faced with the challenge of creating a future nation in which cultural and linguistic diversity are respected, where there is mutual understanding and communication between peoples of different cultures and ethnic histories, and in which poverty, inequality, and exclusion are significantly reduced. The question is whether this can be achieved within the context of democratic governance structures in which indigenous peoples and their organizations can actively participate without regressing to the "exclusive nationalism" and political violence of the past.

Notes

1. The ethnographic and sociological literature on the Mayan and other contemporary indigenous peoples of Guatemala is vast and too lengthy for citation here. However, for an overview of the current situation of indigenous peoples in Guatemala, see Regional Unit for Technical Assistance (RUTA), World Bank, and Guatemalan Ministry of Culture and Sports (2001).

2. On current poverty and human development trends in Guatemala, see United Nations Development Program (UNDP) (2000); and Gobierno de la República de Guatemala (2001).

3. For background on the history of the Guatemalan coffee economy and its relations to the indigenous economy in the western Highlands or Altiplano, see Castellanos Cambranes (1985); and McCreery (1994).

4. On the exclusive nature of the Guatemalan state and its disrespect for the rights and cultures of the Mayan-speaking indigenous population, see Smith (1990); and Taracena Arriola (1999).

5. See Torres Rivas (1971), chapter 2. Much of the historical discussion that follows is taken from a previous publication (Davis 1988).

6. Histories of the growth of coffee production in Guatemala and their effects on indigenous communities are contained in Mosk (1955); Castellanos Cambranes (1985); and McCreery (1994).

7. Batres Jáuregui (1893, 177–78). The latter citation is taken from Grandin (2000, 142, and 284, n. 40). Grandin's book, *The Blood of Guatemala*, is a history of interethnic relations in the K'iche'-speaking highland Indian town of Quezaltenango, the second largest city in Guatemala and a center of the Mayan resurgence both in the late 19th century and currently in Guatemala.

8. For a more detailed discussion of the history of this "exclusionary" notion of citizenship in Guatemala, see Taracena Arriola (1999); and UNDP (2000).

9. For ethnographic research on Mayan communities in the Guatemalan highlands during this period, see LaFarge (1947); Bunzel (1952); and Termer (1957). For a more general discussion of the persistence of Mayan culture and ethnic identity at the local level, see Tax (1937).

10. The argument here draws heavily on the writings of Eric Wolf in relation to the effects of European colonialism and the changing world political economy on indigenous peoples (Wolf 1982).

11. For background on this period, including the response of the United States government to the social reforms of the Arévalo and Arbenz governments, see Gleijeses (1991).

12. For background on the legislative and political changes of this period, especially as they affected the rural indigenous population, see Skinner-Klee (1954); and Silvert (1954).

13. For an overview of some of the results of these studies by the founder and first director of the National Indigenist Institute, see Goubaud Carrera (1959).

14. The nature of these surveys of municipal and communal lands are discussed in Paredes Moreira (1963).

15. More detailed discussions of the content and politics of the Agrarian Re-

form Law are contained in Moreira (1963); Gleijeses (1991); and Handy (1994). The World Bank study referred to in this paragraph is summarized in an article by the head of the World Bank mission, G. E. Britnell (1951).

16. The role of local politics, especially as it related to conflict over municipal lands during the Agrarian Reform are discussed in Handy (1994); Gillin and Silvert (1956); and Wasserstrom (1975).

17. For an analysis of the effects of population growth on land tenure and use in a single Mayan community, see Davis (1997b, 127–56).

18. For a description of the political mobilization that took place in several Indian townships during this period, see Adams (1957).

19. For background on the growth and influence of the Roman Catholic Church in the post-Arbenz period, see Berryman (1984). For anthropological studies of the role of the Catholic Action movement in Indian communities, see Warren (1978); and Falla (1978).

20. The place where Catholic Action took hold most firmly and was ideologically transformed most completely was in the department of El Quiche, where Spanish priests from the Sacred Heart Order had been active since the late 1950s. Throughout the 1960s and 1970s, the Sacred Heart missionaries not only converted large numbers of Indians to the new Catholicism, but they also organized numerous peasant leagues, agricultural cooperatives, and pioneer resettlement schemes. Not surprisingly, it was mainly in this area, especially in the Ixil-speaking region of northern El Quiche, where guerrilla organizing among Indians initially occurred (Fried et al. 1983).

21. The earliest attempts by some Mayas to form an indigenous political party took place during this period, but its leadership was immediately coopted by the traditional political parties (Falla 1978).

22. For background on the 1970s revitalization of the Guatemalan labor movement, see Plant (1978).

23. The significance of the CUC in bringing together farm workers and Indian peasants, as well as in the rise of the guerrilla movement in indigenous areas of the country, is discussed in Handy (1984).

24. For background on the social roots and outcomes of the guerrilla movement and the counterinsurgency campaign that gripped Guatemala in the late 1970s and early 1980s, see Carmack (1988). Since the publication of this book by a group of North American anthropologists who had done field research in Guatemala before the violence, numerous other studies have appeared on the subject, including Commission for Historical Clarification (CEH) (1999).

25. Interestingly, Guillermo Bonfil Batalla was one of the first outside observers to recognize the beginnings of the modern Mayan movement in Guatemala. In his book, he reproduced two articles, one by the Q'eqchi'-speaking Mayan lawyer and intellectual Antonio Pop Caal and the other an excerpt from the first Mayan-language newspaper in Guatemala, *Ixim* (Bonfil Batalla 1981). For more recent accounts in English of the rise, evolution, and philosophical currents within the Mayan movement, see Fischer and Brown (1996); and Warren (1998).

26. Rigoberta Menchú's book, *I, Rigoberta Menchú* (1984), describes her childhood growing up in a remote Maya village in Guatemala and the effects of the in-

creasing repression and military counterinsurgency on her family and other Mayan villagers. The book was written with the assistance of a French anthropologist Elizabeth Burgos-Debray and has been the subject of much debate among both North American and Guatemalan intellectuals. There is little doubt, however, that the publication of the book (originally in French) played an important role in bringing the human rights situation of the Guatemalan Maya to international attention and leading to her winning the Nobel Peace Prize in 1992.

27. For discussions of this heterogeneity within the Mayan movement, see Bastos and Camus (1993); and Choy and Borell (1997).

28. Some of these fears are expressed in the writings of Mario Roberto Morales, a Guatemalan intellectual who was formerly associated with the left, trained in anthropology, and after returning from exile, he began to write regularly about what he saw as some of the philosophical contradictions of the Mayan movement (Morales 1999, 217–72).

29. See Jonas (2000); and Bastos and Camus (1993) for background about the dispute surrounding the ratification of ILO Convention 169.

30. For background on the discussion that took place concerning education reform, see Commisión Nacional Permanente de Reforma Educativa (1998); and Comisión Paritaria de Reforma Educativa (1998).

31. The issue of state recognition of the customary law and legal procedures of indigenous communities had been a central one in the entire debate leading up to and following the ratification of ILO Convention 169 and the implementation of the Indigenous Peoples Accord (Rojas Lima 1995).

32. For background on these land aspects of the Indigenous Peoples Accord, see Davis (1997b).

33. For a detailed analysis of the constitutional reform debate and the May 1999 referendum, see Jonas (2000), chapter 8.

34. For background on the history of the bilingual/intercultural education program in Guatemala and the significance of the educational reform movement promoted by Mayan educators, see Richards and Richards (1996); World Bank (1995); and Comisión Paritaria de Reforma Educativa (1998).

CHAPTER 16

Conclusion:
Implications of a Cultural Lens
for Public Policy and Development Thought

VIJAYENDRA RAO AND MICHAEL WALTON

The articles in this book have provided ways of constructing an interdisciplinary dialogue on culture and public action. Those by economists—Sen, Kuran, Abraham and Platteau, Klamer, and Alkire—show that incorporating cultural notions within an economic framework can lead to new ways of linking economic and social thought that go beyond simplistic notions of culture as a constraint on development. The anthropologists and sociologists—Appadurai, Douglas, Arizpe, Das Gupta and colleagues, Davis, Harragin, Jenkins, and Calderón-Szmukler—demonstrate the potential for a more practical social science that engages constructively with policy and public action, providing both competing and complementary perspectives to more conventional development policy frameworks. Although there are disagreements stemming from different paradigms and perspectives in the book, there is broad agreement that this approach involves two fundamental changes in the way we think about development policy. We label this a shift from equality of opportunity to "equality of agency." First, a change from a focus on individuals to a recognition that relational and group-based phenomena shape and influence individual aspirations, capabilities, and the distribution of power and agency. Second is a shift to provide for debate and decision making when there are several distinct culturally determined perspectives, and in particular, ensure that poorer, subordinate groups have voice and opportunities for redress.

How does a cultural lens relate to ongoing policy and intellectual debates, especially around the role of the state and markets? These debates have primarily gone beyond state versus markets, to questions of understanding the conditions under which both states and markets can effectively support inclusive development in a globalized world. Cultural factors lie at the heart of the functioning of formal and informal institutions that determine nonmarket outcomes in policy decision making, service provision, participation, and conflict management. A theme of almost equal importance, less emphasized in the book but touched on in Sen's contribution and in other work (Bowles 1998; Gudeman 2001), is the contribution of culture to the working of markets via norms of interaction, influences on the competitiveness of firms, and the extent to which market relationships are tilted unequally to groups with "higher" social and cultural capital.

This book acknowledges that cultural diagnoses cannot provide universally applicable answers. Culture is part of the story—part of the formation of agency, of effective markets and institutions—but is often left out. As Sen emphasizes, an integrated account will be necessary for both diagnosis and policy design. In this particular sense, culture is ignored at our peril, in terms of both development effectiveness and understanding. In this chapter, we examine some implications of this for public action and then for the world of thought.

Implications for Public Action

A cultural lens has many implications for the world of action, especially when addressing problems of inequality and empowerment. It implies that interventions need to be shaped in ways that recognize the relative disempowerment of weaker or subordinate groups in cultural, economic, and political terms. This approach involves understanding how context matters in ways that are conditioned by such inequalities[1] and the need to design public action in ways that foster greater "equality of agency" with respect to social hierarchies, including those involving public, private, and international actors.

POLICY DESIGN

For the policy maker, a point of departure is the recognition that actions occur within unequal social, cultural, and political structures. A diagnostic process could involve a range of mechanisms, including socioeconomic assessments, ethnographic investigation, participatory engagement, and ways of discovering the "true" views and preferences of subordinate groups (Kuran, this volume). Because a core concern is the lack of influence or agency of poorer or excluded groups, policy choices to compensate for this are likely to be an important element of strategy.

To understand local conceptions of well-being, and to incorporate "common sense" and "voice," the recipients of public action need to be engaged as central agents in the formation and implementation of policy.[2] This implies that the theory and practice of development will be more difficult and, necessarily, more participatory. However, it also implies that participation in itself is not a panacea precisely because of the social inequities inherent within group-based relations (Abraham and Platteau, this volume; Cooke and Kothari 2001; Mansuri and Rao 2004). This point is illustrated by debates on appropriate ways of combating exclusion, political cultures of clientelism, and inequality. One view is that this is best dealt with by a form of "participatory development" or "deliberative democracy." An alternative view is that participation will only work in exceptional cases because of the existence of culturally embedded elites who will capture increased resources at local levels. If so, approaches from above that are rules and rights based, such as the federal intervention in the civil rights movement in the United States or the rural social security policy of Brazil, may be more effective.[3] The approaches are opposite, but the diagnostic lens for both arguments is fashioned from a recognition of the cultural factors—particularly the nature of Appadurai's "terms of recognition"—that matter to achieve the policy objective. We are consequently led to a proposal that should be self-evident but is rarely put into practice in multilateral agencies: social and historical analysis should inform policy design just as much as economic analysis, and they should be placed on an equal footing (Kanbur 2002; Harriss 2002).

POLICY IMPLEMENTATION

Developing Social Agency / The Capacity to Aspire

How policies are implemented is as important as the design. Building the "capacity to aspire" of subordinate groups—in the specific sense of the concept developed by Appadurai—is a direct implication of a cultural perspective. The capacity to aspire is a forward-looking cultural capacity that is unequally distributed, with the rich having a greater capacity than the poor. Equalizing the capacity to aspire, and changing the terms of recognition, involves creating an enabling environment to provide the poor with the tools, and the voice, to navigate their way out of poverty. A number of activities and processes would fall into this that collectively encourage the inclusive and active participation of the poor. This may require the development of rituals that help support social agency, such as toilet festivals or participatory budgeting, and the identification of key agents—

internal and external—that can facilitate the process of connecting the poor to policy makers. The methods with which such action is undertaken, however, should be shaped by an understanding of the cultural dynamics of groups in ways that recognize potential sources of conflict and the importance of protecting individual agency. The role of government will sometimes be quite specific—for example, in curriculum design in schooling and in the formal recognition of grassroots organizations. At other times, it will be essentially facilitatory because the real public action will take place within the groups involved (as in the interactions of the interlinked associations in Mumbai that Appadurai has documented in his chapter; Appadurai, this volume).

How does "civil society" fit within this? Civil society covers a multitude of organizational forms and cultures, from single-issue activist groups, to broad-based membership associations, to groups concerned with mobilizing difference for destructive purposes, to profit-maximizing organizations whose primary aim is to tap into the gold mine of development aid. Fashioning an important role for civil society groups is intrinsic to building a forward-looking, "aspirational" development orientation for subordinate groups. It also plays a central role in providing checks and balances on state action, improving the terms of recognition, and countering the lack of recognition of abuse by the state and other powerful groups. However, this has to be done with a deep recognition of the heterogeneity of civil society groups, an unpacking of the term, and a careful understanding of the spectrum of interests that fall under that umbrella. The goal would be to foster desirable cultures of grassroots engagement, representative approaches to pluralism, and "federation" between organizations with similar goals.

Learning by Doing and the Incorporation of Context

Culturally informed public action is not easy. The process requires paying close attention to context in shaping interventions both globally and locally. It therefore argues against the idea of "best practice"—that an intervention that worked wonders in one context would do the same in another. Good interventions are very difficult to design ex ante. A cultural lens thus teaches us that public action, particularly when it is participatory, aspiration building, and aware of common sense, requires an element of experimentation and learning. Ironically, the best practice may be the recognition of the absence of a best practice (Mansuri and Rao 2004).

Projects need to be closely monitored and evaluated, not just in terms of the impact but also in the sequence of processes that led to that impact in order to understand how they can be shaped and modified in a manner that matches the diversity inherent in the local cultural context. All projects will make mistakes, but so long as these mistakes are recognized and the lessons incorporated into the next stage of design, common sense can be gradually incorporated into the development process. This may require the integrated use of qualitative and quantitative methods of evaluation because qualitative methods are typically not best suited to assess changes in outcomes for large populations, while quantitative methods are ineffective in gaining a contextual understanding of the processes that lead to particular outcomes (Rao and Woolcock 2003).

A key lesson is that development is not easy. It is, at its core, a social and cultural process that requires a slow process of learning from the ground up in order to be effective and sustainable. A development culture that forces projects to be completed in two or three years before they are either rapidly and meaninglessly scaled up, or abandoned, is not conducive to social change or to learning by doing. A short-term horizon in most circumstances would make it impossible to incorporate a cultural lens. Most interventions that attempt to change the terms of recognition or build the capacity to aspire, therefore, require long-term horizons—sustained efforts spread over many years. Achieving this will require a change in the cultures of donor organizations.

Greater Emphasis on Quality, Behavior, and Training of Street-Level Workers

Another dimension of incorporating context and common sense into project design is the training and behavior of project facilitators and street-level workers. Careful attention to nitty-gritty, ground-level detail necessarily places greater emphasis on these actors, yet they have been neglected as a subject of research and in budgetary allocations—they are, in fact, among the worst-paid workers in the development hierarchy. Poorly trained and compensated street-level workers will tend to be corrupt, poorly motivated, and even abusive. Yet context-sensitive development can place an unduly heavy burden on them—expecting them to be charismatic leaders, trainers, anthropologists, engineers, economists, and accountants.[4] The danger here is that as development shifts to becoming more participatory and bottom up, it does so without recognizing that old mechanisms and models of service delivery and bureaucratic control have to be radically modified lest we end up in simply a new form of "seeing like a state" that Tendler and Serrano (1999) have described as "supply-driven demand-driven development."

Shaping Institutions to Manage Difference

The recognition that societies consist of different groups, often structured in hierarchies with unequal social and cultural capital, suggests that mechanisms of intergroup exchange and deliberation need to be set up in a manner that changes the terms of recognition. In this area, as in many others, there are no magic institutional solutions, as Peter Evans has warned (Evans 2002). One possibility is to use the "deliberative democracy" favored by Calderón and Szmukler, as in the participatory budgeting process developed in Porto Alegre in Brazil, but this has some preconditions. The promotion of democracy is key, but in order for democracy to work at the grass roots, local institutions need to be transparent even to people at the lowest rungs of society.

Similarly, effective education initiatives may need multicultural designs with curricula that are tailored to reflect the reality and lingua franca of students rather than of elites who tend to design curricula. Comparable arguments can be made for the design of health projects, commons management, etc. The recognition that subgroups can often have conflictual interactions leads to the need for effective methods of conflict management—for instance, mechanisms for intergroup dialogue and opportunities for social and cultural interaction, and fair and effective courts that can adjudicate differences and that poor communities can easily access.

It is useful at this point to consider two potential dangers where the state may be implicitly involved in the affirmation of existing cultural practices or group-based identities. The first involves social movements that mobilize difference to the detriment of others—as starkly seen in some fundamentalist movements and ethnic conflicts. The second involves the state itself (or powerful actors within the state) as an active agent in the manipulation of difference in the interest of certain groups. This has been a sadly common feature of history, whether in the form of Serbian nationalism in the former Yugoslavia, chauvinistic religious conflicts encouraged by states around the world for narrow political advantage, or in "tribal" battles for the control of the state (as in the Tsutsi-Hutu conflict in Rwanda). These dangers are precisely why the theme of recognition of different groups with what Charles Taylor (1995) calls the "presumption of equal value"[5] is fundamental. This approach also implies the need for controls on the state, typically through a mixture of constitutional and legal protections—linked to independent judicial and court proceedings, and a vigorous civil society. Closely related to this is understanding how interactions between diverse cultures within a society need to be managed democratically and in a manner that allows for free and fair debate, an important theme of the contributions by Sen and Douglas in this volume.

As Das Gupta et al. show, however, state intervention may be a good thing—to change culturally influenced forms of discrimination by gender, caste, or race, for instance. There may also be cultural practices that are troubling, such as female genital mutilation or forms of slavery. It is within the capacity of the state to implement policies that tackle such practices, whether through affirmative action, directed education interventions, or legislation. However, an important question is who decides whether a particular practice is offensive since one person's offensive practice may be another's sacred belief. There is always dissension on this point, and, as in any disruption of a social equilibrium, changing such practices may result in conflict and hardship and may involve social and economic costs. In such circumstances, the perspective in this book is that, ideally, these normative questions should be decided by a process of internal democratic deliberation. However, processes of internal dialogue can easily be dominated by elites—for reasons of Kuran's "preference falsification" or "constraining preferences" or Bourdieu's "symbolic violence." The process of decision making may be itself subject to cultural inequities. Change may thus have to come from outside, with a role for international agencies or advocacy groups. In this case, it is important, however, that this is preceded by a clear international consensus, determined by a democratic international dialogue, on the status of the cultural "bad" in question.

INTERNATIONAL POLICY AND THE BEHAVIOR OF EXTERNAL AGENTS

How can international action become more culturally attuned? The issue is most commonly framed in terms of the policies and cultures of international agencies, such as the World Bank, the IMF, and the World Trade Organization, though it also applies to the whole range of external actors, from bilateral donors, to UNESCO, international nongovernment agencies such as OXFAM, and multinational companies. In this volume, Alkire explores some of the ethical and practical implications of this. We touch on four areas here.

Supporting Development Design Within Countries

The discussion of implications for local public action applies with equal force to external policy advice. Policy design needs to take account of local conditions, including the interaction between sociocultural, political, and economic structures. This does not mean eschewing generalization from international experience or giving up the documented lessons of history on economic and social change. Indeed a central function of such agencies should precisely be the sharing of knowledge by understanding situations and processes by which policies can be made more effective in improving the conditions of the poor.

However, the debate over what makes effective policy within a country has to be informed by a process of dialogue, deliberation, and continual experimentation within the country—rather than an unthinking application of "best practice" guidelines that are little informed by the social and historical context. Development agencies have a key role to play in sharing the lessons of international experience with other countries, but decisions have to be made within those societies that are the intended beneficiaries of public action. It is of particular importance to have institutionalized mechanisms, at local and national levels, that will foster inclusive debate over the potential consequences of interventions. These discussions should occur both at the time of choosing and designing policies, and in the implementation and evaluation phases. The challenge here is to foster independence, not dependence in a different guise. If such processes of internal deliberation are driven and controlled by external donors, they are likely to be reduced to meaningless rituals.

International Policy Design

A cultural perspective is directly relevant to some areas of international policy. Trade liberalization and foreign investment are typically desirable for income and employment objectives, but the effects of globalization on the living conditions and aspirations of workers can be complex. Typically the diagnostic frame of a cultural lens would not suggest reversing globalization but strengthening the agency of adversely affected domestic groups to influence their capacity to influence, choose, or gain from the consequent economic changes. Thus in arguing for the benefits that may accrue from more open markets, the seismic cultural shifts that would ensue should not be ignored, particularly when they may result in new forms of domination and control. This is not to say that cultural dimensions of integration are always either inequalizing or homogenizing; cross-cultural interactions could also be enriching and productivity enhancing (Cowen 2002).

Support for Cultural Products

Within the UN system support for the preservation of the world's cultural heritage is the mandate of UNESCO. Other bilateral donors may wish to channel assistance for this purpose if their citizens (who provide the taxes to pay for aid) value such assistance. But is there a general case for support for the production or preservation of cultural products by a development agency? The perspective of this book suggests this depends on the relationship between such an activity and the promotion of greater equality of agency. As Sen and Klamer show, cultural products have many effects—they can be a source of affirmation of identity, celebration of a plural history, or symbols of difference and domination. They can also have employment and income effects, as with exports of artisanal production and tourism in cultural sites. All these factors need to be weighed in any assessment, keeping in mind that any investment in cultural goods could reduce investment in alternative means of promoting human agency such as health or education. This can also play out at an international level. Indeed, an important aspect of international trade and legal arrangements is the development of mechanisms that assure that knowledge and pro- duction of indigenous/local aesthetic or scientific activities receives intel- lectual protection (as with the intellectual property rights of inventions in the developed world that have now been integrated into international trading arrangements).

Institutional Cultures

Last, but not least, we need to consider the cultures of the institutions themselves. Tales of arrogance in the interactions between international or bilateral agencies and their "clients" abound. Some would suggest the ease by which borrower countries adopt the ideological fashions of interna- tional development agencies is an example of "symbolic violence" in Bourdieu's sense. Small, less affluent countries eager for a loan are partic- ularly vulnerable to this. However, there is an increasing self-awareness within the organizations of this issue. Recent policies in the World Bank and elsewhere have been seeking to change the asymmetry of dealings with client countries and enable a shift toward a culture of partnership and mutual learning. But although cultures are dynamic, they also take time to change, especially when the international agency is very powerful.

Implications for the World of Thought

A cultural lens also has implications for the world of thought. We have in various places referred to some of the developments in research. It would be foolhardy for us to even sketch a research agenda here. We would conclude with a few points about the kinds of questions that devel- opmentally oriented research can illuminate and some of the method- ological issues that may be faced in the process of investigation.

In terms of research questions, the essays open a range of themes that relate to the broad issue of how the relationality that is at the core of cultural processes interacts with economic processes. How do human beings construct and mobilize identity, and how does this affect inequality and mobility? How do they organize collectively in ways that use cultural constructs to bind people into groups? How does culture work to create conflict in some instances and multicultural debate and dialogue in others? How are preferences formed, and how do they react endogenously to material and social conditions? How are notions of well-being and aspiration conditioned by cultural characterizations? How do cultural exchanges interact with economic exchanges as the world becomes more globalized? How do we measure cultural diversity and polarization? How do we develop meaningful constructs of participation and voice? These are among the numerous questions raised by a cultural lens, which anthropologists and economists[6] have been trying to answer.

In any developmentally oriented research agenda, we would suggest two cross-cutting aspects of these themes. First, and at the risk of repetition, interactions within and between groups have to be at the core of any culturally informed analysis. Dealing seriously with such relational issues implies a conceptual and empirical strategy that can integrate group-based influences with the tradition of individualistic analysis that has proved so powerful within economics. Second, from the perspective of having an influence on development, it will be of great importance to link research on culture to the task of assessing, or disentangling, its influence on development effectiveness. Carefully showing how, and how much, a cultural lens can make a difference to the diagnosis of deprivation and in the design of public action to tackle poverty will be the most powerful means of convincing researchers from different disciplines, policy makers, and development agencies of the importance of the issues raised in this book.

Past work has often involved weak interdisciplinary communication, especially between mainstream economics and anthropology. Work of economists that tries to take culture into consideration is, with a few notable exceptions, relatively ignorant of current thinking in anthropology, sociology, and other related disciplines. Often when anthropologists are read and cited, the work is several decades old and is used because it fits easily within the hypotheses of the economist, rather than because it represents the best the discipline has to offer. Similarly, many anthropological critiques of economics base their understandings on simplistic "Economics 101" models rather than the more sophisticated thinking in the field. These are both undesirable outcomes that could be remedied by more respectful interdisciplinary engagement. Future work may fruitfully be of a multidisciplinary character, with economists and anthropologists collaborating on projects. However, there is no reason for this to be the only way forward. There can be gains from sticking within the training and discourse of one's own discipline, but with a friendly ear open to the discourse of the neighboring discipline. This requires an equality of agency of disciplines—the social sciences do not have "queens" and "kings," but rather many courtiers with diverse voices, all of whom may have useful things to say.

As development agencies have turned more participatory, anthropologists and sociologists have begun to have a bigger say in them. Cernea's work is representative of long-standing efforts by development anthropologists and sociologists to demonstrate how careful social thought can provide a fresh look on policy (Cernea 1984). Sillitoe makes a case for how bottom-up development provides challenging opportunities for anthropologists to use ethnographic methods and understandings to contribute to policy design and evaluation (Sillitoe 1998). A crucial part of this is to learn how to speak to economists, engineers, and natural scientists in ways that facilitate dialogue and collaboration instead of the name-calling that has been the norm for several decades.

An exciting recent trend in anthropology, represented in this volume by the contributions of Appadurai and Harragin, is to conduct ethnographies of development practice that investigate *how* development actually works. One important insight from this work is that development may not be driven by policy as much as by a struggle to maintain coherent representations of the expectations of policy (Mosse 2003). Thus, policy design may matter more for how development is portrayed rather than how it is implemented, which raises difficult questions about whether there is any such thing as "good policy."

Thus anthropologists in this volume, and elsewhere, provide thoughtful examples of how policy-relevant research can be carried forward in various domains, in ways that both facilitate dialogue and fundamentally rework how we think about policy. The sharply increased receptivity to such ideas by economists and development practitioners in recent years has created the right moment for dialogue and understanding. This suggests the need for academic anthropologists and sociologists to move toward a research agenda that is less focused on critique and more on constructive engagement.

At an empirical level, there are important methodological issues, in part associated with different traditions of empirical investigation. Starting, at least, from the work of Bardhan and Rudra and Bliss and Stern, several economists have begun to recognize the value of case studies, and the integration of quantitative and ethnographic methods has become an important topic of research within development (Bardhan 1989; Bliss and

Stern 1982; Kanbur 2003; Rao 2002; White 2002; Rao and Woolcock 2003). Anthropology is perhaps more resistant to the use of statistical and econometric methods, but subfields such as anthropological demography have long recognized their utility (Obermeyer et al. 1997; Kertzer and Fricke 1997; Basu and Aaby 1998), and sociology and political science have diverse traditions, some highly quantitative, others more qualitative. In order to engage with development policy, some element of quantitative empirical analysis is inescapable because development often deals with projects that impact a large number of people, and qualitative methods are ill-equipped to provide a generalizable picture of large populations that can be reliably used by policy makers. On the other hand, quantitative scholars must do better in recognizing the inherent structures of power and control within statistical methodologies such as surveys and censuses (Hacking 1990; Dirks 2001) and their tendency to provide data that lack context and common sense. Integrating qualitative methods with survey methods has the potential value of obtaining both a contextualized understanding and findings that can be generalized.

Thus, at a conceptual level, both theoretical and empirical, a cultural lens gives us directions in which development scholarship should go, and that in many ways it has already begun to go. This will result in better-informed, more contextualized public action that will, we hope, be more immune to the perils of high modernism.

The collection of essays in this volume is by no means the last word on the subject, and certainly not the first. Rather, they seek to represent a thoughtful dialogue across disciplines with the constructive goal of making development policy more effective and inclusive. If the cultural lens teaches us anything, it is that development is not easy and in some ways will always be a game of blindman's bluff. But, blending an understanding of cultural and social dynamics into the mix of economics and politics that have traditionally dominated development thought can shed a little additional light on how to do it better. If we are to adequately respond to the critiques of top-down development—that the domination of development by conventional economics has led to overly bureaucratized cookie-cutter, best practice frameworks that have a tendency toward hegemonic control (Scott 1998; Escobar 1995), we believe that the essays in this volume provide some direction. We expect that they will also generate debate.

Notes

We are grateful to Rajiv Rao and Sita Reddy for helpful comments on an earlier draft. The points of view expressed in this chapter are those of the authors and are not necessarily shared by the World Bank, its executive directors, or member countries.

1. It is consistent with Scott's (1998) emphasis on use of common sense as an alternative to the top-down development designs beloved of high modernism but puts more emphasis on cultural dynamics and inequalities.

2. This is precisely the point made by advocates of participatory development (Chambers 1997).

3. Empirical analysis shows this has highly positive poverty-reducing and -targeting properties.

4. Mansuri and Rao (2004) survey the literature that highlights many problems with facilitation in participatory projects.

5. Which Taylor (1995) emphasizes is not the same thing as the *recognition* of equal value.

6. As noted in the overview, there has been an explosion of interest by mainstream economists on how social and cultural factors relate to economic behavior. These include theories of bounded rationality and evolutionary games (Weibull 1995). Bounded rationality theorists model how culture influences behavior and how cultural norms emerge and are propagated through a society (Boyd and Richerson 1985). Bowles provides a review of the relationship between culture and markets that also surveys his many contributions (along with Gintis) on the interactions between culture and economics (Bowles 1998). Durlauf surveys several empirically grounded models on what he calls "membership theories of inequality," which focus on relational aspects of poverty and income distribution (Durlauf 1997). Esteban and Ray (1994) provide a conceptual foundation for the measurement of social polarization. In another vein, there is now a thriving cultural economics subdiscipline within economics that focuses on the economics of cultural goods such as art and museums. Throsby (2001) provides an admirable survey.

In applications to development economics, Dasgupta (1993) provides an integrative perspective on the causes of destitution; Lal (1998) examines the long-run relationship between culture and economic growth; Basu (2000) makes an eloquent case for the social and political basis of economic behavior; and Basu and Weibull (2002) show that traits considered "cultural," such as a norm for punctuality, could result from strategic interactions where people become punctual because others are punctual rather than an atavistic punctuality preference; and Francois (2002) develops a series of models on the interconnections between culture, trust, social capital, and economic development. In empirical applications, there has been a long tradition in development economics that dates at least as far back as the work of Epstein (1962), followed by Bardhan and Rudra (1978) and Bliss and Stern (1982) of collecting primary data contextualized to reflect local cultures (Udry 2003). More recent work has more explicitly studied how culture affects economic action—Platteau (2000) applies an institutionalist perspective to a variety of phenomena in sub-Saharan Africa and South Asia—with an explicit focus on the relationship between social and economic decisions. A series of experiments in different cultural settings by Henrich et al. (2001) shows that the cultural context affected deviations from the canonical economic model of self-interested individual rationality. Several microdevelopment economists have recently addressed questions of culture and ethnicity. For example, Munshi and Rosenzweig (2003) demonstrate how globalization has affected the relationship between caste and economic mobility differently for men and women in Mumbai; Banerjee and Iyer (2002) demonstrate how laws implemented in colonial India have a path dependent effect on current agricultural productivity; Udry (1996) shows how farms managed by women in Ghana are less efficient than farms managed by men in a manner attributable to differences in their agency; Bloch and Rao (2002) develop and test an ethnographically grounded model of the link between dowry payments and domestic violence in rural India; Fafchamps and Minten (2001) study the informal enforcement of contracts among Malagasy grain traders; Chattopadhyay and Duflo (2001) explore the effects of providing quotas for women in village government in India; and Smith, Barret, and Box (2001) provided a contextualized analysis of risk assessment among East African pastoralists.

References

Abers, R. N. 2000. *Inventing local democracy: Grassroots politics in Brazil.* Boulder, CO: Lynne Rienner Publishers.

Abraham, A., and J.-P. Platteau. 2001. *The dilemma of participation with endogenous community imperfections.* Namur: Centre de Recherche en Economie du Developpement, University of Namur.

———. 2004. Participatory development: Where culture creeps in. In *Culture and public action: A cross-disciplinary dialogue on development policy*, ed. V. Rao and M. Walton. Stanford: Stanford University Press.

Abraham, L., and K. A. Kumar. 1999. Sexual experiences and their correlates among college students in Mumbai City, India. *International Family Planning Perspectives* 25:139–46.

ACSF Investigators. 1992. AIDS and sexual behaviour in France. *Nature* 360:407–9.

Adams, R. N., ed. 1957. *Political changes in Guatemalan Indian communities.* New Orleans: Middle American Research Institute, Tulane University.

Adams, J. 1995. *Risk.* London: University College Press.

Adorno, T. W., ed. 1991. *The culture industry: Selected essays on mass culture.* London: Routledge.

Agarwal, B. 1994. *A field of one's own: Gender and land rights in South Asia.* Cambridge: Cambridge University Press.

Aguirre Beltrán, G. 1961. *Regiones de refugio.* Mexico: Secretaría de Educación Pública.

Ahmad, J. A. 1982. *Plagued by the west (Gharbzadegi).* Trans. P. Sprachman. Delmar, NY: Caravan Books.

Ahmad, J. A., Zubeida, and M. F. Loufti. 1980. Program for rural women. In *Women at work.* Geneva: ILO.

Ahmad, M. 1991. Islamic fundamentalism in South Asia: The Jama'at-i-Islami and the Tablighi Jamaat of South Asia. In *Fundamentalisms observed*, ed. M. M. Marty and R. S. Appleby. Chicago: University of Chicago Press.

Ahmed, A. S., and C. N. Shore. 1995. *The future of anthropology.* Atlantic Highlands, NJ: Athlone Press.

Akerlof, G. 1984. *An economic theorist's book of tales.* Cambridge: Cambridge University Press.

Akerlof, G., and R. Kranton. 2000. Economics and identity. *Quarterly Journal of Economics* 115:715–53.

Alba, R. D. 1990. *Ethnic identity: The transformation of white America*. New Haven, CT: Yale University Press.

Alesina, A., and E. La Ferrera. 2003. Ethnic diversity and economic performance. Mimeograph. Harvard Univ., Cambridge.

Alkire, S. 2002a. Conceptual framework for the commission on human security. Mimeograph. World Bank, Washington, DC.

——. 2002b. Dimensions of human development. *World Development* 30:181–205.

——. 2002c. *Valuing freedoms: Sen's capability approach and poverty reduction*. Oxford: Clarendon Press.

——. 2004. Culture, poverty, and external intervention. In *Culture and public action: A cross-disciplinary dialogue on development policy*, ed. V. Rao and M. Walton. Stanford: Stanford University Press.

All India Institute of Hygiene and Public Health (AIIH&PH). 1997. *A dream, a pledge, a fulfillment: Five year stint at Sonagachi 1992–1997*. Calcutta, India: AIIH&PH.

Almond, G., and S. Verba. 1963. *The civic culture: Political attitudes and democracy in five nations*. Princeton, NJ: Princeton University Press.

Almond, G., and B. Powell. 1992. *Comparative politics today*. New York: Harper Collins

Alverson, H., M. Alverson, and R. Drake. 2000. Addictions services: An ethnographic study of the longitudinal course of substance abuse among people with severe mental illness. *Community Mental Health Journal* 36:557–69.

Anderson, E. 1992. *Streetwise: Race, class, and change in an urban community*. Chicago: University of Chicago Press.

——. 2000. *Code of the street: Decency, violence and the moral life of the inner city*. New York: Norton.

Anderson, E. S. 1993. *Value in ethics and economics*. Cambridge, MA: Harvard University Press.

Anderson, M. 1996. *Do no harm: Supporting local capacities for peace through aid*. Cambridge, MA: Collaboration for Development Action.

Anderson, R. S., and W. Huber. 1988. *The year of the fox: Tropical forests, the World Bank, and indigenous people in central India*. Seattle: University of Washington Press.

Andors, P. 1983. *The unfinished liberation of Chinese women, 1949–1980*. Bloomington: Indiana University Press.

——. 1984. Women's liberation in China: A continuing struggle. *China Notes* 23:287–93.

Anti-Mafia Commission of the Italian Parliament. 1993. *Economia e criminalitá*. Rome, Italy: Camera dei Deputati.

Apffel-Marglin, F., and S. A. Marglin. 1990. *Dominating knowledge: Development, culture, and resistance*. Oxford: Clarendon Press.

——. 1996. *Decolonizing knowledge: From development to dialogue*. Oxford: Clarendon Press.

Appadurai, A. 1986. Introduction: Commodities and the politics of value. In *The social life of things: Commodities and the politics of value*, ed. A. Appadurai. Cambridge: Cambridge University Press.

———. 1989. Smale scale techniques, large scale observations. In *Conversations between economists and anthropologists*, ed. P. Bardhan. Delhi: Oxford University Press.

———. 1990. Technology and the reproduction of values in rural Western India. In *Dominating knowledge: Development, culture and resistance*, ed. F. Apffel-Marglin and S. Apffel-Marglin. Oxford: Clarendon Press.

———. 1996. *Modernity at large: The cultural dimensions of globalization*. Minneapolis: University of Minnesota Press.

———. 2001. Deep democracy: Urban governmentality and the horizon of politics. *Public Culture* 14:22–46.

———. 2004. The capacity to aspire: Culture and the terms of recognition. In *Culture and public action: A cross-disciplinary dialogue on development policy*, ed. V. Rao and M. Walton. Stanford, CA: Stanford University Press.

———, ed. 1986. *The social life of things: Commodities in cultural perspective*. Cambridge: Cambridge University Press.

Appiah, K. A., and H. L. Gates. 1995. *Identities*. Chicago: University of Chicago Press.

Arensberg, C., and S. T. Kimball. 1968. *Family and community in Ireland*. Cambridge, MA: Harvard University Press.

Arizpe, L. 1975. *Indígenas en la ciudad: El caso de las "marías."* Mexico: Sep-Setentas.

———. 1978. *Migración, etnicismo y cambio económico*. Mexico: Colegio de México.

———. 1995. On cultural and social sustainability. *Development* 1:5–11.

———. 2000. Cultural heritage and globalization. In *Values and heritage conservation*, ed. E. Avrami, R. Mason, and M. de la Torre. Los Angeles, CA: Getty Conservation Institute.

———. 2002. No alternatives without diversity. *Development* 45:21–24.

———. 2004. The intellectual history of culture and development institutions. In *Culture and public action: A cross-disciplinary dialogue on development policy*, ed. V. Rao and M. Walton. Stanford: Stanford University Press.

Arizpe, L., and J. Aranda. 1982. The comparative advantage of women's disadvantages: Women workers in the strawberry export agribusiness in Mexico. *Signs* 7:453–70.

Arizpe, L., E. Jelin, M. Rao, and P. Streeten. 2001. Cultural diversity, conflict and pluralism. *World Culture Report* 2:23.

Arneson, R. J. 2000. Perfectionism and politics. *Ethics* 111:37–63.

Arrow, K., R. M. Solow, P. R. Portney, E. E. Leamer, R. Radner, and H. Schuman. 1993. Report of the NOAA Panel on Contingent Valuation. *Federal Register* 58:4602–14.

Asad, T., ed. 1973. *Anthropology and the colonial encounter*. London: Ithaca Press.

Avrami, E., R. Mason, and M. de la Torre, eds. 2000. *Values and heritage conservation*. Los Angeles: Getty Conservation Institute.

Babha, H. 1990. The other question: Difference, discrimination and the discourse of colonialism. In *Out there: Marginalization and contemporary cultures*, ed. R. Ferguson. Cambridge, MA: MIT Press.

Badini, A., 1994, *Naître et grandir chez les Moosé traditionnels*. Paris: Sépia-ADDB.

Baez, J. F., and A. R. B. Felix. 1983. La educación bilingüe y bicultural: Encrucijada de lealtades o conflictos de clase? In *Educación, etnias y descolonización en América Latina*, ed. J. F. Baez and Balderas. México: INI.

Bai, M. K., and W. H. Cho. 1996. Women's employment structure and male-female wage differentials in South Korea. In *Women and industrialization in Asia*, ed. S. Horton. London: Routledge.

Bajos, N., and J. Marquet. 2000. Research on HIV risk: Social relations-based approach in a cross-cultural perspective. *Social Science and Medicine* 50:1533−46.

Baland, J. M., and J.-P. Platteau. 1998. Wealth inequality and efficiency in the commons, part II: The regulated case. *Oxford Economic Papers* 50:1−22.

———. 1999. The ambiguous impact of inequality on local resource management. *World Development* 27:773−88.

Baldwin, J. A., R. T. Trotter, D. Martinez, S. Stevens, D. John, and C. Brems. 1999. HIV/AIDS risks among Native American drug users: Key findings from focus group interviews and implications for intervention strategies. *AIDS Education and Prevention* 11:279−92.

Ball, A. 1999. World Health Organization Programme on Substance Abuse. Paper presented at the 2nd Global Research Meeting on HIV and Injecting Drug Use, at Atlanta, GA.

Ballard, J. 1992. Policy-making on HIV in Australia. In *AIDS in the industrialized democracies: Passions, politics and policies*, ed. D. Kirp and R. Bayer. New Brunswick, NJ: Rutgers University Press.

Banerjee, A., and L. Iyer. 2002. History, institutions and economic performance: The legacy of colonial land tenure in india. Mimeograph. Department of Economics, MIT, Boston.

Banerjee, A., D. Mookherjee, K. Munshi, and D. Ray. 1999. Inequality, control rights and efficiency: A study of sugar cooperatives in western maharashtra. Mimeograph. Boston Univ.

Banfield, E. 1958. *The moral basis of a backward society*. New York: Free Press.

Bank of Korea, The. 1971. *National income statistics yearbook*. Seoul, Korea: Bank of Korea.

Banton, M. 1999. Reporting on race. *Anthropology Today* 15:1−3.

Baptiste, D. A., Jr., K. V. Hardy, and L. Lewis. 1997. Family therapy with English Carribean immigrant families in the United States: Issues of emigration, immigration, culture, and race. *Contemporary Family Therapy* 19:337−59.

Bardhan, P. 2000. Water community: An empirical analysis of cooperation in south India. Mimeograph. Univ. of California at Berkeley.

———, ed. 1989. *Conversations between economists and anthropologists*. Delhi: Oxford University Press.

Bardhan, P., and D. Mookherjee. 1999. *Relative capture of local and central governments: An essay in the political economy of decentralization*. IED Discussion Paper Series No. 97. Boston: Institute of Economic Development, Boston University.

———. 2000a. *Corruption and decentralization of infrastructure delivery in developing countries*. IED Discussion Paper Series No. 104. Boston: Institute of Economic Development, Boston University.

———. 2000b. Decentralizing anti-poverty program delivery in developing countries. Mimeograph. Univ. of California at Berkeley.

Bardhan, P., and A. Rudra. 1978. Interlinkage of land, labour and credit relations: An analysis of village survey data in East India. *Economic and Political Weekly* 13.

Barkow, J. H., L. Cosmides, and J. Tooby. 1992. *The adapted mind: Evolutionary psychology and the generation of culture*. New York: Oxford University Press.

Barrett, W. E. 1962. *The lilies of the field*. Garden City, NJ: Doubleday.

Bartra, R., and G. Otero. 1988. Crisis agraria y diferenciación social en México. *Revista Mexicana de Sociología* 50.

Basch, L., N. Glick-Schiller, and C. Szanton-Blanc. 1994. *Nations unbound: Transnational projects, post-colonial predicaments, and deterritorialized nation-states*. Langhorne, PA: Gordon and Breach.

Bastos, S., and M. Camus. 1993. *Quebrando el silencio: Organizaciones del pueblo maya y sus demandas (1986–1992)*. Guatemala: FLASCO.

Basu, A. 1992. *Culture, the status of women and demographic behavior*. Oxford: Clarendon Press.

Basu, A., and P. Aaby. 1998. *The methods and uses of anthropological demography*. Oxford: Clarendon Press.

Basu, K. 1980. *Revealed preference of government*. Cambridge: Cambridge University Press.

———. 1997. *Analytical development economics: The less developed economy revisited*. Cambridge, MA: MIT Press.

———. 2000. *A prelude to political economy: A study of the social and political foundations of economics*. New York: Oxford University Press.

Basu, K., and J. Weibull. 2002. Punctuality: A cultural trait as equilibrium. Mimeograph. Cornell Univ.

Bates, R. H., J. P. Rui, P. Jr. De Figueiredo, and B. R. Weingast. 1998. The politics of interpretation: Rationality, culture, and transition. *Politics and Society* 26:603–42.

Batres Jáuregui, A. 1893. *Los indios, su historia y su civilización*. Guatemala: Tipográfico La Unión.

Baumann, G. 1996. *Contesting culture: Discourses of identity in multi-ethnic London*. Cambridge: Cambridge University Press.

Baumol, W. J., and W. G. Bowen. 1966. *Performing arts: The economic dilemma*. New York: Twentieth Century Fund.

Bayart, J. F. 1989. *L'Etat en Afrique*. Paris: Fayard.

Bearman, P. S., and H. Bruckner. 2001. Promising the future: Virginity pledges and first intercourse. *American Journal of Sociology* 106:859–912.

Bebbington, A. 1997. New states, new NGOs? Crises and transitions among rural development NGOs in the Andean region. *World Development* 25:1755–65.

Bebbington, A., S. Guggenheim, E. Olson, and M. Woolcock. In press. Exploring social capital debates at the World Bank. *Journal of Development Studies*.

Beck, U. 2000. *What is globalization?* London: Blackwell.

Becker, G. 1996. *Accounting for tastes*. Cambridge, MA: Harvard University Press.

Becker, G., and G. Stigler. 1977. De gustibus non est disputandum. *American Economic Review* 67:76–90.

Begemihl, B. 1999. *Biological exuberance: Animal homosexuality and natural diversity.* New York: St. Martin's Press.

Behar, R. 1993. Brujería sexual, colonialismo y poderes de las mujeres. In *Mujeres invadidas,* ed. V. Stolcke. Madrid: Horas y Horas.

Bell, D., A. Richard, and L. Feltz. 1996. Mediators of drug treatment outcomes. *Addictive Behaviors* 21:597–613.

Ben-Ner, A., and L. Putterman, eds. 1998. *Economics, values and organization.* Cambridge: Cambridge University Press.

Bénabou, R. 1993. The workings of a city: Location, education and production. *Quarterly Journal of Economics* 108:619–52.

Bennett, J. 1988. Anthropology and development: The ambiguous engagement. *Development* 4:6–15.

Benthall, J. 1995. International NGO's and complex political emergencies—conference report. *Anthropology Today* 11:18–19.

Bergensen, H. O., and L. Lunde. 1999. *Dynasaurs or dynamos? The United Nations and the World Bank at the turn of the century.* London: Earthscan Publications.

Bergstrom, T. C. 2002. Evolution of social behavior: Individual and group selection. *Journal of Economic Perspectives* 16:67–88.

Berkes, N. 1998. *The development of secularism in Turkey.* 2nd ed. New York: Routledge.

Berlin, I. 1969. *Two concepts of liberty.* Oxford: Oxford University Press.

Bernheim, D. B. 1994. A theory of conformity. *Journal of Political Economy* 102:841–77.

Berryman, P. 1984. *The religious roots of rebellion: Christians in Central American revolutions.* New York: Orbis Books.

Bierschenk, T., J. P. O. de Sardan, and J. P. Chauveau, eds. 2000. *Courtiers en développement—Les villages africains en quête de projets.* Paris: Karthala.

Bikhchandani, S., D. Hirshleifer, and I. Welch. 1992. A theory of fads, custom and cultural change as informational cascades. *Journal of Political Economy* 100:992–1026.

Bilgrami, A. 1995. What is a Muslim? In *Identities,* ed. A. Appiah and H. L. Gates. Chicago: University of Chicago Press.

Bischoping, K., and H. Schuman. 1992. Pens and polls in Nicaragua: An analysis of the 1990 preelection surveys. *American Journal of Political Science* 36:331–50.

Bisin, A., and T. Verdier. 2001. The economics of cultural transmission and the evolution of preferences. *Journal of Economic Theory* 97:298–319.

Blackburn, J. 2001. Popular participation in Bolivia: Rights versus a clientelistic political culture? "Participacion y empowerment" seminar. Lima, Peru: World Bank.

Blackburn, J., and J. Holland, eds. 1998. *Who changes? Institutionalizing participation in development.* London: Intermediate Technology Publications.

Blau, J. R. 1993. *Social contracts and economic markets.* New York: Plenum Press.

———. 2001a. Bringing in codependence. In *The Blackwell companion to sociology,* ed. J. R. Blau. Oxford, England: Blackwell.

———, ed. 2001b. *The Blackwell companion to sociology.* Oxford, England: Blackwell.

Blaug, M., ed. 1976. *The economics of the arts: Selected readings.* London: Martin Robinson.

Bliss, C. J. 1993. Life-style and the standard of living. In *The quality of life*, ed. M. Nussbaum and A. K. Sen. Oxford: Oxford University Press.

Bliss, C. J., and N. H. Stern. 1982. *Palanpur: The economy of an Indian village.* Delhi: Oxford University Press.

Bloch, F., and V. Rao. 1993. Statistical discrimination, identity selection, and the social transformation of caste and race. Brown University Department of Economics working paper 93-15. Providence, RI: Brown University Department of Economics.

———. 2001. Statistical discrimination and social assimilation. *Economics Bulletin* 10:1–5.

———. 2002. Terror as a bargaining instrument: A case study of dowry violence in rural India. *American Economic Review* 92:1029–43.

Bobbio, N., and N. Matteucci. 1985. *Diccionario de política.* Mexico City: Siglo XXI.

Bockting, W. O., S. Rosser, and E. Coleman. 1999. Transgender HIV prevention: Community involvement and empowerment. *International Journal of Transgenderism* 3.

Bohannan, P., and G. Dalton, eds. 1962. *Markets in Africa.* Evanstone, IL: Northwestern University Press.

Bohman, J., and W. Rehg, eds. 1997. *Deliberative democracy.* Cambridge, MA: MIT Press.

Bonfil Batalla, G., ed. 1981. *Utopía y revolución: El pensamiento político contemporaneo de los indios en América Latina.* Mexico: Editora Nueva Imagen.

———. 1985. *México profundo.* Mexico: SEP.

Boniface, P. 1995. *Managing quality cultural tourism.* London: Routledge.

Boone, C. 1992. *Merchant capital and the roots of state power in Senegal 1930–1985.* Cambridge: Cambridge University Press.

———. 1994. States and ruling classes in postcolonial Africa: The enduring contradictions of power. In *State power and social forces—Domination and transformation in the third world*, ed. J. S. Migdal, A. Kohli, and V. Shue. Cambridge: Cambridge University Press.

Booth, M. 1996. *Opium: A history.* London: Simon and Schuster.

Boserup, E. 1970. *Women's role in economic development.* New York: St. Martin's Press.

Botvin, G. J., E. Baker, L. Dusenbury, and M. Botvin. 1996. Long-term follow-up results of a randomized drug abuse prevention trial in a white, middle-class population. *Journal of the American Medical Association* 273:1106–12.

Bourdieu, P. 1977. *Outline of a theory of practice.* Trans. R. Nice. Cambridge: Cambridge University Press.

———. 1984. *Distinction: A critique of the judgement of taste.* Cambridge, MA: Harvard University Press.

———. 1986. Three forms of capital. In *The handbook of theory and research for the sociology of education*, ed. J. C. Richardson. New York: Greenwood.

———. 1990. *The logic of practice.* Stanford: Stanford University Press.

———. 1998. *Practical reason.* Stanford: Stanford University Press.

Bowles, S. 1998. Endogenous preferences, the cultural consequences of markets and other economic institutions. *Journal of Economic Literature* 36:75–111.

Bowles, S., and H. Gintis. 2002. The inheritance of inequality. *Journal of Economic Perspectives* 16:3–30.

Boyd, R., and P. J. Richerson. 1985. *Culture and the evolutionary process*. Princeton, NJ: Princeton University Press.

Britnell, G. E. 1951. Problems of economic and social change in Guatemala. *Canadian Journal of Economics and Political Science* 17:468–81.

Brittan, S., and A. Hamlin, eds. 1995. *Market capitalism and moral values*. Aldershot, England: Edward Elgar.

Brock, K., and R. McGee, eds. 2002. *Knowing poverty: Critical reflections on participatory research and policy*. Sterling, VA: Earthscan.

Brook, D., J. Brook, L. Richter, M. Whiteman, P. T. Win, J. Masci, and J. Roberto. 1999. Coping strategies of HIV-positive and HIV-negative female injection drug users: A longitudinal study. *AIDS Education and Prevention* 11:373–88.

Brumann, C. 1999. Writing for culture: Why a successful concept should not be discarded. *Current Anthropology* 40:S1–S28.

Bu, W. 1998. Gender and media: Policy and current situation. *Women Studies* 1:15–20.

Buckley, S. 2000. Brazil becomes model in fight against AIDS: Government, activists team to defy epidemic through distribution of drugs. *Washington Post*, September 17, 2000, A22.

Bunzel, R. 1952. *Chichicastenago: A Guatemalan village*. Seattle: University of Washington Press.

Business Wire. 2001. Online pornography usage: A comprehensive snapshot of Hong Kong internet users' demographics, duration, traffic trends and most favoured adult sites. *Hong Kong Business Wire*, February 6, 2001.

Calderón, F. 1995. *Sociedades en atajos: Cultura, política y reestructuración económica en América Latina*. Buenos Aires, Argentina: Paidos.

———. 2002. *La reforma de la política: Deliberación y desarrollo*. Caracas, Venezuela: Nueva Sociedad-ILDIS.

Calderón, F., M. Chiriboga, and D. Pinero. 1992. *Modernización democrática e incluyente de la agricultura en América Latina y el Caribe*. Documento No. 28. San Jose, Costa Rica: IICA.

Calderón, F., and J. Dandler, eds. 1984. *Bolivia: La fuerza histórica del campesinado*. Cochabamba: UNRISD-CERES.

Calderón, F., and M. dos Santos. 1987. Movimientos sociales y democracia: Los conflictos por la constitución de un nuevo orden. In *Los conflictos por la constitución de un nuevo orden*, ed. F. Calderón and M. dos Santos. Buenos Aires, Argentina: CLASCO.

Calderón, F., M. Hopenhayn, and E. Ottone. 1996. *Esa esquiva modernidad*. Caracas, Venezuela: UNESCO-Nueva Sociedad.

Calderón, F., and N. Lechner. 1996. *Modernización y governabilidad democrática: Informe para el Programa de Naciones Unidas para el desarrollo*. La Paz, Bolivia: UNDP.

Calderón, F., and A. Szmukler. 2000. *La política en las calles*. La Paz: Plural.

Carmack, R. M., ed. 1988. *Harvest of violence: The Maya Indians and the Guatemala crisis.* Norman: University of Oklahoma Press.

Carter, P. 2000. Lie of the tiger. *Ecologist* 30:60–61.

Cassen, R. 1986. *Does aid work?* Oxford: Clarendon Press.

Castellanos Cambranes, J. 1985. *Coffee and peasants: The origins of the modern plantation economy in Guatemala, 1853–1897.* Stockholm, Sweden: Institute of Latin American Studies.

Castells, M. 1997. *La era de la información: Económica, sociedad y cultura.* Vol. 1. Madrid, Spain: Alianza.

———. 1998. *La era de la informacion: Económica, sociedad y cultura.* Vols. 2 and 3. Madrid, Spain: Alianza.

Caufield, C. 1996. *Masters of illusion: The World Bank and the poverty of nations.* New York: Henry Holt.

Cavalli-Sforza, L. L., and M. W. Feldman. 1981. *Cultural transmission and evolution: A quantitative approach.* Princeton, NJ: Princeton University Press.

Caves, R. E. 2000. *Creative industries.* Cambridge, MA: Harvard University Press.

Census of India. 2001. Census of India 2001. Available at: http://www.census india.net/index11a.html.

Centers for Disease Control and Prevention (CDC). 2001. Public health and injection drug use. *MMWR Morbidity and Mortality Weekly Report* 50:377.

Cernea, M. 1995. *Primero la gente: Variables sociólogicas en el desarrollo rural.* Mexico: Fondo de Cultura Económica.

———, ed. 1984. *Putting people first: Sociological variables in development.* Washington, DC: Agriculture and Rural Development Department, World Bank.

———, ed. 1991. *Putting people first: Sociological variables in rural development.* Oxford: Oxford University Press/World Bank.

Chambers, R. 1997. *Whose reality counts? Putting the first last.* London: Intermediate Technology.

Chattopadhyay, R., and E. Duflo. 2001. Women as policy makers: Evidence from an India-wide randomized policy experiment. Mimeograph. Deparment of Economics, MIT, Boston.

Chonchol, J. 1990. Modernización agrícola y estrategias campesinas en América Latina. *Revista Internacional de Ciencias Sociales* 124.

Chowdhry, P. 1994. *The veiled women: Shifting gender equations in rural Haryana, 1880–1990.* Dehli: Oxford University Press.

Choy, A. E., and V. G. Borell. 1997. *The Mayan movement today: Issues of indigenous culture and development in Guatemala.* Guatemala: FLASCO.

Chwe, M. S. K. 1999. Structure and strategy in collective action. *American Journal of Sociology* 105:128–56.

———. 2000. Communication and coordination in social networks. *Review of Economic Studies* 67:1–16.

———. 2001. *Rational ritual: Culture, coordination, and common knowledge.* Princeton, NJ: Princeton University Press.

CIETafrica. 2000. *Beyond victims and villains: The culture of sexual violence in South Johannesburg.* Johannesburg, South Africa: CIET International.

Çizakça, M. 2000. *A history of philanthropic foundations: The Islamic world from the seventh century to the present.* Istanbul: Boğaziçi University Press.

Clifford, J., and G. E. Marcus, eds. 1984. *Writing culture: The poetics and politics of ethnography.* Berkeley: University of California Press.

Coleman, J. S. 1988. Social capital in the creation of human capital. *American Journal of Sociology* 94:S95–S120.

Coleman, J. S. 1990. *Foundations of social theory.* Cambridge, MA: Harvard University Press.

Collier, P. 1999. "Aid" dependency: A critique. *Journal of African Economics* 8:528–45.

Collins, R. 2000. Malakal revisited: Britain in the Sudan after fifty years. Paper presented at the 5th Triennial Meeting of the International Sudan Studies Association, at Durham, England.

Comaroff, J., and J. Comaroff. 1991. *Of revelation and revolution.* Chicago: University of Chicago Press.

Comisión Económica para América Latina y el Caribe (CEPAL). 2000. *Panorama social de América Latina 1999–2000.* Santiago de Chile: CEPAL.

———. 2001. *Panorama social de América Latina 2000–2001.* Santiago de Chile: CEPAL.

Comisión Paritaria de Reforma Educativa. 1998. *Diseño de reforma educativa: Runuk'ik Jun K'ak'a Tijonik.* Guatemala: Proyecto de Interculturidad, Políticas Públicas y Desarrollo Humano Sostenible, Q'anil B.

Commission for Historical Clarification (CEH). 1999. *Guatemala: Memory of silence.* Guatemala: United Nations OPS.

Comisión Nacional Permanente de Reforma Educativa. 1998. *Proyecto de reforma educativa desde la perspectiva indígena.* Guatemala: Saqb'ichil COPMAGUA.

Condorcet, M. 1795/1955. *Esquisse d'un tableau historique des progrès de l'esprit human* [Sketch for a historical picture of the progress of the human mind]. Trans. J. Barraclough. London: Weidenfeld and Nicolson.

Congleton, R. 1980. Competitive process, competitive waste, and institutions. In *Toward a theory of the rent-seeking society*, ed. J. Buchanan, R. Tollison, and G. Tullock. Texas: Texas A&M Press.

Conning, J., and M. Kevane. 1999. Community based targeting mechanisms for social safety nets. Mimeograph. Department of Economics, Santa Clara Univ.

Cooke, B., and U. Kothari, eds. 2001. *Participation: The new tyranny?* London: Zed Books.

Cordes, J. J., and R. S. Goldfarb. 1996. The value of public art as public culture. In *The value of culture: On the relationship between economics and arts*, ed. A. Klamer. Amsterdam: Amsterdam University Press.

Cowen, T. 1998. *In praise of commercial culture.* Cambridge, MA: Harvard University Press.

———. 2002. *Creative destruction: How globalization is changing the world's cultures.* Princeton, NJ: Princeton University Press.

Coyle, D. J., and R. J. Ellis, eds. 1994. *Politics, policy and culture.* Boulder, CO: Westview Press.

Crofts, N., and D. Herkt. 1993. A history of peer-based drug-users groups in Australia. *Journal of Drug Issues* 25:599–616.

Croll, E. 1981. *The politics of marriage in contemporary China.* Cambridge: Cambridge University Press.

Cruise-O'Brien, D. B. 1971. *The Mourides of Senegal: Political and economic organization of an Islamic brotherhood.* Oxford: Oxford University Press.

Cummings, W. K. 1980. *Education and equality in Japan.* Princeton, NJ: Princeton University Press.

Daedalus. 2000. The end of tolerance: Engaging cultural differences. *Daedalus* 29, no. 4.

Dahrendorf, R. 1995. *Economic opportunity, civil society and political liberty.* Discussion paper 58. Ginebra: UNRISD.

Danahar, K., ed. 2001. *Democratizing the global economy: The battle against the World Bank and the IMF.* Philadelphia: Common Courage Press.

Dandler, J. 1999. Indigenous peoples and the rule of law in Latin America: Do they have a chance? In *The (un)rule of law and the underprivileged in Latin America*, ed. J. E. Mendez, G. O'Donnell and P. S. Pinheiro. Notre Dame, IN: University of Notre Dame Press.

Darke, S., J. Ross, and W. Hall. 1996. Overdose among heroin users in Sydney, Australia: II. Responses to overdose. *Addiction* 91:413–17.

Das, M. K. 2000. Kerala's decentralised planning-floundering experiment. *Economic and Political Weekly* (December 2): 4300–4303.

Das Gupta, M. 1995. Life course perspectives on women's autonomy and health outcomes. *American Anthropologist* 97:481–91.

Das Gupta, M., and Li Shuzhuo. 1999. Gender bias and the marriage squeeze in China, South Korea and India 1920–1990: The effects of war, famine and fertility decline. *Development and Change* 30:619–52.

Das Gupta, M., J. Zhenghua, X. Zhenming, L. Bohua, N.-H. Cho, W. Chung, and P. N. M. Bhat. 1997. *Gender bias in China, South Korea and India: Causes and policy implications.* Harvard University Center for Population and Development Studies working paper 98.03. Boston: Harvard University Center for Population and Development Studies.

Dasgupta, P. 1993. *An inquiry into well-being and destitution.* Oxford: Clarendon Press.

———. 1999. Economic progress and the idea of social capital. In *Social capital: A multifaceted perspective*, ed. P. Dasgupta and I. Serageldin. Washington, DC: World Bank.

Dasgupta, P., and I. Serageldin, eds. 2000. *Social capital: A multifaceted perspective.* Washington, DC: World Bank.

David, P. A. 1994. Why are institutions the "carriers of history"? Path dependence and the evolution of conventions, organizations and institutions. *Social Change and Economic Dynamics* 5:205–20.

Davin, D. 1976. *Womenwork: Women and the party in revolutionary China.* Oxford: Clarendon Press.

———. 1995. Women, work and property in the Chinese peasant household of the

1980s. In *Male bias in the development process*, ed. D. Elson. Manchester, England: Manchester University Press.

Davis, S. H. 1988. Agrarian structure and ethnic resistance: The Indian in Guatemalan and Salvadoran National Politics. In *Ethnicities and nations: Processes of interethnic relations in Latin America, Southeast Asia, and the Pacific*, ed. R. Guidieri, F. Pellizzi and S. J. Tambiah. Austin: University of Texas Press.

———. 1997a. The Guatemalan peace accords and indigenous communal lands. Paper prepared at the Colloquium Series of the Program in Agrarian Studies. New Haven, CT: Yale University.

———. 1997b. *La tierra de nuestros antepasados: Estudio de la herencia y la tenencia de la tierra en el altiplano de Guatemala.* Antigua, Guatemala: Centro de Investigaciones Regionales de Mesoamerica and Plumsock Mesoamerican Studies.

Davis, S. H., and L. T. Soeftesad. 1995. *Participation and indigenous peoples.* Social Development Papers No. 9. Washington, DC: World Bank.

Davy, G. 1922. *La foi jurée: Étude sociologique du problème du contrat, la formation du lien contractuel.* Paris: Alcan.

Dayton-Johnson, J. 1998. Rules and cooperation on the local commons: theory with evidence from Mexico. Mimeograph. Univ. of California at Berkeley.

de la Torre, M., ed. 2002. *Assessing the values of cultural heritage.* Los Angeles: Getty Conservation Institute.

De Lame, D. 1996. Une Colline Entre Mille ou le Calme avant la Tempête—Transformations et Blocages du Rwanda Rural. *Annales Sciences Humaines du Musée Royal de L'Afrique Centrale* 154:358.

de Leon, M. 2000. Políticas culturales sobre el tapete. *Prensa Libre*, March 16, 2000.

De Waal, A. 1989. *Famine that kills: Darfur, Sudan 1984–5.* Oxford: Oxford University Press.

———. 1990. A re-assessment of entitlement theory in the light of the recent famines in Africa. *Development and Change* 21:469–90.

Deere, C. D., and M. L. Leal. 1982. Peasant production, proletarianization and the sexual division of labour in the Andes. *Signs* 7:338–60.

Deng, L. B. 1999. *Famine in the Sudan: Causes, preparedness and response—A political, social and economic analysis of the 1998 Bahr-El-Ghazal famine.* Sussex, England: IDS.

Des Jarlais, D., M. Marmor, P. Friedmann, S. Titus, E. Aviles, S. Deren, L. Torian, D. Glebatis, C. Murrill, E. Monterroso, and S. Friedman. 2000. HIV incidence among injection drug users in New York City, 1992–1997: Evidence for a declining epidemic. *American Journal of Public Health* 90:352–59.

Dewaraja, R., and Y. Sasaki. 1991. Semen-loss syndrome: A comparison between Sri Lanka and Japan. *American Journal of Psychotherapy* 45:14–20.

Di Tella, T. 1965. Populism and reform in Latin America. In *Obstacles to change in Latin America*, ed. C. Veliz. London: Oxford University Press.

Dirks, N. B. 2001. *Castes of mind: Colonialism and the making of modern India.* Princeton, NJ: Princeton University Press.

Disasters Emergency Committee (DEC). 1999. *Sudan crisis appeal evaluation.* London: DEC.

Disraeli, B. 1845/1998. *Sybil.* Oxford: Oxford Paperbacks.

Dore, R. 1976. Culture revisited. *Institute of Development Studies Bulletin* 8:3.

———. 1987. *Taking Japan seriously: A Confucian perspective on leading economic issues.* Stanford: Stanford University Press.

dos Santos, M., ed. 1987. *Concertación político-social y democratización.* Buenos Aires: CLASCO.

Douglas, M. 1966/1984. *Purity and danger: An analysis of concepts of pollution and taboo.* London: Routledge.

———. 1973/1982. *Natural symbols: Explorations in cosmology.* New York: Pantheon Books.

———. 1978. *Cultural bias.* London: Royal Anthropological Institute of Great Britain and Ireland.

———. 1984. Standard social uses of food: An introduction. In *Food in the social order: Studies of food and festivities in three American communities*, ed. M. Douglas. New York: Russell Sage.

———. 1987. *How institutions think.* London: Routledge.

———. 1992. *Risk and blame: Essays in cultural theory.* London: Routledge.

———. 1996. Prospects for asceticism. In *Thought styles*, ed. M. Douglas. London: Sage Publications.

Douglas, M., and B. Isherwood. 1979/1996. *The world of goods—Towards an anthropology of consumption.* London: Routledge.

Douglas, M., and G. Mars. In press. *Withdrawal, control and violence.*

Douglas, M., and S. Ney. 1998a. Human needs and wants. In *Human choice and climate change*, vol. 1. Edited by S. Rayner and E. Malone. Battelle Press.

———. 1998b. *Missing persons: A critique of personhood in the social sciences.* Berkeley: University of California Press.

Douglas, M., and A. B. Wildavsky. 1982. *Risk and culture: An essay on the selection of technical and environmental dangers.* Berkeley: University of California Press.

Drèze, J., and A. K. Sen. 1990. *The political economy of hunger.* Oxford: Oxford University Press.

———. 1995. *India: Economic development and social opportunity.* Oxford: Oxford University Press.

———. 2002. *India: Development and participation.* Delhi: Oxford University Press.

Drèze, J., and A. M. Z. Hussain. 1995. *The political economy of hunger—Selected essays.* Oxford: Oxford University Press.

Drijver, C. A., and Y. J. J. van Zorge. 1995. With a little help from our friends: The Gouzda case of local resource management in Cameroon. In *Local resource management in Africa*, ed. H. P. M. van den Breemer, C. A. Drijver and L. B. Venema. New York: Wiley.

Dube, L. 1997. *Women and kinship: Comparative perspectives on gender in South and South-East Asia.* New Delhi: Vistaar Publications.

Duffield, M. 1994. The political economy of internal war: Asset transfer, complex emergencies and international aid. In *War and hunger: Rethinking international responses to complex emergencies*, ed. J. Macrae and A. Zwi. London: SCF/Zed.

———. 1998. *Aid policy and post-modern conflict: A critical review.* Occasional Paper 19. Birmingham, England: School of Public Policy, University of Birmingham.

Duffield, M., M. J. Jok, D. Keen, G. Loane, F. O'Reilly, J. Ryle, and P. Winter. 2000.

Sudan: Unintended consequences of humanitarian assistance. Field evaluation study. Report for European Community Humanitarian Office. Dublin, Ireland: Trinity College.

Dumont, L. 1970. *Homo hierarchicus: The caste system and its implications.* Chicago: University of Chicago Press.

Durkheim, E. 1912/1965. *The elementary forms of religious life.* Trans. J. W. Swain. New York: Free Press.

Durlauf, S. N. 1997. The memberships theory of inequality: Ideas and implications. Mimeograph. Univ. of Wisconsin at Madison.

———. 2001. On the empirics of social capital. Mimeograph. Department of Economics, Univ. of Wisconsin at Madison.

———. 2002. Groups, social influences and inequality: A memberships theory perspective on poverty traps. Mimeograph. Department of Economics, Univ. of Wisconsin at Madison.

Dyson-Hudson, N. 1991. Pastoral production systems and livestock development projects: An East African perspective. In *Putting people first,* ed. M. Cernea. New York: Oxford University Press.

Eagleton, T. 1995. *Heathcliff and the Great Hunger: Studies in Irish Culture.* London: Verso.

———. 2000. *The idea of culture.* Oxford, England: Blackwell.

Edgerton, R. B. 1992. *Sick societies: Challenging the myth of primitive harmony.* New York: Free Press.

Eliot, T. S. 1948. *Notes on the definition of culture.* London: Faber and Faber.

Ellen, R. 1984. *Ethnography: A guide to general conduct.* London: Academic Press.

Ellerman, D. 2000. *Must the World Bank have official views?* World Bank internal memo. Washington, DC: World Bank.

———. 2002. Autonomy-respecting assistance: Towards new strategies for development assistance.

Elster, J. 1989. *The cement of society—A study of social order.* Cambridge: Cambridge University Press.

———, ed. 1986. *Rational choice.* Oxford, England: Blackwell.

———, ed. 2001. *La democracia deliberativa.* Barcelona, Spain: Gedisa.

Emmerj, L., R. Jolly, and T. Weiss. 2001. *Ahead of the curve.* Bloomington: Indiana University Press.

Epstein, S. 1962. *Economic development and social change in South India.* Manchester, England: University of Manchester Press.

Escobar, A. 1995. *Encountering development: The making and unmaking of the third world.* Princeton, NJ: Princeton University Press.

Esman, M. J., and N. T. Uphoff. 1984. *Local organizations: Intermediaries in rural development.* Ithaca, NY: Cornell University Press.

Esteban, J.-M., and D. Ray. 1994. On the measurement of polarization. *Econometrica* 62:819–51.

Estebanez, P., N. Russell, M. D. Aguilar, F. Beland, and M. V. Zunzunegui. 2000. Women, drugs and HIV/AIDS: Results of a multicentre European study. *International Journal of Epidemiology* 29:734–43.

Etounga-Manguelle, D. 2000. Comment on Richard Schweder. In *Culture matters:*

How values shape human progress, ed. L. E. Harrison and S. P. Huntington. New York: Basic Books.

Evans, P. 2002. Beyond "institutional monocropping": Institutions, capabilities, and deliberative development. Mimeograph. Univ. of California at Berkeley.

Evans-Pritchard, E. E. 1937. *Witchcraft, oracles and magic among the Azande*. Oxford: Oxford University Press.

———. 1940. *The Nuer: A description of the modes of livelihood and political institutions of a nilotic people*. Oxford: Clarendon Press.

———. 1964. *Closed systems and open minds*. Chicago: Aldine.

Fafchamps, M. 1992. Solidarity networks in preindustrial societies: National peasants with a moral economy. *Economic Development and Cultural Change* 41:147–74.

Fafchamps, M., and B. Minten. 2001. Property rights in a flea market economy. *Economic Development and Cultural Change* 49:229–68.

Falla, R. 1978. El movimiento indígena. *Estudios Centroamericanos* 33:437–61.

Faletto, E. 1988. Cultura política y conciencia democrática. *Revista de la CEPAL* 35.

Faupel, C. E. 1987. Drug availability, life structure and situation ethics of heroin addicts. *Urban Life* 15:395.

Faure, D. 1989. The lineage as cultural invention: The case of the Pearl River Delta. *Modern China* 15:4–36.

Feldstein, M., ed. 1991. *The economics of art museums: A National Bureau of Economic Research conference report*. Chicago: University of Chicago Press.

Ferguson, J. 1990. *The anti-politics machine: development, de-politicisation and bureaucratic power in Lesotho*. Cambridge: Cambridge University Press.

Fernandez, J. 1965. Symbolic consensus in a fang reformative cult. *American Anthropologist* 67:902–27.

———. 1986. *Persuasions and performances: The play of tropes in culture*. Bloomington: Indiana University Press.

Fields, G. S. 2001. *Distribution and development: A new look at the developing world*. Cambridge, MA: MIT Press.

Filmer, D., and L. Pritchett. 1999. Educational enrollment and attainment in India: Household wealth, gender, village and state effects. *Journal of Educational Planning and Administration* 13:135–64.

Fine, B. 2001. *Social capital versus social theory: Political economy and social science at the turn of the millennium*. London: Routledge.

Firth, R. 1951. *Elements of social organization*. London: Watts.

Fischer, E., and R. M. Brown. 1996. *Mayan cultural activism in Guatemala*. Austin: University of Texas Press.

Fitoussi, J., and P. Rosanvallon. 1997. *La nueva era de las desigualdades*. Buenos Aires, Argentina: Manantial.

Forbes, G. 1996. *The new Cambridge history of India: Women in modern India*. Cambridge: Cambridge University Press.

Foucault, M. 1980. *Power/knowledge*. New York: Pantheon Books.

Fox, J. 1993. *The politics of food in Mexico*. Berkeley: University of California Press.

———. 2000. Advocacy research and the World Bank. Paper presented at the American Association of Anthropology Presidential Section.

Franché, M.-A. 2000. Concertación y Acuerdos: La Experiencia de Porto Alegre. *Cuadernos de Futuro* 13.

Francois, P. 2002. *Social capital and economic development.* London: Routledge.

Frank, R. H. 1985. *Choosing the right pond: Human behavior and the quest for status.* New York: Oxford University Press.

———. 1988. *Passions within reason: The strategic role of emotions.* New York: Norton.

———. 1995. *The winner-take-all society.* New York: Martin Kessler Books at the Free Press.

———. 1998. Social norms as positional arms control agreements. In *Economics, values, and organization,* ed. A. Ben-Ner and L. Putterman. Cambridge.

Fraser, N. 2001. *Redistribution, recognition and participation: Toward an integrated conception of justice.* World Culture Report 2. Paris: UNESCO Publications.

Fraser, N., and A. Honneth. 2003. *Redistribution or recognition: A political-philosophical exchange.* London: Verso.

Frey, B. 1997a. The evaluation of cultural heritage: Some critical issues. In *Economic perspectives on cultural heritage,* ed. M. Hutter and I. Rizzo. London: Macmillan.

———. 1997b. *Not just for the money: An economic theory of personal motivation.* Brookfield, Vermont: Edward Elgar.

———. 2000. *Arts and economics: Analysis and policy.* Berlin: Springer Verlag.

Frey, B., and W. W. Pommerehne. 1989. *Muses and markets: Explorations in the economics of the arts.* Oxford, England: Blackwell.

Fried, M. 1969. *Fabric of Chinese society: A study of the social life of a Chinese county seat.* New York: Octagon.

Fried, L., M. E. Gettleman, D. T. Levenson, and N. Peckenham. 1983. *Guatemala in rebellion: Unfinished history.* New York: Grove Press.

Friedlander, J. 1975. *Being Indian in Hueyapan.* New York: Prentice-Hall.

Fujita, M., Y. Hayami, and M. Kikuchi. 1999. The conditions of collective action for local commons management: The case of irrigation in the Philippines. Mimeograph. Aoyama-Gakuin Univ., Tokyo.

Fukuyama, F. 1995. *Trust: The social virtues and the creation of prosperity.* London: Hamish Hamilton.

Galasso, E., and M. Ravallion. 2000. Distributional outcomes of a decentralized welfare program. Mimeograph. World Bank, Washington, DC.

Gamella, J. 1994. The spread of intravenous drug use and AIDS in a neighborhood in Spain. *Medical Anthropology* 8:131–60.

Gandhi, N., and N. Shah. 1992. *The issues at stake: Theory and practice in the contemporary women's movement in India.* New Delhi, India: Kali for Women.

Gardner, B. L. 1990. The United States. In *Agricultural protectionism in the industrialized world,* ed. F. H. Sanderson. Washington, DC: Resources for the Future.

Gardner, K., and D. Lewis. 1996. *Anthropology, development and the postmodern challenge.* London: Pluto Press.

Gasper, D. 1996. Culture and development ethics: Needs, women's rights, and Western theories. *Development and Change* 27:627–61.

Gates, H. L. 1996. *China's motor: A thousand years of petty capitalism*. Ithaca, NY: Cornell University Press.

Gates, G. J., and F. L. Sonenstein. 2000. Heterosexual genital sexual activity among adolescent males: 1988 and 1995. *Family Planning Perspectives* 32:295–97, 304.

Geertz, C. 1973a. Ideology as a cultural system. In *The interpretation of cultures*, ed. C. Geertz. New York: Basic Books.

———. 1973b. Thick description: Toward an interpretative theory of culture. In *The interpretation of cultures: Selected essays*, ed. C. Geertz. New York: Basic Books.

———. 1978. The bazaar economy: Information and search in peasant marketing. *American Economic Review* 68:28–32.

———. 1983. Common sense as a cultural system. In *Local knowledge*, ed. C. Geertz. New York: Basic Books.

Germani, G. 1985. Democracia y autoritarismo en la sociedad moderna. In *Los límites de la democracia*, vol. 1. Buenos Aires, Argentina: Consejo Latinoamericano de Ciencias Sociales (CLASCO).

Geschiere, P. 1994. *Sorcellerie et politique en Afrique—La viande des autres*. Paris: Editions Karthala.

Ghosh, A. 1989. The diaspora in Indian culture. *Public Culture* 2:73–78.

Ghurye, G. S. 1961. *Caste, class, and occupation*. 4th ed. Bombay: Popular Book Depot.

Giddens, A. 1995. *Affluence, poverty and the idea of post-scarcity society*. Discussion paper 63. Geneva, Switzerland: UNRISD.

Gillin, J., and K. H. Silvert. 1956. Ambiguities in Guatemala. *Foreign Affairs* 34:469–82.

Gleijeses, P. 1991. *Shattered hope: The Guatemalan revolution and the United States, 1944–1954*. Princeton, NJ: Princeton University Press.

Glenny, M. 1993. *The fall of Yugoslavia: The third Balkan war*. New York: Penguin Books.

Gluck, C. 1985. *Japan's modern myths: Ideology in the late Meiji period*. Princeton, NJ: Princeton University Press.

Gobierno de la República de Guatemala. 2001. *El drama de la pobreza en Guatemala: Sus rasgos y efectos sobre la sociedad*. Guatemala: Gobierno de la República de Guatemala.

Godelier, M. 1974. Anthropologie et économie: Une anthropologie économique est-elle possible? In *Un domaine conteste: L'anthropologie économique*, ed. M. Godelier. Paris: Mouton.

Goldstein, J. 1998. Scissors, surveys, and psycho-prophylactics: Prenatal health care campaigns and state building in China, 1949–1954. *Historical Sociology* 11:153–84.

Gonzalez, N. L., and C. S. McCommon. 1994. *Conflict, migration and the expressions of ethnicity*. Boulder, CO: Westview Press.

Goody, J. 1996. *The east in the west*. Cambridge: Cambridge University Press.

Gooptu, N. 2000. *Sex workers in Calcutta and the dynamics of collective action*. WIDER working papers, No. 185. Helsinki, Finland: The World Institute for Development Economics Research.

Goubaud Carrera, A. 1959. Adaptación del indígena a la cultura nacional moderna.

In *Cultura indígena de Guatemala: Ensayos de antropología social*, ed. J. L. Arrioa. Guatemala: Seminario de Integración Social Guatemalteca.

Government of Bangladesh. 2001. *Report on the second national expanded HIV surveillance, 1999–2000, Bangladesh*. Dhaka, Bangladesh: Governement of Bangladesh/UNAIDS.

Government of Bolivia. 1970. *Evaluación de la reforma agraria en Bolivia*. La Paz: Servicio Nacional de la Reforma Agraria.

———. 2001. *Pactos democráticos en Bolivia*. La Paz.

Government of India. 1974. *Towards equality: Report of the committee on the status of women in India*. New Delhi, India: Department of Social Welfare.

Grampp, W. 1989. *Princing the priceless: Art, artists and economics*. New York: Basic Books.

Grandin, G. 2000. *The blood of Guatemala: A history of race and nation*. Durham, NC: Duke University Press.

Granovetter, M. 1985. Economic action and social structure: The problem of embeddedness. *American Journal of Sociology* 91:481–510.

Gray, J. 2001. How to achieve sustainability: Learning from successes and mistakes. Paper presented at the 12th International Conference on the Reduction of Drug Related Harm, at Delhi, India.

Greif, A. 1994a. Contract enforceability and economic institutions in early trade: The Maghribi traders' coalition. *American Economic Review* 83:525–48.

———. 1994b. Cultural beliefs and the organization of society: A historical and theoretical reflection on collectivist and individualist societies. *Journal of Political Economy* 102:912–50.

Griffin, K. 1996. *Studies in globalization and economic transitions*. London: Macmillan.

Griffin, K., and J. Knight, eds. 1990. *Human development and the international development strategies for the 1990s*. London: Macmillan.

Grob, C., and M. Dobkin de Rios. 1992. Adolescent drug use in cross-cultural perspective. *Journal of Drug Issues* 22:121–38.

Grondona, M. 2000. Comment on Richard Schweder. In *Culture matters: How values shape human progress*, ed. L. E. Harrison and S. P. Huntington. New York: Basic Books.

Grootaert, C. 1998. Social capital: The missing link? working paper No. 3. In *The social capital initiative*. Washington, DC: World Bank.

Gross, J., and S. Rayner. 1985. *Measuring culture: A paradigm for the analysis of social organization*. New York: Columbia University Press.

Grund, J.-P. 1993. *Drug use as a social ritual: Functionality, symbolism and determinants of self-regulation*. Rotterdam: Institut voor Verslavingsonderzoek.

Gu, L. 1997. Women's workers' rights in joint ventures. *Women of China* 4:6–7.

Gudeman, S. 1978. *The demise of a rural economy: From subsistence to capitalism in a Latin American village*. London: Routledge.

———. 1986. *Economics as culture: Models and metaphors of livelihood*. London: Routledge.

———. 2001. *The anthropology of economy: Community, market, and culture*. Malden, MA: Blackwell.

———. 2002. Comment on Sen and Appadurai. Conference on Culture and Public Action, Washington, DC. Available at: http://www.cultureandpublicaction.org.

Gulliver, P. H. 1955. *The family herds: A study of two pastoral tribes in East Africa, the Jie and Turkana*. London: Routledge and Kegan Paul.

Gupta, D. 2000. *Interrogating caste: Understanding hierarchy and difference in Indian society*. New Delhi, India: Penguin Books.

Gutman, M. 1996. *The meanings of macho: Being a man in Mexico City*. Berkeley: University of California Press.

Gyawali, D. 2001. *Water in Nepal*. Kathmandu: Hirnal Books.

Gyekye, K. 1996. *African cultural values—An introduction*. Accra, Ghana: Sankofa Publishing Company.

Hacking, I. 1990. *The taming of chance*. Cambridge: Cambridge University Press.

Haferkamp, H., and N. Smelser, eds. 1992. *Social change and modernity*. Berkeley: University of California Press.

Hagan, H., and D. Des Jarlais. 2000. HIV and HCV infection among injecting drug users. *Mount Sinai Journal of Medicine* 67:423–28.

Haggis, J., and S. Schech. 2000. *Culture, society, and development: A critical introduction*. Malden, MA: Blackwell.

Hall, S. 1992. Cultural studies and the centre: Some problematics and problems. In *Culture, media, language*, ed. S. Hall. London: Hutchinson.

Hampshire, S. 1983. *Morality and conflict*. Cambridge, MA: Harvard University Press.

Han, W. 1971. *The history of Korea*. Trans. K. Lee. Honolulu: University of Hawaii Press.

Handy, J. 1984. *Gift of the devil: A history of Guatemala*. Boston: South End Press.

———. 1994. *Revolution in the countryside: Rural conflict and agrarian reform in Guatemala 1944–1954*. Chapel Hill: University of North Carolina Press.

Hannerz, U. 1992. *Cultural complexity: Studies in the social organization of meaning*. New York: Columbia University Press.

———. 1996. *Transnational connections: Culture, people, places*. London: Routledge.

Harragin, S., and C. Changath. 1999. *Southern Sudan vulnerability study*. Nairobi, Kenya: Save the Children (UK).

Harrington, M. 1962. *The other America*. New York: Macmillan.

Harrison, L. E., and S. P. Huntington, eds. 2000. *Culture matters: How values shape human progress*. New York: Basic Books.

———. 2000. Introduction: Why culture matters. In *Culture matters: How values shape human progress*, ed. L. E. Harrison and S. P. Huntington. New York: Basic Books.

Harriss, J. 2001. *Depoliticizing development: The World Bank and social capital*. New Delhi, India: LeftWord Books.

———. 2002. The case for cross-disciplinary approaches in international development. *World Development* 30:487–96.

Hart, K. 1973. Informal income opportunities and urban employment in Ghana. *Journal of Modern African Studies* 11:61–89.

———. 2000. *Money in an unequal world*. New York: Texere.

Hausman, D., and M. S. McPherson. 1996. *Economic analysis and moral philosophy*. Cambridge: Cambridge University Press.

Heimsath, C. S. 1964. *Indian nationalism and Hindu social reform.* Princeton, NJ: Princeton University Press.

Heller, P. 1999. *The labor of development: Workers and transformation of capitalism in Kerala, India.* Ithaca, New York: Cornell University Press.

Henrich, J., R. Boyd, S. Bowles, H. Gintis, and E. Fehr. 2001. In search of homo economicus: Experiments in 15 small-scale societies. *American Economic Review* 91:73–78.

Henthorn, W. E. 1971. *A history of Korea.* New York: Free Press.

Herbert, D. T., ed. 1995. *Heritage, tourism and society.* London: Mansell.

Hewitt de Alcántara, C. 1979. La modernización: Las oportunidades de vida de las mujeres de familias rurales de bajos ingresos. *Revista de la CEPAL* 197:15–22.

Hinkelamert, F. 1984. *Crítica a la razón utópica.* San José: DEI.

Hirschman, A. O. 1958. *The strategy of economic development.* New Haven, CT: Yale University Press.

———. 1970. *Exit, voice and loyalty: Responses to decline in firms, organizations, and states.* Cambridge, MA: Harvard University Press.

———. 1977. *Passions and the interests: Political arguments for capitalism before its triumph.* Princeton, NJ: Princeton University Press.

———. 1982. *Shifting involvements.* Princeton, NJ: Princeton University Press.

Hoben, A. 1982. Anthropologists and development. *Annual Review of Anthropology* 11:349–75.

Hoddinott, J., M. Adato, T. Besley, and L. Haddad. 2001. Participation and poverty reduction: Issues, theory, and new evidence from South Africa. FCND Discussion Paper No. 98. Washington, DC: International Food Policy Research Institute.

Hoff, K., and P. Pandey. 2003. Why are social inequalities so durable? An experimental test of Indian caste on performance. Mimeograph. Development Research Group, World Bank, Washington, DC.

Hoff, K., and J. Stiglitz. 2000. Modern economic theory and development. In *Frontiers in development economics*, ed. G. M. Meier and J. Stiglitz. Oxford: Oxford University Press.

Honig, E., and G. Hershatter. 1988. *Personal voices: Chinese women in the 1980s.* Stanford: Stanford University Press.

Hood, C. 1998. *The art of the state: Culture, rhetoric and public management.* Oxford: Clarendon Press.

Horowitz, M. 1996. On not offending the borrower: (self?)-ghettoization of anthropology at the World Bank. *Development Anthropologist* 14:1–12.

Hu, H.-C. 1948. *The common descent group in China and its functions.* New York: Viking Fund.

Hua, C. 2001. *A society without fathers or husbands: The Na of China.* New York: Zone Books.

Hull, T., Sulistyaningsih, and G. Jones. 1998. *Prostitution in Indonesia.* Jakarta, India: Pustaka Sinar Harapan.

Human Rights Watch. 1999. *Broken people: Caste violence against India's "untouchables."* New York: Human Rights Watch.

———. 2001. *Scared at school: Sexual violence against girls in South African schools.* New York: Human Rights Watch.

Hume, D. 1777/1966. *An enquiry concerning the principles of morals.* La Salle, IL: Open Court.

Hunter, G. 1969. *Modernizing peasant societies: A comparative study in Asia and Africa.* Oxford: Oxford University Press.

Huntington, S. P. 1993. The clash of civilizations? *Foreign Affairs* 72, no. 3: 22–50

———. 1998. *The clash of civilizations and the remaking of world order.* New York: Simon and Schuster.

———. 2000. Foreword: Cultures count. In *Culture matters: How values shape human progress,* ed. L. E. Harrison and S. P. Huntington. New York: Basic Books.

Hutter, M., and I. Rizzo. 1997. *Economic perspectives on cultural heritage.* London: Macmillan.

Hutton, J. H. 1963. *Caste in India: Its nature, function, and origins.* 4th ed. Bombay: Oxford University Press.

Ikegami, E. 1995. *The taming of the samurai: Honorific individualism and the making of modern Japan.* Cambridge, MA: Harvard University Press.

Indian Council for Social Science Research. 1977. Report of the International Seminar on Rural Women and Development. Mimeograph. International Seminar on Rural Women and Development, India.

Indian Ministry of Labour. 1964. *Women and development.* India: Ministry of Labour.

Inglehart, R. 1990. *Cultural shift in advanced industrial society.* Princeton, NJ: Princeton University Press.

Innocenti Digest. 2000. Violence against women and girls. *Innocenti Digest* 6.

Isaac, T. 1998. Decentralisation, Democracy and Development: People's Campaign for Decentralised Planning in Kerala. Paper presented at the International Conference on Decentralisation, Devolution and Participation, State Planning Board, Government of West Bengal, at Calcutta, India.

Isaac, T., and K. N. Harilal. 1997. Planning for empowerment. *Economic and Political Weekly* 32:53–58.

Jenkins, C. 1996. The homosexual context of heterosexual practice in Papua New Guinea. In *Bisexualities and AIDS: International perspectives,* ed. P. Aggleton. Social Aspects of AIDS Series. London: Taylor and Francis Publications.

———. 1997. Youth, sexuality, and STD/HIV risk in the Pacific: Results of studies in four island nations. Paper presented at the 4th International Congress on AIDS in Asia and the Pacific, Manila.

———. 1998. Varieties of homosexuality in Bangladesh: Implications for HIV prevention. Paper presented at the 12th World AIDS Conference Record.

———. 2000. *Female sex worker HIV prevention projects: Lessons learnt from Papua New Guinea, India and Bangladesh: UNAIDS case study.* Geneva, Switzerland: UNAIDS.

Jenkins, C., S. Jana, T. Saidel, and H. Rahman. 2001. Measuring impact with behavioral surveillance among injecting drug users in Bangladesh. *AIDS Education and Prevention* 13:452–61.

Jenkins, C., and N. Nahar. 1999. Hijras and HIV risk-transgender communities in

Bangladesh. Paper presented at the 5th International Conference on AIDS in the Asia Pacific Region, at Kuala Lampur.

Jessor, R., A. Colby, and R. A. Shweder, eds. 1996. *Ethnography and human development: Context and meaning in social inquiry.* Chicago: University of Chicago Press.

Jok, M. J. 1998. *Militarisation, gender and reproductive health in south sudan.* Lewiston, NY: Edwin Mellen Press.

Jonas, S. 2000. *Of centaurs and doves: Guatemala's peace process.* Boulder, CO: Westview Press.

Kanbur, R. 2002. Economics, social science and development. *World Development* 30:477–86.

———, ed. 2003. *Qualitative and quantitative poverty appraisal: Complementarities, tensions and the way forward.* Delhi: Permanent Black.

Kane, J. L. 2001. How effective is the current drug policy? Paper presented at the Denver Faculty Forum, at Denver, Colorado.

Kansal, S. M. 1974. *Changes in the per capita income and the per capita availability of essential commodities in India since 1931.* New Delhi, India: Economic and Scientific Research Foundation.

Karahasan, D. 2000. *L'age de sable.* Paris: Robert Laffont.

Karasimeonov, G. 1997. *Human security in Bulgaria.* Sofia, Bulgaria: UNDP.

Karim, A., M. Duffield, S. Jaspars, A. Benini, J. Macrae, M. Bradbury, D. Johnson, G. Larbi, and B. Hendrie. 1996. *Operation Lifeline Sudan: A review.* Final Report for the UN Department of Humanitarian Affairs. Birmingham, England: University of Birmingham.

Karve, I. 1953. *Kinship organization in India.* Poona, India: Deccan College Monograph Series.

Kearney, M. 1995. The local and the global: The anthropology of globalization and transnationalism. *Annual Review of Anthropology* 24:547–65.

Keen, D. 1991. A disaster for whom? Local interests and international donors during famine among the Dinka of Sudan. *Disasters* 15:150–64.

———. 1994. The functions of famine in Southwestern Sudan. In *War and hunger: Rethinking international responses to complex emergencies,* ed. J. Macrae and A. Zwi. London: SCF/Zed.

Keen, D., and J. Ryle. 1996. Introduction: The fate of information in the disaster zone. *Disasters* 20.

Kempadoo, K., and J. Doezema, eds. 1998. *Global sex workers.* London: Routledge.

Kennedy, P. 1976. Cultural factors affecting entrepreneurship and development in the informal economy of Ghana. *Institute of Development Studies Bulletin* 8:17–21.

Kertzer, D. I., and T. Fricke. 1997. *Anthropological demography: Towards a new synthesis.* Chicago: University of Chicago Press.

Kim, E. 1991. *A study of the family law and its reform movement.* Seoul, Korea: Korean Women's Development Institute.

Kim, J.-S. 1993. *Korean family law and its task.* Seoul, Korea: Samyoung-sa.

Kim, K.-K. 1990. Schooling and married women's work in a developing country: The case of the Republic of Korea. Mimeograph. Univ. of Chicago.

Kim, Y.-C. 1986. Women's movement in modern Korea. In *Challenges for women*, ed. S.-W. Chung. Seoul, Korea: Ewha Women's University.

Kim, T. I., J. A. Ross, and G. C. Worth. 1972. *Korea national family planning program*. New York: Population Council.

Kim, Y. Y. 2001. *Becoming intercultural: An integrative theory of communication and cross-cultural adaptation*. Thousand Oaks, CA: Sage Publications.

Kippax, S., R. W. Connell, G. W. Dowsett, and J. Crawford. 1993. *Sustaining safe sex: Gay communities respond to AIDS*. London: Falmer Press.

Kirkpatrick, C. H., and J. Weiss, eds. 1996. *Cost benefit analysis and project appraisal in developing countries*. Cheltenham, England: Edward Elgar.

Klamer, A. 1997. The value of cultural heritage. In *Economic perspectives on cultural heritage*, ed. M. Hutter and I. Rizzo. London: Macmillan.

———. 2004. Cultural goods are good for more than their economic value. In *Culture and public action: A cross-disciplinary dialogue on development policy*, ed. V. Rao and M. Walton. Stanford: Stanford University Press.

———, ed. 1996. *The value of culture: On the relationship between economics and arts*. Amsterdam: Amsterdam University Press.

Klamer, A., and D. Throsby. 2000. Paying for the past: The economics of cultural heritage. In *World culture report, 2000*, ed. UNESCO Publishing. Paris: UNESCO Publishing.

Klamer, A., and P. W. Zuidhof. 1999. The values of cultural heritage: Merging economic and cultural appraisal. In *Economics and heritage conversation*, ed. P. W. Zuidhof. Los Angeles: Getty Conservation Institute.

Klitgaard, R. 1994. Taking culture into account, from let's to how. In *Culture and development in Africa*, ESD Proceedings Series No. 1, ed. I. Serageldin and J. Tabaroff. Washington, DC: World Bank.

———. 1997. Unanticipated consequences in anti-poverty programs. *World Development* 25:1963–72.

Kluckholn, C., and A. L. Kroeber. 1963. *Culture: A critical review of concepts and definitions* (originally published in 1952 as vol. 47, no. 1 of the *Papers of the Peabody Museum of American Archeology and Ethnology, Harvard University*). New York: Vintage Books.

Kolenda, P. 1987. *Regional differences in family structure in India*. Jaipur, India: Rawat Publications.

Koo, H. 1987. The interplay of state, social class, and world system in East Asian development: The cases of South Korea and Taiwan. In *The political economy of the new Asian industrialism*, ed. F. C. Deyo. Ithaca, New York: Cornell University Press.

Kopytoff, I. 1986. The cultural biography of things: Commodization as process. In *The social life of things: Commodities in cultural perspective*, ed. A. Appadurai. Cambridge: Cambridge University Press.

Korean Women's Development Institute. 1999. *Statistical yearbook on women*. Seoul, Korea: Korean Women's Development Institute.

Kreft, I. G. G., and J. H. Brown. 1998. Zero effects of drug prevention programs: Issues and solutions. *Evaluation Review* 22:3–14.

Kreps, D. M. 1990. Corporate culture and economic theory. In *Perspectives on pos-*

itive political economy, ed. J. E. Alt and K. A. Shepsle. Cambridge: Cambridge University Press.

Kroeber, A. L., and C. Kluckholn. 1952. *Culture: A critical review of concepts and definitions.* Cambridge, MA: Peabody Museum of American Archaeology and Ethnology, Harvard University.

Kulick, D. 1998. *Travesti, sex, gender and culture among Brazilian transgendered prostitutes.* Chicago: University of Chicago Press.

Kumar, R. 1993. *The history of doing: An illustrated account of movements for women's rights and feminism in India, 1800–1990.* New Delhi, India: Kali for Women.

Kumon, S., and H. Rosovsky. 1992. *The political economy of Japan,* vol. 3, *Cultural and social dynamics.* Stanford: Stanford University Press.

Kuper, A. 1999. *Culture: The anthropologists' account.* Cambridge, MA: Harvard University Press.

Kuran, T. 1995a. Islamic economics and the Islamic subeconomy. *Journal of Economic Perspectives* 9:155–73.

———. 1995b. *Private truths, public lies: The social consequences of preference falsification.* Cambridge, MA: Harvard University Press.

———. 1997. Islamism and economics: Policy implications for a free society. *International Review of Comparative Public Policy* 9:71–102.

———. 1998a. Ethnic norms and their transformation through reputational cascades. *Journal of Legal Studies* 27:623–59.

———. 1998b. The genesis of Islamic economics: A chapter in the politics of Muslim identity. *Social Research* 64:301–38.

———. 2004. Cultural obstacles to economic development: Often overstated, usually transitory. In *Culture and public action: A cross-disciplinary dialogue on development policy,* ed. V. Rao and M. Walton. Stanford: Stanford University Press.

Kymlicka, W. 1995. *Multicultural citizenship.* Oxford: Oxford University Press.

LaFarge, O. 1947. *Santa Eulalia: The religion of a Cuchumatan Indian town.* Chicago: University of Chicago Press.

Lal, D. 1988. *The Hindu equilibrium,* vol. 1, *Cultural stability and economic stagnation, India c. 1500 BC–AD 1980.* Oxford: Clarendon Press.

———. 1998. *Unintended consequences: The impact of factor endowments, culture and politics on long-run economic performance.* Cambridge, MA: MIT Press.

Landes, D. S. 1998. *The wealth and poverty of nations: Why some are so rich and some are so poor.* New York: Norton.

———. 2000a. Culture makes almost all the difference. In *Culture matters: How values shape human progress,* ed. L. E. Harrison and S. P. Huntington. New York: Basic Books.

———. 2000b. The role of culture in sustainable development. In *Culture counts: Financing, resources and the economics of culture in sustainable development: Proceedings of the conference, Florence, Italy,* ed. J. D. Wolfensohn, L. Dini, G. Bonetti, I. Johnson and J. Martin-Brown. Washington, DC: The World Bank.

Lane, R. E. 1991. *The market experience.* Cambridge: Cambridge University Press.

Laumann, E., J. Gagnon, R. B. Michael, and S. Michaels. 1994. *The social organization of sexuality: Sexual practices in the United States.* Chicago: University of Chicago Press.

Lawson, A. L.-G. 1999. Women and AIDS in Africa: Sociocultural Dimensions of the HIV/AIDS Epidemic. *International Social Science Journal* 161:391–400.

LeBaron, A. 1993. The creation of the modern Maya. In *The rising tide of cultural pluralism: The nation state at bay*, ed. C. Young. Madison: University of Wisconsin Press.

Lechner, N. 1996. *Tres formas de coordinación social: Un esquema*. Santiago de Chile.

Lee, K. 1984. *A new history of Korea*. Trans. E. W. Wagner and E. J. Shultz. Seoul, Korea: Ilchokak.

Lee, K.-S. 1989. Women's images in mass media. *Monthly Women* June:10–15.

Lee, M.-G. 1982. *Sociology and social change in Korea*. Seoul, Korea: Seoul National University Press.

Lee, O.-J. 1980. *Urban-to-rural return migration in Korea*. Seoul, Korea: Seoul National University Press.

Lee, S. 1997. Elite education for career or marriage: The case of female university graduates in South Korea. Mimeograph. Univ. of Chicago.

Leridon, H., G. vanZessen, and M. Hubert. 1998. The Europeans and their sexual partners. In *Sexual behaviour and HIV/AIDS in Europe*, ed. M. Hubert, N. Bajos and T. Sandfort. London: UCL Press.

Levine, N. 1988. *The dynamics of polyandry: Kinship, domesticity and population on the Tibetan border*. Chicago: University of Chicago Press.

LeVine, R. A. 1980. Influences of women's schooling on maternal behavior in the third world. *Comparative Education Review* 24:S78–S105.

Lewis, B. 1968. *The emergence of modern Turkey*. 2nd ed. London: Oxford University Press.

Lewis, O. 1959. *Five families: Mexican case studies in the culture of poverty*. New York: Basic Books.

———. 1964. *Anthropological essays*. New York: Random House.

———. 1968. The culture of poverty. In *On understanding poverty*, ed. D. P. Moynihan. New York: Basic Books.

Lewis, W. A. 1955. *The theory of economic growth*. Homewood II, R. D. Irwin.

Li, X., and X. Zhang. 1994. Creating a space for women: Women's studies in China. *Signs* 20:137–51.

Lim, L. L., ed. 1998. *The sex sector: The economic and social bases of prostitution in Southeast Asia*. Geneva, Switzerland: International Labour Office.

Lomnitz, C. 1998. *Modernidad Indiana*. Mexico: FCE.

London Times. 1988. There is no famine in Sudan yet. *London Times*, April 30.

Loury, G. 1999. Social exclusion and ethnic groups: The challenge to economics. Mimeograph. Boston Univ.

———. 2002a. *The anatomy of racial inequality*. Cambridge, MA: Harvard University Press.

———. 2002b. Commentary on managing difference. Paper presented at the Conference on Culture and Public Action, at Washington, DC.

Lowenthal, D. 1985. *The past is a foreign country*. Cambridge: Cambridge University Press.

Lu, M., and Y. Zhen. 1990. *Chinese women's movement 1840–1921*. Henan, China: The People's Publishing House in Henan.

Lu, Y. 1988. New challenges to women's employment. *Beijing Review* 31:18–21.

Luis Ribeiro, G. 2000. *Cultura e política no mundo contemporaneo.* Brasilia: Universidad Nacional de Brasilia.

Lurie, P., R. Gorsky, S. T. Jones, and L. Shomphe. 1998. An economic analysis of needle exchange and pharmacy-based programs to increase sterile syringe availability for injection drug users. *Journal of Acquired Immune Deficiencies and Human Retrovirology* 18 (Supplement 1):S126–S132.

MacAskill, J. 1994. *An analysis of the present situation in Waat/Jonglei and Akon/Bahr-el-Ghazal.* Unpublished discussion document. Nairobi, Kenya: Save the Children Fund.

Macrae, J. 1998. Purity or political engagement: Issues of food and health security interventions. *Journal of Humanitarian Assistance.* Available at: http://www.jha.ac/articles/a037.htm.

Macrae, J., and A. Zwi. 1992. Contemporary African famines: A review of the evidence. *Disasters* 16:299–321.

Malcolm, N. 1994. *Bosnia: A short history.* New York: New York University Press.

Mane, P., and M. Shubhada. 1992. *AIDS prevention: The socio cultural context in India.* Bombay, India: Tata Institute of Social Sciences.

Mansbridge, J. 1990. *Beyond self-interest.* Chicago: University of Chicago Press.

Mansuri, G., and V. Rao. 2004. Community based (and driven) development: A critical review. *World Bank Research Observer.* Forthcoming.

Manzo, K. 1991. Modernist discourse and the crisis of development theory. *Studies in Comparative Development* 26:3–36.

Marglin, F. A., and S. A. Marglin. 1990. *Dominating knowledge: Development, culture and resistance.* Oxford: Clarendon Press.

Margolis, H. 1982. *Selfishness, altruism, and rationality.* Cambridge: Cambridge University Press.

Mari Bhat, P. N. 1998. Contours of fertility decline in India: An analysis of district-level trends from two recent censuses. In *Reproductive change in India and Brazil,* ed. G. Martine, M. Das Gupta and L. Chen. Oxford: Oxford University Press.

Marshall, A. 1891. *Principles of economics.* London: Macmillan.

Marshall, J. 1991. *Drug wars: Corruption, counterinsurgency and covert operations in the third world.* Berkeley: Cohen and Cohen.

Mata, A. G., and J. S. Jorquez. 1988. Mexican-American intravenous drug users' needle sharing practice: Implications for AIDS prevention. In *Needle sharing among intravenous drug abusers: National and international perspectives,* ed. R. J. Battjes and R. W. Pickens. Rockville, MD: NIDA.

Matos Mar, J. 1968. *Perú problema.* Lima: Instituto de Estudios Peruanos.

Mauss, M. 1997. Essai sur le don, forme et raison de l'échange dans les sociétés archaiques. In *Sociologie et anthropologie,* ed. M. Mauss. Paris: Presse Universitaire de France.

Max-Neef, M. 1993. *Human scale development: Conception, application, and further reflections.* London: Apex Press.

Mbembe, A. 2001. *On the postcolony: Studies on the history of society and culture.* Berkeley: University of California Press.

McCamish, M. 1999. The friends thou hast: Support systems for male commercial sex workers in Pattaya, Thailand. In *Lady boys, tom boys, rent boys: Male and female homosexualities in contemporary Thailand*, ed. P. Jackson and G. Sullivan. New York: Harrington Park Press.

McCloskey, D., N. Donald, and A. Klamer. 1995. One quarter of GDP is persuasion. *American Economic Review* 85, no. 2:191–95.

McCreery, D. 1994. *Rural Guatemala, 1760–1940*. Stanford: Stanford University Press.

McGinn, N., F. Noel, D. R. Sondgrass, Y. B. Kim, S. Kim, and Q. Kim. 1980. *Education and development in Korea*. Cambridge, MA: Council on East Asian Studies, Harvard University Press.

Medina, José. 1980. *Sociología latinoamericana: Consideraciones sociológicas sobre el desarrollo económico de America Latina*. 2nd ed. Buenos Aires: EDUCA.

Meekers, D., and A. E. Calves. 1997. "Main" girlfriends, girlfriends, marriage and money: The social context of HIV risk behavior in Sub-Saharan Africa. *Health Transition Review* 7:361–75.

Melard, C., J.-P. Platteau, and H. Watongoka. 1998. *Étude des incidences socioéconomiques de l'introduction de la technique de pêche au Filet Maillant au Lac Kivu*. Namur, Belgium: Fondation Universitaire pour la Cooperation International au Développement (FUCID), University of Namur.

Meltzer Commission (International Financial Institution Advisory Commission). 2000. International Financial Institutions Reform. Washington, DC: United States Congress.

Meyer, C. A. 1995. Opportunism and NGOs. Entrepreneurship and green north-south transfers. *World Development* 23:1277–89.

Meyer, B. 1999. Commodities and the power of prayer: Pentecostalist attitudes towards consumption in contemporary Ghana. In *Globalization and identity: Dialectics of flow and closure*, ed. B. Meyer and P. Geschiere. Oxford, England: Blackwell.

Meynaud, J. 1963. *Social change and economic development*. Paris: UNESCO Publishing.

Michael, R. B. 1992. *The origins of Virasaiva sects*. New Delhi, India: Motilal Banarsidass Publishers.

Migdal, J. S. 2001. *State in society: Studying how states and societies tranform and constitute one another*. Cambridge: Cambridge University Press.

Mill, J. S. 1859/1974. *On liberty*. Harmondsworth: Penguin.

———. 1861/1962. *Utilitarianism*. London: Collins/Fontana.

Miller, D., and M. Walzer, eds. 1995. *Pluralismo, justicia e igualdad*. Mexico City: FCE.

Ministerio de Cultura y Deportes. 2000a. *Informe final: Congreso nacional sobre lineamientos de políticas culturales*. Guatemala: Ministerio de Cultura y Deportes.

———. 2000b. *Políticas culturales y deportes nacionales*. Guatemala: Ministerio de Cultura y Deportes.

Ministry of Culture and Sports, and SEGEPLAN. 2001. *Seminario taller: Cultura y pobreza—Informe final*. Guatemala: SEGEPLAN.

Mogensen, H. O. 1997. The narrative of AIDS among the Tonga of Zambia. *Social Science and Medicine* 44:431–39.

Mokyr, J. 1983. *Why Ireland starved: A quantitative and analytical history of the Irish economy, 1800–1850.* London: Allen and Unwin.

Montaner, C. A. 2000. Comment on Richard Schweder. In *Culture matters: How values shape human progress,* ed. L. E. Harrison and S. P. Huntington. New York: Basic Books.

Morales, M. R. 1999. Esencialismo "Maya," mestizaje ladino y nación intercultural: Los discursos en debate. In *Racismo en Guatemala? Abriendo el debate sobre un tema tabú,* ed. C. A. Bianchi, C. R. Hale, and G. P. Murga. Guatemala: AVANCSO.

Morishima, M. 1982. *Why has Japan "succeeded"? Western technology and Japanese ethos.* Cambridge: Cambridge University Press.

Mosk, S. A. 1955. The coffee economy of Guatemala, 1850–1918. Development and signs of instability. *Inter-American Economic Affairs* 9:6–20.

Mosse, D. 2001. People knowledge, participation and patronage: Operations and representations in rural development. In *Participation: The new tyranny?,* ed. B. Cooke and U. Kothari. London: Zed Books.

———. 2003. Good policy is unimplementable? Reflections on the ethnography of aid policy and practice. Mimeograph. School of Oriental and African Studies, London.

Mosseto, G. 1993. *Aesthetics and economics.* Dordrecht: Kluwer.

Mourato, S., and M. Mazzanti. 2002. Economic valuation of cultural heritage: Evidence and prospects. In *Assessing the values of cultural heritage,* ed. M. de la Torre. Los Angeles: Getty Conservation Institute.

Mundimbe, V. Y. 1988. *The invention of Africa.* Bloomington: Indiana University Press.

Munshi, K., and M. Rosenzweig. 2003. *Traditional institutions meet the modern world: Caste, gender and schooling choice in a globalizing economy.* Working paper 03-23. Boston: Department of Economics, MIT.

Nair, J. 1996. *Women and law in colonial India: A social history.* New Delhi, India: Kali for Women.

Nakane, C. 1967. *Kinship and economic organization in rural Japan.* London: Athlone Press.

Narayan, D., R. Chambers, M. K. Shah, and P. Petesch. 2001a. *Voices of the poor: Crying out for change.* New York: Published for the World Bank by Oxford University Press.

Narayan, D., and K. Ebbe. 1997. *The design of social funds—Participation, demand orientation, and local organizational capacity.* World Bank Discussion Paper No. 375. Washington, DC: World Bank.

Narayan, D., R. Patel, K. Schafft, A. Rademacher, and S. Koch-Schulte. 2001b. *Voices of the poor: Can anyone hear us?* New York: Published for the World Bank by Oxford University Press.

Nash, J. 2001. *Mayan visions.* London: Routledge.

National Commission on Self-Employed Women and Women in the Informal Sector. 1988. *National commission on self-employed women and women in the informal sector.* New Delhi, India: Shramshakti.

National Institutes of Health (NIH). 1997. NIH Consensus Statement: Interventions to Prevent HIV Risk Behaviors. *NIH Record* 15.

National Sex and Reproduction Research Team, and C. Jenkins. 1994. *National study of sexual and reproductive knowledge and behaviour in Papua New Guinea.* Papua New Guinea Institute of Medical Research Monograph No. 10. Goroka, Papua New Guinea: Papua New Guinea Institute of Medical Research.

National Statistical Office. 1997. *Social indicators in Korea.* Seoul, Korea: National Statistical Office.

Noelle-Neumann, E. 1984. *The spiral of silence: Public opinion—Our social skin.* Chicago: University of Chicago Press.

Nongbri, T. 1993. Gender and the Khasi family structure. In *Family, kinship and marriage in India,* ed. P. Uberoi. New Delhi, India: Oxford University Press.

North, D. C. 1981. *Structure and change in economic history.* New York: Norton.

———. 1990. *Institutions, institutional change and economic performance.* Cambridge: Cambridge University Press.

———. 1993. Institutions and credible commitment. *Journal of Institutional and Theoretical Economics* 149:11–23.

Norton, A., and T. Stephens. 1995. *Participation in poverty assessments.* Environment Department Papers Participation Series No. 20. Washington, DC: World Bank.

Nouwen, H. 1971. *Creative ministry: Beyond professionalism in teaching, preaching, counselling, organizing, and celebrating.* New York: Doubleday.

Nussbaum, M. 1993. Non-relative virtues: An Aristotelian approach. In *The quality of life,* ed. M. Nussbaum and A. K. Sen. Oxford: Clarendon Press.

———. 1998. Public philosophy and international feminism. *Ethics* 108:762–96.

———. 2000. *Women and human development: The capabilities approach.* Cambridge: Cambridge University Press.

Nussbaum, M., and J. Glover, eds. 1995. *Women, culture and development.* Oxford: Clarendon Press.

Nussbaum, M., and A. K. Sen, eds. 1993. *The quality of life.* Oxford: Clarendon Press.

O Grada, C. 1989. *The great Irish famine.* London: Macmillan.

Obermeyer, C. M., S. Greenhaigh, T. Fricke, V. Rao, D. I. Kertzer, and J. Knodel. 1997. Qualitative methods in population studies: A symposium. *Population and Development Review* 23:813–53.

Odets, W. 1994. AIDS education and harm reduction for gay men: Psychological approaches for the 21st century. *AIDS and Public Policy Journal* 9:1–15.

Odzer, C. 1994. *Patpong sisters.* New York: Arcade.

Ortiz, S. 1967. The structure of decision-making among Indians of Colombia. In *Themes in economic anthropology,* ed. R. Firth. London: Tavistock Publications.

Ortner, S. 1995. Domination and the arts of resistance: Hidden transcripts. *Comparative Studies in Society and History* 37:173–93.

Osmani, S. R. 2001. On Inequality. In *The Blackwell companion to economic markets,* ed. J. R. Blau. New York: Plenum Press.

Ostrander, D. 1982. One and two dimensional models of the distribution of beliefs. In *Essays in the sociology of perception,* ed. M. Douglas. London: Routledge.

Ostrom, E. 1990. *Governing the commons: The evolution of institutions for collective action.* Cambridge: Cambridge University Press.

———. 1998. *The comparative study of public economies.* Memphis: P. K. Seidman Foundation.

Pakistan Integrated Household Survey. 1990. *Supervisor manual—Field operations, December.* Islamabad: Federal Bureau of Statistics.

Palley, M. L. 1994. Feminism in a Confucian society: The women's movement in Korea. In *Women of Japan and Korea,* ed. J. Gelb and M. L. Palley. Philadelphia: Temple University Press.

Paraschar, A. 1992. *Women and family law reform in India: Uniform civil code and gender equality.* New Delhi, India: Sage Publications.

Paredes Moreira, J. L. 1963. *Reforma agraria: Una experiencia en Guatemala.* Guatemala: Imprenta Universitaria.

Parish, W. L., and M. K. Whyte. 1980. *Village and family in contemporary China.* Chicago: University of Chicago Press.

Park, M.-H. 1991. Patterns and trends of educational mating in Korea. *Korea Journal of Population and Development* 20:1–15.

Parker, R. 1991. *Bodies, pleasures, and passions: Sexual culture in contemporary Brazil.* Boston: Beacon Press.

Passin, H. 1965. *Society and education in Japan.* New York: Teachers College Press, Columbia University.

Pattanaik, P. 1998. Cultural indicators of well-being: Some conceptual issues. In *World culture report: Culture, creativity and markets,* ed. U. Publishing. Paris: UNESCO Publishing.

Peacock, A., and I. Rizzo, eds. 1994. *Cultural economics and cultural policies.* Dordrecht: Kluwer.

Peacock, A., and R. Weir. 1975. *The composer in the market place: An economic history.* London: Faber.

Pendse, S. 1995. Toil, sweat and the city. In *Bombay: Metaphor for modern India,* ed. S. Patel and A. Thorner. Oxford: Oxford University Press.

Peng, X. 1989. *Demographic transition in China: Fertility trends in China since the 1950s.* Oxford: Oxford University Press.

Peters, P. E. 1994. *Dividing the commons—Politics, policy, and culture in Botswana.* Charlottesville: University Press of Virginia.

Piketty, T. 1995. Social mobility and redistributive politcs. *Quarterly Journal of Economics* 110:551–84.

Pinker, S. 1997. *How the mind works.* New York: Norton.

Pires, V. 1999. *Orçamento participativo: O que e, para que serve, como se faz.* Piracicaba, Brazil: Ed. Do Autor.

Planning Commission—Government of India. 1992. *Eighth five year plan, 1992–97.* New Delhi, India: Planning Commission, Government of India.

Plant, R. 1978. *Guatemala: Unnatural disaster.* London: Latin America Bureau.

Platteau, J.-P. 1991. Traditional systems of social security and hunger insurance: Last achievements and modern challenges. In *Social security in developing countries,* ed. E. Ahmad, J. Drèze, J. Hills, and A. K. Sen. Oxford: Clarendon Press.

———. 2000. *Institutions, social norms and economic development.* Amsterdam: Harwood Academic Publishers.

Platteau, J.-P., and A. Abraham. 2002. *The risk of resource misappropriation in community-based development projects.* Research paper, CRED (Center for Research in the Economics of Development). Namur, Belgium: Department of Economics, Namur, Belgium.

Platteau, J.-P., and Y. Hayami. 1998. Resource endowments and agricultural development: Africa versus Asia. In *The institutional foundations of East Asian economic development*, ed. M. Aoki and Y. Hayami. London: Macmillan.

Platteau, J.-P., and E. Seki. 2001. Coordination and pooling arrangements in Japanese coastal fisheries. In *Community and market in economic development*, ed. M. Aoki and Y. Hayami. Oxford: Clarendon Press.

Pohl, G., and D. Mihaljeck. 1992. Project evaluation and uncertainty in practice: A statistical analysis of rate-of-return divergences of 1,015 World Bank projects. *World Bank Economic Review* 6:255–77.

Polanyi, K. 1944/1965. *The great transformation*. Boston: Beacon Press.

Polanyi, K., and H. W. Pearson. 1977. *The livelihood of man*. New York: Academic Press.

Population Services International. 2000. Position statement on sustainability. Available at: http://www.psi.org.

Portes, A. 1998. Social capital: Its origins, and applications in modern society. *Annual Review of Sociology* 24:1–24.

Powis, B., J. Strang, P. Griffiths, C. Taylor, S. Williamson, J. Fountain, and M. Gossop. 1999. Self-reported overdose among injecting drug users in London: Extent and nature of the problem. *Addiction* 94:471–78.

PRC State Statistical Bureau. 1985. *Statistical yearbook of China, 1985*. Oxford: Oxford University Press.

Presidencia de la Republica Comisión de la Paz. 1996. *Acuerdo sobre identidad y derechos de los pueblos indígenas*. Guatemala: Presidencia de la República Comisión de la Paz.

Price, D. 1989. *Before the bulldozer: The Nambiquara Indians and the World Bank*. Washington, DC: Seven Locks Press.

Prieur, A. 1998. *Mema's house: On machos, queens, and transvestites*. Chicago: University of Chicago Press.

Pronagob/UNDP Bolivia/ILDIS. 1996. *La seguridad humana en Bolivia*. La Paz, Bolivia: Edobol.

Przeworski, A. 1998. Culture and democracy. *World Culture Report* 1:125–46.

———. 2001. Deliberación y dominación ideológica. In *La democracia deliberativa*, ed. J. Elster. Barcelona, Spain: Gedisa.

Putnam, R. D. 1993. The prosperous community: Social capital and public life. *American Prospect* 4, no. 13:1.

Putnam, R. D., R. Leonardi, and R. Y. Nanetti. 1993. *Making democracy work: Civic traditions in modern Italy*. Princeton, NJ: Princeton University Press.

Qizilbash, M. 1996a. Capabilities, well-being and human development: A survey. *Journal of Development Studies* 33:143–62.

———. 1996b. Ethical development. *World Development* 24:1209–21.

Radin, M. J. 2001. *Contested commodities*. Cambridge, MA: Harvard University Press.

Rahman, F. 1964. Ribā and interest. *Islamic Studies* 3:1–43.

Rahnema, M., and V. Bawtree. 2001. *The post-development reader.* London: Zed Books.

Rangasami, A. 1985. The failure of exchange-entitlements theory of famine: A response. *Economic and Political Weekly* 20:1797–1800.

Rao, V. 1997. Wife-beating in rural south India: A qualitative and econometric analysis. *Social Science and Medicine* 44:1169–80.

———. 2001a. Celebrations as social investments: Festival expenditures, unit price variation and social status. *Journal of Development Studies* 38:71–97.

———. 2001b. Poverty and public celebrations in rural India. *The Annals of the American Academy of Political and Social Science* 573:85–104.

———. 2002. Experiments in "participatory econometrics": Improving the connection between economic analysis and the real world. *Economic and Political Weekly* 22, no. 20:1887–1991.

Rao, V., I. Gupta, M. Lokshin, and S. Jana. 2003. Sex workers and the cost of safe sex: The compensating differential for condom use in Calcutta. *Journal of Development Economics* 71:585–603.

Rao, V., and A. M. Ibáñez. 2001. The social impact of social funds in Jamaica: A mixed-methods analysis of participation, targeting and collective action in community driven development. Mimeograph. World Bank, Washington, DC.

Rao, V., and M. Walton, eds. 2004. *Culture and public action: A cross-disciplinary dialogue on development policy.* Stanford: Stanford University Press.

Rao, V., and M. Woolcock. 2003. Integrating qualitative and quantitative approaches in program evaluation. In *Tool kit for evaluating the poverty and distributional impact of economic policies,* ed. F. Bourguignon and L. Pereira Da Silva. Washington, DC: World Bank and Oxford University Press.

Ray, D. 1998. *Development economics.* Princeton, NJ: Princeton University Press.

———. 2003. Aspirations, poverty and economic change. Mimeograph. Department of Economics, New York Univ.

Rayner, S. 1988. The rules that keep us equal: Complexity and costs of egalitarian organization. In *Rules, decisions and inequality in egalitarian societies,* ed. J. Flanagan and S. Rayner. Avebury: Gower Publishing Company.

Redfield, R. 1941. *The folk culture of Yucatan.* Chicago: University of Chicago Press.

———. 1950. *Chan Kom: A village that chose progress.* Chicago: University of Chicago Press.

Regional Unit for Technical Assistance (RUTA), World Bank, and Guatemalan Ministry of Culture and Sports. 2001. *Perfil de los pueblos maya.* Guatemala: Garifuna y Xinka de Guatemala.

Reuters. 2000. Swedes getting ever more liberal in matters of sex. *CDC HIV/STD/TB prevention news update,* April 5, 2000.

Ribeiro, D. 1970. *Os indios e a civilização: A integração das populações indígenas no Brasil moderno.* Rio de Janeiro: UFRJ.

Rich, F. 2001. Naked capitalists: There's no business like porn business. *New York Times,* May 20, 2001.

Richards, J. B., and M. Richards. 1996. Mayan education: An historical and contemporary analysis of Mayan language education policy. In *Mayan cultural ac-*

tivism in Guatemala, ed. E. Fischer and R. M. Brown. Austin: University of Texas Press.

Richards, P. 1996. *Fighting for the rain forest: Youth, resources and war in Sierra Leone*. Oxford, England: James Curry.

Rist, G., ed. 1994. *La culture, hôtage du développement?* Paris: Éditions l'Harmattan.

Rivers, K., and P. Aggleton. 1999. *Adolescent sexuality, gender and the HIV epidemic*. New York: HIV and Development Programme (UNDP).

Roach, J., and J. Roach, eds. 1972. *Poverty: Selected readings*. London: Penguin Press.

Roberts, A. 1994. *Eminent Churchillians*. London: Weidenfeld and Nicolson.

Rodrik, D. 1999. The Asian financial crisis and the virtues of democracy. *Challenge* 42:44–57.

Roemer, J. E. 1998. *Equality of opportunity*. Cambridge, MA: Harvard University Press.

Rofel, L. 1994. Longing: Women and popular culture. In *Gender and China*, ed. X. Li and Z. Hong. Beijing: Sanlian Books.

Rojas Lima, F. 1995. *El derecho consuetudinario en el contexto de la etnicidad guatemalteca*. Guatemala: Procuraduría de los Derechos Humanos.

Ross, M. W. 1989. Gay youth in four cultures: A comparative study. *Journal of Homosexuality* 17:299–314.

Rostow, W. W. 1960. *The stages of economic growth: A non-communist manifesto*. Cambridge: Cambridge University Press.

Rowntree, S. 1901. *Poverty, a study of town life*. London: Macmillan.

Royal Anthropological Institute. 1995. *Report on RAI/ESRC Explanatory Workshop International NGOs and complex political emergencies: Perspectives from anthropology*. London: RAI.

Rwenge, M. 2000. Sexual risk behaviors among young people in Bamenda, Cameroon. *International Family Planning Perspectives* 26:118–23, 130.

Saengtienchai, C., J. Knodel, M. Van Landingha, and A. Pramualratana. 1999. "Prostitutes are better than lovers": Wives' views on the extramarital sexual behavior of Thai men. In *Genders and sexualities in modern Thailand*, ed. P. Jackson and N. Cook. Bangkok, Thailand: Silkworm Books.

Safa, H., and E. Leacock. 1981. Development and the sexual division of labour. *Signs* 7.

Saffioti, H. 1978. *Emprego doméstico e capitalismo*. Petropolis: Vozes.

Sahlins, M. 1972. *Stone Age economics*. Chicago: Aldine-Atherton.

Said, E. W. 1979. *Orientalism*. New York: Vintage Books.

———. 1994. *Culture and imperialism*. New York: Knopf.

Saleem-Murdock, M. 1990. *Anthropology and development in North Africa and the Middle East*. IDA Monographs in Development Anthropology. Boulder, CO: Westview Press.

Salmen, L. 1995. *Beneficiary assessment: An approach described*. Environment Department Papers Social Assessment Series, No. 23. Washington, DC: World Bank.

———. 1999. *Towards a listening bank: A review of best practices and the efficacy of beneficiary assessment*. Draft, Social Policy and Resettlement Division, Environment Department. Washington, DC: World Bank.

Sangari, K., and S.Vaid. 1989. *Recasting women: Essays in colonial history.* New Delhi, India: Kali for Women.

Saqb'ichil COPMAGUA. 2000. *Acciones políticas y organizativas.* Guatemala: Saqb'ichil COPMAGUA.

Saradamoni, K. 1996. Women's rights and the decline of matriliny in southern India. In *Shifting circles of support: Contextualising gender and kinship in South Asia and Sub-Saharan Africa,* ed. R. Palriwala and C. Risseuw. New Delhi, India: Sage Publications.

Sarkar, L. 1999. Reform of Hindu marriage and succession laws: Still the unequal sex. In *From independence towards freedom: Indian women since 1949,* ed. B. Ray and A. Basu. Delhi, India: Oxford University Press.

Sassen, S. 1998. *Globalization and its discontents.* New York: New Press.

———. 1999. *Guests and aliens.* New York: New Press.

Savane, A. 1981. L'emploie des femmes dans une perspective de changements sociaux et de liberation des femmes: Le cas d'Afrique: IFDA.

Scheper-Hughes, N. 1992. *Death without weeping: The violence of everyday life in Brazil.* Berkeley: University of California Press.

Schultz, T. P. 1993. Returns to women's education. In *Women's education in developing countries,* ed. E. M. King and M. A. Hill. Baltimore, MD: Johns Hopkins University Press.

Schurmann,'F. 1968. *Ideology and organization in communist China.* Berkeley: University of California Press.

Schwarz, M., and M. Thompson. 1990. *Divided we stand: Redefining politics, technology and social choice.* Hemel Hempstead: Harvester Wheatsheaf.

Schweder, R. A. 2000. Moral maps, "first world" conceits, and the new evangelists. In *Culture matters: How values shape human progress,* ed. L. E. Harrison and S. P. Huntington. New York: Basic Books.

Scott, J. C. 1985. *Weapons of the weak: Everyday forms of peasant resistance.* New Haven, CT: Yale University Press.

———. 1990. *Domination and the arts of resistance: Hidden transcripts.* New Haven, CT: Yale University Press.

———. 1998. *Seeing like a state: How certain schemes to improve the human condition have failed.* New Haven, CT: Yale University Press.

Seaman, J. 1994. Relief, rehabilitation and development: Are the distinctions useful? *IDS Bulletin* 25:33–36.

SEGEPLAN. 2001a. *El drama de la pobreza en Guatemala: Un informe sobre los rasgos de esta privación y sus efectos sobre la sociedad.* Guatemala: SEGEPLAN.

———. 2001b. *Estrategia de reducción de la pobreza: Un camino para la paz (propuesta para discusión).* Guatemala: SEGEPLAN.

———. 2001c. *Mapas de pobreza de Guatemala: Instrumentos para entender el flagelo de la pobreza en el país.* Guatemala: SEGEPLAN.

Seligman, C. G., and B. Z. Seligman. 1932. *Pagan tribes of the Nilotic Sudan.* London: Routledge.

Sen, A. K. 1970. *Collective choice and social welfare.* Edinburgh: Oliver and Boyd.

———. 1973. Behavior and the concept of preference. *Economica* 40:241–59.

———. 1981. *Poverty and famine: An essay on entitlement and deprivation.* Oxford: Clarendon Press.

———. 1982. *Choice, welfare and measurement.* Oxford, England: Blackwell.

———. 1984. *Resources, values and development.* Oxford, England: Blackwell.

———. 1985a. *Commodities and capabilities.* Amsterdam: Elsevier.

———. 1985b. Well-being, agency and freedom. The Dewey Lectures 1984. *Journal of Philosophy* 82:169–221.

———. 1989. Development as capability expansion. *Journal of Development Planning* 19.

———. 1992. *Inequality reexamined.* Cambridge, MA: Harvard University Press.

———. 1993. Capability and well-being. In *The quality of life,* ed. M. Nussbaum and A. K. Sen. Oxford: Oxford University Press.

———. 1995. *Nuevo examen de la desigualdad.* Madrid, Spain: Alianza.

———. 1996. On the foundations of welfare economics: Utility, capability, and practical reason. In *Ethics, rationality and economic behaviour,* ed. F. Farina, F. Hahn, and S. Vannucci. Oxford: Clarendon Press.

———. 1997a. Human rights and Asian values: What Lee Kuan Yew and Le Peng don't understand about Asia. *New Republic* 217:33–40.

———. 1997b. Indian traditions and Western imagination. *Daedalus* 126:1–26.

———. 1997c. *La libertá individuale come impegno sociale.* Rome, Italy: Literza.

———. 1997d. *Resources, values, and development.* Cambridge, MA: Harvard University Press.

———. 1997e. *On economic inequality: With a substantial annexe "after a quarter century" by J. Foster and A. Sen.* 2nd ed. Oxford: Clarendon Press.

———. 1998a. Culture, freedom and independence. In *UNESCO, world culture report,* ed. UNESCO Publishing. Paris: UNESCO Publishing.

———. 1998b. *Reason before identity.* Oxford: Oxford University Press.

———. 1999. *Development as freedom.* New York: Knopf.

———. 2000. Social exclusion: Concept, application and scrutiny. Social development papers No. 1: Office of Environment and Social Development, Asian Development Bank.

———. In press. *Many faces of gender inequality.*

Sen, G., A. Germain, and L. Chen, eds. 1994. *Population policies reconsidered: Health, empowerment and rights.* Cambridge, MA: Harvard Center for Population and Development/International Women's Health Coalition.

Sen, S. 2000. Towards a feminist politics? The Indian women's movement in historical perspective. Gender policy research report working paper series. Washington, DC: World Bank.

Serageldin, I. 1999. Very special places: The architecture and economics of intervening in historic cities. In *Culture and sustainable development,* ed. I. Serageldin. Washington, DC: World Bank.

Serageldin, I., and J. Tabaroff, eds. 1994. *Culture and development in Africa.* ESD Proceedings Series No. 1. Washington, DC: World Bank.

Sharma, U. 1999. *Caste.* Buckingham, England: Open University Press.

Shiva, M., O. Goyal, and P. Krishnan. 1992. *The state of India's health: Women and health.* New Delhi, India: Voluntary Health Association of India.

Shore, C. N. 1996. Anthropology's identity crisis. *Anthropology Today* 12:2–5.

Sibanda, A. 2000. A nation in pain: Why the HIV/AIDS epidemic is out of control in Zimbabwe. *International Journal of Health Services* 30:717–38.

Sidel, R., and V. Sidel. 1982. *The health of China*. Boston: Beacon Press.

Sieder, R., and M. Mitterauer. 1983. The reconstruction of the family life course: Theoretical problems and empirical results. In *Family forms in historic Europe*, ed. R. Wall, J. Robin and P. Laslett. Cambridge: Cambridge University Press.

Sillitoe, P. 1998. The development of indigenous knowledge: A new applied anthropology. *Current Anthropology* 39:223–52.

Silva, K. T., S. L. Schensul, J. J. Schensul, B. Nastasi, M. W. Amarasiri de Silva, C. Sivayoganathan, P. Ratnayake, P. Wedsinghe, J. Lewis, M. Eisenberg, and H. Aponso. 1997. *Youth and sexual risk in Sri Lanka*. Washington, DC: International Center for Research on Women.

Silverblatt, I. 1990. *Luna, sol y brujas: Género y clases en los Andes prehispánicos y coloniales*. Cusco, Peru: Centro de Estudios Regionales Andinos.

Silvert, K. H. 1954. *A study in government: Guatemala*. Middle American Research Institute publication 21. New Orleans: Tulane University.

Skinner-Klee, J. 1954. *Legislación indigenista de Guatemala*. Mexico: Instituto Indigenista InterAmericano.

Sleightholme, C., and I. Sinha. 1996. *Guilty without trial: Women in the sex trade in Calcutta*. Calcutta: STREE.

Smith, A. 1776/1976. *An inquiry into the nature and causes of the wealth of nations*. Oxford: Clarendon Press.

——. 1790/1976. *The theory of moral sentiments*. Oxford: Clarendon Press.

Smith, C. A., ed. 1990. *Guatemalan Indians and the state: 1540 to 1988*. Austin: University of Texas Press.

Smith, K., C. B. Barret, and P. W. Box. 2001. Not necessarily the same boat: Heterogeneous risk assessment among East African pastoralists. *Journal of Development Studies* 37, no. 5:1–30.

Smith, T. C. 1959. *The agrarian origins of modern Japan*. Stanford: Stanford University Press.

Sorensen, J. L., and A. L. Copeland. 2000. Drug abuse treatment as an HIV prevention strategy: A review. *Drug and Alcohol Dependence* 59:17–31.

SPLM/SSRA-OLS. 1998a. Joint Task Force on Targeting and Vulnerabilities: Final report. Nairobi, Kenya: SPLM/SRRA-OLS.

——. 1998b. Press statement. Nairobi, Kenya.

Srinivas, M. N. 1966. *Social change in modern India*. Berkeley: University of California Press.

Stall, R., L. Pollack, T. C. Mills, J. N. Martin, D. Osmond, J. Paul, D. Binson, T. J. Coates, and J. A. Catania. 2001. Use of antiretroviral therapies among HIV-infected men who have sex with men: A household-based sample of 4 major American cities. *American Journal of Public Health* 91:767–73.

Stavenhagen, R. 1968. *Las clases sociales en las sociedades agrarias*. Mexico: Siglo XXI.

——. 1974. *La sociedad plural en América Latina*. Diálogos.

——. 2001. *La cuestion étnica*. Mexico: Colegio de México.

Stavis, B. 1982. Rural local governance and agricultural development in Taiwan. In *Rural development and local organization in Asia*, ed. N. T. Uphoff. New Delhi: Macmillan.

Steele, C. M. 1999. Thin ice: "Stereotype threat" and black college students. *Atlantic Monthly* 284:44–54.

Steiner, C. B. 1994. *African art in transit.* Cambridge: Cambridge University Press.

Stern, N. H. In press. *Poor people and economic opportunity.* Cambridge, MA: MIT Press.

Stiglitz, J. 1999. Participation and development. Paper presented at the Conference on Democracy, Market Economy and Development, at Seoul, Korea.

———. 2001. Ethics, economic advice, and economic policy. Paper presented at the The Inter-American Develpment Bank Ethics Conference.

———. 2003. Democratizing the International Monetary Fund and the World Bank: Governance and accountability. *Governance* 16, no. 1:111–39.

Stokes, S. 2001. Patologías de la deliberación. In *La democracia deliberativa*, ed. J. Elster. Barcelona, Spain: Gedisa.

Stokes, J. P., and J. Peterson. 1998. Homophobia, self-esteem, and risk for HIV among African American men who have sex with men. *AIDS Education and Prevention* 10:278–92.

Stolcke, V. 1993. Mujeres invadidas. La sangre de la conquista de América. In *Mujeres invadidas*, ed. V. Stolcke. Madrid, Spain: Horas y Horas.

Strathdee, S. 2001. Sex differences in risk factors for HIV seroconversion among injection drug users: A 10–year perspective. Paper presented at the 12th International Congress on Reducing Drug-Related Harm, New Delhi, India.

Sunstein, C. R. 1996. *Legal reasoning and political conflict.* New York: Oxford University Press.

Sunstein, C. R., and E. Ullmann-Margalit. 1997. *Second order decisions.* Public Law and Legal Theory working paper No. 1. Chicago: University of Chicago School of Law.

Swantz, M. L. 1997. *Community and village-based provision of key social services: A case study of Tanzania.* WIDER Research Paper, No. 41. Helsinki, Finland: The World Institute for Development Economics Research.

Swartz, D. 2000. *Culture and power: The sociology of Pierre Bourdieu.* Chicago: University of Chicago Press.

Swift, J. 1981. Rapid appraisal and cost-effective research in West Africa. *Agricultural Administration* 8:485–92.

Sylla, A. 1994. *La philosophie morale des Wolof.* Dakar, Senegal: IFAN, Universite de Dakar.

Szanton, D. L. 1998. Contingent moralities—social and economic investment in a Philippine fishing town. In *Market cultures—Society and morality in the new Asian capitalisms*, ed. R. W. Hefner. Boulder, CO: Westview Press.

Tagore, R. 1928. *Letters to a friend, with essays by C. F. Andrews.* London: Allen and Unwin.

Tang, S. 1992. *Institutions and collective action—Self-governance in irrigation systems.* San Francisco: ICS Press.

Taracena Arriola, A. 1999. Proyecto nacional y nación multicultural. In *Sociedades multiculturales y democracia en América Latina*, ed. J. N. Montesinos. Mexico: UNESCO.

Tax, S. 1937. The Municipios of the Midwestern Highlands of Guatemala. *American Anthropologist* 39:413–44.

———. 1941. World view and social relations in Guatemala. *American Anthropologist* 43:27–42.

Taylor, C. 1992. *Multiculturalism and the politics of recognition: An essay*. Princeton, NJ: Princeton University Press.

———. 1995. The politics of recognition. In *Philosophical arguments*, ed. C. Taylor. Cambridge, MA: Harvard University Press.

Tendler, J. 1997. *Good government in the tropics*. Baltimore, MD: Johns Hopkins University Press.

———. 2000. Why are social funds so popular? In *Local dynamics in the era of globalization: Companion volume of the World Development Report 1999/2000*, ed. S. Yusuf, W. Wu and S. Everett. Oxford: Oxford University Press for the World Bank.

Tendler, J., and R. Serrano. 1999. The rise of social funds: What are they a model of? New York: UNDP.

Termer, F. 1957. *Etnología y etnografía de Guatemala*. Guatemala: Seminario de Integración Guatemalteca.

Thomas, T. 1995. Acculturative stress in the adjustment of immigrant families. *Journal of Social Distress and the Homeless* 4:131–42.

Thompson, M., R. J. Ellis, and A. B. Wildavsky, eds. 1990. *Cultural theory*. Boulder, CO: Westview Press.

Thompson, M., G. Grendstad, and P. Selle. 1999a. Cultural theory as political science. In *Cultural theory as political science*, ed. M. Thompson, G. Grendstad, and P. Selle. London: Routledge.

———, eds. 1999b. *Cultural theory as political science*. London: Routledge.

Throsby, D. 1994. The production and consumption in the arts: A view of cultural economics. *Journal of Economic Literature* 32:1–29.

———. 1999. Cultural capital. *Journal of Cultural Economics* 23:3–12.

———. 2001. *Economics and culture*. Cambridge: Cambridge University Press.

Torres Rivas, E. 1971. *Interpretación del desarollo social Centroamericano: Procesos y estructuras de una sociedad dependiente*. San José, Costa Rica: Editorial Universitaria Centroamericana.

Touraine, A. 1989. *América Latina: Política y sociedad*. Madrid, Spain: Espasa Calpe.

———. 1997. *Pourrons-nous vivre ensemble? Égaux et différents*. Paris: Fayard.

Towse, R. 1993. *Singers in the marketplace: The economics of the singing profession*. Oxford: Clarendon Press.

———, ed. 1997. *Cultural economics: The arts, the heritage and the media industry*. Cheltenham, England: Edward Elgar.

Trautmann, T. R. 1981. *Dravidian kinship*. Cambridge: Cambridge University Press.

Turnbull, C. 1962. *The forest people*. New York: Doubleday.

Turner, V. 1982. Introduction. In *Celebration: Studies in festivity and ritual*, ed. V. Turner. Washington, DC: Smithosian Institution Press.

Turton, D. 1988. Anthropology and development. In *Perspectives on development*, ed. P. F. Leeson and M. M. Minogue. Manchester, England: Manchester University Press.

Tushman, M., and C. A. O'Reilly. 1997. *Winning through innovation: A practical guide to leading organizational change and renewal*. Cambridge, MA: Harvard Business School Press.

US Census Bureau. 2001. Monitoring the Epidemic (MAP): The Status and Trends of HIV/AIDS/STI Epidemic in Asia and the Pacific. Paper presented at the 6th International Congress on AIDS in Asia and the Pacific, at Melbourne, Australia.

Uberoi, P., ed. 1996. *Social reform, sexuality and the state.* New Delhi, India: Sage Publications.

Udry, C. 1996. Gender, agricultural productivity and the theory of the household. *Journal of Political Economy* 104:1010–46.

———. 2003. Fieldwork, economic theory, and research on institutions in developing countries. *American Economic Review Papers and Proceedings* 93:107–11.

UNAIDS. 2000. *Men and AIDS—A gendered approach.* Geneva, Switzerland: UN-AIDS.

United Nations Development Program (UNDP). 1993a. *Country human development indicators: Latin America and the Caribbean.* New York: UNDP.

———. 1993b. *Informe de desarrollo humano 1993.* New York: UNDP.

———. 1994. *Human development report, 1994.* New York: UNDP/Oxford University Press.

———. 1998. *Combating poverty: The Korean experience.* Seoul, Korea: UNDP Seoul.

———. 1999a. *Human development report, 1999: Globalizations with a human face.* New York: UNDP/Oxford University Press.

———. 1999b. *Informe de desarrollo humano 1999.* New York: UNDP.

———. 2000. *Guatemala: La fuerza incluyente del desarrollo humano.* Guatemala: UNDP.

———. 2001. *Informe de desarrollo humano 2001.* New York: UNDP.

United Nations Development Program (UNDP)–Bolivia. 2000. *Informe de desarrollo humano en Bolivia 2000.* La Paz, Bolivia: UNDP.

United Nations Development Program (UNDP)–Chile. 1998. *Informe de desarrollo humano en Chile 1998.* Santiago de Chile: UNDP.

United Nations Educational Scientific and Cultural Organization (UNESCO). 1947. *Les conférences de l'Unesco.* Paris: UNESCO Publishing.

———. 1948. The Program of UNESCO of 1948: Proposed by the Executive Board to Second Session of the General Conference. Paris: UNESCO Publishing.

———. 1969. *Cultural policy: A preliminary study.* Paris: UNESCO Publishing.

———. 1977. *Medium term plan for 1977–1982.* Paris: UNESCO Publishing.

———. 1982. *World conference on cultural policies.* Paris: UNESCO Publishing.

———. 1995. *Our creative diversity: Report of the World Commission on Culture and Development.* Paris: UNESCO Publishing.

———. 1998. *World culture report: Culture, creativity and markets.* Paris: UNESCO publishing.

———. 2000. *World culture report No. 2.* Paris: UNESCO Publishing.

Valentine, C. 1969. Culture and poverty. Chicago: University of Chicago Press.

van Cott, D. L., ed. 1994. *Indigenous peoples and democracy in Latin America.* New York: Saint Martin's Press.

van der Veen, H. T. 2000. *The international drug complex.* Amsterdam: Centre for Drug Research, Universiteit van Amsterdam.

van Puffelen, F. 1992. *De betekenis van impact studies.* Amsterdam: Stichting voor Economisch Onderzoek.

van Staveren, I. 2001. *Caring for economics: An Aristotelian perspective.* London: Routledge.

Velthius, O. 2002. *The story of prices in the art market.* Erasmus University.

Veron, R. 2001. The "new" Kerala model: Lessons for sustainable development. *World Development* 29:601–17.

Vertovec, S., and R. Cohen, eds. 1999. *Migration, diasporas and transnationalism.* London: International Library of Studies on Migration.

Verweij, M. 2004. Appendix: Cultural theory. In *Culture and public action: A cross-disciplinary dialogue on development policy,* ed. V. Rao and M. Walton. Stanford: Stanford University Press.

von Braun, J., and P. J. R. Webb. 1989. The impact of new crop technology on the agricultural division of labor in a West African setting. *Economic Development and Cultural Change* 37:513–34.

Wade, R. 1976. Culture of poverty revisited. *Institute of Development Studies Bulletin* 8:4–7.

———. 1988. *Village republics.* Cambridge: Cambridge University Press.

Walzer, M. 1983. *Spheres of justice: A defense of pluralism and equality.* Oxford, England: Blackwell.

———. 1998. *Traité sur la tólerance.* Paris: Gallimard.

Warman, A. 1988. Los campesinos en el umbral de un nuevo milenio. *Revista Mexicana de Sociología* 50.

Warren, D. M., and D. Brokensha. 1980. *Indigenous knowledge and development.* Washington, DC: University Press of America.

Warren, K. B. 1978. *The symbolism of subordination: Indian identity in a Guatemalan town.* Austin: University of Texas Press.

———. 1998. *Indigenous movements and their critics: Pan-Maya activism in Guatemala.* Princeton, NJ: Princeton University Press.

Wasserstrom, R. 1975. Revolution in Guatemala: Peasants and politics under the Arbenz government. *Comparative Studies in Society and History* 17:443–78.

Weber, M. 1930. *The Protestant ethic and the spirit of capitalism.* Trans. T. Parsons. London: Allen and Unwin.

———. 1951. *The religion of China.* Translated and ed. H. H. Gerth. New York: Free Press.

Weibull, J. 1995. *Evolutionary game theory.* Cambridge, MA: MIT Press.

Wellings, K., J. Field, A. Johnson, and J. Wadsworth. 1994. *Sexual behaviour in Britain.* London: Penguin Books.

Whang, I.-J. 1981. *Management of rural change in Korea.* Seoul, Korea: Seoul National University Press.

White, H. N. 2002. Combining quantitative and qualitative approaches in poverty analysis. *World Development* 30:511–22.

Whitehead, L., and G. Gray-Molina. 2000. Capacidad política a la larga. *Revista Mexicana de Ciencias Políticas y Sociales* 179.

Whyte, M. K., and W. L. Parish. 1985. *Urban life in contemporary China.* Chicago: University of Chicago Press.

Wildavsky, A. B., S. Chai, and B. Swedlow, eds. 1998. *Culture and social theory.* New Brunswick, NJ: Transaction Publishers.

Williams, B. 1993. *Shame and necessity.* Berkeley: University of California Press.

Wolf, E. 1982. *Europe and the people without history.* Berkeley: University of California Press.

Wolf, M. 1985. *Revolution postponed: Women in contemporary China.* Stanford: Stanford University Press.

Wolfensohn, J. D. 1998. Culture and sustainable development: Investing in the promise of societies. Speech given at World Bank Headquarters, September 28, 1998, at Washington, DC.

———. 1999. *A proposal for a comprehensive development framework.* Washington, DC: World Bank.

———. 2000. *Culture counts: Financing, resources, and the economics of culture in sustainable development.* Washington, DC: World Bank.

Woo, M. Y. K. 1994. Chinese women workers: The delicate balance between protection and equality. In *Engendering China: Women, culture and the state*, ed. C. K. Gilmartin, G. Hershatter, L. Rofel, and T. White. Cambridge, MA: Harvard University Press.

Woodham-Smith, C. 1962. *The Great Hunger: Ireland 1845–9.* London: Hamish Hamilton.

Woolcock, M. 1998. Social capital and economic development: Towards a theoretical synthesis and policy framework. *Theory and Society* 27:151–208.

Woolcock, M., and D. Narayan. 2000. Social capital: Implications for development theory, research and policy. *World Bank Research Observer* 15:225–49.

World Bank. 1982. *Bank, tribal peoples and economic development.* Washington, DC: World Bank.

———. 1993. *The East Asian miracle: Economic growth and public policy.* New York: Oxford University Press.

———. 1994. *The World Bank and participation.* Washington, DC: World Bank.

———. 1995. *Guatemala: Basic education strategy: Equity and efficiency in education.* Report No. 12204-GU. Washington, DC: Human Resources Operations Division, Country Department II, Latin America and Caribbean Regional Office.

———. 1996. *Introduction to social assessment (SA): Incorporating participation and social analysis in to the bank's work.* Washington, DC: World Bank, Social Policy and Resettlement Division.

———. 1997. *World development report 1997.* New York: World Bank/Oxford University Press.

———. 1998. *World development indicators.* Washington, DC: World Bank.

———. 2001a. *Cultural heritage and development: A framework for action in the Middle East and North Africa.* Washington, DC: World Bank.

———. 2001b. *World development report 2000/01: Attacking poverty.* New York: World Bank/Oxford University Press.

———. 2001c. Comprehensive development framework questions and answers update. Comprehensive Development Framework Secretariat, March 28, 2001. Washington, DC: World Bank.

———. 2002a. *Empowerment and poverty reduction: A sourcebook.* Washington, DC: World Bank.

———. 2002b. *Globalization, growth and poverty: Building an inclusive world economy.* Washington, DC: World Bank.

———. 2002c. *World development report 2001/02: Building the institutions for markets.* New York: Oxford University Press.

World Food Programme. 1998. Daily bulletin. September 3, 1998.

Wright, R. 1994. *The moral animal—Why we are the way we are: The new science of evolutionary psychology.* New York: Pantheon Books.

Young, H. 1992. *Food security and famine.* Oxfam Practical Health Guide No. 7. Oxford, England: Oxfam.

Zamagni, S., ed. 1993. *Mercati illegali e mafie.* Bologna, Italy: Il Mulino.

———, ed. 1995. *The economics of altruism.* Aldershot: Edward Elgar.

Zelizer, V. 1997. How do we know whether a monetary transaction is a gift, an entitlement, or compensation? In *Economics, values and organization,* ed. A. Ben-Ner and L. Putterman. Cambridge: University of Cambridge Press.

Zhang, H., and L. Xiaojin. 1993. Rescue action in Taihang mountain. *Min Zhu Yu Fa Zhi,* December.

Zhao, Y. 1997. Women's image and gender view in mass media. In *Social change and women's development,* ed. Z. Yan and G. Li. Beijing: Chinese Women Publishing House.

Zhou, M. 1999. Segmented assimilation: Issues, controversies and recent research on the second generation. In *Handbook of immigration: The American experiences,* ed. C. Hirshman, P. Kasinitz, and J. Dewind. New York: Russell Sage.

Index

Aaby, P., 370

Abraham, Anita, 25, 30, 34n30, 96–97, 361

Abraham, L., 265

Accord on the Identity and Rights of
Indigenous Peoples, 344, 345–48, 349–53,
354, 355, 358n31

Adams, J., 110

Adato, M., 210, 226, 230

Afghanistan: Buddhas destroyed by Taliban
in, 138, 140–41, 143, 144–46, 147, 149,
151, 160–61

Africa, 25, 64, 71, 109n, 127–28, 130, 371n6;
beads in, 155, 156; colonialism in, 172–73;
commodities in, 155–56; HIV/AIDS in,
126–27; participatory development in,
210, 211, 219, 220–21, 223, 224, 228, 229,
231; sexual subcultures in, 263, 267, 270.
See also Ghana; South Africa; Sudan

African Americans, 17–18, 34n28, 169

Agarwal, B., 253

Aggleton, P., 264, 269

Aguilar, M. D., 277

Aguirre Beltrán, Gonzalo, 168, 171

Ahmad, A. S., 327n30

Ahmad, J. A., 137n12, 173

AIDS. *See* HIV/AIDS

Akerlof, George, 13, 40, 119

Alba, R. D., 137n6

Albania, 42

Alesina, A., 13

Alkire, Sabina, 19, 28, 57n9, 365

Alliance, the (Mumbai, India), 71–80, 81;
housing exhibitions by, 76–78; politics of
patience within, 73, 74, 81–82; precedent
setting by, 75–76; relations with state
bureaucracy, 72–73, 75–78, 79; and
savings, 73–75; toilet festivals of, 76, 78–
80, 361

All India Institute of Hygiene and Public
Health, 7–8

Almond, G., 282

Alonso, Guiomar, 184n6

Alvarado Ajanel, Virgilio, 351

Alverson, H., 278

Alverson, M., 278

Amarasiri de Silva, M. W., 265, 268

Amish, 152

amphetamines, 278

Anderson, Elijah, 34n29

Anderson, Elizabeth, 146, 148, 157, 159,
162n6

Anderson, M., 307

Anderson, Perry, 167

Anderson, R. S., 208n2

Andors, P., 240, 241, 242

Ang Sang Suu Chi, 184n6

Annan, Kofi, 80

anthropologists, 18–19, 370; attitudes toward
culture, 3, 9, 11–12, 17, 31, 32n5, 32n10,
32n11, 33nn15,23, 60–62, 63–64, 65, 83–

anthropologists *(continued)*
84, 98, 100, 110, 118, 126, 136n, 163, 169–70, 174, 176, 178, 262, 307, 308, 324, 325, 327n28, 334–35, 342, 359, 368; attitudes toward economic development, 9, 19, 32n11, 368–69; attitudes toward racial prejudice, 86; attitudes toward wants, 90; methodological holism among, 14–15, 18; relations with development/relief agencies, 307, 324–25; relations with economists, 11–12, 368–69
apathy, culture of, 41, 87–88, 101; and Cultural Theory, 22, 24, 93, 94, 97, 107–8, 111, 112
Apffel-Marglin, Frederique, 11, 185, 188, 192
Aponso, H., 265, 268
Appadurai, Arjun, 12, 26, 30, 31n1, 153–54, 178, 191, 369; on capacity to aspire, 24–25, 36n41, 59, 64–70, 73–74, 77–78, 80, 81–83, 195, 361; on terms of recognition, 24, 25, 66–67, 70, 76, 77, 80, 81, 83, 361
Arabs, 42
Aranda, J., 173
Arbenz Guzman, Jacobo, 331, 338–39, 340
Arensberg, C., 237, 238
Arévalo, Juan José, 336, 339, 340
Argentina, 329, 334
Aristotle, 40, 86, 153
Arizpe, Lourdes, 9, 16, 18, 34n25, 43, 184nn6,7
Arrow, K., 142
art, 122, 157, 158, 162n12, 167, 209n7
Asad, Talal, 325n1
Asia, 172, 173, 371n6; drug-using subcultures in, 273, 274, 276, 277; the *kothi* in, 266; participatory development in, 211, 224, 225, 229; peasant communities in, 212, 214; sexual subcultures in, 263, 266–67, 270. *See also* Afghanistan; China; India; Korea, South; Sri Lanka
Asia Foundation, 209n5

aspirations, 118–19, 286, 288; capacity to aspire, 24–25, 36n41, 59, 64–70, 73–74, 77–78, 80, 81–83, 195, 361, 362; of the poor, 7, 8, 24–25, 36n41, 59, 64–70, 73–74, 76, 77–78, 80, 81–83, 84, 118, 134, 195, 361, 362; relationship to culture, 4, 15, 24–25, 29, 30, 36n41, 59, 61, 63, 67–70, 73–74, 82–83, 84, 118, 134, 186, 191, 195, 359, 361, 368; of the rich, 36n41, 68–69, 361
Australia, 276, 279, 280; aborigines in, 139, 143, 150, 152, 277
Aviles, E., 276
Aydin, Zulkuf, 324–25

Badini, A., 213
Bajos, N., 270
Baker, E., 275
Baland, J. M., 224, 225
Baldwin, J. A., 277
Balkan wars of 1990s, 119, 124, 134, 135, 137n5, 364; Mostar Bridge destroyed during, 138, 140, 143, 159–60, 161n2
Ball, A., 274
Ballard, J., 280
Bandung Conference of 1955, 173
Banerjee, A., 226–27, 372n
Banfield, Eric, 87, 99
Bangladesh: drug-using subculture in, 276; *hijras* in, 266; sexual subcultures in, 263, 266, 267, 268
Banton, M., 327n26
Baptiste, D. A., Jr., 125
Bardhan, Pranab, 11, 226, 227, 369, 371n6
Barkow, J., 137n2
Barret, C. B., 372n
Barrett, W. E., 93
Barrios, Justo Rufino, 332, 333
Bartra, R., 304n11
Basava, 23
Basu, A., 43, 370

Basu, K., 9, 40, 371n6

Bates, R. H., 137n1

Batres Jáuregui, Antonio, 333–34

Baudrillard, Jean, 162n6

Baumann, G., 177

Bawtree, V., 178

Bayart, J. F., 232n2

Bearman, P. S., 269

Bebbington, A., 34n24, 229

Beck, U., 61–62

Becker, Gary, 14, 24, 33n17, 40, 162n7

Begemihl, B., 264

Behar, R., 284

behaviors, 117–18, 122–24, 165; related to HIV/AIDS, 261–62, 267, 268, 269, 270, 273–78

Beland, F., 277

Belarus, 276; income distribution in, 287

beliefs, 4, 9, 15, 136n, 165; biased interviews experiment, 128; and close observation, 128; hypothetical scenario experiments regarding, 128; as malleable, 116, 120, 131–34, 135, 136; opinion surveys, 125–28, 137n5; private opinion vs. behaviors, 33n21, 117–18, 122–24, 137n5; private opinion vs. public discourse, 22, 30, 116, 118, 120–22, 125–26, 127, 128–29, 132–33, 134, 136, 137nn3,5. *See also* preferences

Bell, D., 278

Bénabou, R., 13

Benini, A., 315

Ben-Ner, A., 40

Bennett, J., 324

Benthall, J., 324

Bergensen, H. O., 208n2

Bergstrom, T. C., 14

Berkes, N., 131

Berlin, I., 104

Bernheim, D. B., 13

Besley, T., 210, 226, 230

Bhaba, Homi, 177

Bierschenk, T., 229

Bikhchandani, S., 13, 316

Bilgrami, Akeel, 54

Binson, D., 267

Bisin, A., 33n17

Blackburn, J., 208n2, 301

Blau, J. R., 43

Bliss, C. J., 91, 369, 371n6

Bloch, F., 35n38, 372n

Bobbio, N., 282

Bockting, W. O., 267

Bohannon, P., 109n

Bolivia: campesino unions in, 285, 305n26; Cochabamba, 305n26; economic development in, 300, 302; Emergency Social Fund (ESF) in, 230; income distribution in, 287; indigenous groups in, 285, 301, 305n26, 306n28, 329, 344, 355; popular participation (PP) in, 300–303, 305nn25,26, 306n27; Potosí, 305n26; Santa Cruz, 305n26; socioeconomic differentiation in, 302; Sucre, 301, 306n27

Bonfil Batalla, Guillermo, 172, 328, 357n25

Boone, C., 223, 232n2

Booth, M., 274

Boserup, Ester, 173

Botswana, 266

Botvin, G. J., 275

Botvin, M., 275

Bourdieu, Pierre, 14–16, 61, 94, 162n6, 214; on cultural capital, 15–16, 28, 30, 151, 152; on *habitus*, 15, 16, 33n19; on social capital, 16, 30; on symbolic violence, 365, 367

Bowles, S., 35n37, 43, 360, 371n6

Box, P. W., 372n

Boyd, R., 118, 371n6

Bradbury, M., 315

Brazil, 36n40, 275, 361; HIV/AIDS policy in, 280; income distribution in, 287;

Brazil *(continued)*
  indigenous groups in, 329; participatory
  budget (PB) process in Porto Alegre, 27,
  298–300, 302, 305nn22,23, 364; partici-
  patory development in, 229; sexual sub-
  cultures in, 266, 268; the *travesti* in, 266
Brems, C., 277
Brittan, S., 40
Brock, K., 35n31
Brokensha, D., 324
Brook, D., 277
Brook, J., 277
Brown, J. H., 275
Brown, R. M., 329
Bruckner, H., 269
Brumann, Christopher, 178
Bu, W., 244
Buckley, S., 280
Buddhism, 42, 49–50, 57nn8,18, 67, 185–86;
  Buddhist statues in Afghanistan, 138, 140–
  41, 143, 144–46, 147, 149, 151, 160–61
buprenorphine, 276
Burgos-Debray, Elizabeth, 358n26
Burkina Faso, 221
Burma, 50, 239
business cultures, 35n33
Business Wire, 271
Butrint, Albania, 42

Cabral, Amilcar, 172–73
Calcutta: sex workers in, 6–9, 23, 26,
  32nn2,4, 272
Calderón, Fernando, 26–27, 364
Calves, A. E., 269
Cambodia, 74
Cameroon, 219, 269
capabilities, 56n3, 136n, 191–92, 198, 203,
  208, 257, 281, 289, 359; political capabili-
  ties, 56, 282, 292, 297, 301, 302, 305n26;
  Sen on, 4, 12–13, 19–20, 28, 32n12,
  36n45, 51, 63, 82, 151, 191, 193–94

capitalism, 20, 32n11, 86, 167–68, 169, 223,
  330, 335; Weber on, 10, 48. *See also*
  globalization; markets
Caribbean, the, 267
Carter, P., 204
Cassen, R., 208n2
Castells, M., 303n6
caste system. *See* India, caste system in
Catania, J. A., 267
Caufield, C., 205, 208n2
Cavalli-Sforza, L. L., 118
Centers for Disease Control and Prevention
  (CDC), 274, 275
Cernea, Michael, 19, 175, 204, 326n13, 369
Cesaire, Aimé, 172
Chai, S., 110
Chambers, Robert, 34n30, 35n31, 65, 190,
  205, 371n2
Changath, C., 314, 327n19
Chattopadhyaya, R., 372n
Chauveau, J. P., 229
Chen, L., 43
Chi, Ang Sang Suu, 184n6
Chile, 334; income distribution in, 287;
  Mapuches in, 303n4
China: Buddhism in, 49, 50, 57n8; Com-
  munist Party of, 239–45, 255–56, 257;
  Constitutional Reform and Moderniza-
  tion movement, 244; Cultural Revolution,
  240, 243–44; drug-using subcultures in,
  276; economic development in, 28, 176,
  234–35, 241, 244, 245; education in, 240,
  244, 245, 255, 256, 258; employment of
  women in, 240–41, 245, 255, 258; family
  law in, 236, 242–43; female child mortality in, 234, 255; income in, 235, 241;
  vs. India, 234–39, 252, 255–58; kinship
  systems in, 234, 235–40, 242, 243, 252,
  258; literacy rate in, 235; the media in,
  236, 243–44; population control in, 242,
  256–57; sexual subcultures in, 263; vs.

South Korea, 234–38, 248, 255–58; state
policies in, 27, 28, 235, 239–45, 252, 255–
56, 257–58; women in, 27, 28, 234–45,
255–58

Chiriboga, M., 289

Chonchol, J., 304n11

Chowdhry, P., 259

Christianity, 144, 152, 176; Calvinism, 10, 48;
Catholicism, 27, 48, 331, 340; in Guatemala, 331, 339, 343, 357n20; in India, 42;
liberation theology, 340; Pentecostalism,
155–56; in South Korea, 49; in Sudan,
327n22

Churchill, Winston, 45, 57n14

Chwe, M. S. K., 22, 32n15, 35n36

CIETafrica, 272

civil society, 114, 364; relationship to the
state, 201, 285, 289, 298–300, 301, 306n28,
362. *See also* nongovernmental
organizations (NGOs)

Çizakça, M., 132

class. *See* social classes

clientelism, 361; in Latin America, 282, 285,
289, 300, 303nn4,5, 306nn26,27; in tribal
communities, 223, 226, 229, 232n1

Clifford, J., 325

Coates, T. J., 267

cocaine, 275, 276, 278

Coleman, E., 267

Coleman, James, 33n18, 162n8

Collier, P., 316, 321

Collins, R., 327n27

Colombia: income distribution in, 287;
indigenous groups in, 329, 344

colonialism, 10, 85, 89, 100, 171–73, 272,
324; in Africa, 172–73; in Guatemala, 330,
356n10; in India, 34n26, 44, 45, 252, 253,
259n7, 273–74; in Korea, 246, 250; in
Latin America, 283–84, 293; in Sudan,
310

Comaroff, J. and J., 61

Comisión Económica para América Latina y
Caribe (CEPAL), 288, 290, 304n14

common good, 282, 291, 295, 297–98, 302

common sense, 8–9, 27, 361, 362, 363, 370,
371n1

community-based development. *See* participatory development

condom use, 8, 32n4, 262, 269, 270

Condorcet, M., 40

conflict, 164, 167; between culture and
economic development, 3–6, 9, 10, 15,
16–17, 20, 26–27, 31, 46–47, 86–88, 98,
100–101, 108–9, 115–17, 118–21, 126,
129–36, 135, 136, 168–70, 186, 187, 191–
98, 202, 209n7, 359, 367; in donor-
beneficiary relations, 4–6, 9, 211–12,
227–29, 307–8, 309, 311, 313–15, 316–
19, 320–22, 323–24, 326nn7,17,18,
327n19; resolution of, 112, 166, 212, 213–
15, 228, 298, 318, 364. *See also* Balkan wars
of 1990s; Guatemala, civil war in; Guatemala, peace accords in; policy design and
implementation, trade-offs in; Sudan, civil
war in

Confucianism, 42, 48, 49–50

Congleton, R., 216

Congo, Republic of, 220

Connell, R. W., 267

Conning, J., 229

consensus, 101; in political cultures, 297, 298,
300, 302, 303, 306n28; role of rituals in,
64, 81, 83; in tribal communities, 217–18

consumerism, 303n4, 304n9

Continental Meeting for Indigenous, Black,
and Popular Resistance, Second, 343

Cooke, B., 34n30, 361

coordination of collective action, 4, 32n15,
91, 94–95, 99–100, 137n1

Coordinator of Organizations of the
Guatemalan Mayan People Saqb'ichil
(COPMAGUA), 345

Copeland, A. L., 276

Cordes, J. J., 160

Cosmides, H. L., 137n2

Costa Rica, 332

Cowen, T., 31n1, 35n34, 141, 148, 366

Coyle, D. J., 110

Crawford, J., 267

Crofts, N., 279

Croll, E., 242

Cruise-O'Brien, D. B., 223

cultural capital, 25, 33nn22,23, 151–53, 160, 162n7, 360; Bourdieu on, 15–16, 28, 30, 151, 152. *See also* values, cultural values

cultural determinism, 20, 38, 43, 46–50, 52, 55

cultural development, 39, 57n9

cultural diversity, 132, 135, 175–77, 179, 180, 182–83, 368; and deliberative politics, 282; in Latin America, 292–93, 294, 295, 328–29, 331, 344, 345–48, 351, 352–54

cultural entrepreneurs, 158

cultural globalization, 38, 52–55

cultural goods, 138–61; commodification resisted by, 156–57, 159, 160; defined, 138, 161n1; economic value of, 142–43, 148, 150–52, 157, 158, 161, 187, 352, 354, 367, 371n6; social value of, 150–51, 160, 367

cultural heritage, 4, 35n36, 39, 60, 150–51, 179, 182, 202, 342; preservation of, 21, 41–42, 57n8, 122, 139, 140, 141, 143, 144, 145, 147, 149, 159, 161, 167, 174, 180, 181, 350–51, 352, 366–67; UNESCO World Heritage List, 18, 139, 140, 141, 144, 145, 147, 159, 174

cultural identity, 4, 9, 15, 20, 54, 116, 117, 119–20, 122, 129, 130, 158, 174, 186, 202, 213, 288, 304n9, 334–36, 342, 344, 367, 368; vs. cultural expression, 35n36, 139–40, 143, 161n1

cultural interaction, 61–62, 181–82, 364–65,

368; learning from, 38, 44, 50–55, 75, 131–32, 166, 366

cultural prejudice, 44–46, 324–25, 327n24

cultural protectionism, 54, 121, 122, 126, 129, 130, 135–36, 137nn11,12, 141–44, 175, 183, 185, 188

cultural relativism, 126

cultural stereotyping, 44–46, 57nn11,14

Cultural Theory, 110–14; and Arun-3 project in Nepal, 112–13, 114; corporatist tendency, 21–22, 91, 92–94, 95–97, 107, 108, 110; and culture of apathy/fatalism, 22, 24, 93, 94, 97, 107–8, 111, 112; and democracy, 111, 112, 113–14; egalitarian tendency, 91, 93, 94, 96, 97, 107, 108, 109, 110, 111–12, 113, 114; and globalization, 110–11; hierarchical tendency, 21–22, 91, 92–94, 95–96, 97–98, 107, 108, 109, 111–12, 113, 114; individualist/entrepreneurial tendency, 21–22, 91, 92–93, 94, 95–98, 107, 108, 110, 111–12, 113, 114; and international community, 109; loner tendency, 91, 93, 94, 107–8, 109, 110, 113; and poverty, 92, 94; and risk, 97–98; and wealth, 96–97

culture: attitudes of anthropologists toward, 3, 9, 11–12, 17, 31, 32n5, 32n10, 32n11, 33nn15,23, 60–62, 63–64, 65, 83–84, 98, 100, 110, 118, 126, 136n, 163, 169–70, 174, 176, 178, 262, 307, 308, 324, 325, 327n28, 334–35, 342, 359, 368; attitudes of economists toward, 3, 9, 10–11, 12–16, 17–18, 19, 31, 32n5, 33n16, 37–38, 48, 60, 83–84, 91, 98–100, 141–43, 146, 162n4, 170–71, 175, 181, 185, 359, 368–69, 371n6; as changing, 4, 20, 23, 27–28, 30, 43–44, 55, 61, 88, 92, 107, 115–16, 117, 120, 171, 180, 186, 191, 260–61, 264–65, 273, 280, 282, 367; consensus in, 64, 81, 83, 101; definitions of, 4, 59–62, 117, 136n, 161n1, 163–65, 167, 183, 260–61;

dissent in, 23−24, 26, 43, 61, 62, 63, 93, 94, 97, 109, 217−18; heterogeneity in, 23−24, 26, 43, 55, 61−62, 63, 93, 94, 97, 109, 117, 193, 197−98, 217−18, 239, 258, 292−93; as identity vs. expression, 35n36, 139−40, 143, 161n1; and internal colonialism, 171−73; as oriented to the future, 60−61, 62−63, 82, 84; as oriented to the past, 60−61, 84; relationality in, 4, 14, 18, 25, 29−30, 61, 62, 67−68, 186, 359, 368; relationship to aspirations, 4, 15, 24−25, 29, 30, 36n41, 59, 61, 63, 67−70, 73−74, 82−83, 84, 118, 134, 186, 191, 195, 359, 361, 368; relationship to deliberative politics, 282; relationship to economic development, 3−4, 9−19, 20, 23, 25−27, 28, 31, 31n1, 32n14, 33n15, 34n24, 35n34, 37−40, 43, 46−50, 55, 59, 60, 62, 82−84, 86−87, 88−89, 98, 99−101, 106−7, 108, 115−17, 118−21, 126, 129−36, 139−40, 143, 152, 163−64, 166, 167−71, 174−77, 178−79, 181−83, 185−98, 200−201, 203−5, 207−8, 208n2, 359, 360, 361, 368, 370, 371n6; role in inequality, 15, 16−17, 21, 23, 25−29, 31, 368

Cummings, W. K., 51

Dalton, G., 109n
Danahar, K., 208
Dandler, J., 285, 344
Darke, S., 279
Das, M. K., 230
Das Gupta, Monica, 27−28, 365
Dasgupta, Partha, 103−5, 106, 113, 114, 371n6
David, P. A., 133
Davin, D., 242
Davis, Shelton, 26, 27, 333
Davy, G., 99
Dayton-Johnson, J., 227
Deere, C. D., 173

De Figueredo, P., 137n1
De Lame, D., 232n1
de Leon, M., 351
deliberative politics, 282, 292, 295−303, 305n19, 361, 364−65
democracy, 26, 29, 47, 121, 143, 181, 304n8; as deliberative, 27, 282, 292, 295−303, 305n19, 361, 364−65; and gender equity, 250−51, 257; in Latin America, 281−82, 284, 288, 290, 291, 294, 298−303, 355; as participatory, 27, 40−41, 53−54, 111, 112, 298−303, 355, 361; and participatory development, 219, 221−22, 225, 228; relationship to capabilities, 281−82; relationship to economic development, 47, 84, 104−5, 113−14, 282, 286; secret ballots in, 121, 129, 137n11, 218; Sen on, 20, 53−54, 55−56, 185, 365; and social capital, 149. *See also* public discussion
Deng, Luka Biong, 312, 313, 316, 319, 320, 323, 326nn5,6,17, 327n25
Deren, S., 276
Des Jarlais, D., 275, 276
De Waal, A., 308, 316, 317, 320, 323, 326n6
Dewaraja, R., 266
DiMaggio, Paul, 162n6
Dione, Emmanuel, 175
Dirks, N. B., 34n26, 370
Disasters Emergency Committee (DEC), 312, 317
Disraeli, Benjamin, 194
Di Tella, T., 303n4
Dobkin de Rios, M., 274
Doezema, J., 270
Donald, N., 162n6
donor-beneficiary relations: and best practice guidelines, 362, 366, 370; inequality in, 9, 28, 200, 205−7, 208, 367; participatory development, 25−26, 210−12, 218−32, 361, 366, 371n2; in Sudan, 4−6, 9, 307−8, 311, 313−15, 316−19, 320−22,

donor-beneficiary relations *(continued)*
323–24, 326nn17,18, 327n19; training and
behavior of street-level workers, 363; in
tribal communities, 211–12, 223–26,
227–29, 232, 232n3
Dore, Ronald, 48, 170, 171
dos Santos, M., 292, 294, 304n9
Douglas, Mary, 11–12, 14, 16, 21–22, 24, 30,
33nn15,20, 43, 64, 130, 162n6, 365
Dowsett, G.W., 267
Draft Declaration on the Rights of
Indigenous Peoples, 343
Drake, R., 278
Drèze, J., 43, 52, 326n14, 326n16
Drijver, C.A., 219
drug users, injecting: in Asia, 273, 274, 276,
277; and HIV/AIDS, 22–23, 261, 263,
273–80; and mental illness, 278; and
poverty, 273; treatment programs for, 276,
278, 279; in United States, 274–75, 276,
278
Dubai, 276
Dube, L., 252
Duffield, M., 232, 313, 315, 316, 318, 319,
321, 326n7, 327n18
Duflo, E., 372n
Dumont, Louis, 17, 34n26
Durkheim, Emile, 14, 30, 35, 67
Durlauf, S. N., 13, 34n24, 371n6
Dusenbury, L., 275
Dyson-Hudson, N., 324

Eagleton, T., 45, 161n1
Earth First!, 111
Ebbe, K., 227
economic capital, 148, 149–50. *See also*
values, economic values
economic development: attitudes of anthropologists toward, 9, 19, 32n11, 368–69; in
China, 28, 176, 234–35, 241, 244, 245; in
India, 52, 130, 234–35, 255; and interest-

based lending, 122–24, 129–30, 133, 134–
35, 137n15; in Japan, 48–49, 50–52; in
Latin America, 282, 284, 291–92, 293–94,
300, 303n4, 304n17, 304nn10,11, 330, 331,
332–35; relationship to culture, 3–4, 9–
19, 20, 23, 25–27, 28, 31, 31n1, 32n14,
33n15, 34n24, 35n34, 37–40, 43, 46–50,
55, 59, 60, 62, 82–84, 86–87, 88–89, 98,
99–101, 106–7, 108, 115–17, 118–21,
126, 129–36, 139–40, 143, 152, 163–64,
166, 167–71, 174–77, 178–79, 181–83,
185–98, 200–201, 203–5, 207–8, 208n2,
359, 360, 361, 368, 370, 371n6; relationship
to democracy, 47, 84, 104–5, 113–14, 282,
286; relationship to HIV/AIDS, 261; in
South Korea, 46–47, 49–50, 234–35, 245.
See also globalization
economists: attitudes toward case studies,
369; attitudes toward culture, 3, 9, 10–11,
12–16, 17–18, 19, 31, 32n5, 33n16, 37–
38, 48, 60, 83–84, 91, 98–100, 141–43,
146, 162n4, 170–71, 175, 181, 185, 359,
368–69, 371n6; attitudes toward flows of
information, 96; attitudes toward institutions, 21; attitudes toward preferences, 87,
148; game theory used by, 12, 13, 22;
methodological individualism among, 14,
18, 21, 22, 40, 67, 68, 87, 91, 98, 368,
371n6; relations with anthropologists, 11–
12, 368–69; and social mobility, 35n37
Ecuador: indigenous groups in, 329, 344, 355
Edgerton, Robert, 126
education, 16, 56, 122, 150, 152, 161, 166,
168, 172, 199–200, 224, 291, 304n15, 362,
364, 367; academic values, 147, 148; and
Buddhism, 50, 57n18; in China, 240, 244,
245, 255, 256, 258; regarding drugs, 275,
276; in Guatemala, 331, 334, 337, 346,
349–50, 355; in India, 52, 251, 254, 255,
256, 258; in Japan, 50–52; regarding sex,
269; and sexual experiences, 265; in South

Korea, 47, 50, 246, 249, 256, 258; for women, 130, 132, 189, 236, 240, 244, 245, 246, 249, 255, 256, 258, 261, 269, 271, 349

Egypt, 131, 141

Eisenberg, M., 265, 268

Ellen, R., 327n28

Ellerman, David, 204, 209n14

Ellis, R. J., 110

El Salvador, 332

Elster, J., 40, 216

Emmerj, Louis, 166, 184n7

employment: job creation, 148, 158; in Latin America, 288, 290, 293–94; for women, 235, 236, 240–41, 245, 246, 250, 251, 254, 255, 258, 286

environmental issues, 179, 207, 354

Epstein, S., 371n6

equality, 3–4, 6, 221–22, 364, 371n5; of agency, 3, 29–31, 359, 360, 367; of opportunity, 3, 28–29, 30, 33n21, 291, 359; in political cultures, 292, 295–96, 301, 302, 303; Sen on, 295, 305n20; for women, 27–28, 122, 179, 188, 235–36, 240–41, 242–44, 246, 247–48, 249, 250–51, 252–54, 256, 257–58, 271. *See also* inequality

Escobar, Arturo, 10, 11, 177–78, 370

Esman, M. J., 228

Esteban, J.-M., 371n6

Estebanez, P., 277

ethnicity, 4, 13, 119–20, 130, 137n6, 164, 263, 283, 334–36; and Balkan wars of 1990s, 119, 124, 134, 135, 137n5, 364; ethnocentrism, 324–25, 327n24

Etounga-Manguelle, D., 126

Etzioni, Michel, 162n6

evaluation, 146, 153, 156; as evolving, 42–43, 143, 144–45, 146–47. *See also* values

Evans, Peter, 364

Evans-Pritchard, E. E., 216

evolution, 14

exit, 63, 69, 83, 195

Fafchamps, M., 215, 372n

Faletto, E., 303n3

Fall, Yoro, 184nn6,7

Falla, R., 357n21

family law: in China, 236, 242–43; in India, 236, 252–53, 258; in South Korea, 236, 247–48, 250

family planning. *See* population control

famine: corruption during, 316, 319; and cultural values, 308; dependency issues during, 316, 320, 321–22, 323, 327n24; early warning of, 308, 314, 315, 326nn14,15; in India, 45; in Ireland, 45, 57n11; political manipulation of, 316, 317–19, 326n17, 327nn19,20; supplementary feeding during, 321, 326n12. *See also* Sudan

Fang, the, 64

Fanon, Frantz, 172

Faupel, C. E., 277

Faure, D., 239

Fehr, E., 371n6

Feldman, M. W., 118

Feldstein, M., 187

Feltz, L., 278

Ferguson, J., 10

Fernandez, James, 64, 81

Field, J., 265

Fields, G. S., 35n37

Filmer, D., 251

Fine, B., 34n24

Firth, Raymond, 215

Fischer, E., 329

Fitoussi, J., 291

Forbes, G., 250

Foucault, Michel, 10, 11, 177, 325n2

Fountain, J., 279

Fox, Jonathan, 36n42, 203

France, 48, 159, 265

Francois, P., 371n6

Frank, R. H., 40, 216

Fraser, N., 63

Frazer, E. Franklin, 169

freedom, 103–5, 136, 148–49, 154, 157, 178, 192; Sen on, 19–20, 56, 56n3, 63, 82, 102, 104, 106, 107, 183, 191, 290

Frey, Bruno, 40, 143, 157, 162n6, 187

Fricke, T., 370

Fried, L., 357n20

Fried, M., 239

Friedlander, Judy, 172

Friedman, Milton, 149

Friedman, S., 276

Friedmann, P., 276

friendship, 149, 154, 157, 159

Fujita, M., 224

Fukuyama, F., 40, 137n1

functionalism, 126, 137n1

fundamentalism: market fundamentalism, 281, 283, 285, 303n1; in religion, 54, 178, 340. *See also* cultural protectionism

Furtado, Celso, 184n6

Gagnon, J., 264, 265

Galasso, E., 225

Galbraith, John Kenneth, 93

Gamella, J., 277

game theory, 12, 13, 22, 33n15

Gandhi, Indira, 66, 79–80

Gandhi, Mahatma, 67, 130, 164, 173

Gandhi, N., 255

Gardner, K., 307, 324, 325n3

Gates, G. J., 268

Gates, H. L., 239

Geertz, Clifford, 9, 12, 33n16, 70, 100–101, 327n24

gender issues, 36n45, 43, 62, 119, 180, 203–4, 293; family law, 236, 242–43, 247–48, 250, 252–53, 258, 271; female child mortality, 234, 235, 255–56, 258; female genital mutilation, 365; gender discrimination, 241, 242, 246, 247, 249, 255–57, 283, 284, 286, 365; gender equity, 27–28, 122, 173–74, 179, 188, 235–36, 240–41, 242–44, 246, 247–48, 249, 250–51, 252–54, 256, 257–58, 271; male dominance and sexual privilege, 261, 272–73; and the media, 236, 243–44, 249–50, 253–54, 256; related to HIV/AIDS, 261; sex-selective abortion, 255, 258; sexual division of labor, 173, 234, 241, 245; son preference, 247, 255–56, 258; and the state, 234–35, 239–35, 245–50, 250–55, 252, 255–56, 257–58, 365; violence against women, 127, 242, 243, 249, 253, 254, 255, 272–73, 372n; women's health care, 236, 241–42, 247, 251–52, 254, 255, 261. *See also* women

Germain, A., 43

Germani, G., 304n8

Germany, 48

Geschiere, P., 216

Gettleman, M. E., 357n20

Ghana, 46–47, 50, 155–56, 171, 372n

Ghosh, A., 177

Ghurye, G. S., 118

Giddens, Anthony, 48

Gintis, H., 35n37, 371n6

Glebatis, D., 276

Glenny, M., 134

globalization, 4, 31n1, 35n34, 61–62, 110–11, 182–83, 202, 263, 303n6, 360, 366, 368, 372n; cultural globalization, 38, 52–55; and Latin America, 282, 286–90, 291–92, 294, 304n9; and political cultures, 286–88, 298; resistance to, 20, 115–16, 130, 188, 192, 204; and the state, 286–87, 289. *See also* capitalism; economic development; markets; trade, international

Gluck, C., 51

Godelier, M., 213

Goldfarb, R. S., 160

Goldstein, J., 241

Goody, J., 43, 44

Gooptu, N., 32n2

Gorsky, R., 276

Goulandris, Niki, 184n6

governments. *See* state, the

Goyal, O., 252

Grampp, W., 141, 148

Gramsci, Antonio, 167

Grandin, G., 356n7

Granovetter, Marc, 40, 162n6

Gray, J., 279

Gray-Molina, G., 301, 305n26

Greece and Elgin Marbles, 139, 143

Greenhaigh, S., 370

Greif, Avner, 13, 21, 22, 40, 137n1

Grendstad, G., 92, 110

Griffin, Keith, 184nn6,7

Griffiths, P., 279

Grob, C., 274

Grondona, M., 126

Grootaert, C., 34n24

Gross, J., 102

Group of 77, 175

Grund, J.-P., 277

Gu, L., 241

Guatemala, 328–55; Association of
Dignitaries of the Nation, 347; Catholic
Action movement in, 339, 340, 357n20;
Center for the Defense of the Constitution, 347; Christian Democratic party,
340; Christianity in, 331, 339, 343,
357n20; Civil Society Assembly, 345; civil
war in, 331, 341–42, 343, 357n20; *cofradías*
in, 336, 340; Committee of Peasant Unity
(CUC), 341; communal lands in, 332,
333–34, 336, 338–39, 346–47; constitution of 1945, 336; constitution of 1985,
344, 347–48, 350, 352; Coordinating
Committee of Agricultural, Commercial,
Industrial and Financial Associations,
347–48; cultural diversity in, 331, 344,
345–48, 351, 352–54; economic development in, 330, 331, 332–35; education in,
331, 334, 337, 346, 349–50, 355; Guatemalan Republican Front, 347; *Ixim* in,
357n25; labor movement in, 340–41;
ladinos in, 26, 330, 333, 335, 336, 337, 342;
land ownership in, 337–39; languages in,
329, 330, 334, 336, 337, 342, 343, 345, 346,
347, 349, 350, 353, 354, 357n25; Maya in,
26, 328–70, 356n7, 357nn20,21,25,
358nn28,31; Ministry of Culture and
Sports, 350–51, 352–54; Ministry of
Education, 337, 350; municipal lands in,
338–39; National Committee for Trade
Union Unity (CNUS), 341; National
Indigenist Institute, 337; nationalism in,
330, 344, 348, 355; national poverty
reduction strategy (NPRS) in, 331,
353–55; National Program of Bilingual/
Intercultural Education (PRONEBI),
346; 1954 coup, 331, 339; Office of the
Presidency's Secretary of Planning and
Programming (SEGEPLAN), 353–54,
355; peace accords in, 331, 345–48, 349–
53, 354, 355, 358n31; political parties in,
340, 347, 357n21; population growth in,
339; poverty in, 330, 331, 353–55; Pro-
Fatherland League, 347; Protestantism in,
339; the state in, 331, 332–33, 334, 336–
39, 340, 346, 350–54, 358n31

Gudeman, Stephen, 32n11, 33n23, 88–89,
360

Guinea Bissau, 220–21; income distribution
in, 287

Gulliver, P. H., 89

Gupta, D., 34n26

Gupta, I., 7

Gutman, M., 267

Gyawali, Dipak, 112–13, 114

Gyekye, K., 213

Hacking, I., 370
Haddad, L., 210, 226, 230
Hagan, H., 275
Haggis, J., 9
Hall, Stuart, 176
Hall, W., 279
Hamlin, A., 40
Hampshire, Stuart, 145
Han, W., 50
Handy, J., 337
Hannerz, U., 61–62
Haq, Mahbub ul, 184n6
Hardy, K.V., 125
Harilal, K. N., 230
Harragin, Simon, 4, 369
Harrington, Michael: *The Other America*, 169
Harrison, Lawrence, 10, 11, 20, 31, 32n6, 37–38, 46, 112
Harriss, J., 34n24, 361
Hart, Keith, 31n1, 32nn8,11
Hausman, D., 40
Hayami, Y., 216, 224
Hayek, Friedrich, 149
health care, 29, 83, 105, 224, 304n15, 305nn22,23, 327n22, 355, 367; for women, 6–9, 236, 241–42, 247, 251–52, 254, 255, 261. *See also* HIV/AIDS
Heimsath, C. S., 250
Heller, P., 24
Hemispheric Fund for Indigenous Peoples, 329
Hendrie, B., 315
Henrich, J., 371n6
Henthorn, W. E., 50
hepatitis B and C, 275
Herkt, D., 279
heroin, 274, 276, 279
Hershatter, G., 240, 243, 244
Hewitt de Alcántara, C., 173

hierarchy, 25–26, 218–19, 231; in Cultural Theory, 21–22, 91, 92–94, 95–96, 97–98, 107, 108, 109, 111–12, 113, 114. *See also* Hinduism, caste system in; kinship systems
high-low procedures, 199–200, 201, 203
Hinduism, 42, 57n18, 251; caste system in, 15, 17, 23, 24, 34nn26,28, 35n39, 36n45, 65, 66, 79–80, 118, 131, 133–34, 135, 230, 250, 259n1, 365, 372n; Hindu Personal Law Code, 253
Hinkelamert, F., 291
Hirschman, Albert, 40, 215, 316; on ego-focused idea of change, 219; on evolutionary individualism, 35n38; *Exit, Voice and Loyalty*, 11, 63, 66, 69–70; on other-regarding norms, 212–13
Hirshleifer, D., 13
HIV/AIDS, 260–80; in Africa, 126–27; behaviors related to, 261–62, 267, 268, 269, 270, 273–78; and condom use, 262, 269, 270; and drug-using subcultures, 22–23, 261, 263, 273–80; and homophobia, 267; and marriage, 269–70; relationship to cultural values, 261–62; relationship to economic development, 261; relationship to sexual subcultures, 263, 264–73; and sex workers, 6–9, 22–23, 32n3, 270–72; state policies related to, 261, 267, 273–76, 280; and vaccine development, 262
Hoben, A., 19
Hoddinott, J., 210, 226, 230
Hoff, K., 13, 34n28
Holland, J., 208n2
Honduras: income distribution in, 287
Honig, E., 240, 243, 244
Honneth, A., 63
Hood, C., 110
Hopenhayn, M., 283
Horowitz, Michael, 204
Hsuan Tsang, 57n8

Hu, H.-C., 239, 270

Hua, C., 239, 252

Huber, W., 208n2

Hubert, M., 269

Hull, T., 270

human capital, 148, 151, 300, 355

human rights, 165, 166, 207, 284, 343

Human Rights Watch, 118, 272

Hume, David, 40

Hunter, G., 215

Huntington, Samuel, 10, 11, 20, 31, 32n6, 37–38, 112, 176; on Ghana vs. South Korea, 46, 50

Hussain, A. M. Z., 326n14

Hutter, Michael, 162nn4,6

Hutton, J. H., 134

hypermodernization, 10, 31

Ibáñez, A. M., 230

identity: collective identity, 4, 9, 15, 20, 35n36, 54, 116, 117, 119–20, 122, 129, 130, 139–40, 143, 149, 158, 161n1, 171n1, 174, 186, 202, 213, 288, 304n9, 334–36, 342, 344, 367, 368; individual identity, 119, 178, 183

IDUs. *See* drug users, injecting

Ikegami, Eiko, 48

IMF. *See* International Monetary Fund

income, 23, 104, 152; in China, 235, 241; in India, 235, 251; in Latin America, 286, 287, 290, 294; in South Korea, 235, 245, 246, 250; in United States, 287

India, 64, 113, 275; Buddhism in, 42, 57n8; caste system in, 15, 17, 23, 24, 34nn26,28, 35n39, 36n45, 65, 66, 79–80, 118, 131, 133–34, 135, 230, 250, 259n1, 365, 372n; chili in, 44, 57n10; vs. China, 234–39, 252, 255–58; Christians in, 42; colonialism in, 34n26, 44, 45, 252, 253, 259n7, 273–74; Congress Party, 173, 252; drug-using subcultures in, 274, 276, 277; economic development in, 52, 130, 234–35, 255; education in, 52, 251, 254, 255, 256, 258; employment of women in, 236, 251, 254, 255, 258; family law in, 236, 252–53, 258; famine in Bengal, 45; female child mortality in, 234, 255; *hijras* in, 266; income in, 235, 251; independence movement, 250–51, 254; Jain culture in, 42; Kerala, 24, 174, 230, 233n4, 239; kinship systems in, 234, 235–39, 252, 258, 259n7; Kolkata (Calcutta), 6–9; literacy rate in, 235; Maharashtra, 71, 72, 226–27; the media in, 236, 253–54; Mumbai, 26, 70–80, 81, 265, 362, 372n; northern vs. southern, 251, 253, 258; opium trade in, 274; Parsees in, 42; participatory development in, 226–27, 230, 233n4; population control in, 252, 254, 256–57; sex workers in, 6–9, 23, 26, 32nn2,4, 272; Sikhism in, 42; vs. South Korea, 234–38, 248, 255–58; state policies in, 27–28, 230, 233n4, 235, 250–55, 257–58, 362; toilet festivals in, 76, 78–80, 361; Virasaiva/Lingayat movement in, 23, 35n39; women in, 27–28, 71, 74, 77, 80, 127, 174, 230, 234, 250–55, 256–58, 259nn1,7, 372n

Indian Council for Social Science Research, 173

Indian Ministry of Labour, 173

indigenous groups, 10, 147, 174–75, 181, 367; Accord on the Identity and Rights of Indigenous Peoples (Guatemala), 344, 345–48, 349–53, 354, 355; Australian aborigines, 139, 143, 150, 152, 277; in Bolivia, 285, 301, 305n26, 306n28, 329, 344, 355; and coffee production, 332–36; Hemispheric Fund for Indigenous Peoples, 329; and International Labour Organization (ILO) Convention 169, 329, 331, 343, 344–45, 358n31; in Latin America, 25, 281, 283, 284, 285, 286, 293,

indigenous groups *(continued)*
301, 305nn19,26, 306n28, 328–55; Maya
in Guatemala, 26, 328–70, 356n7,
357nn20,21,25, 358nn28,31; poverty
among, 330, 353–55; and sexual subcultures, 268; World Bank policies
regarding, 19, 176, 187, 202–3, 204, 208,
209nn11,13
individualism, 13, 35n38, 192; in Cultural
Theory, 21–22, 91, 92–93, 94, 95–98,
107, 108, 110, 111–12, 113, 114; and
markets, 67, 68, 291, 294; vs. other-
regarding norms, 212–13, 218, 219–20,
223
Indonesia, 42, 47, 267, 275–76, 276, 327n24;
Gamelan music, 180
inequality, 36n41, 360, 361; in donor-
beneficiary relationships, 9, 28, 200,
205–7, 208, 367; and globalization, 286–
90; and participatory development, 211,
214, 220–21, 223–27, 228–29, 231, 232;
racial inequality, 17–18; relationship to
poverty, 64, 170, 371n6; between rich and
poor countries, 10, 180, 262, 286, 287,
303n7; role of culture in, 15, 16–17, 21,
23, 25–29, 31, 368; role of political cultures in, 26–28, 281, 282–92; between
westernized and indigenous groups, 10.
See also equality; gender issues
infant survival rate, 104
information: on foreseeable consequences,
187, 195–96, 203–4, 208; information
technologies, 32nn10,11,15, 179, 180, 282,
294, 303n6, 304n9; on probability of
success, 187, 197, 205, 208
information economics, 12
informed participation, 187, 193–98, 200–
208, 209n9
Innocenti Digest, 273
institutions, 32n13, 43; and cultural capital,
16; defined, 13; formal vs. informal, 13,
32n14; institutional cultures, 367

intellectual property and copyright, 167,
181, 367
interest-based lending, 122–24, 128, 129–30,
133, 134–35, 137n15
Intergovernmental Conference on Cultural
Policies for Development, 179
International Forum on Globalization, 111
International Labour Organization (ILO),
173, 176; Convention 169 on Indigenous
and Tribal Peoples, 329, 331, 343, 344–45,
358n31
International Monetary Fund (IMF), 10,
111, 365
international relations, 20
International Rivers Network, 113
Internet, 32nn10,11,15, 180
Iran, 119, 123, 276
Ireland, 44–45, 57n11
Isaac, T., 230
Isar, Raj, 184n6
Isherwood, Baron, 12, 33n15, 64, 90, 99
Islam, 42, 67, 176; in Afghanistan, 138, 140–
41, 143, 144–46, 147, 149, 151, 160–61;
and Balkan wars of 1990s, 119, 124; and
interest-based investments, 122–24, 128,
129–30, 133, 134–35, 137n15; traditional
trust *(waqf)*, 132; and women, 173–74
Italy, 105–6, 159; Anti-Mafia Commission in,
40, 56n6; economic development in, 48
Iyer, L., 372n

Jamaica: Social Investment Fund in, 230
Jana, Smarajit, 7–8, 32n4, 277
Japan: Buddhism in, 49, 50, 141; Charter
Oath, 51; economic development in, 48–
49, 50–52; education in, 50–52; income
distribution in, 287; kinship system in,
237; and Korea, 47, 246, 250; literacy rate
in, 51; peasant communities in, 214;
relations with United States, 51; state
intervention in, 51
Jaspars, S., 315

Java, 327n24

Jelin, Elizabeth, 184nn6,7

Jenkins, Carol, 22–23, 32nn2,3

Jockin, A., 74

John, D., 277

Johnson, A., 265

Johnson, D., 315

Jok, M. J., 313, 319, 321, 323, 327nn18,24

Jolly, R., 166

Jonas, Susanne, 348

Jones, G., 270

Jones, S. T., 276

Jonglei Canal, 309

Jorquez, J. S., 277

Judaism, 176

Kanbur, R., 361, 370

Kane, J. L., 274, 275, 276, 279

Kant, Immanuel, 151

Karahasan, D., 215

Karasimeonov, G., 288

Karim, A., 315

Karve, I., 239

Kazakhstan, 276

Kearney, M., 177

Keen, D., 313, 316, 317, 319, 321, 323, 327nn18,23

Kempadoo, K., 270

Kennedy, Paul, 171

Kertzer, D. I., 370

Kevane, M., 229

Kido Takayoshi, 51

Kikuchi, M., 224

Kim, E., 247, 248, 250

Kim, J.-S., 247

Kim, K.-K, 246, 247

Kim, Q., 47, 50, 246

Kim, S., 47, 50, 246

Kim, T. I., 247

Kim, Y. B., 47, 50, 246

Kim, Y.-C., 250

Kim, Y. Y., 125

Kimball, S. T., 237, 238

kinship systems: in China, 234, 235–40, 242, 243, 252, 258; among European peasants, 237–38; in India, 234, 235–39, 252, 258, 259n7; as matrilineal, 239, 252, 258, 263; as patrilineal, 236–40, 242, 245, 247–48, 252, 258; as patrilocal, 236–40, 248, 258; relationship to gender equity, 235–36; in South Korea, 234, 235–39, 245, 247–48, 258; in Sudan, 5–6, 308, 309–11, 313–14, 319, 322–23, 326nn8,9

Kippax, S., 267

Kirkpatrick, C. H., 208n2

Klamer, Arjo, 20–21, 33n22, 187, 202, 367

Klitgaard, R., 32n5, 230

Kluckholn, C., 4, 136n

Knodel, J., 270, 370

Koch-Schulte, S., 35n31, 65, 190

Kolenda, P., 239

Kolkata (Calcutta): sex workers in, 6–9, 23, 26, 32nn2,4, 272

Koo, H., 245

Kopytoff, I., 154

Korea, South: vs. China, 234–38, 248, 255–58; Civil Code of 1962, 247–48; Confucianism in, 49–50; Constitution of 1948, 247; economic development in, 46–47, 49–50, 234–35, 245; education in, 47, 50, 246, 249, 256, 258; employment for women in, 246, 258; family law in, 236, 247–48, 250; female child mortality in, 234, 255; vs. Ghana, 46–47, 50; income in, 235, 245, 246, 250; vs. India, 234–38, 248, 255–58; Japanese colonialism in, 246, 250; kinship system in, 234, 235–39, 245, 247–48, 258; literacy rate in, 47, 50, 235; the media in, 236, 249–50; population control in, 247, 256–57; state policies in, 27, 46–47, 50, 234–35, 245–50, 257–58; women in, 27, 234, 245–50, 255, 256–58

Korean League of Women Voters, 250

Korean War, 245, 246

Korean Women's Development Institute, 246
Kothari, U., 34n30, 361
Kranton, Rachel, 40, 119
Kreft, I. G. G., 275
Kremer, Michael, 232
Kreps, D. M., 137n1
Krishnan, P., 252
Kroeber, A. L., 4, 136n
Kulick, D., 266
Kumar, K. A., 265
Kumar, R., 255
!Kung, 263
Kuper, A., 11, 98
Kuran, Timur, 22, 30, 123, 360, 365

La Ferrera, E., 13
Lal, D., 31n1, 134, 371n6
Landes, David, 10, 32n7, 224
Lane, R. E., 148
languages, 120, 122, 137n3, 138, 172, 200, 204, 263; in Guatemala, 329, 330, 334, 336, 337, 342, 343, 345, 346, 347, 349, 350, 353, 354, 357n25
Larbi, G., 315
Latin America, 71, 267; campesinos in, 285, 288–89, 293, 305n26; clientelism in, 282, 285, 289, 300, 303nn4,5, 306nn26,27; colonialism in, 283–84, 293; Columbus Discovery celebrations in, 343; cultural heterogeneity in, 292–93, 294, 295, 328–29, 331, 344, 345–48, 351, 352–54; democracy in, 281–82, 284, 288, 290, 291, 294, 298–303, 355; denial of difference in, 283, 284–85, 294; economic development in, 282, 284, 291–92, 293–94, 300, 303n4, 304nn10,11,17, 330, 331, 332–35; employment in, 288, 290, 293–94; exclusion of the other in, 281, 283–84, 290, 294; and globalization, 282, 286–90, 291–92, 294, 304n9; hacienda regimes in, 284, 303n3; income distribution in, 286,

287, 290, 294; indigenous groups in, 25, 281, 283, 284, 285, 286, 293, 301, 305nn19,26, 306n28, 328–55; inequality in, 281, 282–92, 294, 298; labor in, 285, 288, 294, 340–41; land reform in, 294; liberation theology in, 340; markets in, 281, 283, 285, 286, 291–92, 298, 300, 303n1; mestizos/mulattos in, 281, 284, 293; migration from, 125; participatory development in, 211, 224, 225, 229–30; peasant communities in, 212, 214; political cultures in, 27, 281–95, 303nn3,4; political parties in, 289, 291, 294, 302, 340, 347, 357n21; poverty in, 286, 289–90, 300, 301, 304nn13,14, 306n27, 330, 331, 353–55; social mobility in, 288, 294; socioeconomic differentiation in, 286, 288–90, 292–95; the state in, 27, 284–85, 286, 289, 291, 294, 303n4, 304n11, 305n17; urbanization in, 293, 303n4; women in, 173, 281, 283, 284. *See also* Bolivia; Brazil
Latin American Faculty of Social Sciences (FLACSO-Guatemala), 354
Laumann, E., 264, 265
Lawson, A. L.-G., 127
Leacock, E., 173
Leal, M. L., 173
Leamer, E. E., 142
LeBaron, A., 329
Lee, K., 50
Leonardi, R., 34n24, 40, 41, 105, 149
Leoncini, Paula, 184n7
Leridon, H., 269
Lerner, Daniel: *The Uses of Literacy*, 167
Lesaux, Jean-Ives, 184n6
Levenson, D. T., 357n20
Levine, N., 239
LeVine, R. A., 132
Lévi-Strauss, Claude, 61, 184n6
Lewis, B., 131
Lewis, D., 307, 324, 325n3

Lewis, J., 265, 268

Lewis, L., 125

Lewis, Oscar, 34n25, 87, 168–69

Lewis, Sir Arthur, 167

Li, X., 244

life expectancy, 103, 104

Lim, L. L., 271

lineage-based societies: and participatory democracy, 212–13, 214, 217–18, 223, 228, 231; women in, 234, 236–39, 242, 243, 247–48, 252, 258, 263, 322. *See also* kinship systems; Sudan

Lingayat movement, 23, 35n39

literacy rate, 103, 104, 167, 168; and Buddhism, 50; in China, 235; in Guatemala, 349; in India, 235, 251; in Japan, 51; in South Korea, 47, 50, 235

Loane, G., 313, 319, 321, 323, 327n18

Lokshin, M., 7, 32n4

Loufti, M. F., 173

Loury, Glenn, 17–18, 34n27

love, 149, 157

low-high procedures, 199, 200

loyalty, 63, 69, 83, 99, 195

Lu, M., 244

Lubbers, Ruud, 141

Lunde, L., 208n2

Lurie, P., 276

Lux de Coti, Otilia, 351, 352

MacAskill, J., 321

MacMichael, Sir Harold, 324

MacNeice, Louis, 260

Macrae, J., 315, 317, 318

Madagascar, 372n

Mahila Milan, 71–80

Malaysia, 24, 128, 267

Mali, 205

Malraux, André, 166

Mane, P., 266

Mann, Jonathan, 260

Mansbridge, J., 40

Mansuri, G., 361, 362

Marcus, G. E., 325

Marglin, Stephen, 11, 185, 188, 192

Margolis, H., 40

Mari Bhat, P. N., 256

marijuana, 275

markets, 110–11, 114, 153–54, 155–58, 213, 304n15, 360; in China, 28, 235, 241, 244, 245; and individualism, 67, 68, 291, 294; in Latin America, 281, 283, 285, 286, 291–92, 298, 300, 303n1; market test of preferences, 122–24, 130, 131. *See also* capitalism; globalization; trade, international; values, economic values

Marmor, M., 276

Marquet, J., 270

marriage: family law, 236, 242–43, 247–48, 250, 252–53, 258; and HIV/AIDS, 269–70; and sexual subcultures, 269–72; women in, 234, 236–40, 242–43, 244, 245–46, 247–48, 249, 250, 252–53, 258, 259n1, 263, 271, 322. *See also* kinship systems

Mars, G., 96

Marshall, Alfred, 37

Marshall, J., 273

Marshall Plan, 165–66

Martin, J. N., 267

Martinez, D., 277

Marx, Karl, 11, 170; on culture, 167, 183n2

Masci, J., 277

Maslow, Abraham, 139

Mata, A. G., 277

Matteucci, N., 282

Mauritania: slavery in, 204

Mauss, M., 91

Max-Neef, M., 185

Maya, 26, 328–70, 356n7, 357nn20,21,25, 358nn28,31

Mazzanti, M., 143

Mbembe, A., 61–62

McCamish, M., 270

McCloskey, Deirdre, 162nn4,6

McGee, R., 35n31

McGinn, N., 47, 50, 246

McPherson, M. S., 40

Mead, George Herbert, 67

Médecins Sans Frontières, 313, 323

media, the, 122, 167, 179, 180; in China, 236, 243–44; and gender issues, 236, 243–44, 249–50, 253–54, 256; in India, 236, 253–54; in South Korea, 236, 249–50

Medina, José, 303nn3,4

Meekers, D., 269

Melard, C., 220

Meltzer Report, 110–11

memory, collective, 20, 23

Menchú, Rigoberta, 26, 343, 357n26

methodological holism, 14–15, 18, 19, 30

methodological individualism, 14, 18, 21, 22, 30, 33n18, 40, 67, 68, 87, 91, 98, 368, 371n6

Mexico, 36n42, 172, 355; Zapatistas in, 176, 303n4, 329

Meyer, Birgit, 155–56

Meyer, C. A., 229

Meynaud, Mean, 170–71

Michael, R. B., 23, 264, 265

Michaels, S., 264, 265

Middle East, 130, 132

Migdal, J. S., 36n44

migration, 124–25, 130–31, 177, 262–63, 270, 271, 288, 339

Mihaljeck, D., 205

Mikailkov, Nikita, 184n6

Mill, John Stuart, 37, 333

Miller, D., 296

Mills, T. C., 267

Minten, B., 372n

Mitterauer, M., 237, 238

Mogensen, H. O., 266

Mohanty, Chandra, 177

Mokyr, J., 45, 57n11

Mondiacult, 174

Montaner, C. A., 125, 126

Monterroso, E., 276

Mookherjee, D., 226

Morales, Mario Roberto, 358n28

Morishima, Michio, 48

Morocco, 267

Mosse, D., 228, 369

Mostar Bridge, 138, 140, 143, 159–60, 161n2

Mourato, S., 143

Moynihan, Daniel, 169

multiculturalism, 24, 62, 115–16, 117, 176

Mumbai, India, 26, 70–80, 81, 265, 362, 372n

Mundimbe, V. Y., 177

Munshi, K., 226, 372n

Murrill, C., 276

Myanmar, 276

Nahar, N., 266

Nair, J., 250, 252

Nakane, C., 237

Namibia: !Kung in, 263

Nanetti, R. Y., 34n24, 40, 41, 105, 149

Narayan, Deepa, 34n24, 35n31, 65, 227; *Voices of the Poor*, 190, 191

Narmada dam, 204

Nash, June, 181

Nastasi, B., 265, 268

National Institutes of Health (NIH), 276

nationalism, 54, 130, 267, 324, 364; in Guatemala, 330, 344, 348, 355

National Revolutionary Unity (URNG), 331, 345, 347

National Slum Dweller's Foundation, 71–80, 74

Native Americans, 277, 278

Near East, 267

Nepal, 276; Arun-3 project in, 112–13, 114; Pancheswar High Dam in, 114

Netherlands, 159, 279

New Zealand, 276

Ney, S., 14, 90, 93

NGOs. *See* nongovernmental organizations

Nicaragua, 329

Nigeria, 223

Nimeiri, Jafaar, 309

Noel, F., 47, 50, 246

Noelle-Neumann, E., 137n7

Nongbri, T., 252

nongovernmental organizations (NGOs), 76, 78, 188–89, 211, 220–21, 229, 232, 233n3, 244–45, 259n5, 267, 312, 318. *See also* Alliance, the (Mumbai, India); civil society; International Monetary Fund; Oxfam; United Nations; World Bank

North, Douglass, 13, 21, 32nn13,14, 43, 91, 97, 98–100, 133, 208n2

Norton, A., 204

Nouwen, H., 186

Nussbaum, Martha, 102, 162n6

Obermeyer, C. M., 370

Odets, W., 261

Odzer, C., 270

O Grada, C., 45

Operation Lifeline Sudan (OLS), 5, 311–15, 318–19

opinions. *See* beliefs

opium, 274

opportunity costs, 14, 24–25

O'Reilly, C. A., 35n33

O'Reilly, F., 313, 319, 321, 323, 327n18

Ortiz, S., 213

Ortner, S., 61

Osmond, D., 267

Ostrander, D., 96

Ostrom, E., 40, 41, 43

Otero, G., 304n11

Ottone, E., 283

Our Creative Destiny, 178–79

Oxfam, 196, 209n5, 365

Pakistan, 127, 132, 196; caste in, 204; *hijras* in, 266; income distribution in, 287; Islamic banking in, 123, 129–30; Pari Hari, 188–90, 191, 209n5; women in, 188–90

Palley, M. L., 250

Panama, 88–89

Pandey, P., 34n28

Papua New Guinea: sexual subcultures in, 263, 265, 272

Paraguay, 329

Paraschar, A., 253, 267

Parish, W. L., 241

Park, M.-H., 246, 247

Parker, R., 267

Parsons, Talcott, 14–15

participatory development, 19, 25–26, 34n30, 210–12, 218–32, 361, 366, 371n2; and democracy, 219, 221–22, 225, 228; and group-focused idea of change, 219–20; in India, 226–27, 230, 233n4; and inequality, 211, 214, 220–21, 223–27, 228–29, 231, 232; and the poor, 224–27, 230–31; and the state, 210, 212, 226, 227, 229–31, 232; and traditional patterns of authority, 220–23

Patel, R., 35n31, 65, 190

Pattanaik, P., 57n9

Paul, J., 267

Pearson, H. W., 213

peasant communities: in Asia, 212, 214; in Japan, 214; in Latin America, 212, 214; socioeconomic differentiation in, 211, 214

Peckenham, N., 357n20

Pendse, Sandeep, 72

Peng, X., 242

Pérez de Cuéllar, Javier, 178

Peru, 266, 329, 355

Peters, P. E., 232n1

Peterson, J., 267

Petesch, P., 35n31, 65, 190

Philippines, 71, 75; National Irrigation Administration, 224; participatory development in, 224

Piketty, T., 33n21

Pinero, D., 289

Pinker, S., 137n2

Pires, V., 298

Platteau, Jean-Phillipe, 25, 30, 32n14, 34n30, 43, 96–97, 133, 361, 371n6

Pohl, G., 205

Polanyi, Karl, 162n6, 213; *The Great Transformation*, 167–68

policy design and implementation, 360–67; common sense in, 8–9, 27, 361, 362, 363, 370, 371n1; decision-making authority in, 192, 193, 194, 195, 200, 205–7, 208, 225–26, 260, 359, 366; and interest-based lending in Islamic countries, 122–24, 129–30, 133, 134–35; trade-offs in, 20, 116, 131–32, 187, 191–98, 202, 209n7, 367

political cultures: consensus in, 297, 298, 300, 302, 303, 306n28; deliberative political culture, 282, 292, 295–303, 305n19, 361, 364; equality in, 292, 295–96, 301, 302, 303; and globalization, 286–88, 298; inequality in, 26–28, 281, 282–92, 293, 303n4; in Latin America, 27, 281–95, 303nn3,4; popular participation (PP) and the poor, 301, 306n27; reflective capability in, 296–97

political freedom, 103–5, 290

political scientists, 31, 110, 370

political tyranny, 41, 44, 45–46, 55

politics of dignity, 62–63, 78–80

politics of patience, 73, 74, 81–82

politics of recognition, 24, 62–63, 79–80

Pollack, L., 267

Pommerehne, W. W., 187

Ponce, Federico, 336

poor, the, 62, 283, 304n15, 364; aspirations among, 7, 8, 24–25, 36n41, 59, 64–70, 73–74, 76, 77–78, 80, 81–83, 84, 118, 134, 195, 361, 362; and cultural activists, 121; and dominant norms of society, 65–66, 67–68, 81; empowerment of, 64, 70; and participatory development, 224–27, 230–31; resistance among, 23–24, 26, 34n26, 36n40; voice among, 19, 24, 25, 27, 30, 63, 65, 66–67, 69–70, 83, 190, 191, 193, 195, 323, 359, 361, 362, 368. *See also* poverty

Pop Caal, Antonio, 357n25

population control: in China, 242, 256–57; in India, 252, 254, 256–57; in South Korea, 247, 256–57

Population Services International, 262

Portes, A., 34n24

Portillo Cabrera, Alfonso, 351–52

Portney, P. R., 142

Porto Alegre, Brazil, 27, 298–300, 302, 305nn22,23, 364

poverty, 188–92, 371n6; attitudes toward, 85–86; culture of poverty, 16, 17, 34n25, 65, 168–70, 177; definitions of, 85, 89–91, 102, 109; and empowerment, 19; in Latin America, 286, 289–90, 300, 301, 304nn13,14, 306n27, 330, 331, 353–55; North on, 99–100; politics of, 62–63; relationship to inequality, 64, 170, 371n6; Sen on, 101–2, 290, 317; vs. slavery, 85–86, 109; and unhappiness, 102–3. *See also* poor, the

power relations: as asymmetrical, 38, 53, 54, 55; relationship to culture, 31

Powis, B., 279

Pramualratana, A., 270

preferences: and anonymity, 121, 122–24, 125–28, 129; attitudes of economists toward, 87, 148; biased interviewer experiments regarding, 128; and close observation, 128; constraining preferences,

15, 17–18, 22, 24–25, 29, 365; formation of, 14–15, 24–25, 33n16, 33n17, 368; hypothetical scenario experiments regarding, 128; for male children, 247, 255–56, 258; as malleable, 116, 120, 131–34, 135, 136, 144–45, 146–47; market test of, 122–24, 130, 131; migration test of, 124–25, 130–31; preference falsification, 22, 30, 116, 118, 120–22, 125–26, 127, 128–29, 133, 135, 137n3, 217, 365; and voice, 22, 24–25. *See also* beliefs

Preis, Ann-Belinda, 184n7

Price, D., 188, 208n2

Prieur, A., 267

Pritchett, L., 251

property rights, 13, 32n14, 99, 167, 181, 248, 367

prostitution, 6–9, 23, 26, 32nn2,4, 263, 266, 270–72

Przeworski, A., 181

public discussion, 42–43, 53–54, 55–56, 114, 132, 144–45, 359, 364–65; informed participation in, 187, 193–98, 200–208, 209n9; Sen on, 186–87, 193–95, 365. *See also* democracy

purchasing power, 103, 104

Putnam, Robert, 34n24, 40, 41, 105–6, 113, 137n1, 149

Putterman, L., 40

race, 43; racial inequality, 17–18, 34n28, 86, 365

Rademacher, A., 35n31, 65, 190

Radin, M. J., 159

Radner, R., 142

Rafael Landivar University: Institute of Economic and Social Investigation, 354

Rahman, F., 137n15

Rahman, H., 277

Rahnema, M., 178

Rangasami, A., 316

Rao, Mohan, 184n7

Rao, Vijayendra, 7, 35nn38,39, 39, 127, 230, 326n16

rape, 249, 255, 272–73

rational choice theory, 33n18, 97, 98

Ratnayake, P., 265, 268

Ravallion, M., 225

Ray, D., 9, 36n41, 226, 371n6

Rayner, S., 97, 102

Redfield, Robert, 168

redistribution of wealth, 214–16, 218, 219–20, 223

religion, 43, 138, 264–65, 267; fundamentalism in, 54, 178, 340; among the Maya, 26, 336, 340, 343. *See also* Buddhism; Christianity; Hinduism; Islam; Judaism

research agenda, 367–70

revolutions, 24

Ribeiro, Darcy, 172

Rich, F., 271

Richard, A., 278

Richards, Paul, 108

Richerson, P. J., 118, 371n6

Richter, L., 277

Rist, G., 175

rituals, 4, 15, 32n15, 35n36, 36n44, 80, 152, 213, 361; role in consensus building, 64, 81, 83

Rivers, K., 264, 269

Roach, J. and J., 170

Roberto, J., 277

Roberts, A., 57

Rodrik, D., 113

Roemer, J. E., 29

Rofel, L., 244

Rosanvallon, P., 291

Rosenzweig, M., 372n

Ross, J., 279

Ross, J. A., 247

Ross, M. W., 267

Rosser, S., 267

Rostow, W. W., 167

Rowntree, S., 89

Royal Anthropological Institute, 312

Rudra, A., 369, 371n6

Russell, N., 277

Russia, 276

Rwanda: Tsutsi-Hutu conflict in, 364

Rwenge, M., 269

Ryle, J., 313, 319, 321, 323, 324, 327n18, 327n23

Saengtienchai, C., 270

Safa, H., 173

Saffioti, H., 173

Sahlins, M., 90

Said, Edward, 137n12, 177, 325n1

Saidel, T., 277

Saleem-Murdock, M., 307, 325

Salmen, Larry, 204

Sangari, K., 252

Saradamoni, K., 252

Sardan, P. O. de, 229

Sarkar, L., 253

Sasaki, Y., 266

Sassen, S., 31n1, 61–62

Saussure, Ferdinand de, 61

Savane, A., 173

savings, 73–75, 189

Schafft, K., 35n31, 65, 190

Schech, S., 9

Schensul, J. J., 265, 268

Schensul, S. L., 265, 268

Scheper-Hughes, N., 36n40

Schultz, T. P., 132

Schumacher, Ernst, 199

Schuman, H., 142

Schurmann, F., 239

Schwarz, Michiel, 112

Schweder, R. A., 126

Scott, James C., 23–24, 27, 36n40, 61, 128, 308, 370, 371n1; on *metis*, 8–9

SDI. *See* Slum/Shackdwellers International

Seaman, J., 308

Seki, E., 32n14

Seligman, B. Z., 324

Seligman, C. G., 324

Selle, P., 92, 110

Sen, Amartya, 162nn4,6, 236, 296, 326n16; on capabilities, 4, 12–13, 19–20, 28, 32n12, 36n45, 51, 63, 82, 151, 191, 193–94; on cultural values, 20–21, 139, 190–91, 360; on decision-making authority, 194; on democracy, 20, 53–54, 55–56, 185, 365; on distribution, 91; on economic growth, 31n1, 185; on economic value, 20, 21; on ends and means of development, 18, 20, 30; on equality, 295, 305n20; on famine, 316, 317, 326n15; on foreseeable consequences of development, 195–96, 203; on freedom, 19–20, 56, 56n3, 63, 82, 102, 104, 106, 107, 183, 191, 290; on functionings, 14, 191, 194; on globalization, 31n1; on markets, 291, 360; on poverty, 101–2, 290, 317; on public discussion, 186–87, 193–95, 365; on relational deprivation, 4; on social identity, 183, 367; on social welfare, 63; on societal infrastructures, 105; on tolerance, 21; on tourism, 39, 57n8, 367; on valuation, 193–94; on women in India, 250, 254, 255

Sen, G., 43

Senegal, 223, 228

Senghor, Leopold, 172

September 11th attacks, 141, 164

Serageldin, I., 19, 187

Serrano, R., 363

sex education, 269

sexual subcultures, 22–23, 32n3, 264–73; in Africa, 263, 267, 270; anal sex in, 264, 268; in Asia, 263, 266–67, 270; heterosexuality in, 264–65, 268; homosexuality in, 265–

68; and indigenous groups, 268; and marriage, 269–72; oral sex in, 264–65, 268; polyandry, 269; polygyny, 269; and the state, 267–68; in United States, 264–65, 268

sex workers, 26, 32nn2,4, 263, 266; and HIV/AIDS, 6–9, 22–23, 32n3, 270–72

Shah, M. K., 35n31, 65, 190

Shah, N., 255

Sharma, U., 131

Shiva, M., 252

Shomphe, L., 276

Shore, C. N., 324, 327n30

Shubhada, M., 266

Shuzhuo, L., 234, 237, 243

Sibanda, A., 127

Sidel, R., 241, 242

Sidel, V., 241, 242

Sieder, R., 237, 238

Sierra Leone, 108

Sikhism, 42

Sillitoe, P., 3, 369

Silva, K. T., 265, 268

Silverblatt, I., 284

Sinha, I., 7

Sivayoganathan, C., 265, 268

Skok, Vladimir, 184n6

slavery, 85–86, 109, 133, 204, 232n2, 365

Sleightholme, C., 7

Slovakia: income distribution in, 287

Slum/Shackdwellers International (SDI), 70–71, 73, 75, 80

Smith, Adam, 11, 37, 40, 53, 149, 161, 162n6

Smith, K., 372n

Smith, T. C., 214

social capital, 19, 25, 33n23, 34n24, 108, 149–50, 152–53, 160, 182, 301, 302, 306n27, 360, 371n6; Bourdieu on, 16, 30; Coleman on, 162n8; Putnam on, 113, 149; solidarity, 41, 99, 105–6, 109n, 119, 126, 159, 189, 215, 311, 320, 326n9; trust, 21, 35n36, 40,

75, 77–78, 89, 99, 100, 106, 107, 127–28, 149, 197, 282, 300, 305n24, 306n27, 371n6. *See also* values, social values

social classes, 21, 25–26, 34n24, 36nn41,45, 43; in Ghana vs. South Korea, 46; Hindu caste system, 15, 17, 23, 24, 34nn26,28, 35n39, 36n45, 65, 66, 79–80, 118, 131, 133–34, 135, 230, 250, 259n1, 365, 372n; in India, 78, 79–80; oppressive elites, 25–26, 30; socioeconomic differentiation in tribal communities, 211, 214, 220–21, 223–27, 228–29, 231

socialization, 118

social mobility, 23, 35n37, 288, 294, 368

sociologists, 14–15, 18–19, 30, 31, 32n10, 33n18, 35n36, 48, 359, 369, 370

solidarity. *See* social capital, solidarity

Solow, R. M., 142

Somalia, 319

Sonagachi, 6–9, 23, 26, 32n2, 272

Sondgrass, D. R., 47, 50, 246

Sonenstein, F. L., 268

Song Si-yol, 49

Sorensen, J. L., 276

South Africa, 71, 74, 75, 80, 172, 272

South Pacific, 267

SPARC, 71–80

Spender, Stephen, 166

Spenser, Edmund, 45

SPLM/SSRA-OLS, 5

Sri Lanka, 50, 141, 265, 268

Srinivas, M. N., 23, 131

Stall, R., 267

state, the, 9, 36nn42,44, 51, 114, 207, 304n8, 360, 364; in Brazil, 298–300, 361, 364; in China, 27, 28, 235, 239–45, 252, 255–56, 257–58; and drug-using subcultures, 273, 274–76, 279; and gender issues, 234–35, 239–35, 245–50, 250–55, 252, 255–56, 257–58, 365; and globalization, 286–87, 289; in Guatemala, 331, 332–33, 334,

state, the *(continued)*
  336–39, 340, 346, 350–54, 358n31; and
  HIV/AIDS, 261, 267, 273–76, 280; in
  India, 27–28, 230, 233n4, 235, 250–55,
  257–58, 362; in Japan, 51; in Latin
  America, 27, 284–85, 286, 289, 291, 294,
  303n4, 304n11, 305n17; in Mexico,
  36n42; and participatory development,
  210, 212, 226, 227, 229–31, 232; relation-
  ship to civil society, 201, 285, 289, 298–
  300, 301, 306n28, 362; and sexual sub-
  cultures, 267–68; in South Korea, 27,
  46–47, 50, 234–35, 245–50, 257–58;
  subsidies of cultural goods by, 144, 158,
  161
Stavenhagen, Rodolfo, 171–72
Stavis, B., 230
Steele, C. M., 34n28
Steiner, C. B., 156
Stephens, T., 204
Stern, N. H., 33n16, 369, 371n6
Stevens, S., 277
Stigler, G., 14, 24, 114
Stiglitz, Joseph, 13, 186, 208
Stokes, J. P., 267
Stokes, S., 297
Stolcke, V., 284
Strang, J., 279
Strathdee, S., 274
Streeten, Paul, 184n7
subcultures, 22–23, 117, 168–69, 177. *See
  also* Cultural Theory; drug users, injecting;
  sexual subcultures
Sudan, 123, 307–25, 327n27; Bahr-el-
  Ghazal, 317, 318, 319, 323; civil war in,
  309, 312, 313, 326n7; colonialism in, 310;
  Dinka ethnic group, 309–11, 319, 320,
  322, 327n22; donor-beneficiary relations
  in, 4–6, 9, 307–8, 311, 313–15, 316–19,
  320–22, 323–24, 326nn17,18, 327n19;
  kinship system in, 5–6, 308, 309–11, 313–

14, 319, 322–23, 326nnn8,9; 1984–85
  famine in, 317; 1988 famine in, 312, 317,
  318; 1998 famine in, 4–6, 9, 307–8, 311–
  16, 318–23, 326nn6,17, 327nn19,20,25;
  Nuer ethnic group, 309, 310
Sudan People's Liberation Army (SPLA),
  312, 314–15, 319, 327n20
Sudan People's Liberation Movement
  (SPLM), 313, 314–15, 318, 319, 326n11
Sudan Relief and Rehabilitation Association
  (SRRA), 313, 314, 326n11
Sulistyaningsih, 270
Sunstein, C. R., 198, 199
Swantz, M. L., 224
Swartz, David, 15, 16, 33n19
Sweden, 268
Swedlow, B., 110
Swift, Jeremy, 205
Sylla, A., 213
symbols, 4, 15, 36n44
Szanton, David, 232n1
Szmukler, Anita, 26–27, 364

Tabaroff, J., 19
taboos, 11–12, 15, 33n20
Tagore, Rabindranath, 54–55
Taiwan, 49
Tajikistan, 276
Takla, Leila, 184n6
Taliban, 138, 140–41, 143, 144–46, 147, 149,
  151, 160–61
Tang, S., 227
Tax, Sol, 335–36
Taylor, Charles, 24, 62–63, 66, 79, 279, 364,
  371n5
technology, 179, 183, 270, 282, 294, 303n6,
  304n9; Internet, 32nn10,11,15, 180
Tendler, J., 224, 227, 229, 363
terms of recognition, 26, 27, 362, 363, 364;
  Appadurai on, 24, 25, 66–67, 70, 76, 77,
  80, 81, 83, 361

Thailand, 47, 49, 50, 71, 74, 239; sexual
subcultures in, 266, 270
Thomas, T., 125
Thompson, Michael, 92, 110, 112
Throsby, D., 33n22, 35n35, 44, 162n6, 184n7;
on cultural value, 40, 146, 150, 151, 162n4;
on economic value, 142, 148, 160, 371n6
Titus, S., 276
toilet festivals, 76, 78–80, 361
tolerance, 21, 42, 62, 132, 136, 149, 166, 302,
303, 364
Tooby, J., 137n2
Torian, L., 276
Torres Rivas, Edelberto, 332
Touraine, A., 282, 294
tourism, 119, 138, 139, 141, 144, 148, 157,
158, 187, 196; Sen on, 39, 57n8, 367
trade, international, 35n34, 51, 53, 62, 119,
131, 182, 366, 367; protectionism in, 109,
130, 136. *See also* globalization; markets
trade-offs between economic development
and cultural preservation, 20, 116, 131–
32, 187, 191–98, 202, 209n7
transnationalism, 177
Trautmann, T. R., 239
Trevelyan, Charles Edward, 45
tribal communities, 210–32, 263; authority
in, 211, 216–19, 220–23, 223, 225–26,
231; consensus-seeking in, 217–18; other-
regarding norms in, 212–15, 219–20, 231;
participatory development in, 218–32;
patron-client relations in, 223, 226, 229,
232n1; personalized relationships in, 211,
212–16, 218, 223, 231; redistributive
norms in, 214–16, 218, 219–20, 223;
relations with donor agencies, 211–12,
223–26, 227–29, 232, 232n3; social
solidarity in, 215; socioeconomic differentiation in, 211, 214, 220–21, 223–27, 228–
29, 231; witchcraft accusations in, 216
Trotter, R. T., 277

trust. *See* social capital, trust
Turkey, 119, 131–32, 159
Turnbull, C., 90
Turner, V., 35n36
Turton, D., 327n24
Tushman, M., 35n33

Ubico, Jorge, 336
Udry, C., 372n
Uganda, 280
Ukraine, 276
Ullmann-Margalit, E., 199
United Kingdom, 44–45, 48, 51, 57n11, 71,
139, 265, 276, 279
United Nations, 9, 80; Convention for the
Protection of Natural and Cultural
Heritage, 174; Convention of the Child,
174; and culture, 165–67, 174–75; Decade
for Women, 254; Human Rights Commis-
sion, 343; and Operation Lifeline Sudan
(OLS), 311–12; UNAIDS, 265–66, 271;
UNICEF, 312; Universal Declaration of
Human Rights, 165; Volunteer Services,
180; Working Group on Indigenous
Populations, 343; World Commission on
Culture and Development, 163, 178–79,
181, 184n6. *See also* United Nations
Development Program (UNDP); United
Nations Educational, Scientific and
Cultural Organization (UNESCO)
United Nations Development Program
(UNDP), 246, 247, 288, 304n15, 306n28,
352; Human Development Index (HDI),
103, 104, 174–75, 287; Human
Development Reports, 18, 19, 111
United Nations Educational, Scientific and
Cultural Organization (UNESCO), 143,
153, 164, 166–67, 176, 181, 187, 352, 365,
366; and Buddhist statues in Afghanistan,
140, 141, 144, 145, 147; *World Culture
Reports*, 179, 180, 184n7; World Heritage

UNESCO *(continued)*
    List, 18, 139, 140, 141, 144, 145, 147, 159,
    174
United States, 47, 50; African Americans,
    17–18, 34n28, 169; agricultural subsidies
    in, 130; civil rights movement in, 361;
    drug-using subcultures in, 274–75, 276,
    278; ethnicity in, 137n6; and globalization,
    287; income distribution in, 287; Native
    Americans, 277, 278; racial inequalities in,
    17–18, 34n28; relations with Guatemala,
    331; relations with Japan, 51; September
    11th attacks, 141, 164; sexual subcultures
    in, 264–65, 268
Uphoff, N. T., 228
US National Survey of Adolescent Males,
    268

Vaid, S., 252
Valentine, Charles, 170
values: academic values, 147, 148; aesthetic
    values, 116, 138, 146–47; artistic values,
    138, 153, 156, 159; bequest value, 142; and
    choice modeling studies, 143; and contin-
    gent valuation studies, 142–43, 148, 161;
    cultural values, 20, 20–21, 40, 138–47,
    150–53, 154–57, 160, 161, 162n4, 188–
    92, 193–94, 200–201, 202, 203–5, 261,
    267, 271, 308, 309–11, 313–16, 319, 322,
    324–25, 360, 371n6; and demand-supply
    analysis, 148; economic values, 12, 20, 90,
    140, 141–44, 145, 146, 147–49, 150, 151–
    52, 153, 154–55, 156–57, 158, 159, 160,
    161, 162n12, 175, 188–92, 193–94, 200–
    201, 212, 352, 354, 367, 371n6; existence
    value, 142; historical values, 150; measure-
    ment of, 143–45, 148, 150, 153, 157, 158–
    59; option value, 142; other-regarding
    values, 212–16, 218, 219–20, 223, 231;
    political values, 282–83; and public
    discussion, 21–22, 42–43; realization of,
    141–44, 153–55, 157–59; redistributive
    norms, 214–16, 218, 219–20, 223; reli-
    gious/spiritual values, 138, 144, 145–46,
    149, 150, 156, 189; Sen on, 20–21, 139,
    190–91, 193–94, 360; social values, 12, 63,
    98–99, 136, 140, 147, 148–51, 157–59,
    160, 165, 181, 189–92, 212–16; valoriza-
    tion/devalorization, 144, 146–47, 149,
    155, 156–58, 160, 161, 162n7; valuation,
    141–47, 148, 151, 153–55, 156–57, 160,
    161; and willingness to pay studies, 142,
    143, 148
van Cott, D. L., 329
van der Veen, H. T., 274
Van Landingha, M., 270
van Puffelen, F., 142
van Staveren, I., 149, 162n10
van Zessen, G., 269
van Zorge, Y. J. J., 219
Veblen, Thorstein, 162n6
Venezuela, 329
Verdier, T., 33n17
Veron, R., 230, 233n4
Verweij, M., 21, 92, 96
Vietnam, 276
Vinson, Isabelle, 184n7
Virasaiva movement, 23, 35n39
voice. *See* poor, the, voice among
von Braun, J., 213

Wade, Robert, 170, 225
Wadsworth, J., 265
Walton, M., 39
Walzer, Michael, 149, 154, 162n6, 296
Wang Yang-ming, 49
Warman, A., 304n11
Warren, D. M., 324
Warren, K. B., 329
Watongoka, H., 220
Webb, P. J. R., 213
Weber, Max, 11, 33n15, 162n6; on

Calvinism, 10, 48; on capitalism, 10, 48; on Confucianism, 48; *Protestant Ethic and the Spirit of Capitalism*, 10
Wedsinghe, P., 265, 268
Weibull, J., 371n6
Weingast, B. R., 137n1
Weiss, J., 208n2
Weiss, T., 166
Welch, I., 13, 316
Wellings, K., 265
West Samoa, 268
White, J. W., 370
Whitehead, L., 301, 305n26
Whiteman, M., 277
Whyte, M. K., 241
WIDER, 11
Wiesel, Elie, 184n6
Wildavsky, Aaron, 12, 64, 98, 110
Wilde, Oscar, 141
Williams, Bernard, 86
Williamson, S., 279
Win, P. T., 277
Winter, P., 313, 319, 321, 323, 327n18
Wolf, Eric, 168, 171, 356n10
Wolf, M., 240, 241
Wolfensohn, James, 19, 39, 113, 114, 201–2
women: in China, 27, 28, 234–45, 255–58; education for, 130, 132, 189, 236, 240, 244, 245, 246, 249, 255, 256, 258, 261, 269, 271, 349; employment for, 235, 236, 240–41, 245, 246, 250, 251, 254, 255, 258, 286; equality for, 27–28, 122, 179, 188, 235–36, 240–41, 242–44, 246, 247–48, 249, 250, 250–51, 252–54, 256, 257–58, 271; health care for, 6–9, 236, 241–42, 247, 251–52, 254, 255, 261; in India, 27–28, 71, 74, 77, 80, 127, 174, 230, 234, 250–55, 256–58, 259nn1,7, 372n; and Islam, 173–74; in Latin America, 173, 281, 283, 284; in marriage, 234, 236–40, 242–43, 244, 245–46, 247–48, 249, 250, 252–53, 258, 259n1,

263, 271, 322; organizations for, 236, 244–45, 247, 248, 250, 254–55, 256, 257; in Pakistan, 188–90; as sex workers, 6–9, 23, 26, 32nn2,4, 263, 266, 270–72; in South Korea, 27, 234, 245–50, 255, 256–58; violence against, 127, 242, 243, 249, 253, 254, 255, 272–73, 372n. *See also* gender issues
Women's Federation (China), 244–45
Woo, M.Y. K., 241
Wood, Alexander, 274
Woodham-Smith, C., 45
Woolcock, M., 34n24, 363, 370
World Bank, 9, 31n1, 32n13, 34n24, 37, 79, 82, 137n4, 338, 367; comprehensive development framework (CDF), 201–2, 203, 208; criticisms of, 10, 28, 34n24, 111, 112–13, 123, 161, 175, 186, 187–88, 198, 200, 205, 208, 208n2, 227, 325, 365; and cultural issues, 161, 186, 187, 191, 198–208, 202, 208n1; decision-making authority of, 200, 205–7, 208; *Empowerment Sourcebook*, 206; and high-low procedures, 199–200, 201, 203; and informed participation, 200–208, 209n9; Participatory Development Learning Group (PDLG), 209n9; policies on community-driven development, 187; policies on indigenous people, 19, 176, 187, 202–3, 204, 208, 209nn11,13; Poverty Reduction Strategy Papers, 200; poverty reduction strategy programs (PRSPs), 201, 203; *Proposal for a Comprehensive Development Framework*, 114; staff of, 186, 187, 199, 206; Strategy Compact, 208n2; World Development Report on poverty, 19
World Commission on Dams, 207
World Conference on Cultural Policies, 174
World Food Program (WFP), 312, 313, 314, 321
World Trade Organization (WTO), 365

Worth, G. C., 247
Wright, R., 213

Xiaojin, L., 243
Xie Zhenming, 236

Young, H., 321
Yugoslavia, former. *See* Balkan wars of 1990s
Yun Chung, 49

Zamagni, S., 40

Zaoual, Hassan, 175
Zelizer, Viviane, 160, 162n6
Zhao, Y., 244
Zhen, Y., 244
Zhou, M., 177
Zimbabwe, 267
Zubeida, 173
Zuidhof, P.W., 158
Zunzunegui, M.V., 277
Zwi, A., 317